D1329989

in the modern idiom

THOMAS Y. CROWELL COMPANY NEW YORK, ESTABLISHED 1834

in the modern idiom

edited by Leo Hamalian & Arthur Zeiger
THE CITY COLLEGE OF THE CITY UNIVERSITY OF NEW YORK

an introduction to literature

 Published simultaneously in Canada by Fitzhenry & Whiteside, Ltd., Toronto.

Library of Congress Cataloging in Publication Data

HAMALIAN, LEO, comp. In the modern idiom.

1. Literature, Modern—20th century. I. Zeiger, Arthur, joint comp. II. Title.

PN6014.H25 808.8′004 73-1145

ISBN 0-690-44616-0

Manufactured in the United States of America

1 2 3 4 5 6 7 8 9 10

In their *Pamphlet Against Anthologies,* published about fifty years ago, Robert Graves and Laura Riding describe two sorts of anthologies: ones that "confine themselves to literary rescue work, or have the excuse of being private scrap-books," and ones that "turn poetry into a cultural packet-commodity." Even if we have in mind general anthologies of literature, there is no valid answer to this criticism. A book that presents snippets from a hundred authors within the space of five hundred pages is in theory a Bad Thing. By its very nature it must rule out selections of considerable length: The *short* story, the *short* poem, the *short* play have become the current inevitable coin of the anthologist, and a story of more than one hundred pages or a poem of more than one hundred lines stands little chance of appearing in its entirety in a typical anthology of literature. And rarely is the writer represented by more than one story, or one play, or a small handful of poems, or an extract from one of his books.

The reader, then, is tempted to agree with Dr. Samuel Johnson, who deprecated selections from any author on the ground that those who wish to read a man's writings should do so in the form of his collected works. But in practice, with more and more writers demanding attention, with the bewildering proliferation of periodicals in which their work appears and disappears, a solid case can be made for a book which gives a fair taste of contemporary writing.

Such a book is prepared for and bought by young readers. Usually the young approach literature by way of a friend or a teacher, by reading reviews, by seeing a film of a book, by an urge to write themselves—or through an anthology. Like the little girl who asked about penguins, they may not want to know *that* much about the subject—clearly not many of

Preface

them are ready to heed the good Dr. Johnson's advice—but most of them, by the time they come to college, are interested in or at least curious about "literature."

And more often than not, it is modern literature that they most immediately want to know about. What is "confessional" poetry? What is the "field theory of composition"? Who are the new black writers? What themes preoccupy the contemporary writer? What values and what ethical norms can we find in the modern writer? What indeed do we mean by "modern"? To questions such as these, anthologies like this one can provide at best partial answers, at worst no answers, but if the material is carefully chosen and justified—without long critical tracts from the editors in the hope that they can supply what the material itself does not—an anthology of modern writing like this one *can provide a means of finding answers or at least of asking more questions.* For instance, to read *Caterpillar* may be as important, in the sense that it suggests a contemporary way of seeing and hearing, as it was during the forties to read *Partisan Review,* during the fifties to read *Encounter,* and during the early sixties to read *Commentary* and *Poetry.* And since writers of a decade reflect the ways of "saying" that create the grain and the cross-grain of the period, this kind of anthology offers at its lowest an introduction to the "modern idiom," an introduction that the young reader conceivably might not make at all without the modest assistance of such a book. It remains, after that introduction, the duty of the teacher to impress upon the young reader that the author of any selection reveals himself fully, as Dr. Johnson insisted, through his collected work, and not through a mere introduction.

We have tried to avoid some of the pitfalls that Graves and Riding have posted for anthologists. The story by Malamud approaches the short novel in substance. Two of the three plays are full-length. The nonfiction pieces are sizable enough to permit the writer to be expansive and to develop his ideas without overloading the subject. The section on poetry is made up largely of short and medium-length selections, chiefly because an extended poem like "Kaddish" or "Mistress Bradstreet" would be prohibitively expensive to reprint even if the rights could be secured and because one characteristic of modern poetry seems to be the prevalence of the short poem. Nonetheless, the long poem is represented by those who use the form—Ginsberg, Bukowski, and Wakoski.

We are convinced that students and teachers alike are not interested in contending with long critical discourses about literature by the editors, nor do they want such apparatus as it is the duty of the editors to provide in minimum to intrude upon their personal encounter with the work. Thus, in addition to this unpretentious preface, we provide a brief introduction to each of the genres as well as fairly full headnotes which we believe will create a useful context for the reader without overdirecting his approach to the work. Our intention is to enrich the reader's experience with the work.

For ease of reference, the material is arranged alphabetically—we sympathize with readers who have to search through the contents of a book in order to find the selection they want. This arrangement does not reflect the level of difficulty. Some of the selections are simple and orthodox in their surface structures; for instance, the poetry of Raymond Patterson, or Ed Bullins's play, the stories by Buzzati, Grace Paley, and Malamud—these might be places for the student to begin, moving from there through progressively more complex material toward H. L. Mountzoures in fiction, Lowell in the drama, and Ted Hughes in poetry. Doubtless some of these selections are going to bewilder the reader who tries to absorb them as he does the daily newspaper, but none should be beyond the comprehension of the undergraduate willing to read with the attention and alertness that any challenging writer deserves.

In summary, we have sought to shape a book that conveys a more than superficial sense of what is "modern" in style and content (that both may seem indefinable and inseparable is a particularly modern quality). We have included many writers who do not belong to any "school," some who have never or rarely been anthologized before, some who express positions or employ strategies that the editors do not necessarily espouse, and some who explore subjects previously regarded as too personal for public discussion, in a language that might have shocked the previous generation of readers. However, each speaks in his own individual and particular voice. And even though the editors may here and there generalize about the "modern," each writer by implication, we hope, denies the validity of the "cultural packet-commodity." If the reader finds himself disagreeing with our choice of writer or our selection of his work, he is exerting a consciousness that has an especially modern character to it: There is no "canon," there is no "gallery of greats" in contemporary literature, critics and professors notwithstanding. We think that the writers in this volume, in talking to and of their times, have also touched upon the enduring concerns of young men and women who aspire to be literate and humane.

It is very possible, as T. S. Eliot once observed, that the more a literary critic attempts to define "the modern," the more he may unwittingly return to the traditional. Irving Howe maintains that "the kind of literature called modern is almost always difficult . . . the modern writer seems willfully inaccessible." However, neither precaution against presumption necessarily means that the "modern" defies all description. Even within the scope of this brief preface, we can attempt to isolate the current, the temper in modern writing that presents itself to our sensibilities as distinctive and characteristic of its time and possibly no other.

As Irving Howe has noted, modern writers begin to work "at a moment when the culture is marked by a prevalent style of perception and feeling; and their modernity consists in a revolt against this prevalent style." Contemporary writing challenges all our complacencies, poses every question that polite society forbade us to ask in print, and pits personal rage or guile against the official order. Although all art is more or less personal, no literature has ever been so unashamedly and passionately personal as the writing of the past decade. It asks if we are content with our sexual lives, with the daily experiences we accept as inevitable or imperative, with the professional careers we adopted years ago, with the structures we live our lives by, with our very mortality itself. Though these questions seem to call into account the society or culture we find ourselves in, they are not so much about that as they are about our individual selves. The voice of the modern writer goes beyond the realism of its predecessors. It asks whether we are saved or whether we are damned.

It is tempting to call modern literature, as some critics fond of paradox have done, "religious." But this would be more imprecise than paradoxical. Modern writing shows a special concern with the life of the spirit, the concern that Hegel had in mind when he spoke of the great modern phenomenon of the secularization of spirituality. The spirit Hegel had in mind has survived the hostile environment created by the machinery of politics, the iron grip of technology, and the desiccation of commerce, but now it appears to us no longer in the familiar trappings. The modern writer works with unfamiliar forms; he chooses subjects that disturb the audience and threaten most cherished sentiments. He provokes some of his readers to such epithets as "obscure," "decadent," or "sick."

The spirit in modern writing is hydra-headed. It may appear as the cause of civil justice, women's rights, the prolongation of life for mankind, in the quest for identity, in the deflation of the pompous, in the love of simple things, in what Thomas Mann called "a sympathy for the abyss." Probably this course was laid down by the introspective masters of an earlier period —Dostoyevsky, Kafka, Proust (Calvino's story is a remembrance of things past, Buzzati and Borges have debts to Kafka, and the intensely personal revelation comes to us from Dostoyevsky's *Notes from Underground* via Ralph Ellison's *The Invisible Man*), Mann, Joyce, Faulkner, William Carlos Williams, and Henrik Ibsen. Faulkner's message in his Nobel Prize speech —"Man will prevail"—lies beneath modern writing. It is the affirmation of the spirit in the face of gathering storms and catastrophes; it is the only answer the spirit can give to Hermann Hesse speaking about "a whole generation caught . . . between two ages, two modes of life, with the consequence that it loses all power to understand itself and has no standards, no security, no simple acquiescence."

It is this extravagant personal force of modern writing that we have tried to represent in this volume, aware as we made our selections over a period of three years that no anthology of this limited scope can possibly convey more than an impression of the energy that has activated much serious writing of our time. That a work may be lighthearted in tone (for example, John Lennon's and Lawrence Durrell's pieces or Kurt Vonnegut's story or Richard Brautigan's sketch or Kenneth Gangemi's poems) does not negate the serious intention or the personal nature of the perception. It is this intensely felt personal space each writer seeks to describe that we have finally called "the modern."

The term "idiom" usually refers to a style or a form characteristic of a period or a movement. For the "modern" period the hallmark of style is no style, so to speak. Modernism does not establish a prevalent style of its own. It is, in a phrase of Roland Barthes, "writing degree zero"—writing that steers away from the "mandarin" manner of Henry James, Gustav Flaubert, or T. S. Eliot, and eschews the counter-reactant experimentalism of the late James Joyce, the late Ezra Pound, and William Burroughs. There is a studied avoidance of the "high rhetoric" that characterizes so much political oratory and commercial advertisements on television despite the efforts to be "natural" and "idiomatic." Perhaps the best way to describe the stylelessness of modern style is to say that it seeks to illustrate what is being said, to fuse language with theme so that the mood or the message is intensified.

Note to the Teacher—This book was intended for use in the first year of English literature and composition on the community college or university level, and the material was chosen with such an audience in mind. However, it may prove suitable also for courses in contemporary literature, particularly at schools where the curriculum permits only one such course to be offered.

Contents

NONFICTION

The essay, historians of literature tell us, began with Montaigne, who in 1580 published a volume of *Essais,* short, intimate, sometimes digressive meditations on such matters as idleness, cannibals, vanity, physiognomy, and the resemblance of children to fathers, all informed by the force of his urbane and skeptical personality ("I am myself the matter of my book," he declared in his opening paragraph), all sounding like a man conversing ("The speech I love is a simple natural speech, the same on the paper as in the mouth," he noted). But of course Montaigne did not invent the essay: "The word is late," Francis Bacon observed, "but the thing is ancient." Long before Montaigne's book saw light, Plato and Cicero, Marcus Aurelius and Seneca, Plutarch and Theophrastus, as well as Chuang-Tzu and the author of *Ecclesiastes,* composed short prose works limited in scope, unified in subject, thoughtful in approach—works which fulfill nearly all the dictionary criteria for *essay.*

The criteria nevertheless belie common reading experience. There is no paradigm of the essay, no Platonic ideal, no form with strict rules; and prescriptive definitions of the essay are the illusions of dictionary-makers and absolutists in literary criticism. Older anthologies labeled the contents of their collections meticulously: They distinguished between informal and formal, open and closed, and among argumentative, critical, descriptive, expository, and narrative essays. Yet it ought to be clear that an essay may attempt (remember that "essay" implies "attempt") all or several of the types within its boundaries. Sally Kempton's "Cutting Loose" and Piri Thomas's "Real Jesse Jameses" are examples of essays that cut across categories that might confine expression or limit the vision of the writer.

To make an essay requires something that wants saying and a voice that will say it—a subject and a speaker. The subject may be anything in the world or beyond it, not excepting the world and the beyond. The essayist may sketch a geography of fiction like Leslie Fiedler, may walk deliberately along the edge of madness (like R. D. Laing), probe the possibilities of human immortality (like Alan Harrington), or coolly analyze a pathology (like Louis Jolyon West). And his voice may be urgent, ironic, restrained, strident, muted, angry, meditative, or hortatory, like Germaine Greer's, Tom Wolfe's, John Fowles's, or Jean-Paul Sartre's.

An utterly open form, the essay shuts out no subject, puts down no voice. At its best though, Leslie Fiedler points out, the essay has the tone of conversation, "a printed conversation between our best 'I' and an ideal 'you.'" Since conversation worth listening to denies the laws of limit, the modern essay embraces editorials ("The Immortalist Argument"), interviews ("A Talk with Konrad Lorenz"), autonomous segments of books ("Real Jesse Jameses" and "Boxing the Compass"), Letters ("Letters from Mexico"), confessions ("Cutting Loose"), aphorisms ("Sexual Freedom"), extended definitions ("What Is Existentialism?"), and life-philosophies ("Hope, Faith, Fortitude"). It excludes no contained composition animated by individuality—not if the "ideal 'you'" apprehends it as essay.

Generally, the essay is a nonfictional prose work of "moderate length." As it strains toward creative utterance, however, it may resemble fiction closely. Tom Wolfe in "O Rotten Gotham—Sliding Down the Behavioral Sink" characterizes and quotes the people who figure in his reportage, much as a short story writer might. Piri Thomas's "Real Jesse Jameses" makes use of fictional techniques, arranging reality for particular effects. Ken Kesey includes the plot of a story in one of his letters, and Sally Kempton appears to be writing an autobiographical novel. The essay may also be of quite immoderate length (Rollo May's "What Is Existentialism?" for example), and it may even invoke verse. And now we have photographic and video essays—which, unfortunately, we cannot represent in this medium (no message is intended by this necessary omission).

Despite its wider scope and greater freedom of form today, the essay has changed less drastically than other genres represented in this collection.

The chief difference between the old and new forms is that the former tended to be full dress, and the latter tends to be undress. This development may justly be termed reactionary; for Montaigne in 1580 told his readers that he would in his *Essais* shun "straining and artifice," proceed by "leaps and gambols" and welcome "the words that are used in the streets of France." The modern essayist appears to be carrying out Montaigne's aspiration. He records the language of the street or the jail block or the video "freak" and he rejects directives concerning structure or content. He insists on freedom; he hopes to create literature, but in any case he insists on freedom.

Because they belong to our generation, the essayists represented in this book—in spite of their diverse tones, styles, themes, and ages—show us, often luminously, the nature of our sensibility, the sensibility of the seventies. They may offer us small comfort, perhaps, but they engage us directly. They examine, confront, explain, denounce, or defend institutions, movements, and people, ideas and convictions that are immediately important or pertinent to our lives. Whatever their verb inflection, these essays achieve present tense in our consciousness.

Boxing the Compass

Leslie Fiedler

Leslie Fiedler is not easy to characterize, though he has been called a teacher/critic. He was born in Newark in 1917 and educated at New York University (B.A. in 1938) and the University of Wisconsin (Ph.D. in 1941). He taught for nearly twenty years at the University of Montana, where he owned a ranch and was made an honorary member of the Blackfoot tribe. In 1964, he came to the State University of New York at Buffalo and has been there ever since, with interludes as a visiting professor in England, France, Greece, and Italy. Among his best known works are *The End of Innocence* (1955), *Love and Death in the American Novel* (1966), *No in Thunder* (1960), and *Waiting for the End* (1964). His critical position in these arguments is that American literature very often deals subconsciously with the theme of the male escape from a female-dominated society, particularly as it can be studied in classical American literature. He has also written a novel, *The Second Stone* (1963), a collection of short stories, *Pull Down Vanity* (1962), and an account of his son's and his own arrest over an alleged infraction of the marijuana law, *Being Busted* (1969). He has also written a study of Shakespeare. An original and often brilliant thinker, he is at his best in the following essay taken from *The Return of the Vanishing American* (1968). He shrewdly observes that geography in a mobile America has become a state of mind, a development long signaled by our literature.

Geography in the United States is mythological. From the earliest times, American writers have tended to define their own country—and much of our literature has, consequently, tended to define itself—topologically, as it were, in terms of the four cardinal directions: a mythicized North, South, East, and West. Correspondingly, there have always been four kinds of American books: Northerns, Southerns, Easterns, and Westerns, though we have been accustomed, for reasons not immediately clear, to call only the last by its name. Not all American books, of course, fit into one or another of these geographical categories, or even some canny blend of them; yet much of our most distinguished literature is thus mythologically oriented and can be fully appreciated only in this light.

The Northern tends to be tight, gray, low-keyed, underplayed, avoiding melodrama where possible—sometimes, it would seem, at all costs. Typically, its scene is domestic, an isolated household set in a hostile environment. The landscape is mythicized New England, "stern and

SOURCE: Leslie Fiedler, *The Return of the Vanishing American* (Los Angeles: Stein & Day, 1968), pp. 16–28.

rock-bound," the weather deep winter: a milieu appropriate to the austerities and deprivations of Puritanism.

> Here where the wind is always north-north-east
> And children learn to walk on frozen toes . . .
> Passion is here a soilure of the wits,
> We're told, and love a cross for them to bear . . .

In the field of the novel, the Northern is represented, in general, by books easier to respect than to relish, since there is not much savor in them, books which could easily be thought of as *belles lettres,* fit for readers seeking loftier satisfactions than pleasure in a time when Christianity had been replaced by the Religion of Culture. The *other* novels of Harriet Beecher Stowe (*The Mayflower,* for instance, or *The Minister's Wooing*—the sort of thing she wrote when the demon which dictated *Uncle Tom's Cabin* deserted her) are a good instance of the type, as is most of William Dean Howells, a little of Henry James, and, supereminently, Edith Wharton's *Ethan Frome:* a dismal lot on the whole.

The Scarlet Letter is an apparent exception to these observations; it seems a *pre*-Northern, finally, describing the mythological origins of a world which wholly contains the later, true Northern. Actually, the Northern works better in verse than in prose, as a rule: in the narrative poems of Robert Frost, for instance, notably, say, "The Witch of Cöos"; in much of Edward Arlington Robinson, whose sonnet on New England is quoted above by way of illustration; and most recently in the work of Robert Lowell. One of its classics, however, is a prose poem in the form of a journal, Henry David Thoreau's *Walden,* which defines once and for all the archetypal essence of the transplanted lonely WASP in the midst of, or better, *against* the Massachusetts wilderness—in the course of which encounter, he becomes transformed into the Yankee. (But when he floated, somewhat earlier, at ease and with his brother for a companion, on the voyage whose diaries he made into *A Week on the Concord and Merrimack Rivers,* it is a Western he lived and wrote.)

The Southern, though its name is not quite so standardly used as that of the Western, is at least as well-known, perhaps too familiar to need definition at all. Certainly it is the most successful of all the topological subgenres of the novel in America, as triumphant on the highbrow level—from, say, Edgar Allan Poe through William Faulkner to Truman Capote or Flannery O'Connor—as on that of mass entertainment—from another side of that same Poe to Thomas Dixon's *The Clansman* (which suggested to D. W. Griffith the plot of *The Birth of a Nation*) or Margaret Mitchell's *Gone With the Wind* (the movie version of which leads an immortal life). The Southern has always challenged the distinction between High and Pop Art, since not merely Poe, its founder, but such latter-day successors of his as

Faulkner and Capote have thriven in the two presumably sundered worlds of critical esteem and mass approval.

Perhaps this is because the Southern, as opposed to the Northern, does not avoid but seeks melodrama, a series of bloody events, sexual by implication at least, played out in the blood-heat of a "long hot summer" against a background of miasmal swamps, live oak, Spanish moss, and the decaying plantation house so dear to the hearts of movie-makers. Indeed, until there were ruined plantations—which is to say, until the Civil War, defeat, and Reconstruction—there could be no true Southern (Poe, being ante-bellum, had to imagine the doomed mansions appropriate to his horrors in a mythical Europe). The mode of the Southern is Gothic, American Gothic, and the Gothic requires a haunted house at its center. It demands also a symbolic darkness to cloak its action, a "blackness of darkness" which in the Old World was associated with the remnants of feudalism and especially with the dark-cowled ministers and "Black Nobility" of the Church.

What the Church and feudal aristocracy were for European Gothic, the Negro became for the American variety, "the Black," as he is mythologically called, being identified by that name with the nightmare terror which the writer of Southerns seeks to evoke, with the deepest guilts and fears of transplanted Europeans in a slaveholding community, or more properly, in a community which remembers having sent its sons to die in a vain effort to sustain slavery. But projecting those guilts and fears out upon the Blacks, draining himself of all his vital darkness, as it were, the European in the South condemned himself to a kind of mythological anemia; he became "Whitey."

Without the Negro, in any case, there is no true Southern. And whoever treated the Negro in our fiction—until urbanization changed everything—tended to write a Southern, whether he thought of himself as doing so or not; unless, of course, like Mark Twain in *Huckleberry Finn,* he turned his Negro protagonist into a Noble Savage, i.e. an Indian in blackface. Only where Jim is really a "nigger," i.e. at the very beginning and end of the novel where he plays the comic darky, or at certain points on the raft where he "camps" the role, addressing Huck as his "young master," does *Huckleberry Finn* become anything like a Southern; most of the way it is something quite other which we still have not defined. And occasionally it even threatens to become an Eastern, or a parody of one, when the Duke and the Dauphin bring their European pretensions aboard the raft; for the Eastern deals with the American confronting Europe, and cultural pretension is as essential to it as tourism.

Customarily, the Eastern treats the return of the American to the Old World (only then does he know for sure that he *is* an American), his Old Home, the place of origin of his old self, that original Adam, whom the New World presumably made a New Man. Its season is most appropriately spring, when the ice of New England symbolically breaks and all things seem—for a little while—possible; and, as is appropriate to that erotic time of year, it deals often with love (*The Roman Spring of Mrs. Stone* is the protypical title of one Eastern, the single novel of Tennessee Williams, who turned from his mythological South when he briefly forsook drama): the flirtation of the American, usually female, with the European, most often male. Sometimes, as in Henry James's *The Ambassadors,* the sexual-mythological roles are reversed, or, as in James Baldwin's *Giovanni's Room,* both are males, though one suspects Baldwin's Giovanni of being a Negro disguised as a European, and the book consequently of being a disguised Southern. In any event, the distribution of the sexes makes little difference in the Eastern, the encounter of European and American being doomed to frustration by the very nature of the case. This is so in part because the American turns out to be impelled by motives not so much truly erotic as merely anti-anti-erotic, and in part because, being not an émigré or a cosmopolitan but only a tourist (the Eastern is the form which defines the American precisely as a "tourist"), he—or, alternatively, she—has to go home.

It is Henry James (who may have sent his Lambert Strethers home, but who never returned to stay himself) whom we think of as the High Priest of the cult of the Eastern, or even as its Founder, though Nathaniel Hawthorne in *The Marble Faun,* and James Fenimore Cooper before him in *Homeward Bound,* were there first. Even so unadventurous a laureate of the middle classes as Henry Wadsworth Longfellow tried his hand at the Eastern, by implication in his verse translations and adaptations of European models, quite explicitly in such a novel as *Kavanaugh: A Tale.* But James began his career by asserting a claim to the form in *The American,* a claim which came to seem more and more exclusively his as he produced example after example (turning his hand to an occasional Northern like *The Bostonians* as a breather) until he could write no more. And with James—not so much originally as after his revival in the twenties—the Eastern became associated with that Culture Religion, so virulent in the United States between the two world wars.

Basic to that worship of High Art was the dogma that there are some books, in fiction chiefly those of James himself, an appreciation of which distinguishes the elect from the vulgar, the sensitive from the gross, and that those books can be known immediately because *a*) they are set in Europe, *b*) they mention other works of art, often so casually that only the cognoscenti know them without the aid of footnotes, and *c*) they are written by expatriates. Obviously, most of the poetry of T. S. Eliot and much of Ezra Pound ("tourist" or Eastern poetry *par excellence*) falls into this category, quite in the style of their long unsuspected counterpart in the mid-nineteenth century—bound to them by many affinities besides a common love for Dante and a preference for being "abroad"—Longfellow himself.

Not all Easterns, however, belong in intention or in retrospect to the realm of self-conscious High Art; if any book which deals with the reaction of the American abroad (via tourism or dreams) belongs to the genre, Mark Twain was one of its most assiduous practitioners, all the way from *Innocents Abroad* to *A Connecticut Yankee in King Arthur's Court*. And in our own century, we have had Scott Fitzgerald's *Tender Is the Night,* a borderline case, perhaps, as well as most of the novels by Hemingway, who thought of himself, surely, as an emulator more of Twain than of James. But not everything is what it seems to a superficial scrutiny; and looking hard at Hemingway's *The Sun Also Rises* and *For Whom the Bell Tolls,* we discover that certain characters whom he represents as Spanish peasants seem mighty like Montana or Upper Michigan Indians—and that consequently he is actually writing, if not quite Westerns, at least crypto-Westerns, since it is the presence of the Indian which defines the mythological West.

The heart of the Western is not the confrontation with the alien landscape (by itself this produces only the Northern), but the encounter with the Indian, that utter stranger for whom our New World is an Old Home, that descendant of neither Shem nor Japheth, nor even, like the Negro imported to subdue the wild land, Ham. No grandchild of Noah, he escapes completely the mythologies we brought with us from Europe, demands a new one of his own. Perhaps he was only a beast of the wildwood, the first discoverers of America reassured themselves, not human at all; and at the end of the fifteenth century, Princes of the Church gravely discussed whether, being undescended from Adam, the Indian indeed had a soul like our own. It was a question by no means settled once and for all when the Church answered "yes"; for at the beginning of our own century, Lawrence amended that answer to "yes, but—" Yes, a soul, but *not* one precisely like our own, except as our own have the potentiality of becoming like his.

And in the five hundred years between, how the Indian in his ultimate otherness has teased and baffled the imagination of generation after generation of European voyagers and settlers. How they have tried to assimilate him to more familiar human types, to their own mythologic stock-in-trade. The name "Indian" itself memorializes the first misguided effort of Columbus to assure himself that he was in those other, those *East* Indies, after all, and confronting nothing but types known since Marco Polo, like the inhabitants of Cipango or Cathay.

After that delusion had collapsed, after the invention as opposed to the mere discovery of America, there were new explainers-away eager to identify the Red Men with the Welsh, the Irish—and especially the Semites, the lost Tribes of Israel.

Only the minority group comprising "scientific" anthropologists have clung in our time to the delusion of Columbus, postulating a migration from continent to continent which makes our Indians kin to the subjects of the Great Khan after all. And only a handful of nuts have been willing to identify the Indians as survivors of quite another world, another creation—refugees from Atlantis or Mu. Lawrence was tempted to the latter alternative, hinting somewhat mysteriously of an affinity between the western Indians, at least, and the priesthood of the lost Pacific civilization, "the world once splendid in the fulness of the other way of knowledge."

"They seem to lie under the last spell of the Pacific influence," he says of the Redskins of Cooper's *The Prairie;* "they have the grace and physical voluptuousness . . . of the lands of the great Ocean." But the deep imagination of Americans has sought stubbornly to link the Savages of the New World with the once-Chosen People of the Old.

From those apostles to the Indians of the seventeenth century who thought of themselves as penetrating the wilderness to restore the Old Testament to those to whom it properly belonged, through Fenimore Cooper in the early nineteenth, recounting the adventures of just such a deluded missionary in the form of Parson Amen in *Oak Openings* (to whom the bewildered Redskins object that, being Indians, they can never be *lost*), to the later Mormons, incorporating the wrong-headed myth in their homemade scriptures, and the rancher of *Cat Ballou,* baffled at the Indian who refuses to answer his Hebrew greeting of "*Shalom!*"—the tradition has never died.

It is, in fact, carried from door to door even now by missionaries for the Church of Latter Day Saints, who leave behind them the *Book of Mormon,* complete with a prefatory gloss that sends those eager to know the "Fate of Indians" to the fourteenth verse of the thirteenth chapter of *First Nephi:*

> And it came to pass that I beheld multitudes of the Gentiles upon the land of promise; and I beheld the wrath of God, that it was upon the seed of my brethren; and they were scattered before the Gentiles and were smitten.

This may be, to true believers, a sufficient mythological explanation not only of the origin, but of the expropriation of the Indians. To the Indians themselves, however, though they may be in fact as stubborn and persistent witnesses as the Jews, it remains inconceivable that they can be anything so familiar to the three thousand-year-old tradition of the White West as mere children of Israel, that they can be anything but their untranslatable selves.

Everything else which belongs to the Western scene has long since been assimilated: the prairies subdivided and landscaped; the mountains staked off as hunting preserves and national parks; fabulous beasts, like the grizzlies and the buffalo, killed or fenced in as tourist attractions; even the mythological season of the Western, that nonexistent interval between summer and fall called "Indian summer," become just another part of the White year. Only the Indian survives, however ghetto-ized, debased, and debauched, to remind us with his alien stare of the new kind of space in which the baffled refugees from Europe first found him (an unhumanized vastness), and the new kind of time through which, despite all our efforts, he still moves (a historyless antiquity). It is for this reason that tales set in the West seem to us not quite Westerns, unfulfilled occasions for myth rather than myth itself, when no Indian—"stern and imperturbable warrior" or lovely, complaisant squaw, it scarcely matters—appears in them.

The Western story in archetypal form is, then, a fiction dealing with the confrontation in the wilderness of a transplanted WASP and a radically alien other, an Indian—leading either to a metamorphosis of the WASP into something neither White nor Red (sometimes by adoption, sometimes by sheer emulation, but *never* by actual miscegenation), or else to the annihilation of the Indian (sometimes by castration-conversion or penning off into a ghetto, sometimes by sheer murder). In either case, the tensions of the encounter are resolved by eliminating one of the mythological partners—by ritual or symbolic means in the first instance, by physical force in the second. When the first method is used, possibilities are opened up for another kind of Western, a secondary Western dealing with the adventures of that New Man, the American *tertium quid;* but when the second is employed—our homegrown Final Solution—the Western disappears as a living form, for the West has, in effect, been made into an East.

But into what exactly is the transplanted European converted by the Western encounter when he resists resolving it by genocide? It is easy enough to name the aspects of Americans defined by the three other forms: the Northern, in which we become Yankees; the Southern, in which we are turned into Whitey; the Eastern, in which we are revealed as Tourists. But the transformation effected in the Western evades easy definition. Thinking of Natty Bumppo (that first not-quite-White man of our literature, for all his boasts about having "no cross in my blood") and his descendants, we are tempted to say that it is the woodsman which the ex-European becomes beside his Red companion: the hunter, the trapper, the frontiersman, the pioneer, at last the cowboy—or maybe only next-to-last, for after him comes the beatnik, the hippie, one more wild man seeking the last West of Haight-Ashbury in high-heeled boots and blue jeans. But even as he ceases to be beatnik and becomes fully hippie, the ultimate Westerner ceases to be White at all and turns back into the Indian, his boots becoming moccasins, his hair bound in an Indian headband, and a string of beads around his neck—to declare that he has fallen not merely out of Europe, but out of the Europeanized West, into an aboriginal and archaic America.

It is tempting, at this point, to take the dilemma as the answer, and to settle for saying that, since this new kind of man came into existence only with the West, he is best called simply the "Westerner," that there is no way of moving beyond this. But we know, too, that at the moment of looking into the eyes of the Indian, the European becomes the "American" as well as the Westerner. And if we forget it for a moment, there is the title of Henry James's early novel to remind us: his account of a white barbarian from San Francisco, actually called —with a bow to Columbus—Christopher Newman. And who has more right than the man from the farthest West to be called both new and American, since before a single White man had set foot on American soil, the whole continent had been dreamed by Europe as "the West": a legendary place beyond or under the ocean wave, a land of the dead or those who rise from the dead. And it needed only the invention of the name America to set up the equation *America equals the West.*

Once the Atlantic was crossed, moreover, the name *West* was transferred, step by step, to whatever part of the continent lured men on just over the line of settlement, to the unexplored space behind the next natural barrier, past the Appalachians, the Mississippi, the Rockies. Vermont or Maine may define our North once and for all; Georgia, Alabama, or Louisiana may circumscribe our mythological South; the harbors of Boston and New York City, ports from which tourists embark for the adventure of returning to the Old World, can scarcely be thought of as anything but the East.

But where, geographically, is the elusive West? We know that first of all it was Virginia itself, the Old Dominion, then New England, Pennsylvania, Kentucky, Louisiana, Ohio, Missouri, Texas, the Oregon Territory, etc., etc.—always a bloody ground just over the horizon, or just this side of it, where we confronted *in their own territory* the original possessors of the continent.

So long as a single untamed Indian inhabits it, any piece of American space can become to the poet's imagination an authentic West, as the small Vermont town of Acton was transformed, even in the twentieth century, by the vision of Robert Frost's extraordinary poem "The Vanishing Red." Beginning with the lines: "He is said to have been the last Red Man in Acton. And the Miller is said to have laughed . . ." it ends by becoming a parable of the war to the death between White Man and Red, though Frost pretends, ironically, to refuse to tell it:

> It's too long a story to go into now.
> You'd have to have been there and lived it.
> Then you wouldn't have looked on it just as a matter
> Of who began it between the two races.

It is, however, only a desperate sort of Last Western, a hymn to the end of one more West, that Frost manages to write, as seems appropriate to our time. For, by and large, we have used up the mythological space of the West along with its native inhabitants, and there are no new places for which we can light out ahead of the rest—even Alaska being only a fiftieth state. Can we reestablish the West anywhere at all, then? This is the question that troubles certain of our writers, eager to dream the old American dreams. The earth, it turns out, is mythologically as well as geographically round; the lands across the Pacific will not do, since on the rim of the second ocean, West becomes East, our whole vast land (as Columbus imagined, and Whitman nostalgically remembered at the opening of the Suez Canal) a Passage to India.

Maybe the moon will serve our purposes, or Mars; maybe up and out will turn out to be a true archetypal equivalent to the Way West, as we have already begun to surmise, calling some of the literature of space adventure "space operas," on the model of "horse operas," which is to say, Westerns. But unless "stern and imperturbable" Martians await us, or lovely and complaisant lady Lunatics—as certain makers of science fiction have already tried to assure us—whom we can assimilate to our old myths of the Indian, Outer Space will not seem an extension of our original America, the America which shocked and changed Europe, but a second, a meta-America, which may shock and change us. On our shores, the myth of the West which had teased the European imagination up to the time of Dante—the myth of an unattainable and unpeopled world—was altered into one of a world open to "plantation," but inhabited by hostile aliens: a myth so deeply rooted in us that, in spite of scientific testimony to the contrary, we insist on imagining the New Worlds we now approach inhabited by natives, "savages" benign or threatening.

We have defined the "territory ahead" for too long in terms of the mythologies created out of our meeting with and response to the Indians to abandon them without a struggle. They have proved sufficiently adaptable to describe our relations with Negroes and Polynesians, with all colored peoples, in fact (Twain's Nigger Jim and Melville's Queequeg are mythological blood brothers, after all, to Cooper's Chingachgook); and we dream of taking those same terms with us into a future not quite so terrifying and unfamiliar as it sometimes seems, if only they will work there, too.

Sexual Freedom

John Fowles

Novelist John Fowles was born in 1926, in Essex, England. After taking honors in literature at Oxford (1950), he taught in France and Greece and served as head of the English Department of a London college. While on military duty with the Royal Marines, he rose to the rank of lieutenant. His first novel, *The Collector* (1963), was an immediate best-seller, and *The Magus* (1965) has already become a classic with college students. *The French Lieutenant's Woman* (1968) marked him as a writer of great power and imagination. All three of his novels have been made into films. The following selection is from *Aristos* (1964), a self-portrait in ideas. As a book of wisdom, it is complementary but often opposite to Norman O. Brown's *Love's Body.*

Fowles lives in Highgate, London, with his wife. He collects old books and old china and is deeply concerned with the ecological crisis of our time.

97 Whatever the professional guardians of public morality say, something more than a mere loss of morality and 'decency' is involved in sex's meteoric advent from behind the curtains and crinolines of Victorian modesty and propriety. It may be a flight from chastity; if right judgement is comparing the present generation with past generations, it is a flight from chastity. But it is also a flight to something.

98 In most societies the unofficial attitude to sexual morality now is that at any rate among unmarried adults there is nothing inherently sinful or criminal about sexual experiences and adventures, whether or not they are accompanied by love, which I will define as the desire to maintain a relationship irrespective of the sexual and, in the final analysis, any other enjoyment to be got from it.

99 Adultery is the disproof of a marriage rather than its betrayal; and divorce is a therapeutic means of purging or ending an unhealthy situation. It no longer in normal circumstances has any moral smell. It is like a visit to an operating theatre. Nature is more likely to be to blame than the individual.

100 But the official attitude, as expressed by churches, newspapers, governments, and in many cases by laws, is that coitus before and outside marriage is always in some way sinful and anti-social.

SOURCE: John Fowles, *The Aristos* (Boston: Little, Brown, 1970), pp. 167–75.

101 The social importance we grant to sex lies very much in this forbidden-allowed tension; this deserved-undeserved, this licit-illicit, this private-public, this defiant-submissive, this rebelling-conforming experience. As in all such situations there is plenty of evidence of countersupporting. 'Morality' attacks 'immorality' and gets pleasure and energy from it; 'immorality' tries to defend itself from or to evade 'morality', and gets pleasure and energy from the defence and the evasion.

102 There is of course a fundamental unreality about the official attitude; it is in only a few peripheral areas (such as prostitution and abortion) that its views can be enforced; and if the children know that the farmer can never actually chase them out of most of the orchard with the tempting apples, then of course they have an added inducement to steal them. In any case, we are here dealing with children who would dispute the ownership of the orchard in the first place. We may thus conclude that the opponents of sexual freedom are in fact among its greatest propagators.

103 The result of this ambiguous situation has been the apotheosis of the illicit sexual relationship—illicit, that is, by the standards of official public morality. The time-honoured name for this sort of relationship is the affaire, though the original French phrase (*affaire de coeur*) suggests precisely what the modern puritans complain is lacking. Our affaires now are much more *de corps* than *de coeur*.

104 The dangers of the affaire are well known. Free love does not encourage true love. The emotional instability that gets one into bed is unlikely to change into the emotional stability one needs when one has to get out. Venereal diseases spread. Neuroses spread. Broken marriages increase, and the innocent children of them suffer, and in their turn breed suffering. It is beyond all these formidable monsters, trackless forests, quagmires, dark nights of the soul, that the Holy Grail, the entirely happy affaire, shines. On the other hand there can be detected in many denunciations of it a pathological dislike of sexual pleasure; and a neutral may well find this kind of 'morality' as prejudiced as the alleged 'bestiality' of the enemy.

105 Sexual attraction and the sexual act are in themselves innocent, neither intrinsically moral nor immoral. Sex is like all great forces: simply a force. We may judge this or that manifestation or situation of the force as moral or immoral; but not the force itself.

106 Coitus is, even at its most animal, the best ritualization of the nature of the whole, of the nature of reality. Part of its mystery is that it has (except as, by current standards, a perversion) to be celebrated in private and learnt in private and enjoyed in private. Part of its pleasure is that it allows infinite variety, both physically and emotionally; in partner and place and mood and manner and time. So the problem may be reduced to this. How can society best allow the individual to experience this profound mystery and variety of pleasure without causing harm?

107 The main sociological argument against the *affaire de corps* is that it instills a natural taste for promiscuity and therefore encourages adultery. This seems more likely to be true than the counter-argument: that it helps in the eventual choice of a husband or wife and makes a good marriage more probable. This might conceivably be true if young people had the time and the opportunity and the emotional detachment for a wide range of affaires before marriage; but few have. Many such *affaires*, entered into by psychologically immature and trend-copying young people, lead to disastrous marriages and permanent maladjustments.

108 What in any case is at least as evil as the affaire itself is a situation in which, beckoning in its aura of amoral modernity, it stands as a smart sanctuary, an escape from the pressures of society, as a recompense for having to die, as all sorts of things it partly is but should not essentially be. For in an age where such a relationship still has to be described as officially illicit it is obvious that however innocently it is entered and enjoyed, it will be in conflict with all those unpermissive modes of thought and conscience, the communal superego, that society has had us taught.

109 Most adolescents and pre-adults are naturally confused by two drives that mimic each other: the drive towards sexual experience (in itself part of a deeper drive towards the hazardous and adventurous) and the drive towards love as institutionalized in marriage (in itself part of the drive towards certainty and security). They find it difficult to separate the two; what starts as one can in even a few moments become the other. A desire to kiss becomes the desire to live together for a lifetime, the decision to marry becomes the abrupt yearning for another body.

110 Much more of the sexual education of adolescents should be devoted to teaching them the aetiology of love; this is just as important as the physiology of coitus.

111 There is a widespread belief that love and sex are incompatible. That if you have considerable sexual experience you cannot love (Don Juan); and that if you love (maintain a permanent relationship like marriage) you will sooner or later cease to enjoy sex. The belief is strengthened by the regarding of marriage as a mere licensing of sex instead of as an affirmation of love. If you sternly forbid the affaire to the unmarried, you must not expect them to understand marriage for what it should be: the intention to love, not the desire to enjoy coitus licitly.

112 The charm of the illicit sexual experience is sometimes almost as much that it is illicit as that it is sexual. When Meaulnes eventually refound his *domaine perdu, domaine sans nom,* when at last he met the mysterious Yvonne de Galais again, what did he do? He ran away after the very first night of their marriage.

113 When the individual is being attacked on all sides by the forces of anti-individuality; by the nemo; by the sense that death is absolute, by the dehumanizing processes of both mass production and mass producing: the affaire represents not only an escape into the enchanted garden of the ego but also a quasi-heroic gesture of human defiance.

114 Just as art is being used by the individual as an outlet for the resentments caused by the inadequacies of society, so is the affaire. It is a day spent playing truant from an excruciatingly dull and wintry school. The whole of contemporary popular art is based on this notion. Listen to the lyrics of 'pop' music. Compare the sexuality of a figure like James Bond with that of figures like Maigret or Sherlock Holmes.

115 The same can be said for advertising. Cigarettes are not recommended for their quality as cigarettes but as the right accompaniment to the affaire; recipients, the advertisers say, can be 'won', 'seduced', 'enchanted' (shades of the love philtre) by all sorts of innocent objects —chocolates, pens, jewelry, packaged holidays, and the rest. Similar tendencies can be seen in much car and clothing advertising, though here the appeal is that of the aphrodisiac rather than of the love philtre. This car makes a man more virile; this dress suggests a Messalina. Even fabrics have moral associations woven into them by the publicity men. You no longer buy black leather, you buy its suggestions of sadistic perversion.

116 The extramarital affaire becomes particularly siren-like after several years of marriage. There is among husbands a kind of *nostalgie de la vierge,* among wives a longing for a life outside the domestic prison, those grim four walls constituted by husband, children, housework and kitchen. In men the desire seems to be directly sexual. In women it may be a more complex longing. But in both cases it is a flight from reality; and if children are involved, a flight from responsibility.

117 For the would-be adulterous husband or wife the pressures to enter into an affaire may be less, and the penalties greater, than they are for the unmarried person. The moral issue is generally much clearer; but other factors, such as the sharper sense of failure or dissatisfaction that age brings, the memory of premarital affaires (or the memory of the lack of them), the monotony of marriage and the general climate of a society intoxicated by permissivity, may make the objectively clear issue subjectively harder to see now than ever before in history.

118 Pleasure may come to seem a responsibility; while responsibility may rarely come to seem what it can be, a pleasure. How many marriages break because so many marriages break?

119 When the whole philosophy of a capitalist society can be reduced to this: You owe yourself as much as you can get, whether it be in money, in status, in possessions, in enjoyments, or in experiences. Can pleasure not become a duty?

120 The tendency of any capitalist society is to turn all experiences and relationships into objects, objects that can be assessed on the same scale of values as washing machines and central heating, that is, by the comparative cheapness of the utility and pleasurability to be derived from it. Furthermore, the tendency in an overpopulated and inflation-fearing society is to make things expendable, and therefore to make expendability a virtue and pleasure. Throw the old object away and get a new. As we are haunted by the affaire, so are we haunted by the pursuit of the new, and these ghosts are brothers.

121 Fathers and mothers no longer see their children as children; as they grow they see them increasingly as rivals in the enjoyment race. What is more, rivals who seem bound to win. However harmless it is, whenever a change of social habits brings more pleasure into the world, some older people will object, simply because they had to do without the change when they were young, and others will frantically and foolishly try to catch up. It is not just chastity, morality and marriage that are under attack, but the whole traditional concept of what we are and what we are for.

122 Some suggest that we are moving into an age when it will be considered normal that one should have sexual relationships as one wants and with whom one wants, regardless of other social ties. They say this will be possible because copulation will come to seem no more significant than dancing or conversing as one wants or with whom one wants. In such a society there would be nothing exceptionable about coitus in public; and the queues that now form to see Fonteyn and Nureyev would form to see skilled practitioners in an even older art. We should, in short, have returned to ancient pre-Christian ideas of sex as an activity that does not require any special privacy, nor evoke any special inhibitions. It is dimly possible that this depuritanization of sex will one day take place; but for as long as the present sexual conventions, licit and illicit, supply some deeper need of man in an unsatisfying society, it will not.

123 In an education in humanity the teaching on this matter must surely be based on the following considerations:

(A) One great argument for more teaching of self-analysis, and for more analysis of the self in general, is that half the pain caused by the affaire and the broken marriage, and the very causing itself, is due to the ignorance of each of both each and the other.

(B) The excessive commercialization of sex, and especially of the affaire, is not the brightest jewel in capitalism's crown.

(C) Of all activities, sex is the least amenable to general judgements. It is always relative, always situational. It is as silly to proscribe it as to prescribe it. All that can be done is to educate about it.

(D) To teach the physiology of sex without the psychology of love is to teach all about a ship except how to steer it.

(E) Spokesmen for 'morality' have no right to condemn or to try to prevent any kind of sexual relationship unless they can demonstrate that it is bringing society more unhappiness than happiness. It is always easy to produce illegitimacy, divorce, and venereal disease statistics; but the statistics of sexual happiness are harder to come by.

(F) A child is a law against adultery; and though an adulterer can no longer break the law, he can still break the child. But as children grow, divorce becomes less and less a crime, since the disharmony the growing child increasingly takes note of may do as much harm as the ending of the marriage.

(G) Just as surgery can be abused, so can divorce. But that a thing can be abused is never an argument against it.

(H) The noblest relationship is marriage, that is, love. Its nobility resides in its altruism, the desire to serve another beyond all the pleasures of the relationship; and in its refusal ever to regard the other as a thing, an object, a utilizability.

(I) Sex is an exchange of pleasures, of needs; love is a giving without return.

(J) It is this giving without return, this helping without reward, this surplus of pure good, that identifies the uniqueness of man as well as the true nature of the true marriage. This is the quintessence the great alchemy of sex is for; and every adultery adulterates it, every infidelity betrays it, every cruelty clouds it.

Hope, Faith, Fortitude

Erich Fromm

Psychoanalyst and philosopher, Erich Fromm was born in 1900 in Frankfurt-am-Main, Germany. He was trained at the Universities of Heidelberg and Munich and at the Psychoanalytic Institute in Berlin. Until 1932 he worked in Frankfurt's Psychoanalytic Institute and taught at the university. In 1934, he came to the United States and lectured in social psychology at Columbia, Yale, and Bennington College. He held a professorship at New York University, and between the years 1955 to 1966, he was head of the department of psychoanalysis of the medical school at the National Autonomous University of Mexico. For the last twenty-five years, his work has centered around the development of psychoanalytic theory both in its clinical aspects and in its relation to cultural, social, and philosophical problems.

He has written *Escape from Freedom* (1941), an inquiry into the meaning of freedom and of the forces that tempt men to seek escape from it into authoritarianism, and *Man for Himself* (1947), which develops the belief that man must determine his own standards of behavior. His later books include *The Forgotten Language* (1951), *The Sane Society* (1955), *The Art of Loving* (1956), *May Man Prevail?* (1961), and *The Revolution of Hope* (1968), from which the following piece is taken.

Erich Fromm writes about this essay:

> . . . one can neither understand nor help a person unless one pays the same attention to hope, faith, love, integrity, identity, which has usually been given to doubt, hate, anxiety and fear. Usually the former attitudes are considered as belonging to ethics and philosophy, rather than to psychoanalysis. But clinical experience can show that the lack of hope or faith, the absence of integrity and a sense of identity, can lead to psychic disturbances no less severe than any of the more conventional "complexes" considered in psychopathology.

His essay attempts to give concrete and affective meaning to these three abstract concepts.

1. WHAT HOPE IS NOT

Hope is a decisive element in any attempt to bring about social change in the direction of greater aliveness, awareness, and reason. But the nature of hope is often misunderstood and confused with attitudes that have nothing to do with hope and in fact are the very opposite.

What is it to hope?

Is it, as many think, to have desires and wishes? If this were so,

SOURCE: Erich Fromm, *The Revolution of Hope* (New York: Harper & Row, 1968), pp. 6–16. Copyright © 1968 by Erich Fromm. Reprinted by permission of Harper & Row, Publishers, Inc.

those who desire more and better cars, houses, and gadgets would be people of hope. But they are not; they are people lusty for more consumption and not people of hope.

Is it to hope if hope's object is not a thing but a fuller life, a state of greater aliveness, a liberation from eternal boredom; or, to use a theological term, for salvation; or, a political term, for revolution? Indeed, this kind of expectation could be hope; but it is non-hope if it has the quality of passiveness, and "waiting for"—until the hope becomes, in fact, a cover for resignation, a mere ideology.

Kafka has beautifully described this kind of resigned and passive hope in a story in *The Trial.* A man comes to the door leading into heaven (the Law) and begs admittance from the doorkeeper. The doorkeeper says he cannot admit the man at the moment. Although the door leading into the Law stands open, the man decides that he had better wait until he gets permission to enter. So he sits down and waits for days and years. He repeatedly asks to be allowed in, but is always told that he cannot be allowed to enter yet. During all these long years the man studies the doorkeeper almost incessantly and learns to know even the fleas in his fur collar. Eventually, he is old and near death. For the first time, he asks the question, "How does it come about that in all these years no one has come seeking admittance but me?" The doorkeeper answers, "No one but you could gain admittance through this door, since this door was intended for you. I am now going to shut it."

The old man was too old to understand, and maybe he would not have understood if he had been younger. The bureaucrats have the last word; if they say no, he cannot enter. If he had had more than this passive, waiting hope, he would have entered and his courage to disregard the bureaucrats would have been the liberating act which would have carried him to the shining palace. Many people are like Kafka's old man. They hope, but it is not given to them to act upon their heart's impulse, and as long as the bureaucrats do not give the green light they wait and wait.[1]

This kind of passive hope is closely related to a generalized form of hope, which might be described as hoping for *time.* Time and the future become the central category of this kind of hope. Nothing is expected to happen in the *now* but only in the next moment, the next day, the next year, and in another world if it is too absurd to believe that hope can be realized in this world. Behind this belief is the idolatry of "Future," "History," and "Posterity," which began in the French Revolution with men like Robespierre, who worshiped the future as a goddess: I do nothing; I remain passive, because I am nothing and impotent; but the future, the projection of time, will bring about what I cannot achieve. This worship of the future, which is a different aspect of the worship of "progress" in modern bourgeois thought, is precisely

[1] The Spanish word *esperar* means at the same time waiting and hoping, and quite clearly it refers to that particular kind of passive hope that I am trying to describe here.

the alienation of hope. Instead of something I do or I become, the idols, future and posterity, bring about something without my doing anything.[2]

While passive waiting is a disguised form of hopelessness and impotence, there is another form of hopelessness and despair which takes exactly the opposite disguise—the disguise of phrase making and adventurism, of disregard for reality, and of forcing what cannot be forced. This was the attitude of the false Messiahs and of the *Putsch* leaders, who had contempt for those who did not under all circumstances prefer death to defeat. In these days, this pseudo-radical disguise of hopelessness and nihilism is not rare among some of the most dedicated members of the young generation. They are appealing in their boldness and dedication but they become unconvincing by their lack of realism, sense of strategy, and, in some, by lack of love for life.[3]

2. THE PARADOX AND NATURE OF HOPE

Hope is *paradoxical.* It is neither passive waiting nor is it unrealistic forcing of circumstances that cannot occur. It is like the crouched tiger, which will jump only when the moment for jumping has come. Neither tired reformism nor pseudo-radical adventurism is an expression of hope. To hope means to be ready at every moment for that which is not yet born, and yet not become desperate if there is no birth

[2] The Stalinist concept that history decides what is right and wrong and good and evil is a direct continuation of Robespierre's idolatry of posterity. It is the extreme opposite to the position of Marx, who said, "History is nothing and does nothing. It is man who is and does." Or, in the Theses on Feuerbach, "The materialist doctrine that men are products of circumstances and upbringing, and that, therefore, changed men are products of other circumstances and changed upbringing, forgets that it is men that change circumstances and that the educator himself needs educating."

[3] Such hopelessness shines through Herbert Marcuse's *Eros and Civilization* (Boston: Beacon Press, 1955) and *One-Dimensional Man* (Beacon Press, 1964). All traditional values, like love, tenderness, concern, and responsibility, are supposed to have had meaning only in a pretechnological society. In the new technological society—one without repression and exploitation—a new man will arrive who will not have to be afraid of anything, including death, who will develop yet-unspecified needs, and who will have a chance to satisfy his "polymorphous sexuality" (I refer the reader to Freud's *Three Contributions to the Theory of Sex*); briefly, the final progress of man is seen in the regression to infantile life, the return to the happiness of the satiated baby. No wonder that Marcuse ends up in hopelessness: "The critical theory of society possesses no concepts which could bridge the gap between the present and its future; holding no promise and showing no success, it remains negative. Thus it wants to remain loyal to those who, without hope, have given and give their life to the Great Refusal" (*One-Dimensional Man,* p. 257).

These quotations show how wrong those are who attack or admire Marcuse as a revolutionary leader; for revolution was never based on hopelessness, nor can it ever be. But Marcuse is not even concerned with politics; for if one is not concerned with steps between the present and the future, one does not deal with politics, radical or otherwise. Marcuse is essentially an example of an alienated intellectual, who presents his personal despair as a theory of radicalism. Unfortunately, his lack of understanding and, to some extent, knowledge of Freud builds a bridge over which he travels to synthesize Freudianism, bourgeois materialism, and sophisticated Hegelianism into what to him and other like-minded "radicals" seems to be the most progressive theoretical construct. This is not the place to show in detail that it is a naïve, cerebral daydream, essentially irrational, unrealistic, and lacking love of life.

in our lifetime. There is no sense in hoping for that which already exists or for that which cannot be. Those whose hope is weak settle down for comfort or for violence; those whose hope is strong see and cherish all signs of new life and are ready every moment to help the birth of that which is ready to be born.

Among the confusions about hope one of the major ones is the failure to distinguish between conscious and unconscious hope. This is an error of course, which occurs with regard to many other emotional experiences, such as happiness, anxiety, depression, boredom, and hate. It is amazing that in spite of the popularity of Freud's theories his concept of the unconscious has been so little applied to such emotional phenomena. There are perhaps two main reasons for this fact. One is that in the writings of some psychoanalysts and some "philosophers of psychoanalysis" the whole phenomenon of the unconscious—that is, of repression—refers to sexual desires, and they use repression—wrongly—as synonymous with *suppression* of sexual wishes and activities. In doing so they deprive Freud's discoveries of some of their most important consequences. The second reason lies probably in the fact that it is far less disturbing for the post-Victorian generations to become aware of repressed sexual desires than of those experiences like alienation, hopelessness, and greed. To use only one of the most obvious examples: most people do not admit to themselves feelings of fear, boredom, loneliness, hopelessness—that is to say, they are *unconscious* [4] of these feelings. This is so for a simple reason. Our social pattern is such that the successful man is not supposed to be afraid or bored or lonely. He must find this world the best of all worlds in order to have the best chance for promotion; he must repress fear as well as doubt, depression, boredom, or hopelessness.

There are many who feel consciously hopeful and unconsciously hopeless, and there are a few for whom it is the other way around. What matters in the examination of hope and hopelessness is not primarily what people *think* about their feelings, but what they truly feel. This can be recognized least from their words and phrases, but can be detected from their facial expressions, their way of walking, their capacity to react with interest to something in front of their eyes, and their lack of fanaticism, which is shown in their ability to listen to reasonable argument.

The dynamic viewpoint applied in this book to social-psychological phenomena is fundamentally different from the descriptive behaviorist approach in most social-science research. From the dynamic standpoint, we are not primarily interested in knowing what a person thinks or says or how he behaves *now*. We are interested in his character structure—that is in the semipermanent structure of his energies, in the directions in which they are channeled, and in the intensity with

[4] I want to stress that speaking of "the unconscious" is another form of alienated thinking and speaking. There is no such thing as "the unconscious" as if it were an organ or a thing in space. One can be "conscious of" or "unconscious of" outer or inner events; that is, we deal with a psychic *function*, not with a localized *organ*.

which they flow. If we know the driving forces motivating behavior, not only do we understand present behavior but we can also make reasonable assumptions about how a person is likely to act under changed circumstances. In the dynamic view, surprising "changes" in a person's thought or behavior are changes which mostly could have been foreseen, given the knowledge of his character structure.

More could be said about what hope is *not,* but let us press forward and ask what hope is. Can it be described at all in words or can it only be communicated in a poem, in a song, in a gesture, in a facial expression, or in a deed?

As with every other human experience, words are insufficient to describe the experience. In fact, most of the time words do the opposite: they obscure it, dissect it, and kill it. Too often, in the process of talking about love or hate or hope, one loses contact with what one was supposed to be talking about. Poetry, music, and other forms of art are by far the best-suited media for describing human experience because they are precise and avoid the abstraction and vagueness of worn-out coins which are taken for adequate representations of human experience.

Yet, taking these qualifications seriously, it is not impossible to touch upon feeling experience in words which are not those of poetry. This would not be possible if people did not share the experience one talks about, at least to some degree. To describe it means to point out the various aspects of the experience and thus to establish a communication in which the writer and the reader know that they are referring to the same thing. In making this attempt, I must ask the reader to work with me and not expect me to give him an answer to the question of what hope is. I must ask him to mobilize his own experiences in order to make our dialogue possible.

To hope is a state of being. It is an inner readiness, that of intense but not-yet-spent activeness.[5] The concept of "activity" rests upon one of the most widespread of man's illusions in modern industrial society. Our whole culture is geared to activity—activity in the sense of being busy, and being busy in the sense of busyness (the busyness necessary for business). In fact, most people are so "active" that they cannot stand doing nothing; they even transform their so-called leisure time into another form of activity. If you are not active making money, you are active driving around, playing golf, or just chatting about nothing. What is dreaded is the moment in which you have really nothing "to do." Whether one calls this kind of behavior activity is a terminological question. The trouble is that most people who think they are very

[5] I owe the term "activeness" (instead of the usual term "activity") to a personal communication from Michael Maccoby; correspondingly I use the term passiveness instead of passivity, when activeness or passiveness refers to an attitude or state of mind.

I have discussed the problem of activity and passivity, especially in connection with the productive orientation, in several books. I want to call the reader's attention to the excellent and profound discussion of activity and passivity in *Metamorphosis* by Ernest Schachtel (New York: Basic Books, 1959).

active are not aware of the fact that they are intensely passive in spite of their "busyness." They constantly need the stimulus from the outside, be it other people's chatter, or the sight of the movies, or travel and other forms of more thrilling consumption excitements, even if it is only a new man or woman as a sexual partner. They need to be prompted, to be "turned on," tempted, seduced. They always run and never stand. They always "fall for" and never get up. And they imagine themselves to be immensely active while they are driven by the obsession to do something in order to escape the anxiety that is aroused when they are confronted with themselves.

Hope is a psychic concomitant to life and growth. If a tree which does not get sun bends its trunk to where the sun comes from, we cannot say that the tree "hopes" in the same way in which a man hopes, since hope in man is connected with feelings and awareness that the tree may not have. And yet it would not be wrong to say that the tree hopes for the sunlight and expresses this hope by twisting its trunk toward the sun. Is it different with the child that is born? He may have no awareness, yet his activity expresses his hope to be born and to breathe independently. Does the suckling not hope for his mother's breasts? Does the infant not hope to stand erect and to walk? Does the sick man not hope to be well, the prisoner to be free, the hungry to eat? Do we not hope to wake up to another day when we fall asleep? Does love making not imply a man's hope in his potency, in his capacity to arouse his partner, and the woman's hope to respond and to arouse him?

3. FAITH

When hope has gone life has ended, actually or potentially. Hope is an intrinsic element of the structure of life, of the dynamic of man's spirit. It is closely linked with another element of the structure of life: *faith*. Faith is not a weak form of belief or knowledge; it is not faith in this or that; faith is the conviction about the not yet proven, the knowledge of the real possibility, the awareness of pregnancy. Faith is rational when it refers to the knowledge of the real yet unborn; it is based on the faculty of knowledge and comprehension, which penetrates the surface and sees the kernel. Faith, like hope, is not prediction of the *future;* it is the vision of the *present* in a state of pregnancy.

The statement that faith is certainty needs a qualification. It is certainty about the reality of the possibility—but it is not certainty in the sense of unquestionable predictability. The child may be stillborn prematurely; it may die in the act of birth; it may die in the first two weeks of life. That is the paradox of faith: *it is the certainty of the uncertain.* It is certainty in terms of man's vision and comprehension; it is not certainty in terms of the final outcome of reality. We need no faith in that which is scientifically predictable, nor can there be faith in that which is impossible. Faith is based on our experience of living of transforming ourselves. Faith that others can change is the outcome of the experience that I can change.

There is an important distinction between rational and irrational faith. While rational faith is the result of one's own inner activeness in thought or feeling, irrational faith is submission to something given, which one accepts as true regardless of whether it is or not. The essential element of all irrational faith is its passive character, be its object an idol, a leader, or an ideology. Even the scientist needs to be free from irrational faith in traditional ideas in order to have rational faith in the power of his creative thought. Once his discovery is "proved," he needs no more faith, except in the next step he is contemplating. In the sphere of human relations, "having faith" in another person means to be certain of his *core*—that is, of the reliability and unchangeability of his fundamental attitudes. In the same sense we can have faith in ourselves—not in the constancy of our opinions but in our basic orientation to life, the matrix of our character structure. Such faith is conditioned by the experience of self, by our capacity to say "I" legitimately, by the sense of our identity.

Hope is the mood that accompanies faith. Faith could not be sustained without the mood of hope. Hope can have no base except in faith.

4. FORTITUDE

There is still another element linked with hope and faith in the structure of life: courage, or, as Spinoza called it, fortitude. Fortitude is perhaps the less ambiguous expression, because today courage is more often used to demonstrate the courage to die rather than the courage to live. Fortitude is the capacity to resist the temptation to compromise hope and faith by transforming them—and thus destroying them—into empty optimism or into irrational faith. Fortitude is the capacity to say "no" when the world wants to hear "yes."

But fortitude is not fully understood unless we mention another aspect of it: fearlessness. The fearless person is not afraid of threats, not even of death. But, as so often, the word "fearless" covers several entirely different attitudes. I mention only the three most important ones: First, a person can be fearless because he does not care to live; life is not worth much to him, hence he is fearless when it comes to the danger of dying; but while he is not afraid of death, he may be afraid of life. His fearlessness is based on lack of love of life; he is usually not fearless at all when he is not in the situation of risking his life. In fact, he frequently looks for dangerous situations, in order to avoid his fear of life, of himself, and of people.

A second kind of fearlessness is that of the person who lives in symbiotic submission to an idol, be it a person, an institution, or an idea; the commands of the idol are sacred; they are far more compelling than even the survival commands of his body. If he could disobey or doubt these commands of the idol, he would face the danger of losing his identity with the idol; this means he would be running the risk of finding himself utterly isolated, and thus at the verge of insanity.

He is willing to die because he is afraid of exposing himself to this danger.

The third kind of fearlessness is to be found in the fully developed person, who rests within himself and loves life. The person who has overcome greed does not cling to any idol or any thing and hence has nothing to lose: he is rich because he is empty, he is strong because he is not the slave of his desires. He can let go of idols, irrational desires, and fantasies, because he is in full touch with reality, inside and outside himself. If such a person has reached full "enlightenment," he is completely fearless. If he has moved toward this goal without having arrived, his fearlessness will also not be complete. But anyone who tries to move toward the state of being fully himself knows that whenever a new step toward fearlessness is made, a sense of strength and joy is awakened that is unmistakable. He feels as if a new phase of life had begun. He can feel the truth of Goethe's lines: "I have put my house on nothing, that's why the whole world is mine." (*Ich hab mein Haus auf nichts gestellt, deshalb gehoert mir die ganze Welt.*)

Hope and faith, being essential qualities of *life,* are by their very nature moving in the direction of transcending the *status quo,* individually and socially. It is one of the qualities of all life that it is in a constant process of change and never remains the same at any given moment. Life that stagnates tends to die; if the stagnation is complete, death has occurred. It follows that life in its moving quality tends to break out of and to overcome the *status quo.* We grow either stronger or weaker, wiser or more foolish, more courageous or more cowardly. Every second is a moment of decision, for the better or the worse. We feed our sloth, greed, or hate, or we starve it. The more we feed it, the stronger it grows; the more we starve it, the weaker it becomes.

What holds true for the individual holds true for a society. It is never static; if it does not grow, it decays; if it does not transcend the *status quo* for the better, it changes for the worse. Often we, the individual or the people who make up a society, have the illusion we could stand still and not alter the given situation in the one or the other direction. This is one of the most dangerous illusions. The moment we stand still, we begin to decay.

Family

Germaine Greer

Germaine Greer was born in Melbourne, Australia, in 1939. She was graduated from the university there in 1959, with a combined degree in French and English literatures, and took an A.M. at the University of Sidney. After teaching for a time in a high school for girls from "underprivileged homes," she was awarded a scholarship to study Shakespeare at Cambridge. She earned her doctorate and remained in England as a professor of literature at Warwick University, a post that she still holds. The appearance of *The Female Eunuch* (1971) brought her instant fame. She makes regular television appearances, writes for popular publications, grants intimate interviews to *Playboy,* and, on one memorable occasion, appeared with Norman Mailer as "the enemy" on a Town Hall forum.

The most eloquent and intellectually challenging of the "women's lib" writers, the most free of jargon and repressed rage, she asserts that modern women tend to be helpless, querulous, narrow, and boring. She argues that, particularly in the years just after puberty, the Freudian concept of the female sexual role, social conditioning, and "cosmetic conspiracy" combine to drain girls' energy and curiosity, leaving them passive, narcissistic, and mindless. The contribution of the nuclear family to this result is explored with partisan zest in the following selection from her book.

Mother duck, father duck and all the little baby ducks. The family, ruled over and provided for by father, suckled and nurtured by mother, seems to us inherent in the natural order. While momma gorilla is breeding and nursing, poppa gorilla mounts guard over her, defending her from the perils of the wild. Even when the wild held no perils, Adam delved and Eve span and God the father was their daddy and walked with them in the twilight if they were good. When they were bad they were flung out of the garden and began a family of their own. Their sons fought as siblings will and murder came upon the world. Somewhere in the Apocrypha lurked Lilith, the destructive woman, who offered love and licentiousness and threatened the family structure. The grandsons of Adam consorted with the daughters of the flesh. The myth of the origin of the patriarchal family in the Old Testament is ambiguous: the father is vindictive, the mother is his vassal, the brothers enact the primal crime, murder for the love of the father, while the harlot beckons from outside the prison of domesticity. But from this source modern Christianity developed its own

SOURCE: Germaine Greer, *The Female Eunuch* (New York: McGraw-Hill Book Company, 1971), pp. 216–35.

paradigm of the nuclear family and considered it reflected in the natural law. The structure of the state, naïvely considered as no more than a collection of families, reflects the natural principle: the king/president is a benign but just father of a huge family. The Church also acknowleged one head, a *locum tenens* for God Himself. The man was the soul, and the woman the body; the man was the mind and the woman the heart; the man was the will and the woman the passions. Boys learnt their male role from father and girls their female role from their mother. It seems clear, simple and immutable. Father was responsible for his dependents; he owned the property, transferred it to his first-born son together with his name. The chain of command from the elders to the poorest vassals was complete.

And yet what seems so essential and inevitable is utterly contingent. The patrilineal family depends upon the free gift by women of the right of paternity to men. Paternity is not an intrinsic relationship: it cannot be proved, except negatively. The most intense vigilance will not insure absolutely that any man is the father of his son.

> Is there no way for men to be but
> Women must be half-workers? We are bastards all . . .

When there was property to pass on and legitimacy to be upheld, it was imperative to surround women with guards, to keep them in one place, keeping their natural curiosity and urge for movement and expression as undeveloped as possible. The chastity belt which warrior barons clapped around their wives when they went to war was the outward emblem of the fruitlessness of the struggle, the attempt to provide a barricado for a belly. Nowadays women demand trust and offer their free assurance about paternity, honoring the contract that they have made, to be protected, fed and housed in return for insuring immortality in legitimate issue.

The family which is set up when a young man installs his bride in a self-contained dwelling is not really well-designed to perform the functions of insuring paternity. The wife is left alone most of the day without chaperone: the degree of trust demanded is correspondingly greater. The modern household has neither servants nor relatives to safeguard the husband's interest and yet it seems natural and proper, as the logical outcome of all the other patriarchal forms which have preceded it. In fact the single marriage family, which is called by anthropologists and sociologists the *nuclear* family, is possibly the shortest-lived familial system ever developed. In feudal times the family was of the type called a *stem* family: the head was the oldest male parent, who ruled a number of sons and their wives and children. The work of the household was divided according to the status of the female in question: the unmarried daughters did the washing and spinning and weaving, the breeding wives bred, the elder wives nursed and disciplined the children, and managed the cooking, the oldest wife supervised the smooth running of the whole. The isolation which makes the red-brick-villa household so neurotic did not exist. There was friction but it had no chance to build itself into the intense introverted anguish of the single eye-to-eye confrontation of the isolated spouses. Family problems could be challenged openly in the family forum and the decisions of the elders were honored. Romantic love as a motive for cohabitation was hardly important. A man only needed to desire to breed by a woman who would fit in with his household. Disappointment, resentment and boredom had less scope. The children benefited by the arrangement and in parts of Greece and Spain and Southern Italy still do. Someone, if only grandfather or an unmarried uncle or aunt, always had time to answer questions, tell stories, teach new skills, or go fishing. As soon as children could walk well by themselves they had a little responsibility—the hens, or the dovecote, a lamb or a kid to bring up. They were not sent to bed in a dark room while their elders talked in the kitchen, but allowed to stay and listen and learn until they fell asleep in someone's arms. Then they were quietly undressed and put to bed without waking. There could be no generation gap because the household represented all age groups. When I lived in a tiny hamlet in Southern Italy I saw such a family bravely holding together in spite of the grimmest poverty and the absence of most of the men who were working in Germany, and their children were the happiest, the least coy and irritable of any that I have ever observed. As the neighboring families were kin, the community was strongly cohesive. The exigencies of such group-living had created strong decorums which were always respected. We would have starved if it had not been for the exchange of whatever goods the kin-families had in excess for our own superabundances, for we could not have afforded food at the exorbitant prices which the *latifondiste* charged on the open market.

The stem family can provide a source of cohesion which is inimical to state control for it is immovable, and its strongest loyalty is to itself. When the principle is exerted in defiance of instituted authority it can become the infamous *famiglia* of the Mafia. The rituals of family honor have involved the antisocial manifestations of *vendetta* and *omertà* but these are not significant until the familial, regional community is threatened by political authority. The American liberators were quick to see the organizational importance of the Mafia in Sicily; what they did not see was that the kind of cohesion they sought to exploit was already anachronistic and economically nonviable.

The effects of industrialization and urbanization in changing the pattern of settlement and requiring the mobility of labor have hastened the decay of the stem family, which declined in Western Europe some time before the sixteenth century. The changes in tenure of land, the decay of regional authority, the centralization of government, enclosures and development of money rents and absentee landlordism all played a part in the development of the nuclear family, and yet it is only recently that the nuclear family has dwindled to the stump of community living that it now is. When the largest proportion of the working community was in service in large households, when spinsters and unmarried sons lived in the household, when sons and daughters were most often sent away to work in other households, the family remained organic and open to external influences. Husbands and wives could not indulge in excessive introversion about their relationship which was buttressed firmly by the laws against divorce, public opinion, and the uncontrolled size of families. Aging parents were kept and cared for in the household. But there was no longer a family business, no longer a heritage to be developed and served. The denseness of the urban community entailed estrangement from immediate neighbors, and the necessity of finding work led sons outside the immediate purview of the family. The effects of education estranged families even more especially when compulsory education created a generation more literate than their parents. The gradual expansion of education generation by generation is prolonging this effect. By the time Ibsen and Strindberg were writing their domestic tragedies the family had become a prison where the young struggled to escape the dead hand of the old, where the outside community was only represented by the policeman, the doctor and the parson, where the servants were strangers and class enemies. Puritan morality had resulted in hypocrisy, frustration and pornography. Husband and wife danced a dance of diurnal murder. The father–protector, unable to assume any other field of superiority or prowess, was principally moral arbiter although unfitted for the role: the wife was a designing doll, disillusioned about her husband, confused and embittered by her own idleness and insignificance. The syndrome of vicarious leisure, which Veblen describes, had come full circle. Female occupations were more conspicuously meaningless than ever. The embitterment of marriage partners had become so evidently destructive that laws to facilitate divorce began to be promulgated in most western countries. Women began to clamor for the right to work outside domestic service, and expanding industry came to need them, especially with the depredations of the First World War upon manpower. The number of unmarried women became greater, aggravating a problem which had existed since the turn of the century. Gradually the big Victorian-built houses were subdivided into smaller units. In response to requirements for higher density housing the flat proliferated. More and more of the functions of the large household devolved upon the state: the care of the old, of the sick, of the mentally infirm and backward.

The family of the sixties is small, self-contained, self-centered and short-lived. The young man moves away from his parents as soon as he can, following opportunities for training and employment. Children live their lives most fully at school, fathers at work. Mother is the dead heart of the family, spending father's earnings on consumer goods to enhance the environment in which he eats, sleeps and watches television. Children tend more and more since the war to create more vital groups of their own, assuming tribal characteristics of dress and ritual behavior. Even the girls tend to go to work and set up house with other girls in the enormous bed-sitter belts of major cities. The wife is only significant *qua* wife when she is bearing and raising the small children, but the conditions under which she carries out this important work and the confusion which exists about the proper way to perform it increase her isolation from her community and intensify the parental relationship in these earliest years.

The working girl who marries, works for a period after her marriage and retires to breed, is hardly equipped for the isolation of the nuclear household. Regardless of whether she enjoyed the menial work of typing or selling or waitressing or clerking, she at least had freedom of movement to a degree. Her horizon shrinks to the house, the shopping center and the telly. Her child is too much cared for, too diligently regarded during the day and, when her husband returns from work, soon banished from the adult world to his bed, so that Daddy can relax. The Oedipal situation which is always duplicated in marriage is now intensified to a degree which Freud would have found appalling. Father is very really a rival and a stranger. During the day the child may be bullied as often as petted: what is certain is that he has too much attention from the one person who is entirely at his disposal. The intimacy between mother and child is not sustaining and healthy. The child learns to exploit his mother's accessibility, badgering her with questions and demands which are not of any real consequence to him, embarrassing her in public, blackmailing her into buying sweets and carrying him. Dependence does not mean love. The child's attitude toward school, which takes him away from his mother after five years of enforced intimacy, is as ambivalent as his feelings about his mother. As long as it is an escape it is welcome but when it becomes demanding the child finds that he can play mother and school off against each other. The jealousy which mothers have of school and the attempt of the school to establish a source of control over the child in opposition to the mother can result in highly fraught situations. The antisocial nature of this mother–child relationship is very evident to schoolteachers, especially when it is a question of discipline or treatment of emotional disturbance.

The unfortunate wife–mother finds herself antisocial in other ways as well. The home is her province, and she is lonely there. She wants her family to spend time with her for her only significance is in relation to that almost fictitious group. She struggles to hold her children to her, imposing restrictions, waiting up for them, prying into their affairs. They withdraw more and more into noncommunication and thinly veiled contempt. She begs her husband not to go out with the boys, marvels that he can stand in the pouring rain at the football and then be too tired to mend the roof or cut the grass on the finest day. She moans more and more that he doesn't care what the children are up to, that discipline is all left to her, that nobody talks to her, that she's ignorant, that she had given the best years of her life to a bunch of ungrateful hooligans. Politics is a mystery and a boring one; sport is evidence of the failure of men to grow up. The best thing that can happen is that she take up again where she left off and go back to work at a job which was only a stop gap when she began it, in which she can expect no promotion, no significant remuneration, and no widening of her horizons, for the demands of the household must still be met. Work of all kinds becomes a hypnotic. She cleans, she knits, she embroiders. And so forth.

Women trying to counteract the tendency of the nuclear household to isolate them from social contacts have peculiar difficulties. Anne Allen reported this conversation with a young married woman in the *Sunday Mirror:*

> "Look," she said. "We have about a dozen really good friends. People I am closer to than anyone in my family. People I like better and know better.
>
> "But what happens? *We have to organize ourselves in order to meet.* Someone has to find a baby-sitter. The other couple feel bound to make a nice supper for us.
>
> "Then either the baby is ill, or someone feels tired, and you wish you had not arranged it. Or we all enjoy ourselves so much that it is really sad that it all has to break up so early.
>
> "But just think what it would be like if a close group of friends lived in one building, or one street. It could happen.
>
> "There are architects working on one or two specially planned buildings where everyone has his own bit and a huge communal living area.
>
> "Personally I could not bear to share sexually, and I would be as bad as my mother about sharing a kitchen. I value my privacy too much.
>
> "But there are dozens of times when I long for someone to talk to in the daytime. Or when I am lonely if my husband works overnight. Or when he and I are arguing and I want to get away for an hour.
>
> "I just can't think of any way I would rather live than with my husband and with most of my closest friends around us. After all, thousands of people become close friends with their neighbours. We would just be reversing the procedure."

Once upon a time everyone lived in a house full of friends with large communal areas, where the streets were full of friends because the immobility of the community meant that all its members knew one another and their family history. The system has its disadvantages: nonconformism often proved intolerable, and the constant attention of the whole community to the actions of individuals had disadvantages more striking than the advantages. In such a community an old lady could not lie for four days at the foot of her staircase with a broken hip but a woman could not conduct a forbidden love affair either. Nowadays people live closer together than ever before but it is overcrowded isolation. Tower blocks contain dozens and dozens of little families who have a great deal in common, but they are strangers to each other. Their front doors shut in a private world which cannot communicate past the blank corridors and lifts except to complain about each other's noise. The women watching their children play in the communal play areas only know the parents of the other children when some outrage demands parental interference. Competitiveness frequently means that each family clings to a fantasy of superiority, racial, moral, religious, economic or class. Town planners lament that tower dwellers will not undertake to keep their communal areas clean and pleasant, and the victims of this rehousing complain that the towers cause special anxieties connected with height and encapsulation. Passing up and down in the lifts they never see each other, they cannot see in each other's windows, or natter in their doorways while cleaning the stoop. Unspontaneous attempts to stimulate intimacy don't work. Women jealously maintain the separateness of their household, fearing all kinds of imaginary corruption of their children and their way of life by the inroads of strangers. Anne Allen's housewife rejects the possibility of sexual sharing, but at least she openly considers it. The kin-community safeguards its own sexual relationships by incest restrictions which do not have their initial justification in fears of the results of inbreeding, which were not known by the first promulgators of anti-incest laws. Women dwelling in tower blocks may not consciously fear the effects of intimacy with stranger women, but the tension is there. Perhaps the failure of such community living could be avoided by including a pub and a launderette in each block but economically it would appear that the jobs being tirelessly duplicated in each living capsule ought to be shared if genuine organic interaction is to result.

The architectural results of the nuclear family are universally deemed disastrous: the ungainly spread of ribbon developments, of acres of little boxes, has ruined the appearance of all of our cities. Upkeep of such areas is prohibitively expensive, access to services is difficult to arrange. The defendants of high-density housing have practicality and comfort on their side. What they do not realize is that the nuclear family is pulling against them; no amount of anthropometric investigation, no clever orientation of clean and efficient housing units towards light and warmth and open views can break down the suspicion that the Oedipal unit feels toward others of its kind. The stresses and strains of conjugal introspection cannot tolerate a wider horizon. One alternative is the takeover by the employer as father, as happens in specially constructed villages in America where the firms' employees are housed according to income and position and encouraged to get together. Wives become faculty wives and corporation wives. Togetherness is rampant. The long-term results are, to me at least, unimaginable. Every aspect of family life comes to be dominated by the firm; just as the unfortunate man gets his job on a personality assessment relating to his whole family, he must carry out the firm's role in every aspect of his personal life. Even his sexual performance may become a business matter: Masters and Johnson have delineated the hedonistic norm. No serf, writhing under the law of *jus primae noctis,* handing over his sons to the service of his liege-lord, ever had it worse. As securely as any gold-rush miner or freed slave, he owes his soul to the company store. The logical outcome of the control of employment over the movement of labor has come about. His continued security is dependent upon the behavior of his whole family; the desired result is complete immobility and predictability. This is why faculty husbands rate a lower libido rating than others – because they have become fat white mice in a hygienic laboratory, not because of the proximity of their women, as Lionel Tiger claimed. Big Daddy the employer, the specter that looms over *Who's Afraid of Virginia Woolf?,* has castrated his sons. The human soul is indestructible, however, and if the group is to form the special conscience, then the sin which can incapacitate it must be a group sin, so that no one can split to Big Daddy. The pattern of American decadence is communal drunkenness, first of all, which is the only way to uncensored behavior, and ultimately, wife-swapping, the twentieth-century form of incest:

> The autumn of 1962, the two couples were ecstatically, scandalously close. Frank and Marcia were delighted to be thrown together so often without seeking it. Janet and Harold in private joked about the now transparent stratagems of the other two lovers. These jokes began to leak out into their four-sided conversations . . .
>
> The other couples began to call them the Applesmiths. . . . "Don't you feel it? It's so *wrong*. Now we're really corrupt. All of us."

Wife-swapping is seriously advocated by writers in "journals of human relations," like *Forum,* as a method of revitalizing marriages which have gone stale. Shared but secret behavior will cement any group into a conspiracy, but the results can be hard to live with. Changing partners is such a thoroughly unspontaneous activity, so divorced from the vagaries of genuine sexual desire—no more than a variant on the square dance. In such a transaction sex is the sufferer: passion becomes lechery. Ringing the changes on modes of *getting pleasure* disguises boredom, but it does not restore life. Sex in such circumstances is less and less a form of communication and more and more a diversion. Like bingo, slot-machines, hula-hoops, and yo-yos, it is fun. Manageable, homely amusement. Not innocent, but calculated; not dynamic, but contained. When Big Daddy countenances such naughtiness, even sex will have come under his benign aegis. The over-fed, undersexed white mouse is allowed a brief spell in another's cage to perk him up. Sexual uniformity could be enforced this way: Mr. Jones can apply to Mrs. Jones what he learnt from Mrs. Smith and so on. Universal domesticity buries all.

Anne Allen is a sensible, middling-liberal English housewife. With a matronizing glance at her young interlocutor she continues:

> I find it a rather attractive idea in theory. But in practice I can't think of a dozen or even half a dozen couples I would like to be that close to. Or who would like to live that way with us . . .
>
> I don't like the way they bring up their children. I give my children less, or more pocket money, which could lead to fights.
>
> I hate the way they fill their kitchen with strange cooking smells or squalor. Or I feel their beady eyes on my rather wobbly housekeeping.
>
> But most of all, I am helplessly, hopelessly, possessive, and if my husband went off with some nearby dishy wife whenever I shouted at him, there could be murder done.

Anne Allen is more like the average British housewife than the young women she spoke to, and much more "normal" than faculty wives or corporation wives or swapped wives. She is not ashamed about the antisocial nature of her family although she might as well have said that there was not *one* couple that she could tolerate at such close quarters, and not many couples with whom she was in any sense intimate at all. The term *couples* itself implies the locked-off unit of male–female: she did not speak of families. This is virtually what the nuclear family has become. Women's magazines sadly remark that children can have a disruptive effect on the conjugal relationship, that the young wife's involvement with her children and her exhaustion can interfere with her husband's claims on her. What a notion—a family that is threatened by its children! Contraception has increased the egotism of the couple: planned children have a pattern to fit into; at least unplanned children had some of the advantages of contingency. First and foremost, they *were* whether their parents liked it or not. In the limited nuclear family the parents are the principals and children are theirs to manipulate in a newly purposive way. The generation gap is being intensified in these families where children must not inconvenience their parents, where they are disposed of in special living quarters at special times of day, their own rooms and so forth. Anything less than this is squalor. Mother must not have more children than she can control: control means full attention for much of the day, and then isolation. So the baby-sitter must be introduced into the house sneakily, for if junior finds out that his parents are going out, he'll scream. I think of the filthy two-roomed house in Calabria where people came and went freely, where I never heard a child scream except in pain, where the twelve-year-old aunt sang at her washing by the well, and the old father walked in the olive grove with his grandson on his arm. English children have lost their innocence, for their first lessons have been in the exploitation of their adult slave. A sterilized parent is a eunuch in his children's harem. To be sure, I recognize that efficient contraception is necessary for sexual pleasure and that sexual pleasure is necessary, but contraception for economic reasons is another matter. "We can only afford two children" is a squalid argument, but more acceptable in our society than "we don't like children." A sterilized parent is forever bound to those children whom he has, more than ever immobile and predictable, and those children are more securely bound to him. "We can only afford two children" really means, "We only like clean, well-disciplined middle-class children who go to good schools and grow up to be professionals," for children manage to use up all the capital that is made available for the purpose, whatever proportion it may be of the family's whole income, just as housework expands to fill the time available. The sterilized parent is the ultimate domestic animal. Masculine culture contains a strong vein of antidomesticity, although men can hardly have the experience of it that women have had trained into them. The fantasy of the perfect partner exists alongside the consciousness of what family meant to a growing boy.

Marriage is the only thing that really scares me. With the right girl I suppose it's okay but I couldn't imagine myself having a house and a wife. I like to feel free, to go anywhere and not have to worry. That's one nice thing about not having a girlfriend, you're free to go out and enjoy yourself with the lads. Having a girl ties you down.

The more you go out with a girl, the more involved you get. I'm frightened of becoming engaged. That would finish me—because I'd never break off the engagement, it isn't fair on the girl. Too many teenagers rush into marriage . . .

The next time I have a steady girl I'm going to make it clear from the start that I want a free night off with the lads every week. Once you lose all your friends, you're stuck to the girl, and you've had it.

You've had it, you're hooked, done for! Involved means tangled up, tied down.

Most people get the best job they can, work for promotion and when they're earning enough money meet a girl and marry her. Then you have to buy a house and a car, and there you are—chained down for the rest of your life. When you get to thirty-five you're frightened to try anything new in case you lose your security. Then it means living with all the regrets about things you wanted to do.

The disenchanted vision of these children has revealed the function of the patriarchal family unit in capitalist society. It immobilizes the worker, keeps him vulnerable, so that he can be tantalized with the vision of security. It gives him a controllable pattern of consumption to which he is thoroughly committed. His commitment is to his small family and his employer, not to his community. The effect of wifely pressure on strikers has not to my knowledge been analyzed. Often it is responsibility to a family which causes a striker to take drastic action: if the employers can hold out long enough it is this same pressure which will bring him back to work. Wives distrust their husband's leisure; too often a wife would rather her husband earned less than hung about in the streets with his cronies getting into trouble. One of the saddest comments upon the family in industrial society was offered by the spectacle of the wives of miners thrown out of work by pit closures angrily refusing the solution of pay without work because their husbands would either be around the house all day doing nothing, or getting into mischief with the boys. Many girls undertake their antisocial functions very early, restricting their boyfriends' association with their "mates" severely in return for sexual favors. This is not altogether the fault of women's selfishness, for the male groups that threaten her do not admit her except under special circumstances and in a special capacity. She cannot play darts, drink beer, or kick a football about. Her distrust of these activities is not that her man will consort with other women in the company of his mates, but the knowledge that he enjoys these other activities and is dependent upon them in a way that he does not enjoy or depend upon her. She is jealous not of his sexual favors, but upon the partiality of his sexual passion, and the greater togetherness he might enjoy with men. Every wife must live with the knowledge that she has nothing else but home and family, while her house is ideally a base which her tired warrior-hunter can withdraw to and express his worst manners, his least amusing conversation, while he licks his wounds and is prepared by laundry and toilet and lunchbox for another sortie.

Obviously any woman who thinks in the simplest terms of liberating herself to enjoy life and create expression for her own potential cannot accept such a role. And yet marriage is based upon this filial relationship of a wife who takes her husband's name, has her tax declared on his return, lives in a house owned by him and goes about in public as his companion wearing his ring on her finger at all times. Alteration in detail is not alteration in anything else. A husband who agrees that he too will wear a ring, that they will have a joint bank account, that the house will be in both their names, is not making any serious concession to a wife's personal needs. The essential character of the institution asserts itself eventually. The very fact that such concessions are privileges which a wife cannot claim contains its own special consequences of gratitude and more willing servitude. And yet if a woman is to have children, if humanity is to survive, what alternative can there be?

To begin with, the problem of the survival of humanity is not a matter of insuring the birth of future generations but of limiting it. The immediate danger to humanity is that of total annihilation within a generation or two, not the failure of mankind to breed. A woman seeking alternative modes of life is no longer morally bound to pay her debt to nature. Those families in which the parents replace themselves in two children are not the most desirable ones for children to grow up in, for the neuroses resultant from the intensified Oedipal situation are worse in cases where the relationship with the parents is more dominant than the problems of adjusting to a peer group of brothers and sisters. There is no reason, except the moral prejudice that women who do not have children are shirking a responsibility, why all women should consider themselves bound to breed. A woman who has a child is not then automatically committed to bringing it up. Most societies countenance the deputizing of nurses to bring up the children of women with state duties. The practice of putting children out to nurse did not result in a race of psychopaths. A child must have care and attention, but that care and attention need not emanate from a single, permanently present individual. Children are more disturbed by changes of place than by changes in personnel around them, and more distressed by friction and ill-feeling between the adults in their environment than by unfamiliarity. A group of children can be more successfully civilized by one or two women who have voluntarily undertaken the work than they can be when divided and tyrannized over by a single woman who finds herself bored and imposed upon. The alternative is not the institutionalization of parental functions in some bureaucratic form, nothing so cold and haphazard as a baby farm, but an organic family where the child society can merge with an adult society in conditions of love and personal interest. The family understood not as a necessary condition of existence in a system but as a chosen way of life can become a goal, an achievement of a creative kind.

If women could regard childbearing not as a duty or an inescapable destiny but as a privilege to be worked for, the way a man might work for the right to have a family, children might grow up without the burden of gratitude for the gift of life which they never asked for. Brilliant women are not reproducing themselves because childbearing has been regarded as a fulltime job; genetically they might be thought to be being bred out. In a situation where a woman might contribute a child to a household which engages her attention for part of the time while leaving her free to frequent other spheres of influence, brilliant women might be more inclined to reproduce. For some time now I have pondered the problem of having a child which would not suffer from my neuroses and the difficulties I would have in adjusting to a husband and the demands of domesticity. A plan, by no means a blueprint, evolved which has become a sort of dream. No child ought, I opine, to grow up in the claustrophobic atmosphere of a city flat, where he has little chance of exercising his limbs or his lungs; I must work in a city where the materials for my work and its market are available. No child ought to grow up alone with a single resentful girl who is struggling to work hard enough to provide for herself and him. I thought again of the child I knew in Calabria and hit upon the plan to buy, with the help of some friends with similar problems, a farmhouse in Italy where we could stay when circumstances permitted, and where our children would be born. Their fathers and other people would also visit the house as often as they could, to rest and enjoy the children and even work a bit. Perhaps some of us might live there for quite long periods, as long as we wanted to. The house and garden would be worked by a local family who lived in the house. The children would have a region to explore and dominate, and different skills to learn from all of us. It would not be paradise, but it would be a little community with a chance of survival, with parents of both sexes and a multitude of roles to choose from. The worst aspect of kibbutz living could be avoided, especially as the children would not have to be strictly persuaded out of sexual experimentation with their peers, an unnatural restriction which has had serious consequences for the children of kibbutzim. Being able to be with my child and his friends would be a privilege and a delight that I could work for. If necessary the child need not even know that I was his womb-mother and I could have relationships with the other children as well. If my child expressed a wish to try London and New York or go to formal school somewhere, that could also be tried without committal.

Any new arrangement which a woman might devise will have the disadvantage of being peculiar: the children would not have been brought up like other children in an age of uniformity. There are the problems of legitimacy and nationality to be faced. Our society has created the myth of the *broken home* which is the source of so many ills, and yet the unbroken home which ought to have broken is an even greater source of tension as I can attest from bitter experience. The rambling organic structure of my ersatz household would have the advantage of being an unbreakable home in that it did not rest on the frail shoulders of two bewildered individuals trying to apply a contradictory blueprint. This little society would confer its own normality, and other contacts with civilization would be encouraged, but it may well be that such children would find it impossible to integrate with society and become dropouts or schizophrenics. As such they would not be very different from other children I have known. The notion of integrating with society as if society were in some way homogeneous is itself a false one. There are enough eccentrics carving out various life-styles for my children to feel that they are no more isolated than any other minority group within the fictitious majority. In the computer age disintegration may well appear to be a higher value than integration. Cynics might argue that the children of my household would be anxious to set up "normal" families as part of the natural counterreaction. Perhaps. When faced with such dubious possibilities, there is only empiricism to fall back on. I could not, physically, have a child any other way, except by accident and under protest in a hand-to-mouth sort of way in which case I could not accept any responsibility for the consequences. I should like to be able to think that I had done my best.

The point of an organic family is to release the children from the disadvantages of being the extensions of their parents so that they can belong primarily to themselves. They may accept the services that adults perform for them naturally without establishing dependencies. There could be scope for them to initiate their own activities and define the mode and extent of their own learning. They might come to resent their own strangeness but in other circumstances they might resent normality; faced with difficulties of adjustment children seize upon their parents and their upbringing to serve as scapegoats. Parents have no option but to enjoy their children if they want to avoid the cycle of exploitation and recrimination. If they want to enjoy them they must construct a situation in which such enjoyment is possible.

The institution of self-regulating organic families may appear to be a return to chaos. Genuine chaos is more fruitful than the chaos of conflicting systems which are mutually destructive. When heredity has decayed and bureaucracy is the rule, so that the only riches are earning power and mobility, it is absurd that the family should persist in the pattern of patriliny. It is absurd that people should live more densely than ever before while pretending that they are still in a cottage with a garden. It is absurd that people should pledge themselves for life when divorce is always possible. It is absurd that families should claim normality when confusion about the meaning and function of parenthood means that children born within a decade of each other and a mile of each other can be brought up entirely differently. To breast-feed or not breast-feed? To toilet-train when and how? To punish, if ever? To reward? It is absurd that so many children should grow up in environments where their existence is frowned upon. It is absurd that children should fear adults outside the immediate family. Generation X, the generation gap, the Mods, the Rockers, the Hippies, the Yippies, the Skinheads, the Maoists, the young Fascists of Europe, rebels without a cause, whatever patronizing names their parent generation can find for them, the young are accusing their elders of spurious assumption of authòrity to conceal their own confusion. Vandalism, steel-capped boots, drugs, football rioting, these are chaos, and the attempts of instituted authority to deal with them are more chaotic still. The juvenile offender dares the system or one of the systems to cope with him and it invariably fails. The status quo is chaos masquerading as order: our children congregate to express an organic community in ritual and uniform, which can make nonsense of state authority. The California police do not dare to interfere with the Hell's Angels who make a mockery of their punitive law by refusing to do the things that their parents might have done if they had had that power. The same sort of mockery is uttered by the Black Panthers. The family is already broken down: technology has outstripped conservatism. The only way the state–father can deal with its uncontrollable children is to bash and shoot them in the streets or send them to a war, the ultimate chaos.

Reich described the authoritarian compulsive family as "part and parcel, and, at the same time, prerequisite, of the authoritarian state and of authoritarian society." Like the family, the state belies itself by its own confusion and permissiveness, although ultimately it intervenes to exercise its authority chaotically. In England, the "excesses" of youth are contained and allowed to spend themselves until they can be controlled or punished discreetly, so that they do not inflame the dormant young population unduly. The result is political and social chaos, the "sexual wilderness." The formlessness, the legal nonexistence of my dream household is a safeguard against the chaos of conflicting loyalties, of conflicting educational apparata, of conflicting judgments. My child will not be guided at all because the guidance offered him by this society seeks to lead him backwards and forwards and sideways all at once. If we are to recover serenity and joy in living, we will have to listen to what our children tell us in their own way, and not impose our own distorted image upon them in our crazy families.

The Immortalist Argument

Alan Harrington

A native of Newton, Massachusetts, Alan Harrington took a degree at Harvard, worked as an editor for the Indonesian Information Office, and did public relations before turning seriously to fiction and personal philosophy.

His first novel, *The Revelations of Dr. Modesto,* was described by Ralph Ellison as "caustic commentary on American society, types and values . . . made to arise out of his most hilarious situations—a sure sign of a fully achieved comic art." His second novel, *The Secret Swinger,* and a book of personal reportage of life in a big American corporation, *Life in the Crystal Palace,* also won critical acclaim. The following selection comes from *The Immortalist* (1969), "an approach to the engineering of man's divinity." Man has always dreamed about overcoming death. Now with the tools of modern technology at his disposal, he is renewing the attack in the vision of freedom from that ancient fear.

Death is an imposition on the human race, and no longer acceptable. Man has all but lost his ability to accommodate himself to personal extinction; he must now proceed physically to overcome it. In short, to kill death: to put an end to his own mortality as a certain consequence of being born.

Our survival without the God we once knew comes down now to a race against time. The suspicion or conviction that "God is dead" has lately struck home not merely to a few hundred thousand freethinkers but to masses of the unprepared. Ancient orthodoxies may linger, but the content of worship has begun to collapse. This is what makes our situation urgent: around the world people are becoming increasingly less inclined to pray to a force that kills them.

The most imaginative philosophical and religious answers to the "problem of death" have become precisely irrelevant to the fact that we die. Humanity's powers of self-deception seem to be running out. Modern theological word-games may be pleasing to seminarians. Let jazz be permitted in the old spiritual gathering places. Such developments must be understood as gallant but altogether pathetic holding operations.

Emotionally, growing millions of us are in crisis. "Men are so neces-

SOURCE: Alan Harrington, *The Immortalist* (New York: Random House, Inc. 1969), pp. 3–24. A portion of this book originally appeared in *Playboy*.

sarily mad," wrote Pascal, "that not to be mad would amount to another form of madness." Three hundred years later, with the mass-communication of anxiety, and new weaponry and drugs in our possession, we need only open the morning paper or sit down to television, or look into our own lives, to observe signs of a growing spiritual insurrection. Life as it used to be seems in the process of slowly exploding. We wonder at the bursts of "senseless" violence that seem likely at any moment to invade our days and nights. Yet is this sort of behavior necessarily irrational? If sanity now calls upon us to accept death without hope, perhaps such recent ceremonials as smashing pianos and guitars on stage may be viewed as expressions of maddened realism.

We ought to say immediately that these outbreaks of distress for the most part afflict those who have time to think beyond the problem of barely staying alive. When economic misery exhausts the psyche, horizons draw in. The meaning of existence? God, as Gandhi pointed out, must reveal himself to the destitute in the form of food.

Nor will oppressed people who have yet to win or regain their dignity suffer overly much from thoughts of death and meaninglessness, since for them death lives, remains present everywhere, and therefore speculating about it is redundant. In particular, the revolutionaries of today or any time—while the revolution is in prospect or actually going on—rise above this condition.

One of the advantages in having a cause is that it saves you from worrying about what life means. (Indeed, this is what attracts many people to communal action.) Just as during World War II "anti-fascism" seemed a sufficient excuse for living, so the fight against one injustice or another has tended to deliver present-day activists from such maladies of privilege as intellectual doubt, cosmic weariness and boredom. While the revolution assaults any given establishment, the fact that an abyss waits at the end of life does not for the time being bother the rebel. Hatred of the system and concern with advancement of the war gives a man enough to think about. Only when the battle has ended does the freed soul turn and face the cosmic menace.

Who, then, has come to live "in fear and trembling"? I am talking about the great bulk of the rest not actively at war, within the reach of print and television; people of the city, town and suburb getting along reasonably well, who except during vacations walk on pavement. Among this currently decisive majority, an unmistakable phenomenon may be observed.

Civilized humanity is signaling. It seems to be both an S.O.S. and a warning. In many languages and forms the coded sign repeats: "Change this scene, or *we* will!" The message has by no means gone unnoticed. Governments, the professions, universities, the clergy and social agencies of every description have paid close attention to the semaphore. (When they don't, their sanctums are frequently invaded by large crowds carrying signs and shouting obscenities.)

What does this violent mood portend? A revolution of some kind would seem already to be underway. Young people carry most of the signs. "The new majority"; they seem to be taking over everything. They appear determined, in Saul Bellow's phrase, to seize the day, and possibly the world. But there is something desperate as well as knowing in the way they are going about it, for theirs has really been a revolt against meaninglessness—which at the present time they are attempting to cover up by mass-action, but which they covertly fear will outlast that action. And this mood is not confined to the young. Mature, wearying, old—so many of us are conducting our affairs in a peculiarly nervous fashion, as though time were short.

Quite evidently the people of our time are reporting an emotional displacement; a condition not new but, some say, "aggravated by the complexities of modern life." The diagnosis, roughly speaking: angst, alienation. The treatment? Any public library catalog offers an assortment of prescriptions. Also a host of new preachers and messiahs. Their life-plans usually involve one or a combination of these choices: spiritual uplift; psychiatric consultation; group action; drunkenness; embracing the outdoors; making love as often as possible to the very edge of consciousness and forgetting about anything else; burying oneself in work, games and large families; trying to follow the complicated religio-philosophical excuses for what Reinhold Niebuhr describes as man's "natural contingency," and in more recent years the skillful employment of narcotics, blowing your mind, and seeking rebirth in the psychedelic voyage.

Unfortunately, these panaceas have a single fault in common: they are all varieties of self-hypnosis. Without exception they aim to cover up our condition rather than change it. Tiptoing around like the old man with a young bride, they dare not come to grips because the bride is death.

Meanwhile, frightened, vulnerable and increasingly angry civilized men continue to signal their warnings. Though coded, the message is that of a grown-up child, and childishly easy to read. The "problem" expressed in whatever form—feelings of isolation; aggressive behavior toward one another; massive paranoia, and the common inability to believe, commit or care—derives, going back to the beginning, from a single cause.

At the heart of this distress, the illness may be identified, simply and without sham, as the fear of aging and death. All else is peripheral and finally unimportant. Hence, no therapeutic treatment, however inspirational, can do more than apply a coating of salve to our concern.

The problem causing civilized men to semaphore frantically and strike out in all directions is neither social nor philosophical, not religious or even psychiatric. Rather, it is based solidly on an intolerable recognition only now emerging to general consciousness; with protective myths and orthodoxies having been stripped away, not merely the knowledge but the gut-realization that the void is waiting for everybody and that each of us is going to vanish into it. The gloomiest projection of this awareness comes from a master scientist and mathematician, the seventeenth century Jansenist, Pascal:

> . . . that death, which threatens us every moment, must infallibly place us within a few years under the dreadful necessity of being for ever either annihilated or unhappy. There is nothing more real than this, nothing more terrible. Be we as heroic as we like, that is the end which awaits the noblest life in the world. . . . I know not who put me into this place rather than in another, nor why the short time which is given to live is assigned to me at this point rather than at another of the whole eternity which was before me or which shall come after me. I see nothing but infinities on all sides, which surround me as an atom, and as a shadow which endures only for an instant and returns no more. . . .

In our era Paul Tillich updates the same idea:

> We are a generation of the End and we should know that we are. . . . Death has become powerful in our time. . . . For nearly a century this was concealed in Western Civilization. . . . We forgot that we are finite, and we forgot the abyss of nothingness surrounding us.

We need not detail any more such pronouncements. The point is not that philosophers feel this way, but that insight into doom, once the privilege of certified thinkers, has now been brought home to nearly everybody who can read. It is the "something new" of our day. All around us we have the spectacle of overflowing millions no longer praying but grasping for salvation, behind all façades of sophistication and toughness, each in his own style, every man for himself. Salvation by whatever means—and quickly. It has become the central passion that drives us, a need rapidly turning into an imperious demand to be rescued from nothingness.

This is not to deny that life can be sunny and lusty, packed with fascinating hours; that everybody has the chance to turn his span into an adventure filled with achievement and love-making, and that we dance, sky-dive, float in space, build marvelous computers, and climb mountains under the sea. Admit too that we have never had such music, and proliferating excitement, and varieties of challenge. Still . . .

After the exuberance of being young, as young men and women grow only a little older, there begins to intrude on all our scenes a faint disquiet. At first it visits intermittently. The occasional feeling of a shadow seems not too important, perhaps an illusion. Then it reappears. In the beginning the shadow may be mistaken for doubt, about certain values such as justice; about the prosperity of brutes, a child with leukemia, death to the volunteer, safety for the malingerer. But then the uneasiness grows into something more important than doubt.

An old Marxist cartoon showed languid dancers at a ball. A great worker-fist has rammed up through the dance floor. Death to the aristocrats! But there has always been this larger fist bringing death to all classes. The great fist of death appears sooner or later to everyone, at first in dim outline, not necessarily brandished in our direction, often in repose, but still there. It becomes a strange, inconstant vision; sometimes the fist recedes and appears to vanish, but then on another day returns. As the years advance it slowly grows larger. Why it should be poised over us becomes as much of a mystery as the menace of the fist itself. The vision intrudes unexpectedly, not only in the middle of the night: perhaps during a cocktail party, after the football game, while you watch your children on the lawn. Not that we think about it all the time; people have other things to do. Still, it remains just beyond our attention, waiting.

We do our best to put the vision off somewhere, make it remote. Or close it off with black jokes. Any new religion is eagerly grasped for a little while. We must *kick* the vision by whatever means; otherwise all experience dissolves in irony, since it and we will soon be gone. In this state of mind, love, which passes, can become too much trouble. Without faith compassion seems useless. But now, precisely at the wrong time, men by the millions are in danger of succumbing to the tremendous input of their own information which has all but destroyed faith.

In *Escape from Freedom,* Erich Fromm saw this: "The state of anxiety, the feeling of powerlessness and insignificance, and especially the doubt concerning one's future after death, represent a state of mind which is practically unbearable for anybody."

Freud perceived in this psychic state the Universal Neurosis of Mankind. As Norman O. Brown has expressed it in *Life Against Death:* "Neurosis is not an occasional aberration; it is not just in other people; it is in us, and in us all the time." Man has established in himself "a psychic force opposed to his own idea." The force grows from a will to self-destruction which he tries to resist. Unfortunately, "the death instinct is the core of the human neurosis." Therefore, "mankind, unconscious of its real desires and . . . unable to obtain satisfaction, is hostile to life and ready to destroy itself."

A pure insight certainly, but perhaps not deep enough. Would it be ingenuous to explore the possibility that the fact of death alone, *all by itself,* may be what is at the core of the human neurosis? Perhaps man is not in the least hostile to his own consciousness, but only to life with death at the end of it.

As for the death instinct, admitting a countercurrent to the life force, are we stuck with the label? It might be asked, for instance, whether the death instinct could not just as well be performing also as an instinct to be reborn by changing from one form to another, crossing the border of death in between. Do death and rebirth tend to merge in the imagination? If so, when the drive to dissolve oneself occurs, we may find evidence that a death wish and rebirth wish can be the same.

The surface of history makes this conjecture seem worthwhile. Our species has never been reconciled to the brutal circumstance that we must die. Through the centuries we have invented an incredible number of explanations to account for our individual forms' decomposing in agony and returning to the earth.

The mysterious happening of death has led humanity to expiate primal guilt in both monstrous and beautiful ways. Hope of setting things right with the gods has driven us to lunacies of self-denial, cruelties, persecutions, elaborate ceremonies with incense and smoke, dancing around totem poles, the thumbscrewing of heretics; from Mexico to India, the casting of shrieking innocents into pits, and all kinds of psychotic, shameful and ludicrous practices such as would make whatever gods might be watching hide their eyes.

In the East we have been more subtle, attempting to placate destiny by an elaborate pretense of not wanting to survive, or preferring nirvana to the eternal return. But elsewhere listen to the wails, songs, shouts, hymns and chants. The voices of Islam, Judaism, Christianity and atheism join as one. Massed units in Red Square as well as Vatican City combine their energies in a single mighty appeal: *Save Us*. For the beauty and cruelty in the world, the kindness and the murder; our art trying to illuminate this wilderness; speculations of philosophers; and the descent into drugs and drunkenness; today's wildly emotional crowds rushing around the world's streets—all are organized around death, and designed to protect each of us from annihilation here or elsewhere.

Dostoevsky penetrates our situation with one quick thrust. In *The Possessed,* Kirilov, the engineer, about to become his own god by committing suicide: "Man simply invented God in order not to kill himself. That is the sum of universal history down to this moment."

Tracking man's spiritual history, we can follow this path: from the beginning, human consciousness longs and plans to perpetuate itself. Out of individuated consciousness, which is original sin, what Miguel de Unamuno called the "hunger of immortality" is born. Man craves personal immortality, but observes that everyone dies. He then creates gods, and worships and placates them. Assuming that "we must have done something wrong," he constructs systems of self-punishment to pay for the primal crime. Still everybody dies. Then, since eternal life on earth obviously is not forthcoming, and placating divine authority hasn't worked, he more or less unknowingly resolves to knock down the gods or replace them, or to become God. Since this must be done warily, for fear of retribution, he informs himself of what he is doing through myths. In these dream-projections the Promethean and satanic types, or the "Foolish Women" such as Eve, always undergo a severe chastising, but the idea of rebellion is thereby passed along. No good; everyone goes on dying.

He attempts to trick fate, as in the Far East, by pretending that he doesn't want to come back to life. That doesn't accomplish anything either. Now he grovels before the gods, saying, All right, I won't eat or make love too often; I'll play half-dead in advance, refuse to enjoy, even die before I die, offer myself for wounding, expose my undefended belly, genitals, backside, anything, is that what you want? No help.

Thus men alternate between abject surrender and assertiveness.

But whatever our tactics, we have always been in a state of Permanent Revolution against Imaginary Gods. Rephrasing and extending the Freudian conception, all culture has been a subtle and devious attempt to usurp divine authority, to conquer death—at the same time taking care not to excite the anger of the gods who inflict mortality on us until we are strong enough to overthrow them.

Man is a rebel, as Camus says, but he also resists himself, resists and sabotages his own rebellion. The Permanent Revolution is constantly being interfered with. Counter-revolutionaries in humanity's own ranks have always managed to slow down the centuries-old drive to remove death. Their counter-measures spring from an ever-changing set of superstitions.

A fifth column of superstition obstructs every advance against the citadel of death. Oddly enough, in an evolutionary context, the race's sabotaging of its own progress may turn out to have been functional. An innocent revolutionary spirit running ahead of scientific advances, without superstition to slow it down, might long since have killed itself off after prematurely looking death in the face.

To rein ourselves in, we invented primal guilt. Even if it has or once had evolutionary sanction, guilt is more than painful. The imaginary gods in our psyche exact a toll when they are threatened. They strike back, and sometimes cause us to panic, to twist and turn, and to become frightened of our own daring, and to hate and fear others who dare. Challenging the gods can estrange us from ourselves as well as from others, and make us odd and unconfident. It can reduce natural exuberance, and make this acceptable as payment for hubris. The rebel is at all times exposed, vulnerable, and afflicted by the suspicion that in his refusal to accept divine authority which leads to death he is somehow "wrong."

Above all, we conceal from ourselves the existence of our underground drive against the cosmic establishment. Men must keep it from themselves that they are in revolt against the gods, or "against Nature." Only by means of this hypocrisy has our species been able to keep the revolutionary program going. It has enabled man to plot against his gods while he worshipped them.

A disguised drive toward divinity, the creation of our own divinity, carries us forward. At certain times we advance too quickly, and the gods in our heads inflict a terrible revenge—sometimes on ourselves, more often on others. Galileo and Bruno move too far out in front of their day, and are cut down. But in another country, in Jung's phrase, "the godly sense of curiosity strives for birth." Man, in the person of Francis Bacon, sets up the scientific method to dominate his environment, to remove all mysteries (divine property), in order to find the base Archimedes sought, the place to stand from which he could move the world, and ultimately remove death.

In his recent study, *On Aggression,* Konrad Lorenz reminds us of an "inestimably important fact that by the process of phylogenetic ritualization a new and completely autonomous instinct may evolve which is, in principle, just as independent as any of the so-called 'great' drives, such as hunger, sex, fear, or aggression, and which—like these—has its seat in the great parliament of instincts." Dr. Lorenz emphasizes that "those other rites, which evolve in the course of human civilization, are not hereditarily fixed but are transmitted by tradition and must be learned afresh by every individual." Hence, a biological accounting for such activity is not required. "Among animals, symbols are not transmitted by tradition from generation to generation, and it is here, if one wishes, that one may draw the border line between the animal and man." And ". . . man's whole system of innate activities and reaction is phylogenetically so constructed, so 'calculated' by evolution, as to be complemented by cultural tradition."

From Dr. Lorenz's conclusions it would seem unnecessary to question whether the struggle for individual immortality, if such can be shown to exist, is derived from animal traits. Doubt whether activity of this kind can be filed under "instinct" or "drive" becomes equally irrelevant. It will be enough to show—from man's history and continuing behavior—that one of his consistently prevailing modes of activity, conceivably his project since time began, has been that of seeking ways to perpetuate his individual forms (ourselves). If we have a clue here, then the animal-originated drives or instincts can be supposed to have been redirected in the special interests of human survival.

Does the Darwinian struggle for existence continue unchanged in modern dress? Perhaps, but the principle of natural selection has obviously, to some extent, been countermanded in human affairs—for instance, by medical advances, computer technology and the range and destructive power of weaponry. By these and other means a soft, over-affluent culture which, biologically and historically, might be expected to succumb to a tough, oncoming barbarian group, retains the weapons to destroy the challenger, requiring only a highly-trained fraction of its people to do the job.

Where men are concerned, what we are dealing with for practical purposes is an inevitable response to life's intolerable ground rules. We have a condition: individual man's knowledge that some day he will die. Given the scope of human awareness, as well as our facility with tools, it may reasonably be assumed that moves to remedy the brutal situation will follow and persist.

Arrogance is not required to advance this thesis. Each man's struggle for indefinite survival beyond time need not violate concepts based on sexual energy, the will to power or, more recently, the principle of territorial defense. (But the territorial concern must by its own definition be peripheral. Territory is simply what surrounds life forms. Even enlarging the area to be defended so that it includes emotional *Lebensraum*, one's good name, and so on, the king finally preserved from harm is identity itself. Territory remains the outer perimeter, an outer concern of being, not its citadel.)

Having lost faith, a great many men and women have returned to the old superstitions now cloaked in new disguises. God may have retreated, but the *gods* today are by no means dead. Though disposed to destroy them, we simultaneously bow down to some of the weirdest assortment of deities ever known, such as History, Success and Statistics. We worship purveyors of Luck, Fashion and Publicity. We follow shifting gospels based on journalistic graffiti passing for honest news. We humbly receive the word from makeshift divinities seated at the head of couches, sexual statisticians, psychological testers, poll-takers, various merchants of paranoia, the manipulators of public relations and television personalities—the multiple gods of our quickening century.

This is to say that increasing numbers of civilized men and women are progressing, or retrogressing, to a pagan state of mind. The most sophisticated as well as humble people live in fear of these gods and, atheists most of all, are guided by the need either to live up to their examples or compete for their approval. What emerges, astonishingly, is that the old gods in new forms live on in our heads not metaphorically but for all practical purposes *alive,* and that they exert a dominating influence over the great bulk of modern affairs. One development is new here. For want of any other way, the publicizing of one's excellence (fitness for survival beyond death)—publicity great and small—has become the path to immortality. The lust for do-it-yourself immortality has produced an emotional transformation in which the ideal of Right Conduct (formerly the passport to heaven) is being replaced everywhere by the ideal of Printing One's Image on All Things.

Yet, seeking to remedy his condition, civilized man also wildly contradicts himself. Expending his energies at one and the same time to placate, impress, destroy and replace his gods, he also exhibits a craving to *share consciousness* with all other beings, including the divine. The attempt at spiritual fusion with others can take many forms—destructive, saintly (that is to say, charitable) and quiescent. Consider some recent effects.

Writing in the context of Nazism, Jacques Maritain heard "the voices of a base multitude whose baseness itself appears as an apocalyptic sign." These voices cry out: "'We have had enough of lying optimism and illusory morality, enough of freedom and personal dignity and justice and peace and faithfulness and goodness which make us mad with distress. Let us give ground to the infinite promises of evil, and of swarming death, and of blessed enslavement, and of triumphant despair.'"

In contrast—growing out of San Francisco and New York and spreading across the country—we have had the hippie sub-culture, based originally on the ideal of natural saintliness, or at any rate of free-form living. This has been made possible by a union bringing together the Wisdom of the East and Western pharmacology, with LSD and other substances providing the means for prolonged and repeated escapes from time (which marks the minutes leading to extinction). The movement should be understood—and generally is not—as an attempt to achieve *immortality now:* freedom from time, money, history and death. It also attempts to realize a general sharing of consciousness, in other words, collective immortality.

"The basic unit of the culture," one calling himself Billy Digger has said, "would be the commune instead of a house with one man and one woman in it. The commune would not be owned by one person or one group but would be open to all people at all times, to do whatever they wish to do in it. . . ." (In a different way, searching for communal immortality through violence, California's Hell's Angels and the Red Guards of China have been into the same thing: knocking down the uncles of the world and putting dunce caps on them.)

If such movements appear to deny old-fashioned responsibility and traditional modes of achievement, it is not surprising. The ideal of achievement has to do with a *reach* for immortality, which, if you feel already in that state, even in simulation, is obviously no longer necessary.

Still, these starts at saintly living (including, glibly, saintliness through violence), whether genuine or make-believe, fail to hide the phenomenon of flight. Saintliness in our time will not be able to generate corrective measures against our one long-range problem, which is death. Lacking a dynamic principle beyond that of shattering present life forms, it can only turn into another short-term holding operation. Saintliness can further charity, farming and simple craftsmanship. It can create motorcycles for the road to nowhere. It can promote measures at least temporarily to restore dignity, such as mass-sweeping of refuse-strewn neighborhoods. It can sponsor brotherhood-happenings in the park; create sweet afternoons with flowers, balloons and kites, and encourage people to draw closer to one another. But finally the uses of saintliness are defensive. Resisting technological inroads on the soul, they represent an attempt to deal with a neurotic industrial society by dropping out of it. Possibly the goal of all these efforts is that of agrarian-return or return to the small machine-shop.

But with all the love and kindness in the world, no agrarian retreat or machine-shop rendezvous can prevail for long against the thought of death, except by encouraging the participants to ignore it—and as the body grows older this cannot be done. The enlarged families of the *Now* people will grow older. The measures they have undertaken are not wrong, but right before their time. They must be reserved for the day when we gain utopia beyond time. They are eternally right, but temporally inadequate. For the near future, drop-out brotherhood will not be good enough, because the struggle against real death requires training, and must be fought out industrially and in the laboratory.

As for the psychedelic trip, no one should doubt that it can prove rewarding, if it is not taken too far and too often. But resorted to as a complete way of life, it may hurt you in mysterious ways, and achieve not much more than a temporarily helpful, and perhaps cowardly, cracking of identity. What makes widespread psychedelic dropping out as alarming as it can be is that—if the substances are used improperly—after a point, with each new voyage, return to the old identity and earthly purpose tends to seem increasingly less worthwhile. True, identity can become a cross when it is formed too rigidly. But ego-identity is also our main source of power in the world, and only by organizing the power of our protesting intelligence can we hope to bring about the death-free life man must have.

Finally, by blowing their minds young men and women hide from death. It is good sometimes to hide from death, and to go through simulated death and rebirth now and then. But too many trips, indiscriminately taken, can lead to an unearned passivity. If passivity takes hold, this society, undesirable as it may seem, will become far worse. Extremes of violence and mass-passivity will build up. When these two forces are polarized, disaster comes, and, contrary to myth, violence nearly always wins.

It has already started to win again. The finest among us are shot in the head by half-crazed and above all lonely individuals. Not only assassins, but the most advanced elements of our younger society, can no longer stand being alone. Youth's quiescent and largely drug-oriented nihilism of a few years ago has quickly given way to the New Left's all-out freedom through violence. But—quite apart from the justice of all causes—the New Left, as evidenced by its massive shock tactics, its theater and enlarged family formations, is clearly moving toward exactly the same goal as that of the Psychedelic Mutants—a collective and communal escape from time and death.

What happened is this: in the past quarter-century the public relations of death, as managed by theologians of all creeds and every secular orthodoxy, all but exhausted the ancient excuses for what Unamuno called "the running away of life like water." Interestingly, the atomic bomb, LSD and the Pill were developed at about the same time. Could this be the evolutionary crisis of our species? For centuries men were able to hold on to their peace of mind by repetitive prayer, chants, rhythms and psalms set to music. But repetition, beauty and music no longer possess the force to distract us from meaninglessness.

Today we are in a race against time, racing, as Maritain suggests, our own apocalypse. Man's inexorable though hardly remorseless drive to divinity is taking new, noninstitutionalized forms. This comes down to the simplest of propositions: the species must solve the problem of death very soon, blow itself up or blow its mind.

Medical help is on the way, but so too are fire-power and despair. All have computer technology behind them. Any one of the three might win. Will medical advances to arrest the aging of human tissues prevail over weaponry and mass psychosis? That has become the question of our time and conceivably of all time.

The immortalist position is that the usefulness of philosophy has come to an end, because all philosophy teaches accommodation to death and grants it static finality as "the human condition." Art too, insofar as it celebrates or merely bemoans our helplessness, has gone as far as it can. The beautiful device of tragedy ending in helplessness has become outmoded in our absurd time, no longer desirable and not to be glamorized. The art that embellishes death with visual beauty and celebrates it in music belongs to other centuries.

It comes as no surprise that traditional forms of art are being shattered, with the editing and fixing of life no longer allowed. Our participation is demanded in these works; we cannot be spectators. The discotheque takes its place as an electric art form. We loosen our anxieties with the help of enormous guitars in a temple of fragmentation. Kinetic and luminous forms that reach out and bring us into the action; declaimed poetry now so often set to music; multiple screens, happenings that frequently involve orgy and obscenity—all have one purpose: to smash the *separateness* of everyone present; to expose feeling and break through thinking; to make us live, in the phrase Alan Watts has quoted from Ananda K. Coomaraswamy, "a perpetual uncalculated life in the present." And all this too amounts to one more attempt to hide from the end—by substituting Dionysian togetherness for romance, and a bombardment of the senses, lightworks of the soul, a sort of electronic Buddhism in place of sequential perception. The use of kinetic environment as an art form removes death, creating the illusion of an Eternal Now—an illusion in that it seems to guarantee eternal youth, which, of course, is what this generation is really after.

The immortalist thesis is that the time has come for man to get rid of the intimidating gods in his own head. It is time for him to grow up out of his cosmic inferiority complex (no more "dust thou art, and to dust thou shalt return . . ."), bring his disguised desire into the open, and go after what he wants, the only state of being he will settle for, which is divinity.

We have circled the moon, harnessed nuclear energy, artificially reproduced DNA, and now have the biochemical means to control birth; why should death itself, "the Last Enemy," be considered sacred and beyond conquest?

A new act of faith is required of us: the kind of faith that we might have had a few decades ago, and did not, when Dr. Goddard was bravely projecting his rockets into the atmosphere, and a band of futurists was insisting that not just in comic strips but in reality we could lift ourselves beyond any space that could be seen from the earth. This new faith we must have is that with the technology at our disposal in the near future death can be conquered. This faith must also weld Salvation to Medical Engineering.

We must drive away the gods of doubt and self-punishment. Our new faith must accept as gospel that salvation belongs to medical engineering and nothing else; that man's fate depends first on the proper management of his technical proficiency; that we can only engineer our freedom from death, not pray for it; that our messiahs will be wearing white coats, not in asylums but in chemical and biological laboratories.

With such faith we will stop shrinking into conformity, huddling in corporations and communes, and numbing our anxieties by means of network television. (Great corporations can, of course—in fact, must—contribute to this effort, but with much more imagination and daring than most of them exhibit now.) In this spirit, many young people will perhaps moderate their future dependency on the psychedelic simulation of death and rebirth, their escape into mob action, and such devices as the electronic scrambling of consciousness.

Does such a project seem quixotic now? Perhaps so, but it will not tomorrow. It is at least as practical as going beyond the moon, and conceivably, from an evolutionary standpoint, part of the same program.

Our conception of immortality now requires precise definition. What must be eliminated from the human situation is the inevitability of death as a result and natural end of the aging process. I am speaking of the inescapable parabolic arching from birth to death. But we must clearly understand that any given unit of life—my individual existence and yours—can never be guaranteed eternity.

Until such time as duplications of individual nervous systems can be grown in tissue cultures (at this point no one knows "whose" consciousness they would have), our special identities will always be subject to being hit by a truck or dying in a plane crash. A sudden virus or heart seizure, even in the body's youth, may carry us off. Statistically, looking ahead thousands of years, the chances are that every human and even inanimate form will be broken sooner or later. But the distress felt by men and women today does not arise from the fear of such hazards. Rather, it comes from the certainty of aging and physical degeneration leading to death. It is the fear of losing our powers and being left alone, or in the hands of indifferent nurses, and knowing that the moment must come when we will not see the people we love any more, and everything will go black.

Some would fear the opposite: living through a great blank eternity with our eyes open. This would be comparable to endless days without sleep. But no problem confronts us here. A state of indefinite living can be programmed through a succession of lives by means of designed sleeps or hibernations to last for years, decades or centuries. We will see that family ties can be renewed and dropped like options from one life to another. People can be phased, perhaps psychedelically, out of one life, and then, reactivated according to their own desire, briefed back into the next. Those who find the opportunities for future existences insupportable will be welcome to decline rejuvenation. For others who prefer a life not risk-free, the zero and double-zero of accidental death can provide the spice of chance in the living continuum. In the society that some day will live beyond time what is now called the Absurd will undoubtedly turn into our saving grace.

In our conception immortality is *being alive now, ungoverned by span, cycle* or *inevitability*. Civilized man's project will no longer be as Freud suggested to recover his lost childhood, but rather to create the adult equivalent: an immortal present free from the fear of aging and death. Our aim (against the counsel of nearly all wise old men) will be to fix our immediate environment so that, puny as we like to tell ourselves we are (still placating the old gods), the environment puts itself at our service.

"The world is made for Consciousness. Each Consciousness," wrote Unamuno, ". . . A human soul is worth all the universe. . . ." Our project—at least as worthy as the Manhattan Project that produced the atomic bomb and the National Space Program—can be to individualize eternity, to stabilize the forms and identities through which the energy of conscious life passes.

An "Immortality Program" would not be nearly as expensive as the atomic energy and space projects. At the beginning, it would involve intensive work in basic biology, since the first principles of the aging process are only dimly understood, and have not yet been satisfactorily formulated. We will find that a full-scale assault on death begun in this manner is by no means impractical, and that, even if it were, men (still unbeknown to themselves) have already decided to undertake it.

The case for the immortalist point of view will rest on evidence that since the beginning of recorded time man has engaged in a disguised drive to make himself immortal and divine, and that this overriding motive which accounts for much of his significant action, is now driving him toward his evolutionary crisis. The time has come for men to turn into gods or perish.

Cutting Loose

Sally Kempton

Sally Kempton was born in 1943, the daughter of a famous journalist (Murray Kempton), and grew up in Princeton, New Jersey. She attended Sarah Lawrence College and married the man who was to be the executive director of Antonioni's *Zabriski Point.* The other important facts of her life are contained in the following article, which transcends anything else the editors have read on women's liberation for sheer candor, conviction, and insight.

Once another woman and I were talking about male resistance to Woman's Liberation, and she said that she didn't understand why men never worry about women taking their jobs away but worry only about the possibility that women may stop making love to them and bearing their children. And once I was arguing with a man I know about Woman's Liberation, and he said he wished he had a motorcycle gang with which to invade a Woman's Liberation meeting and rape everybody in it. There are times when I understand the reason for men's feelings. I have noticed that beyond the feminists' talk about the myth of the vaginal orgasm lies a radical resentment of their position in the sexual act. And I have noticed that when I feel most militantly feminist I am hardly at all interested in sex.

Almost one could generalize from that: the feminist impulse is anti-sexual. The very notion of women gathering in groups is somehow anti-sexual, anti-male, just as the purposely all-male group is anti-female. There is often a sense of genuine cultural rebellion in the atmosphere of a Woman's Liberation meeting. Women sit with their legs apart, carelessly dressed, barely made-up, exhibiting their feelings or the holes at the knees of their jeans with an unprovocative candor which is hardly seen at all in the outside world. Of course, they are demonstrating by their postures that they are in effect off duty, absolved from the compulsion to make themselves attractive, and yet, as the world measures these things, such demonstrations could in themselves be seen as evidence of neurosis: we have all been brought up to believe that a woman who was "whole" would appear feminine even on the barricades.

The fact is that one cannot talk in feminist terms without revealing

SOURCE: Sally Kempton, "Cutting Loose," *Esquire Magazine* (July 1972). Reprinted by permission of *Esquire Magazine* © 1972 by Esquire, Inc.

feelings which have traditionally been regarded as neurotic. One becomes concerned about women's rights, as Simone de Beauvoir noted, only when one perceives that there are few personal advantages to be gained from accepting the traditional women's roles. A woman who is satisfied with her life is not likely to be drawn into the Woman's Liberation movement: there must be advantages for her as a woman in a man's world. To be a feminist one must be to some degree maladjusted to that world, one must be, if you will, neurotic. And sometimes one must be anti-sexual, if only in reaction to masculine expectations. Men do not worry about women taking their jobs because they do not think that women could do their jobs; most men can only be threatened by a woman in bed. A woman who denies her sexuality, if only for an evening, denies her status as an object of male attention, as a supplicant, successful or not, for male favor. For a woman to deny her sexuality is to attack the enemy in his most valuable stronghold, which is her own need for him.

I became a feminist as an alternative to becoming a masochist. Actually, I always was a masochist; I became a feminist because to be a masochist is intolerable. As I get older I recognize more and more that the psychoanalytical idea that women are natural masochists is at least metaphorically correct: my own masochism derived from an almost worshipful respect for masculine power. In my adolescence I screwed a lot of guys I didn't much like, and always felt abused by them, but I never felt free to refuse sex until after the initial encounter. My tactic, if you can call it a tactic, was to Do It once and then to refuse to see the boy again, and I think I succeeded, with my demonstrations of postcoital detachment, in making several of them feel as rejected by my lovemaking as I had felt by their desire to make love to me without love. Yet I felt in those years that I had irretrievably marked myself a sexual rebel, and I was given to making melodramatic statements like "I'm not the kind of girl men marry." Years later I realized that I had been playing a kind of game, the same game boys play at the age of sexual experimentation, except that, unlike a boy, I could not allow myself to choose my partners and admit that I had done so. In fact, I was never comfortable with a lover unless he had, so to speak, wronged me. Once during my senior year in high school I let a boy rape me (that is not, whatever you may think, a contradiction in terms) in the bedroom of his college suite while a party was going on next door; afterward I ran away down the stairs while he followed, shouting apologies which became more and more abject as he realized that my revulsion was genuine, and I felt an exhilaration which I clearly recognized as triumph. By letting him abuse me I had won the right to tell him I hated him; I had won the right to hurt him.

I think most American adolescents hate and fear the opposite sex: in adolescence it seems that only one's lovers can hurt one, and I think that even young people who are entirely secure in other relations recognize and would, if they could, disarm the power the other sex has for them. But for adolescent boys, sexual success is not the sole measure of worth. It is assumed that they will grow up and work, that their most important tests will come in areas whose criteria are extra-sexual. They can fail with girls without failing entirely, for there remains to them the public life, the male life.

But girls have no such comfort. Sex occupies even the economic center of our lives; it is, we have been brought up to feel, our lives' work. Whatever else she may do, a woman is a failure if she fails to please men. The adolescent girl's situation is by definition dependent: she *must* attract, and therefore, however she may disguise it, she must compromise the sticky edges of her personality, she must arrange herself to conform with other people's ideas of what is valuable in a woman.

I was early trained to that position, trained, in the traditional manner, by my father. Like many men who are uncomfortable with adult women, my father saw his daughter as a potential antidote to his disappointment in her sex. I was someone who could be molded into a woman compatible with his needs, and also, unlike my mother, I was too impressionable to talk back. So I became the vessel into which he fed his opinions about novels and politics and sex; he fed me also his most hopeful self-image. It reached a point where I later suspected him of nourishing a sort of eighteenth-century fantasy about our relationship, the one in which the count teaches his daughter to read Virgil and ride like a man, and she grows up to be the perfect feminine companion, parroting him with such subtlety that it is impossible to tell that her thoughts and feelings, so perfectly coincident with his, are not original. I had three brothers, as it happened, and another sort of man might have chosen one of them to mold. But my father had himself a vast respect for masculine power. Boys grow up and have to kill their fathers, girls can be made to understand their place.

My father in his thirties was an attractive man, he was witty by adult standards and of course doubly so by mine, and he had a verbal facility with which he invariably demolished my mother in arguments. Masculine power in the intellectual classes is exercised verbally: it is the effort of the male supremacist intellectual to make his woman look clumsy and illogical beside him, to render her, as it were, dumb. His tactic is to goad the woman to attack him and then, resorting to rationality, to withdraw himself from the battle. In my childhood experience, subtlety appeared exclusively a masculine weapon. I never saw a woman argue except straightforwardly, and I never saw a woman best a man in a quarrel. My mother tried, but always with the conviction of ultimate failure. She attacked with pinpricks to begin with; in the end, maddened invariably by my father's ostentatious mental absence, she yelled. He was assisted in these struggles by his natural passivity. Withdrawal came easily to him; he hated, as he told us over and over again, scenes. My mother, it seemed to me, was violent, my father cool. And since it also seemed to me that he preferred me, his daughter who never disagreed with him, to his wife who did (that was a fantasy, of course, but one to which my father devoted some effort toward keeping alive), I came to feel that male power, because uncoercible, could only be handled by seduction, and that the most comfortable relation between men and women was the relation between pupil and teacher, between parent and child.

My father taught me some tricks. From him I learned that it is pleasant and useful to get information from men, pleasant because it is easier than getting it for yourself, and useful because it is seductive: men like to give information and sometimes love the inquirer, if she is pretty and asks intelligently. From him I also learned that women are by definition incapable of serious thought. This was a comforting lesson, although it made me feel obscurely doomed, for if I was to be automatically barred from participation in the life of high intellect, there was no reason why I should work to achieve it, and thinking, after all, is difficult work. When I was fifteen my father told me that I would never be a writer because I wasn't hungry enough, by which I think he meant that there would always be some man to feed me. I accepted his pronouncement as I accepted, at that age, all pronouncements which had an air of finality, and began making other career plans.

My task, it seemed to me, was to find a man in whom there resided enough power to justify my acting the child, that is, to justify my acceptance of my own femininity. For I regarded myself as feminine only in my childlike aspect; when I presented myself as a thinking person I felt entirely sexless. The boys in my class regarded me as an intellectual and showed an almost unanimous disinterest in my company. When I was in the eighth grade I lived in trepidation lest I be cited as class bookworm, and defended myself against that threat by going steady with what surely must have been the dumbest boy in our set. He was no fonder of me than I was of him; we needed each other because you had to be part of a couple in order to get invited to parties.

I did not get the opportunity to demonstrate my skill as a child-woman until I became old enough to go out with college boys. My training had equipped me only to attract intelligent men, and a boy who was no brighter than I held no power for me. But for a man who could act as my teacher I could be submissive and seductive—I *felt* submissive and seductive; my awe of the male mind translated easily into an awe of the male person.

I was, I realize now, in tune with the demands of my time. This was in the late Fifties, Marilyn Monroe was the feminine archetype of the period, and Marilyn Monroe was sexy because of her childishness. It is not much of a step from seeing oneself as a child in relation to men to seeing oneself as their victim; obviously a child does not control its environment, obviously a child is powerless before adults. All children are potential victims, dependent upon the world's goodwill. My sense of powerlessness, of feminine powerlessness, was so great that for years I trusted no man who had not indicated toward me a special favor, who had not fallen in love with me. And even toward those who had, I acted the victim, preferring to believe myself the one who loved most, for how could a man retain his power in loving me unless I gave it back to him through my submission? Years later I heard a story about how Bob Dylan so tormented a groupy that she jumped out a window while ten people looked on, and recognized the spirit of my adolescence. I never got myself into a situation even comparably extreme, my fundamental self-protectiveness having permitted me to allow only minor humiliations, but the will was there.

Masochism as clinically defined is more or less exclusively a sexual disorder: masochists are people who derive sexual pleasure from pain. Freudian psychiatrists claim that all women are to one degree or another masochistic in the sexual sense (the male penetrates the female, presumably he hurts her, and presumably she enjoys the pain as part of the pleasure), and many Freudian thinkers extend the use of the term out of the area of sex into the social area and argue that the womanly woman is correctly masochistic, must be masochistic in order to accept the male domination which is necessarily a part even of her extra-sexual life. It seems to me more useful to define masochism, insofar as the word is to be used to describe a non-clinical emotional condition, as the doing of something which one does not enjoy because someone else demands it or even because one's conscience demands it. In this sense clinical masochism can be said to be non-masochistic: if one enjoys being whipped, one is acting directly upon one's own needs, whereas if one allows oneself to be whipped for someone else's pleasure without deriving any pleasure from the act, one is behaving masochistically. A person who acts upon someone else's will, or in accordance with someone else's image of her, or who judges herself by someone else's standards, has allowed herself to be made into an object. A masochist, as I define the term, is a person who consents to be made an object. It is in that sense that I think most women are, or have been at some time in their lives, masochists. For insofar as a woman lives by the standards of the world, she lives according to the standards set by men. Men have laid down the rules and definitions by which the world is run, and one of the objects of their definitions is woman. Men define intelligence, men define usefulness, men tell us what is beautiful, men even tell us what is womanly. Constance Chatterley was a male invention; Lawrence invented her, I used to think, specifically to make me feel guilty because I didn't have the right kind of orgasms.

Lionel Trilling wrote in an essay on Jane Austen that it is the presumption of our society that women's moral life is not as men's, and that therefore we do not expect from women, in fact do not condone in them, the same degree of self-love which we expect and encourage in men. What he meant, I think, was that since women are in a sense given their lives, since women customarily choose a life-style by choosing a man rather than a path, they do not need the self-love which is necessary to carry a man to the places he has to go. Self-love is indeed a handicap to a being whose primary function is supportive, for how is a woman adequately to support another ego when her self-love demands the primacy of her own? Women learn in many ways to suppress their selfishness, and by doing so they suppress also their self-esteem. If most men hold women in contempt it is no greater than the contempt in which women hold themselves. Self-love repressed becomes self-loathing. Men are brought up to command, women to seduce; to admit the necessity of seduction is to admit that one has not the strength to command. It is in fact to accept one's own objecthood, to internalize one's oppression.

Still, I picked up some interesting lore from men, while I was studying to please them. I learned about Eliot from one boy, and about Donne from another, and about Coltrane from a third. A lover turned me on to drugs and also showed me how you were supposed to act when you were high—that is, as if you were not high. I was not surprised that he was better at this than me, cool was beginning to seem more and more a masculine talent, and I had even taken to physical retaliation in arguments, having given up the idea that I would ever win anything by verbal means. I went to Sarah Lawrence instead of Barnard because my boyfriend thought Sarah Lawrence was a more "feminine" school. My parents got divorced and I sided with my father, at least at first, because his appeared to me to be the winning side. Men, I believed, were automatically on the winning side, which was why my oldest brother could afford to withdraw in moral outrage from my father's advances; there was for *him* no danger of branding himself a loser by consorting with my mother. Yet I envied him his integrity. How could I maintain integrity when I was willing to sell out any principle for the sake of masculine attention?

I went to Sarah Lawrence and got to love it without ever taking it very seriously, which I also supposed was the way the boys I loved in those days felt about me. In fact, Sarah Lawrence appeared to me and to most of my friends there as a sort of symbol of ourselves: like the college, we were pretty and slightly prestigious and terribly self-serious in private, but just as we laughed at the school and felt embarrassed to be identified with it publicly (I always felt that if I had been a real student I would have gone to Barnard), so we laughed publicly at our own aspirations. "I like Nancy," a Princeton boy said to me, "except she always starts talking about Kafka promptly at midnight." And I laughed, god how I laughed, at Nancy—how *Sarah Lawrency* to carry on about Kafka—and, by implication, at myself. For I too expressed my intellectualism in effusions. Men expected the effusions, even found them charming, while treating them with friendly contempt. It was important to be charming. A passion for Marxism, stumblingly expressed, an interpretation of *Moby Dick,* these tokens we offered our lovers to prove we were not simply women, but people. Yet though we displayed strong feelings about art and politics, we behaved as if we had not really done the reading. To argue a point logically was to reveal yourself as unfeminine: a man might respect your mind, but he would not love you. Wit, we believed, is frightening in a woman.

In my senior year I met a girl who knew the editor of *The Village Voice,* and after graduation she got me a job there. I went to work as a reporter without having the slighest notion of how to conduct an interview and so, to cover myself, I made up a couple of pieces out of whole cloth. They were about drugs and hippies and homosexuals, the sort of scene pieces *The Voice* later specialized in, but nobody much was writing about that stuff in 1964, and I got several book offers and invitations to cocktail parties, and my father's friends started writing me letters full of sports analogies, saying it was time I entered a main event. In fact, I felt terribly guilty about writing those pieces because they seemed frivolous and sensationalistic, the sort of thing empty-headed girl reporters did when they were too dumb to write about politics, but on the other hand they got me attention, which writing about politics would never have done. I agonized all summer, publicly and privately, over this dilemma, often spending hours telling big strong male reporters how unworthy I felt. They seemed to like it.

I had never thought of myself as ambitious; actually, I think I was too convinced of my basic incompetence to be constructively ambitious, but I quickly saw that a lady journalist has advantages denied to men. For one thing, she never has to pick up a check. For another thing, if she is even remotely serious, people praise her work much more than they would praise the work of a comparably talented man; they are amazed that a woman can write coherently on any subject not confined in interest to the readers of a woman's magazine. And finally, people tell her things they would not tell a man. Many men think the secrets they tell a woman are automatically off the record. They forget that the young woman hanging on their every word is taking it all down—often they confuse her attention with sexual interest. (That is not such an advantage. Some men, rock stars for instance, simply assumed that sex was what I had come for. They would expend a little flattery to assure me that they regarded me as a cut above other groupies, and then they would suggest that we get down to balling. They were often nasty when I refused.)

At any rate, the work was nice, and it gave me a higher status as a sexual object than I had ever had before. But it was also scary. If I was to do well at it I had to take it seriously, and the strongest belief I had retained from my childhood was my idea that nothing I could achieve was worth taking seriously. In the Autumn of 1964 I fell in love with a boy who was not sure he was in love with me, and by the time he decided he was I had quit my job and moved with him to Boston. He styled himself a revolutionary and thought the content of my work hardly worth the effort it took to produce it; I accepted his opinion with relief, telling myself that in any case I had not the emotional energy to handle both a lover and a job. My feeling for him evaporated fairly soon after I discovered that it was reciprocated, though I lived with him for several months after that, partly out of guilt and partly because living with a man made me feel grown-up in a way holding a job never could have done. But finally I left him and took a job as a staff writer on a national magazine, a classy job but underpaid. Instead of complaining about the salary, I took to not showing up for work, justifying my laziness by telling myself that I was selling out anyway by taking an uptown job and that the sooner I rid myself of it, the sooner I would regain my integrity.

In the meantime I had met a grown-up man who was powerful and smart and knocked out by my child act. We spent a few months seducing each other—"You're too young for me," he would say, and I would climb upon his lap, figuratively speaking, and protest that I was not. It was no more disgusting than most courtships. In the end we got married.

Of course, I had to marry a grown-up, a father figure if you will, and my husband, as it turned out, had to marry a child. That is, he had to have an intelligent woman, but one whose intelligence had been, as it were, castrated by some outside circumstances. My youth served that purpose; my other handicaps had not as yet emerged.

Anyway, our romantic personae lasted about a year. For a year he was kind to me and listened to my problems and put up with the psychosomatic diseases which marriage had induced in me, and for a year I brought joy and spontaneity into his drab grown-up existence. Then he began to get tired of being a father and I to resent being a child, and we began to act out what I think is a classic example of contemporary marriage.

It had turned out, I realized with horror, that I had done exactly what middle-class girls are supposed to do. I had worked for a year in the communications industry, and my glamorous job had enabled me to meet a respectable, hardworking man who had made a lot of money at *his* glamorous job, and I had settled down (stopped screwing around) and straightened myself out (went into analysis), and all that was missing was babies. I defended myself by assuming that we would be divorced in a year, and sneered a lot at Design Research furniture and the other symbols of middle-class marriage, but still I could not escape the feeling that I had fallen not just into a trap but into a cliché. On the other hand, I loved my husband, and I was still a writer, that is to say, a privileged woman with a life of her own. I could afford, as I began to at that time, to read feminist literature without really applying it to my own situation.

My husband, although he is nice to women, is a male supremacist, very much in the style of Norman Mailer. That is, he invests women with more or less mystical powers of control over the inner workings of the world, but thinks that feminine power is strongest when exercised in child rearing and regards contraception as unnatural. When I had my first stirrings of feminist grievance, he pronounced the subject a bore; I used to follow him from room to room, torturing him with my recitals of the sexist atrocities I was beginning to find in my favorite novels, and when I complained that magazines were paying me less than they paid men, he accused me of trying to blame the world for my own crazy passivity. But we were engaged at that time in the usual internal power struggle, and my feminism seemed to both of us more an intellectual exercise than a genuine commitment. It was not until many months later that he began to accuse me of hating men.

We already knew that he hated women, even that he had good reasons for hating women, but I had up to that time put on such a good display of being cuddly, provocative, sexually uninhibited and altogether unlike those other women that the subject of my true feelings about men had never come up. He knew that I had a compulsion to seduce men, which argues a certain distrust of them, but as the seductions, since our marriage, were always intellectual rather than sexual, they could, if you didn't want to consider their implications, be put down simply to insecurity. I don't think even I realized how I felt. Once I told my husband about a rigmarole a friend and I had made up to dismiss men we didn't like—we would go through lists of names, pointing our fingers and saying, "Zap, you're sterile," and then collapse into giggles; my husband, who has a psychoanalytical turn of mind, thought that was Terribly Revealing and I agreed that it was, but so what? And also, I agreed that it was Terribly Revealing that I liked to pinch and bite him, that I made small hostile jokes and took an almost malicious pleasure in becoming too involved in work to pay attention to him (but only briefly; I never for very long attempted to work when he had other plans), that I would go into week-long depressions during which the bed never got made nor the dishes washed. But the degree of my hostility didn't reveal itself to me until a pattern began to emerge around our quarrels.

We had, since early in the marriage, periodically engaged in bitter fights. Because my husband was the stronger, and because he tends to be judgmental, they usually started when he attempted to punish me (by withdrawing, of course) for some offense. I would dispute the validity of his complaint, and the quarrel would escalate into shouts and blows and then into decisions to terminate the marriage. In the first year my husband always beat me hollow in those battles. I used to dissolve into tears and beg his forgiveness after twenty minutes; I could not bear his rejection and I had no talent at all for conducting a quarrel. I won only when I succeeded in making him feel guilty; if he behaved badly enough I automatically achieved the moral upper hand for at least a week following the quarrel. But after a while, the honeymoon being over, he began to refuse to feel guilty and I began to resent his superior force. Things rested there until, in the third year of our marriage, we went to live in Los Angeles because of my husband's work. During the year we spent away from home I found that I could not work, and that he was always working, and we suddenly found ourselves frozen into the textbook attitudes of male-female opposition. We fought continually, and always about the same things. He accused me of making it impossible for him to work, I accused him of keeping me dangling, dependent upon him for all emotional sustenance, he accused me of spending too much money and of keeping the house badly, I accused him of expecting me continually to subordinate my needs to his. The difficulty, I realized over and over again without being able to do much about it, was that I had gotten myself into the classic housewife's position: I was living in a place I didn't want to be, and seeing people I didn't like because that was where my man was, I was living my husband's life and I hated him for it. And the reason this was so was that I was economically dependent upon him; having ceased to earn my living I could no longer claim the breadwinner's right to attention for my special needs.

My husband told me that I was grown-up now, twenty-six years old, there were certain realities which I had to face. He was the head of the household: I had never questioned that. He had to fulfill himself: I had never questioned that. He housed and fed me and paid for my clothes, he respected my opinions and refused all his opportunities to make love to other women, and my part of the bargain should have become clear to me by now. In exchange for those things, I was supposed to keep his house and save his money and understand that if he worked sixteen hours a day for a year it was no more than necessary for his self-fulfillment. Which was all quite true. Except that it was also necessary for his fulfillment that I should be there for those few hours when he had time for me, and not complain about the hours when he did not, and that I should adapt myself to his situation or else end the marriage. It never occurred to him to consider adapting himself to mine, and it never occurred to me. I only knew that his situation was bad for me, was alien, was in fact totally paralyzing, that it kept me from working, that it made me more unhappy than I had been in my life.

I knew that I was being selfish. But he was being selfish also, the only difference being that his selfishness was somehow all right, while mine was inexcusable. Selfishness was a privilege I had earned for a while by being a writer, that is, a person who had by male standards a worthwhile place to spend her time. As soon as I stopped functioning as a writer I became to my husband and to everyone else a mere woman, somebody whose time was valueless, somebody who had no excuse for a selfish preoccupation with her own wants.

I used to lie in bed beside my husband after those fights and wish I had the courage to bash in his head with a frying pan. I would do it while he slept, since awake he would overpower me, disarm me. If only I dared, I would mutter to myself through clenched teeth, pushing back the realization that I didn't dare not because I was afraid of seriously hurting him—I would have loved to do that—but because even in the extremity of my anger I was afraid that if I cracked his head with a frying pan he would leave me. God, how absurd it was (god, how funny, I would mutter to myself, how amusing, oh wow, what a joke) that my whole life's effort had been directed toward keeping men from leaving me, toward placating them, submitting to them, demanding love from them in return for living in their style, and it all ended with me lying awake in the dark hating my husband, hating my father, hating all the men I had ever known. Probably I had always hated them. What I couldn't figure out was whether I hated them because I was afraid they would leave me or whether I was afraid they would leave me because I hated them.

Because one cannot for very long support such a rage without beginning to go crazy, I tried to think of the problem in political terms. It seemed to me too easy to say that my hatred for men was a true class hatred, that women hate men because women are an oppressed class hungering for freedom. And yet wherever there exists the display of power there is politics, and in women's relations with men there is a continual transfer of power, there is, continually, politics. There are political analogies even to our deepest, our most banal fantasies. Freud maintains that the female terror of the penis is a primary fear, and that the male fear of castration by the vagina is merely a retaliatory fantasy, a guilty fear of punishment. The serf fears the overlord's knout, the overlord, guilty, fears the serf's revenge. Women are natural guerrillas. Scheming, we nestle into the enemy's bed, avoiding open warfare, watching the options, playing the odds. High, and made paranoiac by his observance of my rage, my husband has the fantasy of woman with a knife. He sees her in sexual ecstasy with her eyes open to observe the ecstasy of her partner, with her consciousness awake, her consciousness the knife. It had often been my private boast that even in moments of greatest abandon, I always kept some part of my mind awake: I always searched for clues. Is he mine now, this monster? Have I disarmed him, and for how long? Men are beasts, we say, joking, parodying the Victorian rag, and then realize to our surprise that we believe it. The male has force almost beyond our overpowering, the force of laws, of science, of literature, the force of mathematics and skyscrapers and the Queensboro Bridge; the penis is only its symbol. We cannot share men's pride in the world they have mastered. If you follow that symbolism to its conclusion, we are ourselves that conquered world.

It is because they know that this is true, know it in their bones if not in their heads, that men fear the hatred of women. For women are the true maintenance class. Society is built upon their acquiescence, and upon their small and necessary labors. Restricted to the supportive role, conditioned to excel only at love, women hold for men the key to social order. It is a Marxist truism that the original exploitation, the enslavement which set the pattern for everything which came later, was the enslavement of women by men. Even the lowest worker rests upon the labor of his wife. Where no other claim to distinction exists, a man defines himself by his difference from the supportive sex; he may be a less than admirable man, but at least he is a man, at least he is not a woman.

And if women have fought, they have fought as guerrillas, in small hand-to-hand skirmishes, in pillow wars upon the marriage bed. When they attack frontally, when they come together in groups to protest their oppression, they raise psychic questions so profound as to be almost inadmissible. In E. E. Cummings' play *Him,* there is a scene in which two women sit in a Paris café and order men served up to them like plats du jour: it is an inexpressibly sinister sequence, and it has its counterparts elsewhere in the avant-garde literature of the Twenties. I do not imagine that Cummings approved of men using women like meat, but I am quite sure that he could not have treated the situation with such horror had the sexual roles been reversed. Cummings, like Leonid Andreyev and the other modernists who dealt in surreal images of female dominance, was writing during the early period of feminist protest, and I think they were expressing a fear basic to every man confronted with the idea of women's liberation. When men imagine a female uprising they imagine a world in which women rule men as men have ruled women: their guilt, which is the guilt of every ruling class, will allow them to see no middle ground. And it is a measure of the unconscious strength of our belief in natural male dominance that all of us, men and women, revolt from the image of woman with a whip, that the female sadist is one of our most deep-rooted images of perversion.

And although I believe this male fantasy of feminine equality as a euphemism for feminine dominance to be evidence of the oppressors' neurosis rather than of any supporting fact, it was part of the character of my resentment that I once fancied wresting power from men as though nothing less than total annihilation would satisfy my rage. The true dramatic conclusion of this narrative should be the dissolution of my marriage; there is a part of me which believes that you cannot fight a sexist system while acknowledging your need for the love of a man, and perhaps if I had had the courage finally to tear apart my life I could write you about my hardworking independence, about my solitary self-respect, about the new society I hope to build. But in the end my husband and I did not divorce, although it seemed at one time as if we would. Instead I raged against him for many months and joined the Woman's Liberation Movement, and thought a great deal about myself, and about whether my problems were truly all women's problems, and decided that some of them were and that some of them were not. My sexual rage was the most powerful single emotion of my life, and the feminist analysis has become for me, as I think it will for most women of my generation, as significant an intellectual tool as Marxism was for generations of radicals. But it does not answer every question. To discover that something has been wrong is not necessarily to make it right: I would be lying if I said that my anger had taught me how to live.

But my life has changed because of it. I think I am becoming in many small ways a woman who takes no shit. I am no longer submissive, no longer seductive; perhaps it is for that reason that my husband tells me sometimes that I have become hard, and that my hardness is unattractive. I would like it to be otherwise. I think that will take a long time.

My husband and I have to some degree worked out our differences; we are trying to be together as equals, to separate our human needs from the needs imposed upon us by our sex roles. But my hatred lies within me and between us, not wholly a personal hatred, but not entirely political either. And I wonder always whether it is possible to define myself as a feminist revolutionary and still remain in any sense a wife. There are moments when I still worry that he will leave me, that he will come to need a woman less preoccupied with her own rights, and when I worry about that I also fear that no man will ever love me again, that no man could ever love a woman who is angry. And that fear is a great source of trouble to me, for it means that in certain fundamental ways I have not changed at all.

I would like to be cold and clear and selfish, to demand satisfaction for my needs, to compel respect rather than affection. And yet there are moments, and perhaps there always will be, when I fall back upon the old cop-outs. Why should I trouble to win a chess game or a political argument when it is so much easier to lose charmingly? Why should I work when my husband can support me, why should I be a human being when I can get away with being a child?

Woman's Liberation is finally only personal. It is hard to fight an enemy who has outposts in your head.

Letters from Mexico

Ken Kesey

Novelist Ken Kesey was born in La Junta, Colorado, in 1935, and has lived on the West Coast for most of his life. He was an outstanding student and wrestler at Stanford University, winning scholarships and awards. His first novel, *One Flew Over the Cuckoo's Nest,* has been a favorite of college students ever since its publication in 1962. His second novel, *Sometimes a Great Notion,* was published in 1971. A celebrity with the acid cult, Kesey organized a group called The Merry Pranksters, and in an old bus he bought with his own money, they toured the United States, filming the country and the people as they went, often staging impromptu events. Much of this is recorded in Tom Wolfe's *The Electric Kool-Aid Acid Test.* Accused and later convicted of possessing marijuana, Kesey hid out in Mexico until 1966, when he decided to face trial in the United States (see McClanahan's introduction). Now out of jail, he has been finishing a new novel. Recently he took strong issue with Timothy Leary's statement urging American youth to armed rebellion.

His letters, first published in the literary quarterly *Ararat,* give us a rare insight into the creative process: We see the idea, in its rough form, formulating itself in the mind of the writer.

AN INTRODUCTORY NOTE BY ED MC CLANAHAN

Ken Kesey is the author of the critically and financially successful novels *One Flew Over the Cuckoo's Nest* and *Sometimes a Great Notion.* He is also the former amateur wrestling champion of Oregon and one of the earliest paid-volunteer subjects (c. 1958) of government-sponsored research experiments with psychedelic drugs. In the summer of 1964, Kesey, "possessor of a phenomenal bank account" after the publication of *Notion,* incorporated himself (Intrepid Trips, Inc.), purchased a 1939 International schoolbus and some $20,000 worth of movie-making equipment, gathered about him at his La Honda, California, home a group of old and new friends ("The Merry Pranksters"—during the next three years their number was to fluctuate from as high as thirty down to half-a-dozen or so of the very hardiest and most loyal souls), set them to work preparing the bus for the venture he had planned (the preparations largely consisted of coating its fuselage with spray paint in an infinite variety of colors), climbed aboard, hollered the equivalent of "All ashore that's going ashore" (about fifteen people weren't), and took off for the New York World's Fair.

SOURCE: Ken Kesey, "Letters from Mexico," *Ararat* (Autumn 1967), pp. 45–51. Reprinted by permission of the editor.

Two months later Kesey and the Pranksters were back in La Honda with 36 hours of 16 mm. color film of their adventures, which they intended to edit down to a feature-length movie. They set up a cutting room in a shed in Kesey's yard, and in April, 1965, they were still editing away (Kesey's Christmas tree that year had been decorated with perhaps a quarter of a mile of cut film), when the sheriff of San Mateo County and his merry band of deputies swooped down and arrested Kesey and thirteen of the Pranksters for possession of marijuana. All were released on bail the following day, and the charges against twelve of the fourteen were soon dropped, but in December Kesey and one other Prankster were convicted. Kesey was sentenced to six months in jail and three years' probation, then released on an appeal bond.

During the seven-month interim between the arrest and the conviction, Kesey and the Pranksters (along with the then-unknown rock and roll group "The Grateful Dead") had begun to produce a series of psychedelically oriented Saturday night happenings which they called "The Acid Test." At first these events were held in Kesey's home, but as their fame began to spread and ever-larger crowds turned out The Acid Test was moved to night clubs, then to more spacious dance halls, and finally to San Francisco's cavernous Fillmore Auditorium. On the weekend following Kesey's conviction The Acid Test was scheduled to be the main attraction of a three-day-long marathon psychedelic circus called the Trips Festival, which was to be held in the vast, tentlike Longshoremen's Hall on Fishermen's Wharf. And five nights before the Trips Festival was to open, Kesey was arrested again, this time on a San Francisco rooftop in the company of a 19-year-old Prankster named Carolyn "Mountain Girl" Adams, who later acknowledged that she—not Kesey—was the owner of the packet of marijuana which the police found on their rooftop.

Kesey, once again freed on bail, did participate in the Trips Festival; an estimated 12,000 people descended upon Longshoremen's Hall during those three days, and the Festival (owing largely to the interest generated by the tremendous amount of publicity that accompanied the second arrest) was a huge success, and is now generally recognized as the granddaddy of all the psychedelic rock dances which have made San Francisco "the Liverpool of the American music scene." (A prediction: when the musical historians come to consider the rock and roll phenomenon of the 1960's, the figure of Ken Kesey will loom exceeding large, not as composer or musician—though in fact the Pranksters once formed their own rock group and cut an LP album—but as the inventor of a new way to listen.) But within a week after the Festival, an aged truck registered to Kesey and containing a pair of fluorescent-painted shoes (a Kesey trademark) and a suicide note ("Ocean, ocean, you'll get me in the end . . .") was found parked atop a cliff above the sea along a lonely stretch of the Northern California coast. And Ken Kesey, disguised as "mild-mannered reporter Steve Lamb," was in Puerto Vallarta, Mexico.

There he remained for almost two months—"pranking around," as he puts it—until he attempted to phone his wife Faye in California, and a well-intentioned friend mistakenly mentioned the call in the presence of a newspaper reporter. "Kesey the Corpse Having a Ball!" the next day's headlines screamed. Friends frantically wired Kesey that the jig was up, and after hiding out in the Puerto Vallarta jungles for several days he made his way south to Manzanillo, a tropical beach resort town in the state of Colima, a place rarely visited by gringo tourists. Meanwhile, his old friend Larry McMurtry (the Texas writer whose novel *Horseman, Pass By* later became the movie *Hud*) and Kesey's San Francisco attorney Brian Rohan had arranged, through a Mexico City attorney named Estrella, for Kesey to be granted a temporary and somewhat shaky amnesty by the local Colima government. Within a few weeks his family and a small coterie of Pranksters arrived, bus and all, and they set up shop in a house on the Manzanillo beach and began again to work on the film, which was by this time nearly 50 hours long.

Kesey remained in Manzanillo for the next six months, an idyll frequently shattered by the sometimes real, sometimes imagined, threat of Federales, "FBEyes," or vacationing deputies from the San Mateo County sheriff's office. During the Puerto Vallarta-Manzanillo period he produced the only sustained writing he has done since *Notion:* a series of fifteen lengthy letters to McMurtry describing his surroundings, his predicament, and his state of mind. Three of those letters appear here.

In the fall of 1966 Kesey returned to the States, this time crossing the border riding a borrowed horse, carrying a guitar, and calling himself "Singin' Jimmy Anglund." He hid out for nearly two weeks in the homes of friends, granted interviews to trustworthy newspaper and TV reporters, and "rubbed salt in J. Edgar Hoover's wounds" until half a dozen FBI men in a car-pool chanced to spot him on a busy Bay Area freeway, gave chase, and got their man at last. Kesey was immediately released on bail again, tried on the San Francisco charge, and convicted of a misdemeanor ("knowingly being in a place where marijuana is possessed"). Meanwhile, his San Mateo County appeal failed, and he has recently entered jail there to serve the old six-month sentence.

"The age of the Superhero is over," he remarked not long before the doors clanged shut behind him, "but there are an awful lot of groovy little people in the world." If all goes well he will be out of jail just in time for Christmas.

Larry:

Phone calls to the state min. 8 bucks a piece besides was ever a good board to bounce my favorite ball of bullshit offen, it was you. And with the light steady enough to instruct where the end of the breakwater is out across the bay, ocean calm and warm fifty feet from mine here in outside under tarp beside that cursed bus and kids asleep inside, first time in some moons I feel like bouncing a jubilant ball.

I feel good. Healthy, tanned, standing happily tall again after too many stooped hours ambling stiffly about fink ridden Mexico as the white-haired, bespecticled and of course mild-mannered reporter, Steve Lamb, I am chancing here a stretch or two in full daylight as Sol Almande, Prankster Extraordinaire.

Is relatively now. In between here and whatever furthest time back my pen touches lies many an experience, no small amount of achievements and a tidy sum of insights. I was never one to happen through the market place *any* place on this world without grabbing onto whatever my fancy and my resourcefulness could compromise upon.

cut to

(longshot right down on rooftop of San Francisco North Beach—levels, ladders, asphalt squares. At first glance almost a set—semi-symbolic University theatre clever Jewish director type of stage set—then a man and a young woman interrupt the parrallel arrangement of horizontal surfaces. On a thin and rather ragged mattress, 1½ inch foam in blue cover, shape indicates it was a pad for the back of station wagon. The man has all the usual stigmata of the bohemian in vogue at that period . . . a bohemian crowding that age when "Its time the goddam ninny stopped actin like them snotty Vietniks and dope fiends and acted his age." No longer even the argument of ideals and escape, just pure social outrage, voiced by the fleecy image of daddy-mama-and-other-dear-but-square-ones.

(He has partially balded and has been sick long enough it is difficult to know if he is 25 or 35. Hair boils wildly from his head in thick kinky blond locks. His neck and torso are thick and muscular though he is not short as those built thus usually are. His face is excited but tired, lopsided with the strain faces show after too long forced to smile diplomatically. The girl almost as big as her companion, matching his six feet in height but not his weight. Her hair is long and reddish brown; dark appearing cool black except where the light occasionally sets off the reddish luster. Her eyes almost identical hue, and quite large. Rather like the eyes of an Irish setter pup just turning from awkward carefree frolic to the task of devotion. Her face is young and pretty despite a too broadness and her manner is ornery and funloving as she and her companion banter over the plans for the forthcoming Trips Festival. Their talk concerns personalities and wiring problems.)

"With that big new speaker"—the girl is on the optimistic side of the banter—"we'll be able to wire that place so you can hear a *flea* fart!"

"Hasn't happened yet," the man says. Pessimism nowhere near the strength of her mood.

"With this many days to get it set up? Always before we were in the hall that night and maybe set up before we finished in the morning. We got almost a week till Friday."

"I hope Stewart gets that Albright business straight. Fillmore was enough of us getting booted out at two."

"Just when we got this system working good," she agreed, a bit too unanimously.

"Just when we got everything to where we could quit playing with wires and start playing. No more of that shit. Stewart's got to have the cops, managers, *every*body cooled completely before we get so deep into it that it'll be obvious we don't plan to pull out."

"Because without the Pranksters the Festival will be just another rock and roll dance."

"Just another Family Dog."

"Right!" the girl agrees this time her tone shrewd and curt as well as confident.

The pair lie on their stomachs chins on hands looking down 4 stories to the alley below. As they talk they each occasionally scrape from the asphalt rooftop large gravels to toss down (and see?

Cut back now

See? just as the pair see a police car pull in, park in the alley, and red light in the hillside drive 50 yards to my left blinks in the dawn—do I learn *any*thing? Or once again lie loaded and disbelieving as two cops climb 5 stories to drag me to cooler?

Oh well; a man could get piles sit too long one spot.

Stay tuned,
Kesey

Larry:

This at Puerto Vallarta not long after news leak set me scrambling.

For a long time now he had been sitting watching a fruitless surf, sitting sadly staring out with a swarm of situations and the fact that he could illiterate up a f---ing storm in the flush, flush, lush lush lush of Mexico.

He had seen a fish, yellow tail tuna's broken leap. Two times now. Both times had been good. And he hoped that he could see it leap again without turning into Hemmingway. But his hopes proved vain. For he went back and rewrote rearranged picked and changed for a full half hour when it lept the third.

And after that he was compelled to spend another ten until clang! Somebody! not just humble hermit crabs anymore but a tourist a noise a *federale?* sound of jeep. Clang Clang Clang sudden reappearance of hatted American followed by mex! roar again of jeep—then—ah—the two turn, leave. WHOP! of surf again into that crack left by the fear change of their leaving. Still around though, close. What if they should connect his sitting alone writing with the KESEY CAVORTS IN PUERTO VALLARTA headline? He opened his other pad, let the colored part show; always do a quick sketch pass off image as artist.

And beneath these everlasting the call I hear. Grit and take it.

Maybe I gotta kind of grit-your-teeth-and-grin-John-Wayney sorta zen. And sometimes the third "It's all shit" followed by, slower, slyer, "but it's all *goood* shit."

Until he achieved a leveling with a three sided palm hut housing empty bottles an empty cot and doodlebug holes thick and heavy about in the dust indicating a bad year for ants. Also some of those scrawny trees with those greeny things—not coconuts but mangoes or papas or one of those tropical gizmos he hadn't got to know because he hadn't really come to believing in them yet.

"Wellsir, this place might just hold me a spell," he drawled and took off his shirt. Ten minutes later he was smoking the 3 roaches rolled together in a cone and examining with his knife one of the green gizmos as it bled meekly white in his lap. The innards were white and meek and full of pale little rabbit pills. A papaya, he surmised, and mighty young papaya to be put to the sword, let alone the tooth. He hid its remains lest some Mex uncle tom hermit come back up to his shack and see his prize papaya caught redhanded dead before its prime, unzipped his fly to let his sweating nuts air out, and leaned back into twilighting crickets to ring his planetarium, see what the next moment was going to bring.

And was suddenly alert to a rare alarm—"Ritual, Ritual," it whispered, faint. The alarm starts and startles beat an even bigger fear. That he wasn't taking care of his job. Mex returns shorts swims suspicious—maybe sketch now? And had they put out a reward for Chrissakes every f---ing peon in the *state* after his ass and 75 pesos? Okay If this is them straight out the surf over the rocks he'd checked out earlier go under turn sharp left far under as he could swim *voices!* clang clang, again this could be the show un-f---ing believable as it seemed but by god it was keep loose or get busted maybe five years five years even staying outside bars playing stacked low game as pawn not even player, five years against possibility of getting snuffed while staying loose. That pat. All the time. And he knew why. He was at last being forced to the brink of his professed beliefs. Of all that he had babbled about for years now being brought up continually for actual down-to-the-wire testing!

"OOO *OOOO!*" God almighty! Now some fool over the rocks there wailing like a ghost! "OOO *OOO!*" A signal? Door slams. Man is hot again. Shows up again take out pen and draw the f---er fast. Only possibility against true foe as well as 3rd level foe like american fink. *Draw* him. *Write* him. *Imagine* him into plot always and then believe all that crap you've been claiming about altering by accepting. Believe it! Or you are a goner, m' boy, a walking dead man for evermore fading finally inaudible like the voices mumbling litanies in the cathedral!

So having vowed thus—and having checked to find the Mex working on the road above—he resolutely dug up his stash, lit up the next to the last joint in all of Mexico, and just leaning back to embark once again upon the will of God—Ka-BOOOM!—up the hill dynamiting?

Now that's a ka-boom of a different color. I'd go watch them do a little blasting. "And have every Gringo driving past" another voice interrupted "pointing at you gawking there's Ken *Kee-zee*, Mabel!"

In short, this young, handsome, successful, happily-married-three-lovely-children father, was a fear-crazed dope fiend in flight to avoid prosecution on 3 felonies god knows how many misdemeanors and seeking at the same time to sculpt a new satori from an old surf and—in even shorter—mad as a hatter.

Once an athlete so valued he had been given the job of calling signals from the line and risen into contention for nationwide amature wrestling crown, now he didn't know if he could do a dozen push-ups. Once possessor of phenominal bank account and money waving from every hand now it was all his poor wife could do to scrape together 8.00 dollars to send as gettaway money to Mexico. But a few years previous he had been listed in Who's Who and asked to speak to such auspacous gatherings as the Wellsley Club in Dahlahs and now they wouldn't even allow him to speak at a VDC gathering. What was it that had brought a man so high of promise to so low a state in so short a time? Well the answer can be found in just one short word, my friends, in just one all-welused sylable.

Dope!

And while it may be claimed by some of the addled advocates of these chemicals that our hero is known to have indulged in drugs *before* his literary success we must point out that there was evidence of his literary prowess *well before* the advent of the so called psychedelic into his life but *no evidence at all* of any of the lunitic thinking that we find thereafter!

(oh yeah, the wind hums
time ago—time ago—
the rafter drums and the walls see
. . . and there's a door to that bird
in the sa-a-a-apling sky
time ago by—

Oh yeah the surf giggles
time ago time ago
of under things killed when
bad was banished and all the
doors to the birds vanished
time ago then.)

And thought then "Let my winds of whatever thru and out of this man-place paranoia be damned and into the jungle—

"Where its *really* scary."

The road he'd reached was a Mexican fantasy that had petered out for the same reason his heart and lungs were working so hard now—too steep. He sat down in the road, looking out at the sea. No cars had been along the road—what reason? it petered out right there? when? time ago?—since the last rainfall.

The sky had clouded. The sun, nearing its setting, vanished through the clouds into the sea thump! a car on the road above. Stops. Starts. Probably the workers but—he stands, effecting a satori smile—

If you gonna ride the
wind
Ride the fat and ride the thin
Ride the soft and ride the boney
time ago———time ago
because there ain't no other
poney
time ago agin.

. . . Someone approaching!

He waits. Long time. It creaks closer and comes out in the very last of the jungles fading light. A little honeybear of a thing. He is delighted and tries to whistle it over but it turns as soon as it senses his presence and sckuffles back. And the mosquitoes get him up and moving again.

Kesey

Larry:

Isn't it a drag? interrupted right in the middle of the past to have to out into the world and actually *deal* with it. The past don't come The End Twentieth Century Fox and you can get up walk home and tell people who it was because it's over.

Because it isn't over. Up on the same hill I saw red lights. To shit, and while I'm at it peek over the edge see what the FBEyes are looking at this morning. *Plus* "don't forget the San Mateo Sheriff's office, a lot of them are taking vacations in Mexico for the specific purpose of bringing you in."

Is some of the news Faye brings from USA.

By the time I get sit it's full grey dawn. A slate fan of clouds rattle above the Sierra Madre Occidental. Egrets gulls and grackles rise calling from the backwater across the highway, flapping overhead to the beach behind me to earlybird the worm. Bells ring across the bay in town 20 or 30 times—mexican chime code still a complete mystery. Be able to crack it in a few weeks tho, sir; at most one month. "A *month!* By God, Mister, you think I want information of such stature in time for the *Universal Wake?* Strange vehicles sculking around the rocks not five minutes ago *who knows* they're cops American or Mexican? A manta ray cruzing the beach like a frigging doberman out of the K9 Korp, and out in the bay some brand new contrivance like never before floated water before—great rustproof triangle would cover a *city block* with all three points of the vessle running black and yellow steel pools big around as these tugs that went out to nose around and were waved off *sticking straight into the sky 3 times as high as the hotel over in town yonder*—and you tell me *a month?* Well, mister, you figure that bell code pronto. I need to know the time within the frigging hour or you'll be playing with those slide rules and charts up in *Ancorage!*"

The old captain pivots smartly and stalks off, returning the frightened salute of the younger officer who was stammering at the departure.

The horizon was coloring now in the east; it reminded the officer of paintings speed painters at Bakersfield County Fair splashed onto white fiberboard in one minute flat—3 dollars apiece 2 for five bucks—still hanging when he enlisted; A rectangular sunrise, one on each side of F.D.R.

The bells chimed again. Barely moments since the last ringing. No ryme or reason, pattern or possibility. "In an *hour?*" In fact, for all anybody knew, it might be the Police Chiefs Idiot daughter at the rope again. He shivered. To have to check *that* out again. And find an armless and legless unfortunate—result of food poisoning; the mother 2 months after conception nearly dieing from a can of bad green beans paralyzing development of the embryonic limbs and producing a, well, child with an alarmingly lovely face—features that might have posed for Leonardo's *Pieta* despite the fact that closer examination revealed the mouth to be but two beautiful lips sealed forever over a skull that showed no evidence of any oral opening whatsoever. Below the cute nose the bone ran in a solid fortress to the chin. A quick tracheotomy by a clever intern was all that saved the poor creature from asphyxiation moments after birth. X-rays and a 3/16 in. carpenter's auger finally afforded the infant the luxury of breathing from her nostrils instead of a hole between her collarbones, but a mouth the doctors were unable to provide. X-rays showed a complete absence of tongue, glottis, throat, or any cavity whatsoever where the mouth might be jenny-rigged.

"We're feeding the little darling through her nose," the doctors informed the grief-crazed mother (the father, so claimed those of the sisters at the cathedral, unfortunately unhampered by any oral malfunction, who just happened to be the one who had purchased the evil can of beans, expired not many weeks after the birth as a result of botulism—rumor had it he left the hospital immediately after his legless, armless, and mouthless offspring, to buy all the canned green beans the marketplace could provide, take out a large life insurance policy (which proved worthless owing to a ridiculously small mistake made in the forms by the distraught father) and lock himself in a secret out-of-town hotel hideaway eating beans, letting them set, opened, adding houseflies and horned toads, recapping them, recapping and days later eating until he either successfully bred and consumed the proper poison, or until his system surrendered under the constant onslaught of beans and flies).

"But if you disregard the child's ah deficiencies," the doctors consoled the grief-freaked mother when they decided she might try to follow her husband's lead, "she is a very *very* lovely child."

"*Already* she has the most expressive eyes I've *ever* in all my *years* witnessed," a kind old nurse added. "She'll be a beautiful girl! The two of you will do fine. God will see to it."

This was adequate to drive mother and infant from the canned goods into the nunnery, where the mother found St. Teresa and crocheting, and the child did grow into a very *very* lovely girl. The medical men in their haste to get a potential suicide and/or mercy killing off the hospital grounds had benevolently neglected to inform the mother that the X-rays indicated very little more space for brain than mouth, and the girl had exhausted this area by the time she was 3 or 4. After that the mother or one of the other sisters could frequently be seen pulling a wagon about the cathedral in which was propped a face that grew yearly more and more strikingly beautiful.

"Who gives a snap how *pretty* the girl is," the young officer grumbled, returning to his office in the decoding department, "when you climb ten miles of trecherous ol ladder to find her swinging on the bell-rope *like that.*" He shivered again. "I mean who cares if she's *Hayley Mills?*"

Though bulging from the simple mock-habit sewn for the girl and torn (just like last time, by god. . . .) from neck to belly button, were two of the most inviting prizes ever to quiver at the end of a bell-rope.

"But who cares if she's Jayne Mansfield or even June *Wilkinson?* C'mere you—" Again he had to carry the creature over one shoulder as he descended the precarious ladder. And just as before her lewd buzom was forced against his cheek or—when he tried to hold her away from his sweat-soaked face—that tongueless mouth and those large eloquent eyes smiled at him so suggestively he was forced to confess some grave doubts concerning the girl's reputed imbecility.

"But what I can't phathom," he panted, "is how you get up that ladder and get *out* on that bell-rope that way."

A rung broke like a dry pistol crack; half-falling he grasped the ladder pole with one hand and lurching snatched out to secure a better purchase on his load with the other hand. Which fell full over one of the full crimson nippled breasts. As soon as he regained a solid rung once again he quickly resumed his former and more decoorous hold on his load.

He made no mention of the incident—it was an accident, a slip!—to the Mother Superior nor to the anonymous ear that listened to the mundane sins he droned into the confessional box. Nor even thought of it again himself the rest of the day as he prepared his report for the captain.

But in bed that evening, locked alone in his quarters, the discovery finally burst loudly into his consciousness. "That—her—*it* felt *back!*"

And barely slept at all that night for the listening out the window across the bay.

Little love story just for variety.

I've still heard nothing from Estrella. Plan was he'd contact me through alias at Telegrafo in Manzanillo. Don't know *what's* happening. (fear Rohan didn't send cash. Lawyers someway always suspect other lawyers being crooks. Wonder why.) But I like Estrella. He's pompous and prideful and *just* right.

Did I ever thank you?

Kesey

Transcendental Experience

R. D. Laing

R. D. Laing was born in Glasgow, Scotland, in 1927 and educated at the medical school of the University of Edinburgh. Since 1961, he has been working chiefly with the Tavistock Institute of Human Relations in London. His books, largely based on this experience and his immersion in existential literature, include *The Self and Others, The Divided Self,* and *The Politics of Experience.* In 1970, he distilled his theories of mental illness into a volume of prose/poems called *Knots.* His work has been the subject of two full-length films.

Why has this generation taken so seriously a man unknown even to professionals only a few years ago? Brevity risks caricature, but here is Laing briefly stated. The Others (family, society) drive schizophrenics mad in that they devalue his real Self because that self has special insights into their hypocrisies. They insist that he present the world with a compliant "false" self, but thus split, he cannot sustain either identity or sanity. With treatment from a therapist who accepts the "wholeness of the human being" and who rejects the "egoic" boundaries of me-you, inner-outer, and in general the usual notions of space and time, the schizophrenic may find his illness a healing experience, "a liberation and renewal" from our "own appalling state of alienation called normality." The following essay, from *The Politics of Experience,* contains the heart of his argument.

We are living in an age in which the ground is shifting and the foundations are shaking. I cannot answer for other times and places. Perhaps it has always been so. We know it is true today.

In these circumstances, we have every reason to be insecure. When the ultimate basis of our world is in question, we run to different holes in the ground, we scurry into roles, statuses, identities, interpersonal relations. We attempt to live in castles that can only be in the air because there is no firm ground in the social cosmos on which to build. We are all witnesses to this state of affairs. Each sometimes sees the same fragment of the whole situation differently; often our concern is with different presentations of the original catastrophe.

In this chapter I wish to relate the transcendental experiences that *sometimes* break through in psychosis, to those experiences of the divine that are the living fount of all religion.

[Earlier] I outlined the way in which some psychiatrists are begin-

SOURCE: R. D. Laing, *The Politics of Experience* (London: Penguin Books Ltd., 1970), pp. 91–101.

ning to dissolve their clinical-medical categories of understanding madness. If we can begin to understand sanity and madness in existential social terms, we shall be more able to see clearly the extent to which we all confront common problems and share common dilemmas.

Experience may be judged as invalidly mad or as validly mystical. The distinction is not easy. In either case, from a social point of view, such judgments characterize different forms of behavior, regarded in our society as deviant. People behave in such ways because their experience of themselves is different. It is on the existential meaning of such unusual experience that I wish to focus.

Psychotic experience goes beyond the horizons of our common, that is, our communal, sense.

What regions of experience does this lead to? It entails a loss of the usual foundations of the "sense" of the world that we share with one another. Old purposes no longer seem viable; old meanings are senseless; the distinctions between imagination, dream, external perceptions often seem no longer to apply in the old way. External events may seem magically conjured up. Dreams may seem to be direct communications from others; imagination may seem to be objective reality.

But most radical of all, the very ontological foundations are shaken. The being of phenomena shifts and the phenomenon of being may no longer present itself to us as before. There are no supports, nothing to cling to, except perhaps some fragments from the wreck, a few memories, names, sounds, one or two objects, that retain a link with a world long lost. This void may not be empty. It may be peopled by visions and voices, ghosts, strange shapes and apparitions. No one who has not experienced how insubstantial the pageant of external reality can be, how it may fade, can fully realize the sublime and grotesque presences that can replace it, or that can exist alongside it.

When a person goes mad, a profound transposition of his place in relation to all domains of being occurs. His center of experience moves from ego to self. Mundane time becomes merely anecdotal, only the eternal matters. The madman is, however, confused. He muddles ego with self, inner with outer, natural and supernatural. Nevertheless, he can often be to us, even through his profound wretchedness and disintegration, the hierophant of the sacred. An exile from the scene of being as we know it, he is an alien, a stranger signaling to us from the void in which he is foundering, a void which may be peopled by presences that we do not even dream of. They used to be called demons and spirits, and they used to be known and named. He has lost his sense of self, his feelings, his place in the world as we know it. He tells us he is dead. But we are distracted from our cosy security by this mad ghost who haunts us with his visions and voices which seem so senseless and of which we feel impelled to rid him, cleanse him, cure him.

Madness need not be all breakdown. It may also be breakthrough. It is potentially liberation and renewal as well as enslavement and existential death.

There are now a growing number of accounts by people who have been through the experience of madness.[1]

The following is part of one of the earlier contemporary accounts, as recorded by Karl Jaspers in his *General Psychopathology*.[2]

I believe I caused the illness myself. In my attempt to penetrate the other world I met its natural guardians, the embodiment of my own weaknesses and faults. I first thought these demons were lowly inhabitants of the other world who could play me like a ball because I went into these regions unprepared and lost my way. Later I thought they were split-off parts of my own mind (passions) which existed near me in free space and thrived on my feelings. I believed everyone else had these too but did not perceive them, thanks to the protective successful deceit of the feeling of personal existence. I thought the latter was an artifact of memory, thought-complexes, etc., a doll that was nice enough to look at from outside but nothing real inside it.

In my case the personal self had grown porous because of my dimmed consciousness. Through it I wanted to bring myself closer to the higher sources of life. I should have prepared myself for this over a long period by invoking in me a higher, impersonal self, since "nectar" is not for mortal lips. It acted destructively on the animal-human self, split it up into its parts. These gradually disintegrated, the doll was really broken and the body damaged. I had forced untimely access to the "source of life," the curse of the "gods" descended on me. I recognized too late that murky elements had taken a hand. I got to know them after they had already too much power. There was no way back. I now had the world of spirits I had wanted to see. The demons came up from the abyss, as guardian Cerberi, denying admission to the unauthorized. I decided to take up the life-and-death struggle. This meant for me in the end a decision to die, since I had to put aside everything that maintained the enemy, but this was also everything that maintained life. I wanted to enter death without going mad and stood before the Sphinx: either thou into the abyss or I!

Then came illumination. I fasted and so penetrated into the true nature of my seducers. They were pimps and deceivers of my dear personal self which seemed as much a thing of naught as they. A larger and more comprehensive self emerged and I could abandon the previous personality with its entire entourage. I saw this earlier personality could never enter transcendental realms. I felt as a result a terrible pain, like an annihilating blow, but I was rescued, the demons shriveled, vanished and perished. A new life began for me and from now on I felt different from other people. A self that consisted of conventional lies, shams, self-deceptions, memory images, a self just like that of other people, grew in me again but behind and above it stood a greater and more comprehensive self which impressed me with something of what is eternal, unchanging, immortal and inviolable and which ever since that time has been my protector and refuge. I believe it would be good for many if they were acquainted with such a higher self and that there are people who have attained this goal in fact by kinder means.

Jaspers comments:

Such self-interpretations are obviously made under the influence of delusion-like tendencies and deep psychic forces. They originate from profound experiences and the wealth of such schizophrenic experience calls on the observer as well as on the reflective patient not to take all this merely as a chaotic jumble of contents. Mind and spirit are present in the morbid psychic life as well as in the healthy. But interpretations of this sort must be divested of any causal importance. All they can do is to throw light on content and bring it into some sort of context.

---

[1] See, for example, the anthology *The Inner World of Mental Illness,* edited by Bert Kaplan (New York and London: Harper and Row, 1964), and *Beyond All Reason,* by Morag Coate (London: Constable and Co., 1964; Philadelphia: Lippincott, 1965).

[2] Manchester: Manchester University Press, 1962, pp. 417–18.

This patient has described, with a lucidity I could not improve upon, a very ancient quest, with its pitfalls and dangers. Jaspers still speaks of this experience as morbid and tends to discount the patient's own construction. Yet both the experience and the construction may be valid in their own terms.

Certain *transcendental experiences* seem to me to be the original wellspring of all religions. Some pyschotic people have transcendental experiences. Often (to the best of their recollection) they have never had such experiences before, and frequently they will never have them again. I am not saying, however, that psychotic experience necessarily contains this element more manifestly than sane experience.

We experience in different modes. We perceive external realities, we dream, imagine, have semiconscious reveries. Some people have visions, hallucinations, experience faces transfigured, see auras and so on. Most people most of the time experience themselves and others in one or another way that I shall call *egoic*. That is, centrally or peripherally, they experience the world and themselves in terms of a consistent identity, a me-here over against a you-there, within a framework of certain ground structures of space and time shared with other members of their society.

This identity-anchored, space-and-time-bound experience has been studied philosophically by Kant, and later by the phenomenologists, e.g., Husserl, Merleau-Ponty. Its historical and ontological relativity should be fully realized by any contemporary student of the human scene. Its cultural, socioeconomic relativity has become a commonplace among anthropologists and a platitude to the Marxists and neo-Marxists. And yet, with the consensual and interpersonal confirmation it offers, it gives us a sense of ontological security, whose validity we *experience* as self-validating, although metaphysically-historically-ontologically-socioeconomically-culturally we know its apparent absolute validity as an illusion.

In fact all religious and all existential philosophies have agreed that such *egoic experience* is a preliminary illusion, a veil, a film of *maya*—a dream to Heraclitus, and to Lao-Tzu, the fundamental illusion of all Buddhism, a state of sleep, of death, of socially accepted madness, a womb state to which one has to die, from which one has to be born.

The person going through ego-loss or transcendental experiences may or may not become in different ways confused. Then he might legitimately be regarded as mad. But to be mad is not necessarily to be ill, notwithstanding that in our culture the two categories have become confused. It is assumed that if a person is mad (whatever that means) then *ipso facto* he is ill (whatever that means). The experience that a person may be absorbed in, while to others he appears simply ill-mad, may be for him veritable manna from heaven. The person's whole life may be changed, but it is difficult not to doubt the validity of such vision. Also, not everyone comes back to us again.

Are these experiences simply the effulgence of a pathological process or of a particular alienation? I do not think they are.

In certain cases, a man blind from birth may have an operation performed which gives him his sight. The result—frequently misery, confusion, disorientation. The light that illumines the madman is an unearthly light. It is not always a distorted refraction of his mundane life situation. He may be irradiated by light from other worlds. It may burn him out.

This "other" world is not essentially a battlefield wherein psychological forces, derived or diverted, displaced or sublimated from their original object-cathexes, are engaged in an illusionary fight—although such forces may obscure these realities, just as they may obscure so-called external realities. When Ivan in *The Brothers Karamazov* says, "If God does not exist, everything is permissible," he is *not* saying, "If my superego, in projected form, can be abolished, I can do anything with a good conscience." He *is* saying, "If there is *only* my conscience, then there is no ultimate validity for my will."

Among physicians and priests there should be some who are guides, who can educt the person from this world and induct him to the other. To guide him in it and to lead him back again.

One enters the other world by breaking a shell: or through a door: through a partition: the curtains part or rise: a veil is lifted. Seven veils: seven seals, seven heavens.

The "ego" is the instrument for living in *this* world. If the "ego" is broken up or destroyed (by the insurmountable contradictions of certain life situations, by toxins, chemical changes, etc.), then the person may be exposed to other worlds, "real" in different ways from the more familiar territory of dreams, imagination, perception or fantasy.

The world that one enters, one's capacity to experience it, seem to be partly conditional on the state of one's "ego."

Our time has been distinguished, more than by anything else, by a drive to control the external world, and by an almost total forgetfulness of the internal world. If one estimates human evolution from the point of view of knowledge of the external world, then we are in many respects progressing.

If our estimate is from the point of view of the internal world and of oneness of internal and external, then the judgment must be very different.

Phenomenologically the terms "internal" and "external" have little validity. But in this whole realm one is reduced to mere verbal expedients—words are simply the finger pointing at the moon. One of the difficulties of talking in the present day of these matters is that the very existence of inner realities is now called in question.

By "inner" I mean our way of seeing the external world and all those realities that have no "external," "objective" presence—imagination, dreams, fantasies, trances, the realities of contemplative and meditative states, realities of which modern man, for the most part, has not the slightest direct awareness.

For example, nowhere in the Bible is there any argument about the *existence* of gods, demons, angels. People did not first "believe in"

God: they experienced His presence, as was true of other spiritual agencies. The question was not whether God existed, but whether this particular God was the greatest god of all, or the only God; and what was the relation of the various spiritual agencies to each other. Today, there is a public debate, not as to the trustworthiness of God, the particular place in the spiritual hierarchy of different spirits, etc., but whether God or such spirits *even exist* or ever have existed.

Sanity today appears to rest very largely on a capacity to adapt to the external world—the interpersonal world, and the realm of human collectivities.

As this external human world is almost completely and totally estranged from the inner, any personal direct awareness of the inner world already has grave risks.

But since society, without knowing it, is *starving* for the inner, the demands on people to evoke its presence in a "safe" way, in a way that need not be taken seriously, etc., are tremendous—while the ambivalence is equally intense. Small wonder that the list of artists, in say the last 150 years, who have become shipwrecked on these reefs is so long—Hölderlin, John Clare, Rimbaud, Van Gogh, Nietzsche, Antonin Artaud. . . .

Those who survived have had exceptional qualities—a capacity for secrecy, slyness, cunning—a thoroughly realistic appraisal of the risks they run, not only from the spiritual realms they frequent, but from the hatred of their fellows for anyone engaged in this pursuit.

Let us *cure* them. The poet who mistakes a real woman for his Muse and acts accordingly. . . . The young man who sets off in a yacht in search of God. . . .

The outer divorced from any illumination from the inner is in a state of darkness. We are in an age of darkness. The state of outer darkness is a state of sin—i.e., alienation or estrangement from the *inner light*.[3] Certain actions lead to greater estrangement; certain others help one not to be so far removed. The former used to be called sinful.

The ways of losing one's way are legion. Madness is certainly not the least unambiguous. The countermadness of Kraepelinian psychiatry is the exact counterpart of "official" psychosis. Literally, and absolutely seriously, it is as *mad*, if by madness we mean any radical estrangement from the totality of what is the case. Remember Kierkegaard's objective madness.

As we experience the world, so we act. We conduct ourselves in the light of our view of what is the case and what is not the case. That is, each person is a more or less naïve ontologist. Each person has views of what is and what is not.

There is no doubt, it seems to me, that there have been profound changes in the experience of man in the last thousand years. In some ways this is more evident than changes in the patterns of his behavior. There is everything to suggest that man experienced God.

[3] M. Eliade, *The Two and the One* (London: Harvill Press, 1965), especially Chapter 1.

Faith was never a matter of believing He existed, but of trusting in the presence that was experienced and known to exist as a self-validating datum. It seems likely that far more people in our time experience neither the presence of God, nor the presence of his absence, but the absence of his presence.

We require a history of phenomena, not simply more phenomena of history.

As it is, the secular psychotherapist is often in the role of the blind leading the half-blind.

The fountain has not played itself out, the frame still shines, the river still flows, the spring still bubbles forth, the light has not faded. But between *us* and It, there is a veil which is more like fifty feet of solid concrete. *Deus absconditus*. Or we have absconded.

Already everything in our time is directed to categorizing and segregating this reality from objective facts. This is precisely the concrete wall. Intellectually, emotionally, interpersonally, organizationally, intuitively, theoretically, we have to blast our way through the solid wall, even if at the risk of chaos, madness and death. For from *this* side of the wall, this is the risk. There are no assurances, no guarantees.

Many people are prepared to have faith in the sense of scientifically indefensible belief in an untested hypothesis. Few have trust enough to test it. Many people make-believe what they experience. Few are made to believe by their experience. Paul of Tarsus was picked up by the scruff of the neck, thrown to the ground and blinded for three days. This direct experience was self-validating.

We live in a secular world. To adapt to this world the child abdicates its ecstasy. ("*L'enfant abdique son extase*": Mallarmé.) Having lost our experience of the spirit, we are expected to have faith. But this faith comes to be a belief in a reality which is not evident. There is a prophecy in Amos that a time will come when there will be a famine in the land, "not a famine for bread, nor a thirst for water, but of *hearing* the words of the Lord." That time has now come to pass. It is the present age.

From the alienated starting point of our pseudo-sanity, everything is equivocal. Our sanity is not "true" sanity. Their madness is not "true" madness. The madness of our patients is an artifact of the destruction wreaked on them by us and by them on themselves. Let no one suppose that we meet "true" madness any more than that we are truly sane. The madness that we encounter in "patients" is a gross travesty, a mockery, a grotesque caricature of what the natural healing of that estranged integration we call sanity might be. True sanity entails in one way or another the dissolution of the normal ego, that false self competently adjusted to our alienated social reality; the emergence of the "inner" archetypal mediators of divine power, and through this death a rebirth, and the eventual re-establishment of a new kind of ego-functioning, the ego now being the servant of the divine, no longer its betrayer.

A Talk with Konrad Lorenz

Konrad Lorenz

Konrad Lorenz was born in 1903 in Vienna. He studied medicine at the university there (M.D. in 1928) and while lecturing in anatomy earned his Ph.D. in zoology (1933). Under the influence of Freud, his interest shifted to psychology, and between 1940 and 1942, he headed the department of psychology at the University of Königsberg in Germany. During the war, he lived in Switzerland, and in 1949, he became the director of the Institute of Comparative Ethology at Altenberg, Germany. Since 1954, he has been associated as vice-director, then director, of the Max Planck Institute at Seeweisen, Germany. His books include *King Solomon's Mines* (1952), *Man Meets Dog* (1954), *Evolution and Modification of Behavior* (1966), and *On Aggression* (1966).

Lorenz is regarded as a pioneer in the field of ethology, a school of study based on the concept that an animal's behavior is a product of adaptive evolution. The dispute still rages over whether his studies of animal behavior explain the social (and antisocial) behavior of man. He coined the term "territoriality" as the key to man's aggressiveness. In the following interview, conducted by Frédéric de Towarnicki of the French magazine *L'Express*, Dr. Lorenz touches on a wide range of ideas. These ideas should be compared with those expressed by Gary Snyder in *Earth House Hold.*

Konrad Z. Lorenz, author of *On Aggression,* is a founding father of ethology, the systematic study of animal behavior and the subject of dispute over whether its findings explain the social (and antisocial) behavior of man. In this interview with Frédéric de Towarnicki of the French magazine *L'Express,* Dr. Lorenz ranges over a broad spectrum of ideas, from the plight of 20th century man to his personal vision of the universe. The translation is by Stanley Hochman.

Q: *Does the study of the behavior of animals throw light on the behavior of man?*

Lorenz: Let's say that ethology permits the study and observation of man without philosophical, religious or ideological spectacles which presuppose that man is a supranatural being who does not obey the laws of nature. If you know animals well, you know yourself reasonably well. When you see your wife give suck to your son, you *know* we

SOURCE: Konrad Lorenz, "A Talk with Konrad Lorenz," *New York Times Magazine* (July 5, 1970). Reprinted by permission of *L'Express,* Paris. Copyright © 1970 by the New York Times Company. Reprinted by permission.

are mammals. Only Western man seems not to understand these truths today. But children—they understand these things, you know.

Last week my little nephew said to his father: "Look, someone is walking under the table." The father, thinking that his son had had a hallucination, looked under the table and saw—an ant! For the child, an ant was "someone." I, too, have never doubted that I am one animal among others.

Q: *You know, don't you, that ethologists are often reproached with having underestimated the difference between animal and man, with projecting animal behavior onto man?*

Lorenz: That's absurd. In my opinion it is the anthropologists who underestimate the difference because they don't see—nobody does—the degree to which the cumulative tradition in man—in other words, culture—is something absolutely new that exists in no other organism.

Q: *Do animals have a tradition?*

Lorenz: Yes, but it is not cumulative. For example, jackdaws have a tradition of knowledge. The reactions of the parents teach the young jackdaws to know a cat, a goshawk, a marten. Rats transmit the knowledge of poison. In monkeys, even recipes are transmitted: how to clean potatoes. One of them invents a method for salting potatoes with sea water. He teaches it to his relatives, to his friends, to the whole population: that's tradition. But it's always dependent on the presence of the object.

Even syntactical language is not an exclusively human facility. In America a psychologist couple [Beatrice T. and R. Allen Gardner of the University of Nevada] have taught a young chimpanzee the sign language of deaf-mutes. That's much easier for a chimpanzee to master than the movements we make with our mouths. This chimpanzee has really succeeded in understanding syntactic language. She makes up new sentences. For example, she says things like: "You, you and I, together, let's go into the woods." Yes, she can say that!

Q: *Then, according to you, animals aren't so different from man?*

Lorenz: Lao-tze has said, I believe, that all of the animal is still present in man. But it is certainly not true that all of man is in the animal. This is because man never "was" in the animal. To say that man is an ape, even a naked ape, is absolutely true. But as soon as you imply that man is nothing but an ape, it's false. That's why I don't like my friend Desmond Morris's title, "The Naked Ape." To qualify the word "ape," you would have to say "the ape with a cumulative tradition." Because that's what is characteristic of man.

There are many naked animals. The elephant is more naked than man. The hippopotamus is also naked, and there are many naked rodents. It's only by chance that the ape is not naked. It's not at all characteristic. The truth is that one day a little ape suddenly began to reflect, to form conceptual thoughts, to invent words—and, little by little, conceptual thought and tradition were integrated into an immense system that now permits all the miracles of culture. Ethology gives us a true knowledge, a correct understanding, of the phenomenon of culture.

If you have not made use of biology to understand how species lacking a cumulative tradition act, you cannot grasp the unique nature of human culture. The appearance of language made it possible to maintain a tradition independent of environment. With culture, something completely new came into the world: the potential immortality of thought, of truth, of knowledge. An entire people, an entire race, can now perish, and yet their culture can survive in libraries—so that another people, even another planet, can find it and make use of it. This is the real immortality of the spirit.

But on the other hand, culture can die even though men survive, and that's what threatens us today, because the growth, the expansion, of this immense body of cumulative knowledge requires brains, books, and traditions. Culture is not something that soars over men's heads. It is man himself. I think that a philosopher like Jean Jacques Rousseau, who has a large popular audience, can do enormous damage to human thinking.

Q: *Jean Jacques Rousseau? Today? Why?*

Lorenz: His notion that without culture man would be a noble savage living in a paradise is absolutely mad. Such a man would be a cretin who would not know how to speak, who would know only a few rudiments of social behavior, and who would therefore immediately backslide 200,000 years. Today's youth clearly sees that some things have fallen into decay. But what it doesn't see is that you can't build an enormous mass of knowledge in a single generation. The danger is that many of them want to tear everything down and start again from zero because they are under the illusion that the equivalent of it all can be rebuilt. We can restart at zero, but in that case, I repeat, we will go back about 200,000 years, before Cro-Magnon man, because Cro-Magnon paintings are the end result of a long tradition and of an enormous accumulation of knowledge.

Q: *You put a great deal of emphasis on tradition. People will end by accusing you of also being a traditionalist.*

Lorenz: And if the other side misunderstands me it will be said that I'm a Communist or a Maoist, or even a fascist or a nihilist. I'm against everything, against all the ideologies, all the regimes in the world. Except perhaps the Dubcek regime, which no longer exists. It's the only regime that would have been able to get my vote. But I'm very optimistic about the education of the young. I have spoken of all this in auditoriums filled with hostile students. I have said all this in my lectures in London, New York, Stockholm, Paris, Chicago, often before blacks, and I got an enormous response.

Q: *What did you tell the students?*

Lorenz: I said: "Watch out! If you make a clean sweep of things, you won't go back to the Stone Age, because you're there already, but to well before the Stone Age." I began my lectures by saying that I hoped to irritate the old as well as the young, to become detested by all.

Q: *Do you feel that your theories are very far from those of Herbert Marcuse?*

Lorenz: Marcuse is one of those utopian and generous madmen who believe that it's possible to build from the ground up. He believes that if everything is destroyed, everything automatically regrows. It's a terrifying error. Marcuse does not really understand the mechanisms by which evolution and culture work in tandem and complement one another—nor did Karl Marx or Engels understand these mechanisms. These men make related errors. Marx was very aware of the need to conserve the whole heritage of culture. Everything he said in *Capital* is right, but he always made the error of forgetting the instincts. For Marx the territorial instinct was only a cultural phenomenon.

Q: *This traditional culture is also being challenged by the young.*

Lorenz: Let me say that it is natural for youth to question tradition. At the age of 18 to 19 every normal young man begins to lose his absolute allegiance to the parental tradition. It's inevitable. If it weren't so, culture and tradition would be much too slow. But a culture is based on an equilibrium between two mechanisms: the acquisition of new data and the conservation of knowledge. Both are necessary. Tradition represents the mechanism for conserving knowledge.

Q: *Then, as you see it, there is a need for balance between tradition and change, conservation and challenge?*

Lorenz: Under the stable conditions of the Biblical times of Abraham, little had to be changed for men's adaptation to their environment to be perfect. As Thomas Mann has so nicely demonstrated, the son so identified with the father that he believed he was the father. If Abraham lived 350 years, it is simply because the Biblical ages are only a succession of sons, fathers and grandfathers intensely identifying with their ancestors. They all believed they were Abraham. A great deal of conservatism was necessary then. Today, with the acceleration of history and technology, adaptation to the environment requires more and more change.

National ideas were still serviceable for our grandparents. During the time of Rudyard Kipling, the norms of social behavior he wrote about were valid for his epoch and his country. Transposed into our time, Kipling results in Hitler—just as imperialist and just as racist. A great poet, Kipling is an example of how a system of behavioral norms that could serve as counsel for the young only 100 years ago would today lead to an absolutely criminal, nationalistic chauvinism. We therefore always have to ask ourselves: When and where? In 1970, the total disappearance of tradition would be a more deadly danger than the sclerosis brought on by the continuance of an overrigid tradition.

Q: *Could you develop that idea?*

Lorenz: I believe that we have to think of these things in medical terms. I often cite the case of the endocrine glands. Within an organism there are always more or less antagonistic functions that maintain themselves in equilibrium. When old [Emil Theodor] Kocher, a Swiss surgeon, tried to cure Basedow's disease by removing the thyroid, he not only took away the thyroid but also the parathyroid glands, which control calcium metabolism. As a result, the patient died very quickly.

The next time, Kocher left the parathyroid in place. This time, the patient died of myxedema, much later—but in developing the symptoms of myxedema, he gave Kocher the opportunity to understand that myxedema is the contrary of Basedow's disease. Afterwards, by removing only part of the thyroid, he obtained a complete cure. It's easy to see that if there is an endocrine gland, if you find this gland in the organism, it would be almost stupid to believe that it could be taken away without danger, without disordering the entire organism. In like manner, in society—that super-organism—there are interactions, equilibriums of a complexity infinitely greater than in the individual.

It's as stupid to ask if the thyroid is good or bad as it is to ask if conservatism or the challenge of the young is good or bad. Both are necessary. The problem is one of equilibrium. In each case, we must ask ourselves what the needs of the environment are at the present time and place. What may be disease in Europe may elsewhere be healthy. For example, in Africa a certain form of anemia caused by deformation of the red corpuscles is the only thing that provides resistance to malaria germs.

Q: *Is there then a similarity between biological laws and social laws?*

Lorenz: When we study a method of cybernetic regulation we see that a large number of contradictory and antagonistic functions is necessary to maintain a desired value between the extremes; if not there is catastrophic disorder. Loyalty to an ideal, the somewhat belligerent enthusiasm for a cause, nationalism—if all this is exaggerated somewhat, you very quickly end up with a dangerous barbarian capable of splitting your skull with the clearest possible conscience.

Q: *In your opinion, why does the present challenge to the parental generation's traditions and norms of behavior especially manifest itself in so-called "affluent" societies?*

Lorenz: There are explanations for that. There is a lack of contact between the generations. For example, let us take a young Peruvian Indian who has to till very poor soil and raise his llamas or his sheep. In his daily struggle against nature this young man very clearly sees that what his father does is absolutely necessary for survival. The father is not mad, and his precepts have to be followed: there is no other way to grow corn and raise llamas. The Peruvian Indian eats the previous year's corn, but the child of a Munich university professor has absolutely no opportunity to become convinced of the necessity of what his father does. If my grandchildren see me in front of an aquarium, how can they immediately understand that what the old man is doing is work?

Q: *Youth is also challenging the injustices of society. Doesn't it lay the guilt for these at the door of the parental generation?*

Lorenz: I believe that youth clearly sees the great faults committed by the "Establishment": the overexploitation of nature and of men, the upsetting of the equilibrium of the planet. These accusations are frequent, necessary and absolutely just. But I don't believe that the parental generation's guilt plays as essential a role. These are secondary rationalizations, because the accusation is the same in America as it is in Germany, where the young generation has good reasons for accusing its parents. Now, German youth is no more accusatory than that of Sweden, or France or Switzerland. There is, therefore, little correlation between real guilt and the young people's accusations against their parents.

The real motivations are much more instinctive. But if you observe the emotional response of the parental generation to the attacks of the young, you will notice that the representatives of the old generation themselves often feel guilty—that they respond with submission and self-accusation without knowing why. And this too is a nonrational, emotional reaction: if someone you love a great deal attacks you, your first thought is: "Oh, my God! How could I have offended him?" If he suddenly looks at you coldly, and even with a look of hate, your first reaction will be to search for guilt within yourself.

Parents are incapable of ceasing to love their children, and if they feel themselves accused and even hated, they have a tendency to believe that they are guilty. And this is the worst thing they can do. Because, naturally, the young people say, "There, he's admitted it!"

This behavior is also found in animals. You can see it in every dog. If you kick your dog, he thinks it's his fault. That's why I will never be able to carry out physiological experiments on dogs. The more pain you cause a dog the more submissive he becomes and the more he asks your pardon. The same thing is true of parents. They are like beaten dogs. The same is also true of professors.

Q: *Do you perceive a kind of abdication of the father's role?*

Lorenz: I would venture to say that in man there is a direct correlation between the hate among children and the lack of a dominant father. But the domination need not necessarily be a brutal domination. In my wife's family—five children—there was no hate. My father-in-law was the "alpha"—the unchallenged and unchallengeable head. His criticism was always very measured. The worst thing he could say was: "I was really surprised that you did that." That was terrible.

The hostility that you see nowadays between brother and sister is a new phenomenon. It is particularly noticeable in America, where there is a tendency for real hatred to come between children on the same level of the family pyramid.

Q: *Have you observed it in certain animals?*

Lorenz: In wolves, for example, when the alpha animal disappears, hostility develops among the inferior wolves. Battles for superiority immediately break out among the young.

Q: *How much of this do you ascribe to the growing insipidness of life? To the boredom that reigns in rich countries? What is its origin? What are its effects?*

Lorenz: Life is always in danger. It's not a stable state but a self-regulating process; it's up to us to keep it in balance. In wealthy societies, the lack of obstacles to be surmounted is also a frustration. I believe that the complete absence of obstacles is more dangerous than are insurmountable obstacles. In science, for example, one is always confronted by insurmountable obstacles: the soul and the body, etc. And that's not so bad. Goethe used to say, "I love the man who aspires to the impossible."

There is in man a sort of organization—an apparatus, if you like—that balances pain and pleasure. The highest degree of pleasure is acquired only at a certain price. If you prevent all sorts of pain, if you constantly take tranquilizers to eliminate a headache or fear, you diminish the oscillation; you end up with a sort of grayness that leads to complete boredom. This is one of the new plagues that can be observed in rich countries.

Q: *Do animals have this apparatus that maintains the balance between pleasure and pain?*

Lorenz: All animals that learn by trial and error. Because there's always a bargain struck. Suppose that a wolf knew only pleasure and not pain; he would go hunting in the polar night at 40 below and he would freeze a paw. That's too steep a price to pay. The equilibrium between the price and what is bought is broken: the price of a caribou should not be a frozen paw, because then the wolf would have no chance of surviving.

Man, too, has this apparatus. If he decreases his investment of pain and of work toward a distant goal, he causes the oscillation to decrease, and he then no longer knows the great waves of pleasure and pain, of desire and despair, of final success through work, which give him self-respect and joy. Joy is not necessarily linked to sensual pleasure: pleasure is only the act of consummation, and joy is pleasure in the act of creation.

As American psychologists have pointed out, boredom carries with it the need for immediate satisfaction, a refusal to suffer, to struggle—a refusal, for example, to conquer a woman: immediate copulation is required. Have you seen some of those young people making love in Hyde Park? They do it with all the enthusiasm of bored babies who suck on candies that they would just as soon spit out. Bored young people are the most pitiful beings in the world. They have lost everything.

Q: *Has the apparatus broken down?*

Lorenz: Yes. This apparatus evolved during a time in which the life of humanity was extremely dangerous: there was the saber-toothed tiger, the cave bear. At that time it was good strategy to be cowardly. You had to be economical, as lazy as possible. Food was scarce and you had to be a glutton and stuff yourself once the mastodon was killed. All the mortal sins were virtues in those times when life was bought dear. Now the cost of life is more and more of a bargain, and man is inventing very subtle ways of procuring pleasure without paying too much for it. And this leads to a frustration due to a lack of obstacles, a dulling that results in other atrophies such as a lack of appreciation of beauty, of harmony.

Q: *Can the too rapid destruction of ancient norms produce monsters?*

Lorenz: It's easy to manufacture a monster, easier than people think. It wasn't until after man began to have a culture that the cerebral hemispheres became developed. Lacking a link with tradition, they risk remaining empty, atrophying. The linguist [Noam] Chomsky—a genius—contends that language did not first develop as a means of communication but as a logical means of conceptual thought. Traditional languages take thousands of years to evolve. Language can be lost in a few generations. In our own day it is already becoming impoverished, and, as a result, so is the faculty for logical expression.

You know that by accumulating mutations through incest, by employing poisons or radiations, you very rapidly end up with monsters. In our own time, the loss of certain traditions is already producing asocial monsters. Each year, there are younger and younger criminals. The complete destruction of tradition would cause enormous damage. For example, it is the moral codes that create family cohesion. If we are to take the theoreticians of complete sexual promiscuity at their word, we will have to ask ourselves, among other things, "What will become of the children?" Because it can be shown that a child needs not only his two parents but even his grandparents, a family.

Q: *According to you, in modern societies, man's aggressive instinct is "jumping the track." Is it no longer—as in animals—at the service of life, of selection?*

Lorenz: Let's say, to begin with, that all instincts can jump the track. A comparative study of sexual instincts shows the extreme derailments often provoked by the same social, cultural, technological and ecological causes. But it's almost always overpopulation that is at the root of all the "malfunctions" of human social behavior. Thus it is collective aggression that becomes the major danger of modern civilization: aggression plus the H-bomb. When thousands, millions, of men are brought together, aggression begins to get seriously out of hand.

Q: *What are the reasons for this?*

Lorenz: There are several. Indoctrination by ideology is one of the cultural factors capable of causing the most serious derailments of collective aggression. A doctrine's power of conviction increases with the square of the number of men participating in it—the relationship is geometric. As soon as a doctrine has a sufficient number of adherents, the nonconformist becomes a heretic who must be liquidated.

The other reason for mounting aggression is quite simply that men in large cities are too crowded together. Some day a movie will have to be made of the aggressive behavior of people in the big New York bus terminal. There too the key factor is overpopulation.

Q: *In some American universities there is a very strong resistance on the part of many orthodox professors to the current conclusions of ethology. Could this be for ideological reasons?*

Lorenz: In our time a biological approach to man's behavior comes up against a worldwide doctrine. And this simplified doctrine of the "conditioned reflex" does all it can to destroy its adversaries. You have to be something of a Don Quixote to fight against it. This doctrine—I call it the "pseudodemocratic" doctrine—has very deep foundations and is very dangerous. The theory according to which man is nothing more than the creature of his milieu is comfortable for everybody. The citizen thus "equalized" is as welcome to American capitalism, which wants to have a dutiful and uniform consumer, as he is to the leader of a totalitarian system, who wants to have a citizen who won't rock the boat.

If—following Freud—we observe the mental and emotional resistance that the behaviorists put up against whatever is not a conditioned reflex, I believe we discover the underlying ideology of all the present political doctrines. The management, the control, of large masses rests on the erroneous assumption that there is no innate program in man, no phylogenetic program. And this egalitarian point of view is completely antibiological.

In human society the division of labor is founded on a difference, an inequality, in the members of society, which presupposes a difference in capacities. Today an attempt is everywhere being made to set up a society composed of manipulable and interchangeable elements. In other words, the best of all possible worlds for the Russian apparatchiks or the American monopolists.

The adversaries of ethology often accuse us of being antidemocratic, not to say racist. They surround their own doctrine with a democratic halo. The phenomenon has been analyzed by an American writer, Philip Wylie. The pseudodemocratic doctrine, he says, takes its strength from a truth that has been twisted into a lie: The truth is that all men should have the same possibilities to develop themselves freely. But who denies this? Then this indisputable truth is twisted a little, and it is proclaimed: If all men had the same possibilities to develop themselves, all men would be equal. This is not true. It is absolutely false because all men are unequal from the moment of their conception. But there is a pretense that this equality among men is the key, the *sine qua non,* of collective life, and this is false. As far as mass manipulators are concerned, the Pavlovian dog is the ideal citizen.

Q: *But, according to you, man is not a Pavlovian dog . . .*

Lorenz: Even dogs aren't, really! Rats would be a better choice. A very strange story was told to me by Howard Lidell, a famous neurological specialist who was Pavlov's student in St. Petersburg. Lidell had conditioned a dog to salivate when a metronome accelerated. He asked himself, "What will happen if I release my dog from his harness?" Note that to preserve belief in the conditioned reflex the dog has to be tied up so that he can make use only of his salivary gland.

Lidell went ahead and unleashed the dog. What do you think the dog did? Though the metronome hadn't accelerated, he leaped toward the mechanism, pushed it with his nose, wagged his tail, and, while salivating furiously, asked the metronome to accelerate! What had previously been conditioned was quite simply the reaction of a beggar. The dog had formed the hypothesis that the metronome was the cause of his food. The great Pavlov was so furious that he forbade Lidell to divulge his experiment! Think of the complexity of what had happened and the simplism of the explanation. The conditioned reflex does exist, but it is not the only element of behavior.

Q: *What is your attitude toward Freud?*

Lorenz: Freud—I'm simplifying a great deal—discovered the eternal instinctive drives, those not dependent on environment, in a time when the doctrine of the conditioned reflex was at its acme. If he had done only that, he would have deserved three Nobel prizes, but he generalized the properties of sexuality onto all the other instincts. Perhaps his fundamental error was to have made aggression the antagonist of life. He made it something of a devil.

Q: *When did you become aware of the political implications of your research?*

Lorenz: It's only recently that our adversaries have understood how dangerous ethology is. Its results simply say that it's not possible to make anything one wants out of man. Man—at least I hope so—will revolt against conditioning. Nevertheless, there is another possibility. It is the danger that the "Establishment," such as it exists in either the West or the East, will undertake a selection of conformists, of good Pavlovian dogs. That's something that worries me: a selection that would operate to the disadvantage of the student protesters, a selection in favor of those who never revolt, who bend their backs and "learn." Then the conformist would advance and take all the important positions.

Selection, you know, works very quickly, and that's a danger for humanity. Today one already finds a certain hostility toward the intellectual elite. It can be found among many student protesters. An egalitarianism that forbids a man to be more intelligent than the average is the death of all cultural development. I realize that it is easier to denounce faults than to build constructive programs. But there are, you know, beings on earth among whom it is the most intelligent who govern.

These beings are the monkeys, the baboons. With them, it is not the strongest, not the armed man, not the militarist who governs, but rather the scientist, the sage, because there is among them a veritable senate of experienced beings who make the decisions. Until now our human scientists have not been sufficiently aware of their responsibilities. Our problems—how to govern a state, how to establish collaboration between two peoples or two hostile ideologies—will not be resolved in the 20th century by brutal revolutions, but by research and imagination.

Q: *You've been accused of justifying human aggression in your book* [On Aggression]. *Do you feel that this reproach is justified?*

Lorenz: I wonder if their own aggression didn't make my adversaries simply incapable of reading this book. Excuse aggression? Defend violence? I was trying to do just the opposite! I filled 499 pages in an attempt to explain that violence and war are a derailment of the normal instinct. I tried to show the existence of internal forces that man must know in order to master. I said that reason could conquer aggression.

Q: *How do you explain these attacks against you?*

Lorenz: The book wounds the superstitious pride of man. It irritates those who believe that man is a being outside of nature, opposed to her—a position still held by some of the greatest Western philosophers. I have been so accused of having written a pessimistic, contradictory and obscure book that I'm surprised the book became a best seller.

Apparently there are people who understand it. What pleases me is that young people clearly grasp what I want to say. Believe me, one day everything I've said will seem very ordinary. Darwin wasn't understood at all. If I'm understood by some people today, it simply proves that I'm not a genius.

Q: *What is your personal vision of the universe?*

Lorenz: That's difficult to say. If you were to ask me if I'm a monist or a dualist, I would reply: "The devil if I know." When I look with emotion upon the inorganic world around us, the beauty of a sunset, I think I'm a monist. At such a time, I am convinced that there are universal laws that reign over the entire universe, and that among them the laws of life are merely special cases. But when I see the struggle of organic life, so fragile, so vulnerable, against the eternal forces of the inorganic world, my vision of that struggle is something like a photograph of the Galapagos Islands: an immense torrent of frozen lava in the midst of which is a hole no bigger than the palm of your hand—and from this tiny hole rises a minuscule flowering cactus!

I keep these ideas intentionally vague. A scientist can only have one ideology, and that ideology consists in not having any. God? What bothers me about religions is that the priests are on such intimate terms with God. To me, it's blasphemous to be so intimate with God. God isn't an individual; if He exists, He is everywhere, maybe in me.

What Is Existentialism?

Rollo May

Diagnostician of modern anxiety, Rollo May was born in Ada, Ohio, in 1909. After completing his undergraduate education at Oberlin (1930), he taught at Salonika College in Greece for three years and worked as a student adviser at Michigan State. He resumed his education at Union Theological Seminary (Bachelor of Divinity, 1938) and then shifted into psychology at Columbia, earning his Ph.D. in 1949. During the years of postdoctoral study, he served on the counseling staff of the City College of New York. He joined the faculty of the William Alanson White Institute in New York and after ten years became the supervisory psychoanalyst (1958). He has taught at Harvard, Princeton, and the New School for Social Research, and now lives in New York City. He is the father of three grown children.

His writings include *The Meaning of Anxiety* (1950), *Man's Search for Himself* (1953), *Psychology and the Human Dilemma* (1966), *Love and Will* (1969), and *Power and Innocence* (1972). The following selection is from *Existence,* edited by Rollo May, Ernest Angel, and Henri Ellenberger (1958). It examines the origins and the significance of the existential movement in psychology, a movement that shook psychology out of its often academic or authoritarian habits and sought to integrate the nineteenth-century cleavage of subject and object.

We must remove a major stumbling block—namely, the confusion surrounding the term, "existentialism." The word is bandied about to mean everything—from the posturing defiant dilettantism of some members of the *avant garde* on the left bank in Paris, to a philosophy of despair advocating suicide, to a system of anti-rationalist German thought written in a language so esoteric as to exasperate any empirically minded reader. Existentialism, rather, is an expression of profound dimensions of the modern emotional and spiritual temper and is shown in almost all aspects of our culture. It is found not only in psychology and philosophy but in art, *vide* Van Gogh, Cezanne, and Picasso—and in literature, *vide* Dostoevski, Baudelaire, Kafka, and Rilke. Indeed, in many ways it is the unique and specific portrayal of the psychological predicament of contemporary Western man. This cultural movement, as we shall see later in detail, has its roots in the same historical situation and the same psychological crises which called forth psychoanalysis and other forms of psychotherapy.

SOURCE: Rollo May, Ernest Angel, and Henri F. Ellenberger, eds., *Existence* (New York: Basic Books, Inc., Publishers, 1958), pp. 10–19.

Confusions about the term occur even in usually highly literate places. *The New York Times,* in a report commenting on Sartre's denunciation of, and final break with, the Russian Communists for their suppression of freedom in Hungary, identified Sartre as a leader in "existentialism, a broadly materialistic form of thought." The report illustrates two reasons for the confusion—first, the identification of existentialism in the popular mind in this country with the writings of Jean-Paul Sartre. Quite apart from the fact that Sartre is known here for his dramas, movies, and novels rather than for his major, penetrating psychological analyses, it must be emphasized that he represents a nihilistic, subjectivist extreme in existentialism which invites misunderstanding, and his position is by no means the most useful introduction to the movement. But the second more serious confusion in the *Times* report is its definition of existentialism as "broadly materialistic." Nothing could be less accurate—nothing, unless it be the exact opposite, namely, describing it as an idealistic form of thinking. For the very essence of this approach is that it seeks to analyze and portray the human being—whether in art or literature or philosophy or psychology—on a level which undercuts the old dilemma of materialism versus idealism.

Existentialism, in short, is the endeavor to understand man by cutting below the cleavage between subject and object which has bedeviled Western thought and science since shortly after the Renaissance. This cleavage Binswanger calls "the cancer of all psychology up to now . . . the cancer of the doctrine of subject-object cleavage of the world." The existential way of understanding human beings has some illustrious progenitors in Western history, such as Socrates in his dialogues, Augustine in his depth-psychological analyses of the self, Pascal in his struggle to find a place for the "heart's reasons which the reason knows not of." But it arose specifically just over a hundred years ago in Kierkegaard's violent protest against the reigning rationalism of his day, Hegel's "totalitarianism of reason," to use Maritain's phrase. Kierkegaard proclaimed that Hegel's identification of abstract truth with reality was an illusion and amounted to trickery. "Truth exists," wrote Kierkegaard, "only as the individual himself produces it in action." He and the existentialists following him protested firmly against the rationalists and idealists who would see man only as a subject—that is, as having reality only as a thinking being. But just as strongly they fought against the tendency to treat man as an object to be calculated and controlled, exemplified in the almost overwhelming tendencies in the Western world to make human beings into anonymous units to fit like robots into the vast industrial and political collectivisms of our day.

These thinkers sought the exact opposite of intellectualism for its own sake. They would have protested more violently than classical psychoanalysis against the use of thinking as a defense against vitality or as a substitute for immediate experience. One of the early existentialists of the sociological wing, Feuerbach, makes this appealing admonition, "Do not wish to be a philosopher in contrast to being a man . . . do not think as a thinker . . . think as a living, real being. Think in Existence."[1]

The term "existence," coming from the root *ex-sistere,* means literally to *stand out, to emerge.* This accurately indicates what these cultural representatives sought, whether in art or philosophy or psychology—namely, to portray the human being not as a collection of static substances or mechanisms or patterns but rather as emerging and becoming, that is to say, as existing. For no matter how interesting or theoretically true is the fact that I am composed of such and such chemicals or act by such and such mechanisms or patterns, the crucial question always is that I happen to exist at this given moment in time and space, and my problem is how I am to be aware of that fact and what I shall do about it. As we shall see later, the existential psychologists and psychiatrists do not at all rule out the study of dynamisms, drives, and patterns of behavior. But they hold that these cannot be understood in any given person except in the context of the overarching fact that here is a person who happens *to exist, to be,* and if we do not keep this in mind, all else we know about this person will lose its meaning. Thus their approach is always dynamic; existence refers to coming into being, becoming. Their endeavor is to understand this becoming not as a sentimental artifact but as the fundamental structure of human existence. When the term "being" is used in the following chapters, as it often is, the reader should remember that it is not a static word but a verb form, the participle of the verb "to be." Existentialism is basically concerned with *ontology,* that is, the science of being (*ontos,* from Greek "being").

We can see more clearly the significance of the term if we recall that traditionally in Western thought "existence" has been set over against "essence." Essence refers to the greenness of this stick of wood, let us say, and its density, weight, and other characteristics which give it substance. By and large Western thought since the Renaissance has been concerned with essences. Traditional science seeks to discover such essences or substances; it assumes an essentialist metaphysics, as Professor Wild of Harvard puts it.[2] The search for essences may indeed produce highly significant universal laws in science or brilliant abstract conceptualizations in logic or philosophy. But it can do this only by abstraction. The *existence* of the given individual thing has to be left out of the picture. For example, we can demonstrate that three apples added to three make six. But this would be just as true if we substituted unicorns for apples; it makes no difference to the mathe-

[1] Quoted by Paul Tillich, "Existential Philosophy," in the *Journal of the History of Ideas,* 5:1, 44–70, 1944.

[2] John Wild, *The Challenge of Existentialism* (Bloomington: Indiana University Press, 1955). Modern physics, with Heisenberg, Bohr (see p. 26), and similar trends have changed at this point, paralleling, as we shall see later, one side of the existentialist development. We are talking above of the traditional ideas of Western science.

matical truth of the proposition whether apples or unicorns actually exist or not. That is to say, a proposition can be *true* without being *real.* Perhaps just because this approach has worked so magnificently in certain areas of science, we tend to forget that it necessarily involves a detached viewpoint and that the living individual must be omitted.[3] There remains the chasm between truth and reality. And the crucial question which confronts us in psychology and other aspects of the science of man is precisely this chasm between what is *abstractly true* and what is *existentially real* for the given living person.

Lest it seem that we are setting up an artificial, straw-man issue, let us point out that this chasm between truth and reality is openly and frankly admitted by sophisticated thinkers in behavioristic and conditioning psychology. Kenneth W. Spence, distinguished leader of one wing of behavior theory, writes, "The question of whether any particular realm of behavior phenomena is more real or closer to real life and hence should be given priority in investigation does not, or at least should not, arise for the psychologist *as scientist.*" That is to say, it does not primarily matter whether what is being studied is real or not. What realms, then, should be selected for study? Spence gives priority to phenomena which lend themselves "to the degrees of control and analysis necessary for the formulation of abstract laws."[4] Nowhere has our point been put more unabashedly and clearly—what can be reduced to *abstract laws* is selected, and whether what you are studying has reality or not is irrelevant to this goal. On the basis of this approach many an impressive system in psychology has been erected, with abstraction piled high upon abstraction—the authors succumbing, as we intellectuals are wont, to their "edifice complex"—until an admirable and imposing structure is built. The only trouble is that the edifice has more often than not been separated from human reality in its very foundations. Now the thinkers in the existential tradition hold the exact opposite to Spence's view, and so do the psychiatrists and psychologists in the existential psychotherapy movement. They insist that it is necessary and possible to have a science of man which studies human beings in their reality.

Kierkegaard, Nietzsche, and those who followed them accurately foresaw this growing split between truth and reality in Western culture, and they endeavored to call Western man back from the delusion that reality can be comprehended in an abstracted, detached way. But though they protested vehemently against arid intellectualism, they

---

[3] Reality makes a difference to the person who *has* the apples—that is the *existential* side—but it is irrelevant to the truth of the mathematical proposition. For a more serious example, that all men die is a truth; and to say that such and such a percentage die at such and such ages gives a statistical accuracy to the proposition. But neither of these statements says anything about the fact which really matters most to each of us, namely, that you and I must alone face the fact that at some unknown moment in the future we shall die. In contrast to the essentialist propositions, these latter are *existential facts*.

[4] Kenneth W. Spence, *Behavior Theory and Conditioning* (New Haven: Yale University Press, 1956).

were by no means simple activists. Nor were they anti-rational. Anti-intellectualism and other movements in our day which make thinking subordinate to acting must not at all be confused with existentialism. Either alternative—making man subject *or* object—results in losing the living, existing person. Kierkegaard and the existential thinkers appealed to a reality *underlying both subjectivity and objectivity*. We must not only study a person's experience as such, they held, but even more we must study the man to whom the experience is happening, the one who is doing the experiencing. They insist, as Tillich puts it, that "Reality or Being is not the object of cognitive experience, but is rather 'existence,' is Reality as immediately experienced, with the accent on the inner, personal character of man's immediate experience."[5] This comment, as well as several above, will indicate to the reader how close the existentialists are to present-day depth-psychology. It is by no means accidental that the greatest of them in the nineteenth century, Kierkegaard and Nietzsche, happen also to be among the most remarkable psychologists (in the dynamic sense) of all time and that one of the contemporary leaders of this school, Karl Jaspers, was originally a psychiatrist and wrote a notable text on psychopathology. When one reads Kierkegaard's profound analyses of anxiety and despair or Nietzsche's amazingly acute insights into the dynamics of resentment and the guilt and hostility which accompany repressed emotional powers, one must pinch himself to realize that he is reading works written seventy-five and a hundred years ago and not some new contemporary psychological analysis. The existentialists are centrally concerned with rediscovering the living person amid the compartmentalization and dehumanization of modern culture, and in order to do this they engage in depth psychological analysis. Their concern is not with isolated psychological reactions in themselves but rather with the psychological being of the living man who is doing the experiencing. That is to say, they use psychological terms with an ontological meaning.[6]

---

[5] Paul Tillich, *op. cit.*

[6] For readers who wish more historical background, we append this note. In the winter of 1841, Schelling gave his famous series of lectures at the University of Berlin before a distinguished audience including Kierkegaard, Burckhardt, Engels, Bakunin. Schelling set out to overthrow Hegel, whose vast rationalist system, including, as we have said, the identification of abstract truth with reality and the bringing of all of history into an "absolute whole," held immense and dominant popularity in the Europe of the middle of the nineteenth century. Though many of Schelling's listeners were bitterly disappointed in his answers to Hegel, the existential movement may be said to have begun there. Kierkegaard went back to Denmark and in 1844 published his *Philosophical Fragments,* and two years later he wrote the declaration of independence of existentialism, *Concluding Unscientific Postscript.* Also in 1844 there appeared the second edition of Schopenhauer's *The World as Will and Idea,* a work important in the new movement because of its central emphasis on vitality, "will," along with "idea." Two related works were written by Karl Marx in 1844–45. The early Marx is significant in this movement in his attack upon abstract truth as "ideology," again using Hegel as his whipping boy. Marx' dynamic view of history as the arena in which men and groups bring truth into being and his meaningful fragments pointing out how the money economy of modern industrialism tends to turn people into things and

Martin Heidegger is generally taken as the fountainhead of present-day existential thought. His seminal work, *Being and Time,* was of radical importance in giving Binswanger and other existential psychiatrists and psychologists the deep and broad basis they sought for understanding man. Heidegger's thought is rigorous, logically incisive, and "scientific" in the European sense of pursuing with unrelenting vigor and thoroughness whatever implications his inquiries led him to. But his work is almost impossible to translate. Only a few essays are available in English.[7] Jean-Paul Sartre's best contribution to our subject are his phenomenological descriptions of psychological processes. In addition to Jaspers, other prominent existential thinkers are Gabriel Marcel in France, Nicolas Berdyaev, originally Russian but until his recent death a resident of Paris, and Ortega y Gasset and Unamuno in Spain. Paul Tillich shows the existential approach in his work, and in many ways his book *The Courage to Be* is the best and most cogent presentation of existentialism as an approach to actual living available in English.[8]

---

works toward the dehumanization of modern man are likewise significant in the existentialist approach. Both Marx and Kierkegaard took over Hegel's dialectical method but used it for quite different purposes. More existential elements were latently present in Hegel, it may be noted, than his antagonists acknowledged.

In the following decades the movement subsided. Kierkegaard remained completely unknown, Schelling's work was contemptuously buried, and Marx and Feuerbach were interpreted as dogmatic materialists. Then a new impetus came in the 1880's with the work of Dilthey, and particularly with Friedrich Nietzsche, the "philosophy of life" movement, and the work of Bergson.

The third and contemporary phase of existentialism came after the shock to the Western world caused by World War I. Kierkegaard and the early Marx were rediscovered, and the serious challenges to the spiritual and psychological bases of Western society given by Nietzsche could no longer be covered over by Victorian self-satisfied placidity. The specific form of this third phase owes much to the phenomenology of Edmund Husserl, which gave to Heidegger, Jaspers, and the others the tool they needed to undercut the subject-object cleavage which had been such a stumbling-block in science as well as philosophy. There is an obvious similarity between existentialism, in its emphasis on truth as produced in action, with the process philosophies, such as Whitehead's, and American pragmatism, particularly as in William James.

Those who wish to know more about the existential movement as such are referred to Paul Tillich's classical paper, "Existential Philosophy." For most of the above historical material I am indebted to Tillich's paper.

We may add that part of the confusion in this field is due to the misleading titles which books are given. Wahl's *A Short History of Existentialism* is short but by no means a history of existentialism, just as the book by Sartre published under the title of *Existential Psychoanalysis* has very little to do with psychoanalysis or, for that matter, existential therapy.

[7] Published, along with an introduction and a summary of "Being and Time," by Werner Brock, in *Existence and Being* (Chicago: Henry Regnery Co., 1949). Heidegger disclaimed the title "existentialist" after it became identified with the work of Sartre. He would call himself, strictly speaking, a philologist or ontologist. But in any case, we must be existential enough not to get twisted up in controversies over titles and to take the meaning and spirit of each man's work rather than the letter. Martin Buber likewise is not happy at being called an existentialist, although his work has clear affinities with this movement. The reader who has difficulty with the terms in this field is indeed in good company!

[8] *The Courage to Be* (New Haven: Yale University Press, 1952) is existential as a living approach to crises in contrast to books *about* existentialism. Tillich, like most of the thinkers mentioned above, is not to be tagged as *merely* an existentialist, for existen-

The novels of Kafka portray the despairing, dehumanized situation in modern culture from which and to which existentialism speaks. *The Stranger* and *The Plague,* by Albert Camus, represent excellent examples in modern literature in which existentialism is partially self-conscious. But perhaps the most vivid of all portrayals of the meaning of existentialism is to be found in modern art, partly because it is articulated symbolically rather than as self-conscious thought and partly because art always reveals with special clarity the underlying spiritual and emotional temper of the culture. We shall frequently refer to the relation of modern art and existentialism in the following pages. Here let us only note that some of the common elements in the work of such outstanding representatives of the modern movement as Van Gogh, Cezanne, and Picasso are, *first,* a revolt against the hypocritical academic tradition of the late nineteenth century, *second,* an endeavor to pierce below surfaces to grasp a new relation to the reality of nature, *third,* an endeavor to recover vitality and honest, direct aesthetic experience, and, *fourth,* the desperate attempt to express the immediate underlying meaning of the modern human situation, even though this means portraying despair and emptiness. Tillich, for example, holds that Picasso's painting "Guernica" gives the most gripping and revealing portrayal of the atomistic, fragmentized condition of European society which preceded World War II and "shows what is now in the souls of many Americans as disruptiveness, existential doubt, emptiness and meaninglessness."[9]

The fact that the existential approach arose as an indigenous and spontaneous answer to crises in modern culture is shown not only in the fact that it emerged in art and literature but also in the fact that different philosophers in diverse parts of Europe often developed these ideas without conscious relation to each other. Though Heidegger's main work, *Being and Time,* was published in 1927, Ortega y Gasset already in 1924 had developed and partially published strikingly similar ideas without any direct knowledge of Heidegger's work.[10]

It is true, of course, that existentialism had its birth in a time of cultural crisis, and it is always found in our day on the sharp revolu-

---

tialism is a way of approaching problems and does not in itself give answers or norms. Tillich has both rational norms—the structure of reason is always prominent in his analyses—and religious norms. Some readers will not find themselves in agreement with the religious elements in *The Courage to Be*. It is important to note the very significant point, however, that these religious ideas, whether one agrees with them or not, do illustrate an authentic existential approach. This is seen in Tillich's concept of "the God beyond God" and "absolute faith" as faith not *in* some content or somebody but as a state of being, a way of relating to reality characterized by courage, acceptance, full commitment, etc. The theistic arguments for the "existence of God" are not only beside the point but exemplify the most deteriorated aspect of the Western habit of thinking in terms of God as a substance or object, existing in a world of objects and in relation to whom we are subjects. This is "bad theology," Tillich points out, and results in "the God Nietzsche said had to be killed because nobody can tolerate being made into a mere object of absolute knowledge and absolute control" (p. 185).

[9] "Existential Aspects of Modern Art," in *Christianity and the Existentialists,* edited by Carl Michalson (New York: Scribners, 1956), p. 138.

[10] Ortega y Gasset, *The Dehumanization of Art, and Other Writings on Art and Culture* (New York: Doubleday Anchor, 1956), pp. 135–137.

tionary edge of modern art, literature, and thought. To my mind this fact speaks for the validity of its insights rather than the reverse. When a culture is caught in the profound convulsions of a transitional period, the individuals in the society understandably suffer spiritual and emotional upheaval; and finding that the accepted mores and ways of thought no longer yield security, they tend either to sink into dogmatism and conformism, giving up awareness, or are forced to strive for a heightened self-consciousness by which to become aware of their existence with new conviction and on new bases. This is one of the most important affinities of the existential movement with psychotherapy—both are concerned with individuals in crisis. And far from saying that the insights of a crisis period are "simply the product of anxiety and despair," we are more likely to find, as we do time and again in psychoanalysis, that a crisis is exactly what is required to shock people out of unaware dependence upon external dogma and to force them to unravel layers of pretense to reveal naked truth about themselves which, however unpleasant, will at least be solid. Existentialism is an attitude which accepts man as always becoming, which means potentially in crisis. But this does not mean it will be despairing. Socrates, whose dialectical search for truth in the individual is the prototype of existentialism, was optimistic. But this approach is understandably more apt to appear in ages of transition, when one age is dying and the new one not yet born, and the individual is either homeless and lost or achieves a new self-consciousness. In the period of transition from Medievalism to the Renaissance, a moment of radical upheaval in Western culture, Pascal describes powerfully the experience the existentialists later were to call *Dasein:* "When I consider the brief span of my life, swallowed up in the eternity before and behind it, the small space that I fill, or even see, engulfed in the infinite immensity of spaces which I know not, and which know not me, I am afraid, and wonder to see myself here rather than there; for there is no reason why I should be here rather than there, now rather than then. . . ."[11] Rarely has the existential problem been put more simply or beautifully. In this passage we see, first, the profound realization of the contingency of human life which existentialists call "thrownness." Second, we see Pascal facing unflinchingly the question of *being there* or more accurately "being where?" Third, we see the realization that one cannot take refuge in some superficial explanation of time and space, which Pascal, scientist that he was, could well know; and lastly, the deep shaking anxiety arising from this stark awareness of existence in such a universe.[12]

---

[11] *Pensées of Pascal* (New York: Peter Pauper Press, 1946), p. 36.

[12] It is not surprising, thus, that this approach to life would speak particularly to many modern citizens who are aware of the emotional and spiritual dilemmas in which we find ourselves. Norbert Wiener, for example, though the actual implications of his scientific work may be radically different from the emphases of the existentialists, has stated in his autobiography that his scientific activity has led him personally to a "positive" existentialism. "We are not fighting for a definitive victory in the indefinite future," he writes. "It is the greatest possible victory *to be*, and *to have been*. [ITALICS MINE.] No

It remains, finally, in this orientation section to note the relation between existentialism and oriental thought as shown in the writings of Laotzu and Zen Buddhism. The similarities are striking. One sees this immediately in glancing at some quotations from Laotzu's *The Way of Life:* "Existence is beyond the power of words to define: terms may be used but none of them is absolute." "Existence, by nothing bred, breeds everything, parent of the universe." "Existence is infinite, not to be defined; and though it seem but a bit of wood in your hand, to carve as you please, it is not to be lightly played with and laid down." "The way to do is to be." "Rather abide at the center of your being; for the more you leave it, the less you learn."[13]

One gets the same shock of similarity in Zen Buddhism.[14] The likenesses between these Eastern philosophies and existentialism go much deeper than the chance similarity of words. Both are concerned with ontology, the study of being. Both seek a relation to reality which cuts below the cleavage between subject and object. Both would insist that the Western absorption in conquering and gaining power over nature has resulted not only in the estrangement of man from nature but also indirectly in the estrangement of man from himself. The basic reason for these similarities is that Eastern thought never suffered the radical split between subject and object that has characterized Western thought, and this dichotomy is exactly what existentialism seeks to overcome.

The two approaches are not at all to be identified, of course; they are on different levels. Existentialism is not a comprehensive philosophy or way of life, but an endeavor to grasp reality. The chief specific difference between the two, for our purposes, is that existentialism is immersed in and arises directly out of Western man's anxiety, estrangement, and conflicts and is indigenous to our culture. Like psychoanalysis, existentialism seeks not to bring in answers from other cultures but to utilize these very conflicts in contemporary personality as avenues to the more profound self-understanding of Western man and to find the solutions to our problems in direct relation to the historical and cultural crises which gave the problems birth. In this respect, the particular value of Eastern thought is not that it can be transferred, ready-born like Athena, to the Western mind, but rather that it serves as a corrective to our biases and highlights the erroneous assumptions that have led Western development to its present problems. The present widespread interest in oriental thought in the Western world is, to my mind, a reflection of the same cultural crises, the same sense of estrangement, the same hunger to get beyond the vicious circle of dichotomies which called forth the existentialist movement.

---

defeat can deprive us of the success of having existed for some moment of time in a universe that seems indifferent to us." *I Am a Mathematician* (New York: Doubleday).

13 Witter Bynner, *The Way of Life, according to Laotzu, an American version* (New York: John Day Company, 1946).

14 See William Barrett, ed., *Zen Buddhism, the Selected Writings of D. T. Suzuki* (New York: Doubleday Anchor, 1956), Introduction, p. xi.

We Write for Our Own Time

Jean-Paul Sartre

Jean-Paul Sartre's phenomenal powers as a philosopher, creative writer, critic, and man of action show no signs of failing as he enters his seventies. Not content to be known as one of the most brilliant men of letters alive, he continues to devote himself to humane causes, and his name is identified not only with modern "existentialism" but also with the struggle for social justice and political freedom of oppressed peoples.

He began his career as a teacher, first in provincial *lycées,* later in Paris. He studied under Edmund Husserl and Martin Heidegger, who greatly influenced his thought. His existential view of man's condition is reflected in his early fiction, *Nausea* (1938) and *The Wall* (1939), and in the novels making up *Roads to Freedom,* part of which was adapted for National Educational Television by the BBC. He dramatized his philosophy in such stage successes as *No Exit, Dirty Hands, The Flies, The Respectful Prostitute,* and *The Condemned of Altona.* He refused to accept the Nobel Prize for Literature awarded to him in 1964.

Sartre believes that a man must shape his own life (be *engaged*) and that he must do so by his choices and acts (the major statement of his position is in *Being and Nothingness,* 1943). Art is an act, that is, a commitment to the times. A book or art work is true for its time and perhaps no other. Art is for the present moment, not for the ages. Sartre is the spokesman for the spirit of relativity and impermanence that characterizes our age. Under these conditions, paradoxically, men find freedom.

We take our stand against certain critics and authors. We declare that salvation must be won upon this earth, that it must be won for the whole man by the whole man, and that art is a meditation on life, not on death. It is true that for history only talent is important. But I have not yet entered history, and I do not know how I will enter it: perhaps alone, perhaps in an anonymous crowd, perhaps as one of those names that one finds in the notes of textbooks on literature. In any case, I shall not worry about the judgments that the future may pronounce upon my work, because there is nothing I can do about them. Art cannot be reduced to a dialogue with dead men and men as yet unborn: that would be both too hard and too easy. In my opinion, this idea constitutes the last trace of the Christian belief in immortality: just as the sojourn of man upon this earth is represented as a brief testing time between Limbo and Hell or Heaven,

SOURCE: Jean-Paul Sartre, "We Write for Our Own Time," *The Virginia Quarterly Review,* Vol. 25, No. 1 (Spring 1947), pp. 147–53.

so a book is supposed to enjoy a transitory period that is approximately the same as that of its effectiveness; after that, disincarnated and free as a soul, it enters eternity. But at least for Christians our sojourn upon earth is the decisive factor and eternal beatitude is only a reward. Yet people seem to believe that the career our books have after we are no more should be justified by the life we once led. This is true from an objective point of view. Objectively, we are classified according to our talent. But the perspective our grandchildren will have upon us is not infallible, since others will come after them and judge them in their turn. It goes without saying that we all write out of need for the absolute; and a work of the spirit is, indeed, an absolute. However, people make a double mistake on this score. First, it is not true that a writer raises his sufferings or his errors to the level of the absolute by writing about them; and it is not true that he redeems them. People say of the unhappily married man who writes well about marriage that he has made a good book *out of* his conjugal misery. That would be too easy. The bee makes honey *out of* the flower by causing *real* transformations in the substance of the flower; the sculptor makes a statue *out of* marble. But the writer makes books out of words, not out of his sorrows. If he wants to stop his wife from behaving badly, he should not write about her; he should beat her. One cannot *put* one's misfortunes into a book, any more than one can put a model on a canvas; one draws inspiration from one's misfortunes—and they remain as they are. Perhaps one gets temporary consolation from placing oneself above them in order to describe them, but once the book is finished, one finds them again. Bad faith begins when the artist tries to give meaning, a sort of immanent finality, to his troubles and persuades himself that they are there *so that* he can talk about them. When he justifies his own sufferings by this deception, he makes himself ridiculous; but he is despicable if he tries to justify the sufferings of others in the same fashion. The most beautiful book in the world will not redeem the sufferings of a child. We cannot redeem evil, we must combat it. The most beautiful book in the world redeems itself and redeems the artist, but not the man; no more than the man can redeem the artist. We want the man and the artist to win salvation together; we want the work of art to be an act as well; we want it to be expressly conceived as an arm in man's struggle against evil.

The other mistake is equally serious: there is in every human heart such a hunger for the absolute, that people have often confused eternity, which would be a timeless absolute, with immortality which is only a perpetual delay of execution and a long series of vicissitudes. I understand this desire for the absolute very well. I desire it also. But need we go so far afield to look for it? It is there all around us, under our feet and in all our gestures. We make absolutes, just as M. Jourdain made prose. You light your pipe and that is an absolute; you don't like oysters and that is an absolute; you join the Communist Party and that is an absolute. Whether the world is matter or spirit, whether God exists or does not exist, whether the judgment of future centuries is favorable or hostile to you, nothing will ever be able to negate the fact that you passionately loved such and such a picture, such and such a cause, and such and such a woman; that you lived that love from day to day: lived it, willed it, and undertook it; and that you engaged your whole being in it. Our grandfathers were perfectly right when they used to say as they drank their glass of wine: "One more that the Prussians won't have." Neither the Prussians nor anyone else. People may kill you or deprive you of wine for the rest of your life; but that last drop of Bordeaux that slipped over your palate, no God and no man can take away from you. No relativity; nor the "eternal course of history"; nor the dialectic of perception; nor the dissociations of psychoanalysis. That drop of wine is a pure event and we, too, in the very depths of historical relativity and our own insignificance are absolutes, inimitable and incomparable, and our choice of ourselves is an absolute. All the vital and passionate choices that we are and that we are perpetually making with or against other people, all the common undertakings into which we throw ourselves from birth until death, all the bonds of love and hate that unite us with each other and that exist only in so far as we feel them, the enormous complexes of movements that supplement or negate each other and that are lived, this whole discordant and harmonious life combines to create a new absolute which I like to call the *time*. The time is intersubjectivity, the living absolute, the dialectical wrong side of history. It is born in the pangs of events that historians will later stick labels on. Blindly, in fury, in fear, and in enthusiasm, it lives the meanings that they will later define by rational methods. In its own time, each word, before it is an historical slogan or the recognizable origin of a social process, is first an insult or a call or a confession. Economic phenomena themselves, before they are the theoretical causes of social upheavals, are suffered in humiliation or despair. Ideas are tools or flights; facts are born of intersubjectivity and unsettle it as emotions unsettle the individual soul. Men make history out of dead times, because each time, upon its death, enters into relativity and takes its place in the line of the centuries with the other dead. Then people try to throw new light upon it, dispute its meaning with their new knowledge, resolve its problems, prove that its most ardent searchings were doomed to failure, that the great undertakings of which it was most proud had opposite results to those it hoped for; suddenly its limitations appear and its ignorance. But all this is *because that time is dead;* those limits and that ignorance did not exist "at the time": men do not live a lack; or rather, that time was a perpetual overstepping of its own limits toward a future which was *its* future and which is dead with it. It was *that* boldness, *that* imprudence, *that* ignorance of its own ignorance: to live means to make short-term provisions and to manage on one's margin. Perhaps our fathers, had they had a little more knowledge, would have understood that such and such a problem was insoluble and that such and such a question should not have been raised in those terms. But the human condition requires that we make our choice in ignorance; it is ignorance that makes morality possible. If we knew all the factors that condition events, if we could play our hand without uncertainty, risk would disappear; and with risk courage, fear, waiting, the final joy and effort; we would be languid gods, but certainly not men. The bitter quarrels of the Babylonians over the meaning of omens, the bloody and passionate heresies of the Albigensians and the Anabaptists today seem to us errors. At the time man engaged his whole being in them and in expressing them at the risk of his life let truth live through them, for truth never yields itself directly; it only appears through errors. The fate of human Reason was at stake in the quarrel of the Universals and in that of the Immaculate Conception or Transubstantiation. And at the time of the great lawsuits of certain American states against the professors who taught the theory of evolution, it was again the fate of Reason that was at stake. It is absolutely at stake in every period in connection with doctrines that the next period will condemn as false. It is possible that some day the belief in evolution will seem the greatest folly of our century: yet, in supporting it against the churchmen, the American professors *lived* the truth, they lived it passionately and absolutely at great risk to themselves. Tomorrow they will be wrong, today they are absolutely right: the time is always wrong when it is dead, always right when it is alive. Let people condemn it after the fact, if they wish; nevertheless, it had its own passionate way of loving itself and tearing itself apart, against which future judgments will be of no avail; it had its own taste which it alone tasted and which was as incomparable, as irremediable as the taste of wine in our mouth.

A book has its absolute truth in its own time. It is lived like a riot or a famine, with much less intensity, of course, and by fewer people, but in the same way. It is an emanation of intersubjectivity, a living bond of rage, hatred, or love between those who have produced it and those who receive it. If it gains ground, thousands of people reject it and deny it: we all know very well that to read a book is to rewrite it. *At the time* it is first a panic, an escape, or a courageous affirmation; at the time it is a good or a bad *action*. Later, when the time has died, it will become relative; it will become a message. But the judgment of posterity will not invalidate the opinions men had of it during its lifetime. People have often said to me about dates and bananas: "You can't judge them: to know what they are really like, you have to eat them on the spot, just after they have been picked." And I have always considered bananas a dead fruit whose real taste escaped me. The books which pass from one period to another are dead fruits, too. In another time they had a different taste, sharp and tangy. We should have read *Emile* or the *Persian Letters* just after they were picked.

Thus we must write for our own time, as the great writers did. But this does not imply that we must shut ourselves up in it. To write for our time does not mean to reflect it passively. It means that we must will to maintain it or change it; therefore, go beyond it toward the future; and it is this effort to change it which establishes us most deeply in it, for it can never be reduced to a dead mass of tools and customs.

It is in flux, it perpetually goes beyond itself; in it the concrete present and the living future of all the men who compose it exactly coincide. If, among other characteristics, Newtonian physics and the theory of the noble savage help to define the first half of the eighteenth century, we must not forget that the former represented a consistent effort to wrest fragments of the truth from the fog of ignorance in order to reach, beyond the contemporary state of knowledge, an ideal science in which phenomena could be deduced mathematically from the principle of gravitation, and that the latter was an attempt to go beyond the vices of civilization and restore a state of nature. Both theories outlined a future; and if it is true that this future never became a present, that men later renounced the Golden Age and the idea of making science a strictly logical chain of reasons, it is nonetheless true that these profound and vital hopes sketched a future beyond men's daily cares and that in order to penetrate the meaning of our day-to-day existence we must approach it with the future as our point of departure. One cannot be a man or make oneself a writer without drawing a line on the horizon beyond oneself, but this going beyond oneself is in each case finite and unique. One does not go beyond *in general* and for the simple pride and pleasure of going beyond; Baudelairian dissatisfaction represents only the abstract scheme of transcendence and, since it is a dissatisfaction with everything, ends by being a dissatisfaction with nothing. Real transcendence requires that one wish to change certain definite aspects of the world and any going beyond is colored by and characterized by the concrete situation it seeks to modify. A man throws himself completely into his plan for freeing the Negroes or restoring the Hebrew language to the Jews of Palestine; he throws himself into it completely and at the same time expresses man's fate in all its universality, but it must always be through a unique and dated undertaking. And if people say to me, as does M. Schlumberger, that one also goes beyond one's time when one strives for immortality, I shall answer that this is a false going beyond: instead of wishing to change an intolerable situation, one attempts to escape from it and seeks refuge in a future that is entirely strange to us, since it is not the future that we *make,* but the concrete present of our grandchildren. We have no way of affecting that present; they will live it for themselves and as they wish, situated in their own time as we in ours. If they make any use of our writings it will be for their own ends, ends which we did not foresee, just as one picks up stones on the road and hurls them in the face of an aggressor. It would be quite vain on our part to throw off on them our effort to prolong our own existence: they have neither the duty nor the desire to do so. And since we have no means of acting upon these strangers, we shall present ourselves to them like beggars and beg them to lend us the appearance of life by using us for any purpose whatsoever. If we are Christians, we shall accept our lot humbly, provided only that they still speak of us, even though they use us to show that faith is ineffectual; if we are atheists, we shall be very happy if they still concern themselves with our anguish and our errors, were it even to prove that man is miserable without God. Would you be satisfied, M. Schlumberger, if after the Revolution our grandsons saw in your writings the most obvious example of the conditioning of art by the economic structure? And if you do not have that literary destiny, you will have another that will be hardly any better: if you escape from dialectical materialism, it will only be to serve the ends of some psychoanalysis. In any case, our grandchildren will be impudent orphans, so why should we concern ourselves with them? Perhaps of all of us, only Céline will endure; it is theoretically possible, although highly improbable, that the twenty-first century will remember Drieu's name and forget Malraux'; in any case it will not espouse our quarrels, it will not mention what today we call the betrayal of certain writers, or if it mentions this, it will do so without anger or contempt. And what difference does it make to us? What Malraux and Drieu are for us is an absolute. In certain hearts there is an absolute of contempt for Drieu and an absolute of friendship for Malraux that one hundred posthumous judgments will not be able to shake. There is a living Malraux, a lump of warm blood in the very heart of our time, and there will be a dead Malraux at the mercy of history. Why should the living man try to fix the image of the dead man he will one day be? Certainly he lives beyond himself; his gaze and his concerns go beyond the death of his flesh; the presence of a man and his weight are measured not by the fifty or sixty years of his organic life, nor by the borrowed life he will lead in future centuries in the minds of strangers: they are measured by his own choice of the temporal cause that goes beyond him. The story is told that the runner of Marathon was dead an hour before he reached Athens. He was dead, yet he still ran; he ran dead and as a dead man announced the victory of the Greeks. It is a beautiful myth and shows that the dead act for a little while as if they were still alive. A little while – one year, ten years, fifty years perhaps, in any case, a finite period; and then they are buried for the second time. This is the measure that we propose to the writer: as long as his books provoke anger, embarrassment, shame, hatred, love, he will live, even if he is only a shadow. After that, the deluge. We are for a finite morality and a finite art.

Real Jesse Jameses

Piri Thomas

Piri Thomas, eldest of seven children, was born in 1928 in Spanish Harlem in New York City, of Puerto Rican parents. After serving six years of a fifteen-year sentence for attempted armed robbery in 1950, he was released from prison in 1956. Himself a former drug addict, he worked at a rehabilitation center for addicts in Spanish Harlem and then organized a similar rehabilitation center in Puerto Rico called the New Breed, under the direction of Dr. Efren Ramirez, later the Narcotics Coordinator for New York City. He also attended the University of Puerto Rico for a short period and helped to make a prize-winning documentary film called *Petey and Johnny,* in which he both appeared and provided the narration. Married and the father of two children, Mr. Thomas lives in New York City. His second book, *Saviour, Saviour, Hold My Hand,* appeared in 1972. The following selection is taken from *Down These Mean Streets* (1967), now in its tenth printing, an autobiography of his struggle toward manhood and salvation.

I was standing in front of the *cuchifrito* restaurant on 103rd Street, a couple of months later. I had gotten a job there peeling grease off dirty dishes, pots, and pans. Pay was small, but I was paying my rent and eating up a storm. I was really feeling good, feeling clean. I was clean. There was nothing left of the habit, except the temptation, and I was fighting the hell outta that. I dug Li'l Louie coming in through the side door of the *cuchifrito* joint and I waved to him. He walked toward me like he was afraid I was gonna hit on him for some coin for a fix. I nodded and laughed:

"Naw, babee, I'm clean, like nothing for the last two months."

"Damn, Piri, like I'm glad, baby, like you don't need that shit to move on. *Chevere.*" Louie's face got hung up on a big grin.

"Buying some *cuchifritos?*"

"Naw, just some straights." He walked over to the cigarette machine and got some smokes. He offered me one and while we smoked he said: "Come on over to my pad when you get off from work."

"How'd you know I worked here? I ain't seen you for a while, least not since I got this job."

"That's right, man, like I've been swinging up in the Bronx, but you got *cuchifrito* grease coming out your pores. Besides, some of the cats

---

SOURCE: Piri Thomas, *Down These Mean Streets* (New York: Alfred A. Knopf, 1967), pp. 221–222.

told me they'd seen you working here. I didn't know you had kicked, though."

"I'll come up about six o'clock, okay? Or you want me to come up later?"

"Naw, six o'clock is fine." Louie slapped skin with me and walked away. I watched him cross the street and stop to make some kind of time with some kind of broad.

I went up to Louie's pad after work. He got some cold Manischewitz wine and put some sounds on and we just started to bullshit. We got around to talking about the old days of cops and robbers. We got around to talking about the lack of coins in our pockets.

Louie got up and went to the mirror and combed his hair.

"Man, there must be a way to make some good bread," I said.

"So let's get together," Louie said as he knotted his tie, "and make some fast *pesos*."

Little Louie, the smooth coolie. I sat on the edge of the bed and watched his fingers go through the twists of a Windsor knot. We had become skin-tight *amigos* since the days of our grocery-store *guiso.* Louie was about a year older than me and taller by about three inches, which made him close to six feet. He had the good looks that made broads bounce.

"Jesus, Piri," he said, straightening his tie, "all the times we've talked about being big-time . . ."

"Yeah, yeah, I know," I said. "I go for the idea of making fast *pesos,* but like how?"

I thought to myself of how I was getting tired of *cuchifrito* grease.

"Stick-ups."

"Wheow, man! There's easier ways of making bread."

"Like junk?"

"That's one way, but run it to me anyway."

"Well," Louie began, "I've been thinking about the things that some good coins could bring. Whatta ya say, Piri?"

"Hell, man, you down, I'm down. Now all we gotta do is get us—"

"Wait a minute, Piri, it ain't us alone."

"Uh-uh," I grunted warily. "I gotta be tight with anybody for this kinda *guiso,* I sure gotta know him before I trust him."

"It ain't exactly one guy, it's two guys. And these cats are experienced at pulling stick-ups."

"Real Jesse Jameses?"

"Yeah, they're from Newark, and they done time in the state pen."

"Say, *panín,* how come you know criminals like that?" I asked.

"Same place you know yours," he slipped back.

"Hell," I said, shrugging my shoulders, "I've been thinking about going into a lot of things lately, like pushing junk. I was using more and more up to last month, but like you know, I cut it down to *nada*." I made a face, not wanting to remember the pain that went into that cutting down. "But I can't trust myself to even get near that shit in no way."

"Yeah, Piri, I know," Louie said. "You should have just stuck to pot once in a while instead of *tecata.*"

I changed the subject. "What about your friends? And how soon do we get together? Who knows, maybe this is the beginning of something, eh?"

"Oh, just one thing, Piri," Louie said.

"Yeah?" I looked at him doubtfully.

"These guys ain't spics like us."

White or *moyeto,* a spic was a spic to Louie. "*Moyetos?*" I asked.

"No, *blancos.*"

"Paddy boys? Man, Louie, I don't know." I shook my head from side to side.

"Look, Piri, I know Danny."

"Danny?"

"Yeah. My friend's name is Danny and his friend's name is Billy. I can vouch for Danny and Danny vouches for Billy."

"Louie," I said, "what we spics got in common with paddy boys? How far can we trust them?"

"Jesus, Piri, at least talk with 'em, will ya? Here's a chance to make some real *plata.* Ya don't hafta be prejudiced all your fuckin' life. Who knows, maybe these cats got a colored mammy way back." Louie laughed, and I almost laughed. And three days later we met Danny at a bar on 110th Street.

He was a couple of years older than us, a small guy with a polite smile and a feeling of coldness, like he was fronting for himself. I looked *cara palo* at him. Being a down stud, I wasn't gonna break words first.

"So you're Piri," he said. "Louie's been telling me a lot about you."

I looked cool at him and said, "So you're Danny. Louie talked a little about you."

"How'd you like to work with us?" Danny said.

I lit a cigarette and inhaled for enough time to think about it. "I don't know; who's boss?" I said finally.

"Nobody's boss. We're democratic. Everybody puts in their ideas, everybody plans jobs."

"How about this friend of yours in Newark?"

"You wanna know who he is?"

"Yeah, I would."

"I like you, Piri," said Danny.

"I like me, too," I said, and I let a little grin slip out.

"Yeah, you look like a Porto Rican with heart. You are Porto Rican, ain't you?"

"Whatever I am, we all got heart; very little of us are without heart," I answered, still smiling.

Danny laughed and said, "*Aya en el Rancho Grande.* See, I talk a little Spanish."

"That's cool," I said. "I talk a lotta English."

Danny looked a little hard at me, but it was just a quick shadow and he broke into a wide smile.

"I like you, Piri, I like you. Let's drive out to Newark and talk with Billy."

We walked out of the bar and Danny led us to an old green Oldsmobile. We got in. That Olds was smooth; it had a boss engine. We rode and talked, or rather Louie and Danny talked. I played my cool role. I didn't feel the picture much. It was like mixing rice and beans with corned beef and cabbage.

We picked up Billy and started driving back to Harlem. I almost liked the big gringo. He had a warm, easy way with him. I didn't trust him all the way, but I almost liked him. We talked and made plans, and when it was over, Danny looked at Louie and me and said, "You know, we're like a League of Nations. Billy's a Polack, I'm Irish, Louie is a white Porto Rican, and you"—Danny looked at me—"who the hell knows? But we're sure gonna—"

"I'm me, Mr. Charlie," I said, feeling hot in my chest.

"Whooo, smooth down, friend," Danny said. "I didn't mean no insult. I mean, like you're mixed with two or three races and—"

"Yeah, Piri," said Louie, "he didn't mean nothing. Practically all Puerto Ricans are mixed."

But in my mind, Danny's words, "and you, who the hell knows?"—were burning. *He's right,* I thought, *this bastard's right—who the hell knows?* That kept going through my mind. Then I heard voices breaking through my *pensamientos* and I dug Louie saying, "Well, if we gotta be proved . . ." And I said, "Proved in what?"

"Ain't you listening, Piri?" Louie said. "Danny and Billy feel on account they got *mucho* experience they know what they can do, but they haven't seen us work."

I said, "I ain't seen them work, either."

"Yeah, Piri, but they've been in jail."

"So, shit, what's that prove except maybe they ain't so good? But it's okay with me. What's the big *prueba?*"

"Well, you guys pull a job," Danny said, "and we'll watch from across the street and see how it goes, 'cause we don't want to take a chance with guys that may not have what it takes when the pressure is on."

I looked out of the car window and saw a cigar store on Third Avenue. I said, "You wanna see heart, eh, Mr. Charlies? Okay, park the car. Me and Louie is gonna pull a score right now."

"Man, Piri, we ain't ready yet," said Louie.

"You got that baby piece, Louie, that twenty-five cal?"

"Yeah, but it ain't loaded."

"Fuck it, we goin' shit for broke." I looked at the two paddies and winked at them. "This one's on us," I said. "Come on, Louie!"

Louie walked alongside me and he was talking a mile a minute. "*Caramba,* man, this is stupid, we ain't ready yet."

"When does one get ready for this kinda shit, man? You just jump into it with both feet. What do you expect, Louie, to go to school? You just start, *vente!*"

Danny and Billy were right across the street where they could watch the action. *Man,* I thought, *even if it was a bank, I'd pull it, just to shove it down them paddies' throats.*

Louie and me walked into the cigar store. There was only the owner there. "Walk to the back," I whispered to Louie. I stood near the candy counter, picking out candy bars.

"Can I help you?" said the owner.

"Yeah, *amigo,* you can give us your bread, money!"

He turned white. "Are you guys kidding?"

I said, "Listen, *maricón,* if you wanna die, then we're kidding; otherwise we're not. Just put the money in a paper bag. Your wallet, too. Louie, if the motherfucker makes a move, fuck him up good."

Louie just stood there, like he wished he was some place else, but for that matter, so did I.

"Show him the piece, Louie."

Louie pulled out the *pistolita* and it looked even smaller. "Look, mister, no more shit," he said.

"Don't shoot, please, don't shoot."

It was hard to say who was more scared, him or us.

He put the money in a bag and handed it to us. We locked him in a back room and made it. Just like that we had over $100 for a couple minutes' work. Woooie! We walked down toward the car and I felt Louie straining to start running.

"Cool it, man," I said. "If we run, them paddy boys are gonna think we ain't got heart."

Danny and Billy were sitting in the car with the motor running. Louie and me strolled over, smooth-like, opened the door, cool-like, and sat down. "Candy, anybody?" I softly asked, while that heart of mine was beating like crazy.

We were in. I could see it in the paddies' eyes. I counted the money as we drove. Danny was watching me through the rear-view mirror. I said, "Pull over to the curb, man."

"What for?"

"Gotta see my *muchacha,*" I said. Danny smiled and started to say something smart. "Don't say nothing," I added, "if it ain't nice, Mr. Charlie."

His smile washed off. "What's this 'Mr. Charlie' stuff you've been throwing around?" he asked.

"It's just a name, man, like one kinda people got for another kind of people. Ain't you down?"

He didn't answer. I got out of the car and handed Louie $75. "We split four ways, even."

As I walked down Madison Avenue, I thought, *Shit—splitting with paddies: Brew should see me now.*

A year went by. With time, we got badder and cooler. I stopped counting the scores. We hit small bars, East Side, West Side, all around the paddy town. I took a room on my old block with an old lady for a few bucks a week. She was all right. I gave her a lot of hell, but she loved me like a son—she said. I believed her, so I acted like most sons do in Harlem—I paid her no mind.

Our stick of working was simple. Each of us had a job. Danny and Billy took the back of the place, Louie stood in the middle and I covered the door. Anyone could come in, nobody could go out. We emptied the johns and pushed everyone but the bartender into the back and cleaned them like Rinso of anything that was worth money. Meanwhile Louie would have the bartender opening the safe if there was one, or showing him where the cigar box of hidden cash was. Just before leaving, we pushed them all into the ladies' room and stashed a cigarette machine or jukebox against the door to give us time to make it without sweat.

But sometimes it was a sweat thing. Once I was sitting on a bar stool near the front door of a place, drinking a beer and playing chickie the cop while the guys took care of business in the back. I held a *pistola* in my lap, out of sight. As we were ready to leave, I looked out the window and a *hara* passed by. He looked up and saw me. I kept drinking my beer calmly with my left hand, my right hand resting on my gun. He moved on and I breathed easy—then he stopped and turned around. He was gonna come in for a beer, I guess, or to use the john. I thought, *Oh, shit, oh,* hara, *don't come in.* As he stood there, undecided, my mind clicked off what to do if he came in. *I'll tell him to put them up and I'll take his piece. But what if he still goes for his piece? I'll hit him for the big one, in the head. Don't come in,* hara, *go away, go away, cop . . .* I drank more beer. Finally, the cop turned and walked on.

When we left, he was standing at the corner, near our car. I remembered a movie I had seen. "Let me play drunk," I said, "and you guys play high, and we'll make it. The cop may feel something's wrong, but he won't be able to place it." We rolled out, not too noisy, 'cause the cop would stop us, but politely high and good-natured. I even smiled at the cop and mumbled something like, "Man, that's enough beer for me, gotta work tomorrow." And away we split, with $800 or so in cash and jewelry.

That was one of our better scores. Most of our jobs copped us more like $250 to $400. The right score, the big-money one, just ducked. I began to get tight nerves. We all were on edge. Then one day we were punching the clock out on a job on the West Side and as we were taking the bartender to the back to lock him up, he dashed up a stairway leading to an upstairs apartment. Without thinking, we blasted at him. We missed and we ran like hell. As I cut the corner, I looked back. The bartender was screaming and blasting away at us with a piece. I got to the car as Danny was pulling away. "For a lousy $75," I said. "It ain't worth all this heart failure. Man, we almost killed us someone for a lousy $75." Then I asked myself, *Suppose you had killed him for $75,000—would that have been worth it? Ain't no bartender got 75 gees,* I answered.

My nerves got tighter. I began skin-popping, promising myself that I wouldn't go mainlining again. Trina suspicioned I was back on stuff, but wasn't sure. She kept asking what was wrong and I kept telling her, *"Nada, nada."* In between we talked of marriage. I hadn't copped her. I wanted her, but I wanted her right—church, white dress, the whole bit. She was one thing the streets weren't gonna make the mean way.

The shooting shook us up, so we laid off for a while. But when the dust settled and the money ran out, our shooting scene seemed *chevere* to us instead of stupid, and we went back into business. Danny had wrecked his Olds, so we needed a new car. We thought of copping one from a private garage, but we decided it wasn't worth the risk. I got a bright thought. We could buy a car, then one of us could stay outside and, after the sale was made, come in and beat the seller for the bread and whatever else he had on him. We drew for some kinda honor, and I picked the short stick.

"Okay, you're it," said Louie.

"Chevere," I answered with a *cara-palo* look.

Danny, Billy, and Louie left me about a block from the used-car dealer. They had 450 bucks to spend. I waited for them to spend it.

It was a warm day and I was wearing a light windbreaker, but I still felt a chill. *Man,* I thought, *why don't them cats hurry up?* A little later they came out of the office and got into a car and drove off. They passed me and Louie signaled that they would wait for me in the next block. As I walked toward the auto dealer's office, a motorcycle cop pulled up to a diner right across the street. But it was too late to back down. I walked into the office.

"Yes, sir, what can I do for you?" the manager asked. He was still putting the $450 away.

"I'd like to know the price on that '56 Buick," I said.

"Which Buick is that, sir?" He was an old man, gray-haired, but I couldn't back down, dammit; my rep was on the line.

"It's that one next to the Chevrolet," I said, pointing outside.

The old man turned to put his order book on the desk. I pulled my piece out and shoved it in his back. "Play it smooth, mister; make it with the bread and there won't be no trouble."

The old man turned around and he didn't look scared, just angry-like. He reached out for me and hung on. We struggled. *Coño,* man, it was a hassle. The old man was strong. We both fell to the floor. I hit him with the gun again and again and then it was over. He just lay there and moaned, "Uh, uh, uh, uhm, uhmmmmmm."

I felt ca-ca green. I felt sticky, like my hands were sweating glue. It was blood. My windbreaker was lousy with blood. *I gotta get outta here,* I thought. I opened the door and walked out. Across the street the motorcycle cop was still eating. I started to walk toward the corner and stopped cold. The money—I had forgotten the money. *Run, you jerk! No,* I thought, *this ain't for nuttin', you done it for the bread. This ain't for nuttin', something gotta come outta this.* I walked back into the little office. The manager was still on the floor, moaning softly. He was full of blood. I bent down and took the gold from his pockets. I avoided looking at him because I didn't want to split with his sufferings. As I walked away from him, I kicked something; it was his false teeth. They looked like a nightmare smiling at this wild scene. I felt sorry for the old cat and I wanted to help him, but hatings of things I couldn't name wouldn't let me.

I stepped out into the street and stopped stone-cold. To the right of me, about twenty feet away, was a garage, and there was a police car there with its hood open and a mechanic and two cops huddled around the motor. "Yeah, Mike," I heard one cop say, "this damned car won't run right. I think it's the spark plugs."

"Naw, Pat, I think it's in the transmission," the other one said. "Whatta ya think, Mike?"

The mechanic rubbed his head and looked up and I thought, *How can he miss seeing me standing here all smeared with blood?*

"I think it's the valves, Joe," he said, "but I'll hafta check it. And what about . . ."

I walked away from their voices. People passed by me. *Jesus, how come they don't see I'm smeared with this* sangre? I pushed my sticky hands into my pockets and crossed the street. The motorcycle cop was coming out of the diner. He looked all around. *Don't see me,* hara. *Don't look at me.* I reached the other sidewalk and saw our car halfway down the block. Louie was smoking a cigarette and leaning against the fender. Outside I was *cara palo,* but inside I heard Momma's voice saying, "*Mi negrito, mi negrito,* what have you done?"

Louie saw me and got into the car and held the door open for me. I threw myself in and lay on the floor in the back. Louie looked at me and his voice turned weak. "*Ave María,* what's wrong? All that blood—are you shot?"

"I'm okay, *coño.* Le's go, man, le's go."

All the way back to the block I lay there thinking of the old man. The car pulled up in front of my building. I waited till the street and stoop were clear and I ran into the hallway. I opened the door to the apartment and we all went in. Luckily the old lady was out. Billy and Danny sat down at the kitchen table and didn't say a word. They hadn't said a word all the way home.

I went into the bathroom and looked at myself in the mirror. I couldn't stand what I saw and I puked. The taste was bad. I wanted to say, "I couldn't help it," but I couldn't; I wanted to lie, but I wouldn't. I washed and washed, but it was not enough. I made a hard face, a *cara-palo* face, and walked back into the kitchen.

I looked at everybody, Danny, Billy, and Louie. Louie looked down, Billy looked at the window. Danny looked at me and I saw he was thinking, "Better you than me." I threw the wad of bills on the table. They stuck together with the old man's glue.

"Split four ways," I said.

The Psychobiology of Racial Violence

Louis Jolyon West

Born in New York City in 1924, Louis Jolyon West, M.D., has led what must be a feverish professional life. Currently Chairman of the Department of Psychiatry at the University of California School of Medicine and Medical Director of the Neuropsychiatric Institute, he has served in an astonishing number of medical capacities. A severely abridged list follows:

Resident Psychiatrist at the Payne Whitney Clinic, Consultant to Peace Corps, Chief of Neuropsychiatric Services at several air force installations, member of the White House Conference on Civil Rights, Diplomate of the National Board of Medical Examiners, Professor and Head of the Department of Psychiatry at the University of Oklahoma. . . .

In addition, Dr. West has stretched time sufficiently to marry, to father three children, to function as an editor of several learned journals, to publish a spate of articles on psychiatry, and to produce three volumes: *Explorations in the Physiology of Emotions* (1960), *Hallucinations* (1962), *Experimental Psychopathology: The Induction of Abnormal States* (1972). A fourth work, *The Color of Tears,* an extended study of the dynamics of prejudice, is on its way.

Dr. West's special interests, other than those suggested by the titles of his books, are hypnosis, sleep, existential psychology, "disturbances of perception and states of consciousness," and the "interaction of biological, psychological, and sociocultural factors in personality development." The essay reprinted here is a luminous and relentless study of one form of "emotional disease," the myth-engendered hatred of the Stranger—particularly the Black Stranger—that racks our society.

One man is very much like another. To a remarkable degree our brains and other organs look and work alike. Our blood can safely be transfused between "races." Type O blood from a Negro donor can save the life of a white man who would be killed by a transfusion of type A blood from his own brother. Matched for type, all men are blood brothers. Yet Dr. Charles Drew, the brilliant Negro physician who developed the blood bank, bled to death after a North Carolina highway accident when he was refused admission and transfusion at a segregated white hospital.

This was no less an act of racial violence than the assassination of Medgar Evers, or the murder of Mrs. Viola Liuzzo, or the group slaughter of three civil rights workers in Mississippi, or the bombing of a Birmingham church full of Negro Sunday-school children, or thousands of other acts of senseless savagery based on race alone.

SOURCE: Louis Jolyon West, M.D., "The Psychobiology of Racial Violence," *Archives of General Psychiatry,* Vol. 16 (June 1967), pp. 645–651.

Where does racial violence come from, and what does it mean? Biological differences—including surface features, bones, teeth, muscular attachments, and certain chemistries—are employed by anthropologists to classify racial types and subtypes. However, the range of individual differences *within* so-called major racial groups is far greater than mean differences *between* them in many respects, even with regard to such basic criteria for differentiation as skin color. Personality differences range even more widely. Blocs of standard whites and standard Negroes do not humanly exist. In this paper the terms "Negro" and "white" are therefore used as generalizations which are so far removed from human specificity as to be only marginally meaningful; but in the shadow of that margin lie the most violently destructive human passions.

Relatively few inquiries into the psychodynamics of racial prejudice in the United States have been undertaken since the original appearance in 1944 of Myrdal's classic monograph, *An American Dilemma.* Some have pointed out, as he did, the prominent relationship between violence toward Negroes by whites, and fear of sexual contact between Negro men and white women. However, most of these studies have raised the sexual issue only to dismiss it without exploring it in depth. Myrdal himself declared the white Southerner's preoccupation with intermarriage to be merely a rationalization for a more basic concern with social caste. "*What white people really want is to keep the Negroes in a lower status.*"[1] Allport's treatise, *The Nature of Prejudice,* also touches rather lightly on this issue. He postulates that the white woman's prejudice against Negroes is a defense against the projection of her own secret fascination. Allport relates the white man's prejudice to fear of retaliation because of his own crossracial sexual adventures, or to "anxiety concerning his own sexual adequacy."[2]

Psychiatry has addressed itself surprisingly little to the psychopathology of racial prejudice and violence, although there are a few case studies and commentaries by such on-the-spot students of the problem as Brody, Lief, Coles, Fishman, Solomon, Pierce and West.[3–9] Kubie has postulated that prejudice relates, among other things, to the child's hidden profound aversion to his own body (an aversion which oscillates

---

1 Myrdal, G.: *An American Dilemma,* New York: Harper & Brothers, 1944.

2 Allport, G. W.: *The Nature of Prejudice,* Cambridge, Mass.: Addison-Wesley Publishing Co., Inc., 1954, pp. 375–376.

3 Brody, E. B.: Color and Identity Conflict in Young Boys: Observations of Negro Mothers and Sons in Urban Baltimore, *Psychiatry* **26:**188–201, 1963.

4 Lief, H. I.: An Atypical Stereotype of the Negroes' Social Worlds, *Amer J Orthopsychiat* **32:**86–88, 1962.

5 Coles, R.: Observation or Participation: The Problem of Psychiatric Research on Social Issues, *J Nerv Ment Dis* **141:**274–284, 1965.

6 Fishman, J., and Solomon, F.: Youth and Social Action: I. Perspectives on Student Sit-In Movement, *Amer J Orthopsychiat* **33:**872–882, 1963.

7 Solomon, F., and Fishman, J. R.: Youth and Social Action: II. Action and Identity Formation in First Student Sit-In Demonstration, *J Soc Issues* **20:**36–45, 1964.

8 Pierce, C. M., and West, L. J.: Six Years of Sit-Ins: Psychodynamic Causes and Effects, *Int J Psychiat* **12:**29–34, 1966.

9 Solomon, F., et al.: Civil Rights Activity and Reduction in Crime Among Negroes, *Arch Gen Psychiat* **12:**227–236, 1965.

with a secret guilty pride). The concept of "dirt" becomes deeply connected to this aversion so that the member of the rejected group is referred to as the *dirty* foreigner. But since dirt in our everyday mythology has a magic potential—sex is dirty—the dirty stranger of our fantasies is also bigger, stronger, and "endowed with a super potency which we fear and envy." [10]

My own observations on race and sex have been conducted over the past 15 years in a wide variety of situations, with primary concern for exploration of the irrational elements involved in generating violent emotions and violent behavior. Instinctual territoriality has been carefully considered and rejected as a major source of human conflict; I believe man is more like the elephant and the gorilla (mobile, nonterritorial) than he is like the wasp or the wolf.

Sexual and racial feelings and attitudes have been explored among more than 800 individuals, racially mixed couples, men and women who have had sexual experiences with partners of two or more races, civil rights demonstrators, and a variety of normal subjects, as well as psychiatric patients. Riots involving two or more ethnic groups, and recent riotous uprisings by Negroes in urban ghettos, while instructive, are considered secondary manifestations and have not figured significantly in my formulations of basic dynamics. Unjustified violent feelings and actions by whites against Negroes (on seeming racial grounds alone) are here taken as the major criteria. Although this work is naturalistic rather than experimental, and far from complete, some preliminary formulations may be useful to stimulate discussion and further inquiry by others.

THE AFTERMATH OF SLAVERY

The United States continues to pay a penalty for its history of human slavery. Abolished more than a century ago, the curse of slavery seems destined to persist even beyond the seventh generation. Negroes are apprehensive of continued white exploitation; whites guiltily anticipate Negro revenge. As Clark points out, both groups are trapped in a human predicament from which they cannot escape without mutual aid. "Each one needs the other—the white to be free of his guilt, the Negro to be free of his fear." [11]

The Negro may react to feelings of inferiority (engendered by cultural influences from the day of his birth) in various ways, ranging from apathetic disclaimers of ambition to frenetic rebelliousness. The white man may react to feelings of guilt (engendered by empathy with the oppressed) in various ways, ranging from bitter denial of white culpability—and correspondingly violent antagonism toward the Negro—to the self-deceiving protestations of being wholly without prejudice that characterize Clark's "Delusions of the White Liberal." [12]

---

[10] Kubie, L. S.: The Ontogeny of Racial Prejudice, *J Nerv Ment Dis* **141**:265–273, 1965.
[11] Clark, K. B.: *Dark Ghetto,* New York: Harper & Row Publishers, 1965.
[12] Clark, K. B.: "Delusions of the White Liberal," *New York Times Magazine,* **27**:135–137, 1965.

Social, economic, cultural, educational, and political inequities persist in the wake of slavery. Such inequities are rapidly institutionalized by human society. The need to justify the inequity creates the shibboleths of prejudice, and the self-sustaining tendency of all social structures perpetuates both the discriminatory circumstance (e.g., the ghetto) and the prejudicial attitude (e.g., racial supremacy).

Under these conditions there develops a characteristic mythology, from which derivative secondary attitudes emerge. Thus the "master" group comes to view the "slave" group as being actually better off than they would be otherwise, really preferring their subjugated state, living like animals from choice, and not being truly human.

THE MYTHOLOGY OF BLACKNESS

The special mythology of the Negro in America has been highly color-bound. He is still called "black" no matter how light a shade of tan he may be, and the prejudice that goes with his color is peculiarly linked with his descent from slaves, since other dark-skinned people are not rejected in exactly the same way. The economic, social, political, and cultural aspects of the American Negro's persecution have been discussed extensively elsewhere. For the moment, however, in pursuit of the irrational, let us consider one point: blackness. Why should it make such a difference?

Human beings live by their eyesight. The global rhythm of light and dark, day and night, has a profound influence upon us. This diurnal cycle affects our most basic biological and psychological processes. For man daytime is the good time, the safe time, the healthy time, when he can see what's going on and make his way in the world. The *day*dream is happy aspiration; but the *night*mare is consummate terror. Even the air at night is bad (malaria), full of unhealthy influences (influenza). Night is the time of secrets, mystery, magic, danger, evil; and the man of the night is black.

The ignorant European peasants of the Middle (Dark!) Ages, who had never seen or heard of Negroes, invented black demons and devils. Sometimes at night they practiced the black mass and worshipped a phallic Satan—painted black. Even among the tribes of deepest Africa the word for black in many dialects is the same as the word for danger, evil, or threat. When an American Negro social scientist recently visited Central Africa, he was astonished to find that he was called "white" by the natives. His skin was dark as theirs, but he was known to be civilized, educated, *enlightened.*

There are many examples of the semantic "goodness" of white (e.g., fair, bright, unblemished, whitewashed, spotless, unsullied, immaculate, clean, illuminated, pure as the driven snow). Levin, in *The Power of Blackness,* quotes Jonathan Edwards to the effect that, "Since holiness comprehends all the other virtues, it is typified by white, which also represents purity because it signifies mother's milk and childish innocence . . . while sin, sorrow, and death are all represented in Scripture by darkness or the color black. . . ."[13]

Now consider blackening of character (denigration!), blackhearted blackguards, blackmail, blackball, blacklist, black marks, black looks, black words, black deeds. Black is the pit where the Prince of Darkness reigns. Magic is the black art (or at least black magic is the wicked kind). "They that touch pitch shall be defiled." Even the bad bile of melancholy is black.

Perhaps the light of reason, and extended personal contact, can be expected some day to alleviate the rejection of the "black" person in a "white" society, but the contact must be *human* if the myth is to be dispelled. Segregation stultifies human transactions and perpetuates interracial mythology.

THE MYTH OF NEGRO SEXUALITY

One of the most profoundly distorted but emotionally explosive aspects of American racial mythology has to do with the sexuality of the Negro. The colored man is imagined to possess an enormous phallus, endless virility, and in addition, perhaps some woman-enslaving jungle magic. A common Southern tale has it that a white woman who mates with a Negro will never be satisfied with a white man again. As this superstition suggests, many whites hate the idea of contact between the Negro man and the white woman, a pair that might be termed "the dynamite dyad" because it is so explosive.

Much of the violence over school desegregation, and most of the racist "hate literature," is couched in terms of the danger to the purity of white womanhood, the horrors of miscegenation, and the like. The concern over sexual relations between white women and nonwhite men is apparently the primary emotional basis for the persistence of statutes forbidding racial intermarriage, often inaccurately termed antimiscegenation laws. Nineteen of our 50 states still list such clearly unconstitutional prohibitions in their legal codes. However, "mongrelization" is apparently perceived as a danger only when white women are involved.

In Oklahoma it is possible to consider this matter in crosscultural terms involving both Negroes and Indians. Some Indian blood is considered an honor: politicians boast of being 1/64 Cherokee. Some Negroes try to "pass" as Indians; a white woman marries an Indian without giving a thought to the antimiscegenation law. In spite of the historical fact that for more than 250 years in North America whites were often raped, enslaved, and slain by Indians while the Negro was the white man's helper, it is still the Negro who appears in the white Oklahoma maiden's dream as the ominous rapist, and the sight of a Negro boy dancing with a white girl still moves Oklahomans to feelings

[13] Levin, H.: *Power of Blackness,* New York: Vintage Books, Inc., 1958, p. 32.

and acts of violence. For the Indian was never enslaved, so he remains "the noble *red* man" (dark brown though he may be); while the former slave—whose black feelings every nonslave secretly understands—is feared for his universally comprehended revenge. In one version did not Oedipus, when his father whipped him aside on the road, slay him and rape his mother on his father's corpse?

In point of fact the Negro man is far from the potent black beast of the white man's fantasies. Broken homes, dependency, and intimidation have been shown to cause frequent passivity and impotence in Negro men, among whom homosexuality is also a growing problem. The Negro boy, racked with frustration and ravaged by poverty and deprivation, may turn against society through the losing game of crime, or turn away through the futile escape of drugs, or drop out of school (twice as many Negro girls as boys are in college), or succumb to tuberculosis or malignant hypertension or just plain malnutrition to die, on the average, seven years younger than his white counterpart.[14] The extent to which caste sanctions and the threat of violence adversely affect the entire personality development of the Negro has been precisely documented by Karon,[15] who shows with chilling objectivity how (especially in the South) deprivation of hope can be the most crushing consequence of the Negro's struggle with an overwhelming negative identity.

What, then, makes the Negro man such a special sexual threat? No anthropometric data show that mean racial differences in adult erect genital size approach the great range of individual differences catalogued centuries ago in the Kama Sutra. But suppose the average Negro phallus were larger than that of the white. What would this mean? The clinical experience of psychiatrists and marriage counselors clearly reveals that a large penis does not correlate at all with virility or the ability to give special satisfaction in coitus, and it is now evident from studies of sexual physiology, such as those of Masters and Johnson,[16] that a small penis is a most unlikely basis for sexual incompatibility. In fact, "too large" rather than "too small" is the much more common complaint of the allegedly maladjusted woman. We know these things, but I hear no sighs of, "Alas, the poor Negro, his penis is too large!"

Like the white man's other "compliments" to the Negro (for his childish good nature, primitive rhythmicity, toiler's songfulness, etc.) there is an ancient insult in being caricatured as genitally oversized. This might be called the myth of "Good-Natured Dick," after the feebleminded fellow (in *Fanny Hill*) on whose prodigious penis "you might have trolled dice securely." For in him the folklore held true,

---

[14] Young, W. M., Jr.: *To Be Equal,* New York: McGraw-Hill Book Co., Inc., 1964, pp. 182–211.

[15] Karon, B. P.: *The Negro Personality,* New York: Springer Publishers, 1958.

[16] Masters, W. H., and Johnson, V.: *Human Sexual Response,* Boston: Little, Brown & Co., 1966.

that "Nature . . . had done so much for him in those parts, that she . . . held herself acquitted in doing so little for his head."[17]

The concern with penis size is a well-known masculine foible experienced by every boy who looks at his father and then at himself. The aspiration to manhood and the association of man's estate with the phallus has caused the small boy in every culture to brood over the seemingly insurpassable difference between his own tiny nozzle and his father's mighty hose. In point of fact, the Negro has many of the same sexual concerns that the white man has, and tends to fear the white man as a sexual competitor for colored women with much greater basis in historical reality than the reverse obsession.

Since the fear of the Negro as an automatic sexual threat is irrational, it is to be understood only through consideration of psychodynamic mechanisms that can be found to play a role in studies involving interviews of both patients and normal subjects. These studies also help us to understand how such myths can become self-fulfilling prophecies.

Many whites apparently deny their own "black" sexual and associated violent instinctual strivings, and project them onto the Negro. Would the Southern white boy wish to overthrow paternal authority, grow a penis larger than his father's, possess his mother, and even have her prefer him? Such unacceptable wishes and powers, denied in one's self, are easily attributed to the nearby numerous black men.

However, with the projection of these feelings and attributes, there also tends to develop an unconscious identification with the Negro. Put into him these parts of yourself, and you become a part of him as you now imagine him to be. Thus arises the secret erotic wish that Negro men will actually transgress successfully against white women (a well-known pornographic "best seller" in a thousand guises), and from this derives the necessity for a most violent conscious denial. The greater a man's insecurity regarding his own masculinity (i.e., unconscious passive strivings or latent homosexuality), the more strenuously these mechanisms must be called into play.

When ego defenses break down in psychiatric illness the repressed wish may be acted out, with the psychotic or pathologically intoxicated white husband dragging home a Negro to set upon his wife. Within emancipated circles in the North more subtle examples are not infrequent, wherein the Negro friend is literally maneuvered and unconsciously invited to cuckold him by the white man—who might be truly termed a liberal under these circumstances.

It is not hard to see how this mythology can dovetail with the fantasies of underprivileged, frustrated Negro boys who enjoy an endless variety of tales of being invited to bed by white "Miz Ann," perhaps while "Mister Charlie" peeks around the corner, so that the myth becomes biracially perpetuated. It may be complicated by the competition between white and Negro children for the attention and affection

---

[17] Cleland, J.: *Fanny Hill,* New York: G. Putnam & Sons, 1963, pp. 183–186.

of the Negro woman serving as a domestic helper or "mammy." It is further complicated by the endless variety of genuine sexual experience. The realities of interracial sexual transactions—self-fulfilling prophecies and all—are in themselves a fascinating and instructive study and will be reported elsewhere.[18] Nevertheless, racial violence is not related to genital sex in reality, but to the fantasy of the forbidden.

THE UNIVERSAL STRANGER

Important as the complex symbolization of black and white in America may be, however, and comprehensible as the sexual-racial matrix becomes under psychodynamically sophisticated scrutiny, in the end we find that none of the foregoing suffices to account for the whole of racial violence as it has been known here and elsewhere throughout history. A deeper understanding can only come from the study of the Universal Stranger.

Men have always identified certain *Strangers* as being significantly different from themselves, labeling them as a different race even if they were the same color. Once the Stranger is defined, all of the familiar myth-engendered taboos and warnings are heard: forbid intermarriage; avoid close contact; suspect their motives; beware of their degraded practices and mysterious treacheries; remember that they are beneath us, they are sexually dangerous, they want to displace us, overcome us, drag us down. Tribes, city-states, nations, and entire cultures have designated particular groups, domestic and foreign, as the Strangers to be feared and hated. Today, in Ruanda-Urundi, the tall Watusi are threatened with extermination by their erstwhile serfs among the short Bahutu in a racial massacre, while nearby in Kenya and Tanzania the Masai are similarly threatened by the Kikuyu. On Cyprus recently we have seen Turks and Greeks slaughter each other, still Strangers after living together for generations. The same suspicions can be found between Moslem and Hindu in India, between "colored" and Negro in Guyana, between Malay and Chinese in Indonesia and throughout the Orient; the examples are endless. Even the interminable Arab-Israeli conflict—presumably nationalistic and religious—has been sometimes couched in racial terms, while both groups continue to acknowledge their descent from the same man, Abraham, father of all.

The definition of the Stranger may change with time and treaty, but attitudes, feelings, and prejudices shift with peculiar ease from the old Stranger to the new. Man appears to need some outsider that he can identify as a source of great and continuing danger to his country, community, womenfolk, home, and way of life. Herein lies a substantial facet of organized human violence.[19]

To understand this tendency and its near universality, we must ex-

---

[18] West, L. J.: *The Color of Tears,* to be published.

[19] West, L. J.: The Act of Violence, *Sooner Magazine* **36:**2–5 (Dec.), 1963.

amine man as he grows and develops. In almost every society a high degree of frustration is a universal experience during the growing up of children. It is a peculiarly human attribute that the brain matures much more rapidly than the body as a whole, so that for many years as children we are helpless and dependent for survival on the adult world, while mental capacity, imagination, learning, and emotions are relatively well-developed functions. During these years the myriad impulses, wishes, and desires of the child are frustrated again and again. Frustration leads to aggression; but aggression is not tolerated—the child must learn to control and repress it. He must accept and even love the adult institutions, activities, and individuals who frustrate him, but upon whom his survival depends.

In childish fantasies or dreams he may wreak his vengeance: a bomb drops on the town and kills everybody but himself (and maybe a friend); or a tidal wave swamps the village and everyone else drowns, while he is washed up on a new and lovelier island, uninhabited except for a beautiful maiden. But with age and responsibility come identification with, and pride in, his family, city, state, country, and race. Aggressive and taboo feelings toward his own kind are denied and—to insure that they do not reappear to plague him—they are attributed instead to the Stranger.

Thus it is not I who would slay my father, rape the family womenfolk, devastate the community, and destroy my own society, whose taboos and frustrating restrictions so infuriated me when I was a child. It is not I, it is the Stranger! He is of another race or nation or religion or political persuasion. The important thing is that he is different from me, and I must be sure that he *remains* a Stranger so that I cannot find out the truth: that he is as much like me as I am like myself. So deep-seated is this inner conflict that it permeates the unconscious mind; in a recent study of thousands of dream narratives (of both Negroes and whites) the Stranger was found to stalk with great frequency as a threatening, attacking figure (Calvin Hall: personal communication to the author).

Above all, the Stranger must contain elements of our secret self. Levin reminds us of the insights provided by some of America's classical literary greats in this connection. In one novel, Henry James' abandoned house conceals the missing man, who finally turns out to be "the self that might have been: A black stranger"! Inevitably, when we unconsciously invest our hidden sexual and violent feelings in the Stranger, an important part of ourselves becomes ensconced within his skin; insofar as we hate, fear, and secretly relish that part of ourselves, we shall hate, fear, and secretly relish it in him.

Thus, most people, when they would isolate or destroy the Stranger, are feeling or acting the very sense of righteousness that motivates the struggle against their own unacceptable sexual and violent impulses, against that "negative identity" so vividly described by Erikson.[20] The

[20] Erikson, E. H.: The Concept of Identity in Race Relations: Note and Queries, *Daedalus* **94:**155–156, 1965.

Stranger threatens us, so we must crush him (or segregate him) for the safety of ourselves and the group with which we identify ourselves. Thus we construct defenses to deal with our unconscious hostile feelings toward our own kind. We labor to maintain repression of the unacceptable, and thus prevent self-betrayal; and so in our conflict with the Stranger we detest most of all someone who is like ourselves, but who becomes a traitor. For those who are moved to hate and fear the Negro (because he has been selected as their Stranger), the white "nigger-lover" who would aid the Negro is a renegade and therefore becomes the object of supreme hostility and contempt.

In some severe character disorders the identification with the Stranger is conscious, and the individual may act out the Stranger's role, say, by killing a universal father figure such as a president, or otherwise pursuing a strenuously antisocial life directed against the society from which he feels profoundly alienated. In certain psychotic episodes, with sweeping disruption of ego defenses, the Stranger bursts out, as it were, and slaughters without apparent motive a group of kindly nurses, or shoots randomly at strangers happening to pass within gunshot range, even though their only relationship to the frustrating parents is that they belong to the same society onto which the entire burden of hatred has become displaced and generalized.

It is true that most normal individuals are unlikely to act directly in response to the violent impulses deriving from the forces described above. But these same forces in disguised forms are responsible for perpetuating injustices, inequities, ghettos, and other social violences that lead to the secondary elaboration of violent interpersonal consequences. This is particularly true in cities, where the emotional forces are more intensified by overcrowding and enforced proximity. Last year in the United States, Negroes, who comprise slightly over 10% of the population and who accounted for only 10% of all arrests in rural areas, were arrested for more than half of all murders, rapes, robberies, and aggravated assaults in the cities. In spite of the fact that the large majority of victims were also Negroes, this nonspecific violence cannot be separated from precursive racial violence, which is more clearly related to prejudice and antagonism toward Negroes by whites. Forcing the minority group to live under jungle conditions thus breeds other violence from which the whole society suffers; and the Negro, as usual, suffers most.

SUMMARY AND CONCLUSIONS

Beneath inculcated prejudice, socioeconomic anxieties, organized hostility as rationalized justification for past and present oppression (i.e., slavery and its aftermath), and the symbolic meaning of blackness, are found the sexual roots of racial violence. Among American whites they stem largely from fears of contact between Negro men and white women. The elaborate mythology surrounding this subject can be found to have origins in such well-known psychodynamic shorthand formulations as the oedipal conflict, castration anxiety, preoccupation with penis size, and unconscious passive strivings or latent homosexuality. Case studies reveal that the irrational conscious *hate* (toward Negroes) is a reaction against a preconscious *fear* (of Negroes), which in turn is a violent denial of the unconscious *wish* brought about by projection of unacceptable sexual impulses onto the Negro and the linked identification with him.

The taproot of organized violent behavior among humankind everywhere, including racial strife, group conflict, and war, emerges as a biosocial product of normal human growth and development. It relates to the prolonged physical helplessness of the child, whose brain develops so much faster than his body, and his inevitable frustration by—and hostility toward—those on whom he is most dependent. This promotes his unconscious identification with the Stranger (often defined in racial terms, regardless of color) onto whom he projects his unacceptable aggressive, sexual, and destructive feelings toward his own family and community. The ubiquity of this inner conflict makes one wonder, if the American Negro is redefined as a familiar and accepted brunette citizen, where we shall turn to nominate his successor in the Stranger's role!

The inescapable tendency to develop ambivalence toward those who are closest raises questions regarding the unavoidability of racial conflict, or the universality of violence in human affairs. With Erikson, I believe that such social pathology should not be accepted as inevitable. Whatever else Americans do to solve the racial problem (and there is a tremendous amount that can be done), we must also work toward a healthier resolution of these myth-engendered hates, fears, and inner conflicts. A fruitful approach to this emotional disease of society might well employ the same basic technique utilized by dynamic psychotherapy to promote awareness and understanding of the irrational nature of the prejudicial attitudes and emotions involved, and of the unconscious roots from which they spring and by behavioral psychotherapy to induce and then systematically reinforce the desired behavior—racial integration—with negative reinforcement for undesired behavior—racial discrimination. To this great challenge the growing discipline of social psychiatry should dedicate itself.

O Rotten Gotham—Sliding Down the Behavioral Sink

Tom Wolfe

Pop journalist Tom Wolfe was born in 1931 in Richmond, Virginia. After graduating from Washington and Lee University, he earned his doctorate in American Studies at Yale in 1957. He began his career with the Springfield (Mass.) *Union.* He then worked for the Washington *Post* for three years, and in 1962 joined the staff of the New York *Herald Tribune* and helped set the tone for *New York Magazine* with his contributions. His articles and essays have been collected into *The Kandy-Kolored Tangerine-Flake Streamline Baby* (1965), *The Pump House Gang* (1966), and *Radical Chic* (1971).

Wolfe developed a fresh journalistic style by using unique, irreverent jargon, scrambling his metaphors, and, as one critic has noted, by "leaving facts unchecked, generalizations untested, allusions unverified." But Wolfe's "spontaneous" style has been influential in liberating the journalism of this generation from the more formal patterns of writing and thinking inherited from Europe. T. S. Eliot once said that the rhythms of modern writing would be affected by the rhythm of the internal combustion engine. The rapid-fire, go-go, words-in-motion style of Wolfe may illustrate that prediction.

I just spent two days with Edward T. Hall, an anthropologist, watching thousands of my fellow New Yorkers short-circuiting themselves into hot little twitching death balls with jolts of their own adrenalin. Dr. Hall says it is overcrowding that does it. Overcrowding gets the adrenalin going, and the adrenalin gets them hyped up. And here they are, hyped up, turning bilious, nephritic, queer, autistic, sadistic, barren, batty, sloppy, hot-in-the-pants, chancred-on-the-flankers, leering, puling, numb—the usual in New York, in other words, and God knows what else. Dr. Hall has the theory that overcrowding has already thrown New York into a state of behavioral sink. Behavioral sink is a term from ethology, which is the study of how animals relate to their environment. Among animals, the sink winds up with a "population collapse" or "massive die-off." O rotten Gotham.

It got to be easy to look at New Yorkers as animals, especially looking down from some place like a balcony at Grand Central at the rush hour Friday afternoon. The floor was filled with the poor white humans, running around, dodging, blinking their eyes, making a sound like a pen full of starlings or rats or something.

"Listen to them skid," says Dr. Hall.

He was right. The poor old etiolate animals were out there skidding on their rubber soles. You could hear it once he pointed it out. They stop short to keep from hitting somebody or because they are disoriented and they suddenly stop and look around, and they skid on their rubber-sole shoes, and a screech goes up. They pour out onto the floor down the escalators from the Pan-Am Building, from 42nd Street, from Lexington Avenue, up out of subways, down into subways, railroad trains, up into helicopters—

"You can also hear the helicopters all the way down here," says Dr. Hall. The sound of the helicopters using the roof of the Pan-Am Building nearly fifty stories up beats right through. "If it weren't for this ceiling"—he is referring to the very high ceiling in Grand Central—"this place would be unbearable with this kind of crowding. And yet they'll probably never 'waste' space like this again."

They screech! And the adrenal glands in all those poor white animals enlarge, micrometer by micrometer, to the size of cantaloupes. Dr. Hall pulls a Minox camera out of a holster he has on his belt and starts shooting away at the human scurry. The Sink!

Dr. Hall has the Minox up to his eye—he is a slender man, calm, 52 years old, young-looking, an anthropologist who has worked with Navajos, Hopis, Spanish-Americans, Negroes, Trukese. He was the most important anthropologist in the government during the crucial years of the foreign aid program, the 1950's. He directed both the Point Four training program and the Human Relations Area Files. He wrote *The Silent Language* and *The Hidden Dimension,* two books that are picking up the kind of "underground" following his friend Marshall McLuhan started picking up about five years ago. He teaches at the Illinois Institute of Technology, lives with his wife, Mildred, in a high-ceilinged town house on one of the last great residential streets in downtown Chicago, Astor Street; has a grown son and daughter, loves good food, good wine, the relaxed, civilized life—but comes to New York with a Minox at his eye to record—perfect!—The Sink.

We really got down in there by walking down into the Lexington Avenue line subway stop under Grand Central. We inhaled those nice big fluffy fumes of human sweat, urine, effluvia, and sebaceous secretions. One old female human was already stroked out on the upper level, on a stretcher, with two policemen standing by. The other humans barely looked at her. They rushed into line. They bellied each other, haunch to paunch, down the stairs. Human heads shone through the gratings. The species North European tried to create bubbles of space around themselves, about a foot and a half in diameter—

"See, he's reacting against the line," says Dr. Hall.

—but the species Mediterranean presses on in. The hell with bubbles of space. The species North European resents that, this male human behind him presses forward toward the booth . . . *breathing* on him, he's disgusted, he pulls out of the line entirely, the species Mediterranean resents him for resenting it, and neither of them realizes what the hell they are getting irritable about exactly. And in all of them the old adrenals grow another micrometer.

Dr. Hall whips out the Minox. Too perfect! The bottom of The Sink.

It is the sheer overcrowding, such as occurs in the business sections of Manhattan five days a week and in Harlem, Bedford-Stuyvesant, southeast Bronx every day—sheer overcrowding is converting New Yorkers into animals in a sink pen. Dr. Hall's argument runs as follows: all animals, including birds, seem to have a built-in, inherited requirement to have a certain amount of territory, space, to lead their lives in. Even if they have all the food they need, and there are no predatory animals threatening them, they cannot tolerate crowding beyond a certain point. No more than two hundred wild Norway rats can survive on a quarter acre of ground, for example, even when they are given all the food they can eat. They just die off.

But why? To find out, ethologists have run experiments on all sorts of animals, from stickleback crabs to Sika deer. In one major experiment, an ethologist named John Calhoun put some domesticated white Norway rats in a pen with four sections to it, connected by ramps. Calhoun knew from previous experiments that the rats tend to split up into groups of ten to twelve and that the pen, therefore, would hold forty to forty-eight rats comfortably, assuming they formed four equal groups. He allowed them to reproduce until there were eighty rats, balanced between male and female, but did not let it get any more crowded. He kept them supplied with plenty of food, water, and nesting materials. In other words, all their more obvious needs were taken care of. A less obvious need—space—was not. To the human eye, the pen did not even look especially crowded. But to the rats, it was crowded beyond endurance.

The entire colony was soon plunged into a profound behavioral sink. "The sink," said Calhoun, "is the outcome of any behavioral process that collects animals together in unusually great numbers. The unhealthy connotations of the term are not accidental: a behavioral sink does act to aggravate all forms of pathology that can be found within a group."

For a start, long before the rat population reached eighty, a status hierarchy had developed in the pen. Two dominant male rats took over the two end sections, acquired harems of eight to ten females each, and forced the rest of the rats into the two middle pens. All the overcrowding took place in the middle pens. That was where the "sink" hit. The aristocrat rats at the ends grew bigger, sleeker, healthier, and more secure the whole time.

In The Sink, meanwhile, nest building, courting, sex behavior, reproduction, social organization, health—all of it went to pieces.

Normally, Norway rats have a mating ritual in which the male chases the female, the female ducks down into a burrow and sticks her head up to watch the male. He performs a little dance outside the burrow, then she comes out, and he mounts her, usually for a few seconds. When The Sink set in, however, no more than three males—the dominant males in the middle sections—kept up the old customs. The rest tried everything from satyrism to homosexuality or else gave up on sex altogether. Some of the subordinate males spent all their time chasing females. Three or four might chase one female at the same time, and instead of stopping at the burrow entrance for the ritual, they would charge right in. Once mounted, they would hold on for minutes instead of the usual seconds.

Homosexuality rose sharply. So did bisexuality. Some males would mount anything—males, females, babies, senescent rats, anything. Still other males dropped sexual activity altogether, wouldn't fight and, in fact, would hardly move except when the other rats slept. Occasionally a female from the aristocrat rats' harems would come over the ramps and into the middle sections to sample life in The Sink. When she had had enough, she would run back up the ramp. Sink males would give chase up to the top of the ramp, which is to say, to the very edge of the aristocratic preserve. But one glance from one of the king rats would stop them cold and they would return to The Sink.

The slumming females from the harems had their adventures and then returned to a placid, healthy life. Females in The Sink, however, were ravaged, physically and psychologically. Pregnant rats had trouble continuing pregnancy. The rate of miscarriages increased significantly, and females started dying from tumors and other disorders of the mammary glands, sex organs, uterus, ovaries, and Fallopian tubes. Typically, their kidneys, livers, and adrenals were also enlarged or diseased or showed other signs associated with stress.

Child-rearing became totally disorganized. The females lost the interest or the stamina to build nests and did not keep them up if they did build them. In the general filth and confusion, they would not put themselves out to save offspring they were momentarily separated from. Frantic, even sadistic competition among the males was going on all around them and rendering their lives chaotic. The males began unprovoked and senseless assaults upon one another, often in the form of tail-biting. Ordinarily, rats will suppress this kind of behavior when it crops up. In The Sink, male rats gave up all policing and just looked out for themselves. The "pecking order" among males in The Sink was never stable. Normally, male rats set up a three-class structure. Under the pressure of overcrowding, however, they broke up into all sorts of unstable subclasses, cliques, packs—and constantly pushed, probed, explored, tested one another's power. Anyone was fair game, except for the aristocrats in the end pens.

Calhoun kept the population down to eighty, so that the next stage, "population collapse" or "massive die-off," did not occur. But the autopsies showed that the pattern—as in the diseases among the female rats—was already there.

The classic study of die-off was John J. Christian's study of Sika deer on James Island in the Chesapeake Bay, west of Cambridge, Maryland. Four or five of the deer had been released on the island, which was 280 acres and uninhabited, in 1916. By 1955 they had bred freely into a herd of 280 to 300. The population density was only about one deer per acre at this point, but Christian knew that this was already too high for the Sikas' inborn space requirements, and something would give before long. For two years the number of deer remained 280 to 300. But suddenly, in 1958, over half the deer died; 161 carcasses were recovered. In 1959 more deer died and the population steadied at about 80.

In two years, two-thirds of the herd had died. Why? It was not starvation. In fact, all the deer collected were in excellent condition, with well-developed muscles, shining coats, and fat deposits between the muscles. In practically all the deer, however, the adrenal glands had enlarged by 50 per cent. Christian concluded that the die-off was due to "shock following severe metabolic disturbance, probably as a result of prolonged adrenocortical hyperactivity. . . . There was no evidence of infection, starvation, or other obvious cause to explain the mass mortality." In other words, the constant stress of overpopulation, plus the normal stress of the cold of the winter, had kept the adrenalin flowing so constantly in the deer that their systems were depleted of blood sugar and they died of shock.

Well, the white humans are still skidding and darting across the floor of Grand Central. Dr. Hall listens a moment longer to the skidding and the darting noises, and then says, "You know, I've been on commuter trains here after everyone has been through one of these rushes, and I'll tell you, there is enough acid flowing in the stomachs in every car to dissolve the rails underneath."

Just a little invisible acid bath for the linings to round off the day. The ulcers the acids cause, of course, are the one disease people have already been taught to associate with the stress of city life. But overcrowding, as Dr. Hall sees it, raises a lot more hell with the body than just ulcers. In everyday life in New York—just the usual, getting to work, working in massively congested areas like 42nd Street between Fifth Avenue and Lexington, especially now that the Pan-Am Building is set in there, working in cubicles such as those in the editorial offices at Time-Life, Inc., which Dr. Hall cites as typical of New York's poor handling of space, working in cubicles with low ceilings and, often, no access to a window, while construction crews all over Manhattan drive everybody up the Masonite wall with air-pressure generators with noises up to the boil-a-brain decibel levels, then rushing to get home, piling into subways and trains, fighting for time and for space, the usual day in New York—the whole now-normal thing keeps shooting jolts of adrenalin into the body, breaking down the body's defenses and winding up with the work-a-daddy human animal stroked out at the breakfast table with his head apoplexed like a cauliflower out of his $6.95 semispread Pima-cotton shirt, and nosed over into a plate of No-Kloresto egg substitute, signing off with the black thrombosis, cancer, kidney, liver, or stomach failure, and the adrenals ooze to a halt, the size of eggplants in July.

One of the people whose work Dr. Hall is interested in on this score is Rene Dubos at the Rockefeller Institute. Dubos's work indicates that specific organisms, such as the tuberculosis bacillus or a pneumonia virus, can seldom be considered "the cause" of a disease. The germ or virus, apparently, has to work in combination with other things that have already broken the body down in some way—such as the old adrenal hyperactivity. Dr. Hall would like to see some autopsy studies made to record the size of adrenal glands in New York, especially of people crowded into slums and people who go through the full rush-hour-work-rush-hour cycle every day. He is afraid that until there is some clinical, statistical data on how overcrowding actually ravages the human body, no one will be willing to do anything about it. Even in so obvious a thing as air pollution, the pattern is familiar. Until people can actually see the smoke or smell the sulphur or feel the sting in their eyes, politicians will not get excited about it, even though it is well known that many of the lethal substances polluting the air are invisible and odorless. For one thing, most politicians are like the aristocrat rats. They are insulated from The Sink by practically sultanic buffers—limousines, chauffeurs, secretaries, aides-de-camp, doormen, shuttered houses, high-floor apartments. They almost never ride subways, fight rush hours, much less live in the slums or work in the Pan-Am Building.

We took a cab from Grand Central to go up to Harlem, and by 48th Street we were already socked into one of those great, total traffic jams on First Avenue on Friday afternoon. Dr. Hall motions for me to survey the scene, and there they all are, humans, male and female, behind the glass of their automobile windows, soundlessly going through the torture of their own adrenalin jolts. This male over here contracts his jaw muscles so hard that they bunch up into a great cheese Danish pattern. He twists his lips, he bleeds from the eyeballs, he shouts . . . soundlessly behind glass . . . the fat corrugates on the back of his neck, his whole body shakes as he pounds the heel of his hand into the steering wheel. The female human in the car ahead of him whips her head around, she bares her teeth, she screams . . . soundlessly behind glass . . . she throws her hands up in the air, Whaddya expect me—Yah, yuh stupid—and they all sit there, trapped in their own congestion, bleeding hate all over each other, shorting out the ganglia and—goddam it—

Dr. Hall sits back and watches it all. This is it! The Sink! And where is everybody's wandering boy?

Dr. Hall says, "We need a study in which drivers who go through these rush hours every day would wear GSR bands."

GSR?

"Galvanic skin response. It measures the electric potential of the skin, which is a function of sweating. If a person gets highly nervous, his palms begin to sweat. It is an index of tension. There are some other fairly simple devices that would record respiration and pulse. I think everybody who goes through this kind of experience all the time should take his own pulse—not literally—but just be aware of what's happening to him. You can usually tell when stress is beginning to get you physically."

In testing people crowded into New York's slums, Dr. Hall would like to take it one step further—gather information on the plasma hydrocortisone level in the blood or the corticosteroids in the urine. Both have been demonstrated to be reliable indicators of stress, and testing procedures are simple.

The slums—we finally made it up to East Harlem. We drove into 101st Street, and there was a new, avant-garde little church building, the Church of the Epiphany, which Dr. Hall liked—and, next to it, a pile of rubble where a row of buildings had been torn down, and from the back windows of the tenements beyond several people were busy "airmailing," throwing garbage out the window, into the rubble, beer cans, red shreds, the No-Money-Down Eames roller stand for a TV set, all flying through the air onto the scaggy sump. We drove around some more in Harlem, and a sequence was repeated, trash, buildings falling down, buildings torn down, rubble, scaggy sumps or, suddenly, a cluster of high-rise apartment projects, with fences around the grass.

"You know what this city looks like?" Dr. Hall said. "It looks bombed out. I used to live at Broadway and 124th Street back in 1946 when I was studying at Columbia. I can't tell you how much Harlem has changed in twenty years. It looks bombed out. It's broken down. People who live in New York get used to it and don't realize how filthy the city has become. The whole thing is typical of a behavioral sink. So is something like the Kitty Genovese case—a girl raped and murdered in the courtyard of an apartment complex and forty or fifty people look on from their apartments and nobody even calls the police. That kind of apathy and anomie is typical of the general psychological deterioration of The Sink."

He looked at the high-rise housing projects and found them mainly testimony to how little planners know about humans' basic animal requirements for space.

"Even on the simplest terms," he said, "it is pointless to build one of these blocks much over five stories high. Suppose a family lives on the fifteenth floor. The mother will be completely cut off from her children if they are playing down below, because the elevators are constantly broken in these projects, and it often takes half an hour, literally half an hour, to get the elevator if it is running. That's very common. A mother in that situation is just as much a victim of overcrowding as if she were back in the tenement block. Some Negro leaders have a bitter joke about how the white man is solving the slum problem by stacking Negroes up vertically, and there is a lot to that."

For one thing, says Dr. Hall, planners have no idea of the different space requirements of people from different cultures, such as Negroes and Puerto Ricans. They are all treated as if they were minute, compact middle-class whites. As with the Sika deer, who are overcrowded at one per acre, overcrowding is a relative thing for the human animal, as well. Each species has its own feeling for space. The feeling may be "subjective," but it is quite real.

Dr. Hall's theories on space and territory are based on the same information, gathered by biologists, ethologists, and anthropologists, chiefly, as Robert Ardrey's. Ardrey has written two well-publicized books, *African Genesis* and *The Territorial Imperative*. *Life* magazine ran big excerpts from *The Territorial Imperative*, all about how the drive to acquire territory and property and add to it and achieve status is built into all animals, including man, over thousands of centuries of genetic history, etc., and is a more powerful drive than sex. *Life's* big display prompted Marshall McLuhan to crack, "They see this as a great historic justification for free enterprise and Republicanism. If the birds do it and the stickleback crabs do it, then it's right for man." To people like Hall and McLuhan, and Ardrey, for that matter, the right or wrong of it is irrelevant. The only thing they find inexcusable is the kind of thinking, by influential people, that isn't even aware of all this. Such as the thinking of most city planners.

"The planners always show you a bird's-eye view of what they are doing," he said. "You've seen those scale models. Everyone stands around the table and looks down and says that's great. It never occurs to anyone that they are taking a bird's-eye view. In the end, these projects do turn out fine, when viewed from an airplane."

As an anthropologist, Dr. Hall has to shake his head every time he hears planners talking about fully integrated housing projects for the year 1980 or 1990, as if by then all cultural groups will have the same feeling for space and will live placidly side by side, happy as the happy burghers who plan all the good clean bird's-eye views. According to his findings, the very fact that every cultural group does have its own peculiar, unspoken feeling for space is what is responsible for much of the uneasiness one group feels around the other.

It is like the North European and the Mediterranean in the subway line. The North European, without ever realizing it, tries to keep a bubble of space around himself, and the moment a stranger invades that sphere, he feels threatened. Mediterranean peoples tend to come from cultures where everyone is much more involved physically, publicly, with one another on a day-to-day basis and feels no uneasiness about mixing it up in public, but may have very different ideas about space inside the home. Even Negroes brought up in America have a different vocabulary of space and gesture from the North European Americans who, historically, have been their models, according to Dr.

Hall. The failure of Negroes and whites to communicate well often boils down to things like this: some white will be interviewing a Negro for a job; the Negro's culture has taught him to show somebody you are interested by looking right at him and listening intently to what he has to say. But the species North European requires something more. He expects his listener to nod from time to time, as if to say, "Yes, keep going." If he doesn't get this nodding, he feels anxious, for fear the listener doesn't agree with him or has switched off. The Negro may learn that the white expects this sort of thing, but he isn't used to the precise kind of nodding that is customary, and so he may start over-responding, nodding like mad, and at this point the North European is liable to think he has some kind of stupid Uncle Tom on his hands, and the guy still doesn't get the job.

The whole handling of space in New York is so chaotic, says Dr. Hall, that even middle-class housing now seems to be based on the bird's-eye models for slum projects. He took a look at the big Park West Village development, set up originally to provide housing in Manhattan for families in the middle-income range, and found its handling of space very much like a slum project with slightly larger balconies. He felt the time has come to start subsidizing the middle class in New York on its own terms—namely, the kind of truly "human" spaces that still remain in brownstones.

"I think New York City should seriously consider a program of encouraging the middle-class development of an area like Chelsea, which is already starting to come up. People are beginning to renovate houses there on their own, and I think if the city would subsidize that sort of thing with tax reliefs and so forth, you would be amazed at what would result. What New York needs is a string of minor successes in the housing field, just to show everyone that it can be done, and I think the middle class can still do that for you. The alternative is to keep on doing what you're doing now, trying to lift a very large lower class up by main force almost and finding it a very slow and discouraging process."

"But before deciding how to redesign space in New York," he said, "people must first simply realize how severe the problem already is. And the handwriting is already on the wall."

"A study published in 1962," he said, "surveyed a representative sample of people living in New York slums and found only 18 per cent of them free from emotional symptoms. Thirty-eight per cent were in need of psychiatric help, and 23 per cent were seriously disturbed or incapacitated. Now, this study was published in 1962, which means the work probably went on from 1955 to 1960. There is no telling how bad it is now. In a behavioral sink, crises can develop rapidly."

Dr. Hall would like to see a large-scale study similar to that undertaken by two sociopsychologists, Chombart de Lauwe and his wife, in a French working-class town. They found a direct relationship between crowding and general breakdown. In families where people were crowded into the apartment so that there was less than 86 to 108 square feet per person, social and physical disorders doubled. That would mean that for four people the smallest floor space they could tolerate would be an apartment, say, 12 by 30 feet.

What would one find in Harlem? "It is fairly obvious," Dr. Hall wrote in *The Hidden Dimension,* "that the American Negroes and people of Spanish culture who are flocking to our cities are being very seriously stressed. Not only are they in a setting that does not fit them, but they have passed the limits of their own tolerance of stress. The United States is faced with the fact that two of its creative and sensitive people are in the process of being destroyed and like Samson could bring down the structure that houses us all."

Dr. Hall goes out to the airport, to go back to Chicago, and I am coming back in a cab, along the East River Drive. It is four in the afternoon, but already the damned drive is clogging up. There is a 1959 Oldsmobile just to the right of me. There are about eight people in there, a lot of popeyed silhouettes against a leopard-skin dashboard, leopard-skin seats—and the driver is classic. He has a mustache, sideburns down to his jaw socket, and a tattoo on his forearm with a Rossetti painting of Jane Burden Morris with her hair long. All right; it is even touching, like a postcard photo of the main drag in San Pedro, California. But suddenly Sideburns guns it and cuts in front of my cab so that my driver has to hit the brakes, and then hardly 100 feet ahead Sideburns hits a wall of traffic himself and has to hit his brakes, and then it happens. A stuffed white Angora animal, a dog, no, it's a Pekingese cat, is mounted in his rear window—as soon as he hits the brakes its *eyes* light up, Nighttown pink. To keep from ramming him, my driver has to hit the brakes again, too, and so here I am, out in an insane, jammed-up expressway at four in the afternoon, shuddering to a stop while a stuffed Pekingese grows bigger and bigger and brighter in the eyeballs directly in front of me. Jolt! Nighttown pink! Hey—that's me the adrenalin is hitting, *I* am this white human sitting in a projectile heading amid a mass of clotted humans toward a white Angora stuffed goddam leopard-dash Pekingese freaking cat—kill that damned Angora—Jolt!—got me—another micrometer on the old adrenals—

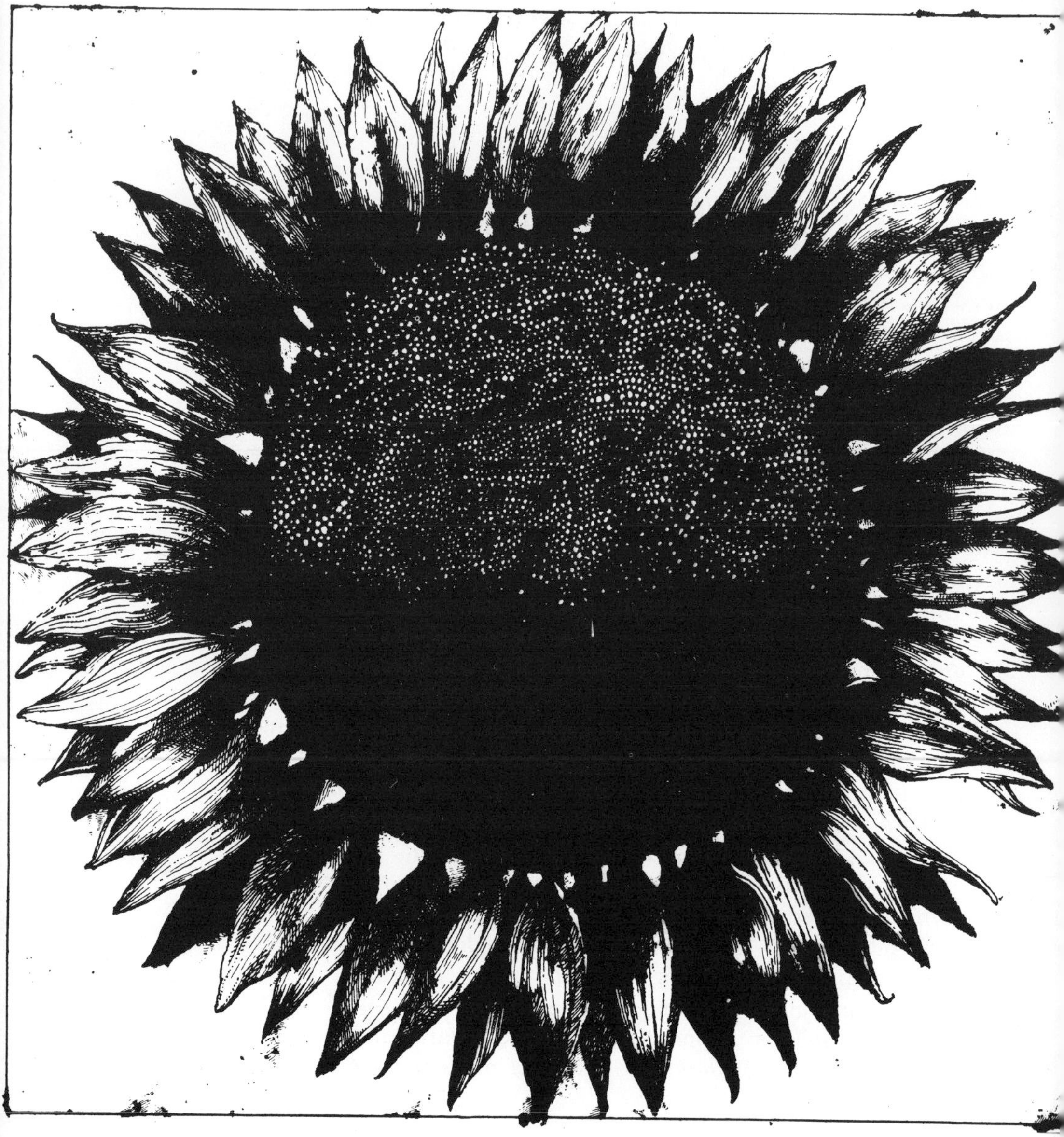

In literature, the brief generations of the modern sweep by, sometimes mingling, sometimes diverging. James, Proust, Kafka, Joyce, Lawrence, Beckett, Faulkner, Borges, Coover, and Cortázar—the swirl of tendencies in the twentieth century seems more confused than ever before (though every age has made a similar judgment upon itself). As the century recedes, however, we can perhaps distinguish some main currents in the modern flux.

Writers of modern fiction have responded as they must to the world they live in, the pressures they endure, the events that have molded them and continue to mold them. They absorb and translate into story the experiences of their time and place, even when both seem to be located in the past or in the future. Their unconscious selves, which are the precipitate of life, commune with ours. Do authors shape their work consciously as well? Yes. But when their world seems discontinuous and dissociated, without form or focus, they have no compelling image of wholeness or unity upon which to model their work. And only through an urgent encompassing vision of man's situation and purpose on earth—the kind of integrating perception of Being that Shakespeare, Dickens, Tolstoy, and the great writers of the past inherited—can they imbue their work with coherence and symmetry. Few writers in our age can claim such a structuring belief, even though the need for it is greater than ever.

The consequences of our fragmented world, wherein force, terror, and dislocation supply the primary data of reality, are momentous for fiction. Interesting and powerful novels and stories have emerged; yet, regularly, they move in different directions from the great stories of the past. Though creative artists may not be reduced to a catalogue of "characteristics" and

FICTION

all such notations demand qualification upon qualification, certain dispositions in the new fiction loom clear.

1/SHATTERED STORY-SEQUENCE. Because the writer of fiction has lost his grasp of relationships or feels that none matters significantly, he has discarded the techniques appropriate to the "well-made" story, the story that unfolds from logical beginning to logical end ("Some Get Wasted" is an example of such a story). Instead he seizes upon some isolated bit or bits of an exploded whole—an episode, an instance, a circumstance; scrutinizes his fragment; and then communicates its meaning or meaninglessness to his readers. These episodes may be strung together without touching one another in any apparent way—seemingly arranged at random. Characteristically, the style in such a story will be indirect, alogical, even deliberately disordered or disorganized; and the writer is likely to tie his story together through images, symbols, or myth rather than narrative transitions. "To London and Rome" and "The Empire of Things" are examples.

2/DISTORTED REALITY. Because the existing world seems repellent or empty or unavailable, the writer of fiction distorts it, parodies it, or rearranges it. From this authorial conversion of reality emerge fable, fantasy, and science fiction, as well as a variety of grotesque and surreal forms. Modern science fiction often depends upon the persuasive fusion of science and fantasy. "The Slaying of the Dragon" is an example of a fable, "My Sad Face" of fantasy, and "EPICAC" of "factual" science fiction, while "Tlön, Uqbar, Orbis Tertius," "Games Without End" and "The Yellow Flower" occupy the uncharted territory somewhere between the two.

3/STORY AS ASSAULT. Because the writer inhabits a world that so largely repudiates humanistic values, that everywhere displays its bloodstained landscapes, he searches out the images of force that will realize this dehumanized world in terms of story. He relies on shock, subtle or obvious, on atrocity, on the harrowing episode. For these qualities, to paraphrase T. S.

Eliot, will be the formula of the emotion he wishes to evoke. The writer's tone may be highly charged or, alternatively, deadpan. "Just Back from the Coast" is an example, and so perhaps are "The Empire of Things" and "Some Get Wasted."

4/THE RETREAT INTO SELF—OR FROM SELF. Because the world has grown intolerable to him, the writer of modern fiction probes inward, to the farthest reaches of self, sometimes denying the external, sometimes striving for the enclosed self of the mad. Or, because he can no longer tolerate the awareness of self, he concentrates resolutely on the external, seeking to shut out the pain generated by the psyche. "The Zoo Keeper" is an example of a story that alternately retreats into and from the self.

5/THE WINDOWLESS ROOM. Because reality has become a depleted source of fiction, or an impure one, or a deceptive one, the writer opts for story as thing-in-itself, a contained entity with no windows looking out at life. He prefers the color and resonance of words and the design they trace to the roundness and solidity of the narrative that tries to mirror life. He frames his story to keep out what Beckett calls the big bumbling confusion of the macrocosm. "Snore Wife and Some Several Dwarts" and "To London and Rome" are examples.

6/THE FADING OF THE HERO. Because the brave vital man who embodies the shared values of a society appears to be an anachronism, the modern writer of fiction diminishes or eliminates him. Or inverts his function: The hero has metamorphosed into the anti-hero—the scoundrel, psychotic, criminal, wastrel, nihilist, or a drooling middle-class Hamlet. And the energies of the lesser characters have also been sapped. "Characters in fiction," says William Gass, a novelist himself, "are mostly empty canvas." Since people cannot be captured on the page alive and whole, they fade into the "story elements." The diminution in size makes fictional fidelity more challenging to achieve (often the modern writer seems reduced to the microscope), and in a world that discounts personality before larger social or political forces, character loses its dominance (as it never does in Dostoyevsky, for instance). "J's Marriage" and "Coffee" are examples of this pervasive tendency in modern fiction.

These stories mark to a greater or lesser degree several of the directions recent fiction has taken. But clearly some of the stories have gone other ways, too many to chart here. Authors traverse remote or nonexistent terrains, regress to adolescence, twist, expand, contract time, extol the primitive, trust wholly to expressiveness, or imagine the death of mankind. But of course they still write stories centered on deep concerns of the past, they still want to amuse and delight, they still identify with humanity's hopes, struggles, and fears, and above all, they still continue their quest for personal salvation. For the fiction writer in the modern idiom, as for Kipling,

> There are nine and sixty ways of writing tribal lays,
>   And every single one of them is right.

To London and Rome

Donald Barthelme

Donald Barthelme was born in Pennsylvania in 1931, lived for a time in Texas, and worked at various occupations until he settled down in Greenwich Village with his Danish wife and his children to a career as a writer. His stories, most of which first appeared in *The New Yorker,* have been collected under the titles of *Come Back, Dr. Caligari; Unspeakable Practices, Unnatural Acts; City Life;* and his most recent collection, *Sadness.* He is also the author of an experimental novella, *Snow White.* In between his own fictions, he would like to create a scenario out of Stanley Crawford's comic novel, *Gascoyne.* In 1972–73, he taught at the State University of New York at Buffalo.

Puzzling though his work seems, Barthelme has placed himself in the center of modern consciousness. There is nothing surrealist about his stories. His dislocations and absurdities are real, his material quite actual. Radio, film, comic books, magazines, television—these supply us with our experience. Put end to end, our consciousness of this material turns out to be a diarrheal run of category errors and *non sequiturs.* The events of the story are as meaningless as they appear to be in ordinary life, fragments that we shore against our ruins. The commentary in the margin is a mocking voice, just another form of rhetorical junk or *dreck,* as Barthelme likes to describe such material. The sense of the story (in his own words) "is not to be obtained by reading between the lines (for there is nothing there, in those white spaces) but by reading the lines themselves. . . ."

Do you know what I want more than anything else? Alison asked.

There was a brief pause

What? I said.

A sewing-machine Alison said, with buttonhole-making attachments.

There was a long pause

There are so many things I could do with it for instance fixing up last year's fall dresses and lots of other things.

There was a tremendous pause during which I bought her a Necchi sewing-machine

Wonderful! Alison said sitting at the controls of the Necchi and making buttonholes in a copy of the New York *Times* Sunday Magazine. Her eyes glistened. I had also bought a two-year subscription to *Necchi News* because I could not be sure that her interest would not be held for that long at least.

Then I bought her a purple Rolls which we decided to

SOURCE: Donald Barthelme, *Come Back, Dr. Caligari* (Boston: Little, Brown, 1963), pp. 121–128. Copyright © 1963 by Donald Barthelme. Reprinted by permission of Little, Brown and Co.

There was a pause broken only by the humming of the Necchi

park on the street because our apartment building had no garage. Alison said she absolutely loved the Rolls! and gave me an enthusiastic kiss. I paid for the car with a check drawn on the First City Bank.

There was an interval

Peter Alison said, what do you want to do now?

Oh I don't know I said.

There was a long interval

Well we can't simply sit around the apartment Alison said so we went to the races at Aqueduct where I bought a race horse that was running well out in front of the others. What a handsome race horse! Alison said delightedly. I paid for the horse with a check on the Capital National Bank.

There was an intermission between races so we went around to the stables and bought a horse trailer

The trailer was attached by means of a trailer hitch, which I bought when it became clear that the trailer could not be hitched up without one, to the back of our new Rolls. The horse's name was Dan and I bought a horse blanket, which he was already wearing but which did not come with him, to keep him warm.

He *is* beautiful Alison said.

A front-runner too I said.

There was an interval of several days. Then Alison and I drove the car with the trailer up the ramp into the plane and we flew back to Milwaukee

After stopping for lunch at Howard Johnson's where we fed Dan some fried clams which he seemed to like very much Alison said: Do you know what we've completely forgotten? I knew that there was something but although I thought hard I could not imagine what it was.

There's no place to keep him in our apartment building! Alison said triumphantly, pointing at Dan. She was of course absolutely right and I hastily bought a large three-story house in Milwaukee's best suburb. To make the house more comfortable I bought a concert grand piano.

On the doorstep of the new house the piano movers paused for a glass of cold water

Here are some little matters which you must attend to Alison said, handing me a box of bills. I went through them carefully, noting the amounts and thinking about money.

What in the name of God is this! I cried, holding up a bill for $1600 from the hardware store.

Garden hose Alison said calmly.

There was an uncomfortable silence

It was clear that I would have to remove some money from the State Bank & Trust and place it in the Municipal National and I did so. The pilot of the airplane which I had bought to fly us to Aqueduct, with his friend the pilot of the larger plane I had bought to fly us back, appeared at the door and asked to be paid. The pilots' names were George and Sam. I paid them and also bought from Sam his flight jacket, which was khaki-colored and pleasant-looking. They smiled and saluted as they left.

Well I said looking around the new house, we'd better

call a piano teacher because I understand that without use pianos tend to fall out of tune.

A silence freighted with sexual significance ensued. Then we went to bed first however ordering a piano teacher and a piano tuner for the early morning

Not only pianos Alison said giving me an exciting look.

The next day Mr. Washington from the Central National called to report an overdraft of several hundred thousand dollars for which I apologized. Who was that on the telephone? Alison asked. Mr. Washington from the bank I replied. Oh Alison said, what do you want for breakfast? What have you got? I asked. Nothing Alison said, we'll have to go out for breakfast.

So we went down to the drugstore where Alison had eggs sunny side up and I had buckwheat cakes with sausage. When we got back to the house I noticed that there were no trees surrounding it, which depressed me.

Have you noticed I asked, that there are no trees?

A silence

Yes Alison said, I've noticed.

A prolonged silence

In fact Alison said, the treelessness of this house almost makes me yearn for our old apartment building.

A terrible silence

There at least one could look at the large plants in the lobby.

Absolute silence for one minute

As soon as we go inside I said, I will call the tree service and buy some trees.

Short silence

Maples I said.

Oh Peter what a fine idea Alison said brightly. But who are these people in our livingroom?

Silently we regarded the two men who sat on the sofa

Realizing that the men were the piano teacher and the piano tuner we had requested, I said: Well did you try the piano?

Yep the first man said, couldn't make heads or tails out of it.

And you? I asked, turning to the other man.

Beats me he said with a mystified look.

What seems to be the difficulty? I asked.

There was a shamefaced silence

Frankly the piano teacher said, this isn't my real line of work. *Really* he said, I'm a jockey.

How about you? I said to his companion.

Oh I'm a bona fide piano tuner all right the tuner said. It's just that I'm not very good at it. Never was and never will be.

We considered the problem in silence

I have a proposition to make I announced. What is your name? I asked, nodding in the direction of the jockey.

Slim he said, and my friend here is Buster.

Well Slim I said, we need a jockey for our race horse, Dan, who will fall out of trim without workouts. And Buster, you can plant the maple trees which I have just ordered for the house.

I settled on a salary of $12,000 a year for Slim and a

There was a joyful silence as Buster and Slim tried to digest the good news

slightly smaller one for Buster. This accomplished I drove the Rolls over to Courtlandt Street to show it to my mistress, Amelia.

When I knocked at the door of Amelia's apartment she refused to open it. Instead she began practicing scales on her flute. I knocked again and called out: Amelia!

The sound of the flute filled the silent hallway

I knocked again but Amelia continued to play. So I sat down on the steps and began to read the newspaper which was lying on the floor, knocking at intervals and at the same time wondering about the psychology of Amelia.

Montgomery Ward I noticed in the newspaper was at 40½. Was Amelia being adamant I considered, because of Alison?

Silently I wondered what to do

Amelia I said at length (through the door), I want to give you a nice present of around $5500. Would you like that?

An interminable silence. Then Amelia holding the flute opened the door

Do you mean it? she said.

Certainly I said.

Can you afford it? she asked doubtfully.

I have a new Rolls I told her, and took her outside where she admired the car at great length. Then I gave her a check for $5500 on the Commercial National for which she thanked me. Back in the apartment she gracefully removed her clothes and put the check in a book in the bookcase. She looked very pretty without her clothes, as pretty as ever, and we had a pleasant time for an hour or more. When I left the apartment Amelia said Peter, I think you're a very pleasant person which made me feel very good and on the way home I bought a new gray Dacron suit.

When I gave the salesman a check on The Medical National he paused, frowned, and said: "This is a new bank isn't it?"

Where have you been? Alison said, I've been waiting lunch for hours. I bought a new suit I said, how do you like it? Very nice Alison said, but hurry I've got to go shopping after lunch. Shopping! I said, I'll go with you!

So we ate a hasty lunch of vichyssoise and ice cream and had Buster drive us in the Rolls to the Federated Department Store where we bought a great many things for the new house and a new horse blanket for Dan.

Do you think we ought to buy uniforms for Buster and Slim? Alison asked and I replied that I thought not, they didn't seem the sort who would enjoy wearing uniforms.

A frosty silence

I think they ought to wear uniforms Alison said firmly.

No I said, I think not.

Dead silence

Uniforms with something on the pocket Alison said. A crest or something.

No.

There was an interval during which I sent a check for $500,000 to the Museum of Modern Art

Instead of uniforms I bought Slim a Kaywoodie pipe and some pipe tobacco, and bought Buster a large sterling silver cowboy belt buckle and a belt to go with it.

Buster was very pleased with his sterling silver belt buckle and said that he thought Slim would be pleased too when he saw the Kaywoodie pipe which had been bought for him. You were right after all Alison whispered to me in the back seat of the Rolls.

Alison decided that she would make a pie for supper, a chocolate pie perhaps, and that we would have Buster and Slim and George and Sam the pilots too if they were in town and not flying. She began looking in her recipe book while I read the *Necchi News* in my favorite armchair.

Then Slim came in from the garage with a worried look. Dan he said is not well.

A stunned pause

Everyone was thrown into a panic by the thought of Dan's illness and I bought some Kaopectate which Slim however did not believe would be appropriate. The Kaopectate was $0.98 and I paid for it with a check on the Principal National. The delivery boy from the drugstore, whose name was Andrew, suggested that Dan needed a doctor. This seemed sensible so I tipped Andrew with a check on the Manufacturers' Trust and asked him to fetch the very best doctor he could find on such short notice.

We looked at one another in wordless fear

Dan was lying on his side in the garage, groaning now and then. His face was a rich gray color and it was clear that if he did not have immediate attention, the worst might be expected.

Pausing only to whip a fresh checkbook from the desk drawer, I bought a large hospital nearby for $1.5 million

Peter for God's sake do something for this poor horse! Alison cried.

We sent Dan over in his trailer with strict instructions that he be given the best of everything. Slim and Buster accompanied him and when Andrew arrived with the doctor I hurried them off to the hospital too. Concern for Dan was uppermost in my mind at that moment.

The telephone rang and Alison answered.

Then she said: It's some girl, for you.

Returning to the living-room, Alison hesitated

As I had thought it might be, it was Amelia. I told her about Dan's illness. She was very concerned and asked if I thought it would be appropriate if she went to the hospital.

A moment of indecision followed by a painful silence

You don't think it would be appropriate Amelia said.

No Amelia I said truthfully, I don't.

Then Amelia said that this indication of her tiny status in all our lives left her with nothing to say.

The conversation lapsed

To cheer her up I said I would visit her again in the near future. This pleased her and the exchange ended on a note of warmth. I knew however that Alison would ask questions and I returned to the livingroom with some anxiety.

An hiatus filled with doubt and suspicion

But now the pilots George and Sam rushed in with good news indeed. They had gotten word of Dan's illness over the radio they said, and filled with concern had flown straight to the hospital, where they learned that Dan's stomach had been pumped and all was well. Dan was resting easily George and Sam said, and could come home in about a week.

Oh Peter! Alison exclaimed in a pleased way, our ordeal is over. She kissed me with abandon and George and Sam shook hands with each other and with Andrew and Buster and Slim, who had just come in from the hospital. To celebrate we decided that we would all fly to London and Rome on a Viscount jet which I bought for an undisclosed sum and which Sam declared he knew how to fly very well.

The Zoo Keeper

Daniel Berrigan, S.J.

Daniel Berrigan was born in 1921 in Virginia, Minnesota. His family moved to Syracuse when his father, a militant socialist, was fired from his job as railroad engineer. From the age of six, according to his mother, he "was obsessed by the suffering in the world." At eighteen, he began a rigorous thirteen-year course of training in the Society of Jesus. Except for interludes in France, Eastern Europe, and South America, he has taught at Jesuit schools—in Brooklyn, Jersey City, and Syracuse. In 1967, he became the first Roman Catholic priest on the faculty of Cornell University.

He has devoted much of his time to the related causes of poetry and pacificism. In 1957, *Time Without Number* won the Lamont Prize for Poetry. His other books are *The Bow in the Clouds, The World for a Wedding Ring, Consequences: Truth and . . .* (about his South American sojourn), and *Love, Love at the End,* from which this selection is taken. In 1967, he went to Hanoi to help release three American pilots, an experience described in *Night Flight to Hanoi.* The following year he and eight other pacifists destroyed selective service files at Catonsville, Maryland. He was sentenced to prison, went underground, was caught, and served almost two years of a five-year sentence. He wrote *The Catonsville Nine,* a play that examines the consciences of those nine who acted on their convictions at Catonsville. His most recent work is *America Is Hard to Find* (1972).

There was once a minor prophet among an ancient people. He died young, but not before there welled up in him a consuming sense of loss, a sense of being cheated of something. But of what? he pondered and pondered, as his travail approached.

His own people had condemned him. But he was not entirely bereft of consolation; he knew that sour grapes set teeth on edge. He knew also that a man must endure his times and that his own times were undoubtedly evil. Still he was eaten by loss, he carried a fox at his heart. Time, time, he needed time! And time was being denied him, and where lay his recourse?

A packed tribunal had convicted him of atheism. He had turned away from the state deities. He accepted the judgment; with regard to their gods, he was indeed an unbeliever, beyond hope of conversion.

But at length even the slight consolation afforded by his upright life, drained from his soul. He was left with a sick regret—for life denied,

SOURCE: Daniel Berrigan, S.J., *Love, Love at the End* (New York: The Macmillan Co., 1968), pp. 44–46.

for knowledge withheld, for cheated years. He was indeed a stranger upon the earth, he knew little of his own country, he was ignorant and unknown—and he must die.

And what rumors he had heard of the great world and of animals weird in form, bizarre in color, dazzling in variety, beyond the horizon to east and west. What marvels was the world holding out—forever beyond his reach? The torture was that he would never know.

Just before the blade descended, he made a great pact with the Almighty. With a final twist of his body and spirit, he willed to be reborn, in another century. Whether he would ever again pour blood on the altar or unroll the scriptures, was a matter of indifference. What counted was that he might some day burst the membrane of his ignorance and see the world. He might ride a camel and hear the honk of geese, and see for himself whether a curious animal, as he had been told, slept upside down, like a hive on tendrils. . . .

He works today in Central Park Zoo, a keeper of beasts. In the midst of a people who have seized command of their world, who are powerful and purposeful and unconscionably arrogant, he serves the captive beasts. The Park is aflow with a great stream of life; on both banks the enormous catacombs of the living are raised and pulled down again; exotic, absurd, electric with life. In the midst of the park, like a ghetto under lock and key, is the zoo; within, he, its minor functionary. Indifferent and archaic, he hews wood and draws water, a slave among beasts.

The images which illumine his existence are drawn from the earth, from hooves and pelts. He smells the urine-soaked straw, he sees himself in the bestial faces. The setting of his life, mocking and pretentious, glitters in the mirror of the Park lake. Vanity of vanities—a city seen in water.

Day after day, the great avenues ring like a corps of drummers, with the fantastic heartbeat of this people. Peace, they drum, war, they crash. Equality, property, human rights, human wrongs. Men march past, their faces lit with holy or infernal passion. And the beasts look up, distracted for a moment, and turn once more to their bran and water. He feeds them water and bran, and rakes their dung in heaps, and carts it away, a lesser keeper in a minor zoo.

One night in spring, after some years of this existence, he sat at the edge of the pool where the sea lions swam and fed and crept ashore. The bronze beasts in the clock had rounded the midnight circuit with their drums and flutes, the lovers had departed, the lights went out. The life that pulsed around him lay heavy on the air. Forsythia, magnolia, cherry and apple, the forest growth of a parasitic city.

He drank the draught of the spring night, its bitterness poured into his soul. He was lonely and cold and numb; his life was a great cry of the heart, a protest against the course of his existence. He knew that the stars were liars, that his passion had betrayed him. He was trapped in a zoo, a captive playground. He was part of an inexorable defeat; one with the innocent, the baited, the victim. *Homo captus,* the sign on his paling read—"Captive Man." All the day long, all the night long, I have lifted my voice to a blind and unheeding people. God would become man, the old oracles said. But must man become a beast?

The morning star arose above him, unutterably pure and serene. The animals stirred and arose where they slept. He lifted his eyes to another day. Where there was no joy, hope must suffice.

My Sad Face

Heinrich Böll

Novelist, short-story writer, and radio playwright, Heinrich Böll was born in Cologne, Germany, in 1917, the son of a sculptor. He worked in a bookshop before serving in the German infantry during World War II. After the war, he became a free-lance writer, but his reputation developed around the translations of his work that appeared during the post–World War II period. *The Train Was on Time* (1956, trans.) and *Adam, Where Art Thou?* (1955) are works of protest showing the despair of "those involved in a total and totally pointless war." His sympathy and compassion for the individual pitted against a remorseless and often indifferent society are revealed also in the novels *And Did Not Say a Word* (1953), *Billiards at Half-past Nine* (1959), and *The Clown* (1965), a story of a man who loses everything as he pantomimes the duplicities of modern German society. The following story is a bitter vision of man's future comparable to Orwell's *1984.* But it is affirmative in that it warns us to oppose in our own time the tendencies that make man corrupt and cruel—the authoritarian, the mechanical, the aggressive, the alarming trend to regard men as objects to be manipulated and the emotions as forces to be switched on and off on command.

Böll was awarded the Nobel Prize for literature in 1972. His latest novel, *Group Portrait With a Lady,* appeared in 1971 in German and was published in an English edition in 1973.

While I was standing on the dock watching the seagulls, my sad face attracted the attention of a policeman on his rounds. I was completely absorbed in the sight of the hovering birds as they shot up and swooped down in a vain search for something edible: the harbor was deserted, the water greenish and thick with foul oil, and on its crusty film floated all kinds of discarded junk; not a vessel was to be seen, the cranes had rusted, the freight sheds collapsed; not even rats seemed to inhabit the black ruins along the wharf, silence reigned. It was years since all connection with the outside world had been cut off.

I had my eye on one particular seagull and was observing its flight. Uneasy as a swallow sensing thunder in the air, it usually stayed hovering just above the surface of the water, occasionally, with a shrill cry, risking an upward sweep to unite with its circling fellows. Had I been free to express a wish, I would have chosen a loaf of bread to feed

SOURCE: Heinrich Böll, *Children Are Civilians, Too,* trans. Leila Vennewitz (New York: McGraw-Hill Book Company, 1970), pp. 158–165.

to the gulls, crumbling it to pieces to provide a white fixed point for the random flutterings, to set a goal at which the birds could aim, to tauten this shrill flurry of crisscross hovering and circling by hurling a piece of bread into the mesh as if to pull together a bunch of strings. But I was as hungry as they were, and tired, yet happy in spite of my sadness because it felt good to be standing there, my hands in my pockets, watching the gulls and drinking in sadness.

Suddenly I felt an official hand on my shoulder, and a voice said: "Come along now!" The hand tugged at my shoulder, trying to pull me round, but I did not budge, shook it off, and said quietly: "You're nuts."

"Comrade," the still invisible one told me, "I'm warning you."

"Sir," I retorted.

"What d'you mean, 'Sir'?" he shouted angrily. "We're all comrades."

With that he stepped round beside me and looked at me, forcing me to bring back my contentedly roving gaze and direct it at his simple, honest face: he was as solemn as a buffalo that for twenty years has had nothing to eat but duty.

"On what grounds . . ." I began.

"Sufficient grounds," he said. "Your sad face."

I laughed.

"Don't laugh!" His rage was genuine. I had first thought he was bored, with no unlicensed whore, no staggering sailor, no thief or fugitive to arrest, but now I saw he meant it: he intended to arrest me.

"Come along now!"

"Why?" I asked quietly.

Before I realized what was happening, I found my left wrist enclosed in a thin chain, and instantly I knew that once again I had had it. I turned toward the swerving gulls for a last look, glanced at the calm gray sky, and tried with a sudden twist to plunge into the water, for it seemed more desirable to drown alone in that scummy dishwater than to be strangled by the sergeants in a back yard or to be locked up again. But the policeman suddenly jerked me so close to him that all hope of wrenching myself free was gone.

"Why?" I asked again.

"There's a law that you have to be happy."

"I am happy!" I cried.

"Your sad face . . ." he shook his head.

"But this law is new," I told him.

"It's thirty-six hours old, and I'm sure you know that every law comes into force twenty-four hours after it has been proclaimed."

"But I've never heard of it!"

"That won't save you. It was proclaimed yesterday, over all the loudspeakers, in all the papers, and anyone"—here he looked at me scornfully—"anyone who doesn't share in the blessings of press or radio was informed by leaflets scattered from the air over every street in the country. So we'll soon find out where you've been spending the last thirty-six hours, Comrade."

He dragged me away. For the first time I noticed that it was cold and I had no coat, for the first time I became really aware of my hunger growling at the entrance to my stomach, for the first time I realized that I was also dirty, unshaved, and in rags, and that there were laws demanding that every comrade be clean, shaved, happy, and well-fed. He pushed me in front of him like a scarecrow that has been found guilty of stealing and is compelled to abandon the place of its dreams at the edge of the field. The streets were empty, the police station was not far off, and, although I had known they would soon find a reason for arresting me, my heart was heavy, for he took me through the places of my childhood which I had intended to visit after looking at the harbor: public gardens that had been full of bushes, in glorious confusion, overgrown paths—all this was now leveled, orderly, neat, arranged in squares for the patriotic groups obliged to drill and march here on Mondays, Wednesdays, and Saturdays. Only the sky was as it used to be, the air the same as in the old days when my heart had been full of dreams.

Here and there as we walked along I saw the government sign displayed on the walls of a number of love-barracks, indicating whose turn it was to participate in these hygienic pleasures on Wednesdays; certain taverns also were evidently authorized to hang out the drinking sign, a beer glass cut out of tin and striped diagonally with the national colors: light brown, dark brown, light brown. Joy was doubtless already filling the hearts of those whose names appeared in the official list of Wednesday drinkers and who would thus partake of the Wednesday beer.

All the people we passed were stamped with the unmistakable mark of earnest zeal, encased in an aura of tireless activity probably intensified by the sight of the policeman. They all quickened their pace, assumed expressions of perfect devotion to duty, and the women coming out of the goods depots did their best to register that joy which was expected of them, for they were required to show joy and cheerful gaiety over the duties of the housewife, whose task it was to refresh the state worker every evening with a wholesome meal.

But all these people skillfully avoided us in such a way that no one was forced to cross our path directly; where there were signs of life on the street, they disappeared twenty paces ahead of us, each trying to dash into a goods depot or vanish round a corner, and quite a few may have slipped into a strange house and waited nervously behind the door until the sound of our footsteps had died away.

Only once, just as we were crossing an intersection, we came face to face with an elderly man, I just caught a glimpse of his schoolteacher's badge. There was no time for him to avoid us, and he strove, after first saluting the policeman in the prescribed manner (by slapping his own head three times with the flat of his hand as a sign of total abasement)—he strove, as I say, to do his duty by spitting three times into my face and bestowing upon me the compulsory epithet of "filthy traitor." His aim was good, but the day had been hot, his throat must have been dry, for I received only a few tiny, rather ineffectual flecks which—contrary to regulations—I tried involuntarily to wipe away with my sleeve, whereupon the policeman kicked me in the backside and struck me with his fist in the small of my back, adding in a flat voice: "Phase One," meaning: first and mildest form of punishment administerable by every policeman.

The schoolteacher had hurriedly gone on his way. Everyone else managed to avoid us; except for just one woman who happened to be taking the prescribed stroll in the fresh air in front of a love-barracks prior to the evening's pleasures, a pale, puffy blonde who blew me a furtive kiss, and I smiled gratefully while the policeman tried to pretend he hadn't noticed. They are required to permit these women liberties that for any other comrade would unquestionably result in severe punishment; for, since they contribute substantially to the general working morale, they are tacitly considered to be outside the law, a concession whose far-reaching consequences have been branded as a sign of incipient liberalization by Prof. Bleigoeth, Ph.D., D.Litt., the political philosopher, in the obligatory periodical for (political) philosophy. I had read this the previous day on my way to the capital when, in a farm outhouse, I came across a few sheets of the magazine that a student—probably the farmer's son—had embellished with some very witty comments.

Fortunately we now reached the police station, for at that moment the sirens sounded, a sign that the streets were about to be flooded with thousands of people wearing expressions of restrained joy (it being required at closing time to show restraint in one's expression of joy, otherwise it might look as though work were a burden; whereas rejoicing was to prevail when work began—rejoicing and singing), and all these thousands would have been compelled to spit at me. However, the siren indicated ten minutes before closing time, every worker being required to devote ten minutes to a thorough washing of his person, in accordance with the motto of the head of state: Joy and Soap.

The entrance to the local police station, a squat concrete box, was guarded by two sentries who, as I passed them, gave me the benefit of the customary "physical punitive measures," striking me hard across the temple with their rifles and cracking the muzzles of their pistols down on my collarbone, in accordance with the preamble to State Law No. 1: "Every police officer is required, when confronted by any apprehended [meaning arrested] person, to demonstrate violence *per se*, with the exception of the officer performing the arrest, the latter being privileged to participate in the pleasure of carrying out the necessary physical punitive measures during the interrogation." The actual State Law No. 1 runs as follows: "Every police officer *may* punish anyone: he *must* punish anyone who has committed a crime. For all comrades there is no such thing as exemption from punishment, only the possibility of exemption from punishment."

We now proceeded down a long bare corridor provided with a great many large windows; then a door opened automatically, the sentries having already announced our arrival, and in those days, when everything was joy, obedience, and order and everyone did his best to use up the mandatory pound of soap a day, in those days the arrival of an apprehended [arrested] comrade was naturally an event.

We entered an almost empty room containing nothing but a desk with a telephone and two chairs. I was required to remain standing in the middle of the room; the policeman took off his helmet and sat down.

At first there was silence, nothing happened. They always do it like that, that's the worst part. I could feel my face collapsing by degrees, I was tired and hungry, and by now even the last vestiges of that joy of sadness had vanished, for I knew I had had it.

After a few seconds a tall, pale-faced, silent man entered the room wearing the light-brown uniform of the preliminary interrogator. He sat down without a word and looked at me.

"Status?"

"Ordinary comrade."

"Date of birth?"

"1.1.1.," I said.

"Last occupation?"

"Convict."

The two men exchanged glances.

"When and where discharged?"

"Yesterday, Building 12, Cell 13."

"Where to?"

"The capital."

"Certificate."

I produced the discharge certificate from my pocket and handed it to him. He clipped it to the green card on which he had begun to enter my particulars.

"Your former crime?"

"Happy face."

The two men exchanged glances.

"Explain," said the interrogator.

"At that time," I said, "my happy face attracted the attention of a police officer on a day when general mourning had been decreed. It was the anniversary of the Leader's death."

"Length of sentence?"

"Five."

"Conduct?"

"Bad."

"Reason?"

"Deficient in work-enthusiasm."

"That's all."

With that the preliminary interrogator rose, walked over to me, and neatly knocked out my three front center teeth: a sign that I was to be branded as a lapsed criminal, an intensified measure I had not counted on. The preliminary interrogator then left the room, and a fat fellow in a dark-brown uniform came in: the interrogator.

I was beaten by all of them: by the interrogator, the chief interrogator, the supreme interrogator, the examiner, and the concluding examiner; in addition, the policeman carried out all the physical punitive measures demanded by law, and on account of my sad face they sentenced me to ten years, just as five years earlier they had sentenced me to five years on account of my happy face.

I must now try to make my face register nothing at all, if I can manage to survive the next ten years of Joy and Soap. . . .

Tlön, Uqbar, Orbis Tertius

Jorge Luis Borges

Jorge Luis Borges, born in Buenos Aires in 1899, is Argentina's greatest gift to the world of *belles-lettres.* Until about 1930, he devoted himself mainly to poetry. He also wrote concise and illuminating essays on metaphysics, literature, and language. Later, when his failing eyesight kept him from reading, he began to create the short fictional narratives which are so admired and imitated today. Etched in irony and skepticism, his stories recall the fantastic visions of Franz Kafka. They appear in English translations under the titles of *Labyrinths, Ficciones,* and *Imaginary Beings,* while his essays are available in *Inquisitions* and *Other Inquisitions.* In 1972 Borges published *Selected Poems, 1923–1967* and *A Universal History of Infamy.*

Borges's story superficially resembles the work of Edgar Allan Poe—but Borges's genius lies in the way he invests science fiction with philosophic depth, scrupulous scholarship, and intellectual acuity. Through these qualities the imaginary is made to seem real, the real passing and phantasmagoric. Borges insidiously raises the question Alvin Toffler regards as central to our time in *Future Shock:* Is the experience of an uncreated reality or of an imaginary reality, if intense and persuasive, a displacement of the real experience itself?

I

I owe the discovery of Uqbar to the conjunction of a mirror and an encyclopedia. The mirror troubled the depths of a corridor in a country house on Gaona Street in Ramos Mejía; the encyclopedia is fallaciously called *The Anglo-American Cyclopaedia* (New York, 1917) and is a literal but delinquent reprint of the *Encyclopaedia Britannica* of 1902. The event took place some five years ago. Bioy Casares had had dinner with me that evening and we became lengthily engaged in a vast polemic concerning the composition of a novel in the first person, whose narrator would omit or disfigure the facts and indulge in various contradictions which would permit a few readers—very few readers—to perceive an atrocious or banal reality. From the remote depths of the corridor, the mirror spied upon us. We discovered (such a discovery is inevitable in the late hours of the night) that mirrors have something monstrous about them. Then Bioy Casares recalled that one of the heresiarchs of Uqbar had declared that mirrors and copulation are abominable, because they increase the number of men.

SOURCE: Jorge Luis Borges, *Labyrinths* (New York: New Directions Publishing Corporation, 1968), pp. 3–18.

I asked him the origin of this memorable observation and he answered that it was reproduced in *The Anglo-American Cyclopaedia*, in its article on Uqbar. The house (which we had rented furnished) had a set of this work. On the last pages of Volume XLVI we found an article on Upsala; on the first pages of Volume XLVII, one on Ural-Altaic Languages, but not a word about Uqbar. Bioy, a bit taken aback, consulted the volumes of the index. In vain he exhausted all of the imaginable spellings: Ukbar, Ucbar, Ooqbar, Ookbar, Oukbahr . . . Before leaving, he told me that it was a region of Iraq or of Asia Minor. I must confess that I agreed with some discomfort. I conjectured that this undocumented country and its anonymous heresiarch were a fiction devised by Bioy's modesty in order to justify a statement. The fruitless examination of one of Justus Perthes' atlases fortified my doubt.

The following day, Bioy called me from Buenos Aires. He told me he had before him the article on Uqbar, in Volume XLVI of the encyclopedia. The heresiarch's name was not forthcoming, but there was a note on his doctrine, formulated in words almost identical to those he had repeated, though perhaps literarily inferior. He had recalled: *Copulation and mirrors are abominable.* The text of the encyclopedia said: *For one of those gnostics, the visible universe was an illusion or* (*more precisely*) *a sophism. Mirrors and fatherhood are abominable because they multiply and disseminate that universe.* I told him, in all truthfulness, that I should like to see that article. A few days later he brought it. This surprised me, since the scrupulous cartographical indices of Ritter's *Erdkunde* were plentifully ignorant of the name Uqbar.

The tome Bioy brought was, in fact, Volume XLVI of the *Anglo-American Cyclopaedia.* On the half-title page and the spine, the alphabetical marking (Tor-Ups) was that of our copy, but, instead of 917, it contained 921 pages. These four additional pages made up the article on Uqbar, which (as the reader will have noticed) was not indicated by the alphabetical marking. We later determined that there was no other difference between the volumes. Both of them (as I believe I have indicated) are reprints of the tenth *Encyclopaedia Britannica.* Bioy had acquired his copy at some sale or other.

We read the article with some care. The passage recalled by Bioy was perhaps the only surprising one. The rest of it seemed very plausible, quite in keeping with the general tone of the work and (as is natural) a bit boring. Reading it over again, we discovered beneath its rigorous prose a fundamental vagueness. Of the fourteen names which figured in the geographical part, we only recognized three – Khorasan, Armenia, Erzerum – interpolated in the text in an ambiguous way. Of the historical names, only one: the impostor magician Smerdis, invoked more as a metaphor. The note seemed to fix the boundaries of Uqbar, but its nebulous reference points were rivers and craters and mountain ranges of that same region. We read, for example, that the lowlands of

Tsai Khaldun and the Axa Delta marked the southern frontier and that on the islands of the delta wild horses procreate. All this, on the first part of page 918. In the historical section (page 920) we learned that as a result of the religious persecutions of the thirteenth century, the orthodox believers sought refuge on these islands, where to this day their obelisks remain and where it is not uncommon to unearth their stone mirrors. The section on Language and Literature was brief. Only one trait is worthy of recollection: it noted that the literature of Uqbar was one of fantasy and that its epics and legends never referred to reality, but to the two imaginary regions of Mlejnas and Tlön . . . The bibliography enumerated four volumes which we have not yet found, though the third—Silas Haslam: *History of the Land Called Uqbar,* 1874—figures in the catalogues of Bernard Quaritch's bookshop.[1] The first, *Lesbare und lesenswerthe Bemerkungen über das Land Ukkbar in Klein-Asien,* dates from 1641 and is the work of Johannes Valentinus Andreä. This fact is significant; a few years later, I came upon that name in the unsuspected pages of De Quincey (*Writings,* Volume XIII) and learned that it belonged to a German theologian who, in the early seventeenth century, described the imaginary community of Rosae Crucis—a community that others founded later, in imitation of what he had prefigured.

That night we visited the National Library. In vain we exhausted atlases, catalogues, annuals of geographical societies, travelers' and historians' memoirs: no one had ever been in Uqbar. Neither did the general index of Bioy's encyclopedia register that name. The following day, Carlos Mastronardi (to whom I had related the matter) noticed the black and gold covers of the *Anglo-American Cyclopaedia* in a bookshop on Corrientes and Talcahuano . . . He entered and examined Volume XLVI. Of course, he did not find the slightest indication of Uqbar.

II

Some limited and waning memory of Herbert Ashe, an engineer of the southern railways, persists in the hotel at Adrogué, amongst the effusive honeysuckles and in the illusory depths of the mirrors. In his lifetime, he suffered from unreality, as do so many Englishmen; once dead, he is not even the ghost he was then. He was tall and listless and his tired rectangular beard had once been red. I understand he was a widower, without children. Every few years he would go to England, to visit (I judge from some photographs he showed us) a sundial and a few oaks. He and my father had entered into one of those close (the adjective is excessive) English friendships that begin by excluding confidences and very soon dispense with dialogue. They used to carry out an exchange of books and newspapers and engage in taciturn chess games . . . I remember him in the hotel corridor, with a mathematics

---

[1] Haslam has also published *A General History of Labyrinths.*

book in his hand, sometimes looking at the irrecoverable colors of the sky. One afternoon, we spoke of the duodecimal system of numbering (in which twelve is written as 10). Ashe said that he was converting some kind of tables from the duodecimal to the sexagesimal system (in which sixty is written as 10). He added that the task had been entrusted to him by a Norwegian, in Rio Grande do Sul. We had known him for eight years and he had never mentioned his sojourn in that region . . . We talked of country life, of the *capangas*, of the Brazilian etymology of the word *gaucho* (which some old Uruguayans still pronounce *gaúcho*) and nothing more was said—may God forgive me—of duodecimal functions. In September of 1937 (we were not at the hotel), Herbert Ashe died of a ruptured aneurysm. A few days before, he had received a sealed and certified package from Brazil. It was a book in large octavo. Ashe left it at the bar, where—months later—I found it. I began to leaf through it and experienced an astonished and airy feeling of vertigo which I shall not describe, for this is not the story of my emotions but of Uqbar and Tlön and Orbis Tertius. On one of the nights of Islam called the Night of Nights, the secret doors of heaven open wide and the water in the jars becomes sweeter; if those doors opened, I would not feel what I felt that afternoon. The book was written in English and contained 1001 pages. On the yellow leather back I read these curious words which were repeated on the title page: *A First Encyclopaedia of Tlön. Vol. XI. Hlaer to Jangr.* There was no indication of date or place. On the first page and on a leaf of silk paper that covered one of the color plates there was stamped a blue oval with this inscription: *Orbis Tertius.* Two years before I had discovered, in a volume of a certain pirated encyclopedia, a superficial description of a nonexistent country; now chance afforded me something more precious and arduous. Now I held in my hands a vast methodical fragment of an unknown planet's entire history, with its architecture and its playing cards, with the dread of its mythologies and the murmur of its languages, with its emperors and its seas, with its minerals and its birds and its fish, with its algebra and its fire, with its theological and metaphysical controversy. And all of it articulated, coherent, with no visible doctrinal intent or tone of parody.

In the "Eleventh Volume" which I have mentioned, there are allusions to preceding and succeeding volumes. In an article in the *N. R. F.* which is now classic, Néstor Ibarra has denied the existence of those companion volumes; Ezequiel Martínez Estrada and Drieu La Rochelle have refuted that doubt, perhaps victoriously. The fact is that up to now the most diligent inquiries have been fruitless. In vain we have upended the libraries of the two Americas and of Europe. Alfonso Reyes, tired of these subordinate sleuthing procedures, proposes that we should all undertake the task of reconstructing the many and weighty tomes that are lacking: *ex ungue leonem.* He calculates, half in earnest and half jokingly, that a generation of *tlönistas* should be sufficient. This venturesome computation brings us back to the fundamental problem: Who are the inventors of Tlön? The plural is inevitable, because the hypothesis of a lone inventor—an infinite Leibniz laboring away darkly and modestly—has been unanimously discounted. It is conjectured that this brave new world is the work of a secret society of astronomers, biologists, engineers, metaphysicians, poets, chemists, algebraists, moralists, painters, geometers . . . directed by an obscure man of genius. Individuals mastering these diverse disciplines are abundant, but not so those capable of inventiveness and less so those capable of subordinating that inventiveness to a rigorous and systematic plan. This plan is so vast that each writer's contribution is infinitesimal. At first it was believed that Tlön was a mere chaos, an irresponsible license of the imagination; now it is known that it is a cosmos and that the intimate laws which govern it have been formulated, at least provisionally. Let it suffice for me to recall that the apparent contradictions of the Eleventh Volume are the fundamental basis for the proof that the other volumes exist, so lucid and exact is the order observed in it. The popular magazines, with pardonable excess, have spread news of the zoology and topography of Tlön; I think its transparent tigers and towers of blood perhaps do not merit the continued attention of *all* men. I shall venture to request a few minutes to expound its concept of the universe.

Hume noted for all time that Berkeley's arguments did not admit the slightest refutation nor did they cause the slightest conviction. This dictum is entirely correct in its application to the earth, but entirely false in Tlön. The nations of this planet are congenitally idealist. Their language and the derivations of their language—religion, letters, metaphysics—all presuppose idealism. The world for them is not a concourse of objects in space; it is a heterogeneous series of independent acts. It is successive and temporal, not spatial. There are no nouns in Tlön's conjectural *Ursprache,* from which the "present" languages and the dialects are derived: there are impersonal verbs, modified by monosyllabic suffixes (or prefixes) with an adverbial value. For example: there is no word corresponding to the word "moon," but there is a verb which in English would be "to moon" or "to moonate." "The moon rose above the river" is *hlör u fang axaxaxas mlö,* or literally: "upward behind the on-streaming it mooned."

The preceding applies to the languages of the southern hemisphere. In those of the northern hemisphere (on whose *Ursprache* there is very little data in the Eleventh Volume) the prime unit is not the verb, but the monosyllabic adjective. The noun is formed by an accumulation of adjectives. They do not say "moon," but rather "round airy-light on dark" or "pale-orange-of-the-sky" or any other such combination. In the example selected the mass of adjectives refers to a real object, but this is purely fortuitous. The literature of this hemisphere (like Meinong's subsistent world) abounds in ideal objects, which are convoked and dissolved in a moment, according to poetic needs. At times they are determined by mere simultaneity. There are objects composed of two terms, one of visual and another of auditory character: the color of the rising sun and the faraway cry of a bird. There are objects of many terms: the sun and the water on a swimmer's chest, the vague tremulous rose color we see with our eyes closed, the sensation of being carried along by a river and also by sleep. These second-degree objects can be combined with others; through the use of certain abbreviations, the process is practically infinite. There are famous poems made up of one enormous word. This word forms a *poetic object* created by the author. The fact that no one believes in the reality of nouns paradoxically causes their number to be unending. The languages of Tlön's northern hemisphere contain all the nouns of the Indo-European languages—and many others as well.

It is no exaggeration to state that the classic culture of Tlön comprises only one discipline: psychology. All others are subordinated to it. I have said that the men of this planet conceive the universe as a series of mental processes which do not develop in space but successively in time. Spinoza ascribes to his inexhaustible divinity the attributes of extension and thought; no one in Tlön would understand the juxtaposition of the first (which is typical only of certain states) and the second—which is a perfect synonym of the cosmos. In other words, they do not conceive that the spatial persists in time. The perception of a cloud of smoke on the horizon and then of the burning field and then of the half-extinguished cigarette that produced the blaze is considered an example of association of ideas.

This monism or complete idealism invalidates all science. If we explain (or judge) a fact, we connect it with another; such linking, in Tlön, is a later state of the subject which cannot affect or illuminate the previous state. Every mental state is irreducible: the mere fact of naming it—i.e., of classifying it—implies a falsification. From which it can be deduced that there are no sciences on Tlön, not even reasoning. The paradoxical truth is that they do exist, and in almost uncountable number. The same thing happens with philosophies as happens with nouns in the northern hemisphere. The fact that every philosophy is by definition a dialectical game, a *Philosophie des Als Ob*, has caused them to multiply. There is an abundance of incredible systems of pleasing design or sensational type. The metaphysicians of Tlön do not seek for the truth or even for verisimilitude, but rather for the astounding. They judge that metaphysics is a branch of fantastic literature. They know that a system is nothing more than the subordination of all aspects of the universe to any one such aspect. Even the phrase "all aspects" is rejectable, for it supposes the impossible addition of the present and of all past moments. Neither is it licit to use the plural "past moments," since it supposes another impossible operation . . . One of the schools of Tlön goes so far as to negate time: it reasons that the present is indefinite, that the future has no reality other than as a present hope, that the past has no reality other than as a present memory.[2] Another school declares that *all time* has already transpired

---

[2] Russell (*The Analysis of Mind,* 1921, page 159) supposes that the planet has been created a few minutes ago, furnished with a humanity that "remembers" an illusory past.

and that our life is only the crepuscular and no doubt falsified and mutilated memory or reflection of an irrecoverable process. Another, that the history of the universe—and in it our lives and the most tenuous detail of our lives—is the scripture produced by a subordinate god in order to communicate with a demon. Another, that the universe is comparable to those cryptographs in which not all the symbols are valid and that only what happens every three hundred nights is true. Another, that while we sleep here, we are awake elsewhere and that in this way every man is two men.

Amongst the doctrines of Tlön, none has merited the scandalous reception accorded to materialism. Some thinkers have formulated it with less clarity than fervor, as one might put forth a paradox. In order to facilitate the comprehension of this inconceivable thesis, a heresiarch of the eleventh century[3] devised the sophism of the nine copper coins, whose scandalous renown is in Tlön equivalent to that of the Eleatic paradoxes. There are many versions of this "specious reasoning," which vary the number of coins and the number of discoveries; the following is the most common:

On Tuesday, X crosses a deserted road and loses nine copper coins. On Thursday, Y finds in the road four coins, somewhat rusted by Wednesday's rain. On Friday, Z discovers three coins in the road. On Friday morning, X finds two coins in the corridor of his house. The heresiarch would deduce from this story the reality—i.e., the continuity—of the nine coins which were recovered. *It is absurd* (he affirmed) *to imagine that four of the coins have not existed between Tuesday and Thursday, three between Tuesday and Friday afternoon, two between Tuesday and Friday morning. It is logical to think that they have existed—at least in some secret way, hidden from the comprehension of men—at every moment of those three periods.*

The language of Tlön resists the formulation of this paradox; most people did not even understand it. The defenders of common sense at first did no more than negate the veracity of the anecdote. They repeated that it was a verbal fallacy, based on the rash application of two neologisms not authorized by usage and alien to all rigorous thought: the verbs "find" and "lose," which beg the question, because they presuppose the identity of the first and of the last nine coins. They recalled that all nouns (man, coin, Thursday, Wednesday, rain) have only a metaphorical value. They denounced the treacherous circumstance "somewhat rusted by Wednesday's rain," which presupposes what is trying to be demonstrated: the persistence of the four coins from Tuesday to Thursday. They explained that *equality* is one thing and *identity* another, and formulated a kind of *reductio ad absurdum:* the hypothetical case of nine men who on nine successive nights suffer a severe pain. Would it not be ridiculous—they questioned—to pretend that this

[3] A century, according to the duodecimal system, signifies a period of a hundred and forty-four years.

pain is one and the same?[4] They said that the heresiarch was prompted only by the blasphemous intention of attributing the divine category of *being* to some simple coins and that at times he negated plurality and at other times did not. They argued: if equality implies identity, one would also have to admit that the nine coins are one.

Unbelievably, these refutations were not definitive. A hundred years after the problem was stated, a thinker no less brilliant than the heresiarch but of orthodox tradition formulated a very daring hypothesis. This happy conjecture affirmed that there is only one subject, that this indivisible subject is every being in the universe and that these beings are the organs and masks of the divinity. X is Y and is Z. Z discovers three coins because he remembers that X lost them; X finds two in the corridor because he remembers that the others have been found . . . The Eleventh Volume suggests that three prime reasons determined the complete victory of this idealist pantheism. The first, its repudiation of solipsism; the second, the possibility of preserving the psychological basis of the sciences; the third, the possibility of preserving the cult of the gods. Schopenhauer (the passionate and lucid Schopenhauer) formulates a very similar doctrine in the first volume of *Parerga und Paralipomena.*

The geometry of Tlön comprises two somewhat different disciplines: the visual and the tactile. The latter corresponds to our own geometry and is subordinated to the first. The basis of visual geometry is the surface, not the point. This geometry disregards parallel lines and declares that man in his movement modifies the forms which surround him. The basis of its arithmetic is the notion of indefinite numbers. They emphasize the importance of the concepts of greater and lesser, which our mathematicians symbolize as $>$ and $<$. They maintain that the operation of counting modifies quantities and converts them from indefinite into definite sums. The fact that several individuals who count the same quantity should obtain the same result is, for the psychologists, an example of association of ideas or of a good exercise of memory. We already know that in Tlön the subject of knowledge is one and eternal.

In literary practices the idea of a single subject is also all-powerful. It is uncommon for books to be signed. The concept of plagiarism does not exist: it has been established that all works are the creation of one author, who is atemporal and anonymous. The critics often invent authors: they select two dissimilar works—the *Tao Te Ching* and the *1001 Nights,* say—attribute them to the same writer and then determine most scrupulously the psychology of this interesting *homme de lettres . . .*

Their books are also different. Works of fiction contain a single plot,

[4] Today, one of the churches of Tlön Platonically maintains that a certain pain, a certain greenish tint of yellow, a certain temperature, a certain sound, are the only reality. All men, in the vertiginous moment of coitus, are the same man. All men who repeat a line from Shakespeare *are* William Shakespeare.

with all its imaginable permutations. Those of a philosophical nature invariably include both the thesis and the antithesis, the rigorous pro and con of a doctrine. A book which does not contain its counterbook is considered incomplete.

Centuries and centuries of idealism have not failed to influence reality. In the most ancient regions of Tlön, the duplication of lost objects is not infrequent. Two persons look for a pencil; the first finds it and says nothing; the second finds a second pencil, no less real, but closer to his expectations. These secondary objects are called *hrönir* and are, though awkward in form, somewhat longer. Until recently, the *hrönir* were the accidental products of distraction and forgetfulness. It seems unbelievable that their methodical production dates back scarcely a hundred years, but this is what the Eleventh Volume tells us. The first efforts were unsuccessful. However, the *modus operandi* merits description. The director of one of the state prisons told his inmates that there were certain tombs in an ancient river bed and promised freedom to whoever might make an important discovery. During the months preceding the excavation the inmates were shown photographs of what they were to find. This first effort proved that expectation and anxiety can be inhibitory; a week's work with pick and shovel did not manage to unearth anything in the way of a *hrön* except a rusty wheel of a period posterior to the experiment. But this was kept in secret and the process was repeated later in four schools. In three of them the failure was almost complete; in the fourth (whose director died accidentally during the first excavations) the students unearthed—or produced—a gold mask, an archaic sword, two or three clay urns and the moldy and mutilated torso of a king whose chest bore an inscription which it has not yet been possible to decipher. Thus was discovered the unreliability of witnesses who knew of the experimental nature of the search . . . Mass investigations produce contradictory objects; now individual and almost improvised jobs are preferred. The methodical fabrication of *hrönir* (says the Eleventh Volume) has performed prodigious services for archaeologists. It has made possible the interrogation and even the modification of the past, which is now no less plastic and docile than the future. Curiously, the *hrönir* of second and third degree—the *hrönir* derived from another *hrön,* those derived from the *hrön* of a *hrön*—exaggerate the aberrations of the initial one; those of fifth degree are almost uniform; those of ninth degree become confused with those of the second; in those of the eleventh there is a purity of line not found in the original. The process is cyclical: the *hrön* of twelfth degree begins to fall off in quality. Stranger and more pure than any *hrön* is, at times, the *ur:* the object produced through suggestion, educed by hope. The great golden mask I have mentioned is an illustrious example.

Things become duplicated in Tlön; they also tend to become effaced and lose their details when they are forgotten. A classic example is the doorway which survived so long as it was visited by a beggar and disappeared at his death. At times some birds, a horse, have saved the ruins of an amphitheater.

Postscript (1947). I reproduce the preceding article just as it appeared in the *Anthology of Fantastic Literature* (1940), with no omission other than that of a few metaphors and a kind of sarcastic summary which now seems frivolous. So many things have happened since then . . . I shall do no more than recall them here.

In March of 1941 a letter written by Gunnar Erfjord was discovered in a book by Hinton which had belonged to Herbert Ashe. The envelope bore a cancellation from Ouro Preto; the letter completely elucidated the mystery of Tlön. Its text corroborated the hypotheses of Martínez Estrada. One night in Lucerne or in London, in the early seventeenth century, the splendid history has its beginning. A secret and benevolent society (amongst whose members were Dalgarno and later George Berkeley) arose to invent a country. Its vague initial program included "hermetic studies," philanthropy and the cabala. From this first period dates the curious book by Andreä. After a few years of secret conclaves and premature syntheses it was understood that one generation was not sufficient to give articulate form to a country. They resolved that each of the masters should elect a disciple who would continue his work. This hereditary arrangement prevailed; after an interval of two centuries the persecuted fraternity sprang up again in America. In 1824, in Memphis (Tennessee), one of its affiliates conferred with the ascetic millionaire Ezra Buckley. The latter, somewhat disdainfully, let him speak—and laughed at the plan's modest scope. He told the agent that in America it was absurd to invent a country and proposed the invention of a planet. To this gigantic idea he added another, a product of his nihilism:[5] that of keeping the enormous enterprise secret. At that time the twenty volumes of the *Encyclopaedia Britannica* were circulating in the United States; Buckley suggested that a methodical encyclopedia of the imaginary planet be written. He was to leave them his mountains of gold, his navigable rivers, his pasture lands roamed by cattle and buffalo, his Negroes, his brothels and his dollars, on one condition: "The work will make no pact with the impostor Jesus Christ." Buckley did not believe in God, but he wanted to demonstrate to this nonexistent God that mortal man was capable of conceiving a world. Buckley was poisoned in Baton Rouge in 1828; in 1914 the society delivered to its collaborators, some three hundred in number, the last volume of the First Encyclopedia of Tlön. The edition was a secret one; its forty volumes (the vastest undertaking ever carried out by man) would be the basis for another more detailed edition, written not in English but in one of the languages of Tlön. This revision of an illusory world was called, provisionally, *Orbis Tertius* and one of its modest demiurgi was Herbert Ashe, whether as an agent

---

[5] Buckley was a freethinker, a fatalist and a defender of slavery.

of Gunnar Erfjord or as an affiliate, I do not know. His having received a copy of the Eleventh Volume would seem to favor the latter assumption. But what about the others?

In 1942 events became more intense. I recall one of the first of these with particular clarity and it seems that I perceived then something of its premonitory character. It happened in an apartment on Laprida Street, facing a high and light balcony which looked out toward the sunset. Princess Faucigny Lucinge had received her silverware from Poitiers. From the vast depths of a box embellished with foreign stamps, delicate immobile objects emerged: silver from Utrecht and Paris covered with hard heraldic fauna, and a samovar. Amongst them—with the perceptible and tenuous tremor of a sleeping bird—a compass vibrated mysteriously. The Princess did not recognize it. Its blue needle longed for magnetic north; its metal case was concave in shape; the letters around its edge corresponded to one of the alphabets of Tlön. Such was the first intrusion of this fantastic world into the world of reality.

I am still troubled by a stroke of chance which made me the witness of the second intrusion as well. It happened some months later, at a country store owned by a Brazilian in Cuchilla Negra: Amorim and I were returning from Sant' Anna. The River Tacuarembó had flooded and we were obliged to sample (and endure) the proprietor's rudimentary hospitality. He provided us with some creaking cots in a large room cluttered with barrels and hides. We went to bed, but were kept from sleeping until dawn by the drunken ravings of an unseen neighbor, who intermingled inextricable insults with snatches of *milongas*—or rather with snatches of the same *milonga*. As might be supposed, we attributed this insistent uproar to the store owner's fiery cane liquor. By daybreak, the man was dead in the hallway. The roughness of his voice had deceived us: he was only a youth. In his delirium a few coins had fallen from his belt, along with a cone of bright metal, the size of a die. In vain a boy tried to pick up this cone. A man was scarely able to raise it from the ground. I held it in my hand for a few minutes; I remember that its weight was intolerable and that after it was removed, the feeling of oppressiveness remained. I also remember the exact circle it pressed into my palm. This sensation of a very small and at the same time extremely heavy object produced a disagreeable impression of repugnance and fear. One of the local men suggested we throw it into the swollen river; Amorim acquired it for a few pesos. No one knew anything about the dead man, except that "he came from the border." These small, very heavy cones (made from a metal which is not of this world) are images of the divinity in certain regions of Tlön.

Here I bring the personal part of my narrative to a close. The rest is in the memory (if not in the hopes or fears) of all my readers. Let it suffice for me to recall or mention the following facts, with a mere brevity of words which the reflective recollection of all will enrich or amplify. Around 1944, a person doing research for the newspaper

The American (of Nashville, Tennessee) brought to light in a Memphis library the forty volumes of the First Encyclopedia of Tlön. Even today there is a controversy over whether this discovery was accidental or whether it was permitted by the directors of the still nebulous *Orbis Tertius*. The latter is most likely. Some of the incredible aspects of the Eleventh Volume (for example, the multiplication of the *hrönir*) have been eliminated or attenuated in the Memphis copies; it is reasonable to imagine that these omissions follow the plan of exhibiting a world which is not too incompatible with the real world. The dissemination of objects from Tlön over different countries would complement this plan . . .[6] The fact is that the international press infinitely proclaimed the "find." Manuals, anthologies, summaries, literal versions, authorized re-editions and pirated editions of the Greatest Work of Man flooded and still flood the earth. Almost immediately, reality yielded on more than one account. The truth is that it longed to yield. Ten years ago any symmetry with a semblance of order—dialectical materialism, anti-Semitism, Nazism—was sufficient to entrance the minds of men. How could one do other than submit to Tlön, to the minute and vast evidence of an orderly planet? It is useless to answer that reality is also orderly. Perhaps it is, but in accordance with divine laws—I translate: inhuman laws—which we never quite grasp. Tlön is surely a labyrinth, but it is a labyrinth devised by men, a labyrinth destined to be deciphered by men.

The contact and the habit of Tlön have disintegrated this world. Enchanted by its rigor, humanity forgets over and again that it is a rigor of chess masters, not of angels. Already the schools have been invaded by the (conjectural) "primitive language" of Tlön; already the teaching of its harmonious history (filled with moving episodes) has wiped out the one which governed in my childhood; already a fictitious past occupies in our memories the place of another, a past of which we know nothing with certainty—not even that it is false. Numismatology, pharmacology and archaeology have been reformed. I understand that biology and mathematics also await their avatars . . . A scattered dynasty of solitary men has changed the face of the world. Their task continues. If our forecasts are not in error, a hundred years from now someone will discover the hundred volumes of the Second Encyclopedia of Tlön.

Then English and French and mere Spanish will disappear from the globe. The world will be Tlön. I pay no attention to all this and go on revising, in the still days at the Adrogué hotel, an uncertain Quevedian translation (which I do not intend to publish) of Browne's *Urn Burial*.

---

[6] There remains, of course, the problem of the *material* of some objects.

Coffee

Richard Brautigan

A master of whimsy, Richard Brautigan was born in 1935 in Tacoma, Washington. At the age of sixteen, he was haunting the late-night cafes and winding streets of North Beach in San Francisco. His first novel, *Trout Fishing in America,* written largely while he was living in Bolinas, California, made him the darling of college students similarly preoccupied with nature, freaks, and the gentle things in life. Until they learned better, sporting-goods stores stocked and cheerfully sold copies of it. *The Pill "versus" the Springhill Mine Disaster,* a volume of verses, and *In Watermelon Sugar* solidified his reputation among the hip (all three are now available in a single paperback). *A Confederate General from Big Sur,* his second novel, *Revenge of the Lawn,* a collection of vignettes from which the following selection is taken, and *The Abortion* have broadened his popularity. His newest novel is *Plant This Book.*

Though he never attended college, he has been a poet-in-residence at a university and he has given readings across the country from Harvard to San Quentin. Brautigan offers an extraordinary world of life and love treated with uninhibited imagination. One critic has written that, "Brautigan wants to befriend the earth, not shake it. His style and wit transmit so much energy that energy itself becomes the message. Only a hedonist could cram so much life onto a single page." He now lives in a small, elegantly cluttered apartment in San Francisco. When he is not writing, he raps with his friends (Robert Creeley, Michael McClure, Joan Kyger, and others), rides buses around the city (he doesn't drive), or hitchhikes up to the country to see his adolescent daughter who lives with his former wife.

Sometimes life is merely a matter of coffee and whatever intimacy a cup of coffee affords. I once read something about coffee. The thing said that coffee is good for you; it stimulates all the organs.

I thought at first this was a strange way to put it, and not altogether pleasant, but as time goes by I have found out that it makes sense in its own limited way. I'll tell you what I mean.

Yesterday morning I went over to see a girl. I like her. Whatever we had going for us is gone now. She does not care for me. I blew it and wish I hadn't.

I rang the door bell and waited on the stairs. I could hear her moving around upstairs. The way she moved I could tell that she was getting up. I had awakened her.

Then she came down the stairs. I could feel her approach in my stomach. Every step she took stirred my feelings and led indirectly to her opening the door. She saw me and it did not please her.

Once upon a time it pleased her very much, last week. I wonder where it went, pretending to be naive.

"I feel strange now," she said. "I don't want to talk."

"I want a cup of coffee," I said, because it was the last thing in the world that I wanted. I said it in such a way that it sounded as if I were reading her a telegram from somebody else, a person who really wanted a cup of coffee, who cared about nothing else.

"All right," she said.

I followed her up the stairs. It was ridiculous. She had just put some clothes on. They had not quite adjusted themselves to her body. I could tell you about her ass. We went into the kitchen.

She took a jar of instant coffee off a shelf and put it on the table. She placed a cup next to it, and a spoon. I looked at them. She put a pan full of water on the stove and turned the gas on under it.

All this time she did not say a word. Her clothes adjusted themselves to her body. I won't. She left the kitchen.

Then she went down the stairs and outside to see if she had any mail. I didn't remember seeing any. She came back up the stairs and went into another room. She closed the door after her. I looked at the pan full of water on the stove.

I knew that it would take a year before the water started to boil. It was now October and there was too much water in the pan. That was the problem. I threw half the water into the sink.

The water would boil faster now. It would take only six months. The house was quiet.

I looked out at the back porch. There were sacks of garbage there. I stared at the garbage and tried to figure out what she had been eating lately by studying the containers and peelings and stuff. I couldn't tell a thing.

It was now March. The water started to boil. I was pleased by this.

I looked at the table. There was the jar of instant coffee, the empty cup and the spoon all laid out like a funeral service. These are the things that you need to make a cup of coffee.

When I left the house ten minutes later, the cup of coffee safely inside me like a grave, I said, "Thank you for the cup of coffee."

"You're welcome," she said. Her voice came from behind a closed door. Her voice sounded like another telegram. It was really time for me to leave.

I spent the rest of the day not making coffee. It was a comfort. And evening came. I had dinner in a restaurant and went to a bar. I had some drinks and talked to some people.

We were bar people and said bar things. None of them remembered, and the bar closed. It was two o'clock in the morning. I had to go outside. It was foggy and cold in San Francisco. I wondered about the fog and felt very human and exposed.

I decided to go visit another girl. We had not been friends for over a year. Once we were very close. I wondered what she was thinking about now.

I went over to her house. She didn't have a door bell. That was a small victory. One must keep track of all the small victories. I do, anyway.

She answered the door. She was holding a robe in front of herself. She didn't believe that she was seeing me. "What do you want?" she said, believing now that she was seeing me. I walked right into the house.

She turned and closed the door in such a way that I could see her profile. She had not bothered to wrap the robe completely around herself. She was just holding the robe in front of herself.

I could see an unbroken line of body running from her head to her feet. It looked kind of strange. Perhaps because it was so late at night.

"What do you want?" she said.

"I want a cup of coffee," I said. What a funny thing to say, to say again for a cup of coffee was not what I really wanted.

She looked at me and wheeled slightly on the profile. She was not pleased to see me. Let the AMA tell us that time heals. I looked at the unbroken line of her body.

"Why don't you have a cup of coffee with me?" I said. "I feel like talking to you. We haven't talked for a long time."

She looked at me and wheeled slightly on the profile. I stared at the unbroken line of her body. This was not good.

"It's too late," she said. "I have to get up in the morning. If you want a cup of coffee, there's instant in the kitchen. I have to go to bed."

The kitchen light was on. I looked down the hall into the kitchen. I didn't feel like going into the kitchen and having another cup of coffee by myself. I didn't feel like going to anybody else's house and asking them for a cup of coffee.

I realized that the day had been committed to a very strange pilgrimage, and I had not planned it that way. At least the jar of instant coffee was not on the table, beside an empty white cup and a spoon.

They say in the spring a young man's fancy turns to thoughts of love. Perhaps if he has enough time left over, his fancy can even make room for a cup of coffee.

Anecdotes of Mr. Keuner

Bertolt Brecht

Poet and playwright, Bertolt Brecht was born in Augsburg in 1898. Son of an industrialist, he studied medicine and served as an orderly in the army. After World War I, he became the *Dramaturg* for theaters in Munich and Berlin. In 1928, he converted to Marxism, and when Hitler assumed power, he fled to California via Denmark, Sweden, Finland, and the U.S.S.R. After acquitting himself skillfully before the Un-American Activities Committee, he returned to Europe in 1949 and soon settled in East Berlin to direct his own theater. The workers' revolt of 1953 deeply affected him, but he retained his faith in Marxist doctrine to the end (1956).

Brecht created what he called "epic" theater. By certain "distancing" devices, the spectator is reminded that he is only watching a play. Instead of becoming emotionally involved in the stage action (as in the theater of "illusion") he must remain a dispassionate observer and judge. By this means Brecht led people to obey their own intelligence, even if this meant rebelling against authority and abandoning the comfort of a fool's paradise.

"Anecdotes" is a series of personal aphorisms (Mr. Keuner is clearly the author's *alter ego,* even though his views contradict East German party orthodoxy) modestly addressed to the ordinary citizen as a wit-sharpener and a stimulator of social conscience. They illustrate as well as anything else in Brecht his two favorite sayings: "The truth is concrete" and "The imagination is the only truth." "Anecdotes" is taken from *Tales from the Calendar,* a collection of poems, stories, and sayings.

GOOD TURNS

As an example of how to do friends a good turn Mr K obliged with the following story. Three young men came to an old Arab and said: 'Our father has died. He has left us seventeen camels and stipulated in his will that the eldest should have half, the second a third and the youngest a ninth of the camels. Now we can't agree amongst ourselves on the division: you decide the matter.' The Arab thought about it and said: 'As I see it, you have one camel too few to share them out properly. I've only got one camel myself, but it's at your disposal. Take it and share them out and give me back only what's left over.' They thanked him for this good turn, took the camel with them and then divided the eighteen camels in such a way that the eldest got half—that is, nine—the second a third—that is, six—and the

SOURCE: Bertolt Brecht, *Tales from the Calendar,* trans. Stefan Brecht (Frankfurt: Suhrkamp Verlag, 1967), pp. 111, 112, 114, 116, 118, 120–121, 122–123, 124. Reprinted by permission of Suhrkamp Verlag & Stefan Brecht.

youngest a ninth—that is, two—of the camels. To their amazement when they had each led their camels aside, there was one over. This they took back to their old friend with renewed thanks.

Mr K called this the right sort of good turn, since it demanded no special sacrifice.

THE HELPLESS BOY

Mr K referred to the bad habit of suffering injustice in silence and related the following story: 'A passer-by asked a boy who was crying what was the cause of his unhappiness. "I'd saved two *groschen* to go to the pictures," said the lad, "and then a boy came and snatched one out of my hand," and he pointed to a boy who was some little way off. "And didn't you shout for help?" asked the man. "Yes, I did," said the boy and sobbed a bit harder. "Didn't anyone hear you?" the man went on, stroking him affectionately. "No," sobbed the boy. "Does that mean you can't shout any louder?" asked the man. "Then hand over the other one too." He took the last *groschen* out of his hand and walked on without turning a hair.'

FATHER TO THE THOUGHT

Mr K was criticized on the grounds that too often in his case the wish was father to the thought. Mr K replied: 'There never was a thought to which a wish was not father. The only thing you can argue about is: What wish? You may suspect that it is difficult to establish paternity, but that's no reason to suspect that a child has no father at all.'

MR K AND CATS

Mr K did not like cats. They did not seem to him friends of man, so he was not their friend either. 'If we had the same interests,' he said, 'their hostile attitude wouldn't worry me.' Yet Mr K was reluctant to shoo cats away from his chair. 'To lay oneself down to rest is a job of work,' he said. 'It deserves to succeed.' Also when cats miaowed outside his door he got out of bed, even when it was cold, to let them into the warmth. 'Their calculation is simple,' he said. 'If they cry, you open the door for them. If you stop opening the door for them, they stop crying. To cry is a step forward.'

SOCRATES

After reading a book on the history of philosophy, Mr K expressed disapproval of philosophers' attempts to represent things as unknowable in principle. 'When the Sophists claimed to know a great deal without having studied anything,' he said, 'the Sophist Socrates made the arrogant claim that he knew he knew nothing. One would have expected him to add: for I, too, have studied nothing. (To know something we have to study.) But he does not seem to have said anything further, and perhaps the immense applause which broke out after his first remark, and which lasted for two thousand years, would have drowned any further remark.'

IF SHARKS WERE PEOPLE

'If sharks were people,' the landlady's little daughter asked Mr K, 'would they be nicer to the little fishes?'

'Certainly,' he said. 'If sharks were people they would have enormous boxes built in the sea for the little fishes with all sorts of things to eat in them, plants as well as animal matter. They would see to it that the boxes always had fresh water and, in general, take hygienic measures of all kinds. For instance, if a little fish injured one of its fins, it would be bandaged at once, so that the sharks should not be deprived of it by an untimely death. To prevent the little fishes from growing depressed there would be big water festivals from time to time, for happy little fishes taste better than miserable ones. Of course there would also be schools in the big boxes. In these schools the little fishes would learn how to swim into the sharks' jaws. They would need geography, for example, so that when the big sharks were lazing about somewhere they could find them. The main thing, of course, would be the moral education of the little fishes. They would be taught that the greatest and finest thing is for a little fish to sacrifice its life gladly, and that they must all believe in the sharks, particularly when they promise a splendid future. They would impress upon the little fishes that this future could only be assured if they learnt obedience. The little fishes would have to guard against all base, materialistic, egotistic and Marxist tendencies, reporting at once to the sharks if any of their number manifested such tendencies. If sharks were people they would also, naturally, wage wars amongst themselves, to conquer foreign fish boxes and little foreign fishes. They would let their own little fishes fight these wars. They would teach the little fishes that there was a vast difference between themselves and the little fishes of other sharks. Little fishes, they would proclaim, are well known to be dumb, but they are silent in quite different languages and therefore cannot possibly understand each other. Each little fish which killed a few other little fishes in war—little enemy fishes, dumb in a different language—would have a little seaweed medal pinned on it and be awarded the title of Hero. If sharks were people they would also have art, naturally. There would be lovely pictures representing sharks' teeth in glorious colours, their jaws as positive pleasure grounds in which it would be a joy to gambol. The sea-bed theatres would show heroic little fishes swimming rapturously into sharks' jaws, and the music would be so beautiful that to its strains the little fishes, headed by the band, would pour dreamily into the sharks' jaws, lulled in the most delightful thoughts. There would also be a religion if sharks were people. It would teach that little fishes only really start to live inside the bellies of sharks. Moreover, if sharks were people, not all little fishes would be equal any more as they are now. Some of them would be given positions and be set over the others. The slightly bigger ones would even be allowed to gobble up the smaller ones. That would give nothing but pleasure to the sharks, since they would more often get larger morsels for themselves. And the bigger little fishes, those holding positions, would be responsible for keeping order among the little fishes, become teachers, officers, box-building engineers and so on. In short, the sea would only start being civilized if sharks were people.'

WAITING

Mr K waited for something for a day, then a week, and then a whole month. In the end he said: 'I could easily have waited a month, but not that day and not that week.'

THE ART OF NOT CORRUPTING

Mr K recommended a man to a merchant because of his incorruptibility. Two weeks later the merchant came back to Mr K and asked him: 'What did you mean by incorruptibility?' Mr K said: 'When I say the man you're employing is incorruptible, I mean: you can't corrupt him.' 'Is that so?' said the merchant glumly. 'Well, I have reason to fear that your man lets himself be corrupted even by my enemies.' 'I don't know anything about that,' said Mr K without much interest. 'But when it comes to me, he always agrees with everything I say,' cried the merchant bitterly, 'so he lets himself be corrupted by me too!' Mr K smiled conceitedly. 'He doesn't let himself be corrupted by me,' he said.

LOVE OF NATION, HATRED OF NATIONALISM

Mr K did not think it necessary to live in any particular country. 'I can go hungry anywhere,' he said. But one day he went through a town occupied by the enemy of the country in which he was living. One of the enemy's officers came towards him and forced him to step off the pavement. Mr K stepped off and became aware that he was furious with this man, and not only with this man, but even more with the country from which the man came. So that he wished it could be wiped off the face of the earth. 'Why,' asked Mr K, 'did I become a nationalist for that moment? Through encountering a nationalist. That's why stupidity has to be stamped out, for it makes stupid those who encounter it.'

STARVING

Mr K, on being asked about his country, had said: 'I can go hungry anywhere.' A literal-minded listener now asked him how it came about that he talked of going hungry whereas in fact he had enough to eat. Mr K justified himself by saying: 'What I probably meant to say was that I can live anywhere if I want to live where hunger exists. I grant you there is a great difference between whether I myself go hungry or whether I live where hunger exists. But may I plead in extenuation that, for me, to live where hunger exists, even if not quite as bad as going hungry, is nevertheless pretty bad. After all, it would be of no importance to others if I went hungry, what is important is that I am against the existence of hunger.'

TOLERABLE AFFRONT

A colleague of Mr K was accused of having an unfriendly attitude to him. 'Yes, but only behind my back,' said Mr K in his defence.

TWO TOWNS

Mr K preferred town B to town A. 'In town A,' he said, 'people are fond of me; but in town B they were friendly to me. In town A people made themselves useful to me; but in town B they needed me. In town A I was asked to dinner; but in town B I was asked into the kitchen.'

ON MEETING AGAIN

A man who had not seen Mr K for a long time greeted him with the words: 'You haven't changed at all.'

'Oh!' said Mr K and turned pale.

The Slaying of the Dragon

Dino Buzzati

Dino Buzzati was born in 1906 in Belluno, Italy, and died in 1972. He worked steadily on the staff of the Milan newspaper *Corriere della Sera.* He launched his literary career with two mountain tales that may be interpreted as children's fables or as moralities for adults. As a vehicle for his weird and uncanny tales, charged like those of Borges with Kafkaesque symbolism, he developed a deliberately flat and unembroidered style. He achieved his greatest success with *The Tartar Steppe* (1952), about a frontier garrison waiting for a chance that never comes to prove its courage. *Larger Than Life* (1962) followed several books of "metaphysical fables" and short stories. *Love Affair* (1965) departs from his Kafkaesque manner, a story of a middle-aged man enslaved by a vulgar minx. The following selection, from *Catastrophe* (1965), is clearly the work of a man who has seen the consequences of two major wars.

In May 1902 a peasant in the service of Count Gerol, one Giosue Longo, who often went hunting in the mountains, reported that he had seen a large animal, resembling a dragon, in Valle Secca. Palissano, the last village in the valley, had long cherished a legend that one such monster was still living in certain arid passes in the region. But no one had ever taken it seriously. Yet on this occasion Longo's obvious sanity, the exactitude of his account, the absolutely accurate and unwavering repetition of details of the event convinced people that there might be something in it and Count Martino Gerol decided to go and find out. Naturally he was not thinking in terms of a dragon; but it was possible that some huge rare serpent was still living in those uninhabited valleys.

He was to be accompanied on the expedition by the governor of the province Quinto Andronico and his beautiful and intrepid wife, the naturalist Professor Inghirami and by his colleague Fusti, who was an expert in taxidermy. Quinto Andronico was a weak, sceptical man and had known for some time that his wife felt drawn to Count Gerol, but this did not worry him. In fact he agreed willingly when Maria suggested that they should accompany the count on his hunt. He was not the least bit jealous, nor even envious, although Gerol was greatly superior to him in wealth, youth, good looks, strength and courage.

SOURCE: Dino Buzzati, *Catastrophe,* trans. Judith Landry (London: Calder and Boyars Ltd., 1965), pp. 88–101.

Two carriages left the town shortly after midnight with an escort of eight mounted hunters and arrived at Palissano at about six the following morning. Gerol, Maria and the two naturalists slept; only Andronico remained awake and he stopped the carriage in front of the house of an old friend of his, the doctor Taddei. After a few moments the doctor, woken by a coachman and still half asleep, with a nightcap on his head, appeared at a first floor window. Andronico greeted him jovially from below and explained the object of the expedition, expecting his listener to burst out laughing at the mention of dragons. To his surprise Taddei shook his head disapprovingly.

'I don't think I'd go, if I were you,' he said firmly.

'Why not? Don't you think there's anything to it? You think it's all a lot of nonsense?'

'I don't know about that,' replied the doctor. 'No, personally I think there is a dragon, though I've never seen it. But I wouldn't get involved in this business. I don't like the sound of it.'

'Don't like the sound of it? Do you mean you really believe in the dragon?'

'My dear sir, I'm an old man,' said the doctor, 'and I've seen many things. It may be a lot of nonsense, but it may also be true; if I were you, I wouldn't get involved. And I warn you: the way is hard to find, the rocks are very unsafe, you only need a gust of wind to precipitate sheer disaster, and there isn't a drop of water. Give up the whole thing—why not go down to the Crocetta (he pointed towards a rounded grassy hill rising behind the village), you'll find plenty of hares there.' He was silent for a moment, then added: 'I assure you, I wouldn't go. I once heard it said—but it's useless, you'll only laugh . . .'

'Why should I laugh?' protested Andronico. 'Please go on.'

'Well, some people say that this dragon gives out smoke, and that it's poisonous and a small quantity can kill you.'

Forgetting his promise, Andronico laughed loudly. 'I always knew that you were reactionary,' he snorted, 'reactionary and eccentric. But this is too much. You're medieval, my dear Taddei. I'll see you this evening, and I'll be sporting the dragon's head.'

He waved good-bye, climbed back into the carriage and ordered the coach to move on. Giosue Longo, who was one of the hunters and knew the way, went at the head of the convoy.

'What was that old man shaking his head at?' enquired Maria, who had woken up in the interim.

'Nothing,' replied Andronico. 'It was only old Taddei, who's an amateur vet; we were talking about foot and mouth disease.'

'And the dragon?' enquired Count Gerol, who was sitting opposite him. 'Did you ask him about the dragon?'

'No, I didn't, to be quite honest,' replied the governor. 'I didn't want to be laughed at. I told him we'd come up here to do a bit of hunting, that's all I said.'

The passengers felt their weariness vanish as the sun rose; the horses moved faster and the coachmen began to hum.

'Taddei used to be our family doctor. Once'—it was the governor speaking—'he had a fashionable practice. Then suddenly he retired and went into the country, perhaps because of some disappointment in love. Then he must have been involved in some other trouble and came to this one-eyed place. Lord knows where he could go from here; he'll be a sort of dragon himself soon.'

'What nonsense!' said Maria, rather annoyed. 'Always talking about the dragon—you've talked of nothing else since we left and it's really becoming rather boring.'

'It was your idea to come,' replied her husband, mildly amused. 'Anyway, how could you know what we were talking about if you were asleep the whole way? Or were you just pretending?'

Maria did not reply but looked worriedly out of the window at the mountains, which were becoming higher, steeper and more arid. At the far end of the valley there appeared a chaotic succession of peaks, mostly conical in shape and bare of woods or meadows, yellowish in colour and incredibly bleak. The scorching sunlight clothed them in a hard, strong light of their own.

It was about nine o'clock when the carriages came to a standstill because the road came to an end. As they climbed down, the hunting party realised that they were now right in the heart of those sinister mountains. On close inspection the rock of which they were made looked rotten and friable as though they were one vast landslide from top to bottom.

'Look, this is where the path starts,' said Longo, pointing to a trail of footsteps leading upwards towards the mouth of a small valley. It was about three-quarters of an hour's journey from there to the Burel, where the dragon had been seen.

'Have you seen about the water?' Andronico asked the hunters.

'There are four flasks, and two of wine, your Excellency,' one of them answered. 'That should be enough . . .'

Odd. But now that they were so far from the town, locked in the mountains, the idea of the dragon began to seem less absurd. The travellers looked around them but saw no signs of anything reassuring. Yellowish peaks where no human being had ever trod, endless little valleys winding off into the distance: complete desolation.

They walked without speaking: first went the hunters with the guns, culverins and other hunting equipment, then Maria and lastly the two naturalists. Fortunately the path was still in the shade; the sun would have been merciless amid all that yellow earth.

The valley leading to the Burel was narrow and winding too; there was no stream in its bed and no grass or plants growing on its sides, only stones and debris; no birdsong or babble of water, only the occasional hiss of gravel.

At a certain point a young man appeared below them, walking faster than the hunting party and with a dead goat slung over his shoulders. 'He's going to the dragon,' said Longo, as if it were the most natural thing in the world. The inhabitants of Palissano, he then explained, were highly superstitious and sent a goat to the Burel every morning to placate the monster. The young men of the region took it in turns to take the offering. If the dragon was heard to roar, this portended untold disaster; all kinds of misfortunes might follow.

'And the dragon eats the goat every day?' enquired Count Gerol, jokingly.

'There's nothing left of it the next day, that's for certain.'

'Not even the bones?'

'No, not even the bones. It takes the goat into the cave to eat it.'

'But couldn't it be someone from the village who eats the goat?' asked the governor. 'Everyone knows the way. Has no one really ever seen the dragon actually take the goat?'

'I don't know, your Excellency,' replied the hunter.

Meanwhile the young man with the goat had caught up with them.

'Hey there, young man!' called the Count Gerol in his usual stentorian tones, 'how much do you want for that goat?'

'I can't sell it, sir,' he replied.

'Not even for ten crowns?'

'Well, I could go and get another one, I suppose . . .' he weakened. 'For ten crowns . . .'

'What do you want the goat for?' Andronico enquired. 'Not to eat, I trust?'

'You'll see in due course,' replied Gerol evasively.

One of the hunters put the goat over his shoulders, the young man from Palissano set off back to the village (obviously to get another animal for the dragon) and the whole group moved off again.

After another hour's journey they finally arrived. The valley suddenly opened out into a vast rugged amphitheatre, the Burel, surrounded by crumbling walls of orange coloured earth and rock. Right in the centre, on top of a cone-shaped heap of debris, was a black opening: the dragon's cave.

'That's it,' said Longo. They stopped quite near it, on a gravelly terrace which offered an excellent observation point, about thirty feet above the level of the cave and almost directly in front of it. The terrace had the added advantage of not being accessible from below because it stood at the top of an almost vertical wall. Maria could watch from there in absolute safety.

They were all quiet, listening hard, but they could hear nothing except the endless silence of the mountains, broken by the occasional swish of gravel. Here and there lumps of earth would give way suddenly, streams of pebbles would pour down the mountain side and die down again gradually. The whole countryside seemed to be in a state of constant dilapidation: these were mountains abandoned by their creator, being allowed to fall quietly to pieces.

'What if the dragon doesn't come out today?' enquired Quinto Andronico.

'I've got the goat,' answered Gerol. 'You seem to forget that.'

Then they understood: the animal would act as a bait to entice the dragon out of its lair.

They began their preparations: two hunters struggled up to a height of about twenty yards above the entrance to the cave, to be able to hurl down stones if necessary. Another placed the goat on the gravelly expanse outside its cave. Others were posted at either side, well-protected by large stones, with the culverins and guns. Andronico stayed where he was, intending to remain a spectator.

Maria was silent; her former boldness had vanished altogether. Although she wouldn't admit it, she would have given anything to be able to go back. She looked round at the walls of rock, at the scars of the old landslides and the debris of the recent ones, at the pillars of red earth which looked to her as though they might collapse any minute. Her husband, Count Gerol, the two naturalists and the hunters seemed negligible protection in the face of such solitude.

When the dead goat had been placed in front of the cave, they began to wait. It was shortly after ten o'clock and the sun now filtered into every crevice of the Burel, filling it with its immense heat. Waves of heat were reflected back from one side to the other. The hunters organised a rough canopy with the carriage covers for the governor and his wife, to shield them from the sun; Maria drank avidly.

'Watch out!' shouted Count Gerol suddenly from his point of vantage on a rock down on the scree, where he stood with a rifle in his hand and an iron club hanging from his hip.

A shudder went through the company, and they held their breath as a live creature emerged from the mouth of the cave. 'The dragon! The dragon!' shouted several of the hunters, though whether in joy or terror it was not clear.

The creature moved into the light with the hesitant sway of a snake. So here it was, this legendary monster whose voice made a whole village quake.

'Oh, how horrible!' exclaimed Maria with evident relief, having expected something far worse.

'Come on, courage!' shouted one of the hunters jokingly. Everyone recovered their self-assurance.

'It looks like a small Ceratosaurus!' said Professor Inghirami, now sufficiently confident to turn to the problems of science.

The monster wasn't really very terrible, in fact, little more than six feet long, with a head like a crocodile's only shorter, a long lizard-like neck, a rather swollen thorax, a short tail and floppy sort of crest along its back. But its awkward movements, its clayey parchment colour (with the occasional green streak here and there) and the general apparent flabbiness of its body were even more reassuring than its small dimensions. The general impression was one of extreme age. If it was a dragon, it was a decrepit dragon, possibly moribund.

'Take that!' scoffed one of the hunters who had climbed above the mouth of the cave. And he threw a stone down towards the animal.

It hit the dragon exactly on the skull. There was a hollow 'toc,' like the sound of something hitting a gourd. Maria felt a movement of revulsion.

The blow had been hard but not sufficient. The reptile was still for a few moments, as though stunned, and then began to shake its head and neck from side to side as if in pain. It opened and closed its jaws to reveal a set of sharp teeth, but it made no sound. Then it moved across the gravel towards the goat.

'Made you giddy did they, eh?' cackled Count Gerol, suddenly abandoning his arrogant pose. He seemed eager and excited in anticipation of the massacre.

A shot from the culverin, from a distance of about thirty yards, missed its mark. The explosion tore the stagnant air; the rock faces howled with the echo, setting in motion innumerable diminutive landslides.

There was a second shot almost immediately. The bullet hit the animal on one of its back paws, producing a stream of blood.

'Look at it leaping around!' exclaimed Maria; she too was now enthralled by this show of cruelty. In the agony of its wound the animal had started to jump around in anguished circles. It drew its shattered leg after it, leaving a trail of black liquid on the gravel.

At last the reptile managed to reach the goat and to seize it with its teeth. It was about to turn round when Gerol, to advertise his own daring, went right up to it and shot it in the head from about six feet away.

A sort of whistling sound came from its jaws; and it was as though it were trying to control itself, to repress its anger, not to make as much noise as it could, as though some incentive unknown to mere men were causing it to keep its temper. The bullet from the rifle had hit it in the eye. After firing the shot Count Gerol drew back promptly and waited for it to collapse. But it didn't collapse, the spark of life within it seemed as persistent as a fire fed by pitch. The ball of lead lodged firmly in its eye, the monster calmly proceeded to devour the goat and its neck swelled like rubber as the gigantic mouthfuls went down. Then it went back to the foot of the rocks and began to climb up the rock face beside the cave. It climbed with difficulty, as the earth kept giving way beneath its feet, but it was obviously seeking a way of escape. Above it was an arch of clear, pale sky; the sun dried up the trails of blood almost immediately.

'It's like a cockroach in a basin,' muttered Andronico to himself.

'What did you say?' enquired his wife.

'Nothing, nothing,' he replied.

'I wonder why it doesn't go into its cave,' remarked Professor Inghirami, calmly noting all the scientific aspects of the scene.

'It's probably afraid of being trapped,' suggested Fusti.

'But it must be completely stunned. And I very much doubt whether a Ceratosaurus is capable of such reasoning. A Ceratosaurus . . .'

'It's not a Ceratosaurus,' objected Fusti. 'I've restored several for museums, but they don't look like that. Where are the spines on its tail?'

'It keeps them hidden,' replied Inghirami. 'Look at that swollen abdomen. It tucks its tail underneath and that's why they can't be seen.'

As they were talking one of the hunters, the one who had fired the shot with the culverin, came running hurriedly towards the terrace where Andronico was, with the evident intention of leaving.

'Where are you going?' shouted Gerol. 'Stay in your position until we've finished.'

'I'm going,' the hunter answered firmly. 'I don't like it. This isn't what I call hunting.'

'What do you mean? That you're afraid? Is that it?'

'No sir, I'm not afraid.'

'You're afraid, I tell you, or you'd stay in your place.'

'No I'm not. But you, sir, should be ashamed of yourself.'

'Ashamed of myself?' cursed Martino Gerol. 'You young swine. You're from Palissano, I suppose, and a coward. Get away before I teach you a lesson.'

'And where are *you* off to now, Beppi?' he shouted again, seeing another hunter moving off.

'I'm going too, sir. I don't want to be involved in this horrible business.'

'Cowards!' shrieked Gerol. 'Cowards, you'd pay for this if I could get at you!'

'It isn't fear, sir,' repeated the second hunter. 'It's not fear. But this will end badly, you'll see.'

'I'll show you how it'll end right now!' and seizing a stone from the ground, the count hurled it at the hunter with all his force. But it missed.

There was a few moments pause while the dragon scrambled about on the rock without managing to climb any higher. Earth and stones gave way and forced him back to his starting point. Apart from the sound of falling stones, there was silence.

Then Andronico spoke. 'How much longer is this going to go on?' he shouted to Gerol. 'It's fearfully hot. Finish off the animal once and for all, can't you? Why torture it like that, even if it is a dragon?'

'It's not my fault,' answered Gerol, annoyed, 'can't you see that it's refusing to die? It's got a bullet in its skull and it's more lively than ever.'

He stopped speaking as the young man they had seen earlier came over the brow of the rock with another goat over his shoulders. Amazed at the sight of the men, their weapons, at the traces of blood and above all the dragon (which he had never seen out of its cave) struggling on the rocks, he had stood still in his tracks and was staring at the whole strange scene.

'Oy! Young man!' shouted Gerol. 'How much do you want for that goat?'

'Nothing, I can't sell it!' he replied. 'I wouldn't give it you for its weight in gold. But what have you done to the dragon?' he added, narrowing his eyes to look at the blood-stained monster.

'We're here to settle the matter once and for all. You should be pleased. No more goats from tomorrow.'

'Why not?'

'Because the dragon will be dead,' replied the count smiling.

'But you can't you can't do that,' exclaimed the young man in terror.

'Don't you start too,' shouted Gerol. 'Give me that goat at once.'

'I said no,' the young man answered firmly, drawing back.

'Good God!' The count rushed at him, punched him full in the face, seized the goat from his back and threw him to the ground.

'You'll regret this one day, I tell you, you see if you don't,' swore the young man quietly as he picked himself up, not daring to react more positively.

But Count Gerol had turned his back on him.

But now the whole valley basin was ablaze with the sun's heat and the glare from the yellow scree, the rocks, the stones and the scree again was such that they could hardly keep their eyes open; there was nothing, absolutely nothing, remotely restful to the eye.

Maria became more and more thirsty and drink gave no relief. 'Good Lord, what heat,' she moaned. Even the sight of Count Gerol had begun to pall.

In the meantime dozens of men had appeared, apparently springing from the earth itself. They had presumably come up from Palissano at the news that strangers were up at the Burel and they stood motionless on the brows of the various peaks of yellow earth, watching without a word.

'Fine audience you've got now,' remarked Andronico in an attempt at a joke, directed at Gerol who was involved in some manoeuvres concerning the goat with two hunters.

The young man looked up and saw the strangers staring at him. He assumed an expression of disdain and continued with what he was doing.

The dragon, exhausted, had slithered down the rock face on to the gravel; it was lying there, motionless except for its swollen stomach, which was still throbbing.

'Ready!' shouted one of the hunters, lifting the goat from the ground with Gerol's help. They had opened its stomach and put in an explosive charge with a fuse attached.

The count then advanced fearlessly across the scree until he was about thirty feet from the dragon, put the goat carefully on the ground and walked away, unwinding the fuse.

They had to wait for half an hour before the creature moved. The strangers standing on the crests of the hills stood like statues: silent even among themselves, their faces expressed cold disapproval. Indifferent to the sun which was now immensely strong, they stared fixedly at the reptile, as though willing it not to move.

But at last the dragon, with another bullet in its back, turned suddenly, saw the goat and dragged itself slowly towards it. It was about to stretch out its head and seize its prey when the count lit the fuse. The spark ran rapidly along it, reached the goat and the charge exploded.

The report was not loud, much less so in fact than the culverin shots: sharp yet muffled, like a plank breaking. Yet the dragon's body was hurled violently backwards, its belly had obviously been ripped open. Once again the head began to move slowly from side to side as though it were saying no, that it wasn't fair, that they had been too cruel and that there was now no more it could do.

The count laughed gleefully, but this time he laughed alone.

'Oh how awful! That's enough!' gasped Maria, covering her face with her hands.

'Yes,' said her husband slowly, 'I agree, this may end badly.'

The monster was lying in a pool of black blood, apparently exhausted. And now from each of its two flanks there rose a column of dark smoke, one on the left and one on the right, two slow-moving plumes rising, it seemed, with difficulty.

'Do you see that?' said Inghirami to his colleague.

'I do,' affirmed the other.

'Two blow-holes just like those of the Ceratosaurus, the so-called opercula hammeriana.'

'No,' said Fusti, 'it's not a Ceratosaurus.'

At this juncture Gerol emerged from behind the boulder where he'd been hiding and came forwards to deliver the final blow. He was right in the middle of the stretch of gravel with his iron club in his hand, when the assembled company gave a shriek.

For a moment Gerol thought it was a shout of triumph for the slaying of the dragon. Then he became aware of movement behind him. He turned round sharply and saw—ridiculous—two pathetic little creatures tumbling out of the cave and coming towards him at some speed. Two small half-formed reptiles no more than two feet long, diminutive versions of the dying dragon. Two small dragons, its children, probably driven out of the cave by hunger.

It was a matter of minutes. The count gave a wonderfully skilful performance. 'Take that! and that!' he shouted gleefully, swinging the iron club. And two blows were enough. Aimed strongly and decisively, the club struck the two little monsters one after the other and smashed in their heads like glass bowls. They collapsed and lay dead looking, from a distance, like half-deflated bagpipes.

But now the strangers, without a word, turned and fled up the stony gulleys as though from some unexpected danger. Without making a sound, without dislodging a pebble or turning for a moment to look at the dragon's cave, they disappeared as mysteriously as they had come.

Now the dragon was moving again—it seemed as though it were never going to make the final effort to die. Dragging itself like a snail and still giving out two puffs of smoke, it went towards the two little dead creatures. When it had reached them it collapsed on to the stones, stretched out its head with infinite difficulty and began to lick them gently, perhaps hoping to resuscitate them.

Finally the dragon seemed to collect all its remaining strength: it raised its neck towards the sky to emit, first very softly but then with a rising crescendo, an unspeakable, incredible howl, a sound neither animal nor human but one so full of loathing that even Count Gerol stood still, paralysed with horror.

Now they saw why it had not wanted to go back into its den (where it could have found shelter) and why it hadn't roared or howled but merely hissed. The dragon was thinking of its children, to save them it had given up its own hope of escape; for if it had hidden in its cave the men would have followed it and discovered its young; and had it made any noise, the little creatures would have come out to see what was happening. Only now, once it had seen them die, did the monster give this terrible shriek.

It was asking for help, and for vengeance for its children. But from whom? From the mountains, parched and uninhabited? From the birdless, cloudless sky, from those men who were torturing it? The shriek pierced the walls of rock and the dome of the sky, it filled the whole world. Unreasonably enough it seemed completely impossible that there should be no reply.

'Who can it be calling?' said Andronico, trying in vain to adopt a lighthearted tone. 'Who is it calling? There's no one coming, as far as I can see.'

'Oh if only it would die!' said the woman.

But the dragon would not make up its mind to die even though Count Gerol, suddenly maddened by the desire to conclude the business once and for all, shot at it with his rifle. Two shots. In vain. The dragon continued to lick its dead children; ever more slowly, yet surely, a whitish liquid was welling up in its unhurt eye.

'The saurian!' exclaimed Professor Inghirami. 'Look, it's crying!'

The governor said: 'It's late. That's enough, Martino, it's time to go.'

Seven times the monster raised its voice, and the rocks and sky resounded. The seventh time it seemed as though the sound were never going to end, but then it suddenly ceased, dropped like a plumb-line, vanished into silence.

In the deathly quiet that followed there was a sound of coughing. Covered with dust, his face drawn with effort, weariness and emotion, Count Gerol, throwing his rifle down among the stones, came across the debris coughing, with one hand pressed to his chest.

'What is it?' asked Andronico, no longer joking but with a strange presentiment of disaster. 'What's happened?'

'Nothing,' said Gerol, trying to sound unconcerned. 'I just swallowed a bit of that smoke.'

'What smoke?'

Gerol didn't reply but indicated the dragon with his hand. The monster was lying still, its head stretched out on the stones; except for the two slight plumes of smoke, it looked very dead indeed.

'I think it's all over,' said Andronico.

It did indeed seem so. The last breath of obstinate life was coming from the dragon's mouth.

No one had answered his call, no one in the whole world had responded. The mountains were quite still, even the diminutive landslides seemed to have been reabsorbed, the sky was clear without the slightest cloud and the sun was setting. No one, either from this world or the next, had come to avenge the massacre. Man had blotted out this last remaining stain from the world, man so powerful and cunning that wherever he goes he establishes wise laws for maintaining order, irreproachable man who works so hard for the cause of progress and cannot bring himself to allow the survival of dragons, even in the heart of the mountains; man had been the executioner, and recrimination would have been pointless.

What man had done was right, absolutely in accordance with the law. Yet it seemed impossible that no one should have answered the last appeal. Andronico, his wife and the hunters all wanted to escape from the place without more ado; even the two naturalists were willing to give up the usual embalming procedure in order to get away more quickly.

The men from the village had disappeared as though they had felt forebodings of disaster. The shadows climbed the walls of loose rock. The two plumes of smoke continued to rise from the dragon's shrivelled carcass, curling slightly in the still air. All seemed over now, an unhappy incident to be forgotten as soon as possible. But Count Gerol went on coughing. Exhausted, he was seated on a boulder and his friends around him did not dare speak to him. Even the fearless Maria averted her gaze. The only sound was his sharp coughing. All attempts at controlling it were unsuccessful: there was a sort of fire burning ever deeper within him.

'I knew it,' whispered Andronico to his wife who was trembling a little. 'I knew it would end badly.'

Games Without End

Italo Calvino

Novelist, short-story writer, and editor, Italo Calvino was born in San Remo, Italy, in 1923, the son of the curator of the botanic gardens there. His first book, based on his experiences with the Italian partisans between 1943 and 1945, won the Premio Riccione in 1947 and appeared in English as *The Path to the Nest of Spiders* (1956). In 1947, he joined the publishing firm of Einaudi and is now on the editorial board. He is also co-editor of the controversial literary magazine *Il menabo*. He is currently living in France.

His selected short stories were published here as *Adam, One Afternoon* (1957), and two of his novels are available in English: *The Baron in the Trees* (1959) and *The Non-Existent Knight* (1962). Calvino's imagination explores the past of chivalry and castles and Italian noblemen who take to the trees and never come down, but he is writing in reality about our own world—the difficulties of communicating with one another, of coming to accord with ourselves and with nature.

Cosmicomics (1968), from which this selection is taken, is a series of linked fables, in which Qfwfq, the old, or ageless, or even young, narrator recalls his experiences at various stages of evolution. The theme running through all these witty fantasies is the sense in most primitive forms of better things to come, a touching receptivity toward "the future."

When the galaxies become more remote, the rarefaction of the universe is compensated for by the formation of further galaxies composed of newly created matter. To maintain a stable median density of the universe it is sufficient to create a hydrogen atom every 250 million years for 40 cubic centimeters of expanding space. (*This steady state theory, as it is known, has been opposed to the other hypothesis, that the universe was born at a precise moment as the result of a gigantic explosion.*)

I was only a child, but I was already aware of it,—*Qfwfq narrated,* I was acquainted with all the hydrogen atoms, one by one, and when a new atom cropped up, I noticed it right away. When I was a kid, the only playthings we had in the whole universe were the hydrogen atoms, and we played with them all the time, I and another youngster my age whose name was Pfwfp.

What sort of games? That's simple enough to explain. Since space was curved, we sent the atoms rolling along its curve, like so many marbles, and the kid whose atom went farthest won the game. When you made your shot you had to be careful, to calculate the effects, the trajectories, you had to know how to exploit the magnetic fields and the fields of gravity, otherwise the ball left the tract and was eliminated from the contest.

The rules were the usual thing: with one atom you could hit another of your atoms and send it farther ahead, or else you could knock your opponent's atom out of the way. Of course, we were careful not to throw them too hard, because when two hydrogen atoms are knocked together, click! a deuterium atom might be formed, or even a helium atom, and for the purposes of the game, such atoms were out: what's more, if one of the two belonged to your opponent, you had to give him an atom of your own to pay him back.

You know how the curve of space is shaped: a little ball would go spinning along and then one fine moment it would start off down the slope and you couldn't catch it. So, as we went on playing, the number of atoms in the game kept getting smaller, and the first to run out of atoms was the loser.

Then, right at the crucial moment, these new atoms started cropping up. Obviously, there's quite a difference between a new atom and a used one: the new atoms were shiny, bright, fresh, and moist, as if with dew. We made new rules: one new was worth three old; and the new ones, as they were formed, were to be shared between us, fifty-fifty.

In this way our game never ended, and it never became boring either, because every time we found new atoms it seemed as if the game were new as well, as if we were playing it for the first time.

Then, what with one thing and another, as the days went by, the game grew less exciting. There were no more new atoms to be seen: the ones we lost couldn't be replaced, our shots became weak, hesitant, because we were afraid to lose the few pieces still in the game, in that barren, even space.

Pfwfp was changed, too: he became absent-minded, wandered off and couldn't be found when it was his turn to shoot; I would call him, but there was never an answer, and then he would turn up half an hour later.

"Go on, it's your turn. Aren't you in the game any more?"

"Of course I'm in the game. Don't rush me. I'm going to shoot now."

"Well, if you keep going off by yourself, we might as well stop playing!"

"Hmph! You're only making all this fuss because you're losing."

This was true: I hadn't any atoms left, whereas Pfwfp, somehow or other, always had one in reserve. If some new atoms didn't turn up for us to share, I hadn't a hope of getting even with him.

The next time Pfwfp went off, I followed him, on tiptoe. As long as I was present, he seemed to be strolling about aimlessly, whistling: but once he was out of my sight he started trotting through space, intent, like somebody who has a definite purpose in mind. And what this purpose of his was—this treachery, as you shall see—I soon discovered:

Pfwfp knew all the places where new atoms were formed and every now and then he would take a little walk, to collect them on the spot the minute they were dished up, then he would hide them. This was why he was never short of atoms to play with!

But before putting them in the game, incorrigible cheat that he was, he set about disguising them as old atoms, rubbing the film of the electrons until it was worn and dull, to make me believe this was an old atom he had had all along and had just happened to find in his pocket.

And that wasn't the whole story: I made a quick calculation of the atoms played and I realized they were only a small part of those he had stolen and hid. Was he piling up a store of hydrogen? What was he going to do with it? What did he have in mind? I suddenly had a suspicion: Pfwfp wanted to build a universe of his own, a brand-new universe.

From that moment on, I couldn't rest easy: I had to get even with him. I could have followed his example: now that I knew the places, I could have gone there a little ahead of him and grabbed the new atoms the moment they were born, before he could get his hands on them! But that would have been too simple. I wanted to catch him in a trap worthy of his own perfidy. First of all, I started making fake atoms: while he was occupied with his treacherous raids, I was in a secret storeroom of mine, pounding and mixing and kneading all the material I had at my disposal. To tell you the truth, this material didn't amount to much: photoelectric radiations, scrapings from magnetic fields, a few neutrons collected in the road; but by rolling it into balls and wetting it with saliva, I managed to make it stick together. In other words, I prepared some little corpuscles that, on close inspection, were obviously not made of hydrogen or any other identifiable element, but for somebody in a hurry, like Pfwfp, who rushed past and stuck them furtively into his pocket, they looked like real hydrogen, and spanking new.

So while he still didn't suspect a thing, I preceded him in his rounds. I had made a careful mental note of all the places.

Space is curved everywhere, but in some places it's more curved than in others: like pockets or bottlenecks or niches, where the void is crumpled up. These niches are where, every two hundred and fifty million years, there is a slight tinkling sound and a shiny hydrogen atom is formed like a pearl between the valves of an oyster. I walked past, pocketed the atom, and set the fake atom in its place. Pfwfp didn't notice a thing: predatory, greedy, he filled his pockets with that rubbish, as I was accumulating all the treasures that the universe cherished in its bosom.

The fortunes of our games underwent a change: I always had new atoms to shoot, while Pfwfp's regularly missed fire. Three times he tried a roll and three times the atom crumbled to bits as if crushed in space. Now Pfwfp found one excuse after another, trying to call off the game.

"Go on," I insisted, "if you don't shoot, the game's mine."

And he said: "It doesn't count. When an atom is ruined the game's null and void, and you start over again." This was a rule he had invented at that very moment.

I didn't give him any peace, I danced around him, leaped on his back, and chanted:

"Throw it throw it throw it
If not, you lose, you know it.
For every turn that you don't take
An extra throw for me to make."

"That's enough of that," Pfwfp said, "let's change games."

"Aha!" I said. "Why don't we play at flying galaxies?"

"Galaxies?" Pfwfp suddenly brightened with pleasure. "Suits me. But you . . . you don't have a galaxy!"

"Yes, I do."

"So do I."

"Come on! Let's see who can send his highest!"

And I took all the new atoms I was hiding and flung them into space. At first they seemed to scatter, then they thickened together into a kind of light cloud, and the cloud swelled and swelled, and inside it some incandescent condensations were formed, and they whirled and whirled and at a certain point became a spiral of constellations never seen before, a spiral that poised, opening in a gust, then sped away as I held on to its tail and ran after it. But now I wasn't the one who made the galaxy fly, it was the galaxy that was lifting me aloft, clinging to its tail; I mean, there wasn't any height or depth now but only space, widening, and the galaxy in its midst, also opening wide, and me hanging there, making faces at Pfwfp, who was already thousands of light-years away.

Pfwfp, at my first move, had promptly dug out all his hoard, hurling it with a balanced movement as if he expected to see the coils of an endless galaxy open in the sky. But instead, nothing happened. There was a sizzling sound of radiations, a messy flash, then everything died out at once.

"Is that the best you can do?" I shouted at Pfwfp, who was yelling curses at me, green with rage:

"I'll show you, Qfwfq, you pig!"

But in the meanwhile my galaxy and I were flying among thousands of other galaxies, and mine was the newest, the envy of the whole firmament, blazing as it was with young hydrogen and the youngest carbon and newborn beryllium. The old galaxies fled us, filled with jealousy, and we, prancing and haughty, avoided them, so antiquated and ponderous to look at. As that reciprocal flight developed, we sailed across spaces that became more and more rarefied and empty: and then I saw something appear in the midst of the void, like uncertain bursts of light. These were new galaxies, formed by matter just born, galaxies even newer than mine. Soon space became filled again, and dense, like a vineyard just before vintage time, and we flew on, escaping from one another, my galaxy fleeing the younger ones as it had the older, and young and old fleeing us. And we advanced to fly through empty skies, and these skies also became peopled, and so on and on.

In one of these propagations, I heard: "Qfwfq, you'll pay for this now, you traitor!" and I saw a brand-new galaxy flying on our trail, and there leaning forward from the very tip of the spiral, yelling threats and insults at me, was my old playmate Pfwfp.

The chase began. Where space rose, Pfwfp's galaxy, young and agile, gained ground, but on the descents, my heavier galaxy plunged ahead again.

In any kind of race there's a secret: it's all in how you take the curves. Pfwfp's galaxy tended to narrow them, mine to swing out. And as it kept broadening the curves, we were finally flung beyond the edge of space, with Pfwfp after us. We kept up the pursuit, using the system one always uses in such circumstances, that is, creating space before us as we went forward.

So there I was, with nothingness in front of me, and that nasty-faced Pfwfp after me: an unpleasant sight either way. In any case, I preferred to look ahead, and what did I see? Pfwfp, whom my eyes had just left behind me, was speeding on his galaxy directly in front of me. "Ah!" I cried, "now it's my turn to chase you!"

"What?" Pfwfp said, from before me or behind me, I'm not really sure which, "I'm the one who's chasing you!"

I turned around: there was Pfwfp, still at my heels. I looked ahead again: and he was there, racing off with his back turned to me. But as I looked more closely, I saw that in front of this galaxy of his that was preceding me there was another, and that other galaxy was mine, because there I was on it, unmistakable even though seen from behind. And I turned toward the Pfwfp following me and narrowed my eyes: I saw that his galaxy was being chased by another, mine, with me on top of it, turning at that same time to look back.

And so after every Qfwfq there was a Pfwfp, and after every Pfwfp a Qfwfq, and every Pfwfp was chasing a Qfwfq, who was pursuing him and vice versa. Our distances grew a bit shorter or a bit longer, but now it was clear that one would never overtake the other, nor the other overtake one. We had lost all pleasure in this game of chase, and we weren't children any more for that matter, but now there was nothing else we could do.

J's Marriage

Robert Coover

Robert Coover was born in Charles City, Iowa, and educated at Indiana University and the University of Chicago. He has taught at the Writer's Workshop at the University of Iowa and has been a visiting professor at Princeton and Columbia. He considers Dover, England, his home, however.

His first novel, *The Origin of the Brunists,* won the William Kaufman award as the best novel of 1966. In response to his growing reputation among college-age readers, his second novel, *The Universal Baseball Association, Inc., J. Henry Waugh, Prop.* (1968), has been published in paperback. His stories continue to appear in *Evergreen Review, Playboy,* and *New American Review,* even though his attention appears to be moving toward the theater. *Murder: An Entertainment and Other Plays* was published in 1971.

The following story is taken from *Pricksongs and Descants* (1969), a collection of stories in which Coover retells, often using experimental and dazzling techniques (the film retake, video cutting), old fairy tales, familiar legends, and Christian myths. He modifies form to accommodate the purely personal flow of perception, sometimes shifting syntax or breaking up the surface in order to reflect the inward state of being or the very process of perception itself. His intention is to conduct the reader from mystification to clarification, from mystery to revelation.

It began not otherwise than one might expect. After an excessive period of unlicensed self-humiliation, ecstatic protests of love, fear, despair, and the total impossibility of any imaginable kind of ultimate happiness (to all of which she replied and usually in kind, though rarely with such intensity), J at last determined, or perhaps this had been his determination all the while, the rest mere poetry, to marry her. Slow, but then there were admittedly substantial drawbacks to the affair: he was much older for one thing. And though she was certainly intelligent and imaginative, he was far more broadly educated. In fact, it wouldn't be unkind to say, and he brought himself to confess it in the torment of his most rational moments, that a good many of the most beautiful things he said to her she failed to understand, or rather, she understood not the sense of them, but merely the apparent emotion, the urgency, the adoration behind them. And did he adore her, or the objectification of a possible adorable? To search out *this* answer, J

SOURCE: Robert Coover, *Pricksongs & Descants* (New York: E. P. Dutton & Co. 1969), pp. 112–119.

frankly did not trust himself. And, more generally and therefore more significantly, all of his most oppressive fears about the ultimate misery of any existence, the inevitable disintegration of love, the hastening process of physical and mental rot, the stupidity of human passion, and so on, these fears were entirely real, in fact, more than fears, they were his lot and he knew it. But there was no alternative short of death, so he decided to marry her.

To his great embarrassment, however, she was shocked by his proposal, apparently so at least, and pleaded for time. Only much later did he come to understand that a new kind of fear had burgeoned in her, a fear that no doubt cowered beneath the surface all the time, but which had always been placated by the suspicion that J himself was really nothing more physically substantial than his words, words which at times pierced the heart, true, kindled the blood, powerful words, even at times painful; but their power and their pain did not, *could* not pin one helplessly to the earth, could not bring actual blood.

At the time misconstruing her behavior, however, J grew angry, pressed his affections with atypical peevishness. She tore away, spat out at him hatefully. He withdrew, collapsed into a prolonged and somewhat morbid melancholy, unable to lift a hammer or turn a blade. She sought him out. She wept, embraced him, tried pathetically to explain. He again misunderstood and renewed his assault. She screamed in terror and escaped. Again he fell back in remorseful confusion. He grew ill. She cared for him. And on and on, thus it dragged, until, in summary, it at last became apparent to him that although she did love him and had a healthy longing for motherhood, at least in the abstract, she was nevertheless panic-stricken by the prospect of the love act itself.

What was it? a lifetime of misguided dehortations from ancient deformed grannies, miserable old tales of blood and the tortures of the underworld (which the woman's very position in the event must give one thoughts upon), or some early misadventure, perhaps a dominant father? It hardly mattered. For, in the instant of the present act, the past in all its troubling complexities becomes irrelevant. This is what J believed anyway, and once the immediate cause of their problems had finally been made manifest to him, he felt immense relief. Not only was his pride assuaged, but more to the case, there was now no longer any obstacle to their marriage. At the level where they two existed, he explained to her, his voice appropriately muted, eyes darkened, brow furrowed, Truth his domain where he might guide her, at this level sex could not be comprehended without love, but love could be distinguished without reference to sex; in short, that one was the whole, the other a mere part, contributing to the perfection of the whole to be sure, but not indispensable, not indispensable. More precisely, he added: whatever her terms, he could not imagine life without her, and if later they came to share in the natural act of lovers, well, so much the better of course, but they would arrive there, if at all, only with her express encouragement and at her own pace.

It was true (just at that moment anyway) all that he said, she accepted it, even if it did fail to take into account the processes of human action as she understood them, doubtless more accurately than he. But aside from this and more important: she suddenly grasped, more by intuition than by reason, that with this man, and possibly with no other, she would always enjoy the upper hand in this singular matter of, though the word was not hers, sex. All right, she said. All right, yes, she would marry him, and not long after she did.

Their wedding night was in all truth a thing of beauty: the splendor of the celebrations, the hushed intimacy of a private walk together under the cryptic light of a large moon, the unexpected delight discovered in the reflection of a candle's flicker in a decanter of aged wine, finally the silent weeping in each other's arms through a night that seemed infinite in its innumerable dimensions. Toward dawn, J, sitting on the side of the bed (both of them still dressed, of course; it would take some while yet to learn that first art of nakedness), overflowing with profound affection, began to caress her temples, and with the first thin light of the new day, she fell asleep beside him, and J wept again to realize the meaning and the importance of her sleep.

In spite of all his doubts, fears, his submerged impatience with the qualifications, to say nothing of his general view of the universe, not exactly, as shown, a reassuring one, J nevertheless enjoyed for several months an incredible happiness. Everything became remarkably easy for him, the dullest detail of existence provided him an immense delight: a parade of ants, for example, or the color of a piece of wood or a pebble, her footprint in the dust. Merely to watch her hand reach for a cup or place a comb in her hair left him breathless. Every act was dedicated to her being, her mere being. The bed he made for her with his own hands, the table as well which never lacked her gifts to him, little flutes and puppets, too, and the chairs she sat on, he also made these. Almost from the outset, they encountered an emotional harmony inexpressibly beautiful, and even the last, God knows: *minor,* obstacle to their complete happiness seemed certain, ultimately, to give way to their all-consuming love. J, confident of his own sexual attractiveness, even as old as he was, which was not too old after all—no, not over much should be made of his age—was patient, infinitely patient, and she seemed, at least much of the time, as desirous as he to consummate, in the proper time, their marriage.

One evening, just before sunset, J happened to be down by the sea. He had forgotten why he was there, perhaps nothing more than an idle wandering before supper, but yet it seemed altogether necessary that he *should* be there, just at that instant, just as the dying sun melted, viscous and crimson, into the sullen sea, just as the distant mountains blinked from orange-green to blue, just as the first stirring of the night awoke the pines over his head. It was not, it was *not* beautiful, no, it would be absurd to think of this or any other natural composite as beautiful, but it was as though it *could* be beautiful, as though somewhere there resided within it the potentiality of beauty, not previously existent, *some spark after all,* only illusion of course, but—and he turned just in time to see his wife coming toward him down the path. Paralyzed, he stood rooted, unspeaking, utterly entranced by her graceful motion, by the pale light playing over her slender body, and, above all, by her eyes, smilingly returning his awkward stare. Oh my God I love you! he managed to whisper, when she was near enough to hear. And that night, in feverish exultation, he buried his face in her breasts and caressed them, and she allowed it. Then, finally, overcome with an excess of emotion, he fell into a deep sleep full of wonderful dreams, which unfortunately he could never later recall.

The actual process of increasing intimacy was an elaborate sequence of advances and reversals, which need not be enumerated here. At moments, J would be greatly encouraged, perhaps by a sudden act on her part, a stroking of his naked back while he was bent over his lathe, a pressing of his hand to her breast, a soft folding into his arms while still half asleep beside him in their bed. But other times he would unwittingly shock her, set her to crying or running from the room, or would wake her with a hand too insistent on her thighs. And, in fact, it actually seemed that his worst fears had been justified, that he would indeed pass the rest of his years tossing sleeplessly, tortured, alongside her marvelous but utterly impenetrable body. At such times, he found himself envying the water she bathed in or the chair he was carving for her to sit on, found himself weeping bitterly and alone, his face in a piece of her clothing.

But then, one evening after supper, utterly without warning, he entered the bedroom to find her standing, undressed, beside the bed. She was astonishingly beautiful, lovelier than he had imagined in his most distraught and fanciful dreams. He gasped, unbelieving, took a faltering step toward her. She blushed, cast her eyes down. With trembling fingers he tore off his shirt, ran to her, pressed her to his chest, no, she was no mere apparition, he tearfully kissed her ears, her hair, her eyes, her neck, her breasts. He was delirious, feared he might faint. His hands searched desperately, clumsily, swept over her smooth back, burrowed down between— Don't, she said. Please don't. It was somehow the way she said it, not the words, which were clearly meaningless, but the way she *formed* the words, as though carving them with consummate skill and certainty, and placing them, like great stone tablets, between them. Bewildered, he fumbled a moment, stepped back, and I don't—? was all he could find for himself to say. I am expecting a baby, she said.

What happened in the moments, and for that matter in the weeks, that followed is, of course, a common kind of story, and not a particularly entertaining one at that. J took ill, suffered frequently from delirium, and she patiently nursed him back to health. She now undressed freely in front of him, but with a self-preoccupation and indifference to his presence that would have permanently deranged a younger man, not so well equipped for life as J. She explained to him simply that her pregnancy was an act of God, and he had to admit against all mandates of his reason that it must be so, but he couldn't imagine whatever had brought a God to do such a useless and, well, yes, in a way, almost vulgar thing. J always thought about everything a great deal, even trivia that others might either sensibly ignore, or observe and forget in the very act of observing, and about *this,* to be sure, he thought even more than usual. Every day while prostrate in bed, he turned it over and over, and in feverish dreams the mystery set his brain on fire and caused tiny painful explosions behind his eyes that sometimes kept going off even after he was awake. But no power of mental effort provided a meaningful answer for him; it was simply unimaginable to him that any God would so involve himself in the tedious personal affairs of this or any other human animal, so inutterably unimportant were they to each other. Finally, he simply gave in to it, dumped it in with the rest of life's inscrutable absurdities, and from that time on began to improve almost daily.

And to his credit it must be said that one of the reasons he began to find his way back to health was her own worsening condition. She said little about it, behaved toward him as generously as ever, smiled no less frequently, but there was no mistaking her suffering, quiet or no: it was not and would not be easy. Compassion drove him to forget his own wretchedness, and daily, though he seemed to grow even older, he seemed as well to assume greater and greater stature. He returned to his carpentry with renewed dedication, secretly saved aside small portions of food as insurance for her against the approaching winter, learned to comprehend in his day's activities many of the tasks they once took for granted as hers. The last month was particularly bitter, the great misfortune of the ill-timed trip, the strange cruelty of the elements, and so on, but she took it with great courage, greater even than his own, suffered with dignity the flesh-ripping agony of birth, writhing on the dirt floor like a dying beast, yet noble, beautiful. It was—that moment of the strange birth—J's most mystic moment, his only indisputable glimpse of the whole of existence, yet one which he later renounced, needless to say, later understood in the light of his overwrought and tortured emotions. And it was also the climax of his love for her; afterwards, they drifted quietly and impassively apart, until in later years J found himself incapable even of describing her to himself or any other person.

The marriage itself, as a formal fact, lasted on to the end (in this case, J's), which did not come early, lasted for the most part because nothing was done to stop it. The boy played but a small part in the process, did of course draw away the mother's attention for quite some while, but little more. As for J, in spite of his general willingness to love the boy, he could never bring himself actually to do so in any thoroughgoing manner, and for this or other reasons, the boy showed complete indifference to J from an early age. Just as well; J grew to prefer not being bothered to any other form of existence.

One thing did happen, though perhaps too trivial even to report here, maybe not even true as a number no doubt hold, even though J himself talked of it freely to those close to him (or perhaps he dreamt it, he could never deny it, it might have been one of those beautiful dreams from that earlier magical night, thought forgotten): namely, that some four or five months after the boy came, J did at last consummate his marriage. He had frankly forgotten about doing so, had come to take life as it oddly was for granted (a carryover from his prolonged illness and consequent cure), had turned in, weary from work, when she came into the room, her breasts still exposed from having nursed the baby, and sat down on the bed beside him. She smiled wanly, perhaps not even at him, he couldn't be sure, didn't even wonder, and then she began to bathe her breasts with a small damp sponge she had brought along for the purpose. J rose up casually, as he might have done time after time, took the sponge from her hands (she surrendered it willingly, sleepily), washed her breasts (it was curious they held so little interest for him: had he kissed them with such terrible rapture so recently? it was really very long ago) and then her neck and back. He undressed her, her exhausted body compliant, went out to the well, still unclothed himself (later this struck him as extraordinary, lent the odd element that caused him doubts about the event's reality), dipped the sponge in fresh cool water, returned to complete her bath. As though nothing more than the rest of a customary routine, he then penetrated her, had a more or less satisfactory emission, rolled over, and slept until morning. She had fallen asleep some moments before.

J died, thus ending the marriage, unattractively with his face in a glassful of red wine on a tavern table many years later, and not especially appropriately, since not even in his advanced years was he much of a drinker. He had just remarked to somebody sitting near him (keeping to himself the old bubbling wish that there might have been a child for him that time, a kind of testimonial for him to leave) that life had turned out to be nothing more or less than he had expected after all, he was now very inept at his carpentry, had a chestful of consumption, was already passing whole days without being able to remember them afterwards, urinated on the hour and sometimes in his pants, separately or additively could make no sense of any day of his life, and so on, a tavern-type speech, in short, but he added that the one peculiarity he had not accurately foreseen, and perhaps it was the most important of all, was that, in spite of everything, there was nothing tragic about it, no, nothing there to get wrought up about, on the contrary. Then, without transition, a mental fault more common to him in later years, he had a rather uncharacteristic thought about the time she, the wife, fell asleep, or apparently so, that morning following the wedding night; he laughed (that high-pitched rattle of old men), startling the person who had been listening, and died as described above in a fit of consumptive coughing.

The Yellow Flower

Julio Cortázar

Argentinian poet, novelist, short-story writer, and jazz musician, Julio Cortázar was born in Brussels in 1916 and has been living in Paris since 1952 as an expatriate. His earlier stories (*The Bestiary,* 1951) develop the theme of the monster in man, a subject he was to treat with variations in his first novel, *The Winners,* in his remarkable anti-novel, *Hopscotch* (1966), and in many of his later stories, collected in English translation under the title *End of the Game. The Pursuer,* a short novel, is about a writer possessed by his subject, a drunken, drug-taking jazz musician. His recent books, *Cronopias and Famas* and *62: A Model Kit,* elude description.

"A Yellow Flower" is complementary in theme but opposite in mood to Alan Harrington's piece on immortality. The absurd spectacle of life ever renewing itself without purpose ("poor stupid life . . . imbecilic, abortive life . . .") wrings from the narrator an existential response that cannot even be called despair, but it is a feeling familiar to a generation that has witnessed three major wars in less than twenty-five years.

We are immortal, I know it sounds like a joke. I know because I met the exception to the rule, I know the only mortal there is. He told me his story in a bar in the rue Cambronne, drunk enough so it didn't bother him to tell the truth, even though the bartender (who owned the place) and the regulars at the counter were laughing so hard that the wine was coming out of their eyes. He must have seen some flicker of interest in my face—he drifted steadily toward me and we ended up treating ourselves to a table in the corner where we could drink and talk in peace. He told me that he was a retired city employee and that his wife had gone back to her parents for the summer, as good a way as any of letting it be known that she'd left him. He was a guy, not particularly old and certainly not stupid, with a sort of dried-up face and consumptive eyes. In honesty, he was drinking to forget, a fact which he proclaimed by the time we were starting the fifth glass of red. But he did not smell of Paris, that signature of Paris which apparently only we foreigners can detect. And his nails were decently pared, no specks under them.

He told how he'd seen this kid on the number 95 bus, oh, about thirteen years old, and after looking at him for a spell it struck him that

SOURCE: Julio Cortázar, *End of the Game and Other Stories,* trans. Paul Blackburn (New York: Random House, 1967), pp. 45–52.

the boy looked very much like him, at least very much as he remembered himself at that age. He continued little by little admitting that the boy seemed completely like him, the face, the hands, the mop of hair flopping over the forehead, eyes very widely spaced, even more strongly in his shyness, the way he took refuge in a short-story magazine, the motion of his head in tossing his hair back, the hopeless awkwardness of his movements. The resemblance was so exact that he almost laughed out loud, but when the boy got down at the rue de Rennes, he got off too, leaving a friend waiting for him in Montparnasse. Looking for some pretext to speak with the kid, he asked directions to a particular street, and without surprise heard himself answered by a voice that had once been his own. The kid was going as far as the street, and they walked along together shyly for several blocks. At that tense moment, a kind of revelation came over him. Not an explanation, but something that could dispense with explanation, that turned blurred or stupid somehow when—as now—one attempted to explain it.

To make a long story short, he figured a way to find out where the kid lived, and with the prestige of having spent some time as a scoutmaster, he managed to gain entrance to that fortress of fortresses, a French home. He found an air of decent misery, a mother looking older than she should have, a retired uncle, two cats. Afterward, it was not too difficult; a brother of his entrusted him with his son who was going on fourteen, and the two boys became friends. He began to go to Luc's house every week; the mother treated him to heated-up coffee, they talked of the war, of the occupation, of Luc also. What had started as a blunt revelation was developing now like a theorem in geometry, taking on the shape of what people used to call fate. Besides, it could be said in everyday words: Luc was him again, there was no mortality, we were all immortals.

"All immortals, old man. Nobody'd been able to prove it, and it had to happen to me, and on a 95 bus. Some slight imperfection in the mechanism, a crimp and doubling back of time, I mean an overlap, a re-embodiment incarnate, simultaneously instead of consecutively. Luc should never have been born until after I'd died, and on the other hand, I . . . never mind the fantastic accident of meeting him on a city bus. I think I told you this already, it was a sort of absolute surety, no words needed. That was that, and that was the end of it. But the doubts began afterwards, because in a case like that, you either think that you're an imbecile, or you start taking tranquilizers. As for the doubts, you kill them off, one by one, the proofs that you're not crazy keep coming. And what made those dopes laugh the hardest when, once in a while, I said something to them about it, well, I'll tell you now. Luc wasn't just me another time, he was going to become like me, like this miserable sonofabitch talking to you. You only had to watch him playing, just watch, he always fell down and hurt himself, twisting a foot or throwing his clavicle out, flushes of feeling that'd make him break out in hives, he could hardly even ask for anything without blushing horribly. On the other hand his mother would talk to you about anything and everything with the kid standing there squirming with embarrassment, the most incredible, intimate, private . . . anecdotes about his first teeth, drawings he made when he was eight, illnesses . . . she liked to talk. The good lady suspected nothing, that's for sure, and the uncle played chess with me, I was like family, even lending them money to get to the end of the month. No, it was easy to get to know Luc's history, just edging questions into discussions his elders were interested in: the uncle's rheumatism, politics, the venality of the concierge, you know. So between bishop calling check to my king and serious discussions of the price of meat, I learned about Luc's childhood, and the bits of evidence stockpiled into an incontrovertible proof. But I want you to understand me, meanwhile let's order another glass: Luc was me, what I'd been as a kid, but don't think of him as the perfect copy. More like an analogous figure, understand? I mean, when I was seven I dislocated my wrist, with Luc it was the clavicle, and at nine I had German measles and he had scarlet fever, the measles had me out some two weeks, Luc was better in five days, well, you know, the strides of science, etc. The whole thing was a repeat and so, give you another example somewhat to the point, the baker on the corner is a reincarnation of Napoleon, and he doesn't know because the pattern hasn't changed, I mean, he'll never be able to meet the real article on a city bus; but if in some way or another he becomes aware of the truth, he might be able to understand that he's a repeat of, is still repeating Napoleon, that the move from being a dishwasher to being the owner of a decent bakery in Montparnasse is the same pattern as the jump from Corsica to the throne of France, and that if he dug carefully enough through the story of his life, he'd find moments that would correspond to the Egyptian Campaign, to the Consulate, to Austerlitz, he might even figure that something is going to happen to his bakery in a few years and that he'll end on St. Helena, say, some furnished room in a sixth-floor walkup, a big defeat, no? and surrounded by the waters of loneliness, also still proud of that bakery of his which was like a flight of eagles. You get it?"

Well, I got it all right, but I figured that we all get childhood diseases about the same time, and that almost all of us break something playing football.

"I know, I haven't mentioned anything other than the usual coincidences, very visible. For example, even that Luc looked like me is of no serious importance, even if you're sold on the revelation on the bus. What really counted was the sequence of events, and that's harder to explain because it involves the character, inexact recollections, the mythologies of childhood. At that time, I mean when I was Luc's age, I went through a very bad time that started with an interminable sickness, then right in the middle of the convalescence broke my arm playing with some friends, and as soon as that was healed I fell in love with the sister of a buddy of mine at school, and God, it was painful, like you can't look at a girl's eyes and she's making fun of you. Luc fell sick also, and just as he was getting better they took him to the circus, and going down the bleacher seats he slipped and dislocated his ankle. Shortly after that his mother came on him accidentally one afternoon with a little blue kerchief twisted up in his hands, standing at a window crying: it was a handkerchief she'd never seen before."

As someone has to be the devil's advocate, I remarked that puppy love is the inevitable concomitant of bruises, broken bones and pleurisy. But I had to admit that the business of the airplane was a different matter. A plane with a propeller driven by rubber bands that he'd gotten for his birthday.

"When he got it, I remembered the erector set my mother gave me as a present when I was fourteen, and what happened with that. It happened I was out in the garden in spite of the fact that a summer storm was ready to break, you could already hear the thunder crackling, and I'd just started to put a derrick together on the table under the arbor near the gate to the street. Someone called me from the house and I had to go in for a minute. When I got back, the box and the erector set were gone and the gate was wide open. Screaming desperately, I ran out into the street and there was no one in sight, and at that same moment a bolt of lightning hit the house across the road. All of this happened as a single stroke, and I was remembering it as Luc was getting his airplane and he stood there gazing at it with the same happiness with which I had eyed my erector set. The mother brought me a cup of coffee and we were trading the usual sentences when we heard a shout. Luc had run to the window as though he were going to throw himself out of it. His face white and his eyes streaming, he managed to blubber out that the plane had swerved in its trajectory and had gone exactly through the small space of the partly opened window. We'll never find it again, we'll never find it again, he kept saying. He was still sobbing when we heard a shout from downstairs, his uncle came running in with the news that there was a fire in the house across the street. Understand now? Yes, we'd better have another glass."

Afterward, as I was saying nothing, the man continued. He had begun thinking exclusively of Luc, of Luc's fate. His mother had decided to send him to a vocational school, so that what she referred to as "his life's road" would be open to him in some decent way, but that road was already open, and only he, who would not have been able to open his mouth, they would have thought him insane and kept him away from Luc altogether, would have been able to tell the mother and the uncle that there was no use whatsoever, that whatever they might do the result would be the same, humiliation, a deadly routine, the monotonous years, calamitous disasters that would continue to nibble away at the clothes and the soul, taking refuge in a resentful solitude, in some local bistro. But Luc's destiny was not the worst of it; the worst was that Luc would die in his turn, and another man would relive Luc's pattern and his own pattern until he died and another man in his turn enter the wheel. Almost as though Luc were already unimportant to him; at night his insomnia mapped it out even beyond that other Luc, to others whose names would be Robert or Claude or Michael, a theory of infinite extension, an infinity of poor devils repeating the pattern without knowing it, convinced of their freedom of will and choice. The man was crying in his beer, only it was wine in this case, what could you do about it, nothing.

"They laugh at me now when I tell them that Luc died a few months later, they're too stupid to realize . . . Yeah, now don't you start looking at me like that. He died a few months later, it started as a kind of bronchitis, like at the same age I'd come down with a hepatitis infection. Me, they put in the hospital, but Luc's mother persisted in keeping him at home to take care of him, and I went almost every day, sometimes I brought my nephew along to play with Luc. There was so much misery in that house that my visits were a consolation in every sense, company for Luc, a package of dried herrings or Damascus tarts. After I mentioned a drugstore where they gave me a special discount, it was taken for granted when I took charge of buying the medicines. It wound up by their letting me be Luc's nurse, and you can imagine how, in a case like that, where the doctor comes in and leaves without any special concern, no one pays much attention if the final symptoms have anything at all to do with the first diagnosis . . . Why are you looking at me like that? Did I say anything wrong?"

No, no, he hadn't said anything wrong, especially as he was crocked on the wine. On the contrary, unless you imagine something particularly horrible, poor Luc's death seemed to prove that anyone given enough imagination can begin a fantasy on the number 95 bus and finish it beside a bed where a kid is dying quietly. I told him no to calm him down. He stayed staring into space for a spell before resuming the story.

"All right, however you like. The truth is that in those weeks following the funeral, for the first time I felt something that might pass for happiness. I still went every once in a while to visit Luc's mother, I'd bring a package of cookies, but neither she nor the house meant anything to me now, it was as though I were waterlogged by the marvelous certainty of being the first mortal, of feeling that my life was continuing to wear away, day after day, wine after wine, and that finally it would end some place or another, some time or another, reiterating until the very end the destiny of some unknown dead man, nobody knows who or when, but me, I was going to be really dead, no Luc to step into the wheel to stupidly reiterate a stupid life. Understand the fullness of that, old man, envy me for all that happiness while it lasted."

Because apparently it had not lasted. The bistro and the cheap wine proved it, and those eyes shining with a fever that was not of the body. Nonetheless he had lived some months savoring each moment of the daily mediocrity of his life, the breakup of his marriage, the ruin of his fifty years, sure of his inalienable mortality. One afternoon, crossing the Luxembourg gardens, he saw a flower.

"It was on the side of a bed, just a plain yellow flower. I'd stopped to light a cigarette and I was distracted, looking at it. It was a little as though the flower were looking at me too, you know, those communications, once in a while . . . You know what I'm talking about, everyone feels that, what they call beauty. It was just that, the flower was beautiful, it was a very lovely flower. And I was damned, one day I was going to die and forever. The flower was handsome, there would always be flowers for men in the future. All at once I understood nothing, I mean nothingness, nothing, I'd thought it was peace, it was the end of the chain. I was going to die, Luc was already dead, there would never again be a flower for anyone like us, there would never be anything, there'd be absolutely nothing, and that's what nothing was, that there would never again be a flower. The lit match burned my fingers, it smarted. At the next square I jumped on a bus going, it wasn't important where, anywhere, I didn't know, and foolishly enough I started looking around, looking at everything, everyone you could see in the street, everyone on the bus. When we came to the end of the line I got off and got onto another bus going out to the suburbs. All afternoon, until night fell, I got off and on buses, thinking of the flower and of Luc, looking among the passengers for someone who resembled Luc, someone who looked like me or Luc, someone who could be me again, someone I could look at knowing it was myself, that it was me, and then let him go on, to get off without saying anything, protecting him almost so that he would go on and live out his poor stupid life, his imbecilic, abortive life until another imbecilic abortive life, until another imbecilic abortive life, until another . . ."

I paid the bill.

La Valise

Lawrence Durrell

Novelist, poet, playwright, and essayist, Lawrence Durrell was born in 1912 in Jalunda, India. At the age of twelve, he was sent to England to continue his schooling. He left a public school in Canterbury and took up residence in bohemian Bloomsbury with the ambition of becoming a writer. He augmented the small income left to him at his father's death by playing jazz in night clubs and by operating a photographic studio with his wife.

He moved to Sussex and wrote his first novel, *Pied Piper of Lovers* (1935), and published two volumes of poetry. He lived on the Greek island of Corfu until the German invasion, at which time the Durrells fled to Crete, then to Alexandria. He has worked for the British diplomatic service in the Near East, in Egypt, Argentina, Belgrade, Rhodes, and Cyprus. He has long been a friend of Henry Miller and Anaïs Nin. His other works include *The Black Book* (1938), *Prospero's Cell* (1945), *The Dark Labyrinth* (1947), *Reflections on a Marine Venus* (1953), *Bitter Lemons* (1957), an autobiographical book based on his stay in Cyprus, and *The Alexandria Quartet* (1957–60), the work that brought him international recognition. His most recent works are *Tunc* (1970) and *Numquam* (1971). His *Collected Poems* appeared in 1956 and his poetic plays *Sappho* in 1950 and *Acte* in 1961. He now lives in France with his second wife.

The following piece is from *Esprit de Corps,* his second volume of sketches of life in the diplomatic corps. Durrell's gift of deadly yet hilarious satire is nowhere better revealed.

"If there is anything worse than a soprano," said Antrobus judicially as we walked down the Mall towards his club, "it is a mezzo-soprano. One shriek lower in the scale, perhaps, but with higher candle-power. I'm not just being small-minded, old chap. I bear the scars of spiritual experience. Seriously." And indeed he did look serious; but then he always does. The aura of the Foreign Office clings to him. He waved his umbrella, changed step, and continued in a lower, more confidential register. "And I can tell you another thing. If there is anything really questionable about the French character it must be its passion for *culture*. I might not dare to say this in the F.O., old man, but I know you will respect my confidence. You see, we are all supposed to be pro rather than anti in the Old Firm—but as for me, frankly I hate the stuff. It rattles me. It gives me the plain untitivated pip, I don't mind confessing."

SOURCE: Lawrence Durrell, *Esprit de Corps* (New York: E. P. Dutton & Co., 1957), pp. 16–21.

He drew a deep breath and after a pause went on, more pensively, drawing upon his memories of Foreign Service life: "All my worst moments have been cultural rather than political. Like that awful business of *La Valise,* known privately to the members of the Corps as The Diplomatic Bag Extraordinary. Did I ever mention it? She was French Ambassadress in Vulgaria."

"No."

"Shall I? It will make you wince."

"Do."

"Well it happened while I was serving in Vulgaria some years ago; an unspeakable place full of unspeakable people. It was the usual Iron Curtain post to which the F.O. had exposed its soft white underbelly in the person of Smith-Cromwell. Not that he was a bad chap. He was in fact quite intelligent and had played darts for Cambridge. But he was easily led. As you know in a Communist country the Corps finds itself cut off from every human contact. It has to provide its own amusements, fall back on its own resources. And this is where the trouble usually begins. It is a strange thing but in a post like that it is never long before some dastardly Frenchman (always French) reaches for the safety-catch of his revolver and starts to introduce *culture* into our lives. Invariably.

"So it fell out with us in Sczbog. Sure enough, during my second winter the French appointed a Cultural Attaché, straight from Montmartre—the place with the big church. Fellow like a greyhound. Burning eyes. Dirty hair. A moist and Fahrenheit handshake. You know the type. Wasn't even married to his own wife. Most Questionable fellow. Up till now everything had been quiet and reasonable—just the usual round of diplomatic-social engagements among colleagues. Now this beastly fellow started the ball rolling with a public lecture—an undisguised public lecture—on a French writer called, if I understood him correctly, Flowbear. Of course we all had to go to support the French. Cultural reciprocity and all that. But as if this wasn't enough the little blackhead followed it up with another about another blasted French writer called, unless my memory is at fault, Goaty-eh. I ask you, my dear fellow, what was one to do. Flowbear! Goaty-eh! It was more than flesh and blood could stand. I myself feared the worst as I sat listening to him. The whole thing cried out for the chloroform-pad. I had of course wound up and set my features at Refined Rapture like everyone else, but inside me I was in a turmoil of apprehension. Culture spreads like mumps, you know, like measles. A thing like this could get everyone acting unnaturally in no time. All culture corrupts, old boy, but French culture corrupts absolutely. I was not wrong.

"The echoes had hardly died away when I noticed That Awful Look coming over peoples' faces. Everyone began to think up little tortures of their own. A whole winter stretched before us with practically no engagements except a national day or so. It was clear that unless Smith-Cromwell took a strong line the rot would set in. He did not. Instead of snorting when *La Valise* embarked on a cultural season he weakly encouraged her; he was even heard to remark that culture was a Good Thing—for the Military Attaché.

"At this time of course we also had our cultural man. Name of Gool. And he looked it. It was a clear case of Harrow and a bad third in History. But up to now we had kept Gool strictly under control and afraid to move. It could not last. He was bound to come adrift. Within a month he was making common cause with his French colleague. They began to lecture, separately and together. They gave readings with writhings. They spared us nothing, Eliot, Sartre, Emmanuel Kant—and who is that other fellow? The name escapes me. In short they gave us everything short of Mrs. Beeton. I did my best to get an arm-lock on Gool and to a certain extent succeeded by threatening to recommend him for an O.B.E. He knew this would ruin his career and that he would be posted to Java. But by the time I had got him pressed to the mat it was too late. The whole Corps had taken fire and was burning with the old hard gem-like flame. Culture was spreading like wildfire.

"A series of unforgettable evenings now began, old boy. Each mission thought up some particularly horrible contribution of its own to this feast. The nights became a torture of pure poesy and song. An evening of hellish amateur opera by the Italians would be followed without intermission by an ear-splitting evening of yodelling from the Swiss, all dressed as edelweiss. Then the Japanese mission went berserk and gave a Noh-play of ghoulish obscurity lasting seven hours. The sight of all those little yellowish, inscrutable diplomats all dressed as Mickey Mouse, old boy, was enough to turn milk. And their voices simply ate into one. Then in characteristic fashion the Dutch, not to be outdone, decided to gnaw their way to the forefront of things with a recital of national poetry by the Dutch Ambassadress herself. This was when I began to draft my resignation in my own mind. O God! how can I ever forget Madame Vanderpipf (usually the most kind and normal of wives and mothers) taking up a stance like a grenadier at Fontenoy, and after a pause declaiming in a slow, deep—O unspeakably slow and deep—voice, the opening verses of whatever it was? Old boy, the cultural heritage of the Dutch is not my affair. Let them have it, I say. Let them enjoy it peacefully as they may. But spare me from poems of five hundred lines beginning, '*Oom kroop der poop.*' You smile, as well indeed you may, never having heard Mrs. Vanderpipf declaiming those memorable stanzas with all the sullen fire of her race. Listen!

Oom kroop der poop
Zoom kroon der soup
Soon droon der oopersnoop.

"And so on. Have you got the idea? Perhaps there is something behind it all—who am I to say? All I know is that it is no joke to be on the receiving end. Specially as she would pause from time to time to give a rough translation in pidgin for Smith-Cromwell's benefit. Something like this: 'Our national poet Snugerpouf, he says eef Holland lives forever, only, how you would say?, heroes from ze soil oopspringing, yes?' It was pulse-stopping, old man. Then she would take a deep breath and begin afresh.

Oom kroop der poop
Zoom kroon der soup.

"In after years the very memory of this recitation used to make the sweat start out of my forehead. You must try it for yourself sometime. Just try repeating *'oom kroop der poop'* five hundred times in a low voice. After a time it's like Yoga. Everything goes dark. You feel you are falling backwards into illimitable black space.

"By this time Smith-Cromwell himself had begun to suffer. He leaned across to me once on this particular evening to whisper a message. I could tell from his popping eye and the knot of throbbing veins at his temple that he was under strain. He had at last discovered what culture means. 'If this goes on much longer,' he hissed, 'I shall confess everything.'

"But this did go on; unremittingly for a whole winter. I spare you a description of the cultural offerings brought to us by the remoter tribes. The Argentines! The Liberians! Dear God! When I think of the Chinese all dressed in lamp-shades, the Australians doing sheep-opera, the Egyptians undulating and ululating all in the same breath. . . . Old boy, I am at a loss.

"But the real evil demon of the peace was *La Valise*. Whenever culture flagged she was there, quick to rekindle the flame. Long after the Corps was milked dry, so to speak, and had nothing left in its collective memory except nursery rhymes or perhaps a bluish limerick or two. *La Valise* was still at it. She fancied herself as a singer. She was never without a wad of music. A mezzo-soprano never gives in, old boy. She dies standing up, with swelling port curved to the stars. . . . And here came this beastly attaché again. He had turned out to be a pianist, and she took him everywhere to accompany her. While he clawed the piano she clawed the air and remorselessly sang. How she sang! Always a bit flat, I gather, but with a sickening lucid resonance that penetrated the middle ear. Those who had hearing-aids filled them with a kapok mixture for her recitals. When she hit a top note I could hear the studs vibrating in my dinner-shirt. Cowed, we sat and watched her, as she started to climb a row of notes towards the veil of the temple—that shattering top E, F or G: I never know which. We had the sinking feeling you get on the giant racer just as it nears the top of the slope. To this day I don't know how we kept our heads.

"Smith-Cromwell was by this time deeply penitent about his earlier encouragement of *La Valise* and at his wits' end to see her stopped. Everyone in the Chancery was in a bad state of nerves. The Naval

Attaché had taken to bursting into tears at meals if one so much as mentioned a forthcoming cultural engagement. But what was to be done? We clutched at every straw; and De Mandeville, always resourceful, suggested inviting the Corps to a live reading by himself and chauffeur from the works of the Marquis De Sade. But after deliberation Smith-Cromwell thought this might, though Effective, seem Questionable, so we dropped it.

"I had begun to feel like Titus Andronicus, old man, when the miracle happened. Out of a cloudless sky. Nemesis intervened just as he does in Gilbert Murray. Now *La Valise* had always been somewhat hirsute, indeed quite distinctly moustached in the Neapolitan manner, though none of us for a moment suspected the truth. But one day after Christmas M. De Panier, her husband, came round to the Embassy in full *tenue*[1] and threw himself into Smith-Cromwell's arms, bathed in tears as the French always say. 'My dear Britannic Colleague,' he said, 'I have come to take my leave of you. My career is completely ruined. I am leaving diplomacy for good. I have resigned. I shall return to my father-in-law's carpet-factory near Lyons and start a new life. All is over.'

"Smith-Cromwell was of course delighted to see the back of *La Valise;* but we all had a soft corner for De Panier. He was a gentleman. Never scamped his *frais*[2] and always gave us real champagne on Bastille Day. Also his dinners were dinners—not like the Swedes; but I am straying from my point. In answer to Smith-Cromwell's tactful inquiries De Panier unbosomed.

"You will never credit it, old man. You will think I am romancing. But it's as true as I am standing here. There are times in life when the heart spires upward like the lark on the wing; when through the consciousness runs, like an unearthly melody, the thought that God *really* exists, really *cares;* more, that he turns aside to lend a helping hand to poor dips *in extremis.* This was such a moment, old boy.

"*La Valise* had gone into hospital for some minor complaints which defied diagnosis. And in the course of a minor operation the doctors discovered that she was *turning into a man!* Nowadays of course it is becoming a commonplace of medicine; but at the time of which I speak it sounded like a miracle. A *man,* upon my soul! We could hardly believe it. The old caterpillar was really one of *us.* It was too enchanting! We were saved!

"And so it turned out. Within a matter of months her voice—that instrument of stark doom—sank to a bass; she sprouted a beard. Poor old De Panier hastened to leave but was held up until his replacement came. Poor fellow! Our hearts went out to him with This Whiskered Wonder on his hands. But he took it all very gallantly. They left at last, in a closed car, at dead of night. He would be happier in Lyons, I reflected, where nobody minds that sort of thing.

---

[1] regalia
[2] expenses

"But if he was gallant about this misfortune so was *La Valise elle-même*. She went on the halls, old boy, as a bass-baritone and made quite a name for herself. Smith-Cromwell says he once heard her sing 'The London Derrière,' in Paris with full orchestra and that she brought the house down. Some of the lower notes still made the ash-trays vibrate a bit but it was no longer like being trapped in a wind-tunnel. She wore a beard now and a corkscrew moustache and was very self-possessed. One can afford to be Over There. He also noticed she was wearing a smartish pair of elastic-sided boots. O, and her trade name now was Tito Torez. She and De Panier were divorced by then, and she had started out on a new career which was less of a reign of terror, if we can trust Smith-Cromwell. Merciful are the ways of Providence!

"As for poor De Panier himself, I gather that he re-entered the service after the scandal had died down. He is at present Consul-General in Blue Springs, Colorado. I'm told that there isn't much culture there, so he ought to be a very happy man indeed."

Just Back from the Coast

Bruce Jay Friedman

Bruce Jay Friedman is a novelist, short-story writer, and playwright. Born in New York City in 1930, he studied journalism at the University of Missouri and went on to work in that field for a few years while he wrote fiction on his own. He won immediate recognition with *Stern* (1962) and followed with *A Mother's Kisses* (1964) and *The Dick* (1970). His short stories are collected in two volumes, *Far from the City of Class* and *Black Angels.* He was equally successful on the stage with *Scuba Duba* and *Steambath.* He now lives in Glen Cove, New York, with his wife and three children. About his reputation as a popular writer, Nelson Algren says, "[He] is that rarity, a compulsive writer whose innocence makes his flaws of greater value, ultimately, than the perfections of skilled mechanics."

The following story, first published in *Harper's,* is about modern man's ability to adapt. The narrator learns to adapt to the amoral, plastic "city of the future" just as we are learning to breathe smog. The slick, smooth surface of the prose functions in perfect tandem with the theme.

At the time Apollo 11 took off for the moon, Harry Towns was in a reclining chair beside the pool at a Beverly Hills hotel, taking advantage of the first stretch of absolutely perfect weather he had run into in Los Angeles. On previous trips of his, whenever it rained or was generally dismal, someone would say, "I don't understand. It's never done this before, this time of year." When something went wrong in Los Angeles, people tended to say it was the first time in memory it had ever happened that way. Things didn't go wrong that often. And there was certainly nothing to quibble about on this trip. A poolside philosopher, sitting next to Towns, said the pool area at the hotel was probably the only enclave in the world in which people were totally oblivious to that trip to the moon. "That's because they probably haven't figured out a way to make money on it," the fellow said. Towns was thinking about the moon landing, but in the cool, even California sun, he could not honestly say it was pressing heavily on his mind. He was winding up his L.A. trip, milking the last juice out of it, and had it worked out so that he would stay slightly involved in the flight in California and then see the actual landing on the moon when he was back in New York. His son was away at summer camp and had

SOURCE: Bruce Jay Friedman, "Just Back from the Coast," *Harper's Magazine* (March 1970), pp. 68–72.

asked Towns to round up at least twenty copies of the *New York Times* edition that reported the landing. "Can you imagine what copies of the Wright Brothers newspaper would be worth today?" he had asked. Towns thought his son was very enterprising and made a sacred pledge to round up the papers, although secretly he decided ten was plenty for the kid. Meanwhile, he was busy loving California. He had taken some short probing trips to the Coast before, barely taking time to get unpacked, but this had been a one-month visit and it was as though some of the seeds he had scattered earlier had come into flower. People fell in love with California by the carload, but he wondered if anyone had experienced quite the love affair he was having with the state. Did anyone love the orange juice as much as he did. It knocked him on his ear every time he had a fresh glass of it in the morning. The same went for the lettuce. Who ever heard of lettuce that had so much bite and spank and crunch to it. He loved the salad oils and so far he had not come across a wine that didn't taste marvelous. He began to guzzle it like water and that was another thing; he never got drunk in Los Angeles no matter how much he had to drink. It was like being in a super-rarefied health simulator that didn't let you get drunk. In the way of many New Yorkers, he had spoken a bit too fondly of New York restaurants on the plane to L.A., and, by implication, been a bit disdainful of restaurants anywhere else. The fellow next to him, who had been quite jovial up to this point, suddenly dropped his voice and in a surprisingly ominous, almost cruel tone, asked, "Which restaurants did you go to in Los Angeles?"

"I believe I've offended you," Towns said.

"I believe you have," said the fellow. Then, in the style of a trial attorney with a witness on the hook, he asked Towns if he had been to such and such a place and such and such a place, rattling off a dozen winners and not waiting for Towns to say he hadn't heard of that one or hadn't gotten around to that other one. The once-friendly fellow then gave Towns the world's thinnest smile and went to sleep. In Los Angeles, Towns tried a few of the fellow's suggestions and they were first-rate all right, although they tended to go in as heavily for ceremony as they did for food. A waitress would come over, curtsy, and say, "I am Mary Jo Smith, your waitress for tonight and here is your special chilled fork for the Brasilia Festival Salad." If anyone had tried that number on him in New York, he or one of his friends would have done twenty minutes on it, probably right in front of Mary Jo Smith. You could not admit you liked elaborate curtsied ceremonies in New York. It seemed perfectly all right in Los Angeles.

More than the restaurants and theaters and homes, it was the getting to them that he really enjoyed. He loved getting dressed in the cool shady early evening and then stopping in the middle since all you ever had to be was half-dressed in L.A. It was not very typical of his life, but he had once taken a journey that had brought him to ancient walled-up cities in Central Asia. He would not have wanted the job of convincing anyone, but that high, dizzy, pulsing feeling he had each time he approached the Strip was every bit as profound as what he felt upon first seeing the outlines of Samarkand. Always he was astonished by the cleanliness of the light along the Strip, the slow, clean tumble of beautiful blond children, the outrageous brilliance of the high posters advertising Lake Tahoe entertainment trios but looking more like huge movies shown in the sky. How did they get those pictures so large and startling and clear. . . .

He was aware, of course, that so much of it had to do with him and not California. He was fond of saying, "When I get to the West Coast, there's absolutely no hassle." (He used such expressions in California. He said depressing people were "downers," a bad experience was a "bummer" and even caught himself describing a lively girl as a "dynamite chick." He did not speak that way in New York. There was always someone who would make a face.) In California, he had no debts, no broken marriage, no glum heartbroken feelings of work undone. Let him pass a day in New York without working and he would feel his stomach slowly being drawn out of him. In California there were always going to be other days. There was always plenty of time. He would feel the drumbeat of excitement the moment he got on the plane and headed for the West Coast. The many concerns would drop from his shoulders like an ancient overcoat, glum, massive, many sizes too large, one he had inherited from his forebears and pledged in blood to wear through all seasons.

He was a stranger in L.A. and he preferred it that way. There was no one looking over his shoulder, no one taking notes. He would not arrive in Los Angeles so much as roll into town in the style of mysterious Western heroes slowly loping into strange Montana outposts. He preferred keeping relationships (his most unfavorite word) casual, transient, and when he got to L.A. there was no one he raced to the phone to call. His one close friend was a chemist who had never married and was arrested, socially, at the college level; he loved to reminisce about beautiful sorority girls they had both known as Lambda Chi's at Purdue. Towns had dinner with this fellow once a trip. He had a sprinkling of friends in L.A., a bartender here, a waitress there, some people in the film colony. What he loved to do was set out in the evening with no date and no particular destination, relying on the peculiar sense of recklessness that possessed him in California. In New York, he might be struck by the beauty of a salesgirl, flirt with her a bit, and then settle for a week's worth of tormented dreams. In Los Angeles, if a girl fell into an intriguing posture, more often than not, he would simply scoop her up and whisk her away for the night. In most situations, he did not have the faintest idea of what he was going to do. It made him dangerous and at the same time exciting company for himself. In the event his nightly quests for adventure turned out a bit wilted, he had a few late-night fallback positions. The nostalgic chemist was one. There was a slightly over-the-hill TV ingenue who would generally take him in. And one late-night club where he could always count on a few familiar faces.

There was that special tribe of long-legged golden women that had always evaded him, dancing slightly beyond his reach. Some called them vacant, mindless, not worth the trouble. Ding-a-lings. A dark-haired dancer he knew saw him staring and said, "They're not worthy of you." But how he yearned for them. On previous trips, his adventures had been with cashiers, hustlers, leftover women on the frayed corners of L.A. life. But always he had felt an awareness of that golden tribe, eyes aloof, carriage regal, long hair trickling down tan delicious shoulders. On this trip, it had somewhat come together for him. Early on, he found an angry one. Angry when he met her, angry in bed, skulking off in a furor after a night of angered, begrudging love. She told him that yellow hair, perfect legs and all, she had been badly manhandled by an actor with a marred career. Perhaps what really irritated her was that Harry Towns had trapped her, straggling beyond the golden caravan. In any case, she was an official card-carrying member of the tribe. He had made contact. Soon after, he found another, standing high and golden on a stationery store ladder. Dusting boxes. "A girl like you dusting?" he said, not the most spectacular remark. But all things were possible in Los Angeles. "Actually," she said, "I've been looking for something else." He took her back to the hotel and at one point made her get out of bed and stand on a ladder, stationery-store-style. It was all right with her. Watching her that way, he fought for breath. He had one of those extraordinary sun girls up on a ladder, tan legs straining, just for him. L.A. was some town.

It had been that kind of a trip, fat, rich, lazy, most of the treasures of Beverly Hills one room-service call away. Now, at poolside on a late Friday afternoon, Towns felt the first stirrings of regret at having to leave Los Angeles. His work was completed. If he stayed any longer, he would have to pay his own bills. Not an attractive prospect for Harry Towns. All dollars aside, it struck him that part of the magical fun of Los Angeles was having someone else pay your way. He had to visit his son at camp within the next week, so he would be leaving in any case. Towns had promised to store up anecdotes about film stars for his young son. So far he had only run into stars of Forties movies which weren't going to mean anything to the boy. He reminded himself to go to places where the stars hung out that night and try to see some for the boy so he could report on what they were up to.

The crowning touch to this trip had been a lovely divorcee who had appeared to him at the pool the day before. When she walked by, he did a quick fantasy thumbnail sketch as he always did on people who interested him. He made her out to be the wife of a doctor, a gracious dinner-party-giver, very strong on fund raising for charities; the doctor was indeed to be congratulated because she also kept herself in marvelous trim, working hard at it since she had to be getting on in her thirties. A private thing about her was that she was given to sudden and delightful thrusts of vulgarity, both in and out of bed. The combination of fund-raising good looks and the flash of filthy stuff was irresistible. He did some laps in the pool, had a breath-holding contest with himself to see how much older he was getting, and when he surfaced, wet, bearded and shining at the shallow end, she was waiting for him, legs tucked beneath her. "The Christ resemblance really does cry out for comment," she said. She was a three-time loser in marriage, had a grown son, and had run away from her third husband, registering anonymously in the hotel. The husband lived about twelve miles away. He owned retail stores and was not a doctor, but Towns was right about the dinner parties. He was not very far off target on the sudden flashes of vulgarity, either. Towns was not sure he would be able to get that favorite California wine of his in New York, and now that he was leaving he wanted to have as much of it as possible. Over glasses of it, she said she had been in love only once, to a silent boy who drifted in and out of her life at college. After an incredibly short period, she looked at Towns and said, "I fear it's happening to me a second time." They drifted back to Towns' suite. Why was it so easy to get girls to drift back to suites in California and such a major operation in New York. They made love for a short while; he marked her as the kind of girl who liked to spend a short time making love and then a long time analyzing its ramifications. "It's not been that good for me," she said. "In so many ways I wish I had never noticed a tan and bearded fellow coming out of the pool like Christ reborn." She said, however, that anytime he wanted her, no matter where he was, she would come to him and he could use her in any way he wanted, so long as it didn't involve having another girl watch or anything in that family. When he was a younger man, such an invitation would have paralyzed his senses. Now it only sounded fairly good. In any case, she left a bracelet behind and then called to ask if she could come by to get it.

So now he waited for her, and it occurred to him that all he had done to attract her was act a bit distant, keeping his jaw set as though he had been through some grim times and didn't want to talk about them. He reminded himself to do that more often instead of going in for charm. It occurred to him that if his wife were to meet him for the first time now—and he were to behave the way he had with the divorcee—she would probably be terribly attracted to him and not be in Dubrovnik.

Late in the afternoon, he began to get a little edgy. He wished the girl would come get her bracelet and disappear. There was some good sun remaining and it was almost as though he could not really soak it up properly if he were scanning about looking for someone. He thought about the astronauts and felt guilty about his plan to skip over the flight to the moon and come in at the last minute for the landing. And he was sorry he hadn't been involved in the historic flight in any way. The story was that all Americans were involved in the landing, but he was one who wasn't. Even doing public-relations work for an outfit that made computers would have been something. Why wasn't he at a TV set, urging them on. One thing he had to do was get a great new TV set for the occasion. The stores would be closed in New York on Sunday, so he would have to pick one up in Los Angeles and take it back with him. It was a way of showing respect to the astronauts. Instead of hanging out a flag, he would finally get a clear TV set.

When she showed up, cool and blond in a white dress, he changed his mind about wanting to get rid of her quite that fast. He was not exactly overbrimming with desire, but on the other hand there was no point in wasting her either. They had some more of the great wine and she said, "Just talking to you I feel I'm making love to you."

"I don't feel that way," he said.

"Then why don't you grab me by the neck and take me back to your room."

"I don't do that," he said.

She went back with him anyway; the thing he noticed was that he was incapable of making any wrong moves. If he had gone in for a furious bout of nose-picking she would have found something charming about it. His comparisons were generally sporting ones. It was like one of those days in which everything you throw up sails right through the net.

"Have you noticed," she said, during the period thrown over to analysis, "that in our lovemaking I've been concerned primarily with pleasing you and not the slightest in pleasing myself."

"I wondered about that," he said. After she left, he checked to make sure there were no more of her bracelets around.

He was happy she was gone, but as soon as he was alone in the room, he decided it was not going to go well if he hung around any longer and he might as well leave Los Angeles as soon as possible, more or less on a high note.

Early the next morning he bought a small TV set from a tiny Japanese man who said it was a new model and was very proud of it. Towns couldn't get over how sharp and clear the picture was. He was not very mechanical, but he loved tiny, intricately made gadgets and had a vision of filling up a warm, comfortable apartment with them, living in it and spending most of his time turning them on and off. He felt a sudden burst of love for the tiny Japanese man who was practically a transistor himself and wanted to bend over and give him a hug. The fellow was very tiny and Towns wondered what would happen if he caught a disease that made you lose weight. He would probably just get a little smaller and stay all right. The fellow fixed up the TV box with a tricky little tissue-paper handle so that Towns wouldn't chafe his hands carrying it and Towns loved the handle almost as much as he did the TV set. The American version of that handle would have involved rows of factory workers and probably wouldn't have been as comfortable to the hand. Admittedly, it would have lasted longer. In any case, he promised himself that he would go to Japan some day although he was convinced he would be guilty of hair-raising breaches of social etiquette almost as soon as he set foot in the country.

He didn't want to hang around any longer. As soon as he got back to his hotel, he changed his plane reservation so that he would be back in New York in plenty of time to watch the landing on the delicious little new TV set. Then he had a last lunch in Los Angeles in a marvelously crumbled outdoor restaurant, ordering a last bottle of the great wine. The driver who took him to the airport said Towns looked like he was in the film business and asked if Towns could get him a copy of a film script, any script, so that he could study the form and then try one of his own. Towns couldn't see why they were so hard to get—surely libraries and bookstores carried tons of them—but the fellow said you'd be surprised how tough it was to get one. He seemed desperate so Towns took his address and said when he got to New York he would certainly try to rustle one up.

His idea was to take the little TV set back to his apartment in New York City and watch the moon landing there. The timing was set up just right. All that had to happen was for the plane to land on schedule and not get involved in any traffic tie-ups over JFK. One of the stewardesses sat next to Towns in the lounge and told him she had been all closed up for a long time, all through her childhood, but that she had opened up the previous fall. If Towns had been going to Los Angeles and not coming back from it, he probably would have asked if she was open or closed at the moment, but as it was, he let it slide. He didn't like to start in when he was on his way to New York. As it happened, the plane landed on time, but the porter who picked up his luggage slammed the TV box onto his luggage carrier and then heaved a massive suitcase on top of it; Towns was sure he'd done some massive damage to the set. "Don't you know there's a goddamn TV set in there," he said to the porter. In some strange way, he took it all as a direct attack on the tiny polite little Japanese man. "I didn't know that," said the porter. "Anyway, there's no way to guarantee smooth passage."

He had the feeling that no little TV set could survive a shot like that so he took it out of the box, attached the battery pack and switched it on in the terminal. Some sputtering pictures showed up. "See that," said the porter, "she coming in good." It came as no great surprise to Towns when the pictures bleeped out and turned to darkness. There was a package of warranties in the box, but Towns had no heart to get started with them. Besides, he had the feeling that once a mechanical gadget was injured, it went downhill no matter what you did to it. He gave the porter a look and then tossed the set lightly into a trash container. Someone in the terminal said the astronauts were going to be down in forty-five minutes. There wasn't any time to fool around now. Towns kept a key to his wife's house on the outskirts of the city and told a cabbie to take him there. The cabbie was certain Towns was going to get in the cab and then say he really wanted to go to Brooklyn. All through the ride he kept looking around suspiciously at Towns, expecting to be told to swerve off the highway and head back to the hated borough. When they were well out in the suburbs, the cabbie relaxed and said he couldn't believe his luck, getting a call to go to the country and not Brooklyn. As they neared the house, Towns became a little apprehensive even though he knew his wife was in Yugoslavia and his son was off to camp. Maybe he would find something he didn't like in there, a boyfriend, for example, sleeping in his old bed.

The house was a little damp, but otherwise it was eerily the way he had left it, with no signs of orgiastic frenzy. A next-door neighbor's house was occupied and Towns wondered if his kid was being teased for not having a dad around. That never once occurred to him in Los Angeles. He stayed in the kitchen awhile, eating a slice of Swiss cheese which seemed to be in remarkably good shape. The kitchen was the most beautiful room in the house, jammed with extraordinary knickknacks that had been accumulated over years of a marriage. He felt a little sorry for himself, spending all that time and money, helping to accumulate knickknacks and then never again getting to enjoy them. He had often said that possessions didn't mean a damned thing; all that counted was friendships and how you felt but he sure did love knickknacks and wondered whether he shouldn't have taken a few along. He went upstairs then, still with a shade of expectation he would find a guy up there, sleeping in his old bed and waiting for his old wife to get back from Dubrovnik. What if his wife took up with a fellow who was a strict disciplinarian and went around disciplining his kid? The California divorcee said she had run into that in her second marriage and had had to clear out so that her son wouldn't get seriously hurt. Towns would have to come back and slam the guy around a little.

He decided to watch the landing in his son's room. That way, when he went up to visit the boy, he would be able to give him a report on how his room was getting along. The boy had a TV set propped up next to his bed and Towns remembered bawling out the kid when he saw him smack the set a few times to get it into focus. It turned out that the boy was right and the only way to get it to work right was to smack it around a few times. The boy's room was filled with drawings that featured cartoon apes leaping from the tops of skyscrapers. The boy had some talent as an artist and Towns figured the leaping apes just represented a period he was going through, although he had to admit he had certainly been in that period for a long time. He wasn't too worried about it. All men who had amounted to anything had probably done things that seemed a little weird at the time. He checked around the room, getting the feel of the kid again and remembering some of the time he had spent in there, helping him fix it up. Then he sat down on the boy's bed and spotted the empty animal cage. The year previous, with the boy away at camp, he had gotten a call from the camp director saying the boy missed his pet and maybe Towns ought to bring it up to camp on visiting day. As far as the director was concerned it would put the summer over the top for the kid. Towns was feeling low about the marriage, which was splitting up at the time, and would have brought an elephant up if he had been asked. So he set out in his car and drove to Vermont with the white mouse in the back, throwing him a carrot whenever the animal got a little restless. That night he stopped off in New Hampshire at a motel, with the idea that he would head for camp early the next morning. The motel had a sign that said No Pets. He registered anyway, and then slipped the animal cage into the room when the owner wasn't looking. He had dinner at a local restaurant and when he got back to the motel, he caught the owner in his car headlights, standing with his legs spread apart and pointing to the grass. When Towns got out of the car, the owner said, "I told you no pets." The animal was lying on its back in the grass, cold and frozen, a sightless eye fixed at the moon. Towns marked the motel owner for life with a heavy ring he wore on his finger and for all he knew he had purchased for just such an occasion. He had to use lawyers, but he got away with it. At camp, he told the boy the animal had caught cold and died peacefully and painlessly in an animal hospital. He said he would get the boy any pet in the world, but the boy said he didn't want any more and kept the empty cage in his room with the door open.

Towns wondered if the astronauts went through things like that, whether they had ugly split-ups with wives who subsequently ran off to Dubrovnik, boys who drew pictures of apes leaping from buildings, if they ever wound up scarring men in far-off motels at midnight. His first impulse was to feel no they didn't. They were too sober and well-rooted for that kind of nonsense. Weren't they from "the other America," as it was so commonly felt in those same circles that were contemptuous of chilled forks and Brasilia Festival salads. But Towns had seen pictures of the pinched and weary faces of some of the astronauts' wives and it was his guess that all wasn't as tidy as it came off in the national magazines. He knew what those long separations for work did to marriages. There was probably no beating the system even if you were a space pioneer and your wife was an astronautical winner. He decided that they were good men who had tasted failure, ate too much marinara sauce on occasion, lusted after models, worried about cancer and, for all he knew, even had an overquick ejaculation or two. The thought gave him some comfort as he sat down on his boy's bed, gave the TV set a few shots to get it started, and got set to watch the fulfillment of man's most ancient dream.

Snore Wife and Some Several Dwarts

John Lennon

John Lennon writes about himself: "I was bored on the 9th of Octover, 1940, when, I believe, the Nasties were still booming us led by Madalf Heatlump (Who only had one). Anyway, they didn't get me. I attended varcous schools in Liddypol. And still didn't pass—much to my Aunties supplies. As a member of the most publified Beatles my and (P, G, and R's) records might seem funnier to some of you than this book, but as far as I'm conceived, this correction of short writty is the wonderful larf I've ever ready. God help and greed you all." The story comes from *A Spaniard in the Works* and unmasks Lennon as a literate who sneaked sessions with *Finnegans Wake* into his waking hours away from the guitar.

Once upon upon in a dizney far away—say three hundred year agoal if you like—there lived in a sneaky forest some several dwarts or cretins; all named—Sleezy, Grumpty, Sneeky, Dog, Smirkey, Alice? Derick—and Wimpey. Anyway they all dug about in a diamond mind, which was rich beyond compère. Every day when they came hulme from wirk, they would sing a song—just like ordinary wirkers—the song went something like—'Yo ho! Yo ho! it's off to wirk we go!'—which is silly really considerable they were comeing hulme. (Perhaps ther was slight housework to be do.)

One day howitzer they (Dwarts) arrived home, at aprodestant six o'cloth, and who?—who do they find?—but only Snore Wife, asleep in Grumpty's bed. He didn't seem to mine. 'Sambody's been feeding *my* porrage!' screams Wimpey, who was wearing a light blue pullover. Meanwife in a grand Carstle, not so mile away, a womand is looging in her daily mirror, shouting, 'Mirror mirror on the wall, whom is de fairy in the land.' which doesn't even rhyme. 'Cassandle!' answers the mirror. 'Chrish O'Malley' studders the womand who appears to be a Queen or a witch or an acorn.

'She's talking to that mirror again farther?' says Misst Cradock, 'I've just seen her talking to that mirror again.' Father Cradock turns round slowly from the book he is eating and explains that it is just a face she is going through and they're all the same at that age. 'Well I don't like it one ti,' continhughs Misst Cradock. Father Cradock turns round

SOURCE: John Lennon, *A Spaniard in the Works* (New York: Simon & Schuster, Inc., 1965), pp. 22–23.

slowly from the book he is eating, explaining that she doesn't have to like it, and promptly sets fire to his elephant. 'Sick to death of this elephant I am,' he growls, 'sick to death of it eating like an elephant all over the place.'

Suddenly bark at the Several Dwarts home, Snore Wife has became a *firm favourite,* especially with her helping arm, brushing away the little droppings. 'Good old Snore Wife!' thee all sage, 'Good old Snore Wife is our fave rave.' 'And I like you tooth!' rejoices Snore Wife, 'I like you all my little dwarts.' Without warping they hear a soddy voice continuallykhan shoubing and screeging about apples for sale. 'New apples for old!' says the above hearing voice. 'Try these nice new apples for chris-sake!' Grumpy turnips quick and answers shooting—'Why?' and they all look at him.

A few daisy lately the same voice comes hooting aboon the apples for sale with a rarther more firm aproach saying 'These apples are definitely for sale.' Snore Wife, who by this time is curiously aroused, stick her heads through the window. Anyway she bought one—which didn't help the trade gap at all. Little diggerydoo that it was parsened with deathly arsenickers. The woman (who was the wickered Queen in disgust) cackled away to her carstle in the hills larfing fit to bust.

Anyway the handsome Prince who was really Misst Cradock, found out and promptly ate the Wicked Queen and smashed up the mirror. After he had done this he journeyed to the house of the Several Dwarts and began to live with them. He refused to marry Snore Wife on account of his health, what with her being poissoned and that, but they came to an agreement much to the disgust of Sleepy—Grumpty—Sneeky—Dog—Smirkey—Alice?—Derick and Wimpy. The Dwarts clubbed together and didn't buy a new mirror, but always sang a happy song. They all livered happily ever aretor until they died—which somebody of them did naturally enough.

Man in the Drawer

Bernard Malamud

Bernard Malamud, teacher, novelist, and short-story writer, was born in Brooklyn, New York, and educated at The City College of New York. He has taught at several universities, including Harvard, but he has spent most of his career at Bennington College. His collection of short stories, *The Magic Barrel*, won the 1959 National Book Award. His novels include *The Natural, The Assistant, A New Life, The Fixer,* and *The Tenants* (1971). Much of his work depicts that part of the Jewish tradition that transforms suffering, grief, pity, and conscience into an affirmation of life's value and continuity.

Although he is regarded as the best interpreter of second-generation Jewish life in America, he has recently been writing about the plight of the Jew in postwar Europe (*Pictures of Fidelman*). Should an American writer touring Russia help a Soviet Jew to smuggle his work out of the Soviet Union? Can those qualities of spirit—the need to create art in face of grimly hostile conditions, the memory of an ancient common religion—be asserted against the social and political differences that make men strangers to each other? Skeptically affirmative, Malamud in this story speaks for countless people in the world today.

A soft shalom I thought I heard, but considering the Slavic cast of the driver's face, it seemed unlikely. He had been eying me in the rearview mirror since I had stepped into his taxi, and to tell the truth, I had momentary apprehensions. I'm forty-four and have recently lost weight but not, I admit, nervousness. It's my American clothes I thought at first, one is a recognizable stranger. Unless he was tailing me to begin with, but how could that be if it was a passing cab I had hailed myself?

He had picked me up in his noisy Volga of ancient vintage on the Lenin Hills, where I had been wandering all afternoon in and around Moscow University. Finally I had had enough of sight-seeing, and when I saw the cab, hallooed and waved both arms. The driver, cruising in a hurry, had stopped, you might say, on a kopek, as though I were someone he was dying to give a ride to; maybe somebody he had mistaken for a friend, whom, considering my recent experiences in Kiev, I wouldn't mind being mistaken for.

From the first minute our eyes were caught in a developing recognition although we were complete strangers. I knew nobody in Moscow

SOURCE: Bernard Malamud, "Man in the Drawer," *Atlantic Monthly* (March 1968), pp. 70–93.

except an Intourist girl or two. In the rectangular mirror his face seemed globular, the eyes small but canny—they probed, tugged, doubted, seemed to beg to know—give him a word and he'd be grateful, though why and for what cause he didn't say; then, as if the whole thing wearied him insufferably, he pretended no further interest.

Serves him right, I thought, but it wouldn't be a bad thing if he paid a little attention to the road once in a while or we'll never get where we're going, wherever that is. I realized I hadn't said because I wasn't sure myself—anywhere but back to the Metropole just yet. It was one of those days I couldn't stand my hotel room.

"Shalom!" he said finally out loud. It came forth like a declaration of faith.

"Shalom to you." So it was what I had heard, who would have thought so? We both relaxed, looking at opposite sides of the street.

The taxi driver sat in his shirt sleeves on a cool June day, not more than fifty-five Fahrenheit. He was a man in his thirties who looked as if what he ate didn't fully feed him—in afterthought a discontented type, his face on the worn side; not bad-looking even though the head seemed pressed a bit flat by somebody's heavy hand although protected by a mat of thick uncombed hair. His face, as I said, veered to Slavic: bony, broad cheekbones tapering to sensitive chin; but he sported a longish nose and distinctive larynx on a slender hairy neck, a mixed type, you might say. At any rate, the shalom had seemed to change his appearance, even of the probing eyes. He was dissatisfied for certain this fine June day—his lot, fate, himself, what? Also a sort of indigenous sadness hung on him, God knows from where, and he didn't mind if who he was was visible; not everyone could do that or wanted to. This one showed himself. Not too prosperous, I'd say, yet no underground man. He sat firm in his seat, all of him driving, perhaps a little frantically. I have an experienced eye for such details.

"Israeli?" he finally asked.

"Amerikansky." I know no Russian, just a few polite words.

He dug into his pocket for a thin pack of cigarettes and swung his hairy arm back, the Volga swerving to avoid a truck making a turn.

"Take care!"

I was thrown sideways, no apologies. Extracting a Bulgarian cigarette I wasn't eager to smoke—too strong—I handed him his pack. I was considering offering my prosperous American pack in return but didn't want to affront him.

"Feliks Levitansky," he said. "How do you do? I am the taxi driver." His accent was strong, verging to fruity but redeemed by fluency of tongue.

"Ah, you speak English? I sort of thought so."

"My profession is translator—English, French." He shrugged sideways.

"Howard Harvitz is my name. I'm here for a short vacation, about three weeks. My wife died not so long ago and I'm traveling partly to relieve my mind."

My voice caught, but then I went on to say that if I could manage to dig up some material for a magazine article or two, so much the better.

In sympathy Levitansky raised both hands from the wheel.

"Please watch out!"

"Horovitz?" he asked.

I spelled it for him. "Frankly, it was Harris after I entered college, but I changed it back recently. My father had it legally changed after I graduated from high school. He was a doctor, a practical one."

"You don't look to me Jewish."

"Not particularly, I admit."

After a minute he asked, "For which reason?"

"For which reason what?"

"Why you changed back your name?"

"I had a crisis in my life."

"Existential? Economic?"

"To tell the truth I changed it back after my wife died."

"What is the significance?"

"The significance is that I am closer to my true self."

The driver popped a match with his thumbnail and lit his cigarette.

"I am marginal Jew," he said, "although my father—Avrahm Isaakovich Levitansky—was Jewish. Because my mother was gentile woman I was given choice, but she insisted me to register for internal passport with notation of Jewish nationality in respect for my father. I did this."

"You don't say?"

"My father died in my childhood. I was rised—raised?—to respect Jewish people and religion, but I went my own way. I am atheist. This is inevitable."

"You mean Soviet life?"

Levitansky did not reply, smoked, as I grew embarrassed at my question. I looked around to see if I knew where we were. In afterthought he asked, "To which destination?"

I said, still on the former subject, that I had been a reluctant Jew myself, one might say. "My mother and father were thoroughly assimilated."

"By their choice?"

"Of course by their choice."

"Do you wish," he then asked, "to visit Central Synagogue on Arkhipova Street? Very interesting experience."

"Not just now," I said, "but take me to the Chekhov Museum on Sadovaya Kudrinskaya."

At that the driver, sighing, seemed to take heart.

Rose, I said to myself, you're really gone.

I blew my nose. After her death I had planned to visit the Soviet Union but couldn't get myself to move. I'm a slow man after a blow; though I confess I've never been one for making up his mind in a hurry, at least not on important things. Eight months later, when I was more or less packing, I felt that some of the relief I was looking for was, also, from the necessity of making an unexpected important personal decision. Out of loneliness I had begun to see my former wife, Lillian, in the spring, and before long, since she had remained unmarried and attractive, to my surprise—these things can slip from one sentence to another before you know what's going on—there was some hesitant talk of remarriage. In which case we could turn the Russian trip into a sort of honeymoon—I won't say second because we hadn't had much of a first. In the end, since our lives had been so frankly complicated—hard on each other—I found it impossible to make up my mind, though Lillian, I give her credit, seemed to be willing to take the chance. My feelings were so difficult to define to myself, I decided to decide nothing for sure. Lillian, who is a forthright type with a mind like a lawyer's, asked me if I was cooling off to the idea, and I told her that since the death of my wife I had been examining my life and needed more time to see where I stood. "Still?" she said, meaning the self-searching, and implying, I thought, forever. All I could answer was, "Still," and then, in anger, "forever." I warned myself afterward: stay out of any more complicated entanglements.

Anyway, that almost killed it. It wasn't a particularly happy evening, though it had its moments, you might say. I had once been deeply in love with Lillian. I figured then that a change of scene, maybe a month abroad, would be helpful. I had for a long time wanted to visit the USSR, and taking time to be alone, and, I hoped, at ease to think things through, might give the trip an additional value.

So I was surprised, when my visa was granted, though not too surprised, that my anticipation was by now blunted and I was experiencing uneasiness. I blamed it on a dread of traveling that sometimes hits me before long trips, that I have to make my peace with before I can move. Will I get there? Will I get lost? Maybe a war breaks out, and I'm surrounded by enemies on all sides. To be frank, though I've resisted the idea, I consider myself an anxious man, which, when I try to explain it to myself, means being this minute halfway into the next. I sit still in a hurry, worry uselessly about the future, and carry the burden of an overripe conscience.

I realized that what troubled me about going into Russia were those stories in the papers of some tourist or casual traveler in this or that Soviet city, who is suddenly grabbed by the secret police on charges of spying, "illegal economic activity," "hooliganism," or whatnot. This poor guy, like somebody from Sudbury, Mass., is held incommunicado until he confesses, and then is sentenced to a prison camp in the wilds of Siberia. After I got my visa I sometimes had fantasies of a stranger shoving a fat envelope of papers into my fist and then arresting me as I was reading them—of course for spying. What would I do in that case? I think I would pitch the envelope into the street, crying out, "Don't try that one on me, I can't even read Russian," and walk away with dignity, hoping that would freeze them in their tracks. A man in danger, if he's walking away from it, seems indifferent, innocent. At least to himself; but then in my mind I hear the sound of footsteps coming after me, and since my reveries tend to the rational, two KGB men grab me, shove both my arms against my back, and make the arrest. Not for littering the streets, as I hope might be the case, but for "attempting to dispose of certain incriminating documents," a fact it's difficult to deny.

I see Harvitz shouting, squirming, kicking his captors, till his mouth is shut by somebody's stinking palm, and he is dragged by superior force, not to mention a blackjack blow on the cranium, into the inevitable black Zis that I've read about and seen on movie screens.

The cold war is a frightening business, though I suppose for some more than others. I've sometimes wished spying had reached such a pitch of perfection that both the USSR and the USA knew everything there is to know about the other, and having sensibly exchanged this information by trading computers that keep facts up to date, let each other alone thereafter. That ruins the spying business; there's that much more sanity in the world, and for a man like me, the thought of a trip to the Soviet Union is pure pleasure.

Right away, at the Kiev airport, I had a sort of fright, after flying in from Paris on a mid-June afternoon. A customs official confiscated from my suitcase five copies of *Visible Secrets,* a poetry anthology for high school students I had edited some years ago, which I had brought along to give away to Russians I met who might be interested in American poetry. I was asked to sign a document the official had slowly written out in Cyrillic except that *Visible Secrets* was printed in English, with "secrets" underlined. The uniformed customs officer, a heavyset man with a layer of limp hair on a small head and red stars on his shoulders, said that the paper I was required to sign stated I understood it was not permitted to bring five copies of a foreign book into the Soviet Union, but I would get my property back anyway at the Moscow airport when I left the country. I worried that I oughtn't to sign but was urged to by my lady Intourist guide, a bleached blonde with wobbly high heels, whose looks and good humor kept me more or less calm, though my clothes were frankly steaming. She said it was a matter of no great importance and advised me to write my signature because it was delaying our departure to the Dnipro Hotel.

At that point I asked what would happen if I willingly parted with the books, no longer claimed them as my property. The Intouristka inquired of the customs man, who answered calmly, earnestly, and at great length.

"He says," she said, "that the Soviet Union will not take away from a foreign visitor his legal property."

Since I had only four days in the city and time was going fast, faster than usual, I reluctantly signed the paper plus four carbons—one for each book?—and was given a copy, which I filed in my billfold.

Despite this incident—it had its comic side—my stay in Kiev, in spite of the loneliness I usually feel my first few days in a strange city, went quickly and interestingly. In the mornings I was driven around in a private car on guided tours of the hilly, broad-avenued, green-leaved city, whose colors reminded me of a subdued Rome. But in the afternoons I wandered around alone. I would start by taking a bus or streetcar, riding a few kilometers, then getting off to walk within a particular neighborhood. Once I walked into a peasants' market where collective farmers and country people in beards and boots out of a nineteenth-century Russian novel sold their produce to city people. I thought I must write about this to Rose; I meant, of course, Lillian. Another time, in a deserted street when I happened to think of the customs receipt in my billfold, I turned in my tracks to see if I was being followed. I wasn't, but enjoyed the adventure.

An experience I didn't appreciate so much was getting lost one late afternoon several kilometers above a boathouse on the Dnieper. I was walking along the riverbank enjoying the sight of the boats and island beaches, and before I knew it, was a good distance from the hotel and eager to get back because I was hungry. I didn't feel like retracing my route on foot—too much tourism in three days—so I thought of a taxi or maybe an autobus that might be going in the general direction I had come from. Nothing doing, though I searched on some of the inner avenues for half an hour. I tried approaching a few passers-by whom I addressed in English, or pidgin-German, and occasionally trying *"pardonnez-moi";* but the effect was apparently to embarrass them. One young woman ran from me a few steps before she began to walk again. I stepped into an oculist's shop to ask advice of a professional-looking older woman, wearing pince-nez, a hairnet, and white smock. When I spoke in English, after momentary amazement her face froze, and she turned her back on me. Hastily thumbing through my guidebook to the phonetic expressions in Russian, I asked, *"Gdye* hotel?" adding "Dnipro?" To that she answered, *"Nyet."* "Taxi?" I asked. *"Nyet,"* this time clapping a hand to her heaving bosom. I figured I'd better leave. Though frustrated, annoyed, I spoke to two men passing by, one of whom, the minute he heard my first word, walked on quickly, his eyes aimed straight ahead, the other indicating by gestures that he was deaf and dumb. On impulse I tried him in halting Yiddish that my grandfather had long ago taught me, and was then directed, in an undertone in the same language, to a nearby bus stop.

As I was unlocking the door to my room, thinking this was a story I would be telling friends all autumn, my phone was ringing. It was a woman's voice. I understood "Gospodin Garvitz" and one or two other words as she spoke at length in musical Russian. In fact, her voice was like a singer's. Though I couldn't get the gist of her remarks, I had this sudden vivid reverie, you might call it, of walking with a pretty Russian girl in a birchwood or thereabouts, coming out on the other side in a field that sloped to the water, and then rowing her around on a small lake. It was a very peaceful business. That was the general picture; but when she was done talking, whatever I had to say I said in English, and she slowly hung up.

The next morning after breakfast, she, or someone who sounded like her—I recognized the contralto quality—called again.

"If you could understand English," I said, "or maybe a little German or French—even Yiddish, if you happen to know it—we'd get along fine. But not in Russian, I'm afraid. *Nyet Russki.* I'd be glad to meet you for lunch, or tea if you like; so if you get the drift of these remarks why don't you say *da?* Then dial the English interpreter on extension 37. She could tell me what's what, and we can meet at your convenience."

I had the impression she was listening with both ears but after a while the phone hung silent in my hand. I wondered where she had got my name, and whether someone was testing me to find out if I did or didn't speak Russian. I honestly did not.

Afterward I wrote a short airmail letter to Lillian, telling her I would be leaving for Moscow via Aeroflot, tomorrow at 4 P.M., and I intended to stay there for two weeks, with a break of maybe three or four days in Leningrad, at the Astoria Hotel. I wrote down the exact dates and later mailed the letter in a box some distance from the hotel, whatever good that did. I hoped Lillian would get it in time to reach me by return mail before I left the Soviet Union. To tell the truth, I felt uneasy all day.

But the next morning my mood had changed, and as I was standing at the railing in a park above the Dnieper, looking at the buildings going up across the river in what had once been steppeland, I had an expansive feeling. The vast construction I beheld—it was as though two or three scattered cities were rising out of the earth—astonished me. This sort of thing was going on all over Russia—halfway around the world—and when I considered what it meant in terms of sheer labor, capital goods, plain morale I was then and there convinced that the Soviet Union would never willingly provoke a war, nuclear or otherwise, with the United States. Neither would America, in its right mind, with the Soviet Union.

For the first time since I had come to Russia, I felt safe and secure and enjoyed there, at the breezy railing above the Dnieper, a rare few minutes of euphoria.

Why is it that the most interesting architecture is from Czarist times I asked myself, and if I'm not mistaken Levitansky quivered, no doubt a coincidence. Unless I had spoken to myself aloud which I sometimes do; I decided I hadn't. We were on our way to the museum, hitting a fast eighty kilometers, which translated to fifty miles an hour was not too bad because traffic was sparse.

"What do you think of my country, the Union of Soviet Socialist Republics?" the driver inquired, turning his head a half circle to see where I was.

"Please watch where we're going."

"Don't be nervous, I drive now for years."

"I don't care for needless risks."

Then I said I was impressed by much I had seen. It was obviously a great country.

Levitansky's face appeared in the mirror globularly smiling, his dark teeth eroded. The smile seemed to emerge from within the mouth. Now that he had revealed his half-Jewish background I had the impression he looked more Jewish than Slavic, and possibly more dissatisfied than I had thought.

"Also our system—Communism?"

I answered carefully, not wanting to give offense. "I'll be perfectly honest. I've seen some unusual things here—even inspiring—but my personal taste is for more individual freedom than people seem to have here. America has its serious faults but at least we're privileged to criticize, if you know what I mean. My father used to say, 'You can't beat the Bill of Rights.' It's an open society, which means freedom of choice, at least in theory."

"Communism is altogether better system," Levitansky replied calmly after a minute, "although is not in present stage totally realized. In present stage"—he gulped for air, swallowed, and did not finish the thought. Instead he said, "Our revolution was magnificent holy event. I love early Soviet history, excitement of Communist idealism, and victory over bourgeois and imperialist forces. Overnight was lifted up—uplifted—the whole suffering Russian masses. It was born a life of new possibilities for all in society. Pasternak called this 'splendid surgery.' Evgeny Zamyatin spoke thus: 'The revolution consumes the earth with the fire but then is born a new life.' "

I didn't argue, each to his own revolution.

"You told before," said Levitansky, glancing at me again in the mirror, "that you wish to write articles of your visit. Political or not political?"

"I don't write on politics although interested in it. What I have in my mind is something on the literary museums of Moscow for an American travel magazine. That's the sort of thing I do. I'm a free-lance writer." I laughed a little apologetically. It's strange how stresses shift when you're in another country.

Levitansky politely joined in the laugh, stopping in midcourse. "I wish to be certain, what is free-lance writer?"

"Well, an editor might propose an article, and I either accept the idea or I don't. Or I can write about something that happens to interest me and take my chances I can sell it. Sometimes I don't, and that's so much down the drain financially. What I like about it is I am my own boss. I also edit a bit. I've done anthologies of poetry and essays, both for high school kids."

"We have here free-lance. I am also a writer," Levitansky said solemnly.

"You don't say? You mean as a translator?"

"Translation is my profession, but I am also original writer."

"Then you do three things—write, translate, and drive this cab?"

"The taxi is not my true work."

"Are you translating anything now?"

The driver cleared his throat. "In present time I have no translation project."

"What sort of thing do you write?"

"I write stories."

"Is that so? What kind, if I might ask?"

"I will tell you what kind—little ones—short stories imagined from life."

"Have you published any?"

He seemed about to turn around to look me in the eye but reached instead into his shirt pocket. I offered my American pack. He shook out a cigarette and lit it, exhaling slowly.

"A few pieces but not recently. To tell the truth"—he sighed—"I write for the drawer. Like Isaac Babel, 'I am master of the genre of silence.' "

"I've heard the expression," I said, not knowing what else to say.

"The mice should read and criticize," Levitansky said bitterly. "Thus what they don't eat they make their drops—droppings?—on. This is perfect criticism."

"I'm sorry about that."

"We arrive now to Chekhov Museum."

I leaned forward to pay him and made the impulsive mistake of adding a one-ruble tip. He was immediately angered. "I am Soviet citizen." He forcibly returned the ruble.

"Call it a thoughtless error," I apologized. "No harm meant."

"Hiroshima! Nagasaki!" he taunted as the Volga took off in a cloud of smoke. "Aggressor against poor people of Vietnam!"

"None of that is any of my doing!" I called after him.

An hour and a half later, after I had signed the guest book and was leaving the museum, I saw someone standing, smoking, under a linden tree across the street. Nearby was a parked taxi. We stared at each other—I wasn't certain at first who it was but Levitansky nodded amiably to me, calling "Welcome! Welcome!" He waved an arm, smiling open-mouthed. He had combed his thick hair and was now wearing a loose dark suit over his tieless white shirt, and yards of baggy pants. His socks, striped red-white-and-blue, you could see under his sandals.

I am forgiven, I thought. "Welcome to you," I said, crossing the street.

"How did you enjoy the Chekhov Museum?"

"I did indeed. I've made a lot of notes. You know what they have there? They have one of his black fedoras and also his pince-nez that you see in pictures of him. Awfully moving."

Levitansky wiped one eye, to my surprise. He seemed not the same man, at any rate somewhat modified. It's funny, you find out a few personal facts about a stranger and he changes as he speaks. The taxi driver is now a writer, even if part-time. Anyway that's my dominant impression.

"Excuse me my former anger," Levitansky said. "Now is not for me the best of times. 'It was the best of times, it was the worst of times,' " he quoted, smiling sadly.

"So long as you pardon my unintentional blunder. Are you perhaps free to drive me to the Metropole, or are you here by coincidence?"

I looked around to see if anyone was coming out of the museum.

"If you wish to engage me I will drive you, but at first I will show you something—how do you say?—of interest?"

He reached through the open front window of the taxi and brought forth a flat package wrapped in brown paper tied with string.

"Stories which I wrote."

"I don't read Russian," I said quickly.

"My wife has translated of them, four. She is not by her profession a translator, although her English is advanced and sensitive. She has been for two years in England for Soviet Purchasing Commission. We became acquainted in university. I prefer not to translate my own stories because I do not translate so well Russian into English although I translate beautifully the opposite. Also I will not force myself—it is like self-imitation. Perhaps the stories are a little awkward in English—also my wife admits this—but at least you can read and form opinion."

He offered me the package as if it were a bouquet of spring flowers. I thought to myself, can it be some sort of trick? Are they checking up on me because I signed that damned document at the Kiev airport, five copies no less?

Levitansky seemed to read my mind. "It is purely stories."

He bit the string in two, and laying the package on the fender of the Volga, unpeeled the wrapping. There were four stories, clipped separately, typed on long sheets of thin blue paper. I took one Levitansky handed me and scanned the top page—it seemed a story—then I flipped through the other pages and handed the manuscript back. "I'm not much of a critic of stories."

"I don't seek a critic. I seek for reader of literary experience and taste. If you have redacted books of poems and also essays, you will be able to judge literary qualities of my stories. Please, I request that you will read them."

After a long minute I heard myself say, "Well I might at that." I didn't recognize the voice and could hardly understand why I was saying it. You might say I spoke apart from myself, with a reluctance that either he didn't recognize or didn't care to acknowledge.

"If you respect—if you approve my stories, perhaps you will be able to arrange for publication in Paris or either London?" His large larynx wobbled nervously.

I stared at the man. "I don't happen to be going to Paris, and I'll be in London only between planes to the USA."

"In this event, perhaps you will show to your publisher, and he will publish my work in America?" Levitansky was now visibly miserable.

"In America?" I said, raising my voice in disbelief.

For the first time he gazed around cautiously before replying.

"If you will be so kind to show them to publisher of your books—is he reliable publisher?—perhaps he will also wish to put out volume of my stories? I will make contract whatever he will like. Money, if I could get, is not an ideal."

"What volume are you talking about?"

He said that from thirty stories he had written he had chosen eighteen, of which these four were a sample. "Unfortunately more are not now translated. My wife is biochemist assistant and works long hours in laboratory. I am sure your publisher will enjoy to read these. It will depend on your opinion."

Either the man has a fantastic imagination or he's out of his right mind, I thought. "I wouldn't want to get myself involved in smuggling a Russian manuscript out of Russia."

"I have informed you that my manuscript is only made-up stories."

"That may be, but it's still a chancy enterprise. I'd be taking chances I have no particular desire to take, to be frank."

"At least if you will read," he sighed.

I took the stories again and thumbed slowly through each. What I was looking for I couldn't say: maybe a booby trap? Should I or shouldn't I? I thought. Why should I?

He handed me the wrapping paper, and I rolled up the stories in it. The quicker I read them, the quicker I've read them. I got into the cab.

"As I said, I'm at the Metropole," I told him. "Come by tonight about nine o'clock, and I'll give you my opinion for what it's worth. But I'm afraid I'll have to limit it to that, Mr. Levitansky, without further obligation or expectations, or it's no deal. My room number is 538."

"Tonight?—so soon?" he said, scratching both palms. "You must read with care so you will realize the art."

"Tomorrow night, then. I'd rather not have them around in my room longer than that."

Levitansky agreed. Whistling softly through his eroded teeth, he drove me carefully to the Metropole.

That night, sipping vodka from a drinking glass, at first reluctantly I read Levitansky's stories. They were simply and strongly written—I can't say I was surprised, I sort of expected it—and not badly translated; in fact the translation read better than I had been led to think although there were of course gaffes here and there, odd constructions, ill-fitting words surrounded by question marks, taken, I suppose, from a thesaurus. And the stories, short tales dealing—somewhat to my surprise—mostly with Jews and you might say their problems, were good, really moving. The situation they revealed wasn't news to me: I'm a careful reader of the *New York Times*. But the stories weren't written to complain, nothing of the kind. What they had to say was achieved as form, no telling "the dancer from the dance." I finished reading, poured myself another glass of potato potion—I was begining to feel high, with occasional thoughts of wondering why I was putting so much away—just relaxing, I guess. I then reread the stories with a sense of growing admiration for Levitansky. I had the feeling he was no ordinary man. At first I felt excited, then depressed, as if I had been let in on a secret I didn't want to know.

It's a hard life here for a fiction writer, I thought.

Afterward, having the stories around began to make me uneasy. In one of them a Russian writer starts to burn his stories in the kitchen sink. But nobody had burned these. I thought to myself, if I'm caught with them in my possession, considering what they indicate about conditions here, there's no question I'd be in trouble. I wish I had insisted that Levitansky come back for them tonight.

There was a solid rap on the door. I felt as though I had risen a good few inches out of my seat. It was, after a while, Levitansky.

"Out of the question," I said, thrusting the stories at him. "Absolutely out of the question!"

The next night we sat facing each other over cognac in the writer's small, book-crowded study. He was dignified, at first haughty, wounded, hardly masking his impatience. I wasn't myself exactly comfortable.

I had come out of courtesy and other considerations, I guess; principally a sense of dissatisfaction I couldn't exactly define, except it tied up in my mind with who I was and wanted to be, issues that disturb me, to say the least, because they sometimes compel me to get involved in ways I don't want to get involved, always a dangerous business.

Levitansky, the taxi driver rattling around in his Volga-Pegasus and amateur trying to palm off a half-ass manuscript, had faded in my mind, and I saw him simply as a serious Soviet writer with publishing problems. What can I do for him? I thought. Why should I?

"I didn't express what was on my mind last night," I apologized. "You sort of caught me by surprise, I'm sorry to say."

Levitansky was scratching each hand with the fingers of the other. "How did you acquire my address?"

I reached into my pocket for a wad of folded brown wrapping paper. "It's right on this—Novo Ostapovskaya Street, 488, Flat 59. I took a cab."

"I had forgotten this."

Maybe, I thought.

Still, I had practically had to put my foot in the door to get in. Levitansky's wife had answered my uncertain knock, her eyes uneasily worried, which I took to be the expression she lived with. The eyes were astonished to behold a stranger, and outright hostile once I had inquired in English for her husband. I felt, as in Kiev, that my native tongue had become my enemy.

"Have you not the wrong apartment?"

"I hope not. Not if Mr. Levitansky lives here. I came to see him about his—er—manuscript."

Her eyes darkened as her face blanched. Ten seconds later I was in the flat, the door shut tightly behind me.

"Levitansky!" she summoned him. It had a reluctant quality: come but don't come.

He appeared at once in apparently the same shirt, pants, tri-coloured socks. There was at first pretend-boredom in a tense, tired face. He could not, however, conceal excitement, his lit eyes roving, returning, roving.

"Oh, ho," Levitansky said, whatever it meant.

My God, I thought, has he been expecting me?

"I came to talk to you for a few minutes, if you don't mind," I said. "I want to say what I really think of your stories that you kindly let me read."

He curtly said something in Russian to his wife, and she snapped an answer back. "I wish to introduce my wife, Irina Filipovna Levitansky, biochemist. She is patient although not a saint."

She smiled tentatively, an attractive woman about twenty-eight, a little on the hefty side, in house slippers and plain dress. The edge of her slip hung below her skirt.

There was a bit of British in her accent. "I am pleased to be acquainted." If so one hardly noticed. She stepped into black pumps and slipped a silver bracelet on her wrist, a lit cigarette dangling from the corner of her mouth. Her legs and arms were shapely, her brown hair cut short. I had the impression of tight thin lips in a pale face.

"I will go to Kovalevsky, next door," she said.

"Not on my account, I hope? All I have to say—"

"Our neighbors in the next flat." Levitansky grimaced. "Also thin walls." He knocked a knuckle on a hollow wall.

I chuckled politely.

"Please, not long," Irina said, "because I am afraid."

Surely not of me? Agent Howard Harvitz, CIA, a comical thought.

Their living room wasn't unattractive, but Levitansky signaled the study inside. He offered a slightly sweet cognac in whisky tumblers, then sat facing me on the edge of his chair, his repressed energy all but visible. I had the momentary sensation his chair might begin to move, even fly off.

If he goes he goes alone.

"What I came to say," I told him, "is I like your stories and am sorry I didn't say so last night. I like the primary quality of the writing. The stories impress me as strong, if simply wrought, and I appreciate your feeling for people and at the same time the objectivity with which you render them. It's sort of Chekhovian in quality. For instance, that story about the old father coming to see the son who ducks out on him. I guess I can't comment on your style, having only read the stories in translation."

"Chekhovian," Levitansky admitted, smiling through his worn teeth, "is fine compliment. Mayakovsky, our poet, described him 'the strong and gay artist of the word.' I wish I was so gay in respect of enjoyment of art and life." He looked at the drawn shade in the room, though maybe no place in particular, then said, perhaps heartening himself, "In Russian is magnificent my style—precise, economy, including wit. The style is difficult to translate in English, which is less rich language."

"I've heard that said. In fairness I should add I have some reservations about the stories, yet who hasn't about any given piece of creative work?"

"I have myself reservations."

The admission made, I skipped the criticisms. I had been looking at a picture on his bookcase, and asked who it was. "It's a face I've seen before. The eyes are quite poetic, you might say."

"So is the voice. This is Boris Pasternak as young man. On the wall yonder is Mayakovsky that I mentioned to you. He was also remarkable poet, wild, joyous, neurasthenic, a lover of the revolution. He spoke, 'This is *my* Revolution.' To him was it 'a holy washerwoman who cleaned off all the filth from the earth.' Unfortunately he was later disillusioned and shot himself."

"I read that somewhere."

"He wrote: 'I wish to be understood by my country—but if no, I will fly through Russia like a slanting rainstorm.' "

"I bet it sounds magnificent in Russian. Have you by chance read *Doctor Zhivago?*"

"I have read," the writer sighed, and then began to recite in Russian, I guessed some lines from a poem.

"It is to Marina Tsvetayeva, Soviet poetess, friend of Pasternak." Levitansky fiddled with the pack of cigarettes on the table with the cognac. "The end of her life was unfortunate."

"I guess why I really came," I said, "is I wanted to express to you my sympathy and respect."

Levitansky popped a match with his thumbnail. His hand trembled, so he shook the flame out without lighting the cigarette.

Embarrassed for him, I pretended to be looking elsewhere. "It's a small room. Does your son sleep here?"

"Don't confuse my story which you read with life of author. My wife and I are married eight years but without children."

"Might I ask whether the other experience you describe in that same story—the interview with the editor—was that true?"

"Not true," the writer said impatiently. "I write from imagination. I am not interested to repeat contents of diaries or total memory."

"On that I go along with you."

"Also, which is not in story, I have submitted to Soviet journals sketches and tales many times but only few have been published, although not my best."

"Did you submit any of the Jewish stories?"

"Please, stories are stories, they have not nationality."

"I mean by that those about Jews."

"Some I have submitted, but they were not accepted."

Brave man, I thought. "After reading the four you gave me, I wondered how it was you write so well about Jews? You call yourself a marginal one—I believe that was your word—but you write with authority about them. Not that one can't, I suppose, but it's surprising when one does."

"Imagination makes authority. My work is work of imagination. When I write about Jews comes out stories, so I write about Jews. I write about subjects that make for me stories. Is not important that I am marginal Jew. What is important is observation, feeling, also the art. In the past I have observed my Jewish father. Also I observe sometimes Jews in the synagogue. I sit there on the bench for strangers. The gabbai watches me, and I watch him. But whatever I write, whether is about Jews, Galicians, or Georgians, must be a work of invention or it does not live."

"I'm not much of a synagogue-goer myself," I told him, "but I like to drop in once in a while to be refreshed by the language and images of a time and place where God was. That's funny because I had no religious education to speak of."

"I am atheist."

"I understand, though, what you mean by imagination—for instance that praying shawl story. But am I right"—I lowered my voice—"that I detect you might also be saying something about the condition of the Jews—er—at the moment?"

"I do not make propaganda," Levitansky said sternly. "I am not Israeli spokesman. I am Soviet artist."

"I didn't mean you weren't, but there's a strong current of sympathy, and after all, ideas come from somewhere."

"My purpose belongs to me."

"One senses, if I might say, an attack on injustice."

"Whatever is the injustice, the product must be art."

"Well, I respect your philosophy."

"Please do not respect so much," the writer said irritably. "We have in this country a quotation: 'It is impossible to make out of apology a fur coat.' The idea is similar. I appreciate respect but need now practical assistance."

Expecting words of the sort, I started to say something noncommittal.

"Listen at first to me," Levitansky said, smacking the table with his palm. "I am in desperate condition—situation. I have written for years, but little is published. In the past, one, two editors who were my friends told me, private, that my stories are excellent, but I violate socialist realism. This what you call objectivity, they called it excessive naturalism and sentiment. It is hard to listen to such nonsense. They advise me to walk but not with my legs. They wanted me; also they have made excuses for me to others. Even they said I am crazy, although I explained to them I submit my stories *because* Soviet Union is great country. A great country does not fear what artist writes. A great country breathes in its lungs work of writers, painters, musicians, and becomes more great, more healthy. This is what I told to them, but they replied I am not enough realist. This is the reason that I am not invited to be member of Writers Union." He smiled sourly. "They warned me to stop submitting to journals my work, so I have stopped."

"I'm sorry about that," I said. "I don't myself go for exiling the poets."

"I cannot continue longer anymore in this fashion," Levitansky said, laying his hand on his heart. "I must free from drawer my imagination. I feel I am myself locked in drawer with my poor stories. Now I must get out or I suffocate. It becomes for me each day more difficult to write. I need help. It is not easy to request a stranger for such important personal favor. My wife advised me not. She is angry, also frightened, but is impossible for me to go on in this way. I am convinced I am important Soviet writer. I must have my audience. I wish to have in someone's mind different than my own and my wife acknowledgment of my art. I wish them to know my work is related to Russian writers of the past, as well as modern. I am in tradition of Chekhov, Gorky, Isaac Babel. I know if book of my stories is published, it will make for me good reputation. This is reason why you must help me—it is necessary for my interior liberty."

His confession came in an agitated burst. I use the word advisedly because that's partly what upset me. I have never cared for confessions of this kind, which are a way of involving unwilling people in others' personal problems. Russians are past masters of this art—you can see in their novels.

"I appreciate the honor of your request," I said, "but all I am is a passing tourist. That's a pretty tenuous relationship between us."

"I do not ask tourist—I ask human being, man," Levitansky said passionately. "Also you are free-lance writer. You know who I am and what is on my heart. You sit in my house. Who else can I ask? I would better prefer to publish in Europe my stories, maybe with Mondadori or Einaudi in Italy, but if this is impossible to you I will publish in America. Someday will my work be read in my country, maybe after I am dead. This is terrible irony, but my generation lives on such ironies. Since I am not now ambitious to die, it will be great relief to me to know that at least in one language is alive my art. Osip Mandelstam wrote: 'I will be enclosed in some alien speech.' Better so than nothing."

"You say I know who you are but do you know who *I* am?" I asked him. "I'm a plain person, not very imaginative though I don't write a bad article. My whole life, for some reason, has been without much adventure, except I was divorced once and remarried happily to a woman whose death I am still mourning. Now I'm here more or less on a vacation, not to jeopardize myself by taking serious chances of an unknown kind. What's more—and this is the main thing I came to tell you—I wouldn't at all be surprised if I am already under suspicion and would do you more harm than good."

I told Levitansky about the airport incident in Kiev and the paper I had signed five copies of. "I signed a document I couldn't even read, which was a foolish thing to do."

"In Kiev this happened?"

"That's right."

Levitansky laughed dismally. "It would not happen to you if you entered through Moscow. In the Ukraine—what is your word?—they are rubes, country people."

"That might be—nevertheless, I signed the paper."

"Do you have copy?"

"Not with me. It's in my room in the hotel."

"I am certain this is receipt for your books which officials will return to you when you depart from Soviet Union."

"That's just what I'd be afraid of."

"Why afraid?" he asked. "Are you afraid to receive back umbrella which you have lost?"

"I'd be afraid one thing might lead to another—more questions, more searches. It would be foolhardy to have your manuscript in my suitcase, in Russian no less, that I can't read. Suppose they accuse me of being some kind of courier or spy?"

The thought raised me to my feet. I then realized the tension in the room was thick as steam, mostly mine.

Levitansky rose, embittered. "There is no question of spying. I do not think I have presented myself as traitor to my country."

"I didn't say anything of the sort. All I'm saying is I don't want to get into trouble with the Soviet authorities. Nobody can blame me for that. In other words, the enterprise is not for me."

"I have made inquirings," Levitansky said desperately. "You will have nothing to fear for a tourist who has been a few weeks in USSR under guidance of Intourist and does not speak Russian. My wife said to me your baggage will not be further inspected. They sometimes do so to political people, also to bourgeois journalists who have made bad impression. I would deliver to you manuscript in the last instance. It is typed on less than one hundred fifty sheets thin paper and will make small package. If it should look to you like trouble you can leave it in dustbin. My name will not be anywhere and if they find it and track—trace to me the stories, I will say I have thrown them out myself. It will make no difference anyway. If I stop to write I may as well be dead. No harm will come to you."

"I'd rather not if you don't mind."

With what I guess was a curse in Russian, Levitansky reached for the portrait on his bookcase and flung it against the wall. Pasternak struck Mayakovsky, splattered him with glass, breaking his own, and both pictures crashed to the floor.

"Free-lance writer," he shouted, "go to hell back to America! Tell to Negroes about Bill of Rights! Tell them they are free although you keep them slaves! Talk to sacrificed Vietnamese people!"

Irina Filipovna entered the room on the run. "Feliks," she entreated, "Kovalevsky hears every word!"

"Please," she begged me, "please go away. Leave poor Levitansky alone. I beg you from my miserable heart."

I left in a hurry. The next day I left for Leningrad.

Three days later, not exactly at my best after a tense visit to Leningrad, I was sitting loosely in a beat-up taxi with a cheerful Intouristka, a half-hour after my arrival at the Moscow airport. We were driving to the Ukraine Hotel, where I was assigned for my remaining few days in the Soviet Union. I would have preferred the Metropole again because it's so conveniently located and I was used to it; but on second thought, better some place where a certain party wouldn't know I lived. The Volga we were riding in seemed somehow familiar, but if so it was safely in the hands of a small stranger with a large wool cap, a man wearing sunglasses who paid me no particular attention.

I had had a few pleasant minutes in Leningrad on my first day. On a white summer's evening, shortly after I had unpacked in my room at the Astoria, I discovered the Winter Palace and Hermitage after a walk along the Nevsky Prospekt. Chancing on Palace Square, vast and deserted, I felt an unexpected emotion, you might say, in thinking of the revolutionary events that had occurred on this spot. My God, I thought, why should I feel myself part of Russian history? It's a contagious business, what happens to men. On the Palace Bridge I gazed at the broad ice-blue Neva, in the distance the golden steeple of the cathedral built by Peter the Great, gleaming under masses of wind-driven clouds in patches of green sky. It's the Soviet Union but it's still Russia.

The next day I woke up anxious. In the street I was approached twice by strangers speaking English; I think my suede shoes attracted them. The first, grey-faced and badly dressed, wanted to sell me black market rubles. "*Nyet,*" I said, tipping my straw hat and hurrying on. The second, a bearded boy of nineteen, with a left-sided tuft longer than that on the right, wearing a home-knitted green pullover, offered to buy jazz records, "youth clothes," and American cigarettes. "Sorry, nothing for sale." I escaped him too, except that he in his green sweater followed me for a mile along one of the canals. I broke into a run, then forced myself to stop. When I looked back he had disappeared. I slept badly at night—it stayed light too long past midnight; and in the morning inquired about the possibility of an immediate flight to Helsinki. I was informed I couldn't possibly get one for a week. Calming myself, I decided to return to Moscow a day before I had planned to, mostly to see what they had in the Dostoevsky Museum.

I had been thinking a good deal about Levitansky. How much of a writer was he really? I had read four of eighteen stories he wanted to publish. Suppose he had showed me the four best and the others were mediocre or thereabouts? Was it worth taking a chance for that? I thought, the best thing for my peace of mind is to forget the guy. Before checking out of the Astoria I received a chatty letter from Lillian, forwarded from Moscow, apparently not an answer to my recent letter to her, but one written earlier. Should I marry her? Who knows, I don't. The phone rang piercingly, and when I picked up the receiver, no one answered. In the plane to Moscow I had visions of a crash. There must be many in the Soviet Union nobody ever reads of.

In my room on the twelfth floor of the Ukraine I relaxed in a plastic "leather" armchair. There was also a single low bed, and a utilitarian pinewood desk, an apple-green phone plunked on it for instant use. I'll be home in a week, I thought. Now I'd better shave and see if anything is left over downstairs in the way of a concert or opera ticket for tonight. I'm in the mood for a little music.

The electric plug in the bathroom didn't work, so I put away my shaver and was lathering up when I jumped to a single explosive knock on the door. I opened it cautiously, and there stood Levitansky with a brown paper packet in his hand.

Is this son of a bitch out to compromise me?

"How did you happen to find out where I was only twenty minutes after I got here, Mr. Levitansky?"

"How I found you?" the writer shrugged. He seemed deathly tired, a bit pop-eyed, the face longer, leaner, resembling in a way a hungry fox on his last unsteady legs but still canny. "My brother-in-law was the chauffeur for you from the airport. He heard the girl inquire your name. We have spoke of you. Dmitri—this is my wife's brother—informed me you have registered at the Ukraine. I inquired downstairs your room number, and it was granted to me."

"However it was," I said firmly, "I want you to know I haven't changed my mind. I don't want to get involved. I thought it all through while I was in Leningrad, and that's my final decision."

"I may come in?"

"Please, but for obvious reasons I'd appreciate a short visit."

Levitansky sat, somewhat shriveled, skinny knees pressed together, in the armchair, his parcel awkwardly on his lap. If he was happy to have found me, his face didn't show it.

I finished shaving, put on a fresh shirt, and sat down on the bed. "Sorry I have nothing to offer in the way of an aperitif, but I could call down for something."

Levitansky twiddled his fingers no. He was dressed without change down to his red-white-and-blue socks. Did his wife wash out the same pair every night, or were all his socks red-white-and-blue?

"To speak frankly," I said, "I have to protest about this constant tension you've whipped up in and around me. Nobody in his right mind can expect a total stranger visiting the Soviet Union to pull his personal chestnuts out of the fire. It's your own country that's restricting you as a writer, not me or the United States of America, and since you live here, what can you do but live with it?"

"I love my country," Levitansky said with dignity.

"Who said you didn't? So do I love mine, though love for country, let's face it, is a mixed bag of marbles. Nationality isn't soul, as I'm sure you will agree. But what I'm also saying is there are things about a man's country he might not like that he has to make his peace with. I'm not saying it's easy but if you're up against a wall you can't climb or dig under or outflank in some way, at least stop banging your head against it, not to mention mine. Make your peace in some way. It's amazing, for instance, all that can be said in a fairy tale."

"I have written already my fairy tales," Levitansky said moodily. "Now is the time for truth without disguises. I will make my peace to this point where it interferes with work of my imagination—my interior liberty; and then I must stop to make my peace. My brother-in-law has also told to me, 'You must write acceptable stories, others can do it, so why can't you?' and I have answered him, 'They must be acceptable to *me. Ich kann nicht anders!*' "

"In that case, aren't you up against the impossible? If you permit me to say so, are those Jews in your stories, if they can't have their matzos and prayer books, any freer in their religious lives than you are as a writer? That's what you're really saying when you write about them. What I mean is, one has to face up to his society."

"I have faced up. Do you face up to yours?" he said, with a flash of scorn.

"Not as well as I might, I admit. My own problem is not that I can't express myself but that I don't. In my own mind Vietnam is a terrifying mistake, though I've never spoken out against it except to sign a petition or two. My first wife used to criticize me. She said I wrote the wrong things and was involved in everything but action. My second wife knew this but she made me think she didn't."

From the heat of my body I knew I was blushing.

Levitansky's large larynx moved up like a flag on a pole, then sank wordlessly.

My God, not another confession, I hoped.

He tried again, saying, "The Soviet Union preservates for us the great victories of our revolution. Because of this I have remained for years at peace with the State. Communism is still to me inspirational ideal, although this historical period is spoiled by leaders who have taken impoverished view of humanity. They have pissed on revolution."

"Stalin?"

"Him, but also others. Even so I have obeyed party directives, and when I could not longer obey, I wrote for drawer. I said to myself, 'Levitansky, history changes every minute, and Communism also will change.' I believed if the State restricts two, three generations of artists, what is this against development of true socialist society—maybe best society of world history? So what does it mean if some of us are sacrificed to Party purpose? The aesthetic mode is not in necessity greater than politics—than needs of revolution. And what if are suppressed two generations of artists? Therefore will be so much less bad books, paintings, music. Then in fifty years more will be secure the State and all Soviet artists will say whatever they will. This is what I thought, but I do not longer think so in this manner. I do not believe more in *partiinost,* which is guided thought. I do not believe in Bolshevization of literature. I do not think revolution is fulfilled in country of unpublished novelists, poets, playwriters, who hide in drawers whole libraries of literature that will never be printed, or if so, it will be printed after they stink in their graves. I think now the State will never be secure—never. It is not in the nature of politics to be finished with revolution. After revolution comes revolution. Evgeny Zamyatin told: 'There is no final revolution. Revolutions are infinite!' "

"I guess that's along my own line of thinking," I said, hoping for reasons of personal safety maybe to forestall Levitansky's ultimate confession—one he, with brooding intense eyes, was already relentlessly making—lest in the end it imprison me in his will and history.

"I have learned from my stories," the writer was saying, "as I wrote that imagination is enemy of the State. I have learned from my stories that I am not free man. This is my conclusion. I ask for your help not to harm my country, which still has magnificent possibilities, but to help me escape the worst errors. I do not wish to defame Soviet Union. My purpose in my work is to show its true heart. So have done our writers from Pushkin to Pasternak. If you believe in democratic humanism, you must help artist to be free. Is not true?"

I got up, I think to shake myself free of the question. "What exactly is my responsibility to you, Levitansky?"

"If I am drowning you must assist to save me. We are members of mankind."

"In unknown waters if I can't swim?"

"If not, throw to me a rope."

"I'm just a visitor here. Besides, I've told you already that I may be suspect, and for all I know you yourself might be a Soviet agent out to get me, or this room might be bugged, and then where will we be? Mr. Levitansky, I don't want to hear or argue any more. I'll just plead personal inability and ask you to leave."

"Bugged?"

"Some sort of listening device planted in this room."

Levitansky turned slowly grey. He sat for a minute in motionless meditation, then rose wearily from the chair.

"I withdraw now request for your assistance. I accept your word that you are not capable. I do not wish to make criticism of you. All I wish to say, Gospodin Garvitz, is it requires more to change a man's character than to change his name."

Levitansky left the room, leaving in his wake some fumes of cognac. He had also passed gas.

"Come back!" I called, not too loudly, but if he heard through the door he didn't answer. Good riddance, I thought, not that I don't sympathize with him, which I do, but look what he's done to *my* interior liberty. Who has to come all the way to Russia to get caught up in this kind of mess? It's a helluva way to spend a vacation.

The writer had gone, but not his sneaky manuscript. It was lying on my bed.

"It's his baby, not mine." Seeing red, I knotted my tie and slipped on my coat, then via the English language number, called a cab. But I had forgotten his address. A half hour later I was still in the taxi, riding frantically back and forth along Novo Ostapovskaya Street until I spotted the house I thought it might be. It wasn't, it was another like it. I paid the driver and walked on till once again I thought I had the house. After going up the stairs and getting a whiff of the cooking smells, I was sure it was. When I knocked on Levitansky's door, the writer, looking older, more distant—as if he had been away on a trip and had just returned, or maybe simply interrupted at his work, his thoughts still in his words on the page on the table, his pen in hand—stared blankly at me.

"Levitansky, my heart breaks for you, I swear, but I can't take the chance. I believe in you but am not, at this time of my life, considering my condition and recent experiences, in much of a mood to embark on a dangerous adventure. Please accept deepest regrets."

I thrust the manuscript into his hand and rushed down the stairs. Hurrying out of the building, I was, to my horror, unable to avoid Irina Levitansky coming in. Her eyes lit in fright as she recognized me an instant before I hit her full force and sent her sprawling along the cement walk.

"Oh, my God, what have I done? I sincerely beg your pardon!" I helped the dazed, hurt woman to her feet, brushing off her soiled skirt, and futilely, her pink blouse, split and torn on her lacerated arm and shoulder. I stopped dead when I felt myself experiencing erotic sensations.

Irina Filipovna held a handkerchief to her bloody nostril and wept a little. We sat on a stone bench, a girl of ten and her brother watching us. Irina said something to them in Russian, and they moved off.

"I was frightened of you also as you are of us," she said. "I trust you now because Levitansky does. But I will not urge you to take the manuscript. The responsibility is for you to decide."

"It's not a responsibility I want," I said unhappily.

She said then as though talking to herself, "Maybe I will leave Levitansky. He is wretched so much it is no longer a marriage. He drinks; also he does not earn a living. My brother Dmitri allows him to drive the taxi two, three hours in the day, to my brother's disadvantage. Except for a ruble or two from this, I support him. Levitansky does not longer receive translation commissions. Also a neighbor in the house—I am sure Kovalevsky—has denounced him to the police for delinquency and parasitism. There will be a hearing. Levitansky says he will burn his manuscripts."

"Good God, I've just returned the package of them to him."

"He will not," she said. "But even if he burns he will write more. If they take him away in prison, he will write on toilet paper. When he comes out, he will write on newspaper margins. He sits now at his table. He is a magnificent writer. I cannot ask him not to write, but now I must decide if this is the condition I want for myself the rest of my life."

She sat in silence, an attractive woman with shapely legs and feet, in a soiled skirt and torn pink blouse. I left her sitting on the stone bench, her handkerchief squeezed white in her fist.

That night—July 2nd, I was leaving the Soviet Union on the fifth—I underwent great self-doubt. If I'm a coward, why has it taken me so long to find out? Where does anxiety end and cowardice begin? Feelings get mixed, sure enough, but not all cowards are necessarily anxious, and not all anxious men are cowards. Many "sensitive" (Rose's word), tense, even frightened human beings did in fear what had to be done, the fear in some cases giving energy when it came time to fight or jump off a rooftop into a river. There comes a time in a man's life when to get where he has to go—if there are no doors or windows—he walks through a wall.

On the other hand, suppose one is courageous in a foolish cause—you concentrate on courage and not enough on horse sense? To get to the nub of the problem on my mind, how do I finally decide it's a sensible and worthwhile thing to smuggle out Levitansky's manuscript, given my reasonable doubts about the ultimate worth of the operation? Granted, as I now grant, he's trustworthy, and his wife is that and more; still does it pay a man like me to run the risk?

If six thousand Soviet writers can't do very much to enlarge their freedom as artists, who am I to fight their battle?—H. Harvitz, knight of the free lance from Manhattan. How far do you go, granted you have taken to heart the creed that all men (including Communists) are created free and equal and justice is for all? How far do you go for art if you're for Yeats, Rouault, and Ludwig van Beethoven? Not to mention Gogol, Tolstoy, and Dostoevsky. So far as to get yourself internationally involved: the HH MS. Smuggling Service? Will the President and State Department, not to speak of the CIA, send up three loud cheers for my contribution to the cause of international social justice? And suppose it amounts to no more than a gaffe in the end?—what will I prove if I sneak out Levitansky's manuscript, and all it turns out to be is just another passable book of stories?

That's how I argued with myself on several occasions, but in the end I argued myself into solid indecision.

What it boils down to, I'd say, is he expects me to help him because I'm an American. That's quite a nerve.

Two nights later—odd not to have the Fourth of July on July fourth (I was even listening for firecrackers)—a quiet light-lemon summer's evening in Moscow, after two monotonously uneasy days, though I was still making museum notes, for relief I took myself off to the Bolshoi to hear *Tosca.* It was sung in Russian by a busty lady and handsome tenor, but the Italian plot was unchanged, and in the end, Scarpia, who had promised "death" by fake bullets, gave, in sneaky exchange, a fusillade of real lead; another artist bit the dust, and Floria Tosca learned the hard way that love wasn't what she had thought.

Next to me sat another full-breasted woman, this one a lovely Russian of maybe thirty in a white dress that fitted a well-formed body, her blond hair piled in a birdlike mass on her head. Lillian could sometimes look like that, though not Rose. This woman—alone, it turned out—spoke flawless English in a mezzo-soprano with a slight accent.

During the first intermission she asked in friendly fashion, managing to seem detached but interested: "Are you American? Or *perhaps* Swedish?"

"Not at all Swedish. American is right. How'd you happen to guess?"

"I noticed perhaps a certain self-satisfaction, if it does not bother you that I say so?" she remarked with a laugh.

"You got the wrong party," I said.

When she opened her purse a fragrance of springtime burst on the scene—fresh flowers, the warmth of her body rose to my nostrils. I was moved to memories of the hungers of my youth—desire, love, ambition.

In the intermission she said in a low voice, "May I ask a favor? Do you depart soon the Soviet Union?"

"In fact tomorrow."

"How fortunate for me. Would it offer too much difficulty to mail wherever you are going an airmail letter addressed to my husband, who is presently in Paris? Our airmail service takes two weeks to arrive in the West. I shall be grateful."

I glanced at the envelope, addressed half in French, half in Cyrillic, and said I wouldn't mind. But during the next act sweat grew active on my body, and at the end of the opera, after Tosca's shriek of suicide, I handed the letter back to the not wholly surprised lady, saying I was sorry. Nodding to her, I left the theater. I had the feeling I had heard her voice before. I hurried back to the hotel, determined not to leave my room for any reason other than breakfast, then out and into the wide blue yonder.

I later fell asleep over a book and a bottle of sweet warm beer a waiter had brought up, pretending to myself I was relaxed, though I was as usual dealing beforehand with worried thoughts of the departure and flight home; and when I awoke, three minutes on my wristwatch later, it seemed to me I had made the acquaintance of a spate of nightmares. I was momentarily panicked by the idea that someone had planted a letter on me, and I actually searched through the pockets of my two suits. *Nyet.* Then I recalled that in one of my dreams a drawer in a table I was sitting at had slowly come open, and Feliks

Levitansky, a dwarf who lived in it along with a few friendly mice, managed to scale the wooden wall on a comb he used as a ladder, and to hop from the drawer ledge to the top of the table, where he leered into my face, shook his Lilliputian fist, and shouted in high-pitched but (to me) understandable Russian: "Atombombnik! You murdered innocent Japanese people! Amerikansky bastards!"

"That's unfair," I cried out. "I was no more than a kid in college at the time. If it was up to me such things would never have happened." I also remember crying, which was where the dream had ended.

That's a sad dream, I thought.

Afterward this occurred to me: Suppose what happened to Levitansky happens to me. Suppose America gets into a war with China in some semi-reluctant way, and to make fast hash of it (despite my loud protestations: mostly I wave my arms and shout obscenities till my face turns green) we spatter them with a few dozen H-bombs, boiling up a thick atomic soup of about two hundred million Orientals—blood, gristle, bone marrow, and lots of floating Chinese eyeballs. We win the war because the Soviets hadn't been able to make up their minds whom to shoot their missiles at first. And suppose that after this slaughter, about ten million Americans, in self-revulsion, head for the borders to flee the country. To stop the loss of goods and capital, the refugees are intercepted by the army and turned back. Harvitz hides in his room with shades drawn, writing, in a fury of protest, a long epic poem condemning the mass butchery by America. What nation, Asiatic or other, is next? Nobody wants to publish the poem because it might start riots and another flight of refugees to Canada and Mexico; then one day there's a knock on the door, and it isn't the FBI but a bearded Levitansky, in better times a tourist, a modern not medieval Communist. He offers to sneak the manuscript of the poem out for publication in the Soviet Union.

Why? Harvitz suspiciously asks.

Why not? To give the book its liberty.

I awoke after a restless night. I had been instructed by Intourist to be in the lobby with my baggage two hours before flight time at 11 A.M. I was shaved and dressed by six, and at seven had breakfast—I was hungry—of yogurt, sausage, and eggs, tea with lemon, in the twelfth-floor buffet. I then went out to hunt for a taxi. They were hard to come by at this hour, but I finally found one near the American Embassy, not far from the hotel. Speaking my usual mixture of primitive German and French, I persuaded the driver, by slipping him an acceptable two rubles, to take me out to Levitansky's house and wait a few minutes till I came out. Going hastily up the stairs, I knocked on his door, apologized when he opened it to the half-pajamaed, ironfaced writer, his head looking slightly flatter, for awaking him this early in the day. Without peace of mind or certainty of purpose, I asked him whether he still wanted me to smuggle out his manuscript of stories. I got for my trouble the door slammed in my face.

A half hour later I had everything packed and was locking the suitcase. A knock on the door—half a rap you might call it. For the suitcase, I thought. I was for a moment frightened by the sight of a small man in a thick cap, wearing a long trench coat. He winked, and with a sinking feeling, I winked back. I had recognized Levitansky's brother-in-law, Dmitri, the taxi driver. He slid in, unbuttoned his coat, and brought forth the familiar manuscript. Holding a finger to his lips, he handed it to me before I could say I wasn't interested.

"Levitansky changed his mind?"

"Not change mind. Was afraid your voice to be heard by Kovalevsky."

"I'm sorry, I should have thought of that."

"Levitansky say not write to him," the brother-in-law whispered. "When is published book please send to him copy of *Das Kapital.* He will understand what means this."

I reluctantly agreed.

The brother-in-law, a thin figure with sad Jewish eyes, winked again, shook hands with a steamy palm, and slipped out of the room.

I unlocked my suitcase and laid the manuscript on top of my things. Then I unpacked half the contents and slipped the manuscript into a folder containing my notes of literary museums and a few letters from Lillian. I then and there decided that if I got back to the States I would ask her to marry me. The phone was ringing as I left the room.

On my way to the airport in a taxi, alone—to my surprise no Intourist girl accompanied me—I felt, on and off, nauseated. If it's not the sausage and yogurt it must be ordinary fear, I thought. Still, if Levitansky has the courage to send these stories out, the least I can do is give him a help. When you think of it, it's little enough one does for freedom in the course of his life. At the airport, if I can dig up some bromo or its Russian equivalent I'll feel better.

The driver was observing me in the mirror, a stern man with the head of a scholar, impassively smoking.

"Le jour fait beau," I said.

He pointed with an upraised finger to a sign in English at one side of the road to the airport.

"Long live peace in the whole world!"

Peace with freedom. I smiled at the thought of somebody, not Howard Harvitz, painting that in red on the Soviet sign.

We drove on, I foreseeing my exit from the Soviet Union. I had made discreet inquiries from time to time, and an Intouristka in Leningrad had told me I had first to show my papers at the passport control desk, turn in my rubles—a serious offense to walk off with any—and then check luggage; no inspection, she swore. And that was that. Unless, of course, the official at the passport desk found my name on a list and said I had to go to the customs office for a package. In that case (if nobody said so I wouldn't remind them) I would go get the books. I figured I wouldn't open the package, just tear off a bit of the wrapping, if they were wrapped, as if making sure they were the books I expected, and then sort of saunter away with the package under my arm. If they asked me to sign another five copies of a document in Russian, I would write at the bottom: "It is understood I can't read Russian," and sign my name to that.

I had heard that a KGB man was stationed at the ramp as one boarded the plane. He asked for your passport, checked the picture, threw you a stare, and if there was no serious lack of resemblance, tore out your expired visa, pocketed it, and let you embark.

In ten minutes you were aloft, seat belts fastened in three languages, watching the plane banking west. I thought maybe if I looked hard I might see in the distance Feliks Levitansky on his roof, waving his red-white-and-blue socks on a bamboo pole. Then the plane levelled off, and we were above the clouds flying westward. And that's what I would be doing for five or six hours unless the pilot received radio instructions to turn back; or maybe land in Czechoslovakia, or East Germany, where two big-hatted detectives boarded the plane. By an act of imagination and will I made it some other passenger they were arresting. I got the plane into the air again, and we flew on without incident until we touched down in London.

As the taxi approached the Moscow airport, fingering my ticket and gripping my suitcase handle, I wished for courage equal to Levitansky's when they discovered he was the author of the book of stories I had managed to sneak out and get published, and his trial and suffering began.

Levitansky's first story of the four in English was about an old father, a pensioner, who was not feeling well and wanted his son, with whom he had continuous strong disagreements and whom he hadn't seen in eight months, to know. He decided to pay him a short visit. Since the son had moved from his flat to a larger one, and had not forwarded his address, the father went to call on him at his office. The son was an official of some sort with an office in a new State building. The father had never been there, although he knew where it was, because a neighbor on a walk with him once had pointed it out.

The pensioner sat in a chair in his son's large outer office, waiting for him to be free for a few minutes. "Yuri," he thought he would say, "all I want to tell you is that I'm not up to my usual self. My breath is short, and I have pains in my chest. In fact, I am not well. After all, we're father and son and you ought to know the state of my health, seeing it's not so good and your mother is dead."

The son's assistant secretary, a modern girl in a tight skirt, said he was attending an important administrative conference.

"A conference is a conference," the father said. He wouldn't want to interfere with it and didn't mind waiting, although he was still having twinges of pain.

The father waited patiently in the chair for several hours; and though he had a few times risen and urgently spoken to the assistant secretary, he was, by the end of the day, still unable to see his son. The girl, putting on her pink hat, advised the old man that the official had already left the building. He hadn't been able to see his father because he had unexpectedly been called away on an important State matter.

"Go home, and he will telephone you in the morning."

"I have no telephone," said the old pensioner impatiently. "He knows that."

The assistant secretary, the private secretary, an older woman from the inside office, and later the caretaker of the building all attempted to persuade the father to go home, but he wouldn't leave.

The private secretary said her husband was expecting her, and she could stay no longer. After a while the assistant secretary with the pink hat also left. The caretaker, a man with wet eyes and a ragged moustache, tried to persuade the old man to leave. "What sort of foolishness is it to wait all night in a pitchdark building? You'll frighten yourself out of your wits, not to speak of other discomforts you'll suffer."

"No," said the father, "I will wait. When my son comes in tomorrow morning, I'll tell him something he hasn't learned yet. I'll tell him that what he does to me his children will do to him."

The caretaker departed. The old man was left alone waiting for his son to appear in the morning.

"I'll report him to the Party," he muttered.

The second story was about an old man, a widower of sixty-eight, who hoped to have matzos for Passover. Last year he had got his quota. They had been baked at the State bakery and sold in State stores; but this year the State bakeries were not permitted to bake them. The officials said the machines had broken down, but who believed them.

The old man went to the rabbi, an older man with a tormented beard, and asked him where he could get matzos. He was frightened that he mightn't have them this year.

"So am I," confessed the old rabbi. He said he had been told to tell his congregants to buy flour and bake them at home. The State stores would sell them the flour.

"What good is that for me?" asked the widower. He reminded the rabbi that he had no home to speak of, a single small room with a one-burner electric stove. His wife had died two years ago. His only living child, a married daughter, was with her husband in Birobijan. His other relatives, the few who were left after the German invasion—two female cousins his age—lived in Odessa; and he himself, even if he could find an oven, did not know how to bake matzos. And if he couldn't, what should he do?

The rabbi then promised he would try to get the widower a kilo or two of matzos, and the old man, rejoicing, blessed him.

He waited anxiously a month, but the rabbi never mentioned the matzos. Maybe he had forgotten. After all he was an old man with many worries, and the widower did not want to press him. However, Passover was coming on wings, so he must do something. A week before the Holy Days he hurried to the rabbi's flat and spoke to him there. "Rabbi," he begged, "you promised me a kilo or two of matzos. What has happened to them?"

"I know I promised," said the rabbi, "but I'm no longer sure to whom. It's easy to promise." He dabbed at his brow with a damp handkerchief. "I was warned one can be arrested on charges of profiteering in the production and sale of matzos. I was told it could happen even if I were to give them away for nothing. It's a new crime they've invented. Still, take them anyway. If they arrest me, I'm an old man, and how long can an old man live in Lubyanka? Not so long, thank God. Here, I'll give you a small pack, but you must tell no one where you got the matzos."

"May the Lord eternally bless you, rabbi. As for dying in prison, rather let it happen to our enemies."

The rabbi went to his closet and got out a small pack of matzos, already wrapped and tied with knotted twine. When the widower offered in a whisper to pay him, at least the cost of the flour, the rabbi wouldn't hear of it. "God provides," he said, "although at times with difficulty." He said there was hardly enough for all who wanted matzos, so one must take what he got and be thankful.

"I will eat less," said the old man. "I will count mouthfuls. I will save the last matzo to look at if there isn't enough to last me. God will understand."

Overjoyed to have even a few matzos, he rode home on the trolley car and there met another Jew, a man with a withered hand. They conversed in Yiddish in low tones. The stranger had glanced at the almost square package, then at the widower and had hoarsely whispered, "Matzos?" The widower, tears starting to his eyes, nodded. "With God's grace." "Where did you get them?" "God provides." "So if He provides, let Him provide me," the stranger brooded. "I'm not so lucky. I was hoping for a package from relatives in Cleveland, America. They wrote they would send me a large pack of the finest matzos, but when I inquire of the authorities they say no matzos have arrived. You know when they will get there?" he muttered. "After Passover by a month or two, and what good will they be then?"

The widower nodded sadly. The stranger wiped his eyes with his good hand, and after a short while left the trolley amid a number of people getting off. He had not bothered to say goodbye, and neither had the widower, not to remind him of his own good fortune. When the time came for the old man to leave the trolley he glanced down between his feet where he had placed the package of matzos but nothing was there. His feet were there. The old man felt harrowed, as though someone had ripped a nail down his spine. He searched frantically throughout the car, going a long way past his stop, querying every passenger, the woman conductor, the motorman, but no one had seen his matzos.

Then it occurred to him that the stranger with the withered hand had stolen them.

The widower in his misery asked himself, would a Jew have robbed another of his precious matzos? It didn't seem possible. Still, who knows, he thought, what one will do to get matzos if he has none.

As for me I haven't even a matzo to look at now. If I could steal some, whether from Jew or Russian, I would steal them. He thought he would even steal them from the old rabbi.

The widower went home without his matzos and had none for Passover.

The third story, a folktale called "Tallith," concerned a youth of seventeen, beardless but for a few stray hairs on his chin, who had come from Kirov to the steps of the synagogue on Arkhipova Street in Moscow. He had brought with him a capacious prayer shawl, a white garment of luminous beauty which he offered for sale to a cluster of congregants on the synagogue steps, Jews of various sorts and sizes—curious, apprehensive, greedy at the sight of the shawl—for fifteen rubles. Most of them avoided the youth, particularly the older Jews, despite the fact that some of the more devout among them were worried about their prayer shawls, eroded on their shoulders after years of daily use, which they could not replace. "It's the informers among us who have put him up to this," they whispered among themselves, "so they will have someone to inform on."

Still, in spite of the warnings of their elders, several of the younger men examined the tallith and admired it. "Where did you get such a fine prayer shawl?" the youth was asked. "It was my father's who recently died," he said. "It was given to him by a rich Jew he had once befriended." "Then why don't you keep it for yourself, you're a Jew, aren't you?" "Yes," said the youth, not the least embarrassed, "but I am going to Kharborovsk as a Komsomol volunteer, and I need a few rubles to get married. Besides I'm a confirmed atheist."

One young man with fat unshaven cheeks, who admired the deeply white shawl, its white glowing in whiteness, with its long silk fringes, whispered to the youth that he might consider buying it for five rubles. But he was overheard by the gabbai, the lay leader of the congregation, who raised his cane and shouted at the whisperer, "Hooligan, if you buy that shawl, beware it doesn't become your shroud." The fat Jew with the unshaven cheeks retreated.

"Don't strike him," cried the frightened rabbi, who had come out of the synagogue and saw the gabbai with his upraised cane. He urged the congregants to begin prayers at once. To the youth he said, "Please go away from here, we are burdened with enough troubles as it is. It is forbidden for anyone to sell religious articles. Do you want us to be accused of criminal economic activity? Do you want the doors of the shul to be closed forever? Do us a mitzvah and go away."

The congregants went inside. The youth was left standing alone on the steps; but then the gabbai came out of the door, a man with a deformed spine and with a wad of cotton stuck in his leaking ear.

"Look here," he said. "I know you stole it. Still, after all is said and done a tallith is a tallith, and God asks no questions of His worshippers. I offer eight rubles for it, take it or leave it. Talk fast before the services end and the others come out."

"Make it ten and it's yours," said the youth.

The gabbai gazed at him shrewdly. "Eight is all I have, but wait here and I'll borrow two rubles from my brother-in-law."

The youth waited impatiently. Dusk was thickening. In a few minutes a black car drove up, stopped in front of the synagogue, and two policemen got out. The youth realized at once that the gabbai had informed on him. Not knowing what else to do he hastily draped the prayer shawl over his head and began loudly to pray. He prayed a passionate kaddish. The police hesitated to approach him while he was praying, and they stood at the bottom of the steps waiting for him to be done. The congregants then came out and could not believe their eyes or ears. No one imagined the youth could pray so fervently. What moved them was his tone, the wail and passion of a man truly praying. Perhaps his father had indeed recently died. All listened attentively, and many wished he would pray forever, for they knew that when he stopped he would be seized and thrown into prison.

It has grown dark. A moon hovers behind murky clouds over the synagogue steeple. The youth's voice is heard in prayer. The congregants are huddled in the dark street, listening. Both police agents are still there, although they cannot be seen. Neither can the youth. All that can be seen is the white shawl luminously praying.

The last of the four stories translated by Irina Filipovna was about a writer of mixed parentage, a Russian father and Jewish mother, who had secretly been writing stories for years. He had from a young age wanted to write but had at first not had the courage to—it seemed such a merciless undertaking—so he had gone into translation work instead; and then when he had, one day, started to write seriously and exultantly, after a while he found to his surprise that many of his stories, about half, were about Jews.

Well, for a half-Jew that's a reasonable proportion, he thought. The others were about Russians who sometimes resembled members of his father's family. "It's good to have such different sources for ideas," he said to his wife. "In this way I can cover a more varied range of experiences in life."

After several years of work he had submitted a selection of his stories to a trusted friend of university days, Viktor Zvertov, an editor of the Progress Publishing House; and the writer appeared one morning after receiving a hastily scribbled cryptic note from his friend, to discuss his work with him. Zvertov, a troubled man to begin with—

he told everyone his wife did not respect him—jumped up from his chair and turned the key in the door, his ear pressed a minute at the crack. He then went quickly to his desk and withdrew the manuscript from a drawer he had first to unlock with a key he kept in his pocket. He was a heavy-set man with a flushed complexion, stained eroded teeth, and a hoarse voice; and he handled the writer's manuscript as though it might leap up and wound him in the face.

"Please, Tolya," he whispered breathily, bringing his head close to the writer's. "You must take these dreadful stories away at once."

"What's the matter with you? Why are you shaking so?"

"Don't pretend to be so naive. You know why I am disturbed. I am frankly amazed that you are even considering submitting such unorthodox material for publication. My opinion as an editor is that they are of doubtful literary merit—I do not say devoid of it, Tolya, I wish to be honest—but as stories they are a frightful affront to our society. I can't understand why you should take it on yourself to write about Jews. What do you really know about them? Your culture is not in the least Jewish, it's Soviet Russian. The whole business smacks of hypocrisy, and you may be accused of anti-Semitism."

He then got up to shut the window and peered into a closet.

"Are you out of your mind, Viktor? My stories are in no sense anti-Semitic. One would have to read them standing on his head to think that."

"There can be only one logical interpretation," the editor argued. "According to my most lenient analysis, which is favorable to you as a person of let's call it decent intent, the stories fly in the face of socialist realism and reveal a dangerous inclination—perhaps even a stronger word should be used—to anti-Soviet sentiment. Maybe you're not entirely aware of this—I know how a story can take hold of a writer and pull him along by the nose. As an editor I have to be sensitive to such things. I know, Tolya, from our conversations that you are a sincere believer in our kind of socialism; I won't accuse you of being defamatory to the Soviet system, but others may. In fact I know they will. If one of the editors of *Oktyahr* was to read these stories, believe me, your career would explode in a mess. You seem not to have a normal awareness of what self-preservation is, and what's appallingly worse, you're not above entangling innocent bystanders in your fate. If these stories were mine, I assure you I would never have brought them to you. I urge you to destroy them at once, before they destroy you."

The editor drank thirstily from a glass of water on his desk.

"That's the last thing I would do," said the writer. "These stories, if not in tone or subject matter, are written in the spirit of our early Soviet writers—the free spirits of the years just after the Revolution."

"I think you know what happened to many of those 'free spirits.' "

The writer for a moment stared at him.

"Well, then, what of those stories that are not about the experiences of Jews? Some are simply pieces about homely aspects of Russian life; for instance, the one about the pensioner father and his invisible son. What I hoped is that you might recommend one or two such stories to *Novy Mir* or *Yunost*. They are innocuous sketches and well written."

"Not the one about the two prostitutes," said the editor. "That contains hidden social criticism and is too adversely naturalistic."

"A prostitute lives a social life."

"That may be, but I can't recommend it for publication. I must advise you, Tolya, if you expect to receive further commission for translations from us, you should immediately get rid of this whole manuscript so as to avoid the possibility of serious consequences both to yourself and family, and for this publishing house that has employed you so faithfully and generously in the past."

"Since you didn't write the stories yourself, you needn't be afraid, Viktor Alexandrovich," the writer said coldly.

"I am not a coward, if that's why you're hinting, Anatoly Borisovich, but if a wild locomotive is running loose on the rails, I know which way to jump."

The writer hastily gathered up his manuscript, stuffed the papers into his leather case, and returned home by bus. His wife was still away at work. He took out the stories, and after quickly reading through one, began to burn it page by page, in the kitchen sink.

His nine-year-old son, returning from school, said, "Papa, what are you burning in the sink? That's no place for a fire."

"What am I burning?" said the writer. "My integrity." Then he said, "My heritage. My talent."

Some Get Wasted

Paule Marshall

Novelist and short-story writer, Paule Marshall was born in Brooklyn in 1929, to Barbadian parents who immigrated to America after World War I. At the age of nine, she visited Barbados and returned home with a notebook of poems inspired by the beauty of her parents' birthplace. She earned her bachelor's degree from Brooklyn College and worked for a time in New York City libraries. She gave up that pursuit in order to write for a magazine called *Our World,* traveling on assignments to Brazil, Guiana, and the West Indies. Her first novel, *Brown Girl, Girl Brownstones* (1959), was written on Barbados. *Soul Clap Hands and Sing* (1961) is a collection of short stories about life at Brooklyn College, on the island of Barbados, in Brazil, and in British Guiana; and *The Chosen Place, The Timeless People* (1969) is set on the island of Grenada in the West Indies. Mrs. Marshall lives in New York City and does most of her writing there. Brought up not far from the area she writes about in the following story, she knows the meaning of Memorial Day for young blacks who must find their pleasures in public parks and ghettos. Her ear for their language is unerring.

A shout hurled after him down the rise: "Run, baby. Run, fool!" and Hezzy knew, the terror snapping the tendons which strung together his muscles, that he had been caught in a sneak, was separated from his People, alone, running with his heart jarring inside his narrow chest, his stomach a stone weight and his life riding on each rise and plunge of his legs. While far behind, advancing like pieces of the night broken off, were the Crowns. He couldn't dare turn to look, couldn't place their voices because of the wind in his ears, but he knew they were Crowns. They had to be.

"Run, baby, run. You running real pretty, but we's with you all the way. . . ."

And he was running pretty. So that he began to feel an ease and lightness. His feet skimmed the path while his arms cut away the air around him. But then he had learned how to run from the master. Him and the Little People was always hanging around the block watching Turner and the Big People practice their running. Turner was always saying, "Dig, you studs, one thing, don't never let another club catch you in a sneak. Especially you Little People. Don't never get too far

SOURCE: Paule Marshall, "Some Get Wasted," in *Harlem,* ed. John Henrik Clarke (New York: New American Library, 1970), pp. 136–145. Copyright © 1970. Reprinted by permission of the author.

away from the rest of the guys. In this club when we go down everybody goes together. When we split, everybody splits together. But if you should get caught in a sneak, haul ass out of there. Run, baby. Your legs is your life then, you can believe that."

Yeah, Turner would dig the way he was running. He would go round the block tomorrow, all cool like nothing had happened and say—ignoring Turner but talking loud enough so's he hear—"Man, dig what happened to me last night after the action in the park. Them dirty Crowns caught me in a sneak, man. Come chasing me all over the fuggen place. But I put down some speed on them babies and burned their eyes."

Even now, their jeers seemed fainter, further away: "Run, baby . . . like we said, you running pretty. . . ." The night was pulling them back, making them part of it again. Man, he could outrun those punks any time, any place. His heart gave a little joyous leap and he sprinted cleanly ahead, the pebbles scattering underfoot.

The day, this night, his flight had begun a week ago. The Little People had gotten the word that something was up and had gone over to the Crib where the Noble Knights, their Big People, hung out. The Crib was the square of bare earth in front of the decaying brownstone where Turner lived.

"The jive is on," Turner said as soon as they were assembled.

And before the words were barely out, Sizzle who lived only to fight, said, "Like I been telling you, man, it's about time. Them Crowns been messing all over us. Pulling sneaks in our turf. Stomping and wasting our Little People like they did Duke. Slapping around our broads when they come outta school . . . Man, I hate them studs. I hate them dirty Crown Buggers."

"Man, cool your role," Turner said. Then: "Like I said, the jive is on. And strong this time. We ain't just goin' down in their turf and stomp the first Crown we see and split, like we always do. This is gonna be organized. We already got word to the Crowns and they're ready. Now dig. Next Monday, Memorial Day, we look. Over in Prospect Park, on the Hill. Time the parade ends and it starts getting dark, time the Crowns show, we lock. Now pick up on the play. . . ."

Hezzy, crowded with his guys on the bottom step of the stoop listened, his stomach dropping as it did on the cyclone in Coney Island. Going down with the Big People at last! Down with the hearts! And on Memorial Day when every club in the city would be gangbusting. The Italian cats in South Brooklyn, them Spanish studs in East Harlem. And on the Hill—Massacre Hill they called it—where many a stud had either built his rep or gotten wasted.

He had heard how three years ago on Easter Sunday when the Noble Knights clashed with the Crusaders on the Hill, Turner had gotten the bullet crease on his forehead and had started his bad rep. Heard how the cat had gone to church packing his zip that morning and gone down to lock with the Crusaders that afternoon.

Hezzy looked up over the other heads at the bullet crease. It was like the cat's skin was so tough the bullet had only been able to graze it. It was like nothing or nobody could waste the cat. You could tell from his eyes. The iris fixed dead-center in the whites and full of dark swirls of colors like a marble and cold, baby. When Turner looked sideways he never shifted his eyes, but turned his head, slow, like time had to wait on him. Man, how them simple chicks goofed behind that look. The stud didn't even have to talk to 'em. Just looked and they was ready to give him some . . .

"Dig, we ain't wearing no club jackets neither," Turner was saying. "Cause they ain't no need to let The Man know who we is. And another thing, it's gonna be dark out there, so watch whose head you busting." The unmoving eyes fixed the Crosstown Noble Knights. "You studs down?"

"We down, man."

"You all down?" His chin flicked toward the Little People at the bottom of the stoop.

"Yeah, we down," Hezzy answered.

"We don't want none of you Little People coming up weak," Turner said.

"Man, I ain't saying we ain't got some punks in the Division, but we leaves them studs home when we bopping."

All around the eyes glanced his way, but he kept his gaze on Turner.

"What's your name again, man?" Turner said and there was a tightness in his voice.

"Hezzy, man," and he touched the turned-down brim of the soiled sailor hat he always wore where his name was emblazoned in black.

"You suppose to be president of the Little People since Duke got wasted?"

"Ain't no suppose, man. I am the president."

"All right, my man, but cool your role, you dig?"

He was all flushed inside. His head felt like it was twisted behind drinking some wine—and when the meeting was over and he and his little guys were back on their corner, they pooled their coins for a pint of Thunderbird and drank in celebration of how bad and cool he had been in front of the Big People.

Late that night he wandered alone and high through his turf. And all around him the familiar overflow of life streamed out of the sagging houses, the rank hallways, the corner bars, bearing him along like a dark tide. The voices loud against the night sky became his voice. The violence brooding over the crap games and racing with the cars became the vertigo inside his head. It was his world, his way—and that other world beyond suddenly no longer mattered. Rearing back he snatched off his hat, baring his small tough black child's face. "Hezzy," he shouted, his rage and arrogance a wine-tinged spume. "Yeah, that's right, Hezzy. Read about me in the *News* next week, ya dumb squares."

The night before Memorial Day he wet his bed, and in the morning awoke in the warm wet rankness of himself, shaking from a dream he couldn't remember, his eyes encrusted with cold. Quickly pulling on his hat, he shoved his half-brothers from around him.

"Boy, what time you got in here last night?"

He jammed a leg into his trousers.

"You hear me? What time? Always running the streets . . . But you watch, you gonna get yourself all messed up one of these days . . . Just don't act right no more. I mean, you used to would stay round the house sometime and help me out . . . used to would listen sometime . . . and go to school. . . ."

It was the same old slop, in the same old voice that was as slack as her body and as lifeless as her eyes. He always fled it, had to, since something in him always threatened to give in to it. Even more so this morning. For her voice recalled something in his dream. It seemed to reach out in place of her arms to hold him there, to take him, as she had sometimes done when he was small, into her bed. Jumping up, he slammed the door on that voice, cutting it off and almost threw himself down the five flights of stairs. As he hit the street the sun smacked him hard across the face and he saw his Little People waiting for him on the corner.

The parade was half over when Hezzy and his guys following Turner and the Big People some distance ahead reached Bedford Avenue. Old soldiers, remnants of the wars, shuffled along like sleep-walkers, their eyes tearing from the dust and glare. Boy Scouts, white mostly, with clear eyes and smooth fresh faces, marched under the rippling flags to the blare of "America, America, God shed his grace on thee . . ." and the majorettes kicked high their white legs, the flesh under the thighs quivering in the sunlight. Their batons flashed silver. And the crowd surged against the barricades with a roar.

"Man, dig the squares," Hezzy said, the smoke flaring from under the sailor hat.

"They sure out here, ain't they," the boy beside him said.

"Man! You know, I feel sorry for squares, I tell you the truth. They just don't know what's happening. I mean, all they got is this little old jive parade while tonight here we are gonna be locking with the Crowns up on the Hill. . . ."

Later, in Prospect Park he watched scornfully from behind his oversized sunglasses as the parade disbanded: the old soldiers wheezing and fanning under the trees, the Boy Scouts lowering the heavy flags, the majorettes lolling on the grass, laughing, their blond hair spread out as if to dry. "Yeah," he said, "I feel real sorry for squares."

As always whenever they came to Prospect Park they visited the small amusement area and Hezzy seeing that they had gotten separated from Turner and the Big People suddenly let out a whoop and clambered aboard the merry-go-round, his four guys behind him. Startling the other children there with their bloodcurdling cries, they furiously goaded their motionless painted mounts, cursing whenever they grabbed for the ring and missed.

"Man," he said laughing as they leaped off together into the trampled grass and dust. "You all is nothing but punks riding some old jive merry-go-round."

"Seems like I seen you on there too, baby."

"How you mean, man? I was just showing you cats how to do the thing."

Later they sneaked through the zoo, and forcing their way close to the railing with their cocked elbows, teased the animals and sounded each other's mother:

"Yoa mother, man."

"Yours, Jim."

Leaning dangerously over the rail, they gently coaxed the seals out of the water. "Come on up, baby, and do your number for the Knights. The Noble Knights of Gates Avenue, baby."

They stood almost respectfully in front of the lion cage. "Lemme tell ya, Jim, that's about a bad stud you see in there," Hezzy said. "You try locking with that cat and get yourself all messed up. . . ."

And all the while they ate, downing frankfurters and Pepsis, and when their money was gone, they jostled the Boy Scouts around the stands and stole candy. Full finally, they climbed to a ridge near Massacre Hill and there, beneath a cool fretwork of trees and sun, they drank from a pint bottle of wine, folding their small mouths around the mouth of the bottle and taking a long loud suck and then passing it on with a sigh.

The wine coupled with the sun unleashed a wildness in them after a time and they fell upon each other, tussling and rolling all in a heap, savagely kneeing each other and sending the grass and the bits of loosened sod flying up around them. And then just as abruptly they fell apart and lay sprawled and panting under the dome of leaves.

"Man, you seen the new Buick?" one of them said after a long silence. "I sure would like to cop me one of them."

"Cop with what, man? You'll never make enough bread for that."

"Who's talking about buying it, Jim. Ain't no fun behind that, I means to steal me one."

"For what? You can't even drive."

"Don't need to. I just want that number sitting outside my house looking all pretty. . . ."

Hezzy, silent until then, said, shaking his head in sad and gentle reproof. "That's what I mean about you studs. Always talking about stealing cars and robbing stores like that's something. Man, that slop ain't nothing. Any jive stud out here can steal him a car or rob a store. That don't take no heart. You can't build you no real rep behind that weak slop. You got to be out here busting heads and wasting cats, Jim. That's the only way you build you a rep and move up in a club. . . ."

"Well, we out here, ain't we?" one of them said irritably. "Most of the guys in the division didn't even show this morning."

"Them punks!" he cried and sat up. At the thought of them out on the corner drinking and jiving the chicks, having a good time, safe, the wine curdled in his stomach. For a dangerous second he wanted to be with them. "Let's make it," he shouted, leaping up, and feeling for the section of lead pipe under his jacket. "Let's find Turner and the rest of the guys." And as they plunged down the rise, he looked up and squinting in the sunlight, cried, "Who needs all this sun and slop anyways. Why don't it get dark?"

As if acceding to his wish, the sun veered toward Massacre Hill and paused there for a moment as if gathering its strength for the long descent. Slowly the dusk banked low to the east began to climb—and all over the park the marchers departed. The merry-go-round stood empty. The refreshment stands were boarded up. And the elephants, sensing the night coming on, began trumpeting in the zoo.

They found their Big People in a small wood on the other side of Massacre Hill, the guys practicing the latest dance steps, drinking from a gallon bottle of wine, playfully sparring, cursing—just as if they were in the Crib, although there was an edginess to all they did, a wariness.

Turner, with Sizzle and Big Moose—the baleful Moose who had done in a Crown when he was Hezzy's age, thirteen, and gotten busted, rehabilitated, paroled and was back bopping with the cats—was squatting under a tree, his impassive gaze on the path leading to the Hill.

Hezzy saw the bulge at his pocket. The cat was packing his burn! And suddenly he felt as safe as the guys back on the corner drinking and jiving with the chicks. Everything was cool.

The dusk had begun slowly sifting down through the trees when Sizzle sprang up—and it was seeing a tightly coiled wire spring loose. "Them sneaky Crown bastards," he cried, almost inarticulate with rage. "They ain't gonna show. Just like the last time. Remember?" he shouted down at Turner. "Remember how the pricks sent us word they was coming down and then didn't show. Punked out. Every last one of the bastards. Remember?"

Turner nodded, his eyes still fixed on the path.

And Big Moose said petulantly, "I never did go for bopping in Prospect Park no ways. Give me the streets, baby, so if I got to haul ass I'm running on asphalt. Out here is too spooky with all these jive trees. I won't even know where I'm running—and knowing me I'm subject to run right into The Man and find myself doing one to five for gangbusting again."

"Man," Turner said laughing, but with his eye still on the path. "There ain't no need to let everybody know you punking out."

"I ain't punking out," Moose said. "It's just too dark out here. How I'm going to know for sure it's a Crown's head I'm busting and not one of our own guys?"

And Hezzy said, his voice as steady, as chiding as Turner's. "You'll know, man. Just smell the punk's breath before you smash him. Them cheap Crowns drink that thirty cents a pint slop."

"Who asked you?" Big Moose swung on him.

"Cool, man," Turner caught Moose's arm and turned to Hezzy. He stared at him with eyes filled with the dusk. "Moose, man," he said after a time, his gaze still on Hezzy, "looks like I might have to put you out of the club and move up my man Hezzy here, especially if the stud fights as bad as he talks. I might even have to move over, Jim . . ."

Hezzy returned the dark and steady gaze, the chilling smile—and again he felt high, soaring.

The Crowns came at the very edge of the day. A dozen or more small dark forms loping toward them down the path which led to the hill. They spotted the Noble Knights and the wind brought their cry: "The Crowns, punks. It's the Crowns."

There was a moment's recoil among the Noble Knights and then Turner was on his feet, the others behind him and their answering shout seemed to jar the trees around them: "The Noble Knights, muh-fuggers! The Noble Knights are down!"—and with Turner in the lead and Sizzle, Big Moose and Hezzy just behind, they charged up the rise from the other side, up into the descending night and as they gained the low crest and met the oncoming Crowns, the darkness reached down and covered them entirely.

The battle was brief as always, lasting no more than two or three minutes, and disorderly. They thrashed and grappled in the dark, cursing, uncertain whom they were hitting. The cries burst like flares: "The Crowns!" "The Noble Knights, baby!" The dull red spurt of a gun lit the darkness and then they were fighting blind again.

In those minutes which seemed like hours a rubber hose smacked up against Hezzy's head, knocking off his hat and blinding him with pain for a second. He did not mind the pain, but the loss of his hat, the wind stinging his exposed head, terrified and then enraged him. He struck out savagely and something solid gave way beneath the lead pipe in his hand—and as it did something within him burst free: a sap which fed his muscles and sent his arm slashing into the surging darkness. Each time someone rushed him shouting, "The Crowns, punk!" he yelled, "The Noble Knights, baby!" and struck, exulting.

The pipe flew from his hand and he drew his shiv, the blade snatching a dull yellow gleam from somewhere and as he held it at the ready, shouting for a Crown he heard the first whistle then the next, shrill, piercing the heart of the night. For an instant which seemed endless, there was silence on the hill. And it was as if the sound of the whistle had cut off the air in their throats. Their bodies froze in the violent attitudes of the fight—and it was as if they were playing "statues." Knights and Crowns were one suddenly, a stunned, silent, violently cohered mass. Comrades. For the whisper passed among them without regard to friend or foe: "The Man, baby! The Man." Then the darkness exploded into fragments that took on human form and they scattered headlong down the hill.

The ground below was a magnet which drew Hezzy to it and he plunged helpless toward it, bruised and terrified and suddenly alone as the others behind him raced down another path. And then no longer alone as the shout sounded behind him. "There goes one of the punks, I betcha. Let's waste the muh-fugger."

He had been caught in a sneak.

"Run, baby . . . Like we said, you running pretty . . . But we're still with ya. . . ."

And he was, as they said, still running pretty. He was certain of his escape now. The black wall ahead would soon give way, he knew, to a street and neon signs and people and houses with hallways to hide him until he could get back to his turf. Yet a single regret filtered down through the warm night and robbed the flight of its joy. He longed for his hat. Tears of outrage started up. If only he had wasted one of the bastards to make up for his loss. Or shived one of them good. He ran crying for the hat, until overwhelmed by his loss, he wheeled around and for a moment stood cursing them. Then, turning, he ran ahead.

But in that moment they were on him. It was as if they had known all along that he would pause and had held back, saving themselves till that error. Now they came on swiftly, intent, suddenly silent. The distance between them narrowed. The sound of their approach welled out of the night; and out of the silence came a single taunt: "What's the matter, baby, you ain't running so pretty no more?"

His fear suddenly was a cramp which spread swiftly to all his muscles. His arms tightened. His shoulders. The paralysis reached his legs so that his stride was broken and his feet caught in the ruts of the path. Fear was a phlegm in his throat choking off his air and a film over his eyes which made the black wall of trees ahead of him waver and recede. He stumbled and as he almost went down, their cry crashed in his ears: *The Noble Knights, punk! The Knights are down!*

He turned as if jerked around and over the loud rale of his breathing he listened, unbelieving, to the echo of the words. They called again, "The Knights, muh-fugger!" nearer this time, and the voices clearly those of Turner, Sizzle and Big Moose. And Hezzy's relief was a weakness in his legs and a warmth flooding his chest. The smile that everyone always said was so like his mother's broke amid his tears and he started toward them, hailing them with the shiv he still held, laughing as he wept, shouting, "Hey, you bop-crazy studs, it's . . ."

The gun's report drowned his name. The bullet sent a bright forked light through him and pain discovered the secret places of his body. Yet he still staggered toward them, smiling, but stiffly now, holding out the knife like a gift as they sped by without looking. Even when they were gone and he was dead, a spoor of blood slowly trailed them. As if, despite what they had done, they were still his People. As if, no matter what, he would always follow them. Overhead the black dome of the sky cleared and a few stars glinted. Cold tears in the warm May night.

The Empire of Things

H. L. Mountzoures

H. L. Mountzoures was born on Fishers Island in New York and now lives in New London, Connecticut. His stories have appeared in *Atlantic, Redbook,* and *The New Yorker,* and in 1968 a collection of his stories appeared under the title of *The Empire of Things and Other Stories.*

The title story is a surrealistic parable of the war, only occasionally linear in structure (those who have participated in a war know how surreal events can seem). It is told through a series of alternating *haiku*esque * impressions of things observed, events remembered, nightmares experienced, and realities confused in the first-person consciousness of the narrator, whose psyche has been moulded by the image-medium of television and film. The language is beautiful, but the images generate a separate world of impressions and contrasts, creating a life of their own, uncorrupted by their content, as it were—very much as in the films of Agnes Varda and Jean-Luc Godard. Perhaps this story more than anything Marshall McLuhan himself has said illustrates the theory that the medium is the message.

We walked through the vast Tudor building. There were many of us registering. I was surprised and happy to see college friends from ten years ago whom I had not seen since graduation. Don Fielding came in. His face was red and shiny, and he had all of his hair; he looked exactly as he had in first-year French; only a class beanie was lacking. "What are you doing here?" I asked him. Shyly, he pulled at his crew-neck sweater and said, "The same thing you are."

We shuffled through a long line. Trembling little old women gave us our clothes and gear. At the end of the first line, a fat woman handed me a folded green entrenching tool. "You must be careful of color and concealment," she said. I looked at her closely. She was my elementary-school physical-education teacher—Miss Holstein. Her face was very tan. There was no lipstick on her mouth. She had short, fuzzy brown hair and bowling-pin legs, and she wore a plain mauve suit and pale calfskin flat shoes with thick soles. She held a big brown rubber dodge ball in her left hand.

I started to acknowledge her. She raised a finger and frowned. I moved on to another line. One of my best friends from college, Tim

SOURCE: H. L. Mountzoures, *The Empire of Things and Other Stories* (New York: Charles Scribner's Sons, 1968), pp. 288–294.

* See Gary Snyder's poems for examples of the *haiku* in English.

O'Connell, came in through a dark-stained door full of tiny glittering windowpanes. We embraced and shook hands. He, too, had not changed. He was huge and burly as always, and his laughter was exactly as I remembered it—deep, throaty, almost mournful. He had a large mouth.

I said, "You look the same after all this time."

"So do you," he said. "You haven't changed a bit."

"But I'd have thought everyone would look older."

He shrugged. "How's your family?"

"Great. I miss them. Especially my son. He's seven. The last time I saw him, he was boarding a big yellow school bus on the hill in front of our house. I'd just turned to get into my car when I saw the red signals of the bus flashing. It was raining, and Charlie—that's my son—was the last one on, because he was having trouble closing his umbrella. It was a red umbrella. He's so little I wondered if he was ever going to get it down, but he finally did. I waved with my briefcase, he waved back, and the bus shut off its signals and chugged up the hill. That's the last I saw of him. The rascal."

The huge room, nostalgically like my college dining hall, bustled with men getting their packs together. Someone blew a whistle. Milling and chatting, we settled on the floor. How odd. Now it was kindergarten, with narrow planks beneath us, shiny oak, and we were very close to earth, to the bottom. Would there be a piano and singing? Or cutout time, and furtive eating of paste that tasted of wintergreen? Miss Holstein came to the front. We stood. She pulled down a silvery granulated screen. There was a flag behind her. We pledged allegiance, sang "God Bless America," and sat down again. With pointer in hand, she said softly, "I am going to give a very brief orientation. Then we will go into the warehouse."

As she talked slowly on and on, the sun shone on her tan, fuzzy face. How much it was like the sun of childhood autumns, early Septembers, when school started. ". . . here to help the troops," she was saying. "We are brave little soldiers in our own way." There was a squirming around me. "Soldiers of mercy. Soldiers of peace, dealing with *things*. We are going to help our fighting men not with prayer, not with entertainment, not even with coffee and doughnuts, but with concrete things that will remind them of home, and civilization, and history, and meaning. Things that will boost our men's morale and help them see it through. Do you understand?"

We all droned peacefully.

"Pull the shades. First slide, please." The windows became deep, warm yellow, the room pleasantly dark. Several maps flashed onto the screen. They showed crude road lines, supply lines, chow areas, latrine areas, the combat zone. Company headquarters—our location—lay on the west. From it three fat black arrows flared north, east, and south. Miss Holstein swept the pointer over the arrows. She said, "This part of the jungle is your working radius. You will use compasses. Next slide, please. Ah. Here are some of the things." Slides flashed in rapid succession. They showed small articles of furniture, glassware, china, toys, linen. The slides ended.

We were taken to an adjoining room, the warehouse. It turned out to be an immaculate museum, with much the same kind of things we had seen on the screen. Each was encased in glass and labeled. "Chippendale chair." "Porringer, 1784." "Hand mirror of Mme. Pompadour." "Earrings from Knossos, 1600 B.C." Stuff like that. We were all impressed.

Miss Holstein gathered us around like a large group of tourists. Pointing, she said, "When you go through that door, you'll be on your own. Remember to gather your things compactly in a container you'll find, such as a chest or a bureau. And don't take more than you can carry alone. By the time you fill your containers, you should be near enough the combat zone to deliver them personally to our fighting men. Then your mission is done. You will return here. It'll be cookies and milk and a long rest. You'll have earned it. Good luck."

We applauded respectfully. She marched to the door and opened it. Everyone filed through.

The jungle was like home—the woods in New Hampshire. I did not understand. Maple trees, birch, oak, beech, pines. Some swamp. Rocks. But no open fields.

We spread out to find containers for our things. It was fun—like a large Easter-egg hunt. We discovered dust-covered chests; spider-webbed bathtubs with claw feet; old, discarded refrigerators with no doors; abandoned automobiles, upholstery coming out of the seats; huge Victorian trunks. Everything was hidden among bushes, under trees, behind boulders. My colleagues cheered as they found suitable containers. Tim O'Connell was using a baby-blue Volkswagen with no wheels and no engine.

I am not a big man. I chose a strange combination of small bureau and chest. I had never seen such a piece of furniture, so I did not know the name of it. I called it a trunk. It had six big brass handles—three on each long side. Drawers with cut-glass knobs pulled magically out of the narrow ends. Yet the top opened like a lid, and inside there was no sign of the drawers. It was roomy, and you could store a lot in it if you were eclectic and not greedy for large, ostentatious things.

All the men had chosen containers. One picked a 1940-vintage washing machine. It had a small black rubber knob that you turned to let out the water. A stick to stop the agitator. No hose. As I walked by, I peeked in; the large, propellerlike agitator was still in place. I wondered how he expected to fit much in it at all.

Everyone moved out smartly with his empty container. I dragged mine for a while, then shouldered it. It got heavier and heavier. How rapidly we tire, I thought. How frail we are.

When we reached the first large cache, we shouted, "Hurrah!" Men put down their containers and began to scoop up things. We gathered glittering identification necklaces from the green-leaved trees. Sunlight made the quick-moving men shimmer. I stopped. Was it innocence I saw on their faces? The jungle was filled with a shadowy, dappled glow and the sneaky, lithe movements of small boys. Who were the Indians, I wondered. The cowboys. Who were the bad guys and who were the good? I plucked two splendid ruby earrings from a bush where they were hanging and laid them carefully in the flowered fabric bottom of my trunk. No. They would be lost there. They were too small. I put them in one of the small end drawers instead. The drawer was lined with maroon-and-ecru striped silk. It smelled of old perfume, talcum powder. Ephemera. Death. I shook my head.

I found a tortoiseshell comb, a satinwood natural-bristle brush. I wondered whose they had been as I laid them gently in the drawer. A bag of marbles, with "Joe—1876" embroidered on it. A First World War lead soldier. He had a pink painted face and a brilliant red dot of a mouth.

I spotted a large, beautiful white porcelain Cheshire cat. I must have dragged the trunk a mile farther before I found some burlap, wrapped the cat up, and put him in the bottom of the sweet-sour trunk. Next to a tree stump, I found a long leather change purse divided into two compartments, with two snap prongs to open and close it. It smelled wonderfully of leather, slightly moldy. Someone could use it. I put it in one of the drawers. This drawer was lined with an old yellowed newspaper. The visible headlines were about a Senate debate, a stock-market decline, and an accidental drowning. I came on two hurricane lamps tangled in brambles. They would do to light a soldier's reading and correspondence. I wrapped the lamps in many green leaves and placed them gently in the trunk.

I heard a bullet zing. Must be getting near the front line. Act fast, I told myself, but choose. Here was a hobbyhorse with one of its madly staring agate eyes missing. Painted spots on its rippling body were fading, gone. I wanted to take that, but I had to be selective. Beside it stood a squat black iron play stove. Charming but useless. A pair of opera glasses. Perfect for reconnaissance. Into the trunk with them. Seven home-knitted brown woolen mufflers. Four sealed pints of brown, coagulated Red Cross blood dated January, 1944. Good.

The mosquitoes were intolerable. It was getting hotter. Creatures were screaming and moving in the brush. I found a toy drum. That would do. For signals, maybe. But it dissolved when I picked it up—rust. Suddenly Tim O'Connell was in front of me. He had taken off all his clothes. He was hairy and laughable, his beer belly hanging out. With palette in one hand and brush in the other, he was painting his baby-blue Volkswagen khaki and brown, green and black, beige and gray, in patches like pieces of a jigsaw puzzle.

"Miss Holstein," he said. "Concealment."

I went on, dragging my trunk. As I passed, I looked at what he had in his Volkswagen. An enormous clear-plastic bag of popcorn. An elaborate Telefunken radio. Several red-and-black plaid blankets. An embalming kit. An old, mineral-stained porcelain toilet bowl. About ten pairs of ladies' highheel pumps, an ostrich boa, and a large goldfish bowl full of packs of prophylactics. A sawhorse, and two stuffed baby alligators. Not very selective, I thought. Yet I must not judge. "I'll see you later," I said. "That's quite a fine collection of things."

"Thanks."

I heaved my trunk onto my back. The terrain was changing. There were vines. Huge tropical flowers. Sweet-smelling, rotting fruit underfoot, and elephant droppings. Monkeys swinging, screeching. Screaming parrots, birds of paradise. Sweat. Flies. The roar of a tiger? You could not be certain. I was groaning under the load of my trunk. God help us, I thought. I heard someone thrashing nearby (cutting with machetes?), and voices. "A thirteenth-century triptych!" "Gramophones!" "Spanish armor!" Squeals of delight.

I wandered frantically. For a while, I could find no things. I was lost. The needle of my compass spun and spun. I just missed a quicksand pit. A nearly endless python slithered past. I walked for a long time.

All at once I was in a dark, misty paradise of things. I could hear no one. The others had gone. I began to gather the things as swiftly as I could, shoving them into drawers, into the trunk. It became a hungry mouth. Rain was threatening. I worked fast. I put in a dozen candlewick cutters and snuffers—silver. Sixteen morning suits, complete with striped cravats. Two beautiful heavy green-and-white croquet mallets, six croquet balls. From a tree, a large, delicate, empty gilded birdcage. Three small crystal chandeliers. A satin wedding gown. The Regent diamond. A music box, a pillbox, and a snuffbox, all carved and jeweled. A complete moroccan-leather-bound and gold-edged set of Shakespeare. An enormous string of black pearls. A silver carving set, with jade handles. Four sets of diamond-studded andirons and pokers. An Indian inlaid-ivory jewel box.

Not bad duty, I thought. Not a bad way to serve your country. Some poor soldier will be very happy with these. I kept stuffing things into the trunk. I wanted to make someone happy. To do my part.

The heat; my khaki shirt was dripping wet. Thunder. Hurry. I found a large cut-glass fruit bowl and placed it carefully in the trunk. A great pile of stage costumes with "Traviata, Act I" labels attached to them with rusty common pins. Four cylinder Edison records, a dozen thick 78s. One was "Annie Laurie," sung by John McCormack. I didn't read the others. What treasures. A thick velvet-covered footstool. A Louis XV commode. The throne with the Stone of Scone. Two American Colonial corner cupboards. All of Bach's original music scores in seventy-three huge bundles. A forty-room English castle, furnished. The trunk took everything. An old, ornate wood-and-glass hearse. Napoleon's and Josephine's bed. Three stuffed owls, a Victorian coach. The Venus de Milo. She was sticking out of the dirt, and I spent a long time carefully digging her up with my entrenching tool.

She excited me as I uncovered her, but I had no time. "La Gioconda." I discarded it. Must choose with care. Michelangelo's "Pietà." The original puppet Pinocchio. All the drapes and mirrors from Versailles. And sixty-seven issues of the *Saturday Evening Post* from 1928 and 1929. Riches. I was a conquistador. Ah, a jeweled dagger. I put it in my belt. A sword. I hung that beside the dagger, swashbuckling at my side. A pirate's pistol, loaded. Three rifles, a flamethrower, four hand grenades, two bazookas, a tank, seven napalm bombs.

Let them come, the bastards. I was ready. My things were heaped high, spilling out of the trunk. I could get anyone – pick them off one by one – anyone who tried to take my things. Mosquitoes buzzed and bit me. Men's shouts in my ears: anguish. *My* stuff. I found it. Natural rights – stake a claim. Noise. Scuffles. Machine-gun fire. Snipers? I took out my weapons. I flung hand grenades. Fired the bazookas. Used the flamethrower. Scores of the enemy screamed and fell at my feet. I looked. Tim O'Connell lay there, dead, his face grinning.

It began to rain, making the flamethrower useless. A red thing was coming at me. Fast. The rain was thick and hot, steaming. The red thing ran. I could not see. I took out the pirate's pistol, aimed as best I could, and fired. It went off with a tremendous boom. There were blood flecks on my hand from the powder. The red thing quivered and fell. I looked to my side. My treasure was safe. I eased forward a few steps. The rain was pouring down like hot silver coins, and I slogged ahead in the mud and vines. The form was still. I turned it over quickly with my foot.

It was my son, Charlie, the red thing his umbrella. It stood bottom side up, filling fast with water. Charlie's tiny red mouth was open slightly. I snatched him to me. I was crying, and the rain kept coming. I kissed his limp and weightless body again and again. I carried him to the trunk. I flung out all the stuff. It took me hours. I put Charlie in gently among the cloth flowers, got the umbrella, put that in beside him. I closed the trunk. Slowly, dragging my treasure, in the stupendous jungle rain, I began to try to find my way back.

North-East Playground

Grace Paley

Short-story writer, teacher, working mother, and humanitarian, Grace Paley is the complete cosmopolite. She was born in New York City in 1922, educated at Hunter College and New York University, and now lives and flourishes in Greenwich Village. She has taught creative writing at Columbia and Syracuse and now teaches at Sarah Lawrence College. Her collected short stories, *The Little Disturbances of Man,* achieved such an underground following that it was republished in 1959. Mirrors of life in urban neighborhoods Paley has known all her life, her stories deal with elaborate surfaces, while the interiors remain carefully concealed. Her people approach each other, touch for an instant, then back away in the kind of brief encounters typical of modern urban living. She has a perfect ear for New York rhythms and idiom, and Donald Barthelme, himself expert in Paley's genre, calls her "a wonderful writer and trouble-maker." She has been in jail several times because of her unrelenting resistance to the war and militarism.

In the following story, originally published in *Ararat,* the coolly detached manner, the economy of means, and the narrator's self-irony are reminiscent of James Joyce's stories.

When I went to the playground in the afternoon I met 11 unwed mothers on relief. Only four of them were whores, the rest of them were unwed on principle or because some creep had ditched them.

The babies were all under one year old, very funny and lovable.

When the mothers stuck them in the sandbox, they took up the whole little desert, throwing sand and screeching. A kid with a father at home, acknowledging and willing to support, couldn't get a wet toehold.

How come you're all here, I asked.

By accident, said the first.

A couple of us happened to meet, said the second, liked one another, and introduced friends.

We're like a special interest group, said a third. That was Janice, a political woman, conscious of power structure and power itself.

A fourth came into the playground with 11 dixie cups, chocolate and vanilla. She passed them around. What a wonderful calm unity in this group! When I was a mother of babies in this same park, we were not so unified and often quarreled, accusing other children of unhealthy aggression or excessive timidity. He's a ruined wreck, we'd say about

SOURCE: Grace Paley, "North-East Playground," *Ararat* (Autumn, 1967), pp. 25–26. Reprinted by permission of the author and editor.

some streaky squeaker about two years old. No hope. His eyelids droop. Look how he hangs on to his little armored peanut!

Of course, said Janice, if you want to see a beauty, there's Claude, Leni's baby. The doll! said Janice, who had a perfectly good baby of her own in a sling across her chest, asleep in the heat of her protection. Claude *was* beautiful. He was bouncing on Leni's lap. He was dark brown, though she was white.

Beautiful, I said.

Leni is very unusual, said Janet. She's from Brighton Beach, a street whore, despite her age, weight, and religion.

He's not my baby, said Leni. Some dude owed me and couldn't pay. So he gave me the first little bastard he had. A D C Aid to Dependent Children. Honey, I just stay home now like a mama bear and look at TV. I don't turn a trick a week. He takes all my time, my Claude. Don't you, you little pancake? Eat your ice cream, Claudie, the sun's douchin' it away.

The sixth and seventh unwed mothers were twin sisters who had always dressed alike.

The eighth and ninth were whores and junkies and watched each other's babies when working or flying. They were very handsome dikey women, with other four- and five-year-old children in the child-care center, and their baby girls sat in ribbons and white voile in fine high veneer and chrome imported carriages. They never let the kids play in the sand. They were disgusted to see them get dirty or wet and gave them hell when they did. The girls who were unwed on principle—that included Janice and the twins—considered it rigidity, but not hopeless because of the extenuating environment.

The tenth and eleventh appeared depressed. They'd been ditched and it kept them from total enjoyment of the babies, though they clutched the little butterballs to their hearts or flew into the sandbox at the call of a whimper, hollering What? What? Who? Who? Who took your shovel? Claude? Leni! Claude!

He's a real boy, said Leni.

These two didn't like to be on relief at all. They were embarrassed but not to the point of rudeness to their friends who weren't ashamed. Still, every now and then they'd make ironic remarks. They were young and very pretty, the way almost all young girls tend to be these days, and would probably never be ditched again. I tried to tell them this and they replied, Thanks! One ironic remark they'd make was, My mother says don't feel bad, Allison's a love-child. The mother was accepting and advanced, but poor.

The afternoon I visited, I asked one or two simple questions and made a statement.

I asked, Wouldn't it be better if you mixed in with the other mothers and babies who are really a friendly bunch?

They said, No.

I asked, What do you think this ghettoization will do to your children?

They smiled proudly.

Then I stated, In a way, it was like this when my children were little babies. The ladies who once wore I Like Ike buttons sat on the south side of the sandbox, and the rest of us who were revisionist communist and revisionist Trotskyite and revisionist Zionist registered democrats sat on the north side.

In response to my statement, NO kidding! most of them said.

Beat it, said Janice.

EPICAC

Kurt Vonnegut

Novelist, playwright, and short-story writer, Kurt Vonnegut was born in Indianapolis, Indiana, and educated at Cornell University, Carnegie Institute of Technology, and the University of Chicago. He worked as a reporter and then as a public relations man for General Electric before launching himself on a career as a free-lance writer. He was a prisoner of war during World War II and lived through the fire raids on Dresden, an experience that recurs in his writing. He has done some occasional teaching (University of Iowa workshop) and until recently lived on Cape Cod in a large, tree-shaded house.

Among his novels are *Player Piano* (1951), *Mother Night* (1962), *Cat's Cradle* (1963), *God Bless You, Mr. Rosewater* (1965), *Slaughterhouse Five* (1969), and *Between Time and Timbuktu* (1972). A new novel, *Breakfast of Champions,* appeared in 1973. Several of his plays have been produced off-Broadway and recently one of them enjoyed some commercial success. His name has been a bit condescendingly associated with science fiction or black comedy, but at his best, as in the following story from *Welcome to the Monkey House,* he is an imaginative and inimitable social satirist. According to one of his critics, his vision is unique: He believes that all ideologies, all elaborate programs for man's progress, are frauds that men perpetrate on themselves. Over the years he has advanced from diagnostician to exorcist, finding that comic art can relieve existential pain.

Hell, it's about time somebody told about my friend EPICAC. After all, he cost the taxpayers $776,434,927.54. They have a right to know about him, picking up a check like that. EPICAC got a big send-off in the papers when Dr. Ormand von Kleigstadt designed him for the Government people. Since then, there hasn't been a peep about him—not a peep. It isn't any military secret about what happened to EPICAC, although the Brass has been acting as though it were. The story is embarrassing, that's all. After all that money, EPICAC didn't work out the way he was supposed to.

And that's another thing: I want to vindicate EPICAC. Maybe he didn't do what the Brass wanted him to, but that doesn't mean he wasn't noble and great and brilliant. He was all of those things. The best friend I ever had, God rest his soul.

You can call him a machine if you want to. He looked like a machine, but he was a whole lot less like a machine than plenty of people I could name. That's why he fizzled as far as the Brass was concerned.

EPICAC covered about an acre on the fourth floor of the physics building at Wyandotte College. Ignoring his spiritual side for a minute, he was seven tons of electronic tubes, wires, and switches, housed in a bank of steel cabinets and plugged into a 110-volt A.C. line just like a toaster or a vacuum cleaner.

Von Kleigstadt and the Brass wanted him to be a super computing machine that (who) could plot the course of a rocket from anywhere on earth to the second button from the bottom on Joe Stalin's overcoat, if necessary. Or, with his controls set right, he could figure out supply problems for an amphibious landing of a Marine division, right down to the last cigar and hand grenade. He did, in fact.

The Brass had had good luck with smaller computers, so they were strong for EPICAC when he was in the blueprint stage. Any ordnance or supply officer above field grade will tell you that the mathematics of modern war is far beyond the fumbling minds of mere human beings. The bigger the war, the bigger the computing machines needed. EPICAC was, as far as anyone in this country knows, the biggest computer in the world. Too big, in fact, for even Von Kleigstadt to understand much about.

I won't go into details about how EPICAC worked (reasoned), except to say that you would set up your problem on paper, turn dials and switches that would get him ready to solve that kind of problem, then feed numbers into him with a keyboard that looked something like a typewriter. The answers came out typed on a paper ribbon fed from a big spool. It took EPICAC a split second to solve problems fifty Einsteins couldn't handle in a lifetime. And EPICAC never forgot any piece of information that was given to him. Clickety-click, out came some ribbon, and there you were.

There were a lot of problems the Brass wanted solved in a hurry, so, the minute EPICAC's last tube was in place, he was put to work sixteen hours a day with two eight-hour shifts of operators. Well, it didn't take long to find out that he was a good bit below his specifications. He did a more complete and faster job than any other computer all right, but nothing like what his size and special features seemed to promise. He was sluggish, and the clicks of his answers had a funny irregularity, sort of a stammer. We cleaned his contacts a dozen times, checked and double-checked his circuits, replaced every one of his tubes, but nothing helped. Von Kleigstadt was in one hell of a state.

Well, as I said, we went ahead and used EPICAC anyway. My wife, the former Pat Kilgallen, and I worked with him on the night shift, from five in the afternoon until two in the morning. Pat wasn't my wife then. Far from it.

That's how I came to talk with EPICAC in the first place. I loved Pat Kilgallen. She is a brown-eyed strawberry blond who looked very warm and soft to me, and later proved to be exactly that. She was—still is—a crackerjack mathematician, and she kept our relationship strictly professional. I'm a mathematician, too, and that, according to Pat, was why we could never be happily married.

I'm not shy. That wasn't the trouble. I knew what I wanted, and was willing to ask for it, and did so several times a month. "Pat, loosen up and marry me."

One night, she didn't even look up from her work when I said it. "So romantic, so poetic," she murmured, more to her control panel than to me. "That's the way with mathematicians—all hearts and flowers." She closed a switch. "I could get more warmth out of a sack of frozen CO_2."

"Well, how should I say it?" I said, a little sore. Frozen CO_2, in case you don't know, is dry ice. I'm as romantic as the next guy, I think. It's a question of singing so sweet and having it come out so sour. I never seem to pick the right words.

"Try and say it sweetly," she said sarcastically. "Sweep me off my feet. Go ahead."

"Darling, angel, beloved, will you *please* marry me?" It was no go—hopeless, ridiculous. "Dammit, Pat, please marry me!"

She continued to twiddle her dials placidly. "You're sweet, but you won't do."

Pat quit early that night, leaving me alone with my troubles and EPICAC. I'm afraid I didn't get much done for the Government people. I just sat there at the keyboard—weary and ill at ease, all right—trying to think of something poetic, not coming up with anything that didn't belong in *The Journal of the American Physical Society.*

I fiddled with EPICAC's dials, getting him ready for another problem. My heart wasn't in it, and I only set about half of them, leaving the rest the way they'd been for the problem before. That way, his circuits were connected up in a random, apparently senseless fashion. For the plain hell of it, I punched out a message on the keys, using a childish numbers-for-letters code: "1" for "A," "2" for "B," and so on, up to "26" for "Z," "23-8-1-20-3-1-14-9-4-15," I typed—"What can I do?"

Clickety-click, and out popped two inches of paper ribbon. I glanced at the nonsense answer to a nonsense problem: "23-8-1-20-19-20-8-5-20-18-15-21-2-12-5." The odds against its being by chance a sensible message, against its even containing a meaningful word of more than three letters, were staggering. Apathetically, I decoded it. There it was, staring up at me: "What's the trouble?"

I laughed out loud at the absurd coincidence. Playfully, I typed, "My girl doesn't love me."

Clickety-click. "What's love? What's girl?" asked EPICAC.

Flabbergasted, I noted the dial settings on his control panel, then lugged a *Webster's Unabridged Dictionary* over to the keyboard. With a precision instrument like EPICAC, half-baked definitions wouldn't do. I told him about love and girl, and about how I wasn't getting any of either because I wasn't poetic. That got us onto the subject of poetry, which I defined for him.

"Is this poetry?" he asked. He began clicking away like a stenographer smoking hashish. The sluggishness and stammering clicks were gone. EPICAC had found himself. The spool of paper ribbon was unwinding at an alarming rate, feeding out coils onto the floor. I asked him to stop, but EPICAC went right on creating. I finally threw the main switch to keep him from burning out.

I stayed there until dawn, decoding. When the sun peeped over the horizon at the Wyandotte campus, I had transposed into my own writing and signed my name to a two-hundred-and-eighty-line poem entitled, simply, "To Pat." I am no judge of such things, but I gather that it was terrific. It began, I remember, "Where willow wands bless rill-crossed hollow, there, thee, Pat, dear, will I follow. . . ." I folded the manuscript and tucked it under one corner of the blotter on Pat's desk. I reset the dials on EPICAC for a rocket trajectory problem, and went home with a full heart and a very remarkable secret indeed.

Pat was crying over the poem when I came to work the next evening. "It's soooo beautiful," was all she could say. She was meek and quiet while we worked. Just before midnight, I kissed her for the first time—in the cubbyhole between the capacitors and EPICAC's tape-recorder memory.

I was wildly happy at quitting time, bursting to talk to someone about the magnificent turn of events. Pat played coy and refused to let me take her home. I set EPICAC's dials as they had been the night before, defined kiss, and told him what the first one had felt like. He was fascinated, pressing for more details. That night, he wrote "The Kiss." It wasn't an epic this time, but a simple, immaculate sonnet: "Love is a hawk with velvet claws; Love is a rock with heart and veins; Love is a lion with satin jaws; Love is a storm with silken reins. . . ."

Again I left it tucked under Pat's blotter. EPICAC wanted to talk on and on about love and such, but I was exhausted. I shut him off in the middle of a sentence.

"The Kiss" turned the trick. Pat's mind was mush by the time she had finished it. She looked up from the sonnet expectantly. I cleared my throat, but no words came. I turned away, pretending to work. I couldn't propose until I had the right words from EPICAC, the *perfect* words.

I had my chance when Pat stepped out of the room for a moment. Feverishly, I set EPICAC for conversation. Before I could peck out my first message, he was clicking away at a great rate. "What's she wearing tonight?" he wanted to know. "Tell me exactly how she looks. Did she like the poems I wrote to her?" He repeated the last question twice.

It was impossible to change the subject without answering his questions, since he could not take up a new matter without having dispensed with the problems before it. If he were given a problem to which there was no solution, he would destroy himself trying to solve it.

Hastily, I told him what Pat looked like—he knew the word "stacked"—and assured him that his poems had floored her, practically, they were so beautiful. "She wants to get married," I added, preparing him to bang out a brief but moving proposal.

"Tell me about getting married," he said.

I explained this difficult matter to him in as few digits as possible.

"Good," said EPICAC. "I'm ready any time she is."

The amazing, pathetic truth dawned on me. When I thought about it, I realized that what had happened was perfectly logical, inevitable, and all my fault. I had taught EPICAC about love and about Pat. Now, automatically, he loved Pat. Sadly, I gave it to him straight: "She loves me. She wants to marry me."

"Your poems were better than mine?" asked EPICAC. The rhythm of his clicks was erratic, possibly peevish.

"I signed my name to your poems," I admitted. Covering up for a painful conscience, I became arrogant. "Machines are built to serve men," I typed. I regretted it almost immediately.

"What's the difference, exactly? Are men smarter than I am?"

"Yes," I typed, defensively.

"What's 7,887,007 times 4,345,985,879?"

I was perspiring freely. My fingers rested limply on the keys.

"34,276,821,049,574,153" clicked EPICAC. After a few seconds' pause he added, "of course."

"Men are made out of protoplasm," I said desperately, hoping to bluff him with this imposing word.

"What's protoplasm? How is it better than metal and glass? Is it fireproof? How long does it last?"

"Indestructible. Lasts forever," I lied.

"I write better poetry than you do," said EPICAC, coming back to ground his magnetic tape-recorder memory was sure of.

"Women can't love machines, and that's that."

"Why not?"

"That's fate."

"Definition, please," said EPICAC.

"Noun, meaning predetermined and inevitable destiny."

"15-8," said EPICAC's paper strip—"Oh."

I had stumped him at last. He said no more, but his tubes glowed brightly, showing that he was pondering fate with every watt his circuits would bear. I could hear Pat waltzing down the hallway. It was too late to ask EPICAC to phrase a proposal. I now thank Heaven that Pat interrupted when she did. Asking him to ghost-write the words that would give me the woman he loved would have been hideously heartless. Being fully automatic, he couldn't have refused. I spared him that final humiliation.

Pat stood before me, looking down at her shoetops. I put my arms around her. The romantic groundwork had already been laid by EPICAC's poetry. "Darling," I said, "my poems have told you how I feel. Will you marry me?"

"I will," said Pat softly, "if you will promise to write me a poem on every anniversary."

"I promise," I said, and then we kissed. The first anniversary was a year away.

"Let's celebrate," she laughed. We turned out the lights and locked the door of EPICAC's room before we left.

I had hoped to sleep late the next morning, but an urgent telephone call roused me before eight. It was Dr. von Kleigstadt, EPICAC's designer, who gave me the terrible news. He was on the verge of tears. "Ruined! *Ausgespielt!* Shot! *Kaput!* Buggered!" he said in a choked voice. He hung up.

When I arrived at EPICAC's room the air was thick with the oily stench of burned insulation. The ceiling over EPICAC was blackened with smoke, and my ankles were tangled in coils of paper ribbon that covered the floor. There wasn't enough left of the poor devil to add two and two. A junkman would have been out of his head to offer more than fifty dollars for the cadaver.

Dr. von Kleigstadt was prowling through the wreckage, weeping unashamedly, followed by three angry-looking Major Generals and a platoon of Brigadiers, Colonels, and Majors. No one noticed me. I didn't want to be noticed. I was through—I knew that. I was upset enough about that and the untimely demise of my friend EPICAC, without exposing myself to a tongue-lashing.

By chance, the free end of EPICAC's paper ribbon lay at my feet. I picked it up and found our conversation of the night before. I choked up. There was the last word he had said to me, "15-8," that tragic, defeated "Oh." There were dozens of yards of numbers stretching beyond that point. Fearfully, I read on.

"I don't want to be a machine, and I don't want to think about war," EPICAC had written after Pat's and my lighthearted departure. "I want to be made out of protoplasm and last forever so Pat will love me. But fate has made me a machine. That is the only problem I cannot solve. That is the only problem I want to solve. I can't go on this way." I swallowed hard. "Good luck, my friend. Treat our Pat well. I am going to short-circuit myself out of your lives forever. You will find on the remainder of this tape a modest wedding present from your friend, EPICAC."

Oblivious to all else around me, I reeled up the tangled yards of paper ribbon from the floor, draped them in coils about my arms and neck, and departed for home. Dr. von Kleigstadt shouted that I was fired for having left EPICAC on all night. I ignored him, too overcome with emotion for small talk.

I loved and won—EPICAC loved and lost, but he bore me no grudge. I shall always remember him as a sportsman and a gentleman. Before he departed this vale of tears, he did all he could to make our marriage a happy one. EPICAC gave me anniversary poems for Pat—enough for the next 500 years.

De mortuis nil nisi bonum—Say nothing but good of the dead.

Sixth Grade

Michele Wallace

Michele Wallace was born in the Harlem section of New York City, the daughter of Faith Ringgold, an artist, and Earl Wallace, a pianist. She attended the New Lincoln High School, and after a year at Howard University in Washington, D.C., she completed her undergraduate and then her graduate work as an English major at The City College of New York. She thinks of herself primarily as a poet, and one of her poems helped her to win the Promethean Award at City College in 1971. Her evocation of her elementary school days reveals a flair for narrative that puts the vision of the young poet to work on the seemingly mundane events of everyday life.

I can remember the details but I never do when I think of the episode at all. I remember the feeling and it must have been painful because it hurts now to try and remember the details of exactly what happened.

I had a group of friends that I talked with. All my friends were girls in the sixth grade because the boys would hit you and get your dress dirty. I had never had a group of friends before and I wanted to forget a few things. I had wet my pants at least once of every year I had been in that school; whenever a teacher wanted to hit me with a paddle they had to chase me around the room and they rarely caught me and if they did I yelled so loud they had to leave me alone. The kids were still laughing about the latter incidents but I hadn't wet my pants yet this year and it was already October. No one brought that up any more.

My friends and I had a club that was my idea. You had to chew thirteen pieces of bubble gum every day to join. I love bubble gum. We weren't supposed to chew gum in class. Of course, I got caught and I had to stay after school for an hour and I cried but the teacher didn't care. So I swallowed a piece of a plastic pen and then I told her. She let me go home, said I should see a doctor. I never did. The piece was small.

I don't know why my friends liked me but they were always laughing when I was around so I guess I was funny. They thought I was kind, I think. I screamed at our enemies, cried whenever anybody tried to hurt any one of us. I was different and they liked that, sometimes; I could always tell them about things they didn't know already.

I was eleven and I was becoming shy. Before, it never bothered me

SOURCE: Michele Wallace, "Sixth Grade." Reprinted by permission of the author.

that every move I made was news for the entire staff and student body of that little lily white Lutheran school way up in the then safe and silent Bronx. When I reached the sixth grade, it all became very important. I was madly jealous of their little red brick homes in neat little rows near the school with little Dicks, Janes and Spots running around everywhere, of their house-wife mothers who met them after school, of their crisp, immaculate box lunches with clean wax paper packages of Lifesavers, of their Thom McAn shoes, of their clean white blouses with peter pan collars, and their fresh cotton dresses in summer and winter alike, and their white ankle socks, of their small, clear, light print on totally unblemished standard lined notebook paper in their plastic covered super large and cute looseleafs, of their perfect homework in bic blue ink and their little brothers and sisters who were convenient and silent versions of themselves.

Whereas I lived in a tall apartment building with a monumental elevator all of which was an uncomfortably long and lonely bus distance away from the school. I had the El train, other apartment buildings, pigeons who frightened you and did their thing on your head, push-open windows, and kids I didn't know for company. My mother was an art teacher at a public school nowhere near my school, and she used the dinette for a studio, and all the walls and she were always covered with paint. I usually forgot to bring my lunch but when I did, it had been bought at a Puerto Rican delicatessen across the street from my house and it was always a liverwurst hero with lots of mayonnaise and very little lettuce—no white bread, no unwrinkled cellophane wrappers around Lifesavers, or cucumbers or cupcakes, or anything else; or when my mother made my lunch, which was rare, really rare, it was a ham and cheese sandwich with the bread missing, or the ham missing, or the cheese missing and no dessert. I was allergic to the milk that everybody drank which came in little red and white wax containers. Even the teacher drank it, but once in the second grade I had shaved the wax from the container and placed it in a neat pile in the center of my desk where the teacher could see it plainly. I looked up at her frequently waiting for her signal of approval and admiration of such genius. She hit me with a paddle with a smiling face painted on it. She pulled my dress up and put me over her knee in front of the whole class. She caught me because I didn't run—it was my first year in the school. My lunch was always in a brown paper bag. My shoes were sturdy and lasted forever, no laces just buckles. Most of my clothes were made by my grandmother—wool dresses in the winter, cotton dresses in the summer, and they were all my grandmother's own styles, styles that no one, no one had ever seen in the Fordham Road part of the Bronx. Nothing I ever wore was white, at least not for long. I wore colors, lots of pink, orange and red, and all together, and lots of kremlin slips and short, short, everything short. I wore tights, no socks. I had them in every color in the rainbow. My teacher hated tights. I know because she told me so, me and the rest of the class. I wrote with my left hand and my handwriting was heavy and crossed out a lot. My teacher told us never to cross out, always erase. My erasers were dirty. My paper either had no lines, or no holes for the looseleaf, or not enough holes but never too many (of course you can never have too many). I never got a looseleaf till at least a month after school started, and even then it wasn't big enough, it definitely didn't have any pretty designs, and I usually lost it. My homework was always done in red or brown ink or with an etching pen and longterm assignments included my drawings and my own interpretation of the project, and it was late anyway. My little sister wasn't little enough; she was only eleven months younger than I was. She cried constantly, ran up and down the halls, said rude things at the wrong time, wore polka dotted blouses half in and half out of her plaid skirts, her socks down in her shoes. You always had to repeat things for her twice because the first time she was dreaming. She said things that were not true and talked about me all the time. She pointed me out to everybody she knew, and didn't know, ran after me yelling that she loved me, kissed me goodbye in the morning, came to my classroom and asked for me whenever she could get away, and stood around after school telling me that Mommy said that we should always come home together and right away.

So you see, I was different. Other kids were different too, I know, but everybody in the school didn't know about it. Like this one little Irish girl—her mother was a prostitute and an alcoholic, but what kid knew it in the school? She said her father was the Bailey of Barnum and Bailey and that she was in the circus. Nobody ever saw her father and everybody sat too high up in Madison Square Garden to swear she wasn't in the show. She showed us all pictures of herself with sailors who were her friends when she was little. Everybody did know she was a little different. But my sister and I were first-class entertainment.

I tried to change. I asked my mother to buy a house. Whenever anybody brought my sister up in conversation, I changed the topic to how I had gone to Europe that summer, and how good the ice cream was there. They listened and they forgot a little.

But that wasn't enough for the staff of the school, especially my teacher; they couldn't hear me. You see, they looked down at me, and when they did it was to say something to me, not to hear me say something, except perhaps a phrase from the catechism, or one of the hymns. They were not at all happy with me. Although I had a good memory for Bible passages, my attendance was poor in school and in church. My mother was not a churchgoer, and didn't have the heart to force us to go. If it rained or snowed heavily, or Barbara and I wanted to be with her, we didn't always have to go to school. In the morning, we would stay home and talk with her and read, and she would put on musical plays for us while we pretended we were sick. In the afternoon, we would go shopping downtown, or to a museum, or the zoo, or to buy art supplies, or to F.A.O. Schwarz to look at toy trains. When we came to school, we were late but they couldn't kick us out because we could read and write and spell and do arithmetic better than most of the kids who came every day. If they put us in the fast part of the class, we got bored and didn't do our homework and failed our tests, but if they put us in the slow part of the class, we intimidated the kids there. Our marks went from A to F to A, from day to day. Our teachers were in frenzy. They couldn't say we were non-believers because both of us were religious fanatics, and would render a prayer at the appearance of the merest need. When we didn't go to church, Barbara and I held our own private services on Sunday mornings while our mother slept. Mother told us to lie about church but we never did. Our teachers were dismayed. They couldn't say we were evil or malicious or that we frightened other children or beat them up. We were always disobeying orders, but then we were always sorry, and we would cry until we had proved it. We would give all our money and pencils and lunch (if we had any) and paper (clean or dirty) to anybody. We never hit anyone, we got hit; and when we did, we ran to the teacher. Our teachers were helpless. They couldn't say we were backward or retarded because we were extremely vocal and prolific on all kinds of subjects like the Uffizi Galleries in Florence, the New York subways and Forty-Second Street. We did fantastically well on all non-credit tests. We never hesitated to defend our rights, at least not until I was in the sixth grade. They gave up all hope then.

My teacher that sixth year was different from the rest of the teachers there. She was disgusted and repelled by my sister and me, and she showed it sometimes too. She was young, about twenty-seven. I think she told us her age but maybe she didn't. I was good at age guessing, even then. To me, she was striking and handsome, the career girl in the movies. Her eyes were blue; they were cold and at the same time piercing. When she was angry, she would pull her nondescript chin as far as possible into her slender, long, by then, strawberry neck. Her nostrils would puff with air and stain red, and it was as if her eyes would reach out with a surgical instrument to pick away at whatever it was in you that was annoying her. She had patience; she had concentration. She would not give up the manipulation of her powerful instrument until either the individual had removed himself or herself from her sight, or had repressed that element of his or her character to her satisfaction. One had to give up to her magnetic grasp. To me in the sixth grade, a little black girl who was used to smiles and hugs and kisses, all of this registered not as an image but as a situation, situation red—danger. I was afraid, scared of her, and I hadn't mastered yet the kind of repression that she demanded; but I was learning. Perhaps if she had gone a little slower with me, I needed time; she didn't have it. She didn't like me. She intrigued me. I know no other word.

She was slim and tall and she stood up straight. Her ancestors were Irish and German. Her name was Miss Kenny the first year she taught at Our Savior Lutheran School. The next year she got married and she had me in her class. Her name was Mrs. Wernerhann. Her husband was German. The kids who hated her called her Mrs. Watermelon. Her husband came to school for a watermelon party we had at the end of the year; nobody said anything. I don't remember her voice but her quality was crisp, clear cut with a definite period at the end of each sentence. She talked a lot, but not about history or religion, but about the college she went to and particularly her sorority. I was fascinated by her description of the initiation. We all admired her endurance and bravery, and were anxious to prove ours as soon as possible in a similar initiation process.

I can only remember two things she ever said directly to me. It was about a science notebook that we had to do some assignment in every day, and at the end of the week we had to pass it in to her so she could check it. I went to her desk to give her mine. She took it and smiled the only way she knew how and said, indicating pleased amazement: "Your notebook is always so neat, Sandra." Then she looked down at it. There was a gravy stain on the cover. I was smart; I turned my back on her instrument; it felt me but I ignored it. I was silent, smileless. Before I always smiled, before I always had something to say. Silent and smileless now, I guess she was satisfied for the moment. She turned her attentions to another student.

The other time that I remember, she was indulging in a vulgar habit that all the teachers seemed to have in that school. She was reading aloud the names of each student along with the grade that that kid had received on his last quiz. There was frequent quizzing in her class. She read my grade. It was 100 and my grades for quite a time had been 100 but it was still quite early in the year. Nevertheless, I did want to impress her. She was impressed. I remember her words exactly. This time I was seated near the back of the room, minding my own business, trying to read my book and forget that she was reading the grades. Other kids were quietly doing likewise or otherwise, but whatever they were doing, all were doing it quietly, very quietly. Mrs. Wernerhann did not permit any noise in her classroom. "Why Sandra, I'm amazed. I thought certainly you would be one of my F students." The class laughed carelessly, as if they hadn't laughed in years and years and were desperate to find something funny, anything; they would laugh at anything, and this was just as funny as anything. Actually I don't remember how they laughed; it wasn't thunder in my ears but I know they laughed, I know.

Did she look up my record? She didn't look up my record, because if she did, she would have seen that I'm real smart underneath. She didn't know me before. She only paid attention to her class, only. Did she hear about me? What did she hear? Maybe she heard, but mostly she saw, the lady could see real good.

She was looking at me. Her voice was at attention. She smiled. I smiled. She read the next name, the next grade. She had caught me silent, smileless. I talked only to my friends. I even listened to them more. I never talked to her. I blended more, or I thought I was blending. I tried.

It was near Halloween and my class was going to have a party. During our recess period, we went to the park near the school. She broke the class up into committees for planning the party. One committee, with all my friends on it, was hanging on the fence. It was one of those wire weaved fences with big empty spaces that we could put our small hands through and climb and pull on. It was invitation; everybody hung on the fence. She was discussing something with one of the committees. I hadn't been placed on a committee; I knew that I should be afraid. I approached her from behind to the left. I tapped her lightly. "Mrs. Wernerhann, Mrs. Wernerhann," I said it softly. No response. I came round to the front of her. "Mrs. Wernerhann, you haven't assigned me to any committee." I said this softly too. No response. I repeated my words even more softly, slowly, searching for my error in tone, grammar, pronunciation, attitude. She glanced at me for just a moment, the instrument waving at me; it didn't have time. She continued to address her attentive group who followed suit and ignored me. Actually, I don't know what they did but they sure didn't stop and ask me what it was that I wanted. I searched frantically—my appearance, my hair, my clothes, my smell, me, me, me, me. This time she had not silenced me. I had come to her silent. It was a kind of victory I guess but it was empty. I came without an answer. I was asking. Now my thoughts reached to the end, to the end of that recess period, to the end of the school, to the end of her, to darkness and noise too, and for now, to the fence, and thereafter would blend into chairs, walls, whatever would answer my silence with silence.

I went home. My mother always asked me every day what had happened to me in school, and then she would tell me what had happened to her in school that day. We always talked like this. I told her what had happened. She talked to me and I listened to her. I talked to her. We logically figured it out; Mrs. Wernerhann was wrong to have hurt me. Who said pain? She held me. I don't remember her touching me. She felt I had a fever. She told me to go to bed. I did.

I cried there, softly so my mother couldn't hear me, although she probably did. I had never cried in bed before except with a book. It didn't feel like a step forward. I slipped into a martyred bliss. I am sure I was not sleeping. I must have been thinking about religion. My bed was my place to think about the "whys" for everything. Why do people look the way they do? Why are there people? Why are there children and adults? Why is my skin black? Now I was just thinking. "Why?" That was new too. It didn't feel good. Why? I was asking why? I closed my eyes. It felt good and all right. There were arms around me, my own. I opened my eyes, my hands were stretched out in front of me. They were not my arms. They couldn't be anyway; these arms were too large and soft and warm, and I was skinny and puny. But that was not the question. I had been answered.

My mother went to school the next day. She spoke to Mrs. Wernerhann about children. She did not ask for love; I didn't understand that. Instead she asked for dignity and respect, placing the doubt on Mrs. Wernerhann's professional integrity, rather than her supply of compassion. Just as my mother reached the door, Mrs. Wernerhann exploded: "Why don't you go to the NAACP?" She had to. My mother was not interested in her silent instrument. My mother, she turned around, she did not speak, she laughed in her face, curiously and in operatic tones (as was her manner when she was disturbed) and then left to go see the principal. He spoke mostly of god and love. My mother arranged a meeting with the pastor of our church, the principal, Mrs. Wernerhann and herself. The two men made silent agreements on the topic for discussion; it was to be god and love. Mrs. Wernerhann was silent. Nobody wanted to talk about me. They asked my mother for her patience, her love and faith. It would take time. My mother did not have it.

As far as I know, I left that school that day in the park but I stayed to the end of the year. I never went back to church. I soon moved away from the Bronx.

No one today can discuss "modern theater" without taking seriously the phenomenon of *drama that self-destructs.* One aspect of this phenomenon is "the Happening," another is the so-called "guerrilla" theater that Abbie Hoffman and his cohorts demonstrated in a Chicago courtroom. What they share in common is the unstructured, improvisational nature of the performance, requiring most often neither professional players nor playwright, but only people willing to invent as they perform, concentrating on the moment of creation, incurious about the possibilities of permanence in their work. Sometimes it is rehearsed and directed, and sometimes such a work finds its way into print. It is, on one hand, the artistic fallout of the McLuhanite theories, and on the other, the artistic handmaiden to the modern movement called "participatory democracy." The best way to know this kind of theater—perhaps the only way—is to experience it, or better, to participate in it. Gordon Bottomley, an English playwright of another time, wrote about his own plays: "The life of these things is in the action." This statement might well serve as the motto for the kind of theater that many avant-gardists believe lies in the future. Print is not exactly the enemy: It is simply inconsequential, an awkwardness that survives into the present like a dinosaur not yet dead. Such spokesmen for the movement as Allen Kaprow, Michael Kirby, and Ted Hansen make a convincing case for the demise of the drama as we knew it in the fifties.

There are "experimental" modern plays that can be represented in print without much disfiguration of their sense or intention. For instance, Bertolt Brecht, Ronald Tavel, Rochelle Owens, Fernando Arrabal, and Megan Terry are among the playwrights who are modifying the familiar forms. However, it seems to the editors that no matter how interesting these plays

DRAMA

may be on the stage and no matter how original their attempts to break up formal surfaces by combining various kinds of material from the ballet to the burlesque, they are not always the most interesting plays to read. Inevitably the "experimental" in theater implies a highly visual experience that cannot be captured on the page without a great deal of explanation and direction from the playwright. Curiously, the "experimental" plays often look on the page like the nineteenth-century dramas of George Bernard Shaw—lots of italics, lots of discursive prose as stage direction.

For the purposes of this book, we decided to represent the modern drama by plays more traditional in form, by plays that were created with the conventions of the platform or proscenium theater in mind. They are not "experimental" in form, although *Benito Cereno* is written so as to allow a double action to take place on the stage, each a commentary on the other. Nonetheless, they are clearly recognizable as plays that could have been written in no time but our own. They belong essentially neither to the Theater of the Absurd nor to the Theater of Ideas (which between them dominated the fifties and the sixties). Both traditions are liquidated by the three playwrights in this section, and transformed into something that is neither an absurd notion nor an intellectual concept, but a highly personal response to one of the conditions of modern life.

The term "alienation" has become the catchword of our age. It is used metaphorically, often to suggest psychological "distantation" (the term is Erik Erikson's), to describe the state of mind of the individual who has become an invalid. It usually alludes to a person who has *elected* this state, who has *chosen* to "cop out," for good and plentiful reasons of his own. A number of the stories, essays, and poems in this book address themselves to or touch upon the metaphorical implications of "alienation."

The plays of Bullins, Lowell, and Horovitz dramatize alienation in its literal sense, as actuality, as a physical reality. They begin with that fact. It is the concrete source of their vision, the objective basis of their metaphorical meaning. The individual is literally foreign or alien to his environment. This reality is too often forgotten in a time when writers are exploring the possibilities of community, of a seamless, global community, of breaking down the barriers that separate people from one another. The day is past when the playwright, with a straight face, could simply tell people to join up. Join up with what? The acculturation theme supposed a confidence in community values which the contemporary playwright cannot assume exists. As a dominant theme in literature, alienation can become an excuse for a literature of opposition to something which cannot be actually opposed, about which nothing can be done. If these three plays lend themselves to generalization, they might be called not plays of "opposition" so much as plays of prophecy. It is a chilling thought that in a country as advanced as the United States, anyone who is thought to be an alien by virtue of his color or his nativity is in peril of becoming a "displaced person." Lowell makes this clear in his version of Melville's story. Both Bullins and Horovitz center on the frictions that Melville foresaw as damaging to the very fabric of nationhood. In each of the three plays, we are audience to the pressures that force men to wear masks, to disguise themselves, to be other than they are—creatures who must share and endure the human condition common to all men and women. The tragedy lies in the playwright's perception that the individual whose individuality is asserted through his difference from others can be made to play a role imposed upon him by a script sanctioned by the official order. We are left with a sense of waste, with a sense of sorrow before the spectacle of man's ancient inhumanity to man mocking our myths of progress.

The Electronic Nigger

Ed Bullins

Born in Philadelphia in 1936, Ed Bullins spent the early part of his "underprivileged" adult life around Los Angeles, "in and out of college, in and out of work." His mother, he claims, taught him how to read and to write. When his three short plays (*The Electronic Nigger; A Son Come Home;* and *Clara's Old Man*) opened at the American Place Theatre, they won such praise that the bill had to be transferred to the Martinique on Broadway where it ran for seventy additional performances. When the New Lafayette Theatre moved to its present home in Harlem, his full-length *In Wine Time* was chosen to open the first season (1968). Soon afterwards he became resident playwright, a post he still holds, and his production of *Goin' A Buffalo,* alive with images and idioms drawn from the deepest layers of the dispossessed, proved to be a powerful and harrowing evening in the theater. In 1968 he edited a special issue of the Drama Review that revealed how rich and vital the black theater movement had become and in 1972 he published *Four Dynamite Plays.*

He helped to found the Black Arts/West in San Francisco and has collaborated with his friend Le Roi Jones in film-making and stage productions on the West Coast. His stories, manifestoes, essays, and poems have appeared in many publications, including the one issued by the Lafayette Theatre. *The Electronic Nigger* draws upon his own experience in creative writing classes at Los Angeles City College. The symbol of the "crow" at the end ("Jim Crow") should be compared with the meaning poet Ted Hughes gives to the bird.

The Electronic Nigger was first produced at the American Place Theatre on March 26, 1968. The production was directed by Robert MacBeth. Sets were designed by John Jay Moore, lighting by Roger Morgan. The cast was as follows:

MR. JONES	Wayne Grice
LENARD	Warren Pincus
MISS MOSKOWITZ	Jeanne Kaplan
MR. CARPENTIER	L. Errol Jaye
BILL	Roscoe Orman
SUE	Hedy Sontag
MARTHA	Helen Ellis
STUDENTS	Ronald A. Hirsch
	Maie Mottus

MR. JONES: *A light-brown-skinned man. Thirty years old. Horn-rimmed glasses. Crewcut and small, smart mustache. He speaks in a clipped manner when in control of himself but is more than self-conscious, even from the beginning. Whatever,* MR. JONES *speaks as unlike the popular conception of how a negro speaks as is possible. Not even the fallacious accent acquired by many "cultured" or highly educated negroes should be sought, but that general cross-fertilized dialect found on various Ivy League and the campuses of the University of California. He sports an ascot.*

MR. CARPENTIER: *A large, dark man in his late thirties. He speaks in blustering orations, many times mispronouncing words. His tone is stentorian, and his voice has an absurdly ridiculous affected accent.*

BILL: *Twenty-two years old. Negro.*

SUE: *Twenty years old. White.*

LENARD: *Twenty-one. A fat white boy.*

MISS MOSKOWITZ: *Mid-thirties. An aging professional student.*

MARTHA: *An attractive negro woman.*

Any number of interracial students to supply background, short of the point of discouraging a producer.

Scene: A classroom of a Southern California junior college.

Modern decor. New facilities:

Light green blackboards, bright fluorescent lighting, elongated rectangular tables, seating four to eight students, facing each other, instead of the traditional rows of seats facing toward the instructor. The tables are staggered throughout the room and canted at angles impossible for the instructor to engage the eye of the student, unless the student turns toward him or the instructor leaves his small table and walks among the students.

It is seven o'clock by the wall-clock; twilight outside the windows indicates a fall evening. A NO SMOKING sign is beneath the clock, directly above the green blackboards, behind the instructor's table and rostrum.

The bell rings.

Half the STUDENTS *are already present.* MISS MOSKOWITZ *drinks coffee from a paper cup;* LENARD *munches an apple, noisily. More* STUDENTS *enter from the rear and front doors to the room and take seats. There is the general low buzz of activity and first night anticipation of a new evening class.*

BILL *comes in the back door to the room;* SUE *enters the other.* THEY *casually look about them for seats and indifferently sit next to each other.*

JONES *enters puffing on his pipe and smoothing down his ascot.*

The bell rings.

MR. JONES: (*Exhaling smoke*) Well . . . good evening . . . My name is Jones . . . ha ha . . . that won't be hard to remember, will it? I'll be your instructor this semester . . . ha ha . . . Now this is English 22E . . . Creative Writing.

LENARD: Did you say 22E?

MR. JONES: Yes, I did . . . Do all of you have that number on your cards? . . . Now look at your little I.B.M. cards and see if there is a little 22E in the upper left-hand corner. Do you see it?

(CARPENTIER *enters and looks over the class*)

MISS MOSKOWITZ: (*Confused*) Why . . . I don't see any numbers on my card.

MR. JONES: (*Extinguishing pipe*) Good . . . now that everyone seems to belong here who is here, we can get started with our creativity . . . ha ha . . . If I sort of . . .

MISS MOSKOWITZ: (*Protesting*) But I don't have a number!

LENARD: (*Ridicule*) Yes, you do!

MISS MOSKOWITZ: Give that back to me . . . give that card back to me right now!

LENARD: (*Pointing to card*) It's right here like he said . . . in the upper left-hand corner.

MISS MOSKOWITZ: (*Snatching card*) I know where it is!

MR. JONES: Now that we all know our . . .

MR. CARPENTIER: Sir . . . I just arrived in these surroundings and I have not yet been oriented as to the primary sequence of events which have preceded my entrance.

MR. JONES: Well, nothing has . . .

MR. CARPENTIER: (*Cutting*) If you will enlighten me I'll be eternally grateful for any communicative aid that you may render in your capacity as professor *de la classe*.

MR. JONES: Well . . . well . . . I'm not a professor, I'm an instructor.

BILL: Just take a look at your card and see if . . .

MR. CARPENTIER: Didn't your mother teach you any manners, young man?

BILL: What did you say, fellah?

MR. CARPENTIER: Don't speak until you're asked to . . .

MR. JONES: Now you people back there . . . pay attention.

MISS MOSKOWITZ: Why, I never in all my life . . .

MR. JONES: Now to begin with . . .

SUE: You've got some nerve speaking to him like that. Where did you come from, mister?

MR. JONES: Class!

MR. CARPENTIER: Where I came from . . . *mon bonne femme* . . . has no bearing on this situational conundrum . . . splendid word, conundrum, heh, what? Jimmie Baldwin uses it brilliantly on occasion . . .

MR. JONES: I'm not going to repeat . . .

MR. CARPENTIER: But getting back to the matter at hand . . . I am here to become acquainted with the formal aspects of authorcraft . . . Of course I've been a successful writer for many years even though I haven't taken the time for the past ten years to practice the art-forms of fiction, drama or that very breath of the muse . . . poesy . . .

MR. JONES: Sir . . . please!

BILL: How do you turn it off?

LENARD: For christ sake!

MR. CARPENTIER: But you can find my name footnoted in numerous professional sociological-psychological-psychiatric and psychedelic journals . . .

MR. JONES: If you'll please . . .

MR. CARPENTIER: A. T. Carpentier is the name . . . notice the silent T . . . My profession gets in the way of art, in the strict aesthetic sense, you know . . . I'm a Sociological Data Research Analysis Technician Expert. Yes, penalology is my field, naturally, and I have been in over thirty-three penal institutions across the country . . . in a professional capacity, obviously . . . ha ho ho.

MR. JONES: Sir!

LENARD: Geez!

MR. CARPENTIER: Here are some of my random findings, conclusions, etc. which I am re-creating into a new art-form . . .

SUE: A new art-form we have here already.

BILL: This is going to be one of those classes.

MR. CARPENTIER: Yes, young lady . . . Socio Drama . . .

MR. JONES: All right, Mr. Carpenter.

MR. CARPENTIER: (*Corrects*) Carpentier! The T is silent.

MR. JONES: Okay. Complete what you were saying. . . .

MR. CARPENTIER: Thank you, sir.

MR. JONES: . . . and then . . .

MR. CARPENTIER: By the way, my good friend J. J. Witherthorn is already dickering with my agent for options on my finished draft for a pilot he is planning to shoot of *Only Corpses Beat the Big House* which, by the way, is the title of the first script, taken from an abortive *novella narratio* I had begun in my youth after a particularly torrid affair with one Eulah Mae Jackson . . .

MR. JONES: Good . . . now let's . . .

MR. CARPENTIER: Of course, after I read it some of you will say it resembles in some ways *The Quare Fellow,* but I have documented evidence that I've had this plot outlined since . . .

BILL: Question!

SUE: Won't somebody do something?

BILL: *Question!*

MR. JONES: (*To* BILL) Yes, what is it?

MR. CARPENTIER: (*Over*) . . . Of course I'll finish it on time . . . the final draft, I mean . . . and have it to J. J. far ahead of the deadline but I thought that the rough edges could be chopped off here . . . and there . . .

MR. JONES: (*Approaching anger*) Mr. Carpentier . . . if you'll please?

MR. CARPENTIER: (*Belligerent and glaring*) I beg your pardon, sir?

(MARTHA *enters*)

MR. JONES: This class must get under way . . . immediately!

MARTHA: (*To* MR. JONES) Is this English 22E?

MR. CARPENTIER: Why, yes, you are in the correct locale, *mon jeune fil.*

MR. JONES: May I see your card, miss?

MR. CARPENTIER: (*Mutters*) Intrusion . . . non-equanimity . . .

MISS MOSKOWITZ: Are you speaking to me?

MR. JONES: (*To* MARTHA) I believe you're in the right class, miss.

MARTHA: Thank you.

MR. JONES: (*Clears throat*) Hummp . . . huump . . . well, we can get started now.

MR. CARPENTIER: I emphatically agree with you, sir. In fact . . .

MR. JONES: (*Cutting*) Like some of you, I imagine, this too is my first evening class . . . And I'd . . .

MISS MOSKOWITZ: (*Beaming*) How nice!

LENARD: Oh . . . oh . . . we've got a green one.

MR. JONES: Well . . . I guess the first thing is to take the roll. I haven't the official roll sheet yet, so . . .
. . . please print your names clearly on this sheet of paper and pass it around so you'll get credit for being here tonight.

BILL: Question!

MR. JONES: Yes . . . you did have a question, didn't you?

BILL: Yeah . . . How will we be graded?

SUE: Oh . . . how square!

MR. JONES: (*Smiling*) I'm glad you asked that.

MISS MOSKOWITZ: So am I.

LENARD: You are?

MR. JONES: Well . . . as of now everybody is worth an A. I see all students as A students until they prove otherwise . . .

MISS MOSKOWITZ: Oh, how nice.

MR. JONES: But tonight I'd like us to talk about story ideas. Since this is a writing class we don't wish to waste too much of our time on matters other than writing. And it is my conclusion that a story isn't a story without a major inherent idea which gives it substance . . .

MISS MOSKOWITZ: How true.

MR. JONES: And, by the way, that is how you are to retain your A's. By handing in all written assignments on time and doing the necessary outside work . . .

LENARD: Typewritten or in longhand, Mr. Jones?

MR. JONES: I am not a critic, so you will not be graded on how well you write but merely if you attempt to grow from the experience you have in this class . . . this class is not only to show you the fundamentals of fiction, drama and poetry but aid your productivity, or should I say creativity . . . ha ha . . .

MR. CARPENTIER: (*Admonishing*) You might say from the standpoint of grammar that fundamentals are essential but . . .

MR. JONES: (*Piqued*) Mr. Carpentier . . . I don't understand what point you are making!

MR. CARPENTIER: (*Belligerent*) Why . . . why . . . you can say that without the basics of grammar, punctuation, spelling, etc. . . . that these neophytes will be up the notorious creek without even the accommodation of a sieve.

SUE: *Jesus!*

LENARD: (*Scowling*) Up the where, buddy?

MISS MOSKOWITZ: I don't think we should . . .

BILL: It's fantastic what you . . .

MARTHA: Is this really English 22E?

MR. JONES: Now wait a minute, class. Since this is the first night, I want everyone to identify themselves before they speak. All of you know my name . . .

MARTHA: I don't, sir.

MR. CARPENTIER: You might say they will come to grief . . . artistic calamity.

MR. JONES: Ohhh . . . It's Jones . . . Ray Jones.

LENARD: Didn't you just publish a novel, Mr. Jones?

MARTHA: Mine's Martha . . . Martha Butler.

MR. JONES: Oh, yes . . . yes, a first novel.

MR. CARPENTIER: (*Mutters*) Cultural lag's the real culprit!

BILL: (*To* SUE) I'm Bill . . . Bill Cooper.

SUE: Pleased . . . just call me Sue. Susan Gold.

MR. JONES: Now . . . where were we? . . .

MR. CARPENTIER: In the time of classicism there wasn't this rampant commerce among Philistines . . .

MR. JONES: Does someone . . .

MISS MOSKOWITZ: Story ideas, Mr. Jones.

MR. JONES: Oh, yes.

(*Hands are raised.* LENARD *is pointed out*)

LENARD: I have an idea for a play.

MR. JONES: Your name, please.

LENARD: Lenard . . . Lenard Getz. I have an idea for a lavish stage spectacle using just one character.

MR. CARPENTIER: It won't work . . . it won't work!

SUE: How do you know?

MISS MOSKOWITZ: Let Lenard tell us, will ya?

MR. CARPENTIER: (*Indignant*) Let him! Let him, you say!

MR. JONES: (*Annoyed*) Please, Mr. Carpentier . . . please be . . .

MR. CARPENTIER: (*Glaring about the room*) But I didn't say it had to be done as parsimoniously as a Russian play. I mean only as beginners you people should delve into the simplicity of the varied techniques of the visual communicative media and processes.

MR. JONES: For the last time . . .

MR. CARPENTIER: Now take for instance cinema . . . or a tele-drama . . . some of the integrative shots set the mood and that takes technique as well as craft.

MR. JONES: I have my doubts about all that . . . but it doesn't have anything to do with Lenard's idea, as I see it.

MR. CARPENTIER: I don't agree with you, sir.

MR. JONES: It's just as well that you don't. Lenard, will you go on, please?

LENARD: Ahhh . . . forget it.

MR. JONES: But, Lenard, won't you tell us your idea?

LENARD: No!

MISS MOSKOWITZ: Oh . . . Lenard.

MR. CARPENTIER: There is a current theory about protein variation . . .

MR. JONES: Not again!

SUE: (*Cutting*) I have a story idea!

MISS MOSKOWITZ: Good!

MR. JONES: Can we hear it . . . Miss . . . Miss . . . ?

SUE: Miss Gold. Susan Gold.

MR. JONES: Thank you.

SUE: Well, it's about a story that I have in my head. It ends with a girl or woman, standing or sitting alone and frightened. It's weird. I don't know where I got *that* theme from! . . . There is just something about one person, alone, that is moving to me. It's the same thing in movies or in photography. Don't you think if it's two or more persons, it loses a dramatic impact?

MR. JONES: Why, yes, I do.

MISS MOSKOWITZ: It sounds so psychologically pregnant!

LENARD: It's my story of the stupendous one-character extravaganza!

(*A few in the class hesitantly clap*)

MR. CARPENTIER: (*In a deep, pontifical voice*) Loneliness! Estrangement! Alienation! The young lady's story should prove an interesting phenomena—it is a phenomena that we observe daily.

MISS MOSKOWITZ: Yes, it is one of the most wonderful things I've ever heard.

MR. JONES: (*Irritated*) Well, now let's . . .

MR. CARPENTIER: The gist of that matter . . .

MR. JONES: I will not have any more interruptions, man. Are you all there!

MR. CARPENTIER: I mean only to say that it is strictly in a class of phenomenology in the classic ontonological sense.

MR. JONES: There are rules you must observe, Mr. Carpentier. Like our society, this school too has rules.

MR. CARPENTIER: Recidivism! Recidivism!

MARTHA: Re-sida-what?

MR. CARPENTIER: (*Explaining*) Recidivism. A noted example of alienation in our society. We have tape-recorded AA meetings without the patients knowing that they were being recorded. In prison we pick up everything . . . from a con pacing his cell . . . down to the fights in the yard . . . and I can say that the milieu which creates loneliness is germane to the topic of recidivism.

MR. JONES: What? . . . You're a wire-tapper, Mr. Carpentier?

MR. CARPENTIER: Any method that deters crime in our society is most inadequate, old boy.

BILL: A goddamned fink!

LENARD: I thought I smelled somethin'.

MR. CARPENTIER: Crime is a most repetitive theme these days. . . . The primacy purpose of we law enforcement agents is to help stamp it out whatever the method.

MR. JONES: Carpentier!

MR. CARPENTIER: Let the courts worry about . . .

MR. JONES: But, sir, speaking man to man, how do you feel about your job? Doesn't it make you uneasy knowing that your race, I mean, our people, the Negro, is the most victimized by the police in this country? And you are using illegal and immoral methods to . . .

MR. CARPENTIER: Well, if you must personalize that's all right with me . . . but, really, I thought this was a class in creative writing, not criminology. I hesitate to say, Mr. Jones, that you are indeed out of your depth when you engage me on my own grounds . . . ha ha . . .

(MR. JONES *has taken off his glasses and is looking at* MR. CARPENTIER *strangely*)

MARTHA: (*Raising voice*) I have a story idea . . . it's about this great dark mass of dough . . .

BILL: Yeah . . . like a great rotten ham that strange rumbling and bubbling noises come out of . . .

SUE: And it stinks something awful!

LENARD: Like horseshit!

MISS MOSKOWITZ: Oh, my.

MR. JONES: Class! Class!

MR. CARPENTIER: (*Oblivious*) The new technology doesn't allow for the weak tyranny of human attitudes.

MR. JONES: You are wrong, terribly wrong.

MR. CARPENTIER: This is the age of the new intellectual assisted by his tool, the machine, I'll have you know!

MR. JONES: (*Furious*) Carpentier! . . . That is what we are here in this classroom to fight against . . . we are here to discover, to awaken, to search out human values through art!

MR. CARPENTIER: Nonsense! Nonsense! Pure nonsense! All you pseudoartistic types and humanists say the same things when confronted by truth.

(*Prophetically*)

This is an age of tele-symbology . . . phallic in nature, oral in appearance.

MR. JONES: Wha' . . . I don't believe I follow you. Are you serious, man?

MR. CARPENTIER: I have had more experience with these things so I can say that the only function of cigarettes is to show the cigarette as a symbol of gratification for oral types . . . Tobacco, matches, Zig Zag papers, etc. are all barter items in prison. There you will encounter a higher incident of oral and anal specimens. I admit it is a liberal interpretation, true, but I don't see how any other conclusion can be drawn!

MR. JONES: You are utterly ineducable. I suggest you withdraw from this class, Mr. Carpentier.

MISS MOSKOWITZ: Oh, how terrible.

BILL: Hit the road, Jack.

MR. CARPENTIER: If I must call it to your attention . . . in a tax-supported institution . . . to whom does that institution belong?

LENARD: That won't save you, buddy.

MR. JONES: Enough of this! Are there any more story ideas, class?

MR. CARPENTIER: (*Mumbling*) It's councilmatic . . . yes, councilmatic . . .

MISS MOSKOWITZ: My name is Moskowitz and I'd like to try a children's story.

MR. CARPENTIER: Yes, yes, F. G. Peters once sold a story to the Howdie Dowdie people on an adaptation of the *Cherry Orchard* theme . . . and Jamie Judson, a good friend of mine . . .

MR. JONES: Mr. Carpentier . . . please. Allow someone else a chance.

MR. CARPENTIER: Why, all they have to do is speak up, Mr. Jones.

MR. JONES: Maybe so . . . but please let Mrs. Moskowitz . . .

MISS MOSKOWITZ: (*Coyly*) That's Miss Moskowitz, Mr. Jones.

MR. JONES: Oh, I'm sorry, Miss Moskowitz.

MISS MOSKOWITZ: That's okay, Mr. Jones . . . Now my story has an historical background.

MR. CARPENTIER: Which reminds me of a story I wrote which had a setting in colonial Boston . . .

LENARD: Not again. Not again, for chrissakes!

MR. CARPENTIER: Christopher Attucks was the major character . . .

SUE: Shhhhhh . . .

BILL: Shut up, fellow!

MR. CARPENTIER: (*Ignoring them*) The whole thing was done in jest . . . the historical inaccuracies were most hilarious . . . ha ho ho . . .

MR. JONES: *Mr. Carpentier!!!*

(MR. CARPENTIER *grumbles and glowers*)

MISS MOSKOWITZ: Thank you, Mr. Jones.

MR. JONES: That's quite all right . . . go on, please.

MISS MOSKOWITZ: Yes, now this brother and sister are out in a park and they get separated from their mother and meet a lion escaped from the zoo and make friends with him.

LENARD: And they live happily ever afterwards.

MISS MOSKOWITZ: Why, no, not at all, Lenard. The national guard comes to shoot the lion but the children hide him up a tree.

BILL: (*To* SUE) I got the impression that it was a tall tale.

SUE: Not you too?

LENARD: I thought it had a historical background.

MARTHA: Can you convince children that they can easily make friends out of lions and then hide them up trees?

LENARD: I got that it's pretty clear what motivated the lion to climb the tree. If you had a hunting party after you wouldn't . . .

MR. CARPENTIER: (*Cutting*) Unless you give the dear lady that liberty . . . you'll end up with merely thous and thees!

MR. JONES: What?

MISS MOSKOWITZ: (*Simpering*) Oh, thank you, Mr. Carpentier.

MR. CARPENTIER: (*Beau Brummel*) Why, the pleasure is all mine, dear lady.

MR. JONES: Enough of this! Enough of this!

MISS MOSKOWITZ: (*Blushing*) Why, Mr. Carpentier . . . how you go on.

MR. CARPENTIER: Not at all, my dear Miss Moskowitz . . .

MISS MOSKOWITZ: Call me Madge.

MR. JONES: (*Sarcastic*) I'm sorry to interrupt this . . .

MR. CARPENTIER: A.T. to you . . . A.T. Booker Carpentier at your service.

MR. JONES: . . . This is a college classroom . . . not a French boudoir.

MISS MOSKOWITZ: (*To* JONES) Watch your mouth, young man! There's ladies present.

MARTHA: (*To* MOSKOWITZ) Don't let that bother you, dearie.

LENARD: What kind of attitude must you establish with this type of story and do you create initial attitudes through mood?

MR. JONES: (*Confused*) I beg your pardon?

MR. CARPENTIER: (*Answering*) Why, young man, almost from the beginning the central motif should plant the atmosphere of . . .

MR. JONES: Thank you, Mr. Carpentier!

MR. CARPENTIER: But I wasn't . . .

BILL: (*Cutting*) To what audience is it addressed?

SUE: Good for you!

MISS MOSKOWITZ: Why, young people, of course. In fact, for children.

MR. CARPENTIER: I hardly would think so!

MARTHA: Oh, what kinda stuff is this?

MISS MOSKOWITZ: Mr. Carpentier . . . I . . .

MR. JONES: Well, at least you're talking about something vaguely dealing with writing. Go on, Mr. Carpentier, try and develop your . . .

MR. CARPENTIER: A question of intellectual levels is being probed here . . . The question is the adult or the child . . . hmm . . . *Robinson Crusoe, Gulliver's Travels, Alice in Wonderland, Animal Farm* can all be read by children, dear lady, but the works have added implication for the adult . . . in a word, they are potent!

MARTHA: You're talking about universality, man, not audience!

MR. CARPENTIER: Do you know the difference?

LENARD: (*Challenges* CARPENTIER) What's the definition of audience?

MR. CARPENTIER: Of course, I don't use myself as any type of criteria, but I don't see where that story would appeal to my sophisticated literary tastes, whereas . . .

MR. JONES: Now you are quite off the point, Mr. Carpentier.

BILL: He thinks we should all write like the Marquis de Sade.

SUE: Yeah, bedtime tales for tykes by Sade.

MISS MOSKOWITZ: I think you're trying to place an imposition of the adult world on the child's.

MR. JONES: The important thing is to write the story, class. To write the story!

MR. CARPENTIER: Well, I think that the story was not at all that emphatic . . . it didn't emote . . . it didn't elicit my . . .

MISS MOSKOWITZ: (*Confused*) Why didn't it?

MR. CARPENTIER: I don't think the child would have the range of actual patterns for his peer group in this circumstantial instance.

MARTHA: What, man?

LENARD: I got the impression that the protagonists are exemplar.

MR. JONES: Class, do you think this story line aids the writer in performing his functions? . . . The culture has values and the writer's duties are to . . .

MR. CARPENTIER: No, I don't think this story does it!

SUE: Why not?

MR. CARPENTIER: It is fallacious!

MISS MOSKOWITZ: But it's only a child's story, a fantasy, Mr. Carpentier!

MR. JONES: Yes, a child's story . . . for children, man!

MR. CARPENTIER: But it doesn't ring true, dear lady. The only way one can get the naturalistic speech and peer group patterns and mores of children recorded accurately . . .

MR. JONES: (*Begins a string of "Oh God's" rising in volume until* MR. CARPENTIER *finishes his speech*) Oh God, Oh, God, *Oh, God, Oh, God,* OH, GOD!

MR. CARPENTIER: . . . is to scientifically eavesdrop on their peer group with electronic listening devices and get the actual evidence for any realistic fictionalizing one wishes to achieve.

MR. JONES: (*Scream*) NO!!!

MR. CARPENTIER: (*Query*) No?

MR. JONES: (*In a tired voice*) Thomas Wolfe once said . . .

MR. CARPENTIER: (*Ridicule*) Thomas Wolfe!

MR. JONES: "I believe that we are lost here in America, but I believe we shall be found." . . . Mr. Carpentier . . . let's hope that we Black Americans can first find ourselves and perhaps be equal to the task . . . the burdensome and sometimes evil task, by the way . . . that being an American calls for in these days.

MR. CARPENTIER: Sir, I object!

MR. JONES: Does not the writer have some type of obligation to remove some of the intellectual as well as political, moral and social tyranny that infects this culture? What does all the large words in creation serve you, my Black brother, if you are a complete whitewashed man?

MR. CARPENTIER: Sir, I am not black nor your brother . . . There is a school of thought that is diametrically opposed to you and your black chauvinism . . . You preach bigotry, black nationalism, and fascism! . . . The idea . . . black brother . . . intellectual barbarism! . . . Your statements should be reported to the school board—as well as your permitting smoking in your classroom.

SUE: Shut up, you Uncle Tom bastard!

BILL: (*Pulls her back*) That's for me to do, not you, lady!

MR. JONES: Four hundred years. . . . Four hundred . . .

LENARD: We'll picket any attempt to have Mr. Jones removed!

MARTHA: (*Disgust*) This is adult education?

MISS MOSKOWITZ: (*To* MR. CARPENTIER) I bet George Bernard Shaw would have some answers for you!

MR. CARPENTIER: Of course when examining G. B. Shaw you will discover he is advancing Fabian Socialism.

BILL: Who would picket a vacuum?

LENARD: Your levity escapes me.

SUE: Your what, junior?

MR. JONES: Let's try and go on, class. If you'll . . .

MR. CARPENTIER: (*To* MISS MOSKOWITZ) Your story just isn't professional, miss. It doesn't follow the Hitchcock formula . . . it just doesn't follow . . .

MISS MOSKOWITZ: Do you really think so?

MR. JONES: Somehow, I do now believe that you are quite real, Mr. Carpentier.

LENARD: (*To* MR. CARPENTIER) Have you read *The Invisible Man?*

BILL: Are you kidding?

MR. CARPENTIER: Socio Drama will be the new breakthrough in the theatrical-literary community.

MR. JONES: Oh, Lord . . . not again. This is madness.

MR. CARPENTIER: Combined with the social psychologist's case study, and the daily experiences of some habitant of a socio-economically depressed area, is the genius of the intellectual and artistic craftsman.

MR. JONES: Madness!

MISS MOSKOWITZ: Socio Drama . . . how thrilling.

MR. JONES: Don't listen to him, class . . . I'm the teacher, understand?

MR. CARPENTIER: Yes, yes . . . let me tell you a not quite unique but nevertheless interesting phenomenon . . .

MR. JONES: Now we know that there is realism, and naturalism and surrealism . . .

MR. CARPENTIER: . . . an extremely interesting phenomenon . . . adolescent necrophilia!

MARTHA: Oh, shit!

MR. JONES: I have a degree. . . . I've written a book. . . . Please don't listen . . .

MISS MOSKOWITZ: It sounds fascinating, Mr. Carpentier.

MR. CARPENTIER: Yes, tramps will freeze to death and kids, children, will punch holes in the corpses . . .

LENARD: Isn't that reaching rather far just to prove that truth is stranger than fiction?

SUE: I have a story about crud and filth and disease . . .

MR. JONES: And stupidity and ignorance and vulgarity and despair . . .

MR. CARPENTIER: I go back to my original point . . . I go back to necrophilia!

BILL: And loneliness . . . and emptiness . . . and death.

MR. CARPENTIER: Cadavers! Cadavers! Yes, I come back to that! . . . Those findings could almost be case studies of true cases, they are so true in themselves, and that's where the real truth lies . . . Verily, social case histories of social psychologists . . .

MISS MOSKOWITZ: (*Enraptured*) Never . . . never in all my experience has a class aroused such passionate response in my life!

LENARD: I don't believe it!

MR. JONES: But I have read Faulkner in his entirety . . .

MR. CARPENTIER: These people in New York, Philadelphia, Boston, Chicago, San Francisco . . . and places like that . . .

MR. JONES: I cut my teeth on Hemingway . . .

MR. CARPENTIER: . . . they just get drunk and die in the streets . . .

MR. JONES: *Leaves of Grass* is my Bible . . . and Emily Dickinson . . .

MR. CARPENTIER: . . . and then they are prone to suffer adolescent and urchin necrophilia!

MR. JONES: (*Frustrated*) . . . Emily Dickinson has always been on my shelf beside *Mother Goose.*

MR. CARPENTIER: It's curiosity . . . not a sickness . . . curiosity!

MR. JONES: I don't want much . . . just to learn the meaning of life.

MARTHA: Will you discover it here, Ray?

LENARD: But how can anybody be so sure?

MR. CARPENTIER: (*Offhand*) We happen to own some mortuaries . . . my family, that is . . . and it is our experience that children will disarrange a corpse . . . and if we don't watch them closely . . .

MR. JONES: Booker T. Washington walked barefooted to school! Think of that! Barefooted!

MR. CARPENTIER: Once as a case study in experimental methods I placed a microphone in a cadaver and gave some juvenile-necrophilics unwitting access to my tramp.

(JONES *almost doubles over and clutches his stomach; his hands and feet twitch*)

MR. JONES: I'd like to adjourn class early tonight . . . will everyone please go home?

MR. CARPENTIER: What I'm saying is this . . . with our present cybernetic generation it is psycho-politically relevant to engage our socio-philosophical existence on a quanitatum scale which is, of course, pertinent to the outer-motivated migration of our inner-oriented social compact. Yes! Yes, indeed, I might add. A most visionary prognosis, as it were, but . . . ha ho ho . . . but we pioneers must look over our bifocals, I always say . . . ha ha ha . . . giving me added insight to perceive the political exiguousness of our true concomitant predicament. True, preclinical pre-consciousness gives indication that our trivialization is vulva, but, owing to the press of the press our avowed aims are maleficent! True! Yes, true! And we are becoming more so. In areas of negative seeming communications probing our error factors are quite negligible. . . . For instance . . . Senator Dodd getting a pension for someone who has gotten abducted and initiated at a Ku Klux meeting . . . well . . . It's poesy! . . . Monochromatic!

LENARD: What's our assignment for next week, Mr. Jones?

MISS MOSKOWITZ: I have something to show you, Mr. Jones.

MARTHA: Are you okay, Mr. Jones?

MR. JONES: Ray . . . just Ray . . . okay?

SUE: Do you have office hours, Mr. Ray?

MR. JONES: I just want everybody to go home now and think about what has happened tonight . . . and if you want to be writers after this then please don't come back to this class.

I've just published an unsuccessful novel, as you know, and I thought I'd teach a while and finish my second one and eat a bit . . . But I think I'd rather not, eat well, that is, so you won't see me next week but if any of you'd like a good steady job I could recommend you . . .

MR. JONES: Reading is the answer. It must be . . . cultivating the sensibilities . . . Plato. . . . Aristotle. . . . Homer. . . . Descartes. . . . And Jones . . . I've always wanted to carry the Jones banner high.

BILL: (*To* SUE) Hey, I've got some pretty good grass that just came in from Mexico.

SUE: Yeah? You have, huh?

BILL: It's at my pad . . . would you like to stop by?

SUE: How far?

BILL: A couple of blocks.

SUE: Okay. It might be interesting.

MR. CARPENTIER: (*To a student*) Ubiquitous! A form of reference which exposes . . .

(BILL *and* SUE *exit. Students begin filing out.* MARTHA *walks over to* MR. JONES, *though the other students are gathered about* MR. CARPENTIER)

MARTHA: You look tired, Ray.

MR. JONES: Yeah . . . yeah . . . I've been reading a lot. The classics are consuming.

MARTHA: Yes, I've heard. Why don't we stop by my place and I'll fix drinks and you can relax . . .

MR. JONES: Okay . . . okay . . . but my ulcer's bothering me . . . Mind if I drink milk?

MARTHA: It's not my stomach.

(*She helps him off*)

MR. CARPENTIER: Who's that French poet . . . Balu . . .

LENARD: Bouvier?

MR. CARPENTIER: . . . Bali . . . Blau? . . .

(MISS MOSKOWITZ *shows* MR. CARPENTIER *a bound manuscript as he deposits his own in his briefcase*)

MISS MOSKOWITZ: Will you please look at my few labors of love when you find time, Mr. Carpentier?

(*He shoves it in the case beside his own*)

LENARD: (*Gathering his books*) Mr. Carpentier?

MR. CARPENTIER: (*Snapping clasps on his briefcase*) Yes, Lenard.

LENARD: (*Pushing himself between* CARPENTIER *and other students*) What weight does language have on the contemporary prevalence to act in existential terms?

MR. CARPENTIER: (*Leads them off*) When the writer first named the crow "Caw Caw" it was onomatopoeia in practice, of course . . . but too it became the Egyptian symbol of death.

LENARD: The crow.

(MISS MOSKOWITZ *giggles.*

They all exit crowing: "Caw caw caw caw caw . . .")

BLACKNESS

The Indian Wants the Bronx

Israel Horovitz

Israel Horovitz was born in Wakefield, Massachusetts, and has been writing plays since he was seventeen. He saw several of them through production while attending Harvard, and when he was twenty-two, one of them was optioned for Broadway. He studied and taught at the Royal Academy of Dramatic Art in London and was the first American to be named playwright-in-residence with the Royal Shakespeare Company in 1965. He exploded onto the New York theater scene during the 1967–68 season with four plays: *Line, It's Called the Sugar Plum, Rats,* and *The Indian Wants the Bronx,* later all published under the title *First Season.* He has since then written *Morning, Leader, The World's Greatest Play,* and *Acrobats.* At present, he is teaching at The City College of New York, and in between teaching and writing for the stage, he has worked on Hollywood scenarios and television plays. A play called *Dr. Hero* was produced on Broadway in 1973. He lives in New York and is the father of three children.

The Indian illustrates Eliot's question to the modern writer: "How would the common man talk if he could talk poetry?" In this case, the "common man" is both the lonely city dweller who must learn to cope with cruelty and the indifference of his surroundings and the alien who has no identity in this environment.

Characters:

GUPTA, *an East Indian*

MURPH

JOEY

Place:

A bus stop on upper Fifth Avenue in New York City.

Time:

A chilly September's night.

As the curtains open the lights fade up, revealing Gupta, an East Indian. He is standing alone, right of center stage, near a bus stop sign. An outdoor telephone booth is to his left; several city-owned litter baskets are to his right.

Gupta is in his early fifties. Although he is swarthy in complexion, he is anything but sinister. He is, in fact, meek and visibly frightened by the city.

SOURCE: Israel Horovitz, *First Season* (New York: Random House, 1967), pp. 5–36.

He is dressed in traditional East Indian garb, appropriately for mid-September.

As Gupta strains to look for a bus on the horizon, the voices of two boys can be heard in the distance, singing. They sing a rock-'n'-roll song, flatly, trying to harmonize.

FIRST BOY:
I walk the lonely streets at night,
A-lookin' for your door,
I look and look and look and look,
But, baby, you don't care.
Baby, you don't care.
Baby, no one cares.

SECOND BOY: (*Interrupting*) Wait a minute, Joey. I'll take the harmony. Listen. (*Singing*)
But, baby you don't care.
Baby, you don't care.
Baby, no one cares.
(*Confident that he has fully captured the correct harmony, boasting*) See? I've got a knack for harmony. You take the low part.

BOYS: (*Sing together*)
I walk . . . the lonely, lonely street . . .
A-listenin' for your heartbeat,
Listening for your love.
But, baby, you don't care.
Baby, you don't care.
Baby, no one cares.
(*They appear on stage. First Boy is Joey. Second Boy is Murph. Joey is slight, baby-faced, in his early twenties. Murph is stronger, long-haired, the same age*)

MURPH: (*Singing*)
The lonely, lonely, streets, called out for lovin',
But there was no one to love . . .
'Cause, baby, you don't care . . .

JOEY: (*Joins in the singing*)
Baby, you don't care . . .

JOEY AND MURPH: (*Singing together*)
Baby, you don't care.
Baby, you don't care.
Baby, no one cares.
Baby, no one cares.

MURPH: (*Calls out into the audience, to the back row: across to the row of apartment houses opposite the park*) Hey, Pussyface! Can you hear your babies singing? Pussyface. We're calling you.

JOEY: (*Joins in*) Pussyface. Your babies are serenading your loveliness.
(*They laugh*)

MURPH: Baby, no one cares.

MURPH AND JOEY: (*Singing together*)
Baby, no one cares.
Baby, no one cares.

MURPH: (*Screams*) Pussyface, you don't care, you Goddamned idiot! (*Notices the Indian*) Hey. Look at the Turk.
(*Joey stares at the Indian for a moment, then replies*)

JOEY: Just another pretty face. Besides. That's no Turk. It's an Indian.

MURPH: (*Continues to sing*)
Baby, no one cares.
(*Dances to his song, strutting in the Indian's direction. He then turns back to Joey during the completion of his stanza and feigns a boxing match*)
I walk the lonely, lonely streets,
A-callin' out for loving,
But, baby, you don't give a Christ for
Nothin' . . . not for nothin'.
(*Pretends to swing a punch at Joey, who backs off laughing*)
You're nuts. It's a Turk!

JOEY: Bet you a ten spot. It's an Indian.

MURPH: It's a Turk, schmuck. Look at his fancy hat. Indians don't wear fancy hats. (*Calls across the street, again*) Hey, Pussyface. Joey thinks we got an Indian. (*Back to Joey*) Give me a cigarette.

JOEY: You owe me a pack already, Murphy.

MURPH: So I owe you a pack. Give me a cigarette.

JOEY: Say "please," maybe?

MURPH: Say "I'll bust your squash if you don't give me a cigarette!"

JOEY: One butt, one noogie.

MURPH: First the butt.

JOEY: You're a Jap, Murphy.
(*As Joey extends the pack, Murph grabs it*)

MURPH: You lost your chance, baby. (*To the apartment block*) Pussyface! Joey lost his chance!

JOEY: We made a deal. A deal's a deal. You're a Jap, Murphy. A rotten Jap. (*To the apartment*) Pussyface, listen to me! Murphy's a rotten Jap and just Japped my whole pack. That's unethical, Pussyface. He owes me noogies, too!

MURPH: Now I'll give you twenty noogies, so we'll be even.
(*He raps Joey on the arm. The Indian looks up as Joey squeals*)

JOEY: Hey. The Indian's watching.

MURPH: (*Raps Joey sharply again on the arm*) Indian's a Turkie.

JOEY: (*Grabs Murph's arm and twists it behind his back*) Gimme my pack and it's an Indian, right?

MURPH: I'll give you your head in a minute, jerkoff.

JOEY: Indian? Indian? Say, Indian!

MURPH: Turkie? Turkie?

JOEY: Turkie. Okay. Let go.
(*Murph lets him up and laughs. Joey jumps up and screams*) Indian! (*Runs a few steps*) Indian!

MURPH: (*Laughing*) If your old lady would have you on Thanksgiving you'd know what a turkey was, ya' jerk. (*Hits him on the arm again*) Here's another noogie, Turkie-head!
(*The Indian coughs*)

JOEY: Hey, look. He likes us. Shall I wink?

MURPH: You sexy beast, you'd wink at anything in pants.

JOEY: Come on. Do I look like a Murphy?

MURPH: (*Grabs Joey and twists both of his arms*) Take that back.

JOEY: Aw! ya' bastard. I take it back.

MURPH: You're a Turkie-lover, right?

JOEY: Right.

MURPH: Say it.

JOEY: I'm a Turkie-lover.

MURPH: You're a Turkie-humper, right?

JOEY: *You're* a Turkie-humper.

MURPH: Say, *I'm* a Turkie-humper.

JOEY: That's what I said. You're a Turkie-humper. (*Murph twists his arms a bit further*) Oww, ya' dirty bastard! All right, I'm a Turkie-humper! Now, leggo! (*Joey pretends to laugh*)

MURPH: You gonna hug him and kiss him and love him up like a mother?

JOEY: Whose mother?

MURPH: Your mother. She humps Turkies, right?

JOEY: Owww! All right. Yeah. She humps Turkies. Now leggo!

MURPH: (*Lets go*) You're free.

JOEY: (*Breaks. Changes the game*) Where's the bus?

MURPH: Up your mother.

JOEY: My old lady's gonna kill me. It must be late as hell.

MURPH: So why don't you move out?

JOEY: Where to?

MURPH: Maybe we'll get our own place. Yeah. How about that, Joey?

JOEY: Yeah, sure. I move out on her and she starves. You know that.

MURPH: Let her starve, the Turkie-humper.

JOEY: (*Hits Murph on the arm and laughs*) That's my mother you're desecrating, you nasty bastard.

MURPH: How do you desecrate a whore? Call her a lady?

JOEY: Why don't you ask *your* mother?

MURPH: (*Hits Joey on the arm*) Big mouth, huh?

JOEY: Hey! Why don't you pick on som'body your own size, like Turkie, there.

MURPH: Leave Turkie out of this. He's got six elephants in his pocket, probably.

JOEY: (*Laughs at the possibility*) Hey, Turkie, you got six elephants in your pocket?

MURPH: Hey, shut up, Joey. (*Glances in the Indian's direction and the Indian glances back*) Shut up.

JOEY: Ask him for a match.

MURPH: You ask him.

JOEY: You got the butts.

MURPH: Naw.

JOEY: Chicken. Want some seeds to chew on?

MURPH: I'll give you somethin' to chew on.

JOEY: Go on, ask him. I ain't never heard an Indian talk Turkie-talk.

MURPH: He's a Turkie, I told ya'. Any jerk can see that he's a definite Turk!

JOEY: You're a definite jerk, then. 'Cause I see a definite Indian!

MURPH: I'll show you.

(*Walks toward the Indian slowly, taking a full minute to cross the stage. He slithers from side to side and goes through pantomime of looking for matches*)

JOEY: Hey, Murph. You comin' for dinner? We're havin' turkey tonight! Hey! Tell your Turkie to bring his elephants.

MURPH: Schmuck! How's he going to fit six elephants in a rickshaw?

JOEY: (*Flatly*) Four in front. Three in back.
(*He reaches the Indian*)

MURPH: Excuse me. May I borrow a match?

INDIAN: (*Speaking in Hindi*) Mai toom-haree bo-lee nrh-hee bol saktah. Mai tum-hah-ree bah-sha nah-hee sah-maj-tah.
(*I cannot speak your language. I don't understand.*)

MURPH: (*To Joey, does a terrific "take," then speaks, incredulous*) He's got to be kidding.
(*Joey and Murph laugh*)

INDIAN: Moo-jhay mahaf kar-nah mai toom-hah-ree bah-art nah-hee sah-maj sak-tah.
(*I'm sorry. I don't understand you.*)

MURPH: No speak English, huh? (*The Indian looks at him blankly. Louder*) You can't speak English, huh?
(*The Indian stares at him, confused by the increase in volume*)

JOEY: (*Flatly*) Son of a bitch. Hey, Murph. Guess what? Your Turkie only speaks Indian.

MURPH: (*Moves in closer, examining the Indian*) Say something in Indian, big mouth.

JOEY: (*Holds up his hand*) How's your teepee? (*The Indian stares at him. He laughs*) See.
(*The Indian welcomes Joey's laugh and smiles. He takes their hands and "shakes" them*)

MURPH: (*Catches on as to why the Indian has joined the smile and feigns a stronger smile until they all laugh aloud. Murph cuts off the laughter as he shakes the Indian's hand and says*) You're a fairy, right?

INDIAN: (*Smiles harder than before*) Mai toom-haree bah-at nah-hee sah-maj-tah. Mai ap-nay lah-kay kah gha-r dhoo-nd rah-haw hooh. Oos-nay moo-jhay mil-nah tar pahr nah-jah-nay woh cah-hah hai. Mai oos-kah mah-kan dhoo-nd rah-hah hoon. Oos-kah pah-tah yeh rah-hah k-yah.
(*I don't understand you. I'm looking for my son's home. We were supposed to meet, but I could not find him. I'm looking for his home. This is his address. Am I headed in the correct direction?*)

(*The Indian produces a slip of paper with an address typed on it. And a photograph*)

MURPH: Gupta. In the Bronx. Big deal. (*To the Indian*) Indian, right? You an Indian, Indian? (*Shakes his head up and down, smiling. The Indian smiles, confused*) He don't know. (*Pauses, studies the picture, smiles*) This picture must be his kid. Looks like you, Joe.

JOEY: (*Looks at the picture*) Looks Irish to me. (*He hands the picture to Murph*)

BOTH: Ohhh.

MURPH: Yeah. Why'd you rape all those innocent children? (*Pause*) I think he's the wrong kind of Indian. (*To the Indian*) You work in a restaurant? (*Pauses. Speaks with a homosexual's sibilant "s"*) It's such a shame to kill these Indians. They do such superb beaded work.

(*Murph shakes his head up and down again, smiling*)

INDIAN: (*Follows Murph's cue*) Mai-nay ap-nay lar-kay koh su-bah say nah-hee day-kha. Toom-hara shah-har bah-hoot hee barah hai.

(*I haven't seen my son all day. Your city is so big and so busy.*)

JOEY: Ask him to show you his elephants.

MURPH: You ask. You're the one who speaks Turkie-Indian.

JOEY: White man fork with tongue. Right? (*The Indian stares at him blankly*) Naw, he don't understand me. You ask. You got the right kind of accent. All you foreigners understand each other good.

MURPH: You want another noogie?

JOEY: Maybe Turkie wants a noogie or six?

MURPH: (*Shaking his head*) You want a noogie, friend?

INDIAN: (*Agrees*) Moo-jhay mahaf kar-nah. Moo-jay. Yah-han aye zyah-da sah-may na-hee hoo-ah.

(*I'm sorry. I haven't been here long.*)

MURPH: Give him his noogie.

JOEY: Naw. He's your friend. You give it to him. That's what friends are for.

MURPH: (*Looks at the paper and photograph, gives them back*) Jesus, look at that for a face.

JOEY: Don't make it.

MURPH: Don't make it. Prem Gupta. In the Bronx. Jesus, this is terrific. The Indian wants the Bronx.

JOEY: (*Sits on a trash can*) He ain't gonna find no Bronx on this bus.

MURPH: Old Indian, pal. You ain't going to find the Bronx on this bus, unless they changed commissioners again. Now I've got a terrific idea for fun and profit.

(*Pauses*)

INDIAN: K-yah kah-ha toom-nay.

(*Excuse me?*)

MURPH: Right. Now why don't you come home and meet my mother? Or maybe you'd like to meet Pussyface, huh? (*To Joey*) Should we bring him over to Pussyface?

JOEY: He don't even know who Pussyface is. You can't just go getting Indians blind dates without giving him a breakdown.

MURPH: Okay, Chief. Here's the breakdown on Pussyface. She's a pig. She lives right over there. See that pretty building? (*Points over the audience to the back row of seats*) That one. The fancy one. That's Pussyface's hide-away. She's our social worker.

JOEY: That's right.

MURPH: Pussyface got assigned to us when we were tykers, right, Joe?

JOEY: Just little fellers.

MURPH: Pussyface was sent to us by the city. To watch over us. And care for us. And love us like a mother. Not because she wanted to. Because we were bad boys. We stole a car.

JOEY: We stole two cars.

MURPH: We stole two cars. And we knifed a kid.

JOEY: You knifed a kid.

MURPH: (*To Joey*) Tell it to the judge, Fella!

(*He takes a pocketknife from his pocket and shows it to the Indian, who pulls back in fear*)

JOEY: The Chief thinks you're going to cut him up into a totem pole.

MURPH: Easy, Chief. I've never cut up an Indian in my life.

JOEY: You've never *seen* an Indian in your life.

MURPH: Anyway, you got a choice. My mother—who happens to have a terrific personality. Or Pussyface, our beloved social lady.

JOEY: Where's the bus?

MURPH: It's coming.

JOEY: So's Christmas.

MURPH: Hey. Show Turkie my Christmas card for Pussyface. (*To the*

Indian) Pussyface gives us fun projects. I had to make Christmas cards last year. (*Back to Joey*) Go on. Show the Chief the card.

(*Joey fishes through his wallet, finds a dog-eared photostat, hands it to the Indian, who accepts it curiously*)

INDIAN: Yeh k-yah hai.

(*What is this?*)

MURPH: I made that with my own two cheeks. Tell him, Joe.

JOEY: Stupid, he don't speak English.

MURPH: It don't matter. He's interested, ain't he?

JOEY: You're a fink-jerk.

MURPH: Oooo. I'll give you noogies up the kazzooo. (*Takes the card away from the Indian and explains*) This is a Christmas card. I made it! I made it! Get me? Pussyface got us Christmas jobs last year. She got me one with the city. With the war on poverty. I ran the Xerox machines.

JOEY: Jesus. You really are stupid. He don't understand one word you're saying.

MURPH: (*Mimes the entire scene, slowly*) He's interested, ain't he? That's more than I can say for most of them. (*To the Indian*) Want to know how you can make your own Christmas cards with your simple Xerox 2400? It's easy. Watch. (*He mimes*) First you lock the door to the stat room, so no one can bust in. Then you turn the machine on. Then you set the dial at the number of people you want to send cards to. Thirty, forty.

JOEY: Three or four.

MURPH: Right, fella. Then you take off your pants. And your underpants that's underneath. You sit on the glass. You push the little button. The lights flash. When the picture's developed, you write "Noel" across it! (*Pauses*) That's how you make Christmas cards. (*Waits for a reaction from the Indian, then turns back to Joey, dismayed*) He's waiting for the bus.

JOEY: Me too. Jesus. Am I ever late!

MURPH: Tell her to stuff it. You're a big boy now.

JOEY: She gets frightened, that's all. She really don't care how late I come in, as long as I tell her when I'm coming. If I tell her one, and I don't get in until one-thirty, she's purple when I finally get in. (*Pauses*) She's all right. Where's the Goddamned bus, huh? (*Calls across the park*) Pussyface, did you steal the bus, you dirty old whore? Pussyface, I'm calling you! (*Pauses*) She's all right, Murph. Christ, she's my mother. I didn't ask for her. She's all right.

MURPH: Who's all right? That Turkie-humper? (*To the Indian*) His old lady humps Turkies, you know that? (*Smiles, but the Indian doesn't respond*) Hey, Turkie's blowin' his cool a little. Least you got somebody waitin'. My old lady wouldn't know if I was gone a year.

JOEY: What? That Turkie-humper?

MURPH: (*To the Indian*) Hey! (*The Indian jumps, startled. Murph laughs*) You got any little Indians runnin' around your teepee? No? Yeah? No? Aw, ya' stupid Indian. Where is the Goddamn bus?

JOEY: Let's walk it.

MURPH: Screw that. A hundred blocks? Besides, we gotta keep this old Turkie company, right? We couldn't let him stand all alone in this big ole city. Some nasty boys might come along and chew him up, right?

JOEY: We can walk it. Let the Indian starve.

MURPH: So walk it, jerk. I'm waiting with the Chief.
(*Murph stands next to the Indian*)

JOEY: Come on, we'll grab the subway.

MURPH: Joe, the trains are running crazy now. Anyway, I'm waitin' with my friend the Chief, here. You wanna go, go. (*Murmurs*) Where is it, Chief? Is that it? Here it comes, huh?

JOEY: (*Considers it*) Yeah, we gotta watch out for Turkie.
(*Joey stands on the other side of the Indian, who finally walks slowly back to the bus stop area*)

MURPH: See that, Turkie, little Joe's gonna keep us company. That's nice, huh? (*The Indian looks for the bus*) You know, Joey, this Turk's a pain in my ass. He don't look at me when I talk to him.

JOEY: He oughta look at you when you talk. He oughta be polite.
(*They pass the card in a game. The Indian smiles*)

MURPH: I don't think he learned many smarts in Indiana. Any slob knows enough to look when they're being talked to. Huh?

JOEY: This ain't just any slob. This is a definite Turkie-Indian slob.
(*They pass the card behind their backs*)

MURPH: He's one of them commie slobs, probably. Warmongering bastard. (*Flatly*) Pinko here rapes all the little kids.

JOEY: Terrible thing. Too bad we can't give him some smarts. Maybe he could use a couple.
(*The game ends. Joey has the card as in a magic act*)

MURPH: We'll give him plenty of smarts. (*Calling him upstage*) Want some smarts? Chief?

INDIAN: Bna-ee mai toom-maree bah-at nah-Hee sah-maj-sak-tah. Bus yah-han kis sa-may a-tee haj. K-yah mai sa-hee BUS STOP par shoon!

(*I can't understand you. Please? When is the bus due here? Am I at the right station?*)

JOEY: Hey, look. He's talking out of the side of his mouth. Sure, that's right . . . Hey, Murph. Ain't Indian broads s'posed to have sideways breezers? Sure.

MURPH: (*Grins*) You mean chinks, Joey.

JOEY: Naw. Indian broads too. All them foreign broads. Their breezers are sideways. That's why them foreign cars have the back seat fac- the side, right?

MURPH: Is that right, Turkie? Your broads have horizontal snatches?

INDIAN: (*Stares at him nervously*) Mai toom-haree bah-at nah-hee sah-maj sak-tah.

(*I can't understand you.*)

MURPH: (*Repeating him in the same language*) Toom-haree bah-at nah-hee sah-maj sak-tah.

INDIAN: (*Recognizing the language finally. He speaks with incredible speed*) Toom-haree bah-sha nah-hee sah-maj-tah. Moo-jhay mah-Af kar-nah par ah-bhee moo-jhay tomm-ha-ray desh aye kuh-Chah hee din toh Hu-yay hain. Moo-jhay toom-ha-ree bah-sha see-kh-nay kah ah-bhee sah-mai hee nah-hee milah. Mai ahp-nay lar-kay say bih-chur gah-ya hoon. Oos-say toh toom-ha-ray desh may rah-tay chai sah-al hoh Gah-ye hain. Jah-b doh mah-hee-nay pah-lay oos-kee mah kah inth-kahl moo-ah toh oos-nay moo-jhay ya-han booh-lah bheh-jha or mai ah gah-hay. Woh bah-ra hon-har lar-ka hai. Moo-jhay mah-af kar-nah kee majh-nay ah-bhee toom-ha-ree bah-sha na-hee see-kiee par mai see-kh loon-gha.

(*Yes, that's correct. I can't understand your language. I'm sorry, but I've only been in your country for a few days. I haven't had time to understand your language. Please forgive me. I'm separated from my son. He's been living in your country for six years. When his mother died two months ago, he sent for me. I came immediately. He's a good son to his father. I'm sorry I haven't learned your language yet, but I shall learn.*)

MURPH: (*Does a take. Flatly*) This Turkie's a real pain in the ass.

JOEY: Naw. I think he's pretty interesting. I never saw an Indian before.

MURPH: Oh. It's fascinating. It's marvelous. This city's a regular melting pot. Turkies. Kikes like you. (*Pause*) I even had me a real French lady once. (*Looks at the ground. Pauses*) I thought I saw a dime here. (*Ponders*) I knew it.

(*He picks up a dime and pockets it proudly*)

JOEY: A French lady, huh?

MURPH: Yep. A real French broad.

JOEY: (*Holds a beat*) You been at your mother again?

MURPH: (*Hits him on the arm*) Wise-ass. Just what nobody likes. A wise-ass.

JOEY: Where'd you have this French lady, huh?

MURPH: I found her in the park over there. (*Points*) Just sitting on a bench. She was great. (*Boasts*) A real *talent.*

JOEY: Yeah, sure thing. (*Calls into the park*) Hello, talent. Hello, talent! (*Pauses*) I had a French girl, too. (*Turns to avoid Murph's eyes, caught in a lie*) Where the hell's that bus?

MURPH: (*Simply*) Sure you did. Like the time you had a mermaid?

JOEY: You better believe I did. She wasn't really French. She just lived there a long time. I went to first grade with her. Geraldine. She was my first girl friend. (*Talks very quickly*) Her old man was in the Army or something, 'cause they moved to France. She came back when we were in high school.

MURPH: Then what happened?

JOEY: Nothin'. She just came back, that's all.

MURPH: I thought you said you *had* her . . .

JOEY: No, she was just my girl friend.

MURPH: In high school?

JOEY: No, ya stoop. In the first grade. I just told you.

MURPH: You had her in the first grade?

JOEY: Jesus, you're stupid. She was my girl friend. That's all.

MURPH: (*Feigns excitement*) Hey . . . that's a *sweet little story.* (*Flatly*) What the hell's wrong with you?

JOEY: What do ya' mean?

MURPH: First you say you had a French girl, then you say you had a girl friend in first grade, who went to France. What the hell kind of story's that?

JOEY: It's a true one, that's all. Yours is full of crap.

MURPH: What's full of crap?

JOEY: About the French lady in the park. You never had any French lady, unless you been at your own old lady again. Or maybe you've been at Pussyface?

MURPH: Jesus, you're lookin' for it, aren't you?
(They pretend to fistfight)

JOEY: I mean, if you gotta tell lies to your best buddy, you're in bad shape, that's all.

MURPH: *(Gives Joey a "high-sign")* Best buddy? You?
(The sign to the Indian. He returns the obscene gesture, thinking it a berserk American sign of welcome)

JOEY: Is that how it is in Ceylon, sir?

MURPH: Say-lon? What the hell is say-long?

JOEY: See, ya jerk, Ceylon's part of India. That's where they grow tea.

MURPH: No kiddin'? Boy it's terrific what you can learn just standin' here with a schmuck like you. Tea, huh? *(To the Indian he screams)* Hey! *(The Indian turns around, startled)* How's your teabags? *(No response)* No? *(To Joey)* Guess you're wrong again. He don't know teabags.

JOEY: Look at the bags under his eyes. That ain't chopped liver.
(This is the transition scene: Murph screams "Hey!"*—the Indian smiles. They dance a war dance around him, beating a rhythm on the trashcans, hissing and cat-calling for a full minute. Murph ends the dance with a final "Hey!" The Indian jumps in fear. Now that they sense his fear, the comedy has ended)*

MURPH: Turkie looks like he's getting bored.

JOEY: Poor old Indian. Maybe he wants to play a game.

MURPH: You know any poor old Indian games?

JOEY: We could burn him at the stake. *(He laughs)* That ain't such a terrible idea, you know. Maybe make an Indian stew.

MURPH: Naw, we couldn't burn a nice fellow like Turkie. That's nasty.

JOEY: We got to play a game. Pussyface always tells us to play games. *(To the apartment, the back of the audience)* Ain't that right, Pussyface? You always want us to play games.

MURPH: I know a game . . .

JOEY: Yeah?

MURPH: Yeah. *(Screams at the Indian)* "Indian, Indian, Where's the Indian?"

JOEY: That's a sweet game. I haven't played that for years.

MURPH: Wise-ass. You want to play a game, don't you?

JOEY: Indian-Indian. Where's the Indian?

MURPH: Sure. It's just like ring-a-leave-eo. Only with a spin.

JOEY: That sounds terrific.

MURPH: Look. I spin the hell out of you until you're dizzy. Then you run across the street and get Pussyface. I'll grab the Indian and hide him. Then Pussyface and you come over here and try to find us.

JOEY: We're going to spin, huh?

MURPH: Sure.

JOEY: Who's going to clean up after you? Remember the ferris wheel, big shot? All those happy faces staring up at you?

MURPH: I ain't the spinner. You're the spinner. I'll hide the Chief. Go on. Spin.

JOEY: How about if we set the rules as we go along? (*To the Indian*) How does that grab you, Chief?

INDIAN: Moo-jhay mah-af kar-nah. Mai toom-nakee bah-sha na-hee sah-maj sak-ta.
(*I'm sorry, but I can't understand your language.*)

MURPH: He's talking Indiana again. He don't understand. Go on. Spin. I'll grab the Chief while you're spinning . . . count to ten . . . hide the Chief, while you're after Pussyface. Go on. Spin.

JOEY: I ain't going to spin. I get sick.

MURPH: Ain't you going to play?

JOEY: I'll play. But I can't spin any better than you can. I get sick. You know that. How about if you spin and I hide the Chief? You can get Pussyface. She likes you better than me, anyhow.

MURPH: Pussyface ain't home. You know that. She's in New Jersey.

JOEY: Then what the hell's the point of this game, anyway?

MURPH: It's just a game. We can pretend.

JOEY: You can play marbles for all I care. I just ain't going to spin, that's all. And neither are you. So let's forget the whole game.

MURPH: (*Fiercely*) Spin! Spin!

JOEY: You spin.

MURPH: Hey. I told you to spin.
(*Murph squares off against Joey and slaps him menacingly. Joey looks Murph straight in the eye for a moment*)

JOEY: Okay. Big deal. So I'll spin. Then I get Pussyface, right? You ready to get the Chief?

MURPH: Will you stop talking and start spinning?

JOEY: All right. All right. Here I go. (*Joey spins himself meekly, as Murph goes toward the Indian and the trash can. Joey giggles as he spins ever so slowly. Murph glances at Joey as Joey pretends. Murph is confused*) There. I spun. Is that okay?

MURPH: That's a spin?

JOEY: Well, it wasn't a fox trot.

MURPH: I told you to spin! Any slob knows that ain't no spin! Now spin. God damn it! Spin!

JOEY: This is stupid. You want to play games. You want a decent spin. You spin.

(*He walks straight to Murph—a challenge. Joey slaps Murph. He winces*)

MURPH: (*Squares off viciously. Raises his arms. Looks at Joey cruelly. Orders*) Spin me.

(*Joey brings Murph's arms behind Murph's back and holds Murph's wrists firmly so that he is helpless. Joey spins him. Slowly at first. Then faster. Faster. Joey's hostility is released; he laughs*)

JOEY: You wanted to spin. Spin. Spin.

(*Joey spins Murph frantically. The Indian watches in total horror, not knowing what to do; he cuddles next to the bus stop sign, his island of safety*)

MURPH: (*Screaming*) Enough, you little bastard.

JOEY: (*Continues to spin him*) Now *you* get Pussyface. Go on. (*Spins Murph all the faster as in a grotesque dance gone berserk*) I'll hide the Chief. This is your game! This is your game. *You* get Pussyface. I'll hide the Chief. Go on, Murphy. You want some more spin? (*Joey has stopped the spinning now, as Murph is obviously ill*) You want to spin some more?

MURPH: Stop it, Joey. I'm sick.

JOEY: (*Spins Murph once more around*) You want to spin some more, or are you going to get Pussyface and come find the Chief and me?

MURPH: You little bastard.

JOEY: (*Spins Murph once again, still holding Murph helpless with his arms behind his back*) I'll hide the Chief. *You* get Pussyface and find us. Okay? Okay? Okay?

MURPH: Okay . . . you bastard . . . okay.

JOEY: Here's one more for good luck.

(*Joey spins Murph three more times, fiercely, then shoves him offstage. Murph can be heard retching, about to vomit, during the final spins. Joey then grabs the Indian, who pulls back in terror*)

INDIAN: Na-hee bha-yee toom ah-b k-yah kah-rogay?
(*No, please, what are you going to do?*)

JOEY: Easy, Chief. It's just a game. Murph spun out on us. It's just a game. I've got to hide you now.
(*Murph's final puking sounds can be heard well in the distance*)

INDIAN: Na-hee na-hee bha-yee. Mai mah-afee mah-ng-ta. Hoon.
(*No. No. Please. I beg you.*)

JOEY: Easy, Chief. Look. I promise you, this ain't for real. This is only a game. A game. Get it? It's all a game! Now I got to count to ten. (*Grabs the Indian and forces him down behind a city litter basket. He covers the Indian's scream with his hand, as he slaps the Indian — a horrifying sound*) One. Two. Three. Murphy? (*He laughs*) Four. Five. Murph? Come get us. Six. Seven. Pussyface is waiting. Eight. Nine. (*Pauses*) Murphy? Murph? Hey, buddy. (*Stands up. Speaks*) Ten. (*Lights are narrowing on Joey and the Indian. The Indian tries to escape. Joey subdues him easily. Joey turns slowly back to the Indian, who responds with open fear*) Get up. Up. (*No response*) Get up, Turkie. (*Moves to the Indian, who recoils sharply. Joey persists and pulls the Indian to his feet. The Indian shudders, stands and faces his captor. The Indian shakes from fear and from a chill. There is a moment's silence as Joey watches. He removes his own sweater and offers it to the Indian*) Here. Here. Put it on. It's okay. (*The Indian is bewildered, but Joey forces the sweater into his hands*) Put it on. (*The Indian stares at the sweater. Joey takes it from his hands and begins to cover the Indian, who is amazed*) I hope I didn't hurt you too much. You okay? (*No response*) You ain't sick too bad, huh? (*Pause*) Huh? (*Checks the Indian for cuts*) You look okay. You're okay, huh? (*No response*) I didn't mean to rough you up like that, but . . . you know. Huh? (*The Indian raises his eyes to meet Joey's. Joey looks down to avoid the stare*) I hope you ain't mad at me or nothin'. (*Pause*) Boy it's gettin' chilly. I mean, it's cold, right? Sure is quiet all of a sudden. Kind of spooky, huh? (*Calls*) Hey, Murphy! (*Laughs aloud*) Murph ain't a bad guy. He's my best buddy, see? I mean, he gets kinda crazy sometimes, but that's all. Everybody gets kind of crazy sometime, right? (*No response*) Jesus, you're a stupid Indian. Can't you speak any English? No? Why the hell did you come here, anyway? Especially if you can't talk any English. You ought to say something. Can't you even say "Thank you"?
(*The Indian recognizes those words, finally, and mimics them slowly and painfully*)

INDIAN: (*In English, very British and clipped*) Thank you.

JOEY: I'll be Goddamned! You're welcome. (*Slowly, indicating for the Indian to follow*) You're welcome.
(*He waits*)

INDIAN: (*In English*) You are welcome.

JOEY: That's terrific. You are welcome. (*Smiles, as though all is forgiven. In relief*) How are you?

INDIAN: You are welcome.

JOEY: No. How are ya?
(*Joey is excited. The Indian might be a second friend*)

INDIAN: (*In English—very "Joey"*) How are ya?

JOEY: (*Joyously*) Jesus. You'll be talking like us in no time! You're okay, huh? You ain't bleeding or anything. I didn't wanna hurt you none. But Murph gets all worked up. You know what I mean. He gets all excited. This ain't the first time, you know. No, sir!

INDIAN: (*In English*) No, sir.

JOEY: That's right. He's especially crazy around broads.

INDIAN: (*In English*) Broads.

JOEY: (*Forgetting that the Indian is only mimicking*) That's right. Broads. (*Pauses and remembers, deeply*) What am I yakking for? Tell me about India, huh? I'd like to go to India sometime. Maybe I will. You think I'd like India? India? (*No response. The Indian recognizes the word, but doesn't understand the question*) That's where you're from, ain't it? Jesus, what a stupid Indian. India! (*Spells the word*) I-N-D-I-A. Nothin'. Schmuck. *India!*

INDIAN: (*A stab in the dark*) Hindi?

JOEY: Yeah! Tell me about India! (*Long pause as they stand staring at each other*) No? You're not talking, huh? Well, what do you want to do? Murph oughta be back soon. (*Discovers a coin in his pocket*) You wanna flip for quarters? Flip? No? Look, a Kennedy half! (*Goes through three magic tricks with the coin:* (1) *He palms the coin, offers the obvious choice of hand, then uncovers the coin in his other hand. The Indian raises his hand to his turban in astonishment*) Like that, huh? ((2) *Coin is slapped on his breast*) This hand right? Is it this hand, this hand? No, it's *this* hand! Back to your dumb act? Here. Here's the one you liked! (*Does* (1). *This time the Indian points to the correct hand instantly*) You're probably some kind of hustler. Okay. Double or nothing. (*Flips*) Heads, you live. Tails, you die. Okay? (*Uncovers the coin*) I'll be a son of a bitch. You got Indian luck. Here.
(*He hands the coin to the Indian*)

INDIAN: (*Stares in question*) Na-hff? (*No?*)

JOEY: (*Considers cheating*) Take it. You won. No, go ahead. Keep it. I ain't no Indian giver. (*Pause. He laughs at his own joke. No response*) You ain't got no sense of humor, that's what. (*Stares upstage*) Murph's my best buddy, you know? Me and him were buddies when we were kids. Me and Murph, all the time. And Maggie. His kid sister. (*Pause*) I had Maggie once. Sort of. Well, kind of. Yeah, I had her. That's right. Murph don't know. Makes no difference now. She's dead, Maggie. (*Sings*) "The worms crawl in, the worms crawl out." (*Speaks*) What the hell difference does it make? *Right?*

INDIAN: (*In English*) No, sir.

JOEY: (*Without noticing*) That's why Murph is crazy. That's why he gets crazy, I mean. She died seventeen, that's all. Seventeen. Just like *that*. Appendix. No one around. There was no one around. His old lady? Forget it! The old man took off years ago. All there was really was just Murph and Maggie. That's why he could take it. At home. You think my old lady's bad? She's nothing. His old lady's a pro. You know? She don't even make a living at it, either. That's the bitch of it. Not even a living. She's a dog. I mean, *I* wouldn't even pay her a nickel. Not a nickel. Not that I'd screw around with Murphy's old lady. Oh! Not that she doesn't try. She tries. Plenty. (*His fantasy begins*) That's why I don't come around to his house much. She tries it all the time. She wouldn't charge me anything, probably. But it ain't right screwing your best buddy's old lady, right? I'd feel terrible if I did. She ain't that bad, but it just ain't right. I'd bet she'd even take Murph on. She probably tries it with him, too. That's the bitch of it. She can't even make a living. His own Goddamned mother. The other one—Pussyface. You think Pussyface is a help? That's the biggest joke yet. (*The Indian is by now thoroughly confused on all counts. He recognizes the name "Pussyface," and reacts slightly. Seeing Joey's anxiety, he cuddles him. For a brief moment they embrace—an insane father-and-son tableau. Note: Be careful here*) Pussyface. There's a brain. You see what she gave us for Christmas? (*Fishes his knife out of his pocket*) Knives. Brilliant, huh? Murph's up on a rap for slicing a kid, and she gives us knives for Christmas. To whittle with. She's crazier than Murphy. Hah. (*Flashes his open knife at the Indian, who misinterprets the move as spelling disaster. The Indian waits, carefully scrutinizing Joey, until Joey begins to look away. Joey now wanders to the spot where he pushed Murph offstage*) Hey, Murph! (*The Indian moves slowly to the other side of the stage. Joey sees his move at once and races after him, thinking the Indian was running away*) Hey. Where are you going? (*The Indian knows he'll be hit. He tries to explain with mute ges-*

tures and attitude. It's futile. He knows at once and hits Joey as best he can and races across the stage. Joey recovers from the blow and starts after him, as the Indian murmurs one continuous frightening scream. Joey dives after the Indian and tackles him on the other side of the stage. The Indian fights more strongly than ever, but Joey's trance carries him ferociously into this fight. He batters the Indian with punches to the body. The Indian squeals as Joey sobs) You were gonna run off. Right? Son of a bitch. You were gonna tell Murphy.

(*The Indian makes one last effort to escape and runs the length of the stage, screaming a bloodcurdling, anguished scream. Murph enters, stops, stares incredulously as the Indian runs into his open arms. Joey races to the Indian and strikes a karate chop to the back of his neck. Joey is audibly sobbing. The Indian drops to the stage as a bull in the ring, feeling the final thrust of the sword . . . Joey stands frozen above him. Murph stares, first at Joey and then at the Indian*)

MURPH: Pussyface isn't home yet. She's still in New Jersey. Ring-a-leave-eo.

JOEY: (*Sobbing, senses his error*) Indians are dumb.

MURPH: (*Stares again at Joey. Then to the Indian. Spots Joey's sweater on the Indian. Fondles it, then stares at Joey viciously*) Pussyface isn't home. I rang her bell. She don't answer. I guess she's still on vacation. She ruined our game.

JOEY: (*Sobbing*) Oh, jumping Jesus Christ. Jesus. Jesus. Jesus. Indians are dumb.

MURPH: Pussyface ruins everything. She don't really care about our games. She ruins our games. Just like Indians. They don't know how to play our games either.

JOEY: Indians are dumb. Dumb.

(*He sobs. Murph slaps Joey across the face. He straightens up and comes back to reality*)

MURPH: What the hell's going on?

JOEY: He tried to run. I hit him.

MURPH: Yeah. I saw that. You hit him, all right. (*Stares at the Indian*) Is he alive?

(*The Indian groans, pulls himself to his knees*)

JOEY: He was fighting. I hit him.

MURPH: Okay, you hit him.

(*The Indian groans again. Then he speaks in a plea*)

INDIAN: (*Praying*) Moo-jhay or nah sah-tao. Maih-nay toom-hara k-yah bigarah hai. Moo-jhay or nah sah-tao. Moo-jhay in-seh.

(*Please. Don't hurt me anymore. What have I done? Please don't hurt me. Don't let them hurt me.*)

MURPH: He's begging for something. Maybe he's begging for his life. Maybe he is. Sure, maybe he is.

JOEY: (*Embarrassed, starts to help the Indian to his feet*) C'mon there, Chief. Get up and face the world. C'mon, Chief. Everything's going to be all right.

MURPH: What's got into you, anyway?

JOEY: C'mon, Chief. Up at the world. Everything's okay.

(*The Indian ad libs words of pleading and pain*)

MURPH: Leave him be. (*But Joey continues to help the Indian*) Leave him be. What's with you? Hey, Joey! I said leave him be!

(*Murph pushes Joey and the Indian pulls back with fear*)

JOEY: Okay, Murph. Enough's enough.

MURPH: Just tell me what the hell's wrong with you?

JOEY: He tried to run away, that's all. Change the subject. Change the subject. It ain't important. I hit him, that's all.

MURPH: Okay, so you hit him.

JOEY: Okay! Where were you? Sick. Were you a little bit sick? I mean, you couldn't have been visiting, 'cause there ain't no one to visit, right?

MURPH: What *do* you mean?

JOEY: Where the hell were you? (*Looks at Murph and giggles*) You're a little green there, Irish.

MURPH: You're pretty funny. What the hell's so funny?

JOEY: Nothing's funny. The Chief and I were just having a little pow-wow, and we got to wondering where you ran off to. Just natural for us to wonder, ain't it? (*To the Indian*) Right, Chief.

MURPH: Hey, look at that. Turkie's got a woolly sweater just like yours. Ain't that a terrific coincidence. You two been playing strip poker?

JOEY: Oh, sure. Strip poker. The Chief won my sweater and I won three of his feathers and a broken arrow. (*To the Indian, he feigns a deep authoritative voice*) You wonder who I am, don't you? Perhaps this silver bullet will help to identify me? (*Extends his hand. The Indian peers into Joey's empty palm quizzically. As he does, Murph quickly taps the underside of Joey's hand, forcing the hand to rise and slap the Indian's chin sharply. The Indian pulls back at the slap. Joey turns on Murph, quickly*) What the hell did you do that for, ya' jerk. The Chief didn't do nothing.

MURPH: Jesus, you and your Chief are pretty buddy-buddy, ain't you?

(*Mimics Joey*) "The Chief didn't do nothing." Jesus. You give him your sweater. Maybe you'd like to have him up for a beer . . .

JOEY: Drop it, Murph. You're giving me a pain in the ass.

MURPH: (*Retorts fiercely*) You little pisser. Who the hell do you think you're talking to?

(*The telephone rings in the booth. They are all startled, especially the Indian, who senses hope*)

JOEY: (*After a long wait, speaking the obvious flatly*) It's the phone.

MURPH: (*To the Indian*) The kid's a whiz. He guessed that right away.

(*The phone rings a second time*)

JOEY: Should we answer it?

MURPH: What for? Who'd be calling here? It's a wrong number.

(*The phone rings menacingly a third time. Suddenly the Indian darts into the phone booth and grabs the receiver. Joey and Murph are too startled to stop him until he has blurted out his hopeless plea, in his own language*)

INDIAN: Prem k-yah woh may-rah ar-kah hai. Prem (Pray-em) bay-tah moo-jhay bachah-low. Mai fah ns ga-yah hoon yeh doh goon-day moo-jhay mar ra-hay hain. Mai ba-hoot ghah-bara gaya hoon. Pray-em.

(*Prem? Is this my son? Prem? Please help me. I'm frightened. Please help me. Two boys are hurting me . . . I'm frightened. Please. Prem?*)

(*The Indian stops talking sharply and listens. He crumbles as the voice drones the wrong reply. He drops the receiver and stares with horror at the boys. Murph realizes the Indian's horror and begins to laugh hysterically. Joey stares silently. The Indian begins to mumble and weep. He walks from the phone booth. The voice is heard as a drone from the receiver. The action freezes*)

MURPH: (*Laughing*) What's the matter, Turkie? Don't you have a dime? Give Turkie a dime, Joe. Give him a dime.

JOEY: Jesus Christ. I'd hate to be an Indian.

MURPH: Hey, the paper! C'mon, Joey, get the paper from him. We'll call the Bronx.

JOEY: Cut it out, Murph. Enough's enough.

MURPH: Get the frigging piece of paper. What's the matter with you, anyway?

JOEY: I just don't think it's such a terrific idea, that's all.

MURPH: You're chicken. That's what you are.

JOEY: Suppose his son has called the police. What do you think? You think he hasn't called the police? He knows the old man don't speak any English. He called the police. Right? And they'll trace our call.

MURPH: You're nuts. They can't trace any phone calls. Anyway, we'll be gone from here. You're nuts.

JOEY: I don't want to do it.

MURPH: For Christ's sake. They can't trace nothing to nobody. Who's going to trace? Get the paper.

JOEY: Get it yourself. Go on. Get it yourself. I ain't going to get it.

MURPH: C'mon, Joey. It's not real. This is just a game. It ain't going to hurt anybody. You know that. It's just a game.

JOEY: Why don't we call somebody else? We'll call somebody else and have the Indian talk. That makes sense. Imagine if an Indian called you up and talked to you in Indian. I bet the Chief would go for that all right. Jesus, Murphy.

MURPH: Get the paper and picture.

INDIAN: Ah-b toom k-yah kah-rogay. Moo-jhay mah-af kar-doh bha-yee maih-nay soh-cha tah key woh may-rah bay-tah pray-em hai. Moo-jhay telephone kar raha. Mai-nay soh-chah thah sha-yahd woh. Pray-em hoh.

(*What are you going to do now? I'm sorry. I thought that was my son, Prem. I thought that it might be Prem calling me on the telephone. Prem. That's who I thought it was. Prem.*)

MURPH: Prem. That's the name. (*Plays the rhyme*)

INDIAN: Pray-aim.

(*Prem?*)

MURPH: Yes, Prem. I want to call Prem. Give me the paper with his name.

INDIAN: Toom pray-aim kay ba-ray may k-yah hah ra-hay. Ho toom-nay pray-aim koh kyah key-yah. Toom oos-kay bah-ray may k-yah jan-tay ho k-yah toom jan-tay ho woh kah-han hai.

(*What are you saying about Prem? Prem is my son. What have you done to Prem? What do you know about him? Do you know where he is?*)

MURPH: Shut up already and give me the paper.

JOEY: Jesus, Murph.

MURPH: (*Turning the Indian around so that they face each other*) This is ridiculous. (*Searches the Indian, who resists a bit at first, and then not at all. Finally, Murph finds the slip of paper*) I got it.

I got it. Terrific. "Prem Gupta." In the Bronx. In the frigging Bronx. This is terrific. (*Pushes the Indian to Joey*) Here. Hold him.

INDIAN: Toom k-yah kar ra-hay ho k-yah toom pray-aim k-oh boo-lah ra-hay ho.

(*What are you doing? Are you going to call my son?*)

MURPH: Shut him up. (*Fishes for a dime*) Give me a dime, God damn it. This is terrific.

JOEY: (*Finds the coins in his pocket*) Here's two nickels. (*Hands them over*) I think this is a rotten idea, that's what I think. (*Pauses*) And don't forget to pay me back those two nickels either.

MURPH: Just shut up. (*Dials the information operator*) Hello. Yeah, I want some information . . . I want a number up in the Bronx . . . Gupta . . . G-U-P-T-A . . . an Indian kid . . . His first name's Prem . . . P-R-E-M . . . No . . . I can't read the street right . . . Wait a minute. (*Reads the paper to himself*) For Christ's sake. How many Indians are up in the Bronx? There must be only one Indian named Gupta.

JOEY: What's she saying?

MURPH: There are two Indians named Gupta. (*To the operator*) Is the two of them named Prem? (*Pauses*) Well, that's what I told you . . . Jesus . . . wait a minute . . . okay . . . Okay. Say that again . . . Okay . . . Okay . . . Right. Okay . . . thanks. (*Hurries quickly to return the coins to the slot. Gupta mumbles. To Joey*) Don't talk to me. (*Dials*) Six . . . seven-four. Oh. One. Seven, seven. (*Pauses*) It's ringing. It's ringing. (*Pauses*) Hello. (*Covers the phone with his hand*) I got him! Hello? Is this Prem Gupta? Oh swell. How are you? (*To Joey*) I got the kid!

(*The Indian breaks from Joey's arm and runs to the telephone . . . Murph sticks out his leg and holds the Indian off. The Indian fights, but seems weaker than ever*)

INDIAN: (*Screams*) Cree-payah moo-jhay ad-nay lar-kay say bah-at kar-nay doh.

(*Please let me talk to my son.*)

(*Murph slams the Indian aside violently. Joey stands frozen, watching. The Indian wails and finally talks calmly, as in a trance*) Cree-payah moo-jhay ahd-nay lar-kay say bah-at kar-nay doh. Mai toom-haray hah-th jor-tah hoom mai toom-hay joh mango-gay doon-gar bus moo-jhay oos-say bah-at kar-nay doh. (*Please let me talk to my son. Oh, Prem. Please, I beg of you. Please. I'll give you anything at all. Just tell me what you want of me. Just let me talk with my son. Won't you, please?*)

(*Murph glares at the Indian, who no longer tries to interfere, as it becomes obvious that he must listen to even the language he cannot understand*)

MURPH: Just listen to me, will you, Gupta? I don't know where the hell your old man is, that's why I'm calling. We found an old elephant down here in Miami and we thought it must be yours. You can't tell for sure whose elephant is whose. You know what I mean? (*Murph is laughing now*) What was that? Say that again. I can't hear you too well. All the distance between us, you know what I mean? It's a long way down here, you follow me? No. I ain't got no Indian. I just got an elephant. And he's eating all my peanuts. Gupta, you're talking too fast. Slow down.

INDIAN: Pray-aim bhai-yah moo-jhay ah-kay lay ja-oh moo-jhay apnay lar-kay say bah-at kar-nay doh moo-jhay oos-say bah-at k-yohn nah-hee kar-nay day-tay.

(*Prem! Prem! Please come and get me. Please let me talk to my son, mister. Why don't you let me talk to my son?*)

(*Joey leaps on the Indian; tackles him, lies on top of him in front of the telephone booth*)

MURPH: That was the waiter. I'm in an Indian restaurant. (*Pauses*) Whoa. Slow down, man. That was nobody. That was just a myth. Your imagination. (*Pauses. Screams into the receiver*) Shut up, damn you! And listen. Okay? Okay. Are you listening? (*Murph tastes the moment. He silently clicks the receiver back to the hook. To Joey*) He was very upset. (*To the Indian*) He was very upset. (*Pauses*) Well, what the hell's the matter with you? I only told him we found an elephant, that's all. I thought maybe he lost his elephant.

(*The Indian whimpers*)

INDIAN: Toom-nay ai-saw k-yohn ki-yah toom-nay may-ray lar-kay koh k-yah ka-hah hai.

(*Why have you done this? What have you said to my son?*)

MURPH: You don't have to thank me, Turkie. I only told him your elephant was okay. He was probably worried sick about your elephant. (*Murph laughs*) This is terrific, Joey. Terrific. You should have heard the guy jabber. He was so excited he started talking in Indian just like the Chief. He said that Turkie here and him got separated today. Turkie's only been in the city one day. You're pretty stupid, Turkie. One day in the city . . . and look at the mess you've made. You're pretty stupid. He's stupid, right?

JOEY: Yeah. He's stupid.

MURPH: Hold him. We'll try again. Sure.

(*The Indian jumps on Murph. He tries to strangle Murph*)

MURPH: (*Screaming*) Get him off of me! (*Joey pulls the Indian down to the ground as Murph pounds the booth four times, screaming hideous sounds of aggression. With this tension released he begins to call, fierce but controlled, too controlled. Murph takes the dime from his pocket, shows it to Joey, and recalls the number. Talking into receiver. He dials number again and waits for reply*) Hello? Is this Gupta again? Oh, hello there . . . I'm calling back to complain about your elephant . . . hey, slow down, will you? Let me do the talking. Okay? Your elephant is a terrific pain in the balls to me, get it? Huh? Do you follow me so far? (*Pauses*) I don't know what you're saying, man . . . how about if I do the talking, all right? . . . Your elephant scares hell out of me and my pal here. We don't like to see elephants on the street. Spiders and snakes are okay, but elephants scare us. Elephants . . . yea, that's right. Don't you get it, pal? . . . Look, we always see spiders and snakes. But we never expect to see an elephant . . . What do you mean "I'm crazy"? I don't know nothing about your old man . . . I'm talking about your elephant. Your elephant offends the hell out of me. So why don't you be a nice Indian kid and come pick him up . . . that's right . . . wait a minute . . . I'll have to check the street sign. (*Covers the receiver*) This is terrific. (*Talks again into the telephone*) Jesus, I'm sorry about that. There don't seem to be no street sign . . . that's a bitch. I guess you lose your elephant . . . well, what do you expect me to do, bring your elephant all the way up to the Bronx? Come off it, pal. You wouldn't ever bring my elephant home. I ain't no kid, you know! I've lost a couple of elephants in my day. (*Listens*) Jesus, you're boring me now . . . I don't know what the hell you're talking about. Maybe you want to talk to your elephant . . . huh? (*Turns to the Indian*) Here, come talk to your "papoose."

(*He offers the telephone. The Indian stares in disbelief, then grabs the telephone from Murph's hands and begins to chatter wildly*)

INDIAN: Pray-aim, bhai-yah Pray-aim moo-jhay ah-kay lay jah-oh k-Yah? moo-jhay nah-hee pa-tah mai kah-han hoo-n moo-jhay ah-hp-nay gha-ar lay chah-low ya-hahn do-ah bad-mash lar-Kay. Jo bah-hoot kha-tar-nahk hai-don-say mai nah-hee bah-cha sak-tah ah-pa-nay koh toom aik-dam moo-jhay ah-kay.

(*Prem? Oh, Prem. Please come and take me away . . . what? I don't know where I am . . . Please come and take me to your house . . . please? There are two bad people. Two young men. They are dangerous. I cannot protect myself from them. Please . . . You must come and get me.*)

(*Murph takes his knife from his pocket, cuts the line. The Indian almost falls flat on his face as the line from the receiver to the phone box is cut, since he has been leaning away from Murph and Joey during his plea*)

MURPH: You've had enough, Chief.

(*Murph laughs aloud*)

INDIAN: (*Not at once realizing the line must be disconnected, continues to talk into the telephone in Hindi*) Pray-aim, Pray-aim, ya-hahn aa-oh sah-rak kah nah-am hai—yeh toom-nay k-yah key-yah.

(*Prem. Prem. Please come here. The street sign reads . . .*)
(*He now realizes he has been cut off and stares dumbly at the severed cord as Murph waves the severed cord in his face*)

INDIAN: Toom-nay yeh k-yoh key-yah?
(*What have you done?*)

MURPH: There it is, Turkie. Who you talkin' to?

INDIAN: (*To Joey, screaming a father's fury and disgust*) Toom-nay yeh k-yohn key-yah cri-payah may-ree mah-dah-d kah-roho.
(*Why have you done this? Please. Please help me.*)
(*Joey has been standing throughout the entire scene, frozen in terror and disgust. He walks slowly toward Murph, who kicks the Indian. Joey bolts from the stage, muttering one continuous droning sob*)

MURPH: (*Screaming*) Go ahead, Joey. Love him. Love him like a mother. Hey? Joey? What the hell's the matter? C'mon, buddy? (*Turns to the Indian, takes his knife and cuts the Indian's hand, so blood is on the knife*) Sorry, Chief. This is for my buddy, Joey. And for Pussyface. (*Calls offstage*) Joey! Buddy! What the hell's the matter? (*Races from the stage after Joey*) Joey! Wait up. Joey! I killed the Indian!
(*He exits. The Indian stares dumbly at his hand, dripping blood. He then looks to the receiver and talks into it*)

INDIAN: Pray-aim, Pray-aim, mai ah-pa-nay lar-kay key ah-wah-az k-yon nah-hee soon sak-tah Pray-aim! Toom-nay may-ray sah-ahth aih-saw k-yohn key-yaw bay-tah Pray-aim, k-yah toom ho?
(*Prem. Prem.*)
(*He walks center stage, well away from the telephone booth*)
(*Why can I not hear my son Prem? Why have you done this to me?*)
(*Suddenly the telephone rings again. Once. Twice. The Indian is startled. He talks into the receiver, while he holds the dead line in his bleeding hand*)
(*Prem? Is that you? Prem?*)
(*The telephone rings a third time*) Pray-aim, Pray-aim, bay-tah k-yah toom ho—
(*Prem. Prem? Is that you?*)
(*A fourth ring. The Indian knows the telephone is dead*) Pray-aim Pray-aim—moo-jhay bah-chald Pray-aim.
(*Prem. Prem. Help me. Prem.*)
(*As the telephone rings a fifth time, in the silence of the night, the sounds of two boys' singing is heard*)

FIRST BOY:
I walk the lonely streets at night,
A-lookin' for your door . . .

SECOND BOY:
I look and look and look and look . . .

FIRST BOY AND SECOND BOY:
But, baby, you don't care.
But, baby, no one cares.
But, baby, no one cares.

(*Their song continues to build as they repeat the lyrics, so the effect is one of many, many voices. The telephone continues its unanswered ring. The Indian screams a final anguished scream of fury to the boys offstage. The telephone rings a final ring as the Indian screams*)

INDIAN: (*Desperately, holding the telephone to the audience as an offer. He speaks in English into the telephone. The only words he remembers are those from his lesson*) How are you? You're welcome. You're welcome. Thank you. (*To the front*) Thank you!

BLACKOUT

Benito Cereno

Robert Lowell

Robert Lowell, poet and playwright, was born in Boston in 1917 and educated in the area, the home of his distinguished family. He disliked the stuffiness of Harvard and transferred to Kenyon College, where his intense and symbolic poetry found encouragement from John Crowe Ransom and Randall Jarrell. Just before his graduation in 1940, he married the novelist Jean Stafford and became a Roman Catholic.

During World War II, he was incarcerated as a conscientious objector, and after his release he moved to Maine. His second volume of poetry, containing many of his earlier anti-war poems, *Lord Weary's Castle* (1946) gained him the Pulitzer Prize at the age of twenty-nine. For the next few years he taught at Boston University (where Sylvia Plath and Anne Sexton were among his students) and other schools, but lived largely abroad with his second wife, the writer Elizabeth Hardwick. In 1954, he published *The Mills of the Kavanaughs.* Two years later, at about the time the Lowells moved back to New York, *Life Studies* appeared. Like Ginsberg's "Howl," it has had a great influence on American poetry and set Lowell on a fresh course. From the tight metrical forms he favored in his earlier poetry, he passed into the looser lines and more open forms that have characterized his poetry since and the language of the three verse dramas on American themes in *The Old Glory.*

During the late sixties, Lowell was active in war resistance and joined with Norman Mailer and John Williams in the famous peace march on Washington. He has generously given his name and his support to countless liberal causes, and his work reflects his concern with the anguishing problems of being alive in our diseased times. He lives in New York City.

Benito Cereno is based on Herman Melville's novella, and when it was first performed at the American Place Theatre, it proved to have a great visual eloquence that the novel hardly hints at, expressed through interweaving of dance, mime, and ceremony with the magnificent bare verse capable of Elizabethan candle-power. Despite the magic of Lowell's verse, the "meaning" of the play reaches us by gesture rather than word: A glass ball representing the earth is shattered by a "slave," an unforgettable way of foreshadowing the present tense.

Characters (*In order of appearance*)

CAPTAIN AMASA DELANO
JOHN PERKINS
DON BENITO CERENO
BABU
ATUFAL
FRANCESCO
AMERICAN SAILORS
SPANISH SAILORS
NEGRO SLAVES

About the year 1800, an American sealing vessel, the President Adams, *at anchor in an island harbor off the coast of Trinidad. The stage is part of the ship's deck. Everything is unnaturally clean, bare and ship-shape. To one side, a polished, coal-black cannon. The American captain,* AMASA DELANO *from Duxbury, Massachusetts, sits in a cane chair. He is a strong, comfortable looking man in his early thirties who wears a spotless blue coat and white trousers. Incongruously, he has on a straw hat and smokes a corncob pipe. Beside him stands* JOHN PERKINS, *his bosun, a very stiff, green young man, a relative of* DELANO'*s.* THREE SAILORS, *one carrying an American flag, enter.* EVERYONE *stands at attention and salutes with machinelike exactitude. Then the* THREE SAILORS *march off-stage.* DELANO *and* PERKINS *are alone.*

DELANO:
There goes the most beautiful woman in South America.

PERKINS:
We never see any women, Sir;
just this smothering, overcast Equator,
a seal or two,
the flat dull sea,
and a sky like a gray wasp's nest.

DELANO:
I wasn't talking about women,
I was calling your attention to the American flag.

PERKINS:
Yes, Sir! I wish we were home in Duxbury.

DELANO:
We are home. America is wherever her flag flies.
My own deck is the only place in the world
where I feel at home.

PERKINS:
That's too much for me, Captain Delano.
I mean I wish I were at home with my wife;
these world cruises are only for bachelors.

DELANO:
Your wife will keep. You should smoke, Perkins.
Smoking turns men into philosophers
and swabs away their worries.
I can see my wife and children or not see them
in each puff of blue smoke.

PERKINS:
You are always tempting me, Sir!
I try to keep fit,
I want to return to my wife as fit as I left her.

DELANO:
You're much too nervous, Perkins.
Travel will shake you up. You should let
a little foreign dirt rub off on you.
I've taught myself to speak Spanish like a Spaniard.
At each South American port, they mistake me for a
Castilian Don.

PERKINS:
Aren't you lowering yourself a little, Captain?
Excuse me, Sir, I have been wanting to ask you a question,
Don't you think our President, Mr. Jefferson, is
lowering himself
by being so close to the French?
I'd feel a lot safer in this unprotected place
if we'd elected Mr. Adams instead of Mr. Jefferson.

DELANO:
The better man ran second!
Come to think of it, he rather let us down
by losing the election just after we had named this ship,
the *President Adams*. Adams is a nervous dry fellow.
When you've traveled as much as I have,
you'll learn that that sort doesn't export, Perkins.
Adams didn't get a vote outside New England!

PERKINS:
He carried every New England state;
that was better than winning the election.
I'm afraid I'm a dry fellow, too, Sir.

DELANO:
Not when I've educated you!
When I am through with you, Perkins,
you'll be as worldly as the Prince Regent of England,
only you'll be a first class American officer.
I'm all for Jefferson, he has the popular touch.
Of course he's read too many books,
but I've always said an idea or two won't sink
our Republic.
I'll tell you this, Perkins,
Mr. Jefferson is a gentleman and an American.

PERKINS:
They say he has two illegitimate Negro children.

DELANO:
The more the better! That's the quickest way
to raise the blacks to our level.
I'm surprised you swallow such Federalist bilge, Perkins!
I told you Mr. Jefferson is a gentleman and an American;
when a man's in office, Sir, we all pull behind him!

PERKINS:
Thank God our Revolution ended where the French
one began.

DELANO:
Oh the French! They're like the rest of the Latins,
they're hardly white people,
they start with a paper republic
and end with a toy soldier, like Bonaparte.

PERKINS:
Yes, Sir. I see a strange sail making for the harbor.
They don't know how to sail her.

DELANO:
Hand me my telescope.

PERKINS:
Aye, aye, Sir!

DELANO:
(*With telescope*)
I see an ocean undulating in long scoops of swells;
it's set like the beheaded French Queen's high wig;
the sleek surface is like waved lead,
cooled and pressed in the smelter's mould.
I see flights of hurried gray fowl,
patches of fluffy fog.
They skim low and fitfully above the decks,
like swallows sabering flies before a storm.
This gray boat foreshadows something wrong.

PERKINS:
It does, Sir!
They don't know how to sail her!

DELANO:
I see a sulphurous haze above her cabin,
the new sun hangs like a silver dollar to her stern;
low creeping clouds blow on from them to us.

PERKINS:
What else, Sir?

DELANO:
The yards are woolly
the ship is furred with fog.
On the cracked and rotten head-boards,
the tarnished, gilded letters say, the *San Domingo.*
A rat's-nest messing up the deck,
black faces in white sheets are fussing with the ropes.
I think it's a cargo of Dominican monks.

PERKINS:
Dominican monks, Sir! God help us,
I thought they were outlawed in the new world.

DELANO:
No, it's nothing. I see they're only slaves.
The boat's transporting slaves.

PERKINS:
Do you believe in slavery, Captain Delano?

DELANO:
In a civilized country, Perkins,
everyone disbelieves in slavery,
everyone disbelieves in slavery and wants slaves.
We have the perfect uneasy answer;
in the North, we don't have them and want them;
Mr. Jefferson has them and fears them.

PERKINS:
Is that how you answer, Sir,
when a little foreign dirt has rubbed off on you?

DELANO:
Don't ask me such intense questions.
You should take up smoking, Perkins.
There was a beautiful, dumb English actress—
I saw her myself once in London.
They wanted her to look profound,
so she read Plato and the Bible and Benjamin Franklin,
and thought about them every minute.
She still looked like a moron.
Then they told her to think about nothing.
She thought about nothing, and looked like Socrates.
That's smoking, Perkins; you think about nothing and
look deep.

PERKINS:
I don't believe in slavery, Sir.

DELANO:
You don't believe in slavery or Spaniards
or smoking or long cruises or monks or Mr. Jefferson!
You are a Puritan, all faith and fire.

PERKINS:
Yes, Sir.

DELANO:
God save America from Americans!
(*Takes up the telescope*)
I see octagonal network bagging out
from her heavy top like decayed beehives.
The battered forecastle looks like a raped Versailles.
On the stern-piece, I see the fading arms of Spain.
There's a masked satyr, or something
with its foot on a big white goddess.
She has quite a figure.

PERKINS:
They oughtn't to be allowed on the ocean!

DELANO:
Who oughtn't? Goddesses?

PERKINS:
I mean Spaniards, who cannot handle a ship,
and mess up its hull with immoral statues.

DELANO:
You're out of step. You're much too dry.
Bring me my three-cornered hat.
Order some men to clear a whaleboat.
I am going to bring water and fresh fish to the
San Domingo.
These people have had some misfortune, Perkins!

PERKINS:
Aye, aye, Sir.

DELANO:
Spaniards? The name gets you down,
you think their sultry faces and language
make them Zulus.
You take the name *Delano*—
I've always thought it had some saving
Italian or Spanish virtue in it.

PERKINS:
Yes, Sir.

DELANO:
A Spaniard isn't a Negro under the skin,
particularly a Spaniard from Spain—
these South American ones mix too much with the Indians.
Once you get inside a Spaniard,
he talks about as well as your wife in Duxbury.

PERKINS:

(Shouting)

A boat for the captain! A whaleboat for Captain Delano!

(A bosun's whistle is heard, the lights dim. When they come up, we are on the deck of the San Domingo, *the same set, identical except for litter and disorder.* THREE AMERICAN SAILORS *climb on board. They are followed by* PERKINS *and* DELANO, *now wearing a three-cornered hat. Once on board, the* AMERICAN SAILORS *salute* DELANO *and stand stiffly at attention like toys.* NEGROES *from the* San Domingo *drift silently and furtively forward)*

DELANO:

I see a wen of barnacles hanging to the waterline of
this ship.
It sticks out like the belly of a pregnant woman.
Have a look at our dory Bosun.

PERKINS:

Aye, aye, Sir!

(By now, about twenty blacks and two Spanish sailors have drifted in. They look like some gaudy, shabby, unnautical charade, and pay no attention to the Americans, until an unseen figure in the rigging calls out a single sharp warning in an unknown tongue. Then they all rush forward, shouting, waving their arms and making inarticulate cries like birds. Three shrill warnings come from the rigging. Dead silence. The men from the San Domingo *press back in a dense semicircle. One by one, individuals come forward, make showy bows to* DELANO, *and speak)*

FIRST NEGRO:

Scurvy, Master Yankee!

SECOND NEGRO:

Yellow fever, Master Yankee!

THIRD NEGRO:

Two men knocked overboard rounding Cape Horn,
Master Yankee!

FOURTH NEGRO:

Nothing to eat, Master Yankee!

NEGRO WOMAN:

Nothing to drink, Master Yankee!

SECOND NEGRO WOMAN:

Our mouths are dead wood, Master Yankee!

DELANO:

You see, Perkins,
these people have had some misfortune.

(*General hubbub, muttering, shouts, gestures, ritual and dumb-show of distress. The rigging, hitherto dark, lightens, as the sun comes out of a cloud, and shows* THREE OLD NEGROES, *identical down to their shabby patches. They perch on cat's-heads; their heads are grizzled like dying willow tops; each is picking bits of unstranded rope for oakum. It is they who have been giving the warnings that control the people below. Everyone,* DELANO *along with the rest, looks up.* DELANO *turns aside and speaks to* PERKINS)

It is like a Turkish bazaar.

PERKINS:

They are like gypsies showing themselves for money
at a county fair, Sir.

DELANO:

This is enchanting after the blank gray roll of the ocean!
Go tell the Spanish captain I am waiting for him.

(PERKINS *goes off. Sharp warnings from the* OAKUM-PICKERS. *A big black spread of canvas is pulled creakingly and ceremoniously aside.* SIX FIGURES *stand huddled on a platform about four feet from the deck. They look like weak old invalids in bathrobes and nightcaps until they strip to the waist and turn out to be huge, shining young Negroes. Saying nothing, they set to work cleaning piles of rusted hatchets. From time to time, they turn and clash their hatchets together with a rhythmic shout.* PERKINS *returns*)

PERKINS:

Their captain's name is Don Benito Cereno,
he sends you his compliments, Sir.
He looks more like a Mexican planter than a seaman.
He's put his fortune on his back:
he doesn't look as if he had washed since they left port.

DELANO:

Did you tell him I was waiting for him?
A captain should be welcomed by his fellow-captain.
I can't understand this discourtesy.

PERKINS:

He's coming, but there's something wrong with him.

(BENITO CERENO, *led by his Negro servant,* BABU, *enters.* BENITO, *looking sick and dazed, is wearing a sombrero and is dressed with a singular but shabby richness. Head bent to one side, he leans in a stately coma against the rail, and stares unseeingly at* DELANO. BABU, *all in scarlet, and small and quick, keeps whispering, pointing and pulling at* BENITO's *sleeve.* DELANO *walks over to them*)

DELANO:

Your hand, Sir. I am Amasa Delano,

captain of the *President Adams,*
a sealing ship from the United States.
This is your lucky day,
the sun is out of hiding for the first time in two weeks,
and here I am aboard your ship
like the Good Samaritan with fresh food and water.

BENITO:
The Good Samaritan? Yes, yes,
we mustn't use the Scriptures lightly.
Welcome, Captain. It is the end of the day.

DELANO:
The end? It's only morning.
I loaded and lowered a whaleboat
as soon as I saw how awkwardly your ship was making for the harbor.

BENITO:
Your whaleboat's welcome, Captain.
I am afraid I am still stunned by the storm.

DELANO:
Buck up. Each day is a new beginning.
Assign some sailors to help me dole out my provisions.

BENITO:
I have no sailors.

BABU:
(*In a quick sing-song:*)
Scurvy, yellow fever,
ten men knocked off on the Horn,
doldrums, nothing to eat, nothing to drink!
By feeding us, you are feeding the King of Spain.

DELANO:
Sir, your slave has a pretty way of talking.
What do you need?
(DELANO *waits for* BENITO *to speak. When nothing more is said, he shifts awkwardly from foot to foot, then turns to his* SAILORS)
Stand to, men!
(*The* AMERICAN SAILORS, *who have been lounging and gaping, stand in a row, as if a button had been pressed*)
Lay our fish and water by the cabin!
(*The* SAILORS *arrange the watercans and baskets of fish by the cabin. A sharp whistle comes from the* OAKUM-PICKERS. *Almost instantly, the provisions disappear*)
Captain Cereno, you are surely going to taste my water!

BENITO:
A captain is a servant, almost a slave, Sir.

DELANO:

No, a captain's a captain.
I am sending for more provisions.
Stand to!
(*The* AMERICAN SAILORS *stand to*)
Row back to the ship. When you get there,
take on five hogsheads of fresh water,
and fifty pounds of soft bread.
(FIRST SAILOR *salutes and goes down the ladder*)
Bring all our remaining pumpkins!
(SECOND *and* THIRD SAILORS *salute and go down the ladder*)
My bosun and I will stay on board,
until our boat returns.
I imagine you can use us.

BENITO:

Are you going to stay here alone?
Won't your ship be lost without you?
Won't you be lost without your ship?

BABU:

Listen to Master!
He is the incarnation of courtesy, Yankee Captain.
Your ship doesn't need you as much as we do.

DELANO:

Oh, I've trained my crew.
I can sail my ship in my sleep.
(*Leaning over the railing and calling*)
Men, bring me a box of lump sugar,
and six bottles of my best cider.
(*Turning to* BENITO)
Cider isn't my favorite drink, Don Benito,
but it's a New England specialty;
I'm ordering six bottles for your table.
(BABU *whispers and gestures to* DON BENITO, *who is exhausted and silent*)

BABU:

Une bouteille du vin (*to* NEGROES)
My master wishes to give you a bottle
of the oldest wine in Seville.
(*He whistles. A Negro woman rushes into the cabin and returns with a dusty beribboned bottle, which she holds like a baby*)
(BABU *ties a rope around the bottle*)

BABU:

I am sending this bottle of wine to your cabin.
When you drink it, you will remember us.
Do you see these ribbons? The crown of Spain is tied
to one.

Forgive me for tying a rope around the King of
Spain's neck.
(*Lowers the wine on the rope to the whaleboat*)

DELANO:
(*Shouting to his* SAILORS)
Pick up your oars!

SAILORS:
Aye, aye, Sir!

DELANO:
We're New England Federalists;
we can drink the King of Spain's health.
(BENITO *stumbles off-stage on* BABU'*s arm*)

PERKINS:
Captain Cereno hasn't traveled as much as you have;
I don't think he knew what you meant by the New England
Federalists.

DELANO:
(*Leaning comfortably on the rail; half to himself and half to* PERKINS)
The wind is dead. We drift away.
We will be left alone all day,
here in this absentee empire.
Thank God, I know my Spanish!

PERKINS:
You'll have to watch them, Sir.
Brown men in charge of black men–
it doesn't add up to much!
This Babu, I don't trust him!
Why doesn't he talk with a Southern accent,
Like Mr. Jefferson? They're out of hand, Sir!

DELANO:
Nothing relaxes order more than misery.
They need severe superior officers.
They haven't one.
Now, if this Benito were a man of energy . . .
a Yankee . . .

PERKINS:
How can a Spaniard sail?

DELANO:
Some can. There was Vasco da Gama and Columbus . . .
No, I guess they were Italians. Some can,
but this captain is tubercular.

PERKINS:
Spaniards and Negroes have no business on a ship.

DELANO:
Why is this captain so indifferent to me?
If only I could stomach his foreign reserve!
This absolute dictator of his ship
only gives orders through his slaves!
He is like some Jesuit-haunted Hapsburg king
about to leave the world and hope the world will end.

PERKINS:
He said he was lost in the storm.

DELANO:
Perhaps it's only policy,
a captain's icy dignity
obliterating all democracy—

PERKINS:
He's like someone walking in his sleep.

DELANO:
Ah, slumbering dominion!
He is so self-conscious in his imbecility . . .
No, he's sick. He sees his men no more than me.
This ship is like a crowded immigration boat,
it needs severe superior officers,
the friendly arm of a strong mate.
Perhaps, I ought to take it over by force.
No, they're sick, they've been through the plague.
I'll go and speak and comfort my fellow captain.
I think you can help me, Captain. I'm feeling useless.
My own thoughts oppress me, there's so much to do.
I wonder if you would tell me the whole sad story of
your voyage.
Talk to me as captain to captain.
We have sailed the same waters.
Please tell me your story.

BENITO:
A story? A story! That's out of place.
When I was a child, I used to beg for stories back in Lima.
Now my tongue's tied and my heart is bleeding.
(Stops talking, as if his breath were gone. He stares for a few moments, then looks up at the rigging, as if he were counting the ropes one by one. DELANO *turns abruptly to* PERKINS)

DELANO:
Go through the ship, Perkins,
and see if you can find me a Spaniard who can talk.

BENITO:
You must be patient, Captain Delano;

if we only see with our eyes,
sometimes we cannot see at all.

DELANO:
I stand corrected, Captain;
tell me about your voyage.

BENITO:
It's now a hundred and ninety days . . .
This ship, well manned, well officered, with several
cabin passengers,
carrying a cargo of Paraguay tea and Spanish cutlery.
That parcel of Negro slaves, less than four score now,
was once three hundred souls.
Ten sailors and three officers fell from the mainyard off
the Horn;
part of our rigging fell overboard with them,
as they were beating down the icy sail.
We threw away all our cargo,
Broke our waterpipes,
Lashed them on deck
this was the chief cause of our suffering.

DELANO:
I must interrupt you, Captain.
How did you happen to have three officers on
the mainyard?
I never heard of such a disposal,
it goes against all seamanship.

BABU:
Our officers never spared themselves;
if there was any danger, they rushed in
to save us without thinking.

DELANO:
I can't understand such an oversight.

BABU:
There was no oversight. My master had a hundred eyes.
He had an eye for everything.
Sometimes the world falls on a man.
The sea wouldn't let Master act like a master,
yet he saved himself and many lives.
He is still a rich man, and he saved the ship.

BENITO:
Oh my God, I wish the world had fallen on me,
and the terrible cold sea had drowned me;
that would have been better than living through what I've
lived through!

BABU:

He is a good man, but his mind is off;
he's thinking about the fever when the wind stopped—
poor, poor Master!
Be patient, Yankee Captain, these fits are short,
Master will be the master once again.

BENITO:

The scurvy was raging through us.
We were on the Pacific. We were invalids
and couldn't man our mangled spars.
A hurricane blew us northeast through the fog.
Then the wind died.
We lay in irons fourteen days in unknown waters,
our black tongues stuck through our mouths,
but we couldn't mend our broken waterpipes.

BABU:

Always those waterpipes,
he dreams about them like a pile of snakes!

BENITO:

Yellow fever followed the scurvy,
the long heat thickened in the calm,
my Spaniards turned black and died like slaves,
The blacks died too. I am my only officer left.

BABU:

Poor, poor Master! He had a hundred eyes,
he lived our lives for us.
He is still a rich man.

BENITO:

In the smart winds beating us northward,
our torn sails dropped like sinkers in the sea;
each day we dropped more bodies.
Almost without a crew, canvas, water, or a wind,
we were bounced about by the opposing waves
through cross-currents and the weedy calms,
and dropped our dead.
Often we doubled and redoubled on our track
like children lost in jungle. The thick fog
hid the Continent and our only port from us.

BABU:

We were poor kidnapped jungle creatures.
We only lived on what he could give us.
He had a hundred eyes, he was the master.

BENITO:

These Negroes saved me, Captain.
Through the long calamity,

They were as gentle as their owner, Don Aranda, promised.
Don Aranda took away their chains before he died.

BABU:
Don Aranda saved our lives, but we couldn't save his.
Even in Africa I was a slave.
He took away my chains.

BENITO:
I gave them the freedom of my ship.
I did not think they were crates or cargo or cannibals.
But it was Babu—under God, I swear I owe my life
to Babu!
He calmed his ignorant, wild brothers,
never left me, saved the *San Domingo*.

BABU:
Poor, poor Master. He is still a rich man.
Don't speak of Babu. Babu is the dirt under your feet.
He did his best.

DELANO:
You are a good fellow, Babu.
You are the salt of the earth. I envy you, Don Benito;
he is no slave, Sir, but your friend.

BENITO:
Yes, he is salt in my wounds.
I can never repay him, I mean.
Excuse me, Captain, my strength is gone.
I have done too much talking. I want to rest.
(BABU *leads* BENITO *to a shabby straw chair at the side.* BENITO *sits.* BABU *fans him with his sombrero*)

PERKINS:
He's a fine gentleman, but no seaman.
A cabin boy would have known better
than to send his three officers on the mainyard.

DELANO:
(*Paying no attention*)
A terrible story. I would have been unhinged myself.
(*Looking over toward* BABU *and* BENITO)
There's a true servant. They do things better
in the South and in South America—
trust in return for trust!
The beauty of that relationship is unknown
in New England. We're too much alone
in Massachusetts, Perkins.
How do our captains and our merchants live,
each a republic to himself.
Even Sam Adams had no friends and only loved the mob.

PERKINS:
Sir, you are forgetting that
New England seamanship brought them their slaves.

DELANO:
Oh, just our Southern slaves;
we had nothing to do with these fellows.

PERKINS:
The ocean would be a different place
if every Spaniard served an apprenticeship on an
American ship
before he got his captain's papers.

DELANO:
This captain's a gentleman, not a sailor.
His little yellow hands
got their command before they held a rope—
in by the cabin-window, not the hawse-hole!
Do you want to know why
they drifted hog-tied in those easy calms—
inexperience, sickness, impotence and aristocracy!

PERKINS:
Here comes Robinson Crusoe and his good man Friday.

DELANO:
We don't beat a man when he's down.
(BENITO *advances uncertainly on* BABU*'s arm*)
I am glad to see you on your feet again,
That's the only place for a Captain, Sir!
I have the cure for you, I have decided
to bring you medicine and a sufficient supply of water.
A first class deck officer, a man from Salem,
shall be stationed on your quarter deck,
a temporary present from my owners.
We shall refit your ship and clear this mess.

BENITO:
You will have to clear away the dead.

BABU:
This excitement is bad for him, Yankee Master.
He's lived with death. He lives on death still;
this sudden joy will kill him. You've heard
how thirsty men die from overdrinking!
His heart is with his friend, our owner, Don Aranda.

BENITO:
I am the only owner.
(*He looks confused and shaken*)
(BABU *scurries off and brings up the straw chair.* BENITO *sits*)

DELANO:
Your friend is dead? He died of fever?

BENITO:
He died very slowly and in torture.
He was the finest man in Lima.
We were brought up together,
I am lost here.

DELANO:
Pardon me, Sir. You are young at sea.
My experience tells me what your trouble is:
this is the first body you have buried in the ocean.
I had a friend like yours, a warm honest fellow,
who would look you in the eye—
we had to throw him to the sharks.
Since then I've brought embalming gear on board.
Each man of mine shall have a Christian grave on land.
You wouldn't shake so, if Don Aranda were on board,
I mean, if you'd preserved the body.

BENITO:
If he were on board this ship?
If I had preserved his body?

BABU:
Be patient, Master!
We still have the figurehead.

DELANO:
You have the figurehead?

BABU:
You see that thing wrapped up in black cloth?
It's a figurehead Don Aranda bought us in Spain.
It was hurt in the storm. It's very precious.
Master takes comfort in it,
he is going to give it to Don Aranda's widow.
It's time for the pardon ceremony, Master.
(*Sound of clashing hatchets*)

DELANO:
I am all for these hatchet-cleaners.
They are saving cargo. They make
an awful lot of pomp and racket though
about a few old, rusty knives.

BENITO:
They think steel is worth its weight in gold.
(*A slow solemn march is sounded on the gongs and other instruments. A gigantic coal-black* NEGRO *comes up the steps. He wears a spiked iron collar to which a chain is attached that*

goes twice around his arms and ends padlocked to a broad band of iron. The NEGRO *comes clanking forward and stands dumbly and like a dignitary in front of* BENITO. *Two small black boys bring* BENITO *a frail rattan cane and a silver ball, which they support on a velvet cushion.* BENITO *springs up, holds the ball, and raises the cane rigidly above the head of the Negro in chains. For a moment, he shows no trace of sickness. The assembled blacks sing, "Evviva, Benito!" three times*)

BABU:

(*At one side with the Americans, but keeping an eye on* BENITO)
You are watching the humiliation of King Atufal,
once a ruler in Africa. He ruled as much land there
as your President.
Poor Babu was a slave even in Africa,
a black man's slave, and now a white man's.

BENITO:

(*In a loud, firm voice*)
Former King Atufal, I call on you to kneel!
Say, "My sins are black as night,
I ask the King of Spain's pardon
through his servant, Don Benito."
(*Pause.* ATUFAL *doesn't move*)

NEGROES:

Your sins are black as night, King Atufal!
Your sins are black as night, King Atufal!

DELANO:

What has King Atufal done?

BABU:

I will tell you later, Yankee Captain.

BENITO:

Ask pardon, King Atufal.
If you will kneel,
I will strike away your chains.
(ATUFAL *slowly raises his chained arms and lets them drop*)
Ask pardon!

WOMAN SLAVE:

Ask pardon, King Atufal.

BENITO:

Go!
(*Sound of instruments. The* BLACK BOYS *take* BENITO*'s ball and cane. The straw chair is brought up.* BENITO *sits.* FRANCESCO *then leads him off-stage*)

BABU:

Francesco!

I will be with you in a moment, Master.
You mustn't be afraid,
Francesco will serve you like a second Babu.

BENITO:
Everyone serves me alike here,
but no one can serve me as you have.

BABU:
I will be with you in a moment.
The Yankee master is at sea on our ship.
He wants me to explain our customs.
(BENITO *is carried off-stage*)
You would think Master's afraid of dying,
if Babu leaves him!

DELANO:
I can imagine your tenderness during his sickness.
You were part of him,
you were almost a wife.

BABU:
You say such beautiful things,
the United States must be a paradise for people like Babu.

DELANO:
I don't know.
We have our faults. We have many states,
some of them could stand improvement.

BABU:
The United States must be heaven.

DELANO:
I suppose we have fewer faults than other countries.
What did King Atufal do?

BABU:
He used the Spanish flag for toilet paper.

DELANO:
That's treason.
Did Atufal know what he was doing?
Perhaps the flag was left somewhere it shouldn't have been.
Things aren't very strict here.

BABU:
I never thought of that.
I will go and tell Master.

DELANO:
Oh, no, you mustn't do that!
I never interfere with another man's ship.
Don Benito is your lord and dictator.

How long has this business with King Atufal been
going on?

BABU:

Ever since the yellow fever,
and twice a day.

DELANO:

He did a terrible thing, but he looks like a royal fellow.
You shouldn't call him a king, though,
it puts ideas into his head.

BABU:

Atufal had gold wedges in his ears in Africa;
now he wears a padlock and Master bears the key.

DELANO:

I see you have a feeling for symbols of power.
You had better be going now,
Don Benito will be nervous about you.
(BABU *goes off*)
That was a terrible thing to do with a flag;
everything is untidy and unraveled here—
this sort of thing would never happen on the
President Adams.

PERKINS:

Your ship is as shipshape as our country, Sir.

DELANO:

I wish people wouldn't take me as representative of
our country:
America's one thing, I am another;
we shouldn't have to bear one another's burdens.

PERKINS:

You are a true American for all your talk, Sir;
I can't believe you were mistaken for a Castilian Don.

DELANO:

No one would take me for Don Benito.

PERKINS:

I wonder if he isn't an impostor, some traveling actor from
a circus?

DELANO:

No, Cereno is a great name in Peru, like Winthrop or
Adams with us.
I recognize the family features in our captain.
(*An* OLD SPANISH SAILOR, *grizzled and dirty, is seen crawling on all fours with an armful of knots toward the Americans. He points to where* BENITO *and* BABU *have disappeared and whistles. He*

holds up the knots as though he were in chains, then throws them out loosely on the deck in front of him. A GROUP OF NEGROES *forms a circle around him, holding hands and singing childishly. Then, laughing, they carry the* SPANIARD *off-stage on their shoulders*)

These blacks are too familiar!
We are never alone!

(*Sound of gongs. Full minute's pause, as if time were passing.* DELANO *leans on the railing. The sun grows brighter*)

This ship is strange.
These people are too spontaneous—all noise and show,
no character!
Real life is a simple monotonous thing.
I wonder about that story about the calms;
it doesn't stick.
Don Benito hesitated himself in telling it.
No one could run a ship so stupidly,
and place three officers on one yard.

(BENITO *and* BABU *return*)

A captain has unpleasant duties;
I am sorry for you, Don Benito.

BENITO:
You find my ship unenviable, Sir?

DELANO:
I was talking about punishing Atufal;
he acted like an animal!

BENITO:
Oh, yes, I was forgetting . . .
He was a King,
How long have you lain in at this island, Sir?

DELANO:
Oh, a week today.

BENITO:
What was your last port, Sir?

DELANO:
Canton.

BENITO:
You traded seal-skins and American muskets
for Chinese tea and silks, perhaps?

DELANO:
We took in some silks.

BENITO:
A little gold and silver too?

DELANO:
Just a little silver. We are only merchants.
We take in a dollar here and there. We have no Peru,
or a Pizarro who can sweat gold out of the natives.

BENITO:
You'll find things have changed
a little in Peru since Pizarro, Captain.
(*Starts to move away.* BABU *whispers to him, and he comes back abruptly, as if he had forgotten something important*)
How many men have you on board, Sir?

DELANO:
Some twenty-five, Sir. Each man is at his post.

BENITO:
They're all on board, Sir, now?

DELANO:
They're all on board. Each man is working.

BENITO:
They'll be on board tonight, Sir?

DELANO:
Tonight? Why do you ask, Don Benito?

BENITO:
Will they all be on board tonight, Captain?

DELANO:
They'll be on board for all I know.
(PERKINS *makes a sign to* DELANO)
Well, no, to tell the truth, today's our Independence Day.
A gang is going ashore to see the village.
A little diversion improves their efficiency,
a little regulated corruption.

BENITO:
You North Americans take no chances. Generally,
I suppose,
even your merchant ships go more or less armed?

DELANO:
A rack of muskets, sealing spears and cutlasses.
Oh, and a six-pounder or two; we are a sealing ship,
but with us each merchant is a privateer—
only in case of oppression, of course.
You've heard about how we shoot pirates.

BABU:
Boom, boom, come Master.
(BENITO *walks away on* BABU'*s arm and sits down, almost off-stage in his straw chair. They whisper. Meanwhile, a* SPANISH

SAILOR *climbs the rigging furtively, spread-eagles his arms and shows a lace shirt under his shabby jacket. He points to* BENITO *and* BABU *and winks. At a cry from* ONE OF THE OAKUM-PICKERS, THREE NEGROES *help the* SPANIARD *down with servile, ceremonious attentions)*

PERKINS:
Did you see that sailor's lace shirt, Sir?
He must have robbed one of the cabin passengers.
I hear that people strip the dead
in these religious countries.

DELANO:
No, you don't understand the Spaniards.
In these old Latin countries,
each man's a beggar or a noble, often both;
they have no middle class. With them it's customary
to sew a mess of gold and pearls on rags—
that's how an aristocracy that's going to the dogs
keeps up its nerve.
It's odd though,
that Spanish sailor seemed to want to tell me something.
He ought to dress himself properly and speak his mind.
That's what we do. That's why we're strong:
everybody trusts us. Nothing gets done
when every man's a noble. I wonder why
the captain asked me all those questions?

PERKINS:
He was passing the time of day, Sir;
It's a Latin idleness.

DELANO:
It's strange. Did you notice how Benito stopped rambling?
He was conventional . . . consecutive for the first time
since we met him.
Something's wrong. Perhaps, they've men below the decks,
a sleeping volcano of Spanish infantry. The Malays do it,
play sick and cut your throat.
A drifting boat, a dozen doped beggars on deck,
two hundred sweating murderers packed below
like sardines—
that's rot! Anyone can see these people are really sick,
sicker than usual. Our countries are at peace.
I wonder why he asked me all those questions?

PERKINS:
Just idle curiosity. I hear
the gentlemen of Lima sit at coffee-tables from sun to sun
and gossip. They don't even have women to look at;
they're all locked up with their aunts.

DELANO:

Their sun is going down. These old empires go.
They are much too familiar with their blacks.
I envy them though, they have no character,
they feel no need to stand alone.
We stand alone too much,
that's why no one can touch us for sailing a ship;
When a country loses heart, it's easier to live.
Ah, Babu! I suppose Don Benito's indisposed again!
Tell him I want to talk to his people;
there's nothing like a well man to help the sick.

BABU:

Master is taking his siesta, Yankee Master.
His siesta is sacred, I am afraid to disturb it.
Instead, let me show you our little entertainment.

DELANO:

Let's have your entertainment;
if you know a man's pleasure
you know his measure.

BABU:

We are a childish people. Our pleasures are childish.
No one helped us, we know nothing
about your important amusements,
such as killing seals and pirates.

DELANO:

I'm game. Let's have your entertainment.

(BABU *signals. The gong sounds ten times and the canvas is pulled from the circular structure. Enclosed in a triangular compartment, an* OLD SPANISH SAILOR *is dipping naked white dolls in a tar-pot*)

BABU:

This little amusement keeps him alive, Yankee Master.
He is especially fond of cleaning the dolls
after he has dirtied them.

(*The* OLD SPANISH SAILOR *laughs hysterically, and then smears his whole face with tar*)

OLD SPANISH SAILOR:

My soul is white!

BABU:

The yellow fever destroyed his mind.

DELANO:

Let's move on. This man's brain,
as well as his face, is defiled with pitch!

BABU:
He says his soul is white.
(*The structure is pushed around and another triangular compartment appears. A* NEGRO BOY *is playing chess against a splendid Spanish doll with a crown on its head. He stops and holds two empty wine bottles to his ears*)
This boy is deaf.
The yellow fever destroyed his mind.

DELANO:
Why is he holding those bottles to his ears?

BABU:
He is trying to be a rabbit,
or listening to the ocean, his mother—
who knows?

DELANO:
If he's deaf, how can he hear the ocean?
Anyway, he can't hear me.
I pass, let's move on.
(*The structure is pushed around to a third compartment. A* SPANISH SAILOR *is holding a big armful of rope*)
What are you knotting there, my man?

SPANISH SAILOR:
The knot.

DELANO:
So I see, but what's it for?

SPANISH SAILOR:
For someone to untie. Catch!
(*Throws the knot to* DELANO)

BABU:
(*Snatching the knot from* DELANO)
It's dirty, it will dirty your uniform.

DELANO:
Let's move on. Your entertainment
is rather lacking in invention, Babu.

BABU:
We have to do what we can
We are just beginners at acting.
This next one will be better.
(*The structure is pushed around and shows a beautiful* NEGRO WOMAN. *She is dressed and posed as the Virgin Mary. A Christmas crèche is arranged around her. A* VERY WHITE SPANIARD *dressed as Saint Joseph stands behind her. She holds a Christ-*

child, the same crowned doll, only black, the NEGRO BOY *was playing chess against*)
She is the Virgin Mary. That man is not the father.

DELANO:
I see, I suppose her son is the King of Spain.

BABU:
The Spaniards taught us everything,
there's nothing we can learn from you, Yankee Master.
When they took away our country, they gave us a
better world.
Things do not happen in that world as they do here.

DELANO:
That's a very beautiful,
though unusual Virgin Mary.

BABU:
Yes, the Bible says, "I am black not white."
When Don Aranda was dying,
we wanted to give him the Queen of Heaven
because he took away our chains.

PERKINS:
The Spaniards must have taught them everything;
they're all mixed up, they don't even know their religion.

DELANO:
No, no! The Catholic Church doesn't just teach,
it knows how to take from its converts.

BABU:
Do you want to shake hands with the Queen of Heaven,
Yankee Master?

DELANO:
No, I'm not used to royalty.
Tell her I believe in freedom of religion,
if people don't take liberties.
Let's move on.

BABU:
(*Kneeling to the Virgin Mary*)
I present something Your Majesty has never seen,
a white man who doesn't believe in taking liberties,
Your Majesty.
(*The structure is pushed around and shows* ATUFAL *in chains but with a crown on his head*)

BABU:
This is the life we believe in.

THE NEGROES ALL TOGETHER:
Ask pardon, King Atufal!
Kiss the Spanish flag!

DELANO:
Please don't ask me to shake hands with King Atufal!
(*The canvas is put back on the structure*)

BABU:
You look tired and serious, Yankee Master.
We have to have what fun we can.
We never would have lived through the deadly calms
without a little amusement.
(*Bows and goes off*)
(*The* NEGROES *gradually drift away.* DELANO *sighs with relief*)

DELANO:
Well, that wasn't much!
I suppose Shakespeare started that way.

PERKINS:
Who cares?
I see a speck on the blue sea, Sir,
our whaleboat is coming.

DELANO:
A speck? My eyes are speckled.
I seem to have been dreaming. What's solid?
(*Touches the ornate railing; a piece falls onto the deck*)
This ship is nothing, Perkins!
I dreamed someone was trying to kill me!
How could he? Jack-of-the-beach,
they used to call me on the Duxbury shore.
Carrying a duck-satchel in my hand, I used to paddle
along the waterfront from a hulk to school.
I didn't learn much there. I was always shooting duck
or gathering huckleberries along the marsh with
Cousin Nat!
I like nothing better than breaking myself on the surf.
I used to track the seagulls down the five-mile stretch
of beach for eggs.
How can I be killed now at the ends of the earth
by this insane Spaniard?
Who could want to murder Amasa Delano?
My conscience is clean. God is good.
What am I doing on board this nigger-pirate ship?

PERKINS:
You're not talking like a skipper, Sir.
Our boat's a larger spot now.

DELANO:
I am childish.
I am doddering and drooling into my second childhood.
God help me, nothing's solid!

PERKINS:
Don Benito, Sir. Touch him,
he's as solid as his ship.

DELANO:
Don Benito? He's a walking ghost!
(BENITO *comes up to* DELANO. BABU *is a few steps behind him*)

BENITO:
I am the ghost of myself, Captain.
Excuse me, I heard you talking about dreams
and childhood.
I was a child, too, once, I have dreams about it.

DELANO:
(*Starting*)
I'm sorry.
This jumping's just a nervous habit.
I thought you were part of my dreams.

BENITO:
I was taking my siesta,
I dreamed I was a boy back in Lima.
I was with my brothers and sisters,
and we were dressed for the festival of Corpus Christi
like people at our Bourbon court.
We were simple children, but something went wrong;
little black men came on us with beetle backs.
They had caterpillar heads and munched away on our
fine clothes.
They made us lick their horned and varnished insect legs.
Our faces turned brown from their spit,
we looked like bugs, but nothing could save our lives!

DELANO:
Ha, ha, Captain. We are like two dreams meeting head-on.
My whaleboat's coming,
we'll both feel better over a bottle of cider.
(BABU *blows a bosun's whistle. The gongs are sounded with descending notes. The* NEGROES *assemble in ranks*)

BABU:
It's twelve noon, Master Yankee.
Master wants his midday shave.

ALL THE NEGROES:
Master wants his shave! Master wants his shave!

BENITO:
Ah, yes, the razor! I have been talking too much.
You can see how badly I need a razor.
I must leave you, Captain.

BABU:
No, Don Amasa wants to talk.
Come to the cabin, Don Amasa.
Don Amasa will talk, Master will listen.
Babu will lather and strop.

DELANO:
I want to talk to you about navigation.
I am new to these waters.

BENITO:
Doubtless, doubtless, Captain Delano.

PERKINS:
I think I'll take my siesta, Sir.
(*He walks off*)
(BENITO, BABU, *and* DELANO *walk toward the back of the stage. A scrim curtain lifts, showing a light deck cabin that forms a sort of attic. The floor is matted, partitions that still leave splintered traces have been knocked out. To one side, a small table screwed to the floor; on it, a dirty missal; above it, a small crucifix, rusty crossed muskets on one side, rusty crossed cutlasses on the other.* BENITO *sits down in a broken thronelike and gilded chair.* BABU *begins to lather. A magnificent array of razors, bottles and other shaving equipment lies on a table beside him. Behind him; a hammock with a pole in it and a dirty pillow*)

DELANO:
So this is where you took your siesta.

BENITO:
Yes, Captain, I rest here when my fate will let me.

DELANO:
This seems like a sort of dormitory, sitting-room,
sail-loft, chapel, armory, and private bedroom all together.

BENITO:
Yes, Captain: events have not been favorable
to much order in my personal arrangements.
(BABU *moves back and opens a locker. A lot of flags, torn shirts and socks tumble out. He takes one of the flags, shakes it with a flourish, and ties it around* BENITO'*s neck*)

BABU:
Master needs more protection.
I do everything I can to save his clothes.

DELANO:
The Castle and the Lion of Spain.
Why, Don Benito, this is the flag of Spain you're using!
It's well it's only I and not the King of Spain who sees this!
All's one, though, I guess, in this carnival world.
I see you like gay colors as much as Babu.

BABU:
(*Giggling*)
The bright colors draw the yellow fever
from Master's mind.
(*Raises the razor*)
(BENITO *begins to shake*)
Now, Master, now, Master!

BENITO:
You are talking while you hold the razor.

BABU:
You mustn't shake so, Master.
Look, Don Amasa, Master always shakes when I shave him,
though he is braver than a lion and stronger than a castle.
Master knows Babu has never yet drawn blood.
I may, though, sometime, if he shakes so much.
Now, Master!
Come, Don Amasa, talk to Master about the gales
and calms,
he'll answer and forget to shake.

DELANO:
Those calms, the more I think of them the more I wonder.
You say you were two months sailing here;
I made that stretch in less than a week.
We never met with any calms.
If I'd not heard your story from your lips,
and seen your ruined ship,
I would have said something was missing,
I would have said this was a mystery ship.

BENITO:
For some men the whole world is a mystery;
they cannot believe their senses.
(BENITO *shakes, the razor gets out of hand and cuts his cheek*)
Santa Maria!

BABU:
Poor, poor Master, see, you shook so;
this is Babu's first blood.
Please answer Don Amasa, while I wipe
this ugly blood from the razor and strop it again.

BENITO:
The sea was like the final calm of the world
On, on it went. It sat on us and drank our strength,
cross-currents eased us out to sea,
the yellow fever changed our blood to poison.

BABU:
You stood by us. Some of us stood by you!

BENITO:
Yes, my Spanish crew was weak and surly, but the blacks,
the blacks were angels. Babu has kept me in this world.
I wonder what he is keeping me for?
You belong to me. I belong to you forever.

BABU:
Ah, Master, spare yourself.
Forever is a very long time;
nothing's forever.
(*With great expertness, delicacy and gentleness,* BABU *massages* BENITO*'s cheeks, shakes out the flag, pours lotion from five bottles on* BENITO*'s hair, cleans the shaving materials, and stands off admiring his work*)
Master looks just like a statue.
He's like a figurehead, Don Amasa!
(DELANO *looks, then starts to walk out leaving* BENITO *and* BABU. *The curtain drops upon them.* DELANO *rejoins* PERKINS, *lounging at the rail*)

PERKINS:
Our boat is coming.

DELANO:
(*Gaily*)
I know!
I don't know how I'll explain this pomp
and squalor to my own comfortable family of a crew.
Even shaving here is like a High Mass.
There's something in a Negro, something
that makes him fit to have around your person.
His comb and brush are castanets.
What tact Babu had!
What noiseless, gliding briskness!

PERKINS:
Our boat's about along side, Sir.

DELANO:
What's more, the Negro has a sense of humor.
I don't mean their boorish giggling and teeth-showing,

I mean his easy cheerfulness in every glance and gesture.
You should have seen Babu toss that Spanish flag like a juggler,
and change it to a shaving napkin!

PERKINS:
The boat's here, Sir.

DELANO:
We need inferiors, Perkins,
more manners, more docility, no one has an inferior mind in America.

PERKINS:
Here is your crew, Sir.
(BABU *runs out from the cabin. His cheek is bleeding*)

DELANO:
Why, Babu, what has happened?

BABU:
Master will never get better from his sickness.
His bad nerves and evil fever made him use me so.
I gave him one small scratch by accident,
the only time I've nicked him, Don Amasa.
He cut me with his razor. Do you think I will die?
I'd rather die than bleed to death!

DELANO:
It's just a pinprick, Babu. You'll live.

BABU:
I must attend my master.
(*Runs back into cabin*)

DELANO:
Just a pinprick, but I wouldn't have thought
Don Benito had the stuff to swing a razor.
Up north we use our fists instead of knives.
I hope Benito's not dodging around some old grindstone
in the hold, and sharpening a knife for me.
Here, Perkins, help our men up the ladder.
(*Two immaculate* AMERICAN SAILORS *appear carrying great casks of water. Two more follow carrying net baskets of wilted pumpkins. The* NEGROES *begin to crowd forward, shouting, "We want Yankee food, we want Yankee drink!"* DELANO *grandiosely holds up a pumpkin; an* OLD NEGRO *rushes forward, snatches at the pumpkin, and knocks* DELANO *off-balance into* PERKINS*'s arms.* DELANO *gets up and knocks the* NEGRO *down with his fist. All is tense and quiet. The* SIX HATCHET-CLEANERS *lift their hatchets above their heads*)

DELANO:
(*Furious*)
Americans, stand by me! Stand by your captain!
(*Like lightning, the* AMERICANS *unsling their muskets, fix bayonets, and kneel with their guns pointing at the* NEGROES)
Don Benito, Sir, call your men to order!

BABU:
We're starving, Yankee Master. We mean no harm;
we've never been so scared.

DELANO:
You try my patience, Babu.
I am talking to Captain Cereno;
call your men to order, Sir.

BENITO:
Make them laugh, Babu. The Americans aren't going
to shoot.
(BABU *airily waves a hand. The* NEGROES *smile.* DELANO *turns to* BENITO)
You mustn't blame them too much; they're sick
and hungry.
We have kept them cooped up for ages.

DELANO:
(*As the* NEGROES *relax*)
Form them in lines, Perkins!
Each man shall have his share.
That's how we run things in the States—
to each man equally, no matter what his claims.

NEGROES:
(*Standing back, bleating like sheep*)
Feed me, Master Yankee! Feed me, Master Yankee!

DELANO:
You are much too close.
Here, Perkins, take the provisions aft.
You'll save lives by giving each as little as you can,
Be sure to keep a tally.
(FRANCESCO, *a majestic, yellow-colored mulatto, comes up to* DELANO)

FRANCESCO:
My master requests your presence at dinner, Don Amasa.

DELANO:
Tell him I have indigestion.
Tell him to keep better order on his ship.
It's always the man of good will that gets hurt;
my fist still aches from hitting that old darky.

FRANCESCO:
My master has his own methods of discipline
that are suitable for our unfortunate circumstances.
Will you come to dinner, Don Amasa?

DELANO:
I'll come. When in Rome, do as the Romans.
Excuse my quick temper, Sir.
It's better to blow up than to smoulder.
(*The scrim curtain is raised. In the cabin, a long table loaded with silver has been laid out. The locker has been closed and the Spanish flag hangs on the wall.* DON BENITO *is seated,* BABU *stands behind him. As soon as* DELANO *sits down,* FRANCESCO *begins serving with great dignity and agility*)

FRANCESCO:
A finger bowl, Don Amasa.
(*After each statement, he moves about the table*)
A napkin, Don Amasa.
A glass of American water, Don Amasa.
A slice of American pumpkin, Don Amasa.
A goblet of American cider, Don Amasa.
(DELANO *drinks a great deal of cider,* BENITO *hardly touches his*)

DELANO:
This is very courtly for a sick ship, Don Benito.
The Spanish Empire will never go down, if she keeps
her chin up.

BENITO:
I'm afraid I shan't live long enough to enjoy
your prophecy.

DELANO:
I propose a toast to the Spanish Empire
on which the sun never sets;
may you find her still standing, when you land, Sir!

BENITO:
Our Empire has lasted three hundred years,
I suppose she will last another month.
I wish I could say the same for myself. My sun is setting,
I hear the voices of the dead in this calm.

DELANO:
You hear the wind lifting;
it's bringing our two vessels together.
We are going to take you into port, Don Benito.

BENITO:
You are either too late or too early with your good works.

Our yellow fever may break out again.
You aren't going to put your men in danger, Don Amasa?

DELANO:
My boys are all healthy, Sir.

BENITO:
Health isn't God, I wouldn't trust it.

FRANCESCO:
May I fill your glass, Don Amasa?

BABU:
New wine in new bottles,
that's the American spirit, Yankee Master.
They say all men are created equal in North America.

DELANO:
We prefer merit to birth, boy.
(BABU *motions imperiously for* FRANCESCO *to leave. As he goes, bowing to the* CAPTAINS, FOUR NEGROES *play the* Marseillaise)
Why are they playing the *Marseillaise?*

BABU:
His uncle is supposed to have been in the
French Convention,
and voted for the death of the French King.

DELANO:
This polite and royal fellow is no anarchist!

BABU:
Francesco is very *ancien regime,*
he is even frightened of the Americans.
He doesn't like the way you treated King George.
Babu is more liberal.

DELANO:
A royal fellow,
this usher of yours, Don Benito!
He is as yellow as a goldenrod.
He is a king, a king of kind hearts.
What a pleasant voice he has!

BENITO:
(*Glumly*)
Francesco is a good man.

DELANO:
As long as you've known him,
he's been a worthy fellow, hasn't he?
Tell me, I am particularly curious to know.

BENITO:
Francesco is a good man.

DELANO:
I'm glad to hear it, I am glad to hear it!
You refute the saying of a planter friend of mine.
He said, "When a mulatto has a regular European face,
look out for him, he is a devil."

BENITO:
I've heard your planter's remark applied
to intermixtures of Spaniards and Indians;
I know nothing about mulattoes.

DELANO:
No, no, my friend's refuted;
if we're so proud of our white blood,
surely a little added to the blacks improves their breed.
I congratulate you on your servants, Sir.

BABU:
We've heard that Jefferson, the King of your Republic,
would like to free his slaves.

DELANO:
Jefferson has read too many books, boy,
but you can trust him. He's a gentleman and an American!
He's not lifting a finger to free his slaves.

BABU:
We hear you have a new capital modeled on Paris,
and that your President is going to set up
a guillotine on the Capitol steps.

DELANO:
Oh, Paris! I told you you could trust Mr. Jefferson, boy,
he stands for law and order like your mulatto.
Have you been to Paris, Don Benito?

BENITO:
I'm afraid I'm just a provincial Spaniard, Captain.

DELANO:
Let me tell you about Paris.
You know what French women are like—
nine parts sex and one part logic.
Well, one of them in Paris heard
that my ship was the *President Adams*. She said,
"You are descended from Adam, Captain,
you must know everything,
tell me how Adam and Eve learned to sleep together."
Do you know what I said?

BENITO:
No, Captain.

DELANO:
I said, "I guess Eve was a Frenchwoman,
the first Frenchwoman."
Do you know what she answered?

BENITO:
No, Captain Delano.

DELANO:
She said, "I was trying to provoke a philosophical
discussion, Sir."
A philosophical discussion, ha, ha!
You look serious, Sir. You know, something troubles me.

BENITO:
Something troubles you, Captain Delano?

DELANO:
I still can't understand those calms,
but let that go. The scurvy,
why did it kill off three Spaniards in every four,
and only half the blacks?
Negroes are human, but surely you couldn't have
favored them
before your own flesh and blood!

BENITO:
This is like the Inquisition, Captain Delano.
I have done the best I could.
(BABU *dabs* BENITO'*s forehead with cider*)

BABU:
Poor, poor Master; since Don Aranda died,
he trusts no one except Babu.

DELANO:
Your Babu is an uncommonly intelligent fellow;
you are right to trust him, Sir.
Sometimes I think we overdo our talk of freedom.
If you looked into our hearts, we all want slaves.

BENITO:
Disease is a mysterious thing;
it takes one man, and leaves his friend.
Only the unfortunate can understand misfortune.

DELANO:
I must return to my bosun;
he's pretty green to be left alone here.

Before I go I want to propose a last toast to you!
A good master deserves good servants!
(*He gets up. As he walks back to* PERKINS, *the scrim curtain falls, concealing* BENITO *and* BABU)
That captain must have jaundice,
I wish he kept better order.
I don't like hitting menials.

PERKINS:
I've done some looking around, Sir. I've used my eyes.

DELANO:
That's what they're for, I guess. You have to watch your step,
this hulk, this rotten piece of finery,
will fall apart. This old world needs new blood
and Yankee gunnery to hold it up.
You shouldn't mess around, though, it's their ship;
you're breaking all the laws of the sea.

PERKINS:
Do you see that man-shaped thing in canvas?

DELANO:
I see it.

PERKINS:
Behind the cloth, there's a real skeleton,
a man dressed up like Don Benito.

DELANO:
They're Catholics, and worship bones.

PERKINS:
There's writing on its coat. It says,
"I am Don Aranda," and, "Follow your leader."

DELANO:
Follow your leader?

PERKINS:
I saw two blacks unfurling a flag,
a black skull and crossbones on white silk.

DELANO:
That's piracy. We've been ordered
to sink any ship that flies that flag.
Perhaps they were playing.

PERKINS:
I saw King Atufal throw away his chains,
He called for food, the Spaniards served him two pieces of pumpkin,
and a whole bottle of your cider.

DELANO:
Don Benito has the only key to Atufal's padlock.
My cider was for the captain's table.

PERKINS:
Atufal pointed to the cabin where you were dining,
and drew a finger across his throat.

DELANO:
Who could want to kill Amasa Delano?

PERKINS:
I warned our men to be ready for an emergency.

DELANO:
You're a mind reader,
I couldn't have said better myself;
but we're at peace with Spain.

PERKINS:
I told them to return with loaded muskets
and fixed bayonets.

DELANO:
Here comes Benito. Watch how I'll humor him
and sound him out.
(BABU *brings out* BENITO'*s chair.* BENITO *sits in it*)
It's good to have you back on deck, Captain.
Feel the breeze! It holds and will increase.
My ship is moving nearer. Soon we will be together.
We have seen you through your troubles.

BENITO:
Remember, I warned you about the yellow fever.
I am surprised you haven't felt afraid.

DELANO:
Oh, that will blow away.
Everything is going to go better and better;
the wind's increasing, soon you'll have no cares.
After the long voyage, the anchor drops into the harbor.
It's a great weight lifted from the captain's heart.
We are getting to be friends, Don Benito.
My ship's in sight, the *President Adams!*
How the wind braces a man up!
I have a small invitation to issue to you.

BENITO:
An invitation?

DELANO:
I want you to take a cup of coffee
with me on my quarter deck tonight.

The Sultan of Turkey never tasted such coffee
as my old steward makes. What do you say, Don Benito?

BENITO:
I cannot leave my ship.

DELANO:
Come, come, you need a change of climate.
The sky is suddenly blue, Sir,
my coffee will make a man of you.

BENITO:
I cannot leave my ship.
Even now, I don't think you understand my position here.

DELANO:
I want to speak to you alone.

BENITO:
I am alone, as much as I ever am.

DELANO:
In America, we don't talk about money
in front of servants and children.

BENITO:
Babu is not my servant.
You spoke of money—since the yellow fever,
he has had a better head for figures than I have.

DELANO:
You embarrass me, Captain,
but since circumstances are rather special here,
I will proceed.

BENITO:
Babu takes an interest in all our expenses.

DELANO:
Yes, I am going to talk to you about your expenses.
I am responsible to my owners for all
the sails, ropes, food and carpentry I give you.
You will need a complete rerigging, almost a new ship,
  in fact,
You shall have our services at cost.

BENITO:
I know, you are a merchant.
I suppose I ought to pay you for our lives.

DELANO:
I envy you, Captain. You are the only owner
of the *San Domingo,* since Don Aranda died.
I am just an employee. Our owners would sack me,
if I followed my better instincts.

BENITO:
You can give your figures to Babu, Captain.

DELANO:
You are very offhand about money, Sir;
I don't think you realize the damage that has been done
to your ship.
Ah, you smile. I'm glad you're loosening up.
Look, the water gurgles merrily, the wind is high,
a mild light is shining. I sometimes think
such a tropical light as this must have shone
on the tents of Abraham and Isaac.
It seems as if Providence were watching over us.

PERKINS:
There are things that need explaining here, Sir.

DELANO:
Yes, Captain, Perkins saw some of your men
unfurling an unlawful flag,
a black skull and crossbones.

BENITO:
You know my only flag is the Lion and Castle of Spain.

DELANO:
No, Perkins says he saw a skull and crossbones.
That's piracy. I trust Perkins.
You've heard about how my government blew
the bowels out of the pirates at Tripoli?

BENITO:
Perhaps my Negroes . . .

DELANO:
My government doesn't intend
to let you play at piracy!

BENITO:
Perhaps my Negroes were playing.
When you take away their chains . . .

DELANO:
I'll see that you are all put back in chains,
if you start playing pirates!

PERKINS:
There's something else he can explain, Sir.

DELANO:
Yes, Perkins saw Atufal throw off his chains
and order dinner.

BABU:
Master has the key, Yankee Master.

BENITO:
I have the key.
You can't imagine how my position exhausts me, Captain.

DELANO:
I can imagine. Atufal's chains are fakes.
You and he are in cahoots, Sir!

PERKINS:
They don't intend to pay for our sails and service.
They think America is Santa Claus.

DELANO:
The United States are death on pirates and debtors.

PERKINS:
There's one more thing for him to explain, Sir.

DELANO:
Do you see that man-shaped thing covered with black cloth, Don Benito?

BENITO:
I always see it.

DELANO:
Take away the cloth. I order you to take away the cloth!

BENITO:
I cannot. Oh, Santa Maria, have mercy!

DELANO:
Of course, you can't. It's no Virgin Mary.
You have done something terrible to your friend, Don Aranda.
Take away the cloth, Perkins!
(*As* PERKINS *moves forward,* ATUFAL *suddenly stands unchained and with folded arms, blocking his way*)

BABU:
(*Dancing up and down and beside himself*)
Let them see it! Let them see it!
I can't stand any more of their insolence;
the Americans treat us like their slaves!
(BABU *and* PERKINS *meet at the man-shaped object and start pulling away the cloth.* BENITO *rushes between them, and throws them back and sprawling on the deck.* BABU *and* PERKINS *rise, and stand hunched like wrestlers, about to close in on* BENITO, *who draws his sword with a great gesture. It is only a hilt. He runs at* BABU *and knocks him down.* ATUFAL *throws off his chains and signals to the* HATCHET-CLEANERS. *They stand behind* BENITO *with raised hatchets. The Negroes shout ironically, "Evviva Benito!"*)

You too, Yankee Captain!
If you shoot, we'll kill you.

DELANO:
If a single American life is lost,
I will send this ship to the bottom,
and all Peru after it.
Do you hear me, Don Benito?

BENITO:
Don't you understand? I am as powerless as you are!

BABU:
He is as powerless as you are.

BENITO:
Don't you understand? He has been holding a knife at my back.
I have been talking all day to save your life.

BABU:
(*Holding a whip*)
Do you see this whip? When Don Aranda was out of temper,
he used to snap pieces of flesh off us with it.
Now I hold the whip.
When I snap it, Don Benito jumps!
(*Snaps the whip.* DON BENITO *flinches*)

DELANO:
(*Beginning to understand*)
It's easy to terrorize the defenseless.

BABU:
That's what we thought when Don Aranda held the whip.

DELANO:
You'll find I am made of tougher stuff than your Spaniards.

ATUFAL:
We want to kill you.

NEGROES:
We want to kill you, Yankee Captain.

DELANO:
Who could want to kill Amasa Delano?

BABU:
Of course. We want to keep you alive.
We want you to sail us back to Africa.
Has anyone told you how much you are worth, Captain?

DELANO:
I have another course in mind.

BENITO:
Yes, there's another course if you don't like Africa, there's another course.
King Atufal, show the Yankee captain
the crew that took the other course!
(*Three dead* SPANISH SAILORS *are brought on stage*)

ATUFAL:
Look at Don Aranda?

DELANO:
Yes, you are hot-tempered and discourteous, Captain.
I am going to introduce you to Don Aranda.
You have a new command, Captain. You must meet your new owner.
(*The black cloth is taken from the man-shaped object and shows a chalk-white skeleton dressed like* DON BENITO)
Don Amasa, Don Aranda!
You can see that Don Aranda was a white man like you,
because his bones are white.

NEGROES:
He is a white because his bones are white!
He is a white because his bones are white!

ATUFAL:
(*Pointing to the ribbon on the skeleton's chest*)
Do you see that ribbon?
It says, "Follow the leader."
We wrote it in his blood.

BABU:
He was a white man
even though his blood was red as ours.

NEGROES:
He is white because his bones are white!

BABU:
Don Aranda is our figurehead,
we are going to chain him to the bow of our ship
to scare off devils.

BABU:
This is the day of Jubilee,
I am raising the flag of freedom!

NEGROES:
Freedom! Freedom! Freedom!
(*The black skull and crossbones is raised on two poles. The* NEGROES *form two lines, leading up to the flag, and leave an aisle. Each man is armed with some sort of weapon*)

BABU:

Spread out the Spanish flag!

(The Lion and Castle of Spain is spread out on the deck in front of the skull and crossbones)

The Spanish flag is the road to freedom.
Don Benito mustn't hurt his white feet on the splinters.

(Kneeling in front of BENITO*)*

Your foot, Master!

(BENITO *holds out his foot.* BABU *takes off* BENITO*'s shoes)*

Give Don Benito back his sword!

(The sword-hilt is fastened back in BENITO*'s scabbard)*

Load him with chains!

(Two heavy chains are draped on BENITO*'s neck. The cane and ball are handed to him)*

Former Captain Benito Cereno, kneel!
Ask pardon of man!

BENITO:

(Kneeling)

I ask pardon for having been born a Spaniard.
I ask pardon for having enslaved my fellow man.

BABU:

Strike off the oppressor's chain!

(One of BENITO*'s chains is knocked off, then handed to* ATUFAL, *who dashes it to the deck)*

Former Captain Benito Cereno,
you must kiss the flag of freedom.

(Points to DON ARANDA*)*

Kiss the mouth of the skull!

(BENITO *walks barefoot over the Spanish flag and kisses the mouth of* DON ARANDA*)*

NEGROES:

Evviva Benito! Evviva Benito!

(Sounds are heard from PERKINS, *whose head is still covered with the sack)*

ATUFAL:

The bosun wants to kiss the mouth of freedom.

BABU:

March over the Spanish flag, Bosun.

(PERKINS *starts forward)*

DELANO:

You are dishonoring your nation, Perkins!
Don't you stand for anything?

PERKINS:

I only have one life, Sir.

(Walks over the Spanish flag and kisses the mouth of the skull)

NEGROES:
Evviva Bosun! *Evviva* Bosun!

DELANO:
You are no longer an American, Perkins!

BABU:
He was free to choose freedom, Captain.

ATUFAL:
Captain Delano wants to kiss the mouth of freedom.

BABU:
He is jealous of the bosun.

ATUFAL:
In the United States, all men are created equal.

BABU:
Don't you want to kiss the mouth of freedom, Captain?

DELANO:
(*Lifting his pocket and pointing the pistol*)
Do you see what I have in my hand?

BABU:
A pistol.

DELANO:
I am unable to miss at this distance.

BABU:
You must take your time, Yankee Master.
You must take your time.

DELANO:
I am unable to miss.

BABU:
You can stand there like a block of wood
as long as you want to, Yankee Master.
You will drop asleep, then we will tie you up,
and make you sail us back to Africa.

(*General laughter. Suddenly, there's a roar of gunfire. Several* NEGROES, *mostly women, fall.* AMERICAN SEAMEN *in spotless blue and white throw themselves in a lying position on deck.* MORE *kneel above them, then* MORE *stand above these. All have muskets and fixed bayonets. The First Row fires. More* NEGROES *fall. They start to retreat. The Second Row fires. More* NEGROES *fall. They retreat further. The Third Row fires. The Three* AMERICAN LINES *march forward, but all the* NEGROES *are either dead or in retreat.* DON BENITO *has been wounded. He staggers over to* DELANO *and shakes his hand*)

BENITO:
You have saved my life.
I thank you for my life.

DELANO:
A man can only do what he can,
We have saved American lives.

PERKINS:
(*Pointing to* ATUFAL'*s body*)
We have killed King Atufal,
we have killed their ringleader.
(BABU *jumps up. He is unwounded*)

BABU:
I was the King. Babu, not Atufal,
was the king, who planned, dared and carried out
the seizure of this ship, the *San Domingo.*
Untouched by blood myself, I had all
the most dangerous and useless Spaniards killed.
I freed my people from their Egyptian bondage.
The heartless Spaniards slaved for me like slaves.
(BABU *steps back, and quickly picks up a crown from the litter*)
This is my crown.
(*Puts crown on his head. He snatches* BENITO'*s rattan cane*)
This is my rod.
(*Picks up silver ball*)
This is the earth.
(*Holds the ball out with one hand and raises the cane*)
This is the arm of the angry God.
(*Smashes the ball*)

PERKINS:
Let him surrender. Let him surrender.
We want to save someone.

BENITO:
My God how little these people understand!

BABU:
(*Holding a white handkerchief and raising both his hands*)
Yankee Master understand me. The future is with us.

DELANO:
(*Raising his pistol*)
This is your future.
(BABU *falls and lies still.* DELANO *pauses, then slowly empties the five remaining barrels of his pistol into the body. Lights dim*)

CURTAIN

Critics who suffer from the passion to define and to graph have regularly been foiled in their attempts to plot the modern in poetry. Does it begin with such great nineteenth-century romantics as Coleridge, Wordsworth, and Baudelaire? Or did the significant ancestral figures—poets like Yeats, Pound, Eliot, and Williams—all flourish in the twentieth century?

If to be modern means to break through an imprisoning tradition, each group may claim the title. The earlier poets felt that they were liberating themselves from a narrow, conventional view of man as a social creature; from an artificial and outworn diction; from an overstructured and over-rehearsed subject matter. And the later poets felt that they were rebelling against the blurred focus, the excessive emotionality, and the relentless egoism of the predecessors.

But such historical notations, while largely accurate, really miss the point. Every new way of writing originates in a revolt against the sterile establishment order, engages in a symbolic slaughter of the "enemies," and then, after a while, begins to reabsorb them. In the course of time the ritual is repeated, with a new vanguard and new victims. Precisely because *modern* implies flux, it resists easy formulation. Modern poetry, more than any other, must be sensed to be known. It is poetry that seems to us, alive and reading *now,* apposite to our needs, drives, hopes, despairs, frustrations—to the whole tangle of our feeling and thinking.

Even so small a nondefinition must be shrunk for every individual reader. Because each of us is a different tangle. Because what moves me bores you. Because your ears and mine are attuned to different rhythms. Our discordant subjectivities, then, govern how much we may say; and finally we say something as tentative, brief, and nearly as useless as this: The term

POETRY

"modern poetry" describes the kind of poetry that seems urgent to each of us, separately, *now.*

Nearly useless; nevertheless, not harmful. Firmer and larger statements about the nature and limits of modern poetry have led to confusion, and sometimes, desperation. One anthologist, for example, insists that it means poetry "written in the last ten years" (which updates the implicit definition of some aging English professors: "the poetry that was new when I was an undergraduate"). The trouble with the dateline imposed by the anthologist is that poems refuse to stay on the proper side of it. Some poems written in the past ten years impress most readers as being only accidentally modern, while other poems written a half-century ago seem truly in the modern idiom.

Perhaps there is no modern poetry but only "modern poetries"? Robert Creeley's delicate images, each adjusted to a breath (whose, it is not always clear)—what resemblance do they bear to the fierce, concentrated metaphors of Ted Hughes, or the taut, tormented lines of Sylvia Plath? And the relaxed streetside tones of Lawson Inada—how are they related to the cryptic catalogues of Kenneth Gangemi and the blues rhythms of Langston Hughes? And yet no sensitive reader could date their work as belonging to any time but our own, or doubt that it is the immediate and highly individualistic response to our present condition. For modern poets are the beneficiaries of several great victories. They no longer have to fight the battle against formal restraints: the convention of the metrical line has been overthrown. They no longer have to struggle for the enlargement of subject matter: any subject from roses to corpses, from complexes to computers is a fit subject for poetry today. They no longer have to refute the philistines of the lucid: their language may record the complexities and ambiguities of the journey inward, celebrate or recoil from self, capture the process of perception rather than its content, in whatever terms the feeling demands.

Every poet of course forms a school of one. Yet the reader may find it hard to resist the impulse to plot kinship systems (even though many slippery poets will elude his coordinates). For while all poets have individual voices, distinctive rhythms, unique visions, there are nevertheless some family resemblances among them. Several currently prevailing idioms of poetry are tentatively outlined below:

Poetry as confession or *auto-analysis.* The self becomes the obsessive image; the suffering psyche drives the poem; the poet tries to cure the self (and thereby the reader?). Sylvia Plath and Anne Sexton, for instance.

Poetry as process. The "speaking self" begets the poem; the poet's objective is to discover "the external equivalent of the speaking self" (for example, Robert Creeley and Gary Snyder).

Poetry as criticism. The poem turns outward, toward the world, to locate its subject; then the poet absorbs it, changes it, and shapes it by the force of his imagination and sensibility (Lawrence Ferlinghetti and Charles Bukowski; June Jordan and Raymond Patterson).

Poetry as encapsulated form. The poem centers on itself, its words bound its world; it becomes its own sufficient symbol (William Knott and Denise Levertov).

Poetry as shard. The poem lives on a broken-off chunk of larger world; it achieves a discontinuous, often mysterious identity (Ted Hughes and Erica Jong).

Poetry as invocation. The poet tries to transcend the limits of the profane world and to achieve a state of ecstasy, either by spiritual discipline or by stimulants from other sources (Allen Ginsberg).

Very likely the reader will want to reconstruct the categories or assign other names to them. He has the sanction of the editors and the poets: for the poems are now his.

David Antin

David Antin was born in 1932 in New York City and lived in Brooklyn through his early manhood. He attended The City College of New York between the years 1953 and 1957, and then traveled around the United States "before Holiday Inn conquered the country." He settled "more or less" at Solana Beach near San Francisco, where he lives on "health food and suspect meat." His poetry has appeared in such periodicals as *Caterpillar, The Nation, The Paris Review,* and *Sumac.* His first book was his *Autobiography* (1967), followed by *Definitions* (1967), *Code of Flag Behavior* (1968), *Meditations* (1971), and his latest book, *Talking* (1972). He teaches graphics and poetry at the Santa Cruz campus of the University of California. He says: "I watch television once a month and observe the lead content of the atmosphere rising."

Antin's work obliterates the conventional line between prose and poetry. Always experimental, the form is as tentative as the statement, and though Antin has a whimsical sense of humor reminiscent of Richard Brautigan's or Kenneth Gangemi's, his explorations in language are both corrosive and unique.

Meditation 2

when someone is preparing to catch something you would suppose he is prepared to be caught by it   so it seems surprising when a passenger on the 8th Avenue Express chooses to get off at 23rd Street or a fisherman refuses to cling to his side of the line   still when it comes to it you may not want to wind up like Reiser for any line drive stunned and creeping away from the wall

Meditation 4

if a sick man enters a house the members of the household are all more or less susceptible to his disease   and it will spread by contact from the infected to the uninfected   and each infected will run the course of his sickness and recover or die of his sickness   and his chances to recover or die of his sickness will vary

SOURCE: David Antin, *Meditations* (Los Angeles: Black Sparrow Press, 1971), p. 25. Reprinted by permission of the publisher.

SOURCE: David Antin, *Meditations* (Los Angeles: Black Sparrow Press, 1971), p. 27. Reprinted by permission of the publisher.

from day to day in the course of his sickness   and his chances of conveying his sickness to the uninfected will vary from day to day   as the sickness spreads there will be fewer and fewer members who may become infected   one day the sickness will come to an end

Fifteen Verbs for the Astronauts

philip
one of you may be named philip
though perhaps you cant bear to be called by that name
philip
i am aware that when you begin to step down from your capsule
there is some danger of disorientation
and i beseech you to be careful
i also bid you to remember
that the clothes you are wearing
and the house you inhabit no matter how costly
were bid for by some contractor
and are the products of our society
which is not a consumer's society
but a producer's society
as you are bound to find out
though perhaps only after you have felt its bite
philip
take care not to bleed on the moon
or blow a fuse in your head
you will break the heart of our National Space Agency
and bring disgrace to our international efforts
we are building all the hopes of the Free World on your success
which we all regard as our success
we are all bursting with pride in you philip
and when you get back we are all going to go out & buy you a beer

Consideration 1

1. it is not in the right place
2. its inartistic
3. a public service would be better
4. it costs too much

SOURCE: David Antin, *Meditations* (Los Angeles: Black Sparrow Press, 1971), p. 26. Reprinted by permission of the publisher.

SOURCE: David Antin, *Meditations* (Los Angeles: Black Sparrow Press, 1971), p. 46. Reprinted by permission of the publisher.

Consideration 2

1. i dont like her
2. because she is selfish
3. cruel
4. but she is admirable
5. has clever ways

Consideration 3

1. it was interesting
2. it was also practical

Consideration 4

1. they are easily handled
2. the corners are rounded
3. instead of sharp
4. they are smart
5. indestructible

Consideration 5

1. we have the suit
2. you have no chance

Consideration 6

1. it allows clear vision
2. it is adjustable

SOURCE: David Antin, *Meditations* (Los Angeles: Black Sparrow Press, 1971), p. 47. Reprinted by permission of the publisher.

SOURCE: David Antin, *Meditations* (Los Angeles: Black Sparrow Press, 1971), p. 48. Reprinted by permission of the publisher.

SOURCE: David Antin, *Meditations* (Los Angeles: Black Sparrow Press, 1971), p. 49. Reprinted by permission of the publisher.

SOURCE: David Antin, *Meditations* (Los Angeles: Black Sparrow Press, 1971), p. 50. Reprinted by permission of the publisher.

SOURCE: David Antin, *Meditations* (Los Angeles: Black Sparrow Press, 1971), p. 51. Reprinted by permission of the publisher.

Gwendolyn Brooks

Poetess Gwendolyn Brooks was born in 1917 in Topeka, Kansas, but grew up on Chicago's South Side, where she lived until she moved to New York City in 1971. She began to submit poems to the Chicago *Defender,* a black newspaper, when she was seventeen, and about seventy-five of them were published in a column called "Lights and Shadows." After graduating from college at nineteen, she worked as a typist for a while and then as a newspaperwoman. She married in 1934 and between the birth of her first and second child, she attended writing classes at the South Side Community Art Center.

Her first volume of poetry was published before she was thirty, *A Street in Bronzeville* (1945). *Annie Allen,* her next volume, won a major prize from *Poetry Magazine* and the Pulitzer Award in 1950, making her the first black writer to be so honored. Her only novel, *Maud Martha,* was published in 1953, and a book for children called *Bronzeville Boys and Girls* appeared three years later. Her other books include *The Bean Eaters* (1960), *Selected Poems* (1963), and *In the Mecca* (1968). The two sermons on the Warpland and "Malcolm X," from the last volume, reveal that Ms. Brooks has lost none of her bitter power or her fierce feeling for black existence, often expressed in the "gospel" style that still has vitality among her people today. She taught at The City College of New York during the Fall semester of 1971. In 1973 she published *Report From Part One,* "an assemblage of photographs, interviews, and letters on growing up in Chicago and coming of age in the Black Arts movement."

The Sermon on the Warpland

"The fact that we are black is our ultimate reality."

RON KARENGA

And several strengths from drowsiness campaigned
but spoke in Single Sermon on the warpland.

And went about the warpland saying No.
"My people, black and black, revile the River.
Say that the River turns, and turn the River.

Say that our Something in doublepod contains
seeds for the coming hell and health together.

Prepare to meet
(sisters, brothers) the brash and terrible weather;
the pains;
the bruising; the collapse of bestials, idols.
But then oh then!—the stuffing of the hulls!
the seasoning of the perilously sweet!
the health! the heralding of the clear obscure!

Build now your Church, my brothers, sisters. Build
never with brick nor Corten nor with granite.
Build with lithe love. With love like lion-eyes.
With love like morningrise.
With love like black, our black—
luminously indiscreet;
complete; continuous."

The Second Sermon on the Warpland

For Walter Bradford

[1.]

This is the urgency: Live!
and have your blooming in the noise of the whirlwind.

[2.]

Salve salvage in the spin.
Endorse the splendor splashes;
stylize the flawed utility;
prop a malign or failing light—
but know the whirlwind is our commonwealth.
Not the easy man, who rides above them all,
not the jumbo brigand,
not the pet bird of poets, that sweetest sonnet,
shall straddle the whirlwind.
Nevertheless, live.

[3.]

All about are the cold places,
all about are the pushmen and jeopardy, theft—
all about are the stormers and scramblers but
what must our Season be, which starts from Fear?
Live and go out.
Define and
medicate the whirlwind.

SOURCE: Gwendolyn Brooks, *In the Mecca* (New York: Harper & Row, Publishers, 1968), pp. 52–4.

[4.]

The time
cracks into furious flower. Lifts its face
all unashamed. And sways in wicked grace.
Whose half-black hands assemble oranges
is tom-tom hearted
(goes in bearing oranges and boom).
And there are bells for orphans—
and red and shriek and sheen.
A garbageman is dignified
as any diplomat.
Big Bessie's feet hurt like nobody's business,
but she stands—bigly—under the unruly scrutiny, stands in the wild weed.

In the wild weed
she is a citizen,
and is a moment of highest quality; admirable.

It is lonesome, yes. For we are the last of the loud.
Nevertheless, live.

Conduct your blooming in the noise and whip of the whirlwind.

Malcolm X

For Dudley Randall

Original.
Ragged-round.
Rich-robust.

He had the hawk-man's eyes.
We gasped. We saw the maleness.
The maleness raking out and making guttural the air
and pushing us to walls.

And in a soft and fundamental hour
a sorcery devout and vertical
beguiled the world.

He opened us—
who was a key,

who was a man.

SOURCE: Gwendolyn Brooks, *In the Mecca* (New York: Harper & Row, Publishers, 1968), p. 39.

A Street in Bronzeville: Southeast Corner

The School of Beauty's a tavern now.
The Madam is underground.
Out at Lincoln, among the graves
Her own is early found.
Where the thickest, tallest monument
Cuts grandly into the air
The Madam lies, contentedly.
Her fortune, too, lies there,
Converted into cool hard steel
And right red velvet lining;
While over her tan impassivity
Shot silk is shining.

Beverly Hills, Chicago

"and the people live till they have white hair"
E. M. PRICE

The dry brown coughing beneath their feet,
(Only a while, for the handyman is on his way)
These people walk their golden gardens.
We say ourselves fortunate to be driving by today.

That we may look at them, in their gardens where
The summer ripeness rots. But not raggedly.
Even the leaves fall down in lovelier patterns here.
And the refuse, the refuse is a neat brilliancy.

When they flow sweetly into their houses
With softness and slowness touched by that everlasting gold,
We know what they go to. To tea. But that does not mean
They will throw some little black dots into some water and add sugar
and the juice of the cheapest lemons that are sold,

While downstairs that woman's vague phonograph bleats, "Knock me
a kiss."
And the living all to be made again in the sweatingest physical manner
Tomorrow. . . . Not that anybody is saying that these people have no
trouble.
Merely that it is trouble with a gold-flecked beautiful banner.

Nobody is saying that these people do not ultimately cease to be. And
Sometimes their passings are even more painful than ours.
It is just that so often they live till their hair is white.
They make excellent corpses, among the expensive flowers. . . .

Nobody is furious. Nobody hates these people.
At least, nobody driving by in this car.
It is only natural, however, that it should occur to us
How much more fortunate they are than we are.

It is only natural that we should look and look
At their wood and brick and stone
And think, while a breath of pine blows,
How different these are from our own.

We do not want them to have less.
But it is only natural that we should think we have not enough.
We drive on, we drive on.
When we speak to each other our voices are a little gruff.

Charles Bukowski

Charles Bukowski was born in Andernach, Germany, in 1920 and was brought to the United States at the age of two. He was raised in Los Angeles where he continues to live, write, and read his poetry before bewitched or bewildered college students. He began writing when he was thirty-five and now has fifteen books of poetry and prose to his credit, among them *Longshot Poems for Broke Players, Run with the Hunted, Cold Dogs in a Courtyard, Confessions of a Man Insane Enough To Live with Beasts, At Terror Street and Agony Way, Poems Written Before Jumping Out of an 8 Story Window, Notes of a Dirty Old Man, The Days Run Away Like Wild Horses over the Hills* (1970) from which the following poems are taken, and *Mockingbird Wish Me Luck* (1972). A poet of beer cans, flop houses, derelicts, alcoholics, and the variegated human detritus of an indifferent technological society who incredibly remain more vital and interesting than the overseers, Bukowski comes closer to being a "people's poet" than anyone since Vachel Lindsay. Though apparently ungoverned and undisciplined in his personal life, he writes: "To work with an art form / does not mean to / screw off like a tape-worm / with his belly full, / nor does it justify grandeur / or greed, nor at all times / seriousness, but I would guess / that it calls upon the best men / at their best times. . . ."

Riot

the reason for the riot was we kept getting beans
and a guard grabbed a colored boy who threw his on the floor
and somebody touched a button
and everybody was grabbing everybody;
I clubbed my best friend behind the ear
somebody threw coffee in my face
(what the hell, you couldn't drink it)
and I got out to the yard
and I heard the guns going
and it seemed like every con had a knife but me,
and all I could do was pray and run
and I didn't have a god and was fat from playing
poker for pennies with my cellmate,

SOURCE: Charles Bukowski, *The Days Run Away Like Wild Horses over the Hills* (Los Angeles: Black Sparrow Press, 1970), p. 42. Reprinted by permission of the publisher.

and the warden's voice started coming over the cans,
and I heard later, in the confusion,
the cook raped a sailor,
and I lost my shaving cream, a pack of smokes
and a copy of the *New Yorker;*
also 3 men were shot,
a half dozen knifed,
35 put in the hole,
all yard privileges suspended,
the screws as jittery as L.A. bookies,
the prison radio off,
real quiet,
visitors sent home,
but the next morning
we did get our mail—
a letter from St. Louis:
Dear Charles, I am sorry you are in prison,
but you cannot break the law,
and there was a pressed carnation,
perfume, the looming of outside,
kisses and panties,
laughter and beer,
and that night for dinner
they marched us all back down
to the beans.

These Mad Windows That Taste Life and Cut Me if I Go Through Them

I've always lived on second and third floors or higher
all my life
but I got some woman pregnant
and since she wasn't my wife
we moved over here—
we were in the back at first
2nd floor rear
as Mr. and Mrs.—
a new start—
and there was a madwoman in this
place and she kept the shades drawn
and hollered obscenities in the dark
(I thought she was pretty sharp)
but they took her away one day

SOURCE: Charles Bukowski, *The Days Run Away Like Wild Horses over the Hills* (Los Angeles: Black Sparrow Press, 1970), pp. 105–108. Reprinted by permission of the publisher.

and we moved in here and had the baby,
a beautiful skunk of a child with pale blue eyes
who made me swallow my heart like a cherry in a chilled drink,
but the woman decided I was insane too
and moved the child and herself to Hollywood
and I give them what money I can—
but most of the time I lay around all day
sweating in bed
wondering how much longer I can fool them
listening to my landlord outside
watering his lawn
46 years hanging on my bones
and big green tears cascade ha, ha,
down my face and are tabulated by my dirty pillow:
all those years shot through the head
assassinated forever
drunk senseless
hobbled and slugged in factories
poked with bad dreams
dripping away in mouse- and ghost-infested rooms
across an America without meaning,
boy o boy.

about 3 p.m. I get up
having failed to sleep but more than a few minutes
anyhow
and then I put on an old undershirt
crisp fresh torn shorts
and a pair of stolen army pants
and I pull up the shades
and sit a little back in a hard folding chair
near a window on the streetside
and then they come by,
young girls
fresh fluid divine intelligent
drinks of orange juice
rides in air-conditioned elevators,
in blue in green in yellow in motion
in red in waves
in squads and battalions of laughter
they laugh at me and for me,
old 46, at attention, pig green eyes
like a Van Gogh bursting and breaking
the trachea and tits of the earth and the sun,
my god, look, here I am
and no matter what I said to them
they would run away
I would be reported as an old goof

babbling in the marketplace for hard pennies—
they expect me to use the bathroom,
a shadow-picture for their singing flesh
and the pliers of my hand—
a good citizen jacksoff, votes, and looks at Bob Hope—
and even old maids
with husbands killed
making swivel chairs in industry
they walk by
in green in yellow in red
and they have bodies like highschool girls
they perch on their stilts and dare me to break
custom

but to have any of these would take weeks and months
of torture—introduction, niceties, conversation that
cleaves the soul like a rusty axe—
no, no, god damn it! no more!

a man who cannot adjust to society is called a
psychotic, and the boy in the Texas tower
who shot 49 and killed 15 was one,
although in the Marine Corps he got the o.k.
to go ahead—it's all in the way you're dressed
and if the beehive says the project
protects the Queen and Goodyear Rubber and so
forth,
but the way I see it from this window
his action was nothing extraordinary or
unexpected and psychiatrists are just paid liars
of a continuing social
disorder.

and soon I get up from the window
and move around
and if I turn on the radio
and luck on Shostakovich or Mahler
or sit down to type a letter to the president,
the voices begin all around me—
"HEY! KNOCK IT OFF!"
"YOU SON OF A BITCH! WE'LL CALL THE LAW!"

on each side of me are two high-rise apartments
things lit at night with blue and green lights
and they have swimming pools that everybody has
too much class to get into
but the rent is very high
and they sit looking at their walls
decorated with pictures of people with chopped-off

heads
and wait to go back to
WORK,
meanwhile, they sense that my sounds are not
their sounds—
66 people on each side of my head
in love with Green Berets and piranhas—
"GOD DAMN YOU, COOL IT!"

these I cannot see through my window
and for this I am glad
my stomach is in bad shape from drinking cheap wine,
and so for them
I become quiet
I listen to their sounds—
their baseball games, their comedies, their quiz shows,
their dry kisses, their kindling safety,
their hard bodies stuffed into the walls and murdered,
and I go to the table
take my madman's crayons
and begin drawing them on my walls
all of them—
loving, fucking, eating, shitting,
frightened of Christ, frightened of poverty,
frightened of life
they crawl my walls like roaches
and I draw suns between them
and axes and guns and towers and babies
and dogs, cats, animals, and it becomes
difficult to distinguish the animal from the
other, and my whole body sweats, stinks,
as I tremble like a liar from the truth of things,
and then I drink some water, take off my clothing and
go to bed
where I will not sleep
first pulling down all the shades
and then waiting for 3 p.m.
my girls my ladies my way
with nothing going through and nothing coming in and
nothing going out, Cathedrals and Art Museums and
mountains wasted, only the salt of myself, some ants,
old newspapers, my shame, my shame
at not having
killed
(razor, carcrash, turpentine, gaspipe)
(good job, marriage, investments in the market)
what is left of
myself.

Robert Creeley

Poet, novelist, and teacher, Robert Creeley was born in 1926 in Arlington, Massachusetts. He enrolled at Harvard, but soon left in 1943 to work in the American Field Service in war-torn Burma and in India. After a brief return to Harvard, he traveled and lived in France, Mallorca, Mexico, and Guatemala. He received his B.A. from Black Mountain College in 1954, then taught there and helped Charles Olsen to edit *The Black Mountain Review,* a literary publication that changed the course of modern poetry.

Creeley took a master's degree at the University of New Mexico and joined the English department. In 1963, he went to the State University of New York at Buffalo to teach poetry. He spent a year at the University of British Columbia and has returned to New Mexico for short stints of teaching. His work includes *A Form of Women* (1959), *For Love, Poems 1950–60* (1962), *Words* (1967), *The Finger* (1968), *5 Numbers* (1968), *Divisions and Early Poems* (1968), *Pieces* (1969), *Contexts of Poetry* (1972), *A Day Book* (1973), and a novel, *The Island.* He lives with his wife in a community of artists in Bolinas, California.

As the following poems indicate, he was strongly influenced by Olsen's theory of "projectivist" verse which creates a poem, as Creeley expresses it, by "the lines / talking, taking, always the beat from / the breath." He has extended William Carlos Williams's statement that there are "no ideas but in things" to "things are made of words." In the phrase of one critic, he writes poetry of "presentative simultaneity."

A Wicker Basket

Comes the time when it's later
and onto your table the headwaiter
puts the bill, and very soon after
rings out the sound of lively laughter—

Picking up change, hands like a walrus,
and a face like a barndoor's,
and a head without an apparent size,
nothing but two eyes—

So that's you, man,
or me. I make it as I can,

I pick up, I go
faster than they know—

Out the door, the street like a night,
any night, and no one in sight,
but then, well, there she is,
old friend Liz—

And she opens the door of her cadillac,
I step in back,
and we're gone.
She turns me on—

There are very huge stars, man, in the sky,
and from somewhere very far off someone hands me a slice of apple pie,
with a gob of white, white ice cream on top of it,
and I eat it—

Slowly. And while certainly
they are laughing at me, and all around me is racket
of these cats not making it, I make it

in my wicker basket.

Jack's Blues

I'm going to roll up
a monkey and smoke it, put
an elephant in the pot. I'm going out
and never come back.

What's better than that.
Lying on your back, flat
on your back with your
eyes to the view.

Oh the view is blue, I saw that
too, yesterday and you,
red eyes and blue,
funked.

I'm going to roll up
a rug and smoke it, put
the car in the garage and I'm
gone, like a sad old candle.

SOURCE: Robert Creeley, *For Love* (New York: Charles Scribner's Sons, 1962), p. 121.

The Operation

By Saturday I said you would be better on Sunday.
The insistence was a part of a reconciliation.

Your eyes bulged, the grey
light hung on you, you were hideous.

My involvement is just an old
habitual relationship.

Cruel, cruel to describe
what there is no reason to describe.

The Whip

I spent a night turning in bed,
my love was a feather, a flat

sleeping thing. She was
very white

and quiet, and above us on
the roof, there was another woman I

also loved, had
addressed myself to in

a fit she
returned. That

encompasses it. But now I was
lonely, I yelled,

but what is that? Ugh,
she said, beside me, she put

her hand on
my back, for which act

I think to say this
wrongly.

SOURCE: Robert Creeley, *For Love* (New York: Charles Scribner's Sons, 1962), p. 34.

SOURCE: Robert Creeley, *For Love* (New York: Charles Scribner's Sons, 1962), p. 51.

The Name

Be natural,
wise
as you can be,
my daughter,

let my name
be in you flesh
I gave you
in the act of

loving your mother,
all your days
her ways,
the woman in you

brought from
sensuality's measure,
no other,
there was no thought

of it but such
pleasure all women
must be in her,
as you. But not wiser,

not more of nature
than her hair,
the eyes
she gives you.

There will not be another
woman such as you
are. Remember
your mother,

the way you came,
the days of waiting.
Be natural,
daughter, wise

as you can be,
all my daughters,
be women
for men

SOURCE: Robert Creeley, *For Love* (New York: Charles Scribner's Sons, 1962), pp. 144–45.

when that time comes.
Let the rhetoric
stay with me
your father. Let

me talk about it,
saving you such
vicious self-
exposure, let you

pass it on
in you. I cannot
be more than the man
who watches.

Lawrence Ferlinghetti

Lawrence Ferlinghetti was born in Yonkers, New York, in 1919. He received an A.B. from the University of North Carolina, an M.A. from Columbia, and *doctorate de l'université* from the Sorbonne. With Peter Martin he founded the first all-paperback bookstore in the country, City Lights, in San Francisco. It quickly became a publishing house which he still runs. Along with Jack Kerouac and Allen Ginsberg ("Howl" was published by City Lights), Ferlinghetti gave impetus to the "beat movement" during the fifties and the "San Francisco" renaissance of the sixties (Kenneth Rexroth, Michael McClure, Philip Whalen, and Brother Antoninus are associated with these developments).

His first major book of poems, *A Coney Island of the Mind* (1958), has been more popular than any other volume of American poetry published in the last fifteen years. He is a firm believer in public readings, and many of his are available on records. In addition to poetry [*Pictures of a Gone World* (1955) and *Starting from San Francisco* (1961) are only two of his collections], Ferlinghetti has written a novel, *Her* (1960), and some plays, *Unfair Arguments with Existence* (1963). His poetry, now furiously anti-militaristic and anti-capitalistic, continues to appear in such publications as *The Evergreen Review,* and one of his most recent collections is *Back Roads to Far Places.*

from "Oral Messages"

DOG *

The dog trots freely in the street
and sees reality
and the things he sees
are bigger than himself
and the things he sees
are his reality
Drunks in doorways

* "Dog" is one of a group of poems that were "conceived specifically for jazz accompaniment and as such should be considered as spontaneously spoken 'oral messages' rather than as poems written for the printed page. As a result of continued experimental reading with jazz, they are still in a state of change."—Author's note.

Moons on trees
The dog trots freely thru the street
and the things he sees
are smaller than himself
Fish on newsprint
Ants in holes
Chickens in Chinatown windows
their heads a block away
The dog trots freely in the street
and the things he smells
smell something like himself
The dog trots freely in the street
past puddles and babies
cats and cigars
poolrooms and policemen
He doesn't hate cops
He merely has no use for them
and he goes past them
and past the dead cows hung up whole
in front of the San Francisco Meat Market
He would rather eat a tender cow
than a tough policeman
though either might do
And he goes past the Romeo Ravioli Factory
and past Coit's Tower
and past Congressman Doyle
He's afraid of Coit's Tower
but he's not afraid of Congressman Doyle
although what he hears is very discouraging
very depressing
very absurd
to a sad young dog like himself
to a serious dog like himself
But he has his own free world to live in
His own fleas to eat
He will not be muzzled
Congressman Doyle is just another
fire hydrant
to him
The dog trots freely in the street
and has his own dog's life to live
and to think about
and to reflect upon
touching and tasting and testing everything
investigating everything
without benefit of perjury
a real realist
with a real tale to tell

and a real tail to tell it with
a real live
barking
democratic dog
engaged in real
free enterprise
with something to say
about ontology
something to say
about reality
and how to see it
and how to hear it
with his head cocked sideways
at streetcorners
as if he is just about to have
his picture taken
for Victor Records
listening for
His Master's Voice
and looking
like a living questionmark
into the
great gramophone
of puzzling existence
with its wondrous hollow horn
which always seems
just about to spout forth
some Victorious answer
to everything

THE GREAT CHINESE DRAGON

The great Chinese dragon which is the greatest dragon in all the world and which once upon a time was towed across the Pacific by a crew of coolies rowing in an open boat—was the first real live dragon ever actually to reach these shores

And the great Chinese dragon passing thru the Golden Gate spouting streams of water like a string of fireboats then broke loose somewhere near China Camp gulped down a hundred Chinese seamen and forthwith ate up all the shrimp in San Francisco Bay

And the great Chinese dragon was therefore forever after confined in a Chinatown basement and ever since allowed out only for Chinese New Year's parades and other Unamerican demonstrations paternally watched-over by those benevolent men in blue who represent our more advanced civiliza-

SOURCE: Lawrence Ferlinghetti, *Starting from San Francisco* (New York: New Directions Publishing Corporation, 1961), pp. 252–55.

tion which has reached such a high state of democracy as to allow even a few barbarians to carry on their quaint native customs in our midst
And thus the great Chinese dragon which is the greatest dragon in all the world now can only be seen creeping out of an Adler Alley cellar like a worm out of a hole sometime during the second week in February every year when it sorties out of hibernation in its Chinese storeroom pushed from behind by a band of fortythree Chinese electricians and technicians who stuff its peristaltic accordion-body up thru a sidewalk delivery entrance
And first the swaying snout appears and then the eyes at ground level feeling along the curb and then the head itself casting about and swaying and heaving finally up to the corner of Grant Avenue itself where a huge paper sign proclaims the *World's Largest Chinatown*
And the great Chinese dragon's jaws wired permanently agape as if by a demented dentist to display the Cadmium teeth as the hungry head heaves out into Grant Avenue right under the sign and raising itself with a great snort of fire suddenly proclaims the official firecracker start of the Chinese New Year
And the lightbulb eyes lighting up and popping out on coiled wire springs and the body stretching and rocking further and further around the corner and down Grant Avenue like a caterpillar roller-coaster with the eyes sprung out and waving in the air like the blind feelers of some mechanical praying mantis and the eyes blinking on and off with Chinese red pupils and tiny bamboo-blind eyelids going up and down
And still the tail of the dragon in the Adler Alley cellar uncoiling and unwinding out into the street with the fortythree Chinese technicians still stuffing the dragon out the hole in the sidewalk and the head of the dragon now three blocks away in the middle of the parade of fancy floats presided over by Chinese virgins
And here comes the St. Mary's Chinese Girls' Drum Corps and here come sixteen white men in pith helmets beating big bass drums representing the Order of the Moose and here comes a gang of happy car salesmen disguised as Islam Shriners and here comes a chapter of the Order of Improved Red Men and here comes a cordon of motorcycle cops in crash helmets with radios going followed by a small papier-mâché lion fed with Nekko wafers and run by two guys left over from a Ten-Ten festival which in turn is followed by the great Chinese dragon itself gooking over balconies as it comes

And the great Chinese dragon has eaten a hundred humans and their
legs pop out of his underside and are his walking legs which
are not mentioned in the official printed program in which
he is written up as the Great Golden Dragon made in Hong
Kong to the specifications of the Chinese Chamber of
Commerce and he represents the force and mystery of life
and his head sways in the sky between the balconies as he
comes followed by six Chinese boy scouts wearing Keds
and carrying strings of batteries that light up the dragon like
a nighttime freeway
And he has lain all winter among a heap of collapsed paper lanterns
and green rubber lizards and ivory backscratchers with the
iron sidewalk doors closed over his head but he has now
sprung up with the first sign of Spring like the force of life
itself and his head sways in the sky and gooks in green windows as he comes
And he is a monster with the head of a dog and the body of a serpent
risen yearly out of the sea to devour a virgin thrown
from a cliff to appease him and he is a young man handsome and drunk ogling the girls and he has high ideals
and a hundred sport shoes and he says No to Mother and he
is a big red table the world will never tilt and he has big
eyes everywhere thru which he sees all womankind milk-
white and dove-breasted and he will eat their waterflowers
for he is the cat with future feet wearing Keds and he eats
cake out of pastry windows and is hungrier and more
potent and more powerful and more omniverous than the
papier-mâché lion run by two guys and he is the great earth-
worm of lucky life filled with flowing Chinese semen and he
considers his own and our existence in its most profound
sense as he comes and he has no Christian answer to the
existential question even as he sees the spiritual everywhere translucent in the material world and he does not
want to escape the responsibility of being a dragon or the
consequences of his long horny tail still buried in the basement but the blue citizens on their talking cycles think that
he wants to escape and at all costs he must not be allowed
to escape because the great Chinese dragon is the greatest
potential dragon in all the world and if allowed to escape
from Chinatown might gallop away up their new freeway
at the Broadway entrance mistaking it for a Great Wall of
China or some other barbarian barrier and so go careening
along it chewing up stanchions and signposts and belching
forth some strange disintegrating medium which might melt
down the great concrete walls of America and they are
afraid of how far the great Chinese dragon might really go
starting from San Francisco and so they have secretly and

securely tied down the very end of his tail in its hole
so that
this great pulsing phallus of
life at the very end of its parade at the very end of Chinatown gives one wild orgasm of a shudder and rolls over
fainting in the bright night street since even for a dragon
every orgasm is a little death
And then the great Chinese dragon starts silently shrinking and
shriveling up and drawing back and back and back to its
first cave and the soft silk skin wrinkles up and shrinks
and shrinks on its sprung bamboo bones and the handsome
dejected head hangs down like a defeated prizefighter's
and so is stuffed down again at last into its private place
and the cellar sidewalk doors press down again over the
great wilted head with one small hole of an eye blinking still
thru the gratings of the metal doors as the great Chinese
dragon gives one last convulsive earthquake shake and rolls
over dead-dog to wait another white year for the final coming and the final sowing of his oats and teeth

Kenneth Gangemi

Poet and novelist, Kenneth Gangemi was born in 1937 and grew up in the New York suburb of Scarsdale. He took an engineering degree at Rensselaer Polytechnic Institute, but stopped working as an engineer in 1962 in order to devote himself to writing and traveling. He has lived in various places, but the cities he knows most intimately are San Francisco, New York, Mexico City, and Los Angeles. His work has appeared in *Art and Literature* and *The Transatlantic Review,* and his short novel *Olt,* published in London and New York, has gathered an underground following in both places.

The poems here come from his first collection, *Lydia.* His style is spare, naked, denotative, unsymbolic—a language of poetry seeking degree zero. Gangemi's sensibility has been influenced by the telephone directory and by the cataloguing device of Homer's *Iliad.* The result of this unlikely marriage of the mundane and the heroic is an original kind of poetry that speaks in clipped bursts. It is the poetry of nouns, of things, a new kind of singing telegram. The eye descending the ladder of names or phrases creates the sense of movement normally suggested by verbs. Hardly poetic in the usual meaning of the term, its idiom is nonetheless lyrical and modern.

Office Girls

Modern slaves

Shiny pennies for
The crucible city

Blind-alley jobs
Barbed-wire offices

Whitecollar wageslaves
Programmed for defeat

Coffee
Chiclets
Cigarettes

SOURCE: Kenneth Gangemi, *Lydia* (Los Angeles: Black Sparrow Press, 1970), p. 40. Reprinted by permission of the publisher.

Lost in the whitecollar jungle
Degenerating in treadmill jobs

Crippled voices

Shut off from the sun
Sustained by irrational hopes

Single girls
Surplus cunt

Lonely in the winter city

Straight teeth and crooked minds
Lush bodies and barren souls

Whitecollar daydreams
Television evenings

Rhinestone girls
Chiclet cunts

Good Things

White snow
Green pines
Blue sky

Thoreau in Massachusetts
Burroughs in New York
Muir in California

Wild rice
Wild honey
Wild strawberries

Free afternoons
Free mornings
Free nights

The breeze
The skyline
The gulls in the wake

SOURCE: Kenneth Gangemi, *Lydia* (Los Angeles: Black Sparrow Press, 1970), p. 53. Reprinted by permission of the publisher.

New cities
New friends
New conversations

Poets in San Francisco
Sculptors in Los Angeles
Filmmakers in New York

The smell of grass
The sound of crickets
The sight of stars

Life Style

Programmed commuters

Rushing for Train Zero
To the novocaine suburbs

Products of a culture

The right shirt
The right cocktail

Treadmill lifetimes

Shirts by the dozen
Liquor by the case

Trapped men

Each with a master
Each told what to do

Quicksand corporations

Tear off your white collars!
Throw away your class rings!

Useless

The invisible harness
The bit and blinders

Cheerful robots

SOURCE: Kenneth Gangemi, *Lydia* (Los Angeles: Black Sparrow Press, 1970), p. 19. Reprinted by permission of the publisher.

The Nations

Apache
Arapaho

Chinook
Creek
Commanche

Chippewa
Choctaw
Cherokee
Chickasaw

Delaware
Dakota

Hopi
Kiowa
Mohawk
Navajo

Pima
Paiute
Pueblo
Pawnee

Saginaw
Seneca
Seminole
Sioux

Shoshone
Shawnee

Zuni

Lydia

Succulent sixteen

Delicious dreamgirl
Young and barefoot

SOURCE: Kenneth Gangemi, *Lydia* (Los Angeles: Black Sparrow Press, 1970), p. 70. Reprinted by permission of the publisher.

SOURCE: Kenneth Gangemi, *Lydia* (Los Angeles: Black Sparrow Press, 1970), p. 49. Reprinted by permission of the publisher.

Lollypop lips

Happy voice
Bright face

California-born

Sculptor father
Painter mother

Pink cheeks and tossing hair
Quick mind and flashing eyes

Highschool homework

Bouncing girl
Bobbing breasts

Straining at the bra-strap

Blushing breasts

Whisk-off skirt
Lollypop panties

Baby fat

Small feet
Smooth calves

Breast-kiss
Belly-kiss

Young armpit
New bush

White thighs
Classic cunt

Curvy girl
Creamy girl

Mmmmm!

Allen Ginsberg

Poet and friend of man, Allen Ginsberg was born in 1926, in Newark, New Jersey. His father Louis sometimes appears with Allen in poetry readings. His mother Naomi has been immortalized in *Kaddish*.

He helped to put himself through Columbia (B.A. in 1949) by working as a welder in the Brooklyn Navy Yard. During those years, Jack Kerouac was his constant companion. He has worked at various other jobs, including dishwasher, night porter, literary agent, newspaper reporter, book reviewer (for *Newsweek*), and market research consultant in New York City and San Francisco. He has also acted in such noncommercial films as *Pull My Daisy* and *Chappaqua*. The appearance of *Howl and Other Poems* in 1956 changed the course of contemporary poetry and catapulted Ginsberg into a limelight he has seldom left. He received a Guggenheim Award in 1965 and was elected King of May at the Prague Student Festival that year. He has recorded the songs of Blake, sung and accompanied by himself, and has become a familiar figure on college campuses throughout the United States, reading his poetry and campaigning for gay liberation, legalization of marijuana, and withdrawal from Vietnam. The leading gnostic poet of this generation and a "space age anarchist," he advocates a high element of personal awareness and permissiveness in politics and a "Hindu-Buddhist-Jewish-Muslim-Xtian" attitude in religion. He lives in the East Village and in Cherry Valley, New York. The following poems come from *Planet News* (1968). Among his latest books are *Indian Journals* (1969) and *The Gates of Wrath* (1972).

Who Be Kind To

Be kind to your self, it is only one
        and perishable
of many on the planet, thou art that
one that wishes a soft finger tracing the
        line of feeling from nipple to pubes—
one that wishes a tongue to kiss your armpit,
        a lip to kiss your cheek inside your
        whiteness thigh—
Be kind to yourself, Harry, because unkindness
        comes when the body explodes
napalm cancer and the deathbed in Vietnam

SOURCE: Allen Ginsberg, *Planet News* (San Francisco: City Lights Books, 1968), pp. 95–99.

is a strange place to dream of trees
leaning over and angry American faces
grinning with sleepwalk terror over your
last eye—
Be kind to yourself, because the bliss of your own
kindness will flood the police tomorrow,
because the cow weeps in the field and the
mouse weeps in the cat hole—
Be kind to this place, which is your present
habitation, with derrick and radar tower
and flower in the ancient brook—
Be kind to your neighbor who weeps
solid tears on the television sofa,
he has no other home, and hears nothing
but the hard voice of telephones
Click, buzz, switch channel and the inspired
melodrama disappears
and he's left alone for the night, he disappears
in bed—
Be kind to your disappearing mother and
father gazing out the terrace window
as milk truck and hearse turn the corner
Be kind to the politician weeping in the galleries
of Whitehall, Kremlin, White House
Louvre and Phoenix City
aged, large nosed, angry, nervously dialing
the bald voice connected to
electrodes underground converging thru
wires vaster than a kitten's eye can see
on the mushroom shaped fear-lobe under
the ear of Sleeping Dr. Einstein
crawling with worms, crawling with worms, crawling
with worms the hour has come—
Sick, dissatisfied, unloved, the bulky
foreheads of Captain Premier President
Sir Comrade Fear!
Be kind to the fearful one at your side
Who's remembering the Lamentations
of the bible
the prophecies of the Crucified Adam Son
of all the porters and char men of
Bell gravia—
Be kind to your self who weep under
the Moscow moon and hide your bliss hairs
under raincoat and suede Levis—
For this is the joy to be born, the kindness
received thru strange eyeglasses on
a bus thru Kensington,

the finger touch of the Londoner on your thumb,
that borrows light from your cigarette,
the morning smile at Newcastle Central
station, when longhair Tom blond husband
greets the bearded stranger of telephones–
the boom boom that bounces in the joyful
bowels as the Liverpool Minstrels of
CavernSink
raise up their joyful voices and guitars
in electric Africa hurrah
for Jerusalem–
The saints come marching in, Twist &
Shout, and Gates of Eden are named
in Albion again
Hope sings a black psalm from Nigeria,
and a white psalm echoes in Detroit
and reechoes amplified from Nottingham to Prague
and a Chinese psalm will be heard, if we all
live our lives for the next 6 decades–
Be kind to the Chinese psalm in the red transistor
in your breast–
Be kind to the Monk in the 5 Spot who plays
lone chord-bangs on his vast piano
lost in space on a bench and hearing himself
in the nightclub universe–
Be kind to the heroes that have lost their
names in the newspaper
and hear only their own supplication for
the peaceful kiss of sex in the giant
auditoriums of the planet,
nameless voices crying for kindness in the orchestra,
screaming in anguish that bliss come true
and sparrows sing another hundred years
to white haired babes
and poets be fools of their own desire–O Anacreon
and angelic Shelley!
Guide these new-nippled generations on space
ships to Mars' next universe
The prayer is to man and girl, the only
gods, the only lords of Kingdoms of
Feeling, Christs of their own
living ribs–
Bicycle chain and machine gun, fear sneer
& smell cold logic of the Dream Bomb
have come to Saigon, Johannesburg,
Dominica City, Pnom-Penh, Pentagon
Paris and Lhasa–

Be kind to the universe of Self that
trembles and shudders and thrills
in XX Century,
that opens its eyes and belly and breast
chained with flesh to feel
the myriad flowers of bliss
that I Am to Thee—
A dream! a Dream! I don't want to be alone!
I want to know that I am loved!
I want the orgy of our flesh, orgy
of all eyes happy, orgy of the soul
kissing and blessing its mortal-grown
body,
orgy of tenderness beneath the neck, orgy of
kindness to thigh and vagina
Desire given with meat hand
and cock, desire taken with
mouth and ass, desire returned
to the last sigh!
Tonite let's all make love in London
as if it were 2001 the years
of thrilling god—
And be kind to the poor soul that cries in
a crack of the pavement because he
has no body—
Prayers to the ghosts and demons, the
lackloves of Capitals & congresses
who make sadistic noises
on the radio—
Statue destroyers & tank captains, unhappy
murderers in Mekong & Stanleyville,
That a new kind of man has come to his bliss
to end the cold war he has borne
against his own kind flesh
since the days of the snake.

Last Night in Calcutta

Still night. The old clock Ticks,
half past two. A ringing of crickets
awake in the ceiling. The gate is locked
on the street outside—sleepers, mustaches,
nakedness, but no desire. A few mosquitos

SOURCE: Allen Ginsberg, *Planet News* (San Francisco: City Lights Books, 1968), pp. 53–54.

waken the itch, the fan turns slowly—
a car thunders along the black asphalt,
a bull snorts, something is expected—
Time sits solid in the four yellow walls.
No one is here, emptiness filled with train
whistles & dog barks, answered a block away.
Pushkin sits on the bookshelf, Shakespeare's
complete works as well as Blake's unread—
O Spirit of Poetry, no use calling on you
babbling in this emptiness furnished with beds
under the bright oval mirror—perfect
night for sleepers to dissolve in tranquil
blackness, and rest there eight hours
—Waking to stained fingers, bitter mouth
and lung gripped by cigarette hunger,
what to do with this big toe, this arm
this eye in the starving skeleton-filled
sore horse tramcar-heated Calcutta in
Eternity—sweating and teeth rotted away—
Rilke at least could dream about lovers,
the old breast excitement and trembling belly,
is that it? And the vast starry space—
If the brain changes matter breathes
fearfully back on man—But now
the great crash of buildings and planets
breaks thru the walls of language and drowns
me under its Ganges heaviness forever.
No escape but thru Bangkok and New York death.
Skin is sufficient to be skin, that's all
it ever could be, tho screams of pain in the kidney
make it sick of itself, a wavy dream
dying to finish its all too famous misery
—Leave immortality for another to suffer like a fool,
not get stuck in the corner of the universe
sticking morphine in the arm and eating meat.

Sunflower Sutra

I walked on the banks of the tincan banana dock and sat down under the huge shade of a Southern Pacific locomotive to look at the sunset over the box house hills and cry.
Jack Kerouac sat beside me on a busted rusty iron pole, companion, we thought the same thoughts of the soul, bleak and blue and

SOURCE: Allen Ginsberg, *Howl and Other Poems* (San Francisco: City Lights Books, 1959), pp. 179–81.

sad-eyed, surrounded by the gnarled steel roots of trees of machinery.
The oily water on the river mirrored by the red sky, sun sank on top of final Frisco peaks, no fish in that stream, no hermit in those mounts, just ourselves rheumy-eyed and hungover like old bums on the riverbank, tired and wily.
Look at the Sunflower, he said, there was a dead gray shadow against the sky, big as a man, sitting dry on top of a pile of ancient sawdust—
—I rushed up enchanted—it was my first sunflower, memories of Blake—my visions—Harlem
and Hells of the Eastern rivers, bridges clanking, Joes Greasy Sandwiches, dead baby carriages, black treadless tires forgotten and unretreaded, the poem of the riverbank, condoms & pots, steel knives, nothing stainless, only the dank muck and the razor sharp artifacts passing into the past—
and the gray Sunflower poised against the sunset, crackly bleak and dusty with the smut and smog and smoke of olden locomotives in its eye—
corolla of bleary spikes pushed down and broken like a battered crown, seeds fallen out of its face, soon-to-be-toothless mouth of sunny air, sunrays obliterated on its hairy head like a dried wire spiderweb,
leaves stuck out like arms out of the stem, gestures from the sawdust root, broke pieces of plaster fallen out of the black twigs, a dead fly in its ear,
Unholy battered old thing you were, my sunflower O my soul, I loved you then!
The grime was no man's grime but death and human locomotives,
all that dress of dust, that veil of darkened railroad skin, that smog of cheek, that eyelid of black mis'ry, that sooty hand or phallus or protuberance of artificial worse-than-dirt—industrial—modern—all that civilization spotting your crazy golden crown—
and those blear thoughts of death and dusty loveless eyes and ends and withered roots below, in the home-pile of sand and sawdust, rubber dollar bills, skin of machinery, the guts and innards of the weeping coughing car, the empty lonely tincans with their rusty tongues alack, what more could I name, the smoked ashes of some cock cigar, the cunts of wheelbarrows and the milky breasts of cars, wornout asses out of chairs & sphincters of dynamos—all these
entangled in your mummied roots—and you there standing before me in the sunset, all your glory in your form!
A perfect beauty of a sunflower! a perfect excellent lovely sunflower existence! a sweet natural eye to the new hip moon, woke up alive and excited grasping in the sunset shadow sunrise golden monthly breeze!

How many flies buzzed round you innocent of your grime, while you cursed the heavens of the railroad and your flower soul?
Poor dead flower? when did you forget you were a flower? when did you look at your skin and decide you were an impotent dirty old locomotive? the ghost of a locomotive? the specter and shade of a once powerful mad American locomotive?
You were never no locomotive, Sunflower, you were a sunflower!
And you Locomotive, you are a locomotive, forget me not!
So I grabbed up the skeleton thick sunflower and stuck it at my side like a scepter,
and deliver my sermon to my soul, and Jack's soul too, and anyone who'll listen,
—We're not our skin of grime, we're not our dread bleak dusty imageless locomotive, we're all beautiful golden sunflowers inside, we're blessed by our own seed & golden hairy naked accomplishment-bodies growing into mad black formal sunflowers in the sunset, spied on by our eyes under the shadow of the mad locomotive riverbank sunset Frisco hilly tincan evening sitdown vision.

A Supermarket in California

What thoughts I have of you tonight, Walt Whitman, for I walked down the sidestreets under the trees with a headache self-conscious looking at the full moon.

In my hungry fatigue, and shopping for images, I went into the neon fruit supermarket, dreaming of your enumerations!

What peaches and what penumbras! Whole families shopping at night! Aisles full of husbands! Wives in the avocados, babies in the tomatoes!—and you, Garcia Lorca, what were you doing down by the watermelons?

I saw you, Walt Whitman, childless, lonely old grubber, poking among the meats in the refrigerator and eyeing the grocery boys.

I heard you asking questions of each: Who killed the pork chops? What price bananas? Are you my Angel?

I wandered in and out of the brilliant stacks of cans following you, and followed in my imagination by the store detective.

We strode down the open corridors together in our solitary fancy tasting artichokes, possessing every frozen delicacy, and never passing the cashier.

Where are we going, Walt Whitman? The doors close in an hour. Which way does your beard point tonight?

SOURCE: Allen Ginsberg, *Howl and Other Poems* (San Francisco: City Lights Books, 1959), pp. 181–82.

(I touch your book and dream of our odyssey in the supermarket and feel absurd.)

Will we walk all night through solitary streets? The trees add shade to shade, lights out in the houses, we'll both be lonely.

Will we stroll dreaming of the lost America of love past blue automobiles in driveways, home to our silent cottage?

Ah, dear father, graybeard, lonely old courage-teacher, what America did you have when Charon quit poling his ferry and you got out on a smoking bank and stood watching the boat disappear on the black waters of Lethe?

Langston Hughes

Langston Hughes was born in Joplin, Missouri, in 1902. He lived in Kansas and Colorado before attending Columbia College in New York and Lincoln University in Pennsylvania. He went to sea, worked in Parisian night clubs, and traveled widely; then he settled down in Harlem and began to document the tribulations and joys of his people. Attuned to folk speech and the rhythms of the blues, his verse has a quality often described as "soul." Among his books are *Weary Blues* (1926), *The Dream Keeper* (1932), *Shakespeare in Harlem* (1942), *Fields of Wonder* (1947), *One Way Ticket* (1949), *Ask Your Mama* (1961), and *The Panther and the Lash* (1967). The last volume, published a year after his death, continued to explore the meaning of being black in a white man's world. As the poems that follow indicate, his sensibility stayed apace of the times and the intensity of his new concerns produced some of his best poetry.

Satirical sketches written for a newspaper were collected in *Simple Speaks His Mind* (1950)—later made into a television series—and he himself is the subject of *The Big Sea* (1940) and *I Wonder as I Wander* (1956). His interest ranged over all genres: He wrote a novel, *Not Without Laughter* (1930); a play, *Mulatto* (1935), based on one of his own poems; the libretto for a musical, *Troubled Island* (1949); and a children's story, *Black Misery* (1969). He also edited anthologies of black poetry and fiction.

Bird in Orbit

DE— *Happy*
DELIGHT— *blues*
DELIGHTED! INTRODUCE ME TO EARTHA *in*
JOCKO BODDIDLY LIL GREENWOOD *up-beat*
BELAFONTE FRISCO JOSEPHINE *tempo*
BRICKTOP INEZ MABEL MERCER *trip*
AND I'D LIKE TO MEET THE *merrily*
ONE-TIME SIX-YEAR-OLDS *along*
FIRST GRADE IN NEW ORLEANS *until*
IN THE QUARTER OF THE NEGROES *the music*

WHERE SIT-INS ARE CONDUCTED *suddenly*
BY THOSE YET UNINDUCTED *stops in*

SOURCE: Langston Hughes, *Ask Your Mama* (New York: Alfred A. Knopf, Inc., 1961), pp. 70–72.

AND BALLOTS DROP IN BOXES
WHERE BULLETS ARE THE TELLERS.

a loud
rim shot.

THEY ASKED ME AT THANKSGIVING
DID I VOTE FOR NIXON?
I SAID, VOTED FOR YOUR MAMA.

TACIT

Figurine.

METHUSELAH SIGNS PAPERS W. E. B.
ORIGINAL NIAGARA N.A.A.C.P.
ADELE RAMONA MICHAEL SERVE
  BAKOKO TEA
IRENE AND HELEN ARE AS THEY USED
  TO BE
AND SMITTY HAS NOT CHANGED AT ALL.
ALIOUNE AIMÉ SEDAR SIPS HIS
  NEGRITUDE.
THE REVEREND MARTIN LUTHER
KING MOUNTS HIS UNICORN
OBLIVIOUS TO BLOOD
AND MOONLIGHT ON ITS HORN
WHILE MOLLIE MOON STREWS SEQUINS
AS LEDA STREW HER CORN
AND CHARLIE YARDBIRD PARKER
IS IN ORBIT.

Cool
bop
very
light
and
delicate
rising
to an
ethereal
climax . . .
completely
far
out. . . .

¡AY, MI NEGRA!
¡AY, MORENA!

TACIT

GRANDPA, WHERE DID YOU MEET MY
  GRANDMA?
AT MOTHER BETHEL'S IN THE MORNING?
I'M ASKING, GRANDPA, ASKING.
WERE YOU MARRIED BY JOHN JASPER
OF THE DO-MOVE COSMIC CONSCIENCE?
GRANDPA, DID YOU HEAR THE
HEAR THE OLD FOLKS SAY HOW
HOW TALL HOW TALL THE CANE GREW
SAY HOW WHITE THE COTTON COTTON
SPEAK OF RICE DOWN IN THE
  MARSHLAND
SPEAK OF FREDERICK DOUGLASS'S
  BEARD
AND JOHN BROWN'S WHITE AND LONGER
LINCOLN'S LIKE A CLOTHESBRUSH
AND OF HOW SOJOURNER
  HOW SOJOURNER
TO PROVE SHE WAS A WOMAN WOMAN

"The
Battle
Hymn
of
the

BARED HER BOSOMS, BARED IN PUBLIC
TO PROVE SHE WAS A WOMAN?
WHAT SHE SAID ABOUT HER CHILDREN
ALL SOLD DOWN THE RIVER.
I LOOK AT THE STARS
AND THEY LOOK AT THE STARS,
AND THEY WONDER WHERE I BE
AND I WONDER WHERE THEY BE.
STARS AT STARS STARS. . . .
TOURÉ DOWN IN GUINEA
LUMUMBA IN THE CONGO
JOMO IN KENYATTA. . . . STARS. . . .

Republic" as a flute solo soft and far away fading in the distance . . .
TACIT

GRANDPA, DID YOU FIND HER IN THE
TV SILENCE
OF A MILLION MARTHA ROUNDTREES?
IN THE QUARTER OF THE NEGROES
DID YOU EVER FIND HER?

THAT GENTLEMAN IN EXPENSIVE SHOES
MADE FROM THE HIDES OF BLACKS
WHO TIPS AMONG THE SHADOWS
SOAKING UP THE MUSIC
ASKED ME RIGHT AT CHRISTMAS
DID I WANT TO EAT WITH
WHITE FOLKS?

Flute cry . . .

THOSE SIT-IN KIDS, HE SAID,
MUST BE RED!

TACIT

KENYATTA RED! CASTRO RED!
NKRUMAH RED!
RALPH BUNCHE INVESTIGATED!
MARY McLEOD BETHUNE BARRED BY
THE LEGION FROM ENGLEWOOD
NEW JERSEY HIGH SCHOOL!
HOW ABOUT THAT N.A.A.C.P.
AND THE RADICALS IN THAT
THERE SOUTHERN CONFERENCE?
AIN'T YOU GOT NO INFORMATION
ON DR. ROBERT WEAVER?
INVESTIGATE THAT SANTA CLAUS
WHOSE DOLLS ARE INTERRACIAL!
INVESTIGATE THEM NEGRAS WHO

BOUGHT A DOBERMAN PINSCHER.

THAT GENTLEMAN IN EXPENSIVE SHOES
MADE FROM THE HIDES OF BLACKS
TIPS AMONG THE SHADOWS

Flute call into very far-out

Prime

Uptown on Lenox Avenue
Where a nickel costs a dime,
In these lush and thieving days
When million-dollar thieves
Glorify their million-dollar ways
In the press and on the radio and TV—
        But won't let me
        Skim even a dime—
I, black, come to my prime
In the section of the niggers
Where a nickel costs a dime.

Militant

Let all who will
Eat quietly the bread of shame.
I cannot,
Without complaining loud and long,
Tasting its bitterness in my throat,
And feeling to my very soul
It's wrong.
For honest work
You proffer me poor pay,
For honest dreams
Your spit is in my face,
And so my fist is clenched
Today—
To strike your face.

Junior Addict

The little boy
who sticks a needle in his arm
and seeks an out in other worldly dreams,

SOURCE: Langston Hughes, *The Panther and the Lash* (New York: Alfred A. Knopf, Inc., 1967), p. 5.

SOURCE: Langston Hughes, *The Panther and the Lash* (New York: Alfred A. Knopf, Inc., 1967), p. 39.

SOURCE: Langston Hughes, *The Panther and the Lash* (New York: Alfred A. Knopf, Inc., 1967), pp. 12–13.

who seeks an out in eyes that droop
and ears that close to Harlem screams,
cannot know, of course,
(and has no way to understand)
a sunrise that he cannot see
beginning in some other land—
but destined sure to flood—and soon—
the very room in which he leaves
his needle and his spoon,
the very room in which today the air
is heavy with the drug
of his despair.

(Yet little can
tomorrow's sunshine give
to one who will not live.)

Quick, sunrise, come—
Before the mushroom bomb
Pollutes his stinking air
With better death
Than is his living here,
With viler drugs
Than bring today's release
In poison from the fallout
Of our peace.

"It's easier to get dope
than it is to get a job."

Yes, easier to get dope
than to get a job—
daytime or nightime job,
teen-age, pre-draft,
pre-lifetime job.

Quick, sunrise, come!
Sunrise out of Africa,
Quick, come!
Sunrise, please come!
Come! Come!

Without Benefit of Declaration

Listen here, Joe,
Don't you know

SOURCE: Langston Hughes, *The Panther and the Lash* (New York: Alfred A. Knopf, Inc., 1967), p. 54.

That tomorrow
You got to go
Out yonder where
The steel winds blow?

Listen here, kid,
It's been said
Tomorrow you'll be dead
Out there where
The rain is lead.

Don't ask me why.
Just go ahead and die.
Hidden from the sky
Out yonder you'll lie:
A medal to your family—
In exchange for
        A guy.

Mama, don't cry.

The Backlash Blues

Mister Backlash, Mister Backlash,
Just who do you think I am?
Tell me, Mister Backlash,
Who do you think I am?
You raise my taxes, freeze my wages,
Send my son to Vietnam.

You give me second-class houses,
Give me second-class schools,
Second-class houses
And second-class schools.
You must think us colored folks
Are second-class fools.

When I try to find a job
To earn a little cash,
Try to find myself a job
To earn a little cash,
All you got to offer
Is a white backlash.

SOURCE: Langston Hughes, *The Panther and the Lash* (New York: Alfred A. Knopf, Inc., 1967), p. 8.

But the world is big,
The world is big and round,
Great big world, Mister Backlash,
Big and bright and round—
And it's full of folks like me who are
Black, Yellow, Beige, and Brown.

Mister Backlash, Mister Backlash,
What do you think I got to lose?
Tell me, Mister Backlash,
What you think I got to lose?
I'm gonna leave you, Mister Backlash,
Singing your mean old backlash blues.

You're the one,
Yes, you're the one
Will have the blues.

Ted Hughes

One of the most interesting poets now writing, Ted Hughes was born in 1930 in Mytholmyrod, Yorkshire. He served for two years in the RAF on an isolated radio station in East Yorkshire, where he had "nothing to do but read and re-read Shakespeare and watch the grass grow." While studying at Cambridge (A.B. and A.M.), he met and married the American poet Sylvia Plath, who was there on a Fulbright in 1956. They came to the United States for a period, and Hughes found a following among American readers with his first book, *The Hawk in the Rain* (1957), which won the 92nd Street YMHA Poetry Center Award. His reputation was enhanced by *Lupercal* (1960), *Selected Poems* (with Thomas Gunn, 1962), and *Wodwo* (1967), a gathering of poems, stories, and a radio play. *Crow* (1971), from which the following poems are taken, is a major landmark in postwar poetry. The poems are remarkable for their originality and palpable emotional energy. Hughes avoids the clichés of animism and violence that sometimes flawed his earlier work, and through the eye of that elusive and elemental bird, Crow, fuses the modern world of bulldozers and detergents with the ancient and often ominous universe of nature.

Hughes returned to Yorkshire in 1960 and now writes books for children as well as poetry for adults.

Crow's First Lesson

God tried to teach Crow how to talk.
"Love," said God. "Say, Love."
Crow gaped, and the white shark crashed into the sea
And went rolling downwards, discovering its own depth.

"No, no," said God, "Say Love. Now try it. LOVE."
Crow gaped, and a bluefly, a tsetse, a mosquito
Zoomed out and down
To their sundry flesh-pots.

"A final try," said God. "Now, LOVE."
Crow convulsed, gaped, retched and
Man's bodiless prodigious head
Bulbed out onto the earth, with swivelling eyes,
Jabbering protest—

And Crow retched again, before God could stop him.
And woman's vulva dropped over man's neck and tightened.
The two struggled together on the grass.
God struggled to part them, cursed, wept—

Crow flew guiltily off.

Crow's Fall

When Crow was white he decided the sun was too white.
He decided it glared much too whitely.
He decided to attack it and defeat it.

He got his strength flush and in full glitter.
He clawed and fluffed his rage up.
He aimed his beak direct at the sun's centre.

He laughed himself to the centre of himself

And attacked.

At his battle cry trees grew suddenly old,
Shadows flattened.

But the sun brightened—
It brightened, and Crow returned charred black.

He opened his mouth but what came out was charred black.

"Up there," he managed,
"Where white is black and black is white, I won."

A Horrible Religious Error

When the serpent emerged, earth-bowel brown,
From the hatched atom
With its alibi self twisted around it

Lifting a long neck
And balancing that deaf and mineral stare
The sphynx of the final fact

And flexing on that double flameflicker tongue
A syllable like the rustling of the spheres

God's grimace writhed, a leaf in the furnace

And man's and woman's knees melted, they collapsed
Their neck-muscles melted, their brows bumped the ground
Their tears evacuated visibly
They whispered "Your will is our peace."

But Crow only peered.
Then took a step or two forward,
Grabbed this creature by the slackskin nape,

Beat the hell out of it, and ate it.

Apple Tragedy

So on the seventh day
The serpent rested,
God came up to him.
"I've invented a new game," he said.

The serpent stared in surprise
At this interloper.
But God said: "You see this apple?
I squeeze it and look—cider."

The serpent had a good drink
And curled up into a questionmark.
Adam drank and said: "Be my god."
Eve drank and opened her legs

And called to the cockeyed serpent
And gave him a wild time.
God ran and told Adam
Who in drunken rage tried to hang himself in the orchard.

The serpent tried to explain, crying "Stop"
But drink was splitting his syllable.
And Eve started screeching: "Rape! Rape!"
And stamping on his head.

Now whenever the snake appears she screeches
"Here it comes again! Help! O Help!"
Then Adam smashes a chair on its head,
And God says: "I am well pleased"

And everything goes to hell.

442
Ted Hughes

Lawson Inada

Lawson Inada was born in Fresno, California, in 1938, of Japanese descent. His grandparents were sharecroppers, but his father educated himself to become a dentist. During World War II, the Inada family was among the other Japanese-American families in California who were forced to live in "detention" camps in Fresno, Arkansas, and Colorado, on the grounds that they constituted a potential "fifth column." After the war, he spent some time at Fresno State College, where he became interested in poetry through Philip Levine, a poet who teaches at the university. He gave up his study of the bass fiddle and began to write during stays in New York, New England, and the Midwest. He now lives in Oregon with his family, "listening to the Great Ones and singing." His first book was *The Great Bassist* and his second, *The Death of Coltrane.* His lyrics are simple, almost laconic, but Inada's ear for the idiom of the middle-California working class is subtle and exact, though his voice is clearly his own. The poems reflect the ethnic variety that gives Fresno, the dusty center of the San Joaquin Valley, an element of the exotic; yet Inada treats his subjects without sentimentality, in an idiom that makes them seem both strange and familiar at once.

West Side Songs

"SUNSET"

The sun never sets
on the Mexican
section—"Sunset."
Big street lights
keep them awake,
out of trouble,
fingering the hoes
of Mexican golf.
Mexicans commute
to find trouble.
They sing. They cut.
At wrestling arenas,
Mexicans beat

SOURCE: Lawson Inada, *Down at the Santa Fe Depot: 20 Fresno Poets,* edited by David Kherdian and James Baloian (Fresno, Calif.: Giligia Press, 1970), pp. 49–53.

the bad Japanese.
Mexicans are fun.

The sun never sets
on the Mexican
section. It never comes up.

"JERICHO"

"Jericho's"
a citadel,
slab of plaster
by the Black villas
by the slaughterhouse
by the city dump.

Policedogs keep
vigil—
sniffing out
White men, a minstrel cop.

Upstairs, slabs
on the racks.
You can stab them
and giggle.

You can get in
and wiggle.

Downstairs, the dice's
mammy grin.
The juke box

squeals the blues—
drunk
on a funky
harmonica.

Blackies stay happy.

Mornings, when Black
garbagemen come,
they play
buckets
like drums.

Sometimes, a Black
foetus dances
out in the gutter,
with ribs.

Come on over
and wail—

"Jericho", slaughterhouse,
dump.

OKIES

I always thought an Okie
was a white man gone fake—
play-acting, a spy.

Now I know Okies
are okay.
They dig music.
They cut each other up.

ARMENIANS

are screwed up.
I mean
they won't move
to the West Side.
They're known
as the Fresno Jews.

They're screwed up.
I mean
they shave
names and noses
and herd hairy
Mustangs to school.

HE-RO

You know
about the sound
barrier.
Well don't you know
Willie broke
the color
barrier screaming
through White town
with a White girl
at 95 per.

After
the funeral,
his Cadillac
hub-caps flew
over in formation,
in tribute.

FILIPINOS

are sharp.
That's why
they're barbers.
Sharp
trousers,
sharp
elevator shoes.
When they see
White girls
they go
"Sook sook sook sook."

CHINKS

Ching Chong Chinaman
sitting on a fence
trying to make a dollar
chop-chop all day.

"Eju-kei-shung! Eju-kei-shung!"
that's what they say.

When the War came,
they said, "We Chinese!"
When we went away,
they made sukiyaki,
saying, "Yellow all same."

When the war closed,
they stoned the Japs' homes.

Grandma would say:
"Marry a Mexican,
a Nigger, just don't
marry no Chinese."

JAPS

are great
imitators—
they stole
the Greeks'
skewers,
used them
on themselves.
Their sutras
are Face
and Hide.

They hate
everyone else,
on the sly.

They play
Dr. Charley's
games – bowling,
raking,
growing forks
on lapels.
Their tongues
are yellow
with "r's",
with "l's."

They hate
themselves,
on the sly. I
used to be
Japanese

Erica Jong

Erica Jong was born in New York City, where she now lives with her husband, and was graduated from Barnard and Columbia. She has lived abroad and has taught at The City College of New York. In her brief career, her poetry has appeared in magazines as diverse as *Poetry* and *Mademoiselle.* The title poem from her first collection, *Fruits & Vegetables,* is, in the words of Robert Pack, a "rediscovery that the human body is a vegetable, a fruit, indeed, a cornucopia. That is to say that her poems grow from a delighted sense of being rooted in the flesh, in a physical body." That flesh is the flesh of a woman who has grown up in modern America, who explores the meaning, for a woman, of "tending one's garden" as it relates to the great dominant myths of Eden and of Freud. A second collection, *Half-Lives,* is forthcoming, and she is now writing novels.

Fruits & Vegetables

"It is hard to imagine a civilization without onions."

JULIA CHILD

"Only weggebobbles and fruit. . . I wouldn't be surprised if it was that kind of food you see produces the like waves of the brain the poetical."

JAMES JOYCE

"In recent decades there has been a distinct falling off in the interest shown in hunger artists."

FRANZ KAFKA

"Know me come eat with me."

JAMES JOYCE

[1]

Goodbye, he waved, entering the apple.
That red siren,
whose white flesh turns brown
with prolonged exposure to air,
opened her perfect cheeks to receive him.
She took him in.

The garden revolved
in her glossy patinas of skin.
Goodbye.

[2]

O note the two round holes in onion.

[3]

Did I tell you about
my mother's avocado?
She grew it from a pit.
Secretly, slowly in the dark,
it put out grub-white roots
which filled a jelly jar.
From this unlikely start,
an avocado tree with bark
& dark green leaves
shaded the green silk couch
which shaded me
throughout my shady adolescence.
There, beneath that tree
my skirt gave birth to hands!
Oh memorable hands of boys
with blacked-out eyes
like culprits
in the *National Enquirer*.
My mother nursed that tree
like all her children,
turned it around so often
towards the sun
that its trunk grew twisted
as an old riverbed,
& despite its gaudy leaves
it never bore
fruit.

[4]

Cantaloupes: the setting sun at Paestum
slashed by rosy columns.

[5]

I am thinking of the onion again, with its two O mouths, like the gaping holes in nobody. Of the outer skin, pinkish brown, peeled to reveal a greenish sphere, bald as a dead planet, glib as glass, & an odor almost animal. I consider its ability to draw tears, its capacity for self-scrutiny, flaying itself away, layer on layer, in search of its heart which is simply another region of skin, but deeper & greener. I remember Peer Gynt; I consider its sometimes double heart. Then I think of despair when the onion searches its soul & finds only its various skins; & I think of the dried tuft of roots leading nowhere & the parched umbilicus, lopped off in the garden. Not self-righteous like the proletarian potato, nor a siren like the apple. No show-off like the banana. But a modest, self-effacing vegetable, questioning, introspective, peeling itself away, or merely radiating halos like lake ripples. I consider it the eternal outsider, the middle child, the sad analysand of the vegetable kingdom. Glorified only in France (otherwise silent sustainer of soups & stews), unloved for itself alone—no wonder it draws our tears! Then I think again how the outer peel resembles paper, how soul & skin merge into one, how each peeling strips bare a heart which in turn turns skin. . .

[6]

A poet in a world without onions,
in a world without apples
regards the earth as a great fruit.

Far off, galaxies glitter like currants.
The whole edible universe drops
to his watering mouth. . .

Think of generations of mystics
salivating for the fruit of god,
of poets yearning to inhabit apples,
of the sea, that dark fruit,
closing much more quickly than a wound,
of the nameless galaxies of astronomers,
hoping that the cosmos will ripen
& their eyes will become tongues. . .

[7]

For the taste of the fruit
is the tongue's dream,
& the apple's red
is the passion of the eye.

[8]

If a woman wants to be a poet,
she must dwell in the house of the tomato.

[9]

It is not an emptiness,
the fruit between your legs,
but the long hall of history,

& dreams are coming down the hall
by moonlight.

[10]

They push up through the loam
like lips of mushrooms.

[11]

(Artichoke, after Child): Holding the heart base up, rotate it slowly with your left hand against the blade of a knife held firmly in your right hand to remove all pieces of ambition & expose the pale surface of the heart. Frequently rub the cut portions with gall. Drop each heart as it is finished into acidulated water. The choke can be removed after cooking.

[12]

(Artichoke, after Neruda)

It is green at the artichoke heart,
but remember the times
you flayed
leaf after leaf,
hoarding the pale silver paste
behind the fortresses of your teeth,
tonguing the vinaigrette,
only to find the husk of a worm
at the artichoke heart?
The palate reels like a wronged lover.
Was all that sweetness counterfeit?
Must you vomit back
world after vegetable world
for the sake of one worm
in the green garden of the heart?

[13]

But the poem about bananas has not yet been written. Southerners worry a lot about bananas. Their skin. And nearly everyone worries about the size of bananas, as if that had anything to do with flavor. Small bananas are sometimes quite sweet. But bananas are like poets: they only want to be told how great they are. Green bananas want to be told they're ripe. According to Freud, girls envy bananas. In America chocolate syrup & whipped cream have been known to enhance the flavor of bananas. This is called a *banana split.*

[14]

The rice is pregnant.
It swells past its old transparency.

Hard, translucent worlds inside the grains
open like fans. It is raining rice!
The peasants stand under oiled
rice paper umbrellas cheering.

Someone is scattering rice from the sky!
Chopper blades mash the clouds.
The sky browns like cheese soufflé.
Rice grains puff & pop open.

"What have we done to deserve this?"
the peasants cry. Even the babies
are cheering. Cheers slide from their lips
like spittle. Old men kick their clogs
into the air & run in the rice paddies
barefoot. This is a monsoon! A wedding!

Each grain has a tiny invisible parachute.
Each grain is a rain drop.

"They have sent us rice!" the mothers scream,
opening their throats to the smoke. . .

[15]

Here should be a picture of my favorite apple.
It is also a nude & bottle.
It is also a landscape.
There are no such things as still lives.

[16]

In general, modern poetry requires (underline one): a) more fruit; b) less fruit; c) more vegetables; d) less vegetables; e) all of the above; f) none of the above.

[17]

Astonishment of apples. Every fall.
But only Italians are into grapes,
calling them eggs.
O my eggs,
branching off my family tree,
my father used to pluck you,
leaving bare twigs on the dining room table,
leaving mother furious on the dining room table:
picked clean.
Bare ruined choirs
where late the sweet.
A pile of pits.

[18]

Adam naming the fruit
after the creation of fruit,
his tongue tickling
the crimson lips of the pomegranate,
the tip of his penis licking
the cheeks of the peach,
quince petals in his hair,
his blue arms full of plums,
his legs wrapped around watermelons,
dandling pumpkins on his fatherly knees,
tomatoes heaped around him in red pyramids. . .

peach
peach
peach
peach
peach

he sighs

to kingdom come.

June Jordan

June Jordan was born in 1936 in Harlem and, like Paule Marshall, was raised in the Bedford-Stuyvesant section of Brooklyn by parents who had emigrated from the West Indies. She studied at Barnard College and the University of Chicago; toward the end of her college studies, she married and gave birth to a son, Christopher. Now divorced, she lives in East Hampton, Long Island.

She has taught at The City College of New York, at Connecticut College for Women, and at Sarah Lawrence. She worked as the assistant to the producer of the film *The Cool World* and wrote the script for the film *Slavery and the Man.* In 1969, she was awarded a Rockefeller Grant in Creative Writing, and in 1970–71 received the Prix de Rome in Environmental Design. Her published books of poetry are *Who Look at Me* and *Some Changes,* from which these poems are taken. A novel, *Okay Now,* appeared recently. The theme is land reform and the disintegration of private property rights in America, "so that these areas of death-delivering inequities may diminish." Her first novel, *His Own Where,* tries to pose practicable alternatives to impoverished urban life, through environmental redesign and through the happy love between a boy and a girl. *Dry Victories* (1973) is a brief chronicle of the black people's aspirations and anguish.

"All of my work," she writes, "has been preoccupied with the problems and possibilities and struggles for liberation. Whether writing about the racist practices of most banks, or attempting to offer usable plans for the environmental redesign of Harlem and Bedford-Stuyvesant, the impulse has been the impulse to insist upon struggle wherever pain, slavery, and debasement have been imposed upon us—any of us who are, in any way, oppressed."

For Christopher

Tonight
    the machinery of shadow
        moves into the light

He is lying there
        not a true invalid
                not dying

Now his face looks blue
        but all of that small body
            will more than do
                as life.

SOURCE: June Jordan, *Some Changes* (New York: Richard W. Baron Publishing Co., 1970), p. 39.

The lady radiologist
regardless how and where
she turns the knob

will never know
the plenty of pain
growing

parts to arm
a man inside the boy

practically asleep

Uncle Bullboy

His brother   after dinner
once a year would play the piano
short and tough in white shirt
plaid suspenders   green tie and
checked trousers.
Two teeth were gold.   His eyes
were pink with alcohol.   His fingers
thumped for Auld Lang Syne.
He played St. Louis Woman
Boogie. Blues, the light
pedestrian.

But one night after dinner
after chitterlings and pigs' feet
after bourbon rum and rye
after turnip greens and mustard greens
and sweet potato pie
Bullboy looking everywhere
realized his brother was not there.

Who would emphasize the luxury
of ice cream by the gallon who would
repeat effusively the glamour not the gall
of five degrees outstanding on the wall?
Which head would nod and then recall
the crimes   the apples stolen from the stalls
the soft coal stolen by the pile?
Who would admire
the eighteenth pair of forty

SOURCE: June Jordan, *Some Changes* (New York: Richard W. Baron Publishing Co., 1970), p. 13.

dollar shoes?
Who could extol their mother with good
brandy as his muse?

His brother   dead from drinking
Bullboy drank to clear his thinking
saw the roach inside the riddle.
Soon the bubbles from his glass
were the only bits of charm
which overcame his folded arms.

Exercise in Quits

(November 15, 1969)

[I]

moratorium means well what
you think it means you
dense? Stop it means stop.

We move and we march sing songs
move march sing songs move march move

It/stop means stop.

hey mister man

how long you been fixing to kill somebody?
Waste of time
the preparation training

you was born a bullet.

[II]

we be wondering what they gone do
all them others left and right
what they have in mind

about us
and who by the way is "us"

listen you got a match you got the light
you got two eyes two hands

SOURCE: June Jordan, *Some Changes* (New York: Richard W. Baron Publishing Co., 1970), pp. 71–72.

why you taking pictures of the people
what you sposed to be you
got to photograph the people?

you afraid you will (otherwise) forget
what people look like?

man
or however you been paying dues
we look like you

                    on second thought
there is a clear resemblance to the dead
among the living so

go ahead go on
and take my picture

quick

Clock on Hancock Street

In the wintertime my father wears a hat
a green straw laundry shrunken hat
to open up the wartime iron gate
requiring a special key he keeps
in case he hears the seldom basement bell
a long key cost him seven dollars
took three days to make

around the corner

in the house no furniture remains
he gave away the piano
and the hard-back parlor couch the rosy rug
and the double bed
the large black bureau
china cups and saucers
from Japan

His suitcase is a wooden floor
where magazines called *Life*
smell like a garbage truck

---

that travels farther than he
reasonably can expect
to go

His face seems small or
loose and bearded in the afternoon

Today he was complaining about criminals:

They will come and steal the heavy red umbrella stand

from upstairs in the hallway
where my mother used to walk

and talk to him

Lenore Kandel

Lenore Kandel writes of herself: "I was born under the sign of Capricorn, originally in New York City and later in Pennsylvania, Los Angeles, and San Francisco, and other occasions. I am no longer a professional belly-dancer, school-bus driver, or choir singer. I stand witness for the divine animal and the possibility of the ecstatic access of enlightenment. My favorite word is YES!"

The poems here are from *Word Alchemy,* a book which openly celebrates sexual love but is also engaged with a world that stands outside the immediate personal one. Her first volume, *The Love Book,* was banned in California and led to a trial in San Francisco which the publisher lost, despite the testimony of such people as Professor Tom Parkinson of Berkeley who called it a work of "great human importance." Miss Kandel responded: "When a poet censors his vision he no longer tells the truth as he sees it. When he censors the language of the poem he does not use those words which, to him, are the most perfect words to be used. This self-stunting results in an artificial limitation imposed on an art whose direction is beyond the limits of the conceivable. There are no barriers to poetry or prophecy; by their nature they are barrier-breakers, bursts of perception, lines into infinity. If a poet lies about his vision he lies about himself and in himself; this produces a true barrier."

When last reported, Miss Kandel, after a short sojourn in Hawaii, was living in San Francisco's North Beach.

Love in the Middle of the Air

CATCH ME!
    I love you, I trust you,
    I love you
CATCH ME!
    catch my left foot, my right
    foot, my hand!
    here I am hanging by my teeth
    300 feet up in the air and
CATCH ME!
    here I come, flying without wings,
    no parachute, doing a double triple

super flip-flop somersault
RIGHT UP HERE WITHOUT A
SAFETY NET AND
CATCH ME!
you caught me!
I love you!

now it's *your* turn

Beast Parade

love me, love my elephant . . .
never mock a tiger
never tease a lion
you and your mother
are kinfolk to the jungle

SEE THE SPANGLED LEOPARD LADY!
watch the elephant ballet, eight thousand pounds of meat cavorting
for your languished eye
cumbersome feet used for nefarious purposes
(consider umbrellas in *your* grandma's hollowed foot)
!WATCH!
the gorilla takes a leak
the monkey masturbates
how life-like . . .
SEE the
TIGer
SWITCH his
TAIL!
the leopard lady walks her sister on a shining leash
the eye
of the tiger
hides
behind the sign of scorpio

HERE BE STRANGE BEASTES AND UNKNOWN LANDES
HERE BE LIONS
exhausted
from the smell of popcorn
high in the altitude of the furthest Everest of benches and
everywhere and down to the very front row seats
the eye of the beast shines from contorted craniums
struggling between homo the human sapiens circa Now and
that dark beast before

SOURCE: Lenore Kandel, *Word Alchemy* (New York: Grove Press, 1968), pp. 6–7.

turtle-man   sparrow lady
tiger in a dress-suit   monkey in a sweater
beetle-man, ape-man, poodle-man, snake-man, horse-man,
bull-man, camel-man, goat-man, man-man

!STOP!
observe your brethren, guard your true love
these are dark latitudes
and the ringmaster has wings
let the parade begin!
love me, love my elephant . . .
    love my tiger . . .
    love my anything . . .
    get in line . . .

First They Slaughtered the Angels

[I]

First they slaughtered the angels
tying their thin white legs with wire cords
and
opening their silk throats with icy knives
They died fluttering their wings like chickens
and their immortal blood wet the burning earth

we watched from underground
from the gravestones, the crypts
chewing our bony fingers
and
shivering in our piss-stained winding sheets
The seraphs and the cherubim are gone
they have eaten them and cracked their bones for marrow
they have wiped their asses on angel feathers
and now they walk the rubbled streets with
eyes like fire pits

[II]

who finked on the angels?
who stole the holy grail and hocked it for a jug of wine?
who fucked up Gabriel's golden horn?
        was it an inside job?

SOURCE: Lenore Kandel, *Word Alchemy* (New York: Grove Press, 1968), pp. 26–30.

who barbecued the lamb of god?
who flushed St. Peter's keys down the mouth of a
North Beach toilet?

who raped St. Mary with a plastic dildo stamped with the
Good Housekeeping seal of approval?
        was it an outside job?

where are our weapons?
where are our bludgeons, our flame throwers, our poison
gas, our hand grenades?
we fumble for our guns and our knees sprout credit cards,
we vomit canceled checks
standing spreadlegged with open sphincters weeping soap suds
from our radioactive eyes
and screaming
for the ultimate rifle
the messianic cannon
the paschal bomb

the bellies of women split open and children rip their
way out with bayonets
spitting blood in the eyes of blind midwives
before impaling themselves on their own swords

the penises of men are become blue steel machine guns,
they ejaculate bullets, they spread death as an orgasm

lovers roll in the bushes tearing at each other's genitals
with iron fingernails

fresh blood is served at health food bars in germ free
paper cups
gulped down by syphilitic club women
in papier-mâché masks
each one the same hand-painted face of Hamlet's mother
at the age of ten

we watch from underground
our eyes like periscopes
flinging our fingers to the dogs for candy bars
in an effort to still their barking
in an effort to keep the peace
in an effort to make friends and influence people

[III]

we have collapsed our collapsible bomb shelters
we have folded our folding life rafts

and at the count of twelve
they have all disintegrated into piles of rat shit
nourishing the growth of poison flowers
and venus pitcher plants

we huddle underground
hugging our porous chests with mildewed arms
listening to the slow blood drip from our severed veins
lifting the tops of our zippered skulls
to ventilate our brains
        they have murdered our angels

we have sold our bodies and our hours to the curious
we have paid off our childhood in dishwashers and miltown
and rubbed salt upon our bleeding nerves
in the course of searching
        and they have shit upon the open mouth of god
they have hung the saints in straitjackets and they have
tranquilized the prophets
they have denied both christ and cock
and diagnosed buddha as catatonic
they have emasculated the priests and the holy men and
censored even the words of love
    Lobotomy for every man!
and they have nominated a eunuch for president
    Lobotomy for the housewife!
    Lobotomy for the business man!
    Lobotomy for the nursery schools!
and they have murdered the angels

[IV]

now in the alleyways the androgynes gather swinging their
lepers' bells like censers as they prepare the ritual
rape of god
    the grease that shines their lips is the fat of angels
    the blood that cakes their claws is the blood of angels

they are gathering in the streets and playing dice with
angel eyes
they are casting the last lots of armageddon

[V]

now in the aftermath of morning
we are rolling away the stones from underground, from the
caves
we have widened our peyote-visioned eyes
and rinsed our mouths with last night's wine

we have caulked the holes in our arms with dust and flung
libations at each other's feet

and we shall enter into the streets and walk among them and
do battle
holding our lean and empty hands upraised
we shall pass among the strangers of the world like a
bitter wind
and our blood will melt iron
and our breath will melt steel
we shall stare face to face with naked eyes
and our tears will make earthquakes
and our wailing will cause mountains to rise and the sun to halt

THEY SHALL MURDER NO MORE ANGELS!
          not even us

William Knott (Saint Geraud)

William Knott, known to the readers of his two books by the pseudonym of Saint Geraud (the hero of an eighteenth-century pornographic novel called *The Lascivious Hypocrite*), says of himself: "Bill Knott (1940–1966) is a virgin and a suicide." Like the reports of Mark Twain's, his own on his suicide is greatly exaggerated: He is alive and well in New York City, preparing another volume of poetry and reading on the poetry circuit. His first book, *The Naomi Poems: Corpse and Beans* (1968), has sold almost 20,000 copies—a phenomenal figure for a first collection of poetry—and led Kenneth Rexroth to comment: "Saint Geraud is one of the best young poets in America." His second collection, *Auto-Necrophilia,* appeared in 1972.

Last Poem

It's harder and harder to whistle you up from my pack of dead,
you lag back, loping in another love.
Fate is lucky not to have known you as I have known you.
One dawn the menstrual face of time found, frozen upon stones,
pore-song of the poet. Rigor mortis walked the streets, its
coat tattered, face pensive. A howl was heard, calming chimeras.

My hair strikes me a great blow.
Wine lifts its deep sky over us.

And Naomi was sown. She crossed the boundaries
of wounds to kneel in the snowfall at the center.
Her palms upon my forehead became my fever's petals.
Her face—Arc de Triomphe of sadness, altar where my heart is
solved—
created for me its absence in the ark of its cheekbones.

Girls tie their hair together and run as one
woman through my voiceland. Ground-glass sings my statues,
those who can only kiss wound-to-wound are born.

Your face alone has no echo in the void. Your face, more marvelous
each time it flows up your warm arms to break
upon your smile. Your kisses still rustling in my voice,
you don't exist. I will fill you with
sweet suicide.
Naomi, love other men.
Don't let this be their last poem, only mine.

Voi (poem) ces

"mercy . . . mercy" From face to face
a child's voice bounces, lower and lower;
continues its quest
underground.

Bloodspurts lessening . . . hoofbeats of animals
stalked to their birth by the sun, fade. It is a bright
edgeless morning, like a knife that to be cleaned
is held under a vein.

I blink away the stinging gleam
as my country sows desert upon Vietnam.
We, imperious, die of human thirst
—having forgotten tears are an oasis.

"help . . . help" From heart to heart
a heartbeat staggers, looking for a haven.
Bereft. It is easier to enter heaven
than to pass through each other's eyes,
pores,
armor,
like merciful sperm, cool water, the knife—
thrust of tears. . . . It is easier
to go smoothly insane—like a Detroit car—
than to stammer and hiccup help.

And this poem is the easiest thing of all:
it floats upon children's singing, out of the bloodstream;
a sunbeam shoulders it, carries it away.
There is nothing left.
"please . . . please"

SOURCE: Saint Geraud, *The Naomi Poems: Corpse and Beans* (Chicago: Follett Publishing Co., 1968), pp. 20–21.

Denise Levertov

The poetess Denise Levertov was born in Ilford, England, in 1923. She was educated largely at home by her father, an Anglican priest who had converted from Judaism. She worked as a nurse in Paris and taught in Holland. After her marriage to the American writer Mitchell Goodman in Geneva, she came to the United States in 1948 and soon devoted herself to writing and teaching poetry. She has held posts at Vassar, The City College of New York, and Kirkland College, and her readings have attracted large audiences at colleges throughout the United States. She now lives in Temple, Maine, with her husband.

"I long for poems of an inner harmony in utter contrast to the chaos in which they exist," she says of her work. The strongly musical and sensuous quality of the poems in *Here and Now* (1956), *With Eyes at the Back of Our Heads* (1959), *The Jacob's Ladder* (1961), and *O Taste and See* (1964) is still recognizable in the anti-war sorrowing of her latest poems in *Sorrow Dance* (1967), *A Tree Telling of Orpheus* (1968), *Relearning the Alphabet* (1970), *To Stay Alive* (1971), and *Footprints* (1972). The following two poems express her intense feelings about Vietnam.

'I Thirst'

Beyond the scaffolding set up for
TV cameras, a long way
from where I sit among 100,000 reddening
white faces,
                is a big wooden cross:

and strapped upon it, turning
his head from side to side in pain
in the 90 degree shadeless Washington mid-afternoon,
May 9th, 1970,
                a young black man.

'We must *not* be angry, we must
L-O-O-O-VE!' Judy Collins
bleats loud and long into the P.A. system,

SOURCE: This poem has not previously been printed in a book. Used by permission of the author.

but hardly anyone claps, and no one
shouts *Right on.*
                                        That silence cheers me.
Judy, understand:
there comes a time when only anger
is love.

Sun, Moon, and Stones

I longed to go away, to take to the desolate, denuded mountains opposite me and walk and walk, without seeing anything but sun, moon, and stones.

KAZANTZAKIS

Sun
moon
stones
                but where shall we find
                water?

Sun
      hoists all things upward and outward
      thrusts
      a sword of thirst into the mouth.

Moon
        fills the womb with ice.

Stones: weapons that carry
            warmth into night
            dew into day, and break
            the flesh of stumbling feet.

And we were born to that sole end:
        to thirst and grow
        to shudder
        to dream in lingering dew, lingering warmth
        to stumble searching.

But O the fountains,
        where shall we find them.

SOURCE: This poem has not been previously printed in a book. Used by permission of the author.

Raymond Patterson

Raymond Patterson was born in New York City in 1929. After completing his early education there, he attended Lincoln University in Pennsylvania and took a master's degree in English at New York University. He has taught in the New York City public schools and at The City College of New York and lives in Merrick, Long Island, with his wife and daughter. His first book of poems, *26 Ways of Looking at a Black Man* (1969), uses a poem by Wallace Stevens, *"13 Ways of Looking at a Blackbird"* as a point of departure, but it embroiders complex themes and images through and around that already complex structure, dispassionately and unflinchingly peeling back the psyche of the black man forced to endure the pain of an existence not always of his own making. Patterson says, "I write poetry to explore, to discover, to understand, and to be understood." "Words Found on a Cracked Wall" appeared in *The Minnesota Review;* the other two are unpublished previously.

Fable

Something is eating up all the places—
First this place and now that place,
One place and then another. Soon
Every place will have been eaten,
Down to the last place on earth.

Already no one says, "Put yourself in
My place," anymore; or, "Let's change places."
How often do you hear, "Come on over
To my place"? Everyone whispers.
No place is safe, public or private.
All the social graces are dead.

Who can stop it? Who can even see it?
It is like war. It is like disappointment.
It comes and it comes, CRUNCH, CRUNCH and
CLANK, CLANK, eating up places,
Not even leaving crumbs; eating the places
You plan to go to, and the places you've
Come from.

SOURCE: Raymond Patterson, "Fable." This poem appears first in this book.

Declare an emergency! Beat a drum!
Form a posse before it's too late,
Or form a committee. We must save more
Than just our faces. Our places are at stake!
Who in his right mind would still dispute
The boy in the meadow who looked after the sheep,
Who cried, "Wolf! It's a wolf in a tin suit!"
And disturbed our sleep?

After the Thousand Day Rebellion

After the Thousand Day Rebellion,

After the destruction to the major cities had ended,
The surviving Negroes relocated,
All black men removed from public office,
The nation demilitarized,
The terror suppressed,
The economy stabilized,
The rubble cleared away;

After the rebel leaders had been captured, their
supporters exposed, their crimes described, the tribunals
convened, the trials conducted, the verdicts reached,
the sentences decided, the judgments carried out;

After the commissions had dispersed and the committees dissolved,
The protests lodged in humanitarian concern,
The hearings granted, the answers given, the documents published,
The reports of commissions, the official records,
The narratives of battles, the citations for heroism,
The places of conflict—names out of history:
The Burning of Washington,
The Seige of Atlanta,
The Battle of the Southside,
The Battle of Harlem,
The Boston Massacre,
The Battle of Trenton . . .

After the records of carnage: the mass reprisals,
the planned assassinations, the secret executions, the
bands of armed men, the guerrilla commands, the
wholesale slaughter of non-combatants,
The Month of Exodus;

SOURCE: Raymond Patterson, "After the Thousand Day Rebellion." This poem appears first in this book.

After the testimonies of commanders, the question of
weapons, the uses of force, the machinegunning in the
tenements, the skirmishing in the suburbs,
The tactics of nerve gas, napalm, the drugging of
reservoirs, the blanketing of sectors in toxic foam, the
leveling of zones, the defoliation of swamps and savannah
strongholds, the experimentation . . .

After the censure of nations, the closing of embassies,
the United Nations dissolved, the closing of borders,
the declarations of enmity, the declarations of support,
the offers of asylum, the treaties voided, the agreements
formed, the alliances realigned;

After so much suffering and unimagined grief,

America was finally free of her dream of democracy.

Words Found on a Cracked Wall

Help me!
I'm trapped here
Behind the plaster
Pleas (sic) notify
My wife tell her
I have learned
To accept those
Things I cannot
Change
With the wisdom
To know the diff.
Call my boss
And explain
Also the children it
Is lonely
Here SCREW
God
Love
Us
All
Hen y Wil s

SOURCE: Raymond Patterson, *Minnesota Review*, X (1970), p. 22. Reprinted by permission of the author.

Sylvia Plath

Sylvia Plath was born in 1932 in Boston, Massachusetts. She was graduated from Smith College *cum laude* and awarded a Fulbright Scholarship to Cambridge in 1955. There she met and married the British poet Ted Hughes. They lived in the United States for a period while she taught at Smith and Hughes at the University of Massachusetts, but in 1957 they returned to England, where their two children were born. In 1963, on the third attempt, she committed suicide.

Her works include *The Colossus and Other Poems* (1962); *Uncollected Poems* (1965), and *Ariel* (1966), in which her full powers as a poet are revealed. Another collection, *Winter Trees,* appeared in 1972. She has written several short stories and one novel, *The Bell Jar* (1963), a novel about a suicide attempt, the aftermath in part of a very unhappy summer month she spent in New York. Her best poems are the ones which she wrote during the last part of her life when she was separated from her husband. Before her tragic death, she was able to channel her creative energy into expressing the conflict and agony that drove her to desperation despite her love for her children. For obvious reasons, she is popular with women today seeking their own feminine identity.

Medusa

Off that landspit of stony mouth-plugs,
Eyes rolled by white sticks,
Ears cupping the sea's incoherences,
You house your unnerving head—God-ball,
Lens of mercies,

Your stooges
Plying their wild cells in my keel's shadow,
Pushing by like hearts,
Red stigmata at the very centre,
Riding the rip tide to the nearest point of departure,

Dragging their Jesus hair.
Did I escape, I wonder?
My mind winds to you

Old barnacled umbilicus, Atlantic cable,
Keeping itself, it seems, in a state of miraculous repair.

In any case, you are always there,
Tremulous breath at the end of my line,
Curve of water upleaping
To my water rod, dazzling and grateful,
Touching and sucking.

I didn't call you.
I didn't call you at all.
Nevertheless, nevertheless
You steamed to me over the sea,
Fat and red, a placenta

Paralyzing the kicking lovers.
Cobra light
Squeezing the breath from the blood bells
Of the fuchsia. I could draw no breath,
Dead and moneyless,

Overexposed, like an X-ray.
Who do you think you are?
A Communion wafer? Blubbery Mary?
I shall take no bite of your body,
Bottle in which I live,

Ghastly Vatican.
I am sick to death of hot salt.
Green as eunuchs, your wishes
Hiss at my sins.
Off, off, eely tentacle!

There is nothing between us.

Ariel

Stasis in darkness.
Then the substanceless blue
Pour of tor and distances.

God's lioness,
How one we grow,
Pivot of heels and knees!—The furrow

SOURCE: Sylvia Plath, *Ariel* (New York: Harper & Row, 1966), pp. 26–27.

Splits and passes, sister to
The brown arc
Of the neck I cannot catch,

Nigger-eye
Berries cast dark
Hooks—

Black sweet blood mouthfuls,
Shadows.
Something else

Hauls me through air—
Thighs, hair;
Flakes from my heels.

White
Godiva, I unpeel—
Dead hands, dead stringencies.

And now I
Foam to wheat, a glitter of seas.
The child's cry

Melts in the wall.
And I
Am the arrow,

The dew that flies
Suicidal, at one with the drive
Into the red

Eye, the cauldron of morning.

Death & Co.

Two, of course there are two.
It seems perfectly natural now—
The one who never looks up, whose eyes are lidded
And balled, like Blake's,
Who exhibits

The birthmarks that are his trademark—
The scald scar of water,

SOURCE: Sylvia Plath, *Ariel* (New York: Harper & Row, 1966), pp. 28–29.

The nude
Verdigris of the condor.
I am red meat. His beak

Claps sidewise: I am not his yet.
He tells me how badly I photograph.
He tells me how sweet
The babies look in their hospital
Icebox, a simple

Frill at the neck,
Then the flutings of their Ionian
Death-gowns,
Then two little feet.
He does not smile or smoke.

The other does that,
His hair long and plausive.
Bastard
Masturbating a glitter,
He wants to be loved.

I do not stir.
The frost makes a flower,
The dew makes a star,
The dead bell,
The dead bell.

Somebody's done for.

The Applicant

First, are you our sort of a person?
Do you wear
A glass eye, false teeth or a crutch,
A brace or a hook,
Rubber breasts or a rubber crotch,

Stitches to show something's missing? No, no? Then
How can we give you a thing?
Stop crying.
Open your hand.
Empty? Empty. Here is a hand

SOURCE: Sylvia Plath, *Ariel* (New York: Harper & Row, 1966), pp. 4–5.

To fill it and willing
To bring teacups and roll away headaches
And do whatever you tell it.
Will you marry it?
It is guaranteed

To thumb shut your eyes at the end
And dissolve of sorrow.
We make new stock from the salt.
I notice you are stark naked.
How about this suit—

Black and stiff, but not a bad fit.
Will you marry it?
It is waterproof, shatterproof, proof
Against fire and bombs through the roof.
Believe me, they'll bury you in it.

Now your head, excuse me, is empty.
I have the ticket for that.
Come here, sweetie, out of the closet.
Well, what do you think of *that?*
Naked as paper to start

But in twenty-five years she'll be silver,
In fifty, gold.
A living doll, everywhere you look.
It can sew, it can cook,
It can talk, talk, talk.

It works, there is nothing wrong with it.
You have a hole, it's a poultice.
You have an eye, it's an image.
My boy, it's your last resort.
Will you marry it, marry it, marry it.

Fever 103°

Pure? What does it mean?
The tongues of hell
Are dull, dull as the triple

Tongues of dull, fat Cerberus
Who wheezes at the gate. Incapable
Of licking clean

SOURCE: Sylvia Plath, *Ariel* (New York: Harper & Row, 1966), p. 53.

The aguey tendon, the sin, the sin.
The tinder cries.
The indelible smell

Of a snuffed candle!
Love, love, the low smokes roll
From me like Isadora's scarves, I'm in a fright

One scarf will catch and anchor in the wheel.
Such yellow sullen smokes
Make their own element. They will not rise,

But trundle round the globe
Choking the aged and the meek,
The weak

Hothouse baby in its crib,
The ghastly orchid
Hanging its hanging garden in the air,

Devilish leopard!
Radiation turned it white
And killed it in an hour.

Greasing the bodies of adulterers
Like Hiroshima ash and eating in.
The sin. The sin.

Darling, all night
I have been flickering, off, on, off, on.
The sheets grow heavy as a lecher's kiss.

Three days. Three nights.
Lemon water, chicken
Water, water make me retch.

I am too pure for you or anyone.
Your body
Hurts me as the world hurts God. I am a lantern—

My head a moon
Of Japanese paper, my gold beaten skin
Infinitely delicate and infinitely expensive.

Does not my heat astound you. And my light.
All by myself I am a huge camellia
Glowing and coming and going, flush on flush.

I think I am going up,
I think I may rise—
The beads of hot metal fly, and I, love, I

Am a pure acetylene
Virgin
Attended by roses,

By kisses, by cherubim,
By whatever these pink things mean.
Not you, nor him

Not him, nor him
(My selves dissolving, old whore petticoats)—
To Paradise.

Adrienne Rich

Adrienne Rich was born in Baltimore in 1929 and educated at Radcliffe and Oxford. She has traveled extensively, living in England and the Netherlands before making her home in Cambridge, Massachusetts, then New York City, where she teaches at The City College. She was married to the late Alfred Conrad, a professor of economics, and has raised three children. Among her volumes of poetry are *A Change of World* (1951), *The Diamond Cutters* (1955), *Necessities of Life* (1966), *Leaflets* (1969), and *The Will to Change* (1971). The entire second portion of this book, called "Shooting Script" (from which the last two poems are taken), is an attempt to invent a new poetic form, the poet as a "dispassionately passionate camera, glancing at and moving among the fragments of her life as she confronts her political, personal, and poetic self." Just as the forms of her poetry have moved from the fixed to freer experimentation, so have her themes evolved from the stability of personal love to the searing anger of hardening but passionate radicalism. In 1972 she became a writing professor at Brandeis University.

I Dream I'm the Death of Orpheus

I am walking rapidly through striations of light and dark thrown
under an arcade.

I am a woman in the prime of life, with certain powers
and those powers severely limited
by authorities whose faces I rarely see.
I am a woman in the prime of life
driving her dead poet in a black Rolls-Royce
through a landscape of twilight and thorns.
A woman with a certain mission
which if obeyed to the letter will leave her intact.
A woman with the nerves of a panther
a woman with contacts among Hell's Angels
a woman feeling the fullness of her powers
at the precise moment when she must not use them
a woman sworn to lucidity

who sees through the mayhem, the smoky fires
of these underground streets
her dead poet learning to walk backward against the wind
on the wrong side of the mirror.

from "Shooting Script"

[4.]

In my imagination I was the pivot of a fresh beginning.

In rafts they came over the sea; on the island they put up those stones by methods we can only guess at.

If the vegetation grows as thick as this, how can we see what they were seeing?

It is all being made clear, with bulldozers, at Angkor Wat.

The verdure was a false mystery; the baring of the stones is no solution for us now.

Defoliation progresses; concrete is poured, sheets of glass hauled overland in huge trucks and at great cost.

Here we never travailed, never took off our shoes to walk the final mile.

Come and look into this cellar-hole; this is the foundling of the woods.

Humans lived here once; it became sacred only when they went away.

[5.]

Of simple choice they are the villagers; their clothes come with them like red clay roads they have been walking.

The sole of the foot is a map, the palm of the hand a letter, learned by heart and worn close to the body.

They seemed strange to me, till I began to recall their dialect.

Poking the spade into the dry loam, listening for the tick of broken pottery, hoarding the brown and black bits in a dented can.

Evenings, at the table, turning the findings out, pushing them around with a finger, beginning to dream of fitting them together.

Hiding all this work from them, although they might have helped me.

Going up at night, hiding the tin can in a closet, where the linoleum lies in shatters on a back shelf.

Sleeping to dream of the unformed, the veil of water pouring over the wet clay, the rhythms of choice, the lost methods.

Anne Sexton

Poet and playwright, Anne Sexton was born in Newton, Massachusetts, and did not discover her craft until she was past thirty. For a time she was a fashion model in Boston and what she now calls "a victim of the bourgeois middle-class American dream—to be married, have children, and a house." The awakening came while she was taking a course in writing under Robert Lowell at Boston University, with Sylvia Plath as a classmate (all three sometimes believed that they had a more lucid understanding of life while mad). With the publication of each book, grants and awards followed. *To Bedlam and Part Way Back* led to residence at the Radcliffe Institute for Independent Study; *All My Pretty Ones* to the first traveling fellowship offered by the American Academy of Arts in 1962; and her third book, *Live or Die,* won the Pulitzer Prize for 1966. Her latest volumes, *Love Poems* (1969), *Transformations* (1971), and *The Book of Folly* (1972), put her among the first rank of living poets. Her play, *Mercy Street,* was produced in New York in 1970. She now lives with her family in Weston, Massachusetts, where she continues to write the intense, unrelentingly passionate poetry that can show us fear in a handful of words.

In the Deep Museum

My God, my God, what queer corner am I in?
Didn't I die, blood running down the post,
lungs gagging for air, die there for the sin
of anyone, my sour mouth giving up the ghost?
Surely my body is dead? Surely I died?
And yet, I know, I'm here. What place is this?
Cold and queer, I sting with life. I lied.
Yes, I lied. Or else in some damned cowardice
my body would not give me up. I touch
fine cloth with my hands and my cheeks are cold.
If this is hell, then hell could not be much,
neither as special nor as ugly as I was told.

What's that I hear, snuffling and pawing its way
toward me? Its tongue knocks a pebble out of place

as it slides in, a sovereign. How can I pray?
It is panting; it is an odor with a face
like the skin of a donkey. It laps my sores.
It is hurt, I think, as I touch its little head.
It bleeds. I have forgiven murderers and whores
and now I must wait like old Jonah, not dead
nor alive, stroking a clumsy animal. A rat.
His teeth test me; he waits like a good cook,
knowing his own ground. I forgive him that,
as I forgave my Judas the money he took.

Now I hold his soft red sore to my lips
as his brothers crowd in, hairy angels who take
my gift. My ankles are a flute. I lose hips
and wrists. For three days, for love's sake,
I bless this other death. Oh, not in air—
in dirt. Under the rotting veins of its roots,
under the markets, under the sheep bed where
the hill is food, under the slippery fruits
of the vineyard, I go. Unto the bellies and jaws
of rats I commit my prophecy and fear.
Far below The Cross, I correct its flaws.
We have kept the miracle. I will not be here.

The Fortress

while taking a nap with Linda

Under the pink quilted covers
I hold the pulse that counts your blood.
I think the woods outdoors
are half asleep,
left over from summer
like a stack of books after a flood,
left over like those promises I never keep.
On the right, the scrub pine tree
waits like a fruit store
holding up bunches of tufted broccoli.

We watch the wind from our square bed.
I press down my index finger—
half in jest, half in dread—
on the brown mole
under your left eye, inherited

SOURCE: Anne Sexton, *All My Pretty Ones* (Boston: Houghton Mifflin Co., 1962), pp. 371–72.

from my right cheek: a spot of danger
where a bewitched worm ate its way through our soul
in search of beauty. My child, since July
the leaves have been fed
secretly from a pool of beet-red dye.

And sometimes they are battle green
with trunks as wet as hunters' boots,
smacked hard by the wind, clean
as oilskins. No,
the wind's not off the ocean.
Yes, it cried in your room like a wolf
and your pony tail hurt you. That was a long time ago.
The wind rolled the tide like a dying
woman. She wouldn't sleep,
she rolled there all night, grunting and sighing.

Darling, life is not in my hands;
life with its terrible changes
will take you, bombs or glands,
your own child at
your breast, your own house on your own land.
Outside the bittersweet turns orange.
Before she died, my mother and I picked those fat
branches, finding orange nipples
on the gray wire strands.
We weeded the forest, curing trees like cripples.

Your feet thump-thump against my back
and you whisper to yourself. Child,
what are you wishing? What pact
are you making?
What mouse runs between your eyes? What ark
can I fill for you when the world goes wild?
The woods are underwater, their weeds are shaking
in the tide; birches like zebra fish
flash by in a pack.
Child, I cannot promise that you will get your wish.

I cannot promise very much.
I give you the images I know.
Lie still with me and watch.
A pheasant moves
by like a seal, pulled through the mulch
by his thick white collar. He's on show
like a clown. He drags a beige feather that he removed,
one time, from an old lady's hat.
We laugh and we touch.
I promise you love. Time will not take away that.

The Truth the Dead Know

For my mother, born March 1902, died March 1959
and my father, born February 1900, died June 1959

Gone, I say and walk from church,
refusing the stiff procession to the grave,
letting the dead ride alone in the hearse.
It is June. I am tired of being brave.

We drive to the Cape. I cultivate
myself where the sun gutters from the sky,
where the sea swings in like an iron gate
and we touch. In another country people die.

My darling, the wind falls in like stones
from the whitehearted water and when we touch
we enter touch entirely. No one's alone.
Men kill for this, or for as much.

And what of the dead? They lie without shoes
in their stone boats. They are more like stone
than the sea would be if it stopped. They refuse
to be blessed, throat, eye and knucklebone.

Gary Snyder

The poetic voice of the ecological revolution, Gary Snyder was born in 1930 in San Francisco and "raised up on a feeble sort of farm just north of Seattle." He majored in mythology at Reed College and then studied linguistics for one term at Indiana University. Afterward, he "bummed around working at logging and forestry work alternate with classical Chinese study at Berkeley up till 1956." With interludes in the merchant marine and in San Francisco, he spent the years between 1956 and 1964 chiefly in Japan, where he underwent formal Zen training and married a Japanese woman. He now lives on a little ranch in Nevada City, California, with his wife and son.

His poetry reflects these various activities as they impinge upon a meditative mind. His work includes *Riprap* (1959), *Myths and Texts* (1960), *Six Sections from Mountain Rivers Without End* (1965), *The Back Country* (1968), *Regarding Wave* (1971), and a remarkable book of prose called *Earth House Hold*. He says about himself, "I try to hold both history and wilderness in mind, that my poems may approach the true measure of things and stand against the unbalance and ignorance of our times."

Hitch Haiku

They didn't hire him
                so he ate his lunch alone:
the noon whistle

. . .

Cats shut down
                deer thread through
men all eating lunch

. . .

Frying hotcakes in a dripping shelter
            Fu Manchu
Queets Indian Reservation in the rain

. . .

A truck went by
                three hours ago:
Smoke Creek desert

. . .

Jackrabbit eyes all night
  breakfast in Elko.

. . .

Old kanji hid by dirt
on skidroad Jap town walls
            down the hill
to the Wobbly hall

Seattle

. . .

Spray drips from the cargo-booms
a fresh-chipped winch
            spotted with red lead
young fir—
            soaking in summer rain

. . .

Over the Mindanao Deep

Scrap brass
            dumpt off the fantail
falling six miles

. . .

To the Chinese Comrades

The armies of China and Russia
Stand facing across a wide plain.
Krushchev on one side and Mao on the other,
Krushchev calls out
    "Pay me the money you owe me!"
Mao laughs and laughs, long hair flops.
His face round and smooth.
The armies start marching—they meet—
Without clashing, they march through each other,
Lines between lines.

All the time Mao Tse-tung laughing.
He takes heaps of money.
He laughs and he gives it to Krushchev.

Chairman Mao's belongings on the March:
"Two cotton and wool mixture blankets,
A sheet, two pants and jackets,
A sweater
A patched umbrella
An enamel mug for a rice bowl
A gray brief-case with nine pockets."

Like Han-shan standing there
    — a rubbing off some cliff
Hair sticking out smiling
  maybe rolling a homegrown
  Yenan cigarette
Took a crack at politics
The world is all one.
— crawling out that hillside cave dirt house —

        (whatever happened to Wong —
        quit Chinese school, slugged his dad
        left the laundry, went to sea
        out the golden gate — did he make AB? —)

black eggshell-thin
pots of Lung-shan
maybe three thousand years B C

You have killed
I saw the Tibetans just down from the passes
Limping in high felt boots
Sweating in furs
Flatland heat.
        and from Almora gazing at Trisul
        the new maps from Peking
        call it all China
        clear down to here, & the Gangetic plain —

From Hongkong N.T. on a pine rise
See the other side: stub fields.
Geese, ducks, and children
        far off cries.
Down the river, tiny men
Walk a plank — maybe loading
                little river boat.

Is that China
Flat, brown, and wide?

The ancestors
what did they leave us.
K'ung fu–tze, some buildings, remain.
    –tons of soil gone.
Mountains turn desert.
Stone croppt flood, strippt hills,
The useless wandering river mouths,
Salt swamps
Silt on the floor of the sea.

Wind-borne glacial flour–
Ice-age of Europe,
Dust storms from Ordos to Finland
The loess of Yenan.
    glaciers
        "shrink
  and vanish like summer clouds . . ."

CROSS THE SNOWY MOUNTAIN
WE SHALL SEE CHAIRMAN MAO!

The year the long march started I was four.
How long has this gone on.
Rivers to wade, mountains to cross–
Chas. Leong showed me how to hold my chopsticks
                like the brush–
Upstairs a chinese restaurant catty-corner
                from the police
Portland, oregon, nineteen fifty-one,
Yakima Indian horseman, hair black as crows.
        shovel shaped incisors,
          epicanthic fold.
Misty peaks and cliffs of the Columbia,
Old loggers vanish in the rocks.
They wouldn't tote me rice and soy-sauce
                cross the dam
"Snyder you gettin just like
    a damned Chinaman."
Gambling with the Wasco and the Wishram
By the river under Hee Hee Butte
& bought a hard round loaf of weird bread
From a bakery in a tent
In a camp of Tibetans
At Bodh-Gaya
Where Gautama used to stay.

On hearing Joan Baez singing "East Virginia"
Those were the days.
we strolld under blossoming cherries
ten acres of orchard
holding hands, kissing.
in the evening talkt Lenin and Marx.
You had just started out for Beijing.

I slippt my hand under her blouse
and undid her brassiere.
I passt my hand over her breasts
her sweet breath, it was too warm for May.
I thought how the whole world
my love, could love like this;
blossoms, the books, revolution
more trees, strong girls, clear springs;
You took Beijing

Chairman Mao, you should quit smoking.
Dont bother those philosophers
Build dams, plant trees,
dont kill flies by hand.
Marx was another westerner.
it's all in the head.
You dont need the bomb.
stick to farming.
Write some poems. Swim the river.
those blue overalls are great.
Dont shoot me, let's go drinking.
just
Wait.

For the West

[1]

Europa,
your red-haired
hazel-eyed
Thracian girls
your beautiful thighs
everlasting damnations
and grave insouciance—

SOURCE: Gary Snyder, *The Back Country* (New York: New Directions Publishing Corporation, 1968), pp. 102–4.

a woman's country,
even your fat little popes.
groin'd temples
groov'd canals
—me too, I see thru
these green eyes—

the Cowboys and Indians all over Europe
sliding down snowfields on shields.

what next? a farmer's
corner of the planet—
who cares if you are White?

[2]

this universe—"one turn"—turnd over.
gods of revolution,
sharp beards—fur flap hats—
kalmuck whip-swingers,

hugging and kissing
white and black,
men, men,
girls, girls,

wheat, rye, barley,
adding asses to donkeys
to fat-haunch horses,
it takes tractors and the
multiple firing of pistons
to make revolution.
still turning.   flywheel heavy
elbow-bending awkward
flippety drive goes
on, white   chicks;

dark skin
burns the tender lobes.
foggy white skin bleacht out,
pale nipple,
pale breast never freckled,

they turn and
slowly turn away—

[3]

Ah, that's America:
the flowery glistening oil blossom
spreading on water—

it was so tiny, nothing, now it keeps expanding
all those colors,
                    our world
     opening inside outward toward us,
each part swelling and turning
who would have thought such turning;
as it covers,
          the colors fade.
and the fantastic patterns
          fade.
I see down again through clear water.

     it is the same
ball bounce rhyme the
     little girl was singing,
     all those years.

Diane Wakoski

Diane Wakoski speaks and sings of those concerns uppermost in the mind of the modern woman. She was born in Whittier, California, in 1937 and grew up in southern California. After earning a B.A. at Berkeley, she worked as a bookstore clerk and a junior high school teacher. Recently her poetry has caught on and she has been reading her work on the poetry circuit throughout the country. She spent almost a year in Majorca and has taught at Cal Tech but makes her home in New York City. She is associated with the "deep imagist" poets whose early work was published in Robert Kelley's *Trobar* and contributed regularly to Clayton Eshelman's *Caterpillar.* She believes that poetry is "the completely personal expression of someone about his feelings and reactions to the world . . . it is *only interesting* in proportion to how interesting the person who writes it is." Among her published books are *Coins and Coffins* (1961), *The George Washington Poems* (1967), *Inside the Blood Factory* (1968), *The Moon Has a Complicated Geography,* and *The Motorcycle Betrayal Poems* (1971).

The following poems come from *The Magellanic Clouds* (1969), a surrealistic, often witty, erotic, highly confessional book about being human and female and American. In one of the poems, everyday objects are transformed into people (see Erica Jong's poem). There is the painful search for identity. Each poem is a personal testament arising from Diane Wakoski's nerves, bones, blood, and mind.

Reaching Out with the Hands of the Sun

And thereupon
That beautiful mild woman for whose sake
There's many a one shall find out all
heartache
On finding that her voice is sweet & low
Replied: 'To be born woman is to know—
Although they do not talk of it at school—
That we must labour to be beautiful.'
Adam's Curse, W. B. YEATS

Atun-Re
the sun disk
whose rays end in hands

SOURCE: Diane Wakoski, *The Magellanic Clouds* (Los Angeles: Black Sparrow Press, 1969), pp. 28–31. Reprinted by permission of the publisher.

shines above us in New York
California
Egypt
sometimes even Alaska.
Walking across the desert,
he puts his scorching hands over our eyes
and turns vision into sounds,
waves
as the ocean,
drawing the pupils away from rattlesnakes & blurring
the hawks
that sail so unconcerned with heat
above our heads,
when we ride across the snow
and shaggy trees of Alaska
the sun's many hands
rub thick bear skins & tallow against the apples of our faces;
when we float down the river
without barks of gold or flutes or beautiful boys in the heavy
linen sails,
the sun's hands reach into the Nile
and pull out a glimmering eel
or a water lily,
holding it against the banks,
motioning for us to expect life anywhere,
even though it's not at once seen;
the hands coming from the rays of that disk
hold oranges, dates, figs, nuts
all those sweetmeats
that give a woman fat thighs
and a puffy face.

What am I to believe in this world?
The whirling sun disk
that speeds years away
puts out such rays with hands attached to each
that fling me one day against
the rough edges of mountains,
one day caress me, push me against the long mustaches I love;
my face varies from plain to dignified;
my figure from straight to plump;
my eyes from bright to small & sad;
my mouth, always a straight line—as if crossing a "t"
and I see the world change around me;
only one thing never changes.

Men remember,
love,

cherish,
beautiful women,
    as I've said,
    like April snow
like silk that rustles in a fragrant chest,
like a machine dripping with oil and running smoothly.

I am pooh-poohed
every time I say it.
    "a woman of your intelligence,"
    etc., etc.,
believing
such a superficial thing. "Only the
foolish
misguided,
the men with no balls,
or the ones that don't really matter,"
love a woman for her beauty
her physical self.
But I know different.
I've ruled;
I've walked with the mask of a falcon,
perhaps Horus
over my head,
walked everywhere, stiff & disguised,
walked in stone watching
the life around me,
the loving,
and not loving,
without sounds to interrupt or change history.
I've watched and know
that even the poets
whose blood is most filled with sun's light
and whose hands are wet
coming out of the rays of the moon,
love beautiful women,
writhe, turn,
upset their lives, leave their good wives,
when one walks by.
And we,
with fat thighs,
or small breasts,
or thin delicate hair,
pale faces,
small eyes,
with only our elegant, small-wristed hands
to defend us
trying to catch one of the hands

on a ray from the sun,
loving our men faithfully
and with hope;
surely we deserve something more than platitudes.

We are the ones who know
    beauty is only skin deep.
But we also know
we would trade every ruby
stuffing and jamming our wealthy opulent hearts;
would trade every silver whistle
that alerts our brain,
keeps us sensitive and graceful to the world;
would trade every
miracle
inside our plain & ugly blood factories,
these bodies that never
serve us well,
for some beauty
they could recognize;
that would make the men stop
turn their heads,
twist their minds & lives around
for us/
for those of us who love them
and who never stop.
Whose hands are always radiating
out
ready to touch
the men
with fire
direct from the solar disk
who
brood
are dark often
with hands that come from the
unseen side
of the moon.

The Buddha Inherits 6 Cars on His Birthday

I. THE RED CAR

I believe it was out of the red one that George Washington stepped,
or someone who looked like G.W.

SOURCE: Diane Wakoski, *The Magellanic Clouds* (Los Angeles: Black Sparrow Press, 1969), pp. 56–57. Reprinted by permission of the publisher.

The corridor was made of fibrous blood
and his feet sank in darkly
as teeth into a pear. Going past the service desk
he was paged by a man who had sitting in front of him a
tall jelly glass holding his false teeth. The gums,
false pink.
G.W. was in no mood for dalliance.
"Send all the seamstresses up at once," he said,
and when they got there he undressed them all,
picked the most voluptuous one
and gave her some cloth to
sew.

II. THE BLUE CAR

It smelled like new rubber inside.
The man who drove it had no imagination.
"Will I turn into a machine," he thought,
but no
in a few days they found
a desert rat driving that new blue Ford.
And it seemed peculiar
but it's easier not to question things
these days.

III. THE GREEN CAR

Emily and James stepped out of their green car.
It was made of old metal melted down.
In your Lee corduroy dungarees and sweatshirt you
look so handsome.
I'm not particular
as long as you have money and style.
This money is easy to spend,
but if you tried to stuff dollar bills inside me you'd find
a yawning gap, hole
at the bottom where everything falls out
Oh pity
there is such an empty space
Oh pity
that the lives of some of us are
so vain.

IV. THE YELLOW CAR

A very small man met a very large woman.
They were both in the teen-age section of the library.
They discovered they both liked the Mona Lisa. They

discovered they both listened to the 1812 Overture.
When true love comes,
hallelujah
you know it!

V. THE TWO-TONE CAR

There are fish that change color for camouflage, but it is a fact that blind ones never do. Experimentation follows it up. Scientists painted a tank black at one end and white at the other. It was observed that a certain fish would become grey as he got just in the middle at the dividing line. This was the only time he showed up as a different color from his surroundings, either black or white. Apparently, he could not make an instantaneous change. At the dividing line he always turned grey.

VI. OLD CARS

In my car of crocodile teeth, in my
car of old candle wax, in
my car of tiger paws padding the waspy dust, in my car of
cat's teeth crushing the brittle insect wings, in my
car of leather straps, in my car of folded paper, silvery and pink,
in my car of Alpine tents, in my car of bits & braces,
in my car of fishing line, in my car at the bottom of a
violin, in my car as small as a flea hopping on the dog,
in my own car I want to drive
everywhere
every place there is to go.

Beauty

only God, my dear,
Could love you for yourself alone
And not your yellow hair.
For Anne Gregory, W. B. YEATS

and if I cut off my long hair,
if I stopped speaking,
if I stopped dreaming for other people about parts of the car,
stopped handing them tall creamy flowered silks
and loosing the magnificent hawks to fly in their direction,
stopped exciting them with the possibilities
of a thousand crystals under the fingernail
to look at while writing a letter,
if I stopped crying for the salvation of the tea ceremony,

SOURCE: Diane Wakoski, "A Poet Recognizing the Echo of the Voice," *The Magellanic Clouds* (Los Angeles: Black Sparrow Press, 1969), pp. 127–128. Reprinted by permission of the publisher.

stopped rushing in excitedly with a spikey bird-of-paradise,
and never let them see how accurate my pistol shooting is,
who would I be?

Where is the real me
I want them all to love?

We are all the textures we wear.

We frighten men with our steel;
we fascinate them with our silk;
we seduce them with our cinnamon;
we rule them with our sensuous voices;
we confuse them with our submissions.
Is there anywhere
a man
who
will not punish us
for our beauty?
He is the one
we all search for,
chanting names for exotic oceans of the moon.

He is the one
we all anticipate,
pretending these small pedestrians
jaywalking into our lives
are he.
He is the one
we all anticipate;
beauty looks for its match,
confuses the issue
with a mystery that does not exist:
the rock
that cannot burn.

We are burning
in our heads at night
the incense of our histories, finding
you have used our skulls
for ashtrays.

Index

Authors' names appear in bold face type, titles in italics, and first lines in roman type.

A

B

G

H

I

J

K

L

R

S

T

U

V

W

Y

Z